A Functional Theory
of Cognition

A Functional Theory
of Cognition

Norman H. Anderson

LAWRENCE ERLBAUM ASSOCIATES, PUBLISHERS
1996   Mahwah, New Jersey

Lawrence Erlbaum Associates, Inc., Publishers
10 Industrial Avenue
Mahwah, New Jersey 07430

Library of Congress Cataloging-in-Publication Data

Anderson, Norman H.
    A functional theory of cognition / Norman H. Anderson.
        p.   cm.
    Includes bibliographical references and indexes.
    ISBN 0-8058-2244-5 (alk. paper)
    1. Human information processing. 2. Integration (Theory of
knowledge) 3. Cognition. 4. Psychometrics. I. Title.
    [DNLM: 1. Cognition. 2. Psychological Theory. BF 311 A548 1996]
BF444.A53 1996
153--dc20
DNLM/DLC   96-1834

Books published by Lawrence Erlbaum Associates are printed
on acid-free paper, and their bindings are chosen
for strength and durability.

Printed in the United States of America

10 9 8 7 6 5 4 3 2 1

DEDICATION

The work summarized in this book owes much to many men and women. Some are gratefully acknowledged at the end of certain chapters. Others, to whom I am especially indebted, are listed here.

James Alexander
James Anderson
Margaret Armstrong
Michael Birnbaum
Donald Blankenship
Richard Bogartz
Jerome Busemeyer
Clifford Butzin
Edward Carterette
John Clavadetscher
Diane Cuneo
Mary Dozier
Arthur Farkas
Cheryl Graesser Stecher
Reid Hastie
Samuel Himmelfarb
Wilfried Hommers
Steven Hubert
Clyde Hendrick
James Jaccard
Ann Norman Jacobson
Martin Kaplan
Michael Klitzner
Anita Lampel
Manuel Leon
Irwin Levin

Lola Lopes
Jordan Louviere
Dominic Massaro
Robert McBride
Etienne Mullet
Kent Norman
Gregg Oden
Mary Pendery
Peter Petzold
Winifred Riney
Barbara Sawyers Maze
Anne Schlottmann
James Shanteau
Joseph Sidowski
Ramadhar Singh
Lennart Sjöberg
Ralph Stewart
Colleen Surber Moore
John Verdi
David Weiss
Friedrich Wilkening
Yuval Wolf
William Wright
James Zalinski
Shu-Hong Zhu

FOREWORD

This book is intended to be readable by psychologists in all fields of specialization. The theory of information integration (IIT) covers many substantive areas, from psychophysics through memory and person cognition to language processing. This work forms a theoretical whole, based on the same concepts and methods in each area. Foremost is a new theory of psychological measurement, empirically successful in many areas. This theoretical unification contrasts with the increasing fragmentation that has characterized the development of psychology.

Workers in one area, however, are not often cognizant of associated work on IIT that has been done in other areas. Crossing areas presents problems, of course, but IIT cannot be fully understood within its applications to a single area. The contrast between internal and external structure, for example, takes on different forms in different areas, as does the issue of meaning invariance. For these and other issues, results in one area often buttress results in other areas.

The purpose of this book, accordingly, is to give an overview of IIT that will be accessible to workers in all areas. This is possible because the theory is unified in concept and method. Each empirical chapter presents illustrative experiments to cover a set of basic issues in one area. Each chapter revolves around a contrast between a traditional conceptual framework and a new way of thinking.

To cover this range of content in a book intended for the general reader has imposed several constraints. Each empirical chapter is largely self-contained, requiring only Chapter 1 and part of Chapter 2. Some redundancy will thus appear across chapters. References have been omitted from the main text as much as possible. Some issues are detailed in chapter notes, which also refer back to the original literature. Various general issues could be covered only in a cursory way. To relate IIT to other functional theories, for example, would have required a book in itself. Similarly, much other work on cognitive theory of everyday life, which is a primary ground for IIT, has perforce gone unmentioned. I hope to amend these limitations in future work.

CONTENTS

PREFACE

The axiom of purposiveness is a foundation for the present theory. Purposiveness entails a functional perspective, embodying the goal-oriented character of thought and action. Thereby, purposiveness also entails a notable simplification: Goal approach and avoidance impose a one-dimensional value representation of complex processes. This value representation is a key to theory.

The organism is considered an active processor of information in pursuit of ever-changing goals. *Valuation* is one primary process, as stimulus and memory informers are processed into goal valences of approach or avoidance. *Integration* is a second primary process, for multiple determinants are typically involved with any goal or course of action. Following valuation of the separate determinants, therefore, they must be integrated into a net effective value for action. Valuation and integration are both dynamic processes, reflecting the ever-changing situation and motivation of the organism.

Integration operations have structure. This structure has provided a base and frame for theory development. This approach focuses directly on the fundamental problem of integration of multiple determinants. A central result is that valuation and integration are independent in many cases. By virtue of this independence, a simultaneous solution is possible for both primary problems, valuation as well as integration.

This theory of information integration (IIT) has established a general cognitive algebra. A few algebraic rules—averaging, multiplying, adding—have been revealed in virtually every area of psychology, from judgment–decision and cognitive development to language processing. This cognitive algebra is the base and frame of IIT.

Although conjectures about algebraic rules have long been popular in psychology, establishing these rules was not possible without a theory for measuring psychological values on true metric scales. Despite many attempts, metric theory of psychological measurement had made little progress. IIT succeeded through a new direction—by making the algebraic rules themselves the base and frame for measurement.

Measurement is thus integral to and derivative from algebraic structure of substantive laws. This *functional measurement theory* provided the first effective, general solution to the problem of psychological metrics.

One major difficulty in establishing cognitive algebra and functional measurement was the averaging rule. Many situations that had been conjectured to obey adding rules instead obeyed averaging rules. The averaging rule is nonadditive in general, however, one reason why it was difficult to put on solid ground (see Chapters 2 and 4).

A new avenue of inquiry thus opened up. Integration is basic for general theory, but integration analysis had been severely handicapped by lack of psychological metrics. Even the simple additive rule cannot be established without measurement capability. Previous approaches, accordingly, developed other lines of inquiry that allowed progress with available measurement tools. Although much has been learned in this way, bypassing the two primary problems of valuation and integration has fragmented the field. Promising new advances typically led to complications; the more that was learned, the farther prospects of unified theory receded. Functional measurement, in contrast, led to unified theory—cumulative science demonstrated in the diverse areas covered in this book.

Several characteristics of IIT deserve consideration. Foremost, as befits its functional perspective, IIT has a primary concern with phenomenology of everyday life. The terms and concepts of the algebraic rules are typically taken from everyday experience and language. Affective concepts, in particular, provide a unifying theme for goal-oriented behavior, indeed, for life itself, from perception of the external world to social communication and self-concepts.

Furthermore, IIT aims to be self-sufficient near the level of everyday phenomenology. This is possible because cognitive algebra can help provide validational assessment of the everyday concepts that appear in the algebraic rules. Phenomenology is a priceless source of knowledge, but it can be obstinately mistaken, as it was with the issue of meaning invariance. Cognitive algebra can help assay and refine phenomenology as a base for substantive theory.

Phenomenology is not enough; nonconscious concepts are essential. Functional measurement can handle nonconscious concepts under certain conditions, thereby making possible self-sufficient theory that embraces phenomenology. Deeper, more detailed process analysis has great interest and importance, but it is not necessary for general theory of everyday life. The unitization principle allows the resultants of detailed processing to be treated as molar units near the level of everyday thought and action.

IIT builds on structure of the internal world. This internalist focus contrasts with a reliance on structure of the external world throughout psychology. The externalist focus appears in the near-total reliance on reproductive tasks in memory research, on accuracy criteria in language analysis, on reinforcement concepts in learning, in the predominance of normative approaches in judgment–decision, in bias–distortion concepts in social cognition, in the classical concept of psychophysical law, in modern theories of direct perception, and in the internal–external isomorphism that underlies Piaget's theory of formal operations. Such externalist approaches are attractive, and useful, because the internal world has evolved for survival in the external world.

The internal world, however, has its own structure and order, essentially different from those of the external world. These need to be addressed in their own terms. In each of the cited areas, the externalist focus has obstructed the way to general theory. Functional memory, for example, central in everyday life, requires concepts and methods outside the scope of traditional reproductive conceptions of memory. In each of its various forms, the assumption of internal–external congruence foreclosed the development of concepts and methods necessary for unified theory. The unity of cognition has revealed itself in cognitive algebra, a framework for general theory, founded on structure of the internal world.

IIT is primarily an inductive theory, grounded in empirical analysis. This inductive character is reflected in the heavy emphasis on experimental studies in Chapters 4–12. In a real sense, the theory resides and manifests itself in these empirical applications. In this inductive view, the functional theory is more than the abstract principles, for it includes the empirical details that govern its application and reveal its reality.

Among other characteristics, the inductive approach places less emphasis on critical tests of competing hypotheses, more on empirical exploration of phenomena. The worth of this inductive approach is demonstrated by the new way of thinking it has produced in each of these empirical area.

IIT is a unified, general theory. It is unified through the applicability of the same concepts and methods across all the substantive areas considered in this book. It is general in the success of the same concepts and methods across all these areas. In place of the increasing compartmentalization that has characterized the development of psychology, IIT offers simplicity and unity. It has led to a new conceptual framework and to new lines of inquiry in every area to which it has been applied.

IIT is incomplete in important respects. To put cognitive algebra and functional measurement on solid ground, the scope of inquiry had to be limited. As a consequence, knowledge systems, operating memory, and other nonalgebraic aspects of cognition have been treated in cursory manner. Now that it has been reasonably established, however, cognitive algebra can be employed for analysis of nonalgebraic structure.

Indeed, the conceptual implications of the work to date are in many ways more important than the algebraic structure. A new way of thinking appears in each empirical chapter, as shown in the conceptual shift away from traditional approaches in each area. The studies of cognitive algebra have thus led beyond themselves to conceptual restructuring. Much of what has been learned from cognitive algebra consists of qualitative conceptions itemized on the last page of Chapter 13.

Past work on IIT, it seems fair to say, represents cumulative science. It is hoped this approach will continue helpful in these further problems.

PREFACE

The conscious purposiveness so prominent in our everyday life has been perennially attractive as a base for psychological science—and has proved perennially disappointing. Much cognition is nonconscious; what is accessible to consciousness has failed to provide a base for theory. Purposiveness itself has been much condemned, like teleological concepts in physics.

This book presents a functional theory of cognition, founded on the axiom of purposiveness and grounded in cognitive algebra. The functional nature of cognition manifests itself in an approach–avoidance axis of thought and action. This axis provides a one-dimensional representation of cognition in terms of value, positive and negative. Functional value pervades cognition and provides a unifying base for analysis.

Cognitive algebra gives a cutting edge to the axiom of purposiveness. Multiple determinants, and hence multiple values, typically operate in thought and action. These multiple values are integrated by the organism, and these integrations often follow algebraic rules: averaging, multiplying, and adding.

Empirical reality of cognitive algebra has been demonstrated through a new theory of psychological measurement. The effectiveness of this functional measurement theory is illustrated in this chapter by an experimental study of person cognition and in later chapters by experimental studies in many different domains of psychology.

Cognitive algebra addresses everyday cognition in everyday terms. It can also penetrate more deeply to measure nonconscious sensation and affect, a necessity for transforming everyday cognition into scientific theory.

The axiom of purposiveness embodies a functional perspective, in which cognition is represented in goal-directed function. Purposiveness becomes a scientific concept through representation as measurable, personal value. This functional perspective entails a new approach to many issues in mainstream cognitive psychology. Functional memory, for example, differs markedly from traditional conceptions of reproductive memory. Affect and motivation, hostile terrain to much current cognitive psychology, are organic components of functional cognition. New directions appear in every area.

The theory of information integration is a unified, general theory. Generality appears in empirical applications across nearly all domains of psychology. Unity appears in the utility of the same concepts and methods across all these domains. The theory of information integration is not another promissory note; it is not only a manifesto but a working reality. Contributions so far are modest but real; they open onto a new horizon of psychological science.

Chapter 1

COGNITIVE THEORY OF EVERYDAY LIFE

Everyday life is characterized by conscious purposiveness. From reaching for food to designing an experiment, our actions are directed at goals. This purposiveness reveals itself partly in our conscious awareness, partly in the organization of our thought and action. Everyday life is thus an obvious, seemingly ideal place to begin, filled with promise for development of cognitive theory.

This promise has been tantalizing in the original Greek sense of that term: Tantalos, a son of Zeus and a king, was condemned in the afterlife to stand, racked with hunger and thirst, amid fruit-laden boughs in water up to his chin—with the fruit and water receding at each attempt to eat and drink. Many present-day psychologists feel like Tantalos. Our awareness of our feelings, desires, and goals ought to have shown the way to deeper understanding. Our immediate experience ought to have lighted a path to scientific theory. Many writers have sought to develop psychological theory on the basis of conscious experience. But, as with Tantalos, the sought-for understanding has receded at each attempt to eat and drink.

This recalcitrance of everyday experience to scientific development caused the dissolution of the original school of introspection. The main successor, the behaviorist movement, reacted against introspection by exiling consciousness. The psychoanalytic movement, otherwise very different, moved the prime locus of mental life to an unconscious realm, generally inaccessible to conscious awareness. The modern cognitive movement has welcomed consciousness home from exile, but has been deaf to affect and emotion. Since affect and emotion are central in our daily experience, these cognitive theories cannot say much about everyday life.

The theme of this volume is that scientific theory can be constructed around the concepts of everyday life. Everyday concepts are thus the focus of study, with the expectation that they can be established as scientific concepts. A partial list of everyday concepts will illustrate the broad field for study:

Psychophysical sensations such as sweetness and loudness.
Perceptual judgments such as size, distance, and movement.
Physical concepts such as time and torque.
Decision concepts such as cost, benefit, and probability.
Physiological reactions such as thirst, fatigue, and pain.
Emotional reactions such as joy and fear.
Interpersonal reactions such as admiration and envy, love and hate.
Moral judgments such as fairness and blame.
Goal experiences such as failure and success.
Self-concepts such as pride and ability.
Ego defenses such as excuses and self-pity.
And many more.

A good beginning has been made in the theory of information integration (IIT). IIT provides a unified, general theory of everyday life. Its generality appears in the spectrum of chapter titles, from person cognition and cognitive development to decision theory and language processing. Its unity appears in the applicability of the same concepts and methods across all these domains.

Moreover, IIT has a solid empirical foundation. It is not another promissory note. It is not only a manifesto but a working reality. It opens onto a new horizon in psychological science.

INFORMATION INTEGRATION THEORY

Two characteristics are basic to IIT. First is the functional perspective, which focuses on purposiveness of thought and action. Second is cognitive algebra. These two are interlinked: Purposiveness imposes a value representation that makes cognitive algebra possible; cognitive algebra provides effective analysis of value and hence of purposiveness.

This chapter gives a conceptual overview of IIT. This first part begins with the unifying theme of purposiveness. Purposiveness leads to two fundamental problems, *multiple determination* and *personal value*, and thence to concepts summarized in the integration diagram of Figure 1.1, collectively called the *problem of the three unobservables*.

The second part of the chapter illustrates method and theory with an experimental study of cognitive algebra in person cognition. The third part amplifies the functional perspective with topical discussions of meaning invariance, nonconsciousness, motivation, functional memory, and knowledge systems. The chapter concludes with a discussion of strategy of theory construction.

AXIOM OF PURPOSIVENESS[1]

Purposiveness is the prime axiom of psychology. The purposiveness of behavior has two main implications for IIT. The first is a functional perspective: Thought and action are conceptualized in terms of their functions in goal-directed behavior. This functional perspective entails sometimes substantial changes from customary views. Everyday life requires a functional conception of memory, for example, which is very different from the traditional conception of reproductive memory. Again, nonconscious emotion, which is virtually defined into nonexistence in traditional emotion theories, is an integral part of functional cognition.

The second implication of purposiveness, derived from the first, provides a means for its analysis. This is a one-dimensional representation of cognition. Thought and action have a basic approach—avoidance character; they are directed toward or away from goals. This is clear with affective senses, such as taste, temperature, and sex. These senses embody approach— avoidance polarity, which has evolved for goal-relevant function.

In everyday life, also, approach—avoidance is a fundamental axis of thought and action. Sports are typically centered on winning and losing, and similar success—failure dimensions appear in work and achievement. Our reactions to other persons exhibit a basic like—dislike dimension. An overall dimension of satisfaction—dissatisfaction pervades married life. These approach—avoidance continua represent purposiveness in a dimensional form.

This one-dimensional representation is encapsulated in the concept of value. Values embody and represent goal-directed thought and action. Although a one-dimensional value representation omits much of importance, it captures something of first importance, namely, goal directedness. Approach and avoidance are represented by positive and negative values associated with goals. With this one-dimensional representation, quantitative analysis of complex behavior becomes thinkable.

But values must be measured. Measurement is necessary to quantify goal directedness. Measurement is necessary to actualize the value representation.

Measurement of values has long been controversial in psychology, even for simple sensations such as sweetness and loudness. We have no sucrometer to place on your tongue to measure your sensation of sweetness, nor any audiometer to implant in your auditory cortex. Even more problematic is measurement of feelings of affection, blame, unfairness, and other everyday experiences. Without a solution to this problem of value measurement, the one-dimensional representation of goal directedness has limited usefulness.

By a blessing of Nature, the measurement problem has a solution. The key came with the discovery of cognitive algebra. Work on IIT has revealed algebraic rules in nearly every domain. The stimulus terms in these algebraic rules embody one-dimensional values; the response term embodies the one-dimensional character of goal directedness. Stimulus and response measurement are both possible with cognitive algebra.

Moreover, cognitive algebra can operate at the level of conscious phenomenology, yet still analyze nonconscious concepts. Cognitive algebra thus provides a key to unlock the promise of conscious purposiveness.

MULTIPLE DETERMINATION

Virtually all judgment and action depend on more than one determinant. This is obvious in our social behavior. When we discipline a child, our action depends not only on the transgression, but also on our attribution about the child's intent, our desire to punish or instruct, and so on. When we meet a woman, we are influenced by her facial appearance and makeup, smile and gesture, dress, qualities of voice and language, and content and style of conversation. Marriage satisfaction depends on personal appreciation and quality of sex from your spouse and also on finances and children. Small moral problems, such as admitting fault or lying to save face, are everyday examples of conflicting factors. Such multiple determination is basic throughout the social–personality domain.

Multiple determination is equally important in other domains. In psychophysics, the taste of our food and drink depends not only on several sensations of the tongue, but also on visual cues and odor. Purchase decisions depend on cost–benefit analysis, taking account of price, quality, appearance, and other attributes. Understanding language depends on syntactic and semantic elements and also on contextual variables. Opinions on any professional issue, from education of graduate students to promising and unpromising problems for research, involve multiple pros and cons.

Development of general cognitive theory rests squarely on capability for analysis of multiple determination. This problem has resisted attack. Many psychological experiments, it is true, manipulate two or more variables and obtain multivariable tables of data. Such data tables, however, are generally descriptive and situation-specific. Sometimes they represent important phenomena; sometimes they are useful in testing local hypotheses. However, they do not lead to general theory.

Indeed, the disheartening but common conclusion of an extensive research program is that "it all depends." Each new variable requires qualification of previous generalizations. The pattern of results grows more complicated with each new study. The more that is learned, the farther away theoretical unification recedes.

Cognitive algebra provides a new approach to multiple determination. It focuses on integration, that is, the rules whereby the various determinants are integrated into a unitary response. This can provide a foundation for theory because the same integration rules can apply to varied sets of determinants. Cognitive algebra can thus provide an underlying order and unifying framework for the surface complications of the innumerable determinants of thought and action. The effectiveness of this line of attack will be demonstrated in each later empirical chapter.

The development of cognitive algebra, however, involved a second basic problem. This is the problem of psychological measurement, considered next.

PSYCHOLOGICAL MEASUREMENT

The concept of value, as already emphasized, offers a fundamental simplification of purposiveness. But values are personal. The importance and promise you attach to your own research often differ from the opinions of reviewers and colleagues. A wife's feelings of affection for her husband differ in many ways from his for her. Values differ across cultures; across social groups within each culture; and across individuals within each social group.

This basic fact of individual differences has been a quagmire for psychological science. How can general truths be established when individuals may differ sharply in the values that govern their thought and action? And how can individuals be understood without capability for measuring their personal values?

Both questions can be answered by cognitive algebra. Individuals may exhibit similar rules of multiple determination even though they differ in the personal values operative in these rules (see Figure 1.2). Some of these rules have algebraic form—this cognitive algebra provides a grounded theory of psychological measurement, with the needed capability for measuring personal values. The concepts and methods of this approach are outlined next.

INTEGRATION DIAGRAM

A conceptual overview of IIT appears in the simplified integration diagram of Figure 1.1. The organism is considered to reside in a multivariable field of observable stimuli, denoted by S_1, S_2, . . . , at the left of the diagram. These multiple stimuli are determinants of the observable response, R, at the right of the diagram. Between the observable stimuli and the observable response intervene three processing operators: *valuation*, *integration*, and *action*, denoted by **V**, **I**, and **A**, respectively.

Also represented in the integration diagram is the operative goal, which controls all three processing operations. The purposiveness of thought and action is thus explicitly incorporated in the integration diagram. All three operators, accordingly, embody the construction principle discussed later.

The valuation operator, **V**, extracts information from stimuli. In the integration diagram, it refers to processing chains that lead from the observable stimuli, S_i, to their psychological representations, denoted by ψ_i. Valuation may be as simple as tasting the sweetness of a drink or as difficult as interpreting the complaints of your spouse.

INTEGRATION   DIAGRAM

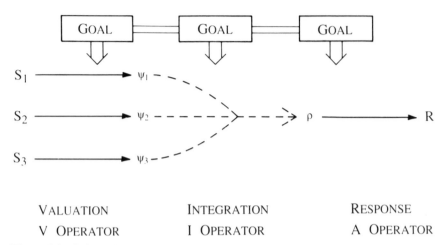

Figure 1.1. Information integration diagram. Chain of three operators, $\mathbf{V} - \mathbf{I} - \mathbf{A}$, leads from observable stimulus field, $\{S_i\}$, to observable response, R. Valuation operator, $\mathbf{V}$, transforms observable stimuli, S_i, into subjective representations, ψ_i. Integration operator, $\mathbf{I}$, transforms subjective stimulus field, $\{\psi_i\}$, into implicit response, ρ. Action operator, $\mathbf{A}$, transforms implicit response, ρ, into observable response, R. (After N. H. Anderson, *Foundations of Information Integration Theory.* Academic Press, 1981.)

The goal has major influences in valuation. This goal influence holds even in early sensory links in the processing chain, in which motivational and attentional factors can influence the effective stimulus field. Goal influence increases in later links, as motivation and memory increase in importance. This is as it should be, for values are not in the stimuli, but are constructed by the organism.

Valuation may thus seem too fluid to pin down. An effective grip is possible, fortunately, by virtue of the unitization principle and $\mathbf{V} - \mathbf{I}$ independence.

The integration operator, $\mathbf{I}$, combines the several discrete psychological stimuli, ψ_i, into a unitary response, denoted by ρ. Integration thus represents multiple determination—the focus of IIT.

Multiple determination can be difficult to analyze. When even two factors are at work, each pushing in different directions, their combined effect is not generally predictable without quantitative theory. It is indeed a blessing of Nature, therefore, that some integration operators have simple algebraic forms. And this, as will be seen, carries the associated blessing of a foundation for theory of psychological measurement.

The action operator, $\mathbf{A}$, transforms the implicit response, ρ, into the observable response, R. This $\rho \to R$ distinction is clearest with simple sensations: ρ could be your private feeling of the loudness of a sound, for example, and R could be your rating of loudness on a 1–20 scale. As a more complex example, ρ could be a feeling of irritation with your spouse, and R could be a verbal retort, facial grimace, or sullen silence.

The three operators are portrayed as independent and successive in the diagram. **V–I** independence is a fundamental empirical finding, discussed in a later section. A more general diagram is necessary for many situation, but this simple version sets out the basic problem of the three unobservables.[2]

THE THREE UNOBSERVABLES

The most important entities in the integration diagram are unobservable. The integration operator is clearly unobservable, generally beyond the reach of introspection. The physical stimuli, S_i, are observable, but the corresponding psychological stimuli, ψ_i, are inside the body, often nonconscious. The implicit response, ρ, may be conscious, but it also is inside the body; the observable R may be severely biased as a measure of ρ (see, e.g., Figure 3.1). These three unobservables are the focus of IIT.

The problem of the three unobservables seems formidable. To illustrate, suppose you are told that some person is *level-headed* and *humorless*, and asked to rate that person on a 1–20 scale of likableness. In a simple theoretical model, you would have to evaluate each given trait to determine its separate likableness value, then integrate these separate values to arrive at an overall judgment of likableness. Almost the simplest integration rule is addition. In words:

$$\text{Liking} = \text{Level-headed} + \text{Humorless}.$$

More formally, in the notation of the integration diagram:

$$\rho_{\text{Liking}} = \psi_{\text{Level-headed}} + \psi_{\text{Humorless}}.$$

This addition rule may well be false, of course, but the problem is to test it. This might seem straightforward: Measure the three terms, ρ_{Liking}, $\psi_{\text{Level-headed}}$, and $\psi_{\text{Humorless}}$, and see if they add up.

Some form of this direct approach has been tried by various workers, but the test has generally failed. The three terms did not add up. Unfortunately, this outcome is ambiguous. The addition rule might still be true; the failure might result merely from a faulty measure of the response.

For what we measure is R, the observable rating, whereas the addition rule applies to the unobservable ρ. A valid test requires that R be a veridical measure of ρ. You may believe that your rating is a veridical measure of your feeling, but we cannot take your word for this. More definite evidence is needed. At the same time, veridical measures of the unobservable stimulus values, $\psi_{\text{Level-headed}}$ and $\psi_{\text{Humorless}}$, would also be needed.

This measurement problem is fundamental. Unless it can be solved, even the simple addition rule—wrong or right—will remain generally untestable. And if this simple rule cannot be tested, neither proved nor disproved, little hope appears for studying multiple determination of more complex form.

One reaction is that of behaviorism: Stick to the observables. Only unresolvable argument can come from trying to develop theories based on unobservable quantities. This behavioristic reaction has much to be said for it, but it foregoes all hope of developing a theory of everyday experience.

A second reaction is to try to divide and conquer. The integration problem can be avoided by using only a single stimulus. With no integration, ψ and ρ become equivalent. This effectively reduces the three unobservables to one, which would seem easier to handle. This reaction is embodied in classical psychophysics, which sought to measure simple sensations such as sweetness and loudness. Avoiding the integration problem seemed altogether sensible, but it turned out to be self-defeating (Chapter 9).

Fortunately, there is a way to solve the problem of the three unobservables. In fact, it turns out to be rather simple. This was the foundation for cognitive algebra, as indicated next.

COGNITIVE ALGEBRA
AND FUNCTIONAL MEASUREMENT

It is striking how simply the problem of the three unobservables can be solved. In the foregoing task of person cognition, manipulate the trait adjectives in a factorial design, plot the likableness judgments as a factorial graph, and inspect the pattern in this graph. A little overstated,

A pattern of parallelism solves the problem of the three unobservables.

Parallelism supports the hypothesized addition rule. At the same time, parallelism supports the working hypothesis that the observable R is a veridical measure of the unobservable ρ. An additional analysis yields the ψ values. All three unobservables thus have a solution. This *functional measurement methodology* is illustrated in the subsequent discussion of Figure 1.2.

It may seem surprising that so simple a methodology was not exploited much earlier. Conjectures about algebraic rules abound in psychology. Aristotle presented a ratio rule for fairness that is psychologically superior to a popular modern model (Chapter 7). Summation rules for warmth, loudness, and other sensations have often been suggested in psychophysics. In judgment–decision, degree of preference between two objects should obey a difference rule; expectancy for an outcome should multiply the value of the outcome. But virtually all these conjectures remained hopeful verbalisms, lacking mathematical backbone and psychological substance.

Several causes held back the discovery of cognitive algebra. First, the traditional approach to psychological measurement had to be inverted. Traditionally, measurement has been seen as a methodological preliminary to substantive inquiry, as with Thurstone's method of pair comparison scaling (Chapter 3). In the functional approach, in contrast, measurement is carried on as part of substantive study of the integration rule. Functional measurement is thus an organic component of empirical investigation.

A second obstacle to cognitive algebra concerned the rating response, which has been a mainstay of the experimental studies. The simplicity of parallelism analysis depends on the observable response being a veridical measure of the unobservable feeling. The rating method, however, has been generally condemned in other approaches to psychological measurement (Chapter 3). To obtain a veridical rating method requires certain experimental precautions, which, although not difficult in themselves, took time to establish. One contribution of IIT has been to put the rating method on a solid measurement-theoretical foundation, usable even with little children (Chapters 6 and 8).

A third obstacle to cognitive algebra was that many expected rules turned out to be incorrect, especially addition rules. Many tasks in which addition rules seemed indicated instead turned out to obey averaging rules. This markedly complicated the theoretical analysis, a matter discussed under *Parallelism and Nonparallelism* in Chapter 2.

A fourth obstacle was ways of thinking that have evolved to produce useful results while bypassing the fundamental problem of multiple determination. These ways of thinking came to define the nature of the field, but they were inherently inadequate for unified, general theory. Instead, they are a major cause of the fragmentation of the field.

Cognitive algebra represents a new way of thinking. This provides a unifying theme that runs through virtually all psychology.

COGNITIVE ALGEBRA IN PERSON COGNITION

Person cognition is central in everyday life. Interpersonal interactions dominate family life: wife–husband, child–parent, siblings, relatives, and family friends. In most work situations, also, interpersonal relations have substantial roles, usually routine, occasionally crucial. Political and social knowledge systems often revolve around person cognition, as in U. S. history and in current civic issues. Abstract issues may take on new life when personified. This centrality of person cognition is underscored in drama and the novel.

EXPERIMENTAL ANALYSIS

Personality Adjective Task. In this experimental task, subjects received a short list of adjectives that described a hypothetical person and judged this person on likableness. This task has ecological validity. Our jugments of persons are often influenced by what others say about them. Letters of reference, for example, typically consist of strings of adjectives cast into sentence form. This task also has cognitive validity; it taps into cognitive processes continually ingrained in everyday life. In other ways, also, this task is ideal for experimental analysis (see Chapter 4).

The adjective lists were constructed from the Row × Column *factorial design* illustrated for Subject F. F. in the left panel of Figure 1.2. Each of the nine data points represents F. F.'s judgment about likableness of one person, described by the two adjectives listed for the corresponding row and column (see also figure legend). Each subject judged a complete set of person descriptions on each of five successive days; this allowed separate analysis for each individual subject.

Theoretical Hypotheses. What should the results look like? A perennially popular hypothesis is that the adjectives interact with one another to form a unified conception of a person. Each adjective has various shades of meaning. Thus, *bold* may range from *courageous* to *foolhardy*; *unsophisticated* may range from *gullible* to *unspoiled*. The subject selects shades of meaning so that the adjectives in each description fit best together, thereby forming a person gestalt. This is one form of consistency principle, which asserts that subjects seek to maximize consistency in their perceptions of entities (Chapter 4).

This interaction hypothesis is called the *meaning change hypothesis* because it asserts that the effective meaning of each adjective will change, depending on which other adjectives it is combined with. Introspection endows this meaning change hypothesis with compelling face plausibility.

An alternative hypothesis is that the adjectives simply add without any interaction. This is a strong hypothesis; it assumes not only *meaning invariance*, but also specifies the exact form of the integration rule.

This addition hypothesis makes a strong prediction: The curves in both factorial graphs of Figure 1.2 should be parallel. The meaning change hypothesis, in contrast, predicts nonparallelism. Nonparallelism is not a strong prediction, of course, because its locus is not specified. This would depend on semantic and pragmatic relations among the adjectives in each description. The rationale for these two predictions will be given under the *Parallelism Theorem* of Chapter 2. Here it need only be noted that the addition hypothesis makes a much stronger prediction than the meaning change hypothesis.

A strong test between the two hypotheses is thus provided by this experiment. Visual inspection will show whether the data are parallel or nonparallel. More interesting, perhaps, is the potential for analysis of interaction and meaning change. The locus of any nonparallelism should reflect which adjectives interacted and the nature of their interaction.

RESULTS: THE THREE UNOBSERVABLES

The results supported meaning invariance and the addition hypothesis. This follows from the near-parallelism observable in Figure 1.2, both for Subject F. F. in

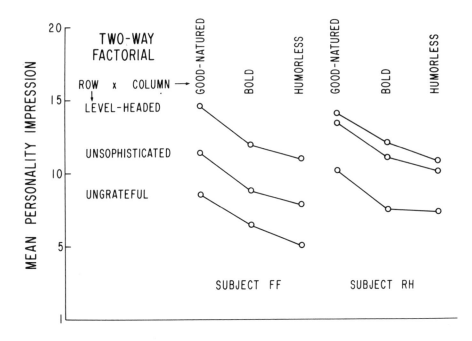

Figure 1.2. Parallelism pattern supports adding-type rule in person cognition. Subjects judged likableness of hypothetical persons described by two trait adjectives listed in the Row × Column design: row adjectives of *level-headed*, *unsophisticated*, and *ungrateful*; column adjectives of *good-natured*, *bold*, and *humorless*. Each of these 3 × 3 = 9 person descriptions corresponds to one data point. (Data averaged over third trait for simplicity; see Figure 1.4 of Anderson, 1982). (After N. H. Anderson, 1962, Application of an additive model to impression formation, *Science*, *138*, 817-818. Copyright 1962 by American Association for Advancement of Science. Adapted with permission.)

the left panel and for Subject R. H. in the right panel. This parallelism pattern solves the problem of the three unobservables. The implications of parallelism are discussed in the following three subsections, one for each unobservable.

Integration. Parallelism points to an adding-type rule. It is as though the subject assigns values to each adjective and adds them to determine the likableness of the person. Ten other subjects served in this experiment, with five additional sets of adjectives for stimulus generality. Similar parallelism was observed in all but three of the subjects. Only one of these, however, appeared to present any serious difficulty for the simple integration rule.

One qualification needs notice. The actual integration rule turns out to be averaging, not adding. Both can account for the parallelism observed here. The adding rule, however, fails in critical tests shown in Figures 2.4 and 4.4.

The disagreement of this result with introspection is notable. To phenomenology and introspection, the adjectives seem in dynamic interaction, each taking on different meanings depending on which other adjectives it is combined with. To phenomenology, person cognition appears to involve interactive organizing processes, in which the final outcome is a gestalt, not any simple sum of the separate adjectives.

But phenomenology was wrong. Functional measurement revealed a very different picture of person cognition. Valuation and integration both involve organizing processes, but their nature is very different from the claims of introspection. A theory of everyday cognition must thus be able to operate at a deeper level than phenomenology. This application of functional measurement showed that this must be done—and how it can be done.

Valuation. The second unobservable concerns the subjective values of the personality adjectives. Inspection of Figure 1.2 shows different values for the two subjects. For F. F., the equidistant vertical spacing of the three curves means that *unsophisticated* lies halfway between *ungrateful* and *level-headed* in likableness value. For R. H., however, *unsophisticated* is much closer to *level-headed* than to *ungrateful*. The values of the two subjects are thus essentially different. This value difference illustrates how parallelism analysis takes cognizance of the personal values of each individual subject.

Allowance for individual values is an obvious necessity for general theory of person cognition. We cannot predict F. F.'s judgments using R. H.'s values; these values are visibly different in Figure 1.2. Neither can we predict F. F.'s judgments if we have biased measurement of F. F.'s values. By providing valid measures of individual values, the theory of functional measurement serves an essential function in development of general theory.

Action. The last unobservable is the internal feeling of likableness. Our problem is that the observed response may not be a veridical measure of the internal feeling. This is the $R-\rho$ distinction, discussed in relation to Figure 1.1. The observed parallelism, however, could hardly happen by accident. Hence it is encouraging support for response veridicality, in accord with the parallelism theorem of Chapter 2.

This issue is more important than might appear. Parallelism depends squarely on response veridicality. An adding-type rule will not yield parallelism unless the response is veridical. And in fact, there was ample reason to distrust the rating method (see discussion of Figure 3.1). With some simple experimental procedures, however, the rating method can provide veridical scales in many diverse tasks. This matter is discussed in Chapter 3, which also summarizes the interlocking network of evidence that supports the rating method. The veridicality of the rating methodology developed in IIT is an essential and integral component of cognitive algebra.

IMPLICATIONS

Developing a cognitive theory of everyday life involves a number of problems that are pointed up by the outcome of the foregoing experiment. Some of these are discussed in the following subsections.

Meaning Invariance. A recurrent claim in psychology has been that stimuli change their meaning in context. In the personality adjective task, for example, the quality of *level-headed* would be different in a *bold* person than in a *humorless* person. This meaning change hypothesis has been strongly advocated in this task, and indeed as a general characteristic of cognitive integration.

Parallelism is strong evidence against meaning change. If adjectives did change meaning, taking on different values in different person descriptions, then parallelism would generally fail. The observed parallelism implies that value, and hence meaning, is the same in all descriptions. Within this task, therefore, each adjective has invariant meaning.

Phenomenologically, meaning change seems beyond doubt. Subjects and experimenters alike swear to it. But this phenomenological truth is a cognitive illusion. The methods of IIT can penetrate below phenomenology to reach a truer understanding of the nature of conscious experience. The present finding of meaning invariance has been extensively supported in other areas, most notably in psycholinguistics (Chapter 12).

Nomothetic–Idiographic Unity. The *nomothetic* approach seeks general laws that hold across individuals; the *idiographic* approach recognizes the uniqueness of each individual and seeks meaningfulness at an individual level. The nomothetic approach has been predominant in experimental analysis; its practitioners tend to consider it the only proper method of science. The idiographic approach has been predominant in personality psychology; its advocates tend to consider it the only meaningful psychological way. These two approaches generally have been in sharp disagreement.

IIT combines the nomothetic and idiographic approaches into a working unity. The valuation operation allows for individual differences, including the many heredity and environmental factors that make one individual different from another. Moreover, the valuation operation also allows variable motivation within the same individual over time.

The integration operation, in contrast, has some uniformity over individuals. The averaging rule, in particular, has proved ubiquitous. The idiographic nature of value is thus unified with the nomothetic generality of cognitive algebra. Indeed, this nomothetic algebra provides the foundation for true measurement of idiographic value.

Psychological Measurement. Cognitive algebra demonstrates the necessity for a theory of psychological measurement through the act of providing such a theory. This has been seen in the contrast between the personal values of F. F.

and R. H. in Figure 1.2. Parallelism analysis reveals this value difference by actually measuring the personal values. Without this measurement capability, the integration rule could not have been established.

No other theory has solved this measurement problem. Individual differences hardly have been denied, but cognitive psychology has massively ignored them. Nomothetic progress is possible by selecting amenable problems, as with testing typical single process hypotheses or assessing generality of interesting phenomena. Without idiographic measurement capability, however, general nomothetic theory is not possible.

Some idiographic progress is similarly possible by selecting qualitative problems that do not require measurement analysis. The two main idiographic approaches, however, have made limited progress. One approach relies on verbal reports, which can be seriously misleading, as with the meaning change hypothesis, and at best are fundamentally insufficient (e.g., Chapter 6). The other approach rests on crude forms of measurement that are inadequate for general theory of person cognition, as in popular trait theories and in attempts at measurement in judgment–decision theory (Chapter 10).

Expert Judgment. Person cognition is ubiquitous, not only in family and social life, but also in professional settings. For counselors and clinical psychologists, diplomats and politicians, chair of the board and leader of the street gang, person cognition is part of their way of life. Many consider themselves expert judges of others, but assessing the accuracy of such judgments is notoriously difficult. The present experiment does not assess accuracy, but it does reveal a strong cognitive illusion in self-report about such judgments. The common belief of expert judges, that their thinking is too subtle, contingent, and configural to be reduced to any simple formula, thus comes under question.

Other workers in judgment–decision have made a stronger argument, claiming that expert judgment can be mimicked by a linear, additive model for integration of information, and hence is not configural. Their evidence, however, suffers fatal defects—shown by the fact that the additive rule is generally false (see Chapter 10). Functional measurement methodology has instead found extensive evidence for the averaging rule, including findings of opposite effects that eliminate additive rules (e.g., Figures 10.2 and 10.3).

Cognitive Theory of Everyday Life. The cognitive illusion noted in the discussion of meaning invariance implies that phenomenology cannot be adequately understood at its own level and in its own terms. A deeper foundation is required. Much previous work, of course, has shown that people may be unaware of the effects of certain stimuli on their thought and action. The present result goes farther, however, for it shows that awareness may be subject to strong self-error.

This error of phenomenology points up a two-fold advantage of IIT. The success of the algebraic rule demonstrated the cognitive illusion and continued on to explain it (Chapter 4). Of more general importance, the algebraic rule provided capability for assaying the claims of phenomenology at their true worth. Theory centered on everyday life thus becomes possible.

Unified Theory. This experiment was the harbinger of cognitive algebra. It has been supported and extended in subsequent work. It has led to concepts and methods that have provided a fundamentally new approach to general cognitive theory. Difficult problems still had to be overcome, as discussed in Chapter 4, but they were overcome.

Previous approaches were inherently too narrow to provide a base for general theory. They could not measure personal value, nor could they solve the integration problem. Even the conceptual distinction between valuation and integration has been a frequent source of confusion.

IIT, in contrast, has solved the twin problems of valuation and integration. This solution is general: It applies not only in person cognition (Chapter 4), but also in attitude theory and attribution (Chapter 5) and social development (Chapter 6). This solution is unified: The same concepts and methods have been productive across all these areas. Further generality and unity appear in later chapters on other areas, including judgment–decision theory and psycholinguistics. Although person cognition initially appeared unpromising as a field for cognitive algebra, it has turned out to be exceptionally fruitful.

FUNCTIONAL PERSPECTIVE

Purposiveness entails a functional perspective, in which thought and action are viewed in relation to their functions in the organism's goal-oriented behavior. Functional perspectives are not new; they typify everyday experience. More formal attempts at functional theory have often appeared in psychology, but their attractiveness has not been matched by effectiveness.

Cognitive algebra, through its capabilities for analysis of values and goal-directedness, has contributed to effective functional analysis. A variety of implications are discussed in the following sections.

MEANING INVARIANCE

Meaning invariance is an important implication of cognitive algebra, first demonstrated in the experiment of Figure 1.2. To introspection, it seems overwhelmingly clear that the adjectives in a person description influence one another's meanings. Experimental analysis, however, demonstrated that the judgment obeyed an averaging rule—with invariant meanings of the adjectives.

Meaning invariance provides a novel opening for cognitive analysis. Measurement of values becomes potentially possible; their constancy means they can be pinned down. This potential can be actualized through cognitive algebra. Operating together, therefore, valuation–integration operations embody an idiographic–nomothetic harmony.

Meaning invariance is a general implication of cognitive algebra. Meaning invariance reappears in each domain covered in later empirical chapters, from moral development to language perception. In each domain, it reveals something about the nature of cognition and provides a base for further analysis.

V–I INDEPENDENCE

The independence of valuation and integration is a corollary implication of cognitive algebra. Valuation itself is sensitive to the dimension of judgment. The same adjective, *happy-go-lucky*, for example, may have quite different values depending on whether the goal is to judge likableness, say, or reliability of the person. Given this goal, however, the adjectives are insensitive to one another. They do not ordinarily interact. It follows that valuation and integration are independent operators, as represented in the integration diagram.

V–I independence is a significant finding about information processing. Information processing theories often run into trouble because the hypothesized processing stages appear to interact. At best, this makes interpretation difficult; at worst, it vitiates the presumed reality of the stages. Although **V–I** interaction can occur, as when some informers are sharply inconsistent, for example, a normal mode is independence. It follows that **V** and **I** are distinct operators, representing distinct cognitive processes.

V–I independence infirms some current views of information processing. Some theories of semantic memory, for example, represent meaning as a set of features. Integration, they would argue, is accomplished by conjunction of the sets of features activated by the separate adjectives. This view implies that valuation and integration would be essentially similar. Hence this view cannot be generally correct.

V–I independence has functional utility. Meaning invariance requires less processing than would meaning interaction. This is not mere insensitivity; the meanings are very sensitive to the goal through the valuation operation. Integration is analogously sensitive to the situation because the integrated output embodies multiple informers operative in the situation. Taken together, therefore, valuation and integration constitute an efficient and adaptive system.

V–I independence provides a key to cognitive analysis, for it represents a factoring of the two operations. This makes functional measurement possible. Because the integration operator is factorable from valuation operator, it can be used as the base and frame for measurement—measurement functional in its dependence on task and goal.

CONSCIOUS AND NONCONSCIOUS

The immediacy of experience gives the impression that everyday life is lived essentially at a conscious level. Our everyday experience seems understandable in its own terms of purposes and feelings, an impression powerfully reinforced by human proclivities for verbal rationalization.

Much the same view underlies most phenomenological approaches. Current theories of action, in particular, typically rest on the foundation assumption that a theory of everyday experience can be developed within its own framework and in its own terms. Conscious experience thus cu..stitutes what is to be explained—together with the means for explaining it.

Such phenomenological approaches exemplify the Tantalos metaphor with which this chapter began. Immediate experience continually promises a clear explanatory framework for thought and action. The idea that some way can yet be found to exploit this promise becomes an overwhelming temptation. Memory of the last failure dies away; hope kindles anew.

But nonconscious explanatory concepts are essential. Everyday experience is not comprehensible solely at its own level. A theory of everyday life must possess capability for analysis of nonconscious concepts. Nonconscious sensation, nonconscious affect, and nonconscious emotion must be accommodated within any general theory of everyday experience.

Nonconscious processes are well-known, of course, especially in perception. In the psychophysical study of the size−weight illusion of Figure 9.2, for example, the heaviness ψ value for the cue of size was beyond the grasp of consciousness. Such nonconscious processes do not, however, preclude self-contained theory operating at the level of immediate experience.

Meaning invariance, in contrast, does indicate an essential need for nonconscious concepts. The strong phenomenological belief in meaning change was a cognitive illusion; consciousness was in self-error. This cognitive illusion is not a matter of empirical fact, however, as is the size−weight illusion, but a matter of theory. To demonstrate this illusion required development of a theory that could analyze nonconscious determinants of conscious experience.

Conscious experience is a priceless source of information. People can tell us invaluable truths about their mental states. In cognitive theory of everyday life, most concepts, from loudness to blame, derive from conscious experience. Furthermore, veridical quantitative self-reports of these experiences can be obtained with functional measurement methodology.

At the same time, conscious report is sometimes obstinately wrong, as with the illusion of meaning change. Functional measurement makes it possible to analyze nonconscious determinants of conscious experience. In this way, it offers a validational criterion for conscious report. It provides a unique, bilevel analysis of conscious and nonconscious, a necessity for cognitive theory of everyday life.

MOTIVATION, AFFECT, AND EMOTION

Motivations, in a functional view, may be considered biosocial knowledge systems. Biologically, motivations are survival systems; they represent biological knowledge developed in the course of evolution. In human societies, such biological bases are amplified and transformed. Food preferences and sexual behavior, for example, are heavily overlaid by social learning. Other human motivations, related to achievement and morality, for example, are far removed from biological drives, embodying knowledge developed through social evolution and assimilated through social learning.

All motivations, however, have a similar function: They place values, positive or negative, on aspects of the environment. This one-dimensional, goal-oriented value representation is a vital simplification and opening for analysis.

A single goal, of course, typically involves multiple motivations, as with approach–avoidance conflict. Understanding motivation thus involves problems of multiple determination and measurement of coactive values.

Integration analysis provides a new approach to motivation. Under certain conditions, the two problems of multiple determination and value measurement can be solved. Values represent motivation in a functional mode, as organism–goal interaction, or as drive–incentive interaction in traditional learning theory. Value measurement furnishes a rigorous approach to the teleological problem of defining motivation in terms of its consequences. Moreover, diverse kinds of motivation, both biological and social, can be treated jointly in comparable terms.

Affect is information. Quality and intensity of affect guide action. Biological examples appear in sensory systems. Taste is affective information to guide ingestion; temperature senses provide affective information that helps to maintain the internal environment. Social affects include moral feelings of right and shame and virtues of pride and submission, which help stabilize society and maintain the individual within society. Play and sex involve more complex affective systems that have informational and adaptive functions.

In this informational view, affect is an organic part of cognition. This view is reinforced by two integration considerations, relating to operating memory and long-term memory, respectively. Affect in operating memory depends generally on integration of nonaffective, "cognitive" factors, such as expectancy or social context. What reaches consciousness is an integrated unity. Such cognitive–affective reactions may then be stored in long-term knowledge systems. Social affects, in particular, thus depend on knowledge systems that include affect integrated into cognition.

Mainstream cognitive psychology has largely passed over affect, considering it qualitatively different from cognition. This narrowness has begun to be recognized, but it has constricted the conceptual framework. Affect cannot be tacked on at the end; it must be incorporated from the beginning. Cognitive theory of everyday life must give affect a central role. Cognitive algebra does this in fields as far apart as morality, psychophysics, and memory (see Chapters 7, 9, and 11).

Emotion is motivation with affect. This informational view reverses the popular arousal theories which claim nonaffective, "cognitive" information is essential to label and define the phenomenal quality of emotional experience. Far from requiring information to specify its own quality, affective experience constitutes information that is utilized in goal-oriented thought and action. In its simplest form, this informational function is analogous to that of sensory experience and makes equal biological sense.

Discussions of emotion have often stressed their disorganizing effects, in anger and panic reactions, for example, as though these were wholly irrational. This partial truth neglects the biosocial heuristic. A number of writers have indeed argued that emotions have useful, organizing roles, and greater attention has lately been given to positive emotions. A similar view is adopted here, but with a shift in focus. The most common focus has been taxonomic, seeking to define a set of basic emotions, especially in terms of biological need systems. The present focus is on multiple determination. Problems of motivation integration provide a new base for theory development.

The need for an integrationist base for emotion theory is underscored by the consideration that emotions cannot be analyzed solely in their own terms. Nonemotional determinants are integrated into emotional reactions. Phobic reactions, for example, may depend on nearness, expectancy, and even verbal labels, determinants that are themselves nonemotional. The same holds for hope and envy, two important emotions of everyday life. "Emotion" and "cognition" cannot be well separated. General theory must be able to treat both in a unified way.

BIOSOCIAL HEURISTIC

The nature of human thought and action depends jointly on their biological foundation and on their social development. The human biosocial inheritance includes an array of motivational systems, ranging from ingestion and affection to perceptual, intellectual, and moral, that is efficient and adaptable. This adaptability may be seen in the continuing evolution of society and especially in its continuous reconstruction from new-born organisms.

Society, like biology, is concerned with survival. It has done remarkably well, on the whole, considering the unpromising origins and small size of the human brain. One key to success, as various writers have noted, lies in general purpose processes that can determine rough-and-ready action in diverse situations. A small brain can thus do reasonably well with simple means in many situations, even though it may do poorly in a few. These considerations reflect the *biosocial heuristic* for understanding behavior (Anderson, 1991a).

Social stereotypes furnish an apt application of the biosocial heuristic. Social stereotypes, in the present view, are adaptive knowledge systems that facilitate functioning in varied social situations. Stereotypes have long had a bad name as irrational and pernicious, almost by definition, because they were studied in relation to ethnic prejudice. That stereotypes are often superficial and inaccurate is certainly true, but they also furnish social stability. Society could not exist if its members did not have capabilities for forming and using stereotypes. To treat them as irrational and pernicious stems from lack of appreciation of the biosocial heuristic (Chapter 5).

The concept of *biases* in judgment–decision theory makes the same point. The standard normative approach prescribes optimal behavior, relative to which actual judgment–decision generally falls short; these shortcomings are considered biases, faults, and flaws of the organism. Instead, they may be optimal relative to limited processing capacities of a small brain. The faults and flaws seem instead to be in normative theory, which obstructs the development of functional theory (Chapter 10).

Despite its generality, the biosocial heuristic can be effective. It brings out the cognitive significance of affect and emotion, already discussed. It agrees with a functional conception of memory, considered later. In these and other ways, it leads to better appreciation of functioning cognition.

UNITIZATION PRINCIPLE

Cognitive algebra can treat complex stimuli as unitary. Exact theory is thus possible at a molar level, independent of more molecular structure of processing. Unitization potentiates self-sufficient theory of everyday cognition.

In the attitude experiment of Figure 5.1, for example, the stimuli were biographical paragraphs about American presidents, who were judged on statesmanship. Valuation of each paragraph involved a chain of processing that began with a distribution of light energy on the retina and continued with identification of these retinal stimuli as words and sentences, understanding the content of each sentence, evaluating its implications relative to the assigned goal, and integrating across the several sentences in each paragraph. The end result of this extended chain of processing was representable as a single number: the value of the paragraph. This value constituted a complete and exact summary of all the processing. This value is thus a molar unit. This principle of molar unitization holds generally, from intuitive physics (Chapter 8) to language processing (Chapter 12).

Unitization relates to $\mathbf{V}-\mathbf{I}$ independence. In an alternative view, interaction would occur continuously along the processing chain from stimulus to response. In this flux, units would not be well defined. Valuation and integration would not be factorable, perhaps not distinct. Cognitive algebra thus affirms the principle of molar unitization and goes further to define and measure molar units.

Moreover, **V–I** independence and the unitization principle may still apply when no simple algebraic rule holds. On this basis, theoretical analysis can proceed at intermediate levels of information processing without having to await explication of prior levels.

Unitization is a key to cognitive theory of everyday experience. The diverse concepts of everyday experience, from psychophysical sensation to social affect, are potential concepts of scientific theory. A self-sufficient theory of everyday cognition is potentially attainable. Cognitive algebra helps convert this potential into actuality.[3]

Unitization can also help analyze more molecular processing: It provides boundary conditions that such processing must obey. Any molecular theory of valuation processing must agree with the molar values determinable with functional measurement. Similarly, any molecular theory of integration must agree with the rules established in cognitive algebra. Such boundary conditions can provide a unique window into the mind.

CONSTRUCTION PRINCIPLE

That cognition is constructive is an explicit premise of IIT. The construction principle applies to each operator—valuation, integration, and action—in the integration diagram of Figure 1.1.

The constructive nature of integration is self-evident: To combine multiple determinants into a unitary response *is* construction. The ubiquity of multiple determination is one sign of the importance of the construction principle.

The constructive nature of valuation is shown by its dependence on the goal as well as on the stimulus. Value is not a constant property of the stimulus, but a variable that depends on the operative goal. Treating value as a variable is necessary for handling motivational states, in particular. These are primary determinants of value, but they change with time and circumstance.

Many values, of course, also involve integration. Indeed, molar values generally result from chains of more molecular **V–I→V–I→** ... operations. In such processing chains, the integrated output of one link constitutes an input value for the next link. Essentially the same point appeared in the preceding discussion of unitization.

The constructive nature of action appears most clearly in goal dynamics, as in constructing a plan to attain some goal. But even the rating response, beneath its simplicity, involves a rather sophisticated construction of correspondence between unobservable ρ and observable R (Chapter 3).

The construction principle is also prominent in assemblage of operating memory, discussed in following sections. Overall, the construction principle goes hand in hand with the functional perspective. Purposive behavior is adaptive behavior. Adaptive behavior requires construction as the organism utilizes its limited capabilities to function in diverse situations.

FUNCTIONAL MEMORY

The functional perspective entails a corresponding conception of memory, that is, memory as it functions in everyday life. One function of memory lies in construction of values relative to the operative goal. Another function lies in the development of knowledge systems that store experience for later use in goal-directed thought and action.

Traditionally, memory is reproductive—epitomized as recall. This reproductive conception of memory has seemed almost its definition. Associated with this has been the reliance on accuracy measures, whose great usefulness has reinforced the reproductive conceptualization. But reproductive memory is insufficient, often barely relevant to memory function in everyday life.

The need for something more than reproductive memory was brought home in an early experiment on person memory. In this study, a hypothetical person was described by a list of trait adjectives; the subject judged overall likableness of the person and also recalled the adjectives. These two tasks are quite different: Recall pertains to the separate adjectives, whereas the person judgment involves an integration of all the adjectives into a unitary response.

According to the *verbal memory hypothesis*, recall probabilities would measure importance in the person judgment. If the initial adjectives were more important, for example, a primacy effect would be expected both in recall and in person judgment. This assumption that thought and action are determined by what is recalled from the given stimulus materials has been one base for the traditional reproductive conception of memory.

The results, however, revealed the operation of a person memory distinct from the verbal memory. Relevant meaning about the person was extracted from each adjective informer as it was received, and this meaning was integrated into a cumulative, on-line memory of the person. Once processed, the adjective was no longer needed, and in fact was forgotten or stored in a different memory. This was the origin of the *functional memory representation*.

Traditional, reproductive memory theory says little about memory function in everyday thought and action; reproduction of given stimulus materials is not the normal function of memory. Everyday memory typically deals with entities such as persons, objects, and events. Entity memory generally depends on integration of meanings or implications of multiple informers. These meanings are not usually in the stimulus informers per se. Instead, they arise from valuation of those informers relative to operative goals. Traditional memory theory, having virtually no place for goal-directed valuation—or integration—has limited relevance to these primary memory functions.

Functional memory requires a new way of thinking. Its analysis requires new kinds of experimental tasks, tasks that embody the valuation and integration operations of everyday judgment–decision. This and other issues of functional memory are taken up in Chapter 11.

SCHEMAS

Algebraic integration rules are schemas. They exhibit the primary characteristic of schemas, namely, organization that may be applied to more or less complex stimulus fields. As schemas, they go deeper than the algebraic form to emphasize qualitative aspects of the mental model of the task and goal at hand. This qualitative aspect appears more explicitly in specific schemas: the behavior–motivation–ability schemas of Chapter 5, for example, the blame schema of Chapter 6, the expectancy–value schema of Chapter 10, and especially the time–speed–distance schemas of Chapter 8.

Algebraic integration schemas are a singular exception to the vagueness of current schema formulations. Schema concepts flourished in the 1970s as psychologists gave greater attention to questions of organization. Mostly, however, the term *schema* was presented as an explanation, whereas it was what needed to be explained. Although the concept of schema pointed to important problems, analytical capabilities were lacking. Most formulations remain stuck little ahead of where they started. IIT, in contrast, has established exact structure of schemas in several domains.

This point may be illustrated with the concept of default values for missing information. For example, attributing causal responsibility for some harmful action depends not only on the harmfulness of the action, but also on the intention of the actor and/or situational constraints. If these latter factors are unknown, some value may be imputed to them in making the causal attribution. Imputation processes are important because pertinent information is often missing in everyday judgment–decision.

The concept of default values claimed to handle this problem of missing information. Schemas were considered to have *slots*, corresponding to relevant variables, filled with *default values* to be used when needed information was missing. This idea of slot-and-default value became almost a defining property of schemas in some prominent formulations.

Cognitive algebra furnishes an ideal proving ground for formulations based on slot-and-default value. The stimulus variables of any algebraic rule correspond to the slots; the default value is what should be used when information about some variable is not specified. This problem of missing information has been extensively studied in IIT.

The experimental data, however, disagree with the concept of slot-and-default value. People often do not impute any value to an unspecified variable. When they do, the value might be nonconstant, dependent on the situation. The concept of slot-and-default value cannot handle such results (e.g., Chapter 7).

In retrospect, it is clear that the slot-and-default value formulations were mainly armchair analogies to computer programs, without serious foundation in psychological science. Schema concepts need to be substantially more flexible to represent thought and action. Cognitive algebra has this flexibility.

ASSEMBLAGE

Thought and action typically require assemblage of diverse contents into an operating memory for the task at hand. Assemblage is explicit in the constructive nature of valuation and inherent in the concept of integration. These are only aspects of operating memory, however, which will generally include representations of goals, some mental model of the task, together with activated background knowledge that is utilized in thought and action. Operating memory thus consists of heterogeneous contents assembled and joined together in relation to operative goal directions—qualitative integration, in other words, to which the term *assemblage* may be appropriately applied.

The concept of assemblage unifies the construction principle and functional memory. The necessity for a concept of assemblage appears in the multiplicity of possible goals. Assemblage relates the mass of background knowledge to the active operating memory that represents momentary purposiveness. Assemblage goes beyond the reproductive conception of memory retrieval to the functional role of memory in constructive processes.[4]

KNOWLEDGE SYSTEMS

A concept of knowledge system, more general than schema, is also needed to represent organization in memory. Some properties of knowledge systems may be illustrated with four concepts taken from the social–personality domain: attitudes, roles, traits, and persons.

In attitude theory, IIT distinguishes *attitude* as a knowledge system from *attitudinal responses*, which are functional manifestations of that knowledge system in thought and action. In the study of attitudes toward U. S. presidents of Figure 5.1, for example, the knowledge system about any president will contain information from history courses and general reading, additional information given in the experiment, as well as affective-valuational information relating to ideals for presidents and social–political issues. This knowledge system is processed to help construct specific attitudinal responses, as with the judgment of statesmanship. Attitude as knowledge system thus differs qualitatively from attitudinal response.

Most attitude theories, in contrast, have defined attitude as a one-dimensional evaluative reaction. This is only an attitudinal response, in IIT, and indeed only one class thereof. Such attitudinal responses should not be confused with attitudes as knowledge systems, which may subserve many different attitudinal responses.

This view also clarifies the common finding of low correlations between attitudes and behavior, which has been perplexing to traditional theories. This perplexity reflects a too-narrow concept of attitude. To obtain high correlation would require the same one-dimensional measure of attitude to be a good predictor in many different situations. As a knowledge system, however, an attitude can function adaptively in many situations. Almost necessarily, therefore, any one-dimensional index of attitude will yield low correlation because behavior depends also on components of the knowledge system whose activation in operating memory reflects situational specifics.

Roles are knowledge systems organized for action. For many social roles, the main content consists of prescriptions for speech and behavior appropriate to particular situations. In the present functional view, role enactments on particular occasions obey the construction principle. As with attitudes, accordingly, a qualitative distinction is needed between roles as knowledge systems and particular role enactments subserved by that knowledge system.

It may seem odd to consider traits such as honesty, perseverance, and sociability as knowledge systems. A traditional conception, especially in trait theories of personality, treats traits as one-dimensional properties of the person much as a physical object may be specified by its mass, velocity, temperature, and so on. In the present functional view, in contrast, traits represent general organization of personal functioning.

A long-standing embarrassment of trait theories of personality is that traits have low correlations with behavior. This embarrassment stems from a too-narrow conception of *trait*, exactly like that just discussed for attitudes.

The trait of honesty, for example, is a functional system that helps guide behavior in diverse social situations. Reducing this system to a one-dimensional trait score can sometimes have practical usefulness. This score, however, should not be confused with the underlying knowledge system.

Traits as knowledge systems include situational information for social functioning. Honesty is not absolute; acceptable and even meritorious standards of dishonesty depend on the situation. Conflicts of honesty are not uncommon and need to be resolved by reference to strengths of particular obligations. It is such knowledge systems that constitute honesty and other personal traits.[5]

Knowledge systems reach a culmination in *person cognition*. Our memory representation of a particular person includes both generic and particular elements organized in ways that partially embody perceived regularities in that person's behavior. The behavior–motivation–ability schemas of Chapter 5 and other generic schemas may thus become particularized into the knowledge systems that constitute our memory of a person. Similar general–particular processes hold for trait, role, and attitude components of memory of individual persons.

Specific interactions with the person, imagined or actual, involve assemblage that takes account of the immediate goal and situation. This is an operating complex that includes not only contributions from specific person memory, but also from general person cognition, as well as from nonpersonal knowledge systems (e.g., Chapters 10 and 11).

From these four examples, the concept of knowledge system may seem too flexible and too complex to be useful. This flexible complexity, however, reflects cognitive reality. It is preferable to recognize this complexity in the conceptual framework than to obscure or deny it, as in traditional theories of attitudes and personality traits.

Knowledge systems and assemblage involve qualitative integration. Although qualitative integration represents a major incompleteness in IIT, cognitive algebra can make useful contributions. Reflected in the value representation of purposiveness, much qualitative integration leads to quantitative response. In turn, these quantitative responses can furnish helpful clues and tracers for analysis of qualitative structure. Some qualitative, conceptual implications of cognitive algebra are itemized in the final section of this book, *Beyond Cognitive Algebra.*

STRATEGY OF THEORY CONSTRUCTION

Theory construction in information integration theory follows a strategy that may be described as inductive and molar. This inductive, molar strategy gives the theory a different character from the most popular alternatives, as noted in the following sections.

MOLAR THEORY AND MICRO THEORY

The functional perspective adopted in IIT leads naturally to a molar approach. Goals, as represented in phenomenology, are themselves molar. It is desirable to represent these concepts at their own level—without necessary concern for the complex chains of processing that underlie them.

Cognitive algebra has this molar capability, as noted in the earlier discussions of molar unitization and **V–I** independence. Moreover, cognitive algebra provides validational criteria to establish itself. A self-sufficient theoretical framework for phenomenology thus becomes available.

A parallel may be seen in thermodynamics. Thermodynamics is a self-sufficient theory, independent of an explanatory base in statistical mechanics. Of course, cognitive algebra does not begin to compare with the grandeur of thermodynamics, but it does claim to be self-sufficient at a molar level. This claim rests on an extensive base of experimental analysis.

Molecular theories, or micro theories, seek some primitive level of elements, typically hypothetical, as a foundation for theory. Micro strategy appears in the classical associationist views and remains overwhelmingly popular today. Micro strategy has done well in physics and even in physiology. In social science, however, its reductionist promise remains unfulfilled.

Given the validity of the averaging rule, for example, it is not difficult to hypothesize micro entities that exhibit an averaging process, and thereby purport to "explain" averaging. Several such micro hypotheses are noted in Chapter 2. Such exercises are specious as explanations, however, until they have been expanded into interlocking theory. Until then, the effective direction of explanation is just the reverse: from known to unknown, that is, from macro to micro. Overtly or covertly, it is the macro results that determine the micro assumptions.

Only by finessing the micro level was it possible to establish cognitive algebra. Now these algebraic rules provide a base and frame for self-sufficient theory at the functional level of everyday experience.

IIT does not disregard micro approaches. It places high importance on more molecular processes in mental models and assemblage. It argues for a functional conception of memory distributed through diverse knowledge systems. In conjunction therewith, it assumes parallel processing as a means of similarity assessment in the valuation operation.

Moreover, cognitive algebra can help micro theories by providing boundary conditions for their development. One boundary condition is the algebraic structure of the averaging model, just discussed. Meaning invariance, similarly, is a boundary condition of ramified importance.

GENERAL THEORY AND MINI–THEORY

Theory construction in IIT contrasts in a different way with another alternative, which may be called mini-theory strategy. Although mini-theories are often molar, they are not general but specific, focused on particular issues. The attractiveness and undoubted usefulness of mini-theory strategy needs to be balanced against serious shortcomings.

A common complaint about mini-theories is lack of development; their expansion is often just complication. It is often easy to postulate concepts and processes that ostensibly account for most known results on particular issues. Typically, however, further tests run into difficulties that require additional assumption or qualification. Such complications multiply, with concomitant decrease in theoretical scope and power.

A major reservation about mini-theories is their responsibility for the compartmentalization and fragmentation that characterize contemporary psychology. Except for occasional fads, each mini-theory typically has a mini-group of proponents, who have minimal interaction with other mini-theories.

This fragmentation is pervasive. Curiously, it is more or less accepted as the normal state of affairs. This should not be. A shift in strategy of theory construction is needed. This requires substantial change in the conceptual framework that currently guides research.

A major reason for fragmentation and limited progress may be seen in the character of most mini-theories. Without realizing it, they have usually been concerned with determinants of values and with valuation processes in particular tasks. Mini-theories sometimes address integration, it is true, but for this they have generally been inadequate. Indeed, they typically become confused from confounding the concepts of valuation and integration, as in many cognitive consistency theories. Mini-theories of valuation are important, but order and law will continue elusive with standard strategy because of the innumerable determinants of value.

Integration theory often seems strange, almost atheoretical, to workers accustomed to standard mini-theories. Concepts and processes of mini-theories usually seem psychologically real and pregnant, having concrete situational meaning. This phenomenal reality seems lacking in such trans-situational concepts as informer, value, and integration used in IIT.

A more general theory, however, can be at once simpler and more powerful than special theories. Examples include the analysis of schemas, previously mentioned, the cognitive consistency theories discussed in Chapter 4, developmental processes in knowledge of the external world (Chapter 8), grounded cognitive framework for judgment–decision (Chapter 10), and contextual interaction in psycholinguistics (Chapter 12). In all these cases, the concepts and methods of IIT were effective with simple analyses.

Mini-theories are important and essential. They are at their best when exploring new phenomena, an activity that underlies the vitality and fascination of current psychological research. They also have the great merit of seeking careful, detailed explication of particular tasks rather than vague generalities. What is needed is a shift in strategy, in which the mini-theory trees do not obscure the forest of general theory.

INDUCTIVE STRATEGY AND DEDUCTIVE STRATEGY

In the inductive mode of theory construction, generalizations are sought as emergents from experimental analysis. The deductive mode, in contrast, begins with postulates and seeks to test discriminative predictions therefrom. Both modes are important, and both appear in any scientific inquiry.

It makes a big difference, however, which mode is taken as primary. The inductive mode is primary in IIT, whereas the deductive mode is primary in most mini-theory and micro approaches. Many of the foregoing differences between IIT and these two approaches stem from this inductive–deductive orientation.

This difference may be illustrated with cognitive algebra, as with the averaging model at issue in the experiment of Figure 1.2. In a narrow sense, this parallelism test of the model might seem a fine example of the classical hypothetico-deductive strategy. In actuality, matters were considerably more complicated.

Altogether, seven basic theoretical issues had to be resolved to put the averaging model on firm ground, as will be detailed in Chapter 4.

The analyses of Chapter 4 did involve essential deductive elements, but this should not obscure the primarily inductive nature of this investigation. The solidity of the theoretical structure depends on the network of results, especially as concerns the basic issue of response measurement, covered in Chapter 3. The empirical procedures developed for response measurement are thus an essential component of the theory. The question of where the averaging model holds, moreover, remains primarily a question of empirical generalization.

Cognitive algebra rests on empirical demonstrations of algebraic rules common across diverse domains. Its validity resides in these experimental analyses, not in hypotheses or axioms, but distributed through the empirico–theoretical network. As said previously (Anderson, 1981a, pp. 82-83):

> Many psychological theories claim to operate in the deductive mode. It is often considered to be the ideal, sometimes the only, truly scientific way of thinking. Workers in the deductive mode often have difficulty comprehending inductive theory; to them, it appears formless and uncertain. To workers in the inductive mode, however, the deductive mode appears simplistic, not to say specious, beyond the local level. Among other reasons, what passes for deductive theory in psychology is typically an awkward form of inductive theory.

> For the plain fact is that deductive theories are rarely abandoned when their deductions fail. Instead, they are modified, first in their auxiliary simplifying assumptions, later in their basic conceptual assumptions. Deductive theories in psychology typically exhibit a short, initial period of deductive flourish, followed by slow, grudging assimilation of inductive change. Open acceptance of a more inductive approach as a basic research orientation would seem developmentally more truthful, not to say more efficient.

> Inductive theory views science not as formalized knowledge, but as living inquiry. It recognizes and incorporates background thinking and experimental lore, including pesky problems of apparatus and organism, that are obscured or lost in deductive formalizations. And is is more open to nature, which continually reveals new riches to surprise and delight her students.

The prominence of hypothetico-deductive strategy stems in large part from its utility in physical science. In social science, however, hypothetico-deductive strategy has done poorly, as is illustrated with mini-theories. The lack of cumulative progress, noted by various writers, is a consequence of adopting a strategy that is inappropriate to the nature of the phenomena.

The effectiveness of the inductive approach will be demonstrated by its applications across diverse fields of psychology, generally considered quite different and unrelated, in the later empirical chapters. This effectiveness depended substantially on cognitive algebra and functional measurement, which have transformed the axiom of purposiveness into a working principle. With these concepts and methods, the data often speak for themselves. This is more effective than the hypothesis testing typical of mini-theories and micro approaches. By seeking order at the level of integration, it was possible to avoid bogging down in the swamp of multiple determinants of valuation.

INTERNAL WORLD AND EXTERNAL WORLD

Psychology is unique in its concern with an inner world distinct from the external world studied in other sciences, such as physics and physiology. The existence of this inner world is self-evident in conscious experience, but it has resisted analysis.

IIT is founded on structure in the inner world. Internal structure provides the base and frame for theory construction. Most other theories, in contrast, place essential reliance on the external world. Some even deny meaningfulness or relevance to the internal world. This internal–external difference leads to qualitative differences in the nature of theory and direction of inquiry.

Reliance on the external world is certainly sensible. Attempts to exploit the internal world through introspection have repeatedly been disappointing, as noted in the Tantalos metaphor at the beginning of this chapter. Moreover, the internal world has a biological function of survival in the external world, and so should mirror—and be mirrored in—its structure.

This is clear in visual perception. We take for granted that our visual world is a replica of the external world. Indeed, some theories, modern as well as ancient, consider visual perception to be direct apprehension of the external world. This approach failed, however, in measuring simple psychophysical sensations. Integration psychophysics, in contrast, was able to measure sensation in the internal world (Chapter 9).

Reliance on the external world appears everywhere in psychology. Memory, for example, has virtually been defined in terms of the external standard of accuracy of reproduction of given stimulus materials. This reliance on the external world, although extremely useful for certain purposes, has quite obscured the functional character of memory in thought and action (see *Functional Memory* above and in Chapter 11).

A different kind of reliance on the external world appears in the dominant normative orientation in judgment–decision theory. There thought and action are conceptualized in a framework of optimal behavior—defined by objective standards in the external world. This normative approach is contradicted by cognitive algebra, which differs qualitatively from normative algebra. The prime example is the averaging model, which yields a nonprobabilistic disproof of the sure-thing axiom, once considered a cornerstone for judgment–decision theory (Chapter 10). The decision averaging model, moreover, has proved superior to the analogous normative Bayesian decision model.

A similar case history appears in developmental analysis of intuitive physics. Here the external world sets a standard in the form of physical laws of simple algebraic form. These laws control reinforcement in the external world of daily experience, so it was an attractive assumption that children would learn them. This isomorphism assumption proved a false alley. Intuitive physics does obey algebraic rules, but these cognitive rules often differ from those of the external physical world (Chapter 8).

This argument of nonisomorphism is pertinent to learning theories, from operant to connectionist, that rely on external reinforcement. The ability of organisms to learn something about reinforcement structure in the external world has furnished valuable leverage for psychological analysis. This is not sufficient, however, as shown by the cited examples of nonisomorphic rules from cognitive algebra. And regardless of cognitive algebra, the insufficiency of traditional memory theory follows simply from recognition of memory function in everyday life.

A priori, reliance on internal structure seems unattractive. Formidable difficulties appeared in the problem of the three unobservables of Figure 1.1. In this diagram, internal structure has three aspects, one corresponding to each unobservable. Two are metric structures, for the stimulus variables and for the response; the third is qualitative structure of the integration function. A divide-and-conquer strategy naturally seems more sensible than trying to solve all three unobservables together. As it happened, divide-and-conquer did not solve even one unobservable. Instead, it misdirected the path of inquiry.

The potential of internal structure as a foundation for theory was illustrated in the parallelism theorem and its empirical application in Figure 1.2. Internal structure of additivity allows a simple solution to all three unobservables together. More important, as it turned out, this method of structural analysis also holds for the general averaging rule, despite the real difficulties in the theoretical development (see *Parallelism and Nonparallelism* in Chapter 2).

In the end, cognitive algebra was found to be a general characteristic of thought and action. This internal algebraic structure provided a base and frame for a general functional theory of cognition.

PHENOMENOLOGY

Cognitive algebra provides a base for self-sufficient theory of phenomenology of everyday life. Self-sufficient theory is not obviously attainable, for multiple levels or stages are usually operative. In the study of person cognition of Figure 1.2, for example, the valuation process for each single adjective represents an intricate chain that begins with sensory stimulation, leads on to identification of letter, word, and lexical meaning, to goal-directed similarity comparisons with distributed memory for constructing task-relevant values, to incorporation in an operating memory, and perhaps to further interaction in the integration process. This partial view of the chain indicates the terrible complexity of complete process analysis of valuation, let alone integration and action.

Within this flux of processing, cognitive algebra provides an Archimedean fulcrum of stability. No matter how intricate the chain of valuation, the net result is typically a single value, as discussed under unitization. The validity and usefulness of this unitization principle rest heavily on the twin findings of meaning invariance and **V**–**I** independence in cognitive algebra.

The development of cognitive algebra has relied heavily on phenomenology. The terms or concepts of the algebraic rules studied so far have mostly been taken from everyday experience. The idea of algebraic rules of cognition has a similar origin in everyday thinking. In both respects, phenomenology provided a priceless beginning.[6]

Phenomenology is not by itself a sufficient base for theory. Nonconscious concepts are essential. Moreover, phenomenology can make stubborn errors, as in the meaning change controversy and in certain forms of ego defense.

Cognitive algebra can remedy both shortcomings of phenomenology. Algebraic structure constitutes a criterion to assay and refine ideas and concepts of everyday experience. Capitalizing on phenomenology in this manner seems more effective in many ways than seeking a primitive micro level of explanation. Moreover, cognitive algebra explicitly incorporates a functional perspective with its focus on the purposiveness of everyday thought and action.

UNIFIED THEORY

IIT aims to develop a unified, general theory that treats everyday experience in something like its own terms. The terrain for investigation is broad: Sensory–perceptual reactions that direct our movements in the world around us; biosocial motivations that guide our approach–avoidance; memory functions that incorporate learning from experience; judgment–decision capabilities utilized in our thought and action; and moral–social knowledge systems that operate in our interactions with other persons. Of special significance are the feelings, strivings, thoughts, skills, and actions that characterize that central entity, our self.

The potential for unification lies in purposiveness. To actualize this potential requires resolution of two fundamental problems: measurement and multiple determination. The concept of value, as noted in the introduction, provides a basic simplification for analysis of purposiveness. Values differ across persons, however, so general theory must provide capability for measurement of personal values. The companion problem of multiple determination arises because any one goal typically involves multiple values.

By a blessing of Nature, the two problems can be solved jointly with cognitive algebra. Cognitive algebra is general, applying across nearly all domains of psychology. It appears to be a biosocial universal. Cognitive algebra is unified, for the same concepts and methods apply in all these domains.

An integration approach involves a new way of thinking that is sometimes hard to comprehend from traditional perspectives. This new way of thinking is epitomized in the present approach to multiple determination and psychological measurement, discussed further in Chapter 3. This way of thinking ramifies through all aspects of inquiry, from choice of experimental question, task, response measure, and design, from conceptions of memory, affect, and knowledge systems, to the structure of theory itself. Some aspects of this new way of thinking have been indicated in this chapter and will be amplified in later chapters. Indeed, each later chapter revolves around a clash between old and new ways of thinking.[7]

The contributions of this work are modest, but they are real. Beyond the establishment of exact algebraic laws of cognition, this approach also yields conceptual implications for qualitative cognition (see *Beyond Cognitive Algebra* at end of Chapter 13). This work, it seems fair to say, constitutes a good beginning on unified theory of everyday cognition.

NOTES

Two source books on the theory of information integration are the *Foundations* and *Methods* volumes (Anderson, 1981a, 1982). More recent developments by a number of workers are summarized in three *Contributions* volumes (Anderson, 1991b,c,d), respectively reviewed by Sjöberg (1994), Pratkanis (1994), and Bogartz (1994).

1. Purposiveness deserves the status of an axiom since it has been considered self-evident even by most of those who disown it theoretically. Although the main lines of psychological science have shunned purposiveness, many writers have attempted to develop formulations based on goal concepts and functional perspectives. Among these are the neglected Darwinian purposive behaviorism of McDougall (e.g., 1928; see also Tolman, 1959) and a variety of functional perspectives stemming from James and Dewey, also based on Darwinian ideas. Comparison of IIT with these formulations is beyond the scope of this book; useful references are Boring (1950), Vygotsky (1978), McGuire (1983), Bandura (1986), Frese and Sabini (1985), and Pervin (1989).

All the concepts of this chapter have been considered by other writers. The construction principle, for example, was primary in the formulation of Helmholtz. The complex lineage of ideas in emotion theory is covered in the learned volume of Mandler (1984). To attempt to relate the manifold indebtedness of the present discussion to this and other previous work would require at least another volume. The present treatment aims to show how these concepts arise and function within IIT in a simple way, with no claim for originality in most of what is said.

The main claims for originality in IIT are two: Development of capabilities for solving the two basic problems of multiple determination and psychological measurement; and experimental application of these capabilities to develop an interlocking framework across many psychological domains. Functional measurement theory has thus made purposiveness a legitimate theoretical construct, properly deserving the status of an axiom.

2. The integration diagram of Figure 1.1 is useful for setting out the problem of the three unobservables, but it represents only a simple case. Stimuli may be internal as well as external, and the valuation operation, here treated as a molar unit, may consist of a chain of valuation–integration operations. Valuation and integration will not always be independent, moreover, as with inconsistency and redundancy (see Chapter 11). In addition, action evolves temporally with feedback. Hence the stimulus field will change over time, reflecting interaction between action and valuation operations, as the organism approaches the goal.

3. Unitization seems similar and related to categorization as a fundamental ability, but it has received relatively little directed analysis. One line of inquiry would consider cases in which unitization does not occur. Examples appear in inconsistency reactions (Chapter 11) and in comparing hypotheses of input integration and equity integration (Chapter 7). More extreme examples are sometimes found with information overload, conflict, and emotional reactions, in which normal integration processes seem to fail. Another line of inquiry concerns unitization as a result of integration across different sense modalities, as in psychophysics and psycholinguistics.

4. Experimental analysis of assemblage in operating memory seems promising in intuitive physics. In the study of Figure 8.1 of Chapter 8, for example, the children's judgments rested on a qualitative assemblage representing the physical structure of the task. This assemblage is more important, and more interesting, than the algebraic rule that it subserves (see also *Assemblage Theory* in Anderson & Wilkening, 1991, pp. 20-24).

5. The trait, *honesty*, is used in tribute to Hartshorne and May (1928), who showed that honest–dishonest behavior of school children depended very much on situation and circumstance. Honesty could not be considered a general personality trait, therefore, an implication long neglected in personality theory. Instead, honesty, and by inference other personality traits, involved person–situation interaction and indeed constituted some kind of knowledge system. The research program of Hartshorne and May commands admiration and still stands out as a model for other workers (see Mischel, 1968).

6. Some philosophers (e.g., Churchland, 1979; Stich, 1983) have argued that everyday concepts and beliefs, so-called folk psychology, are totally lacking in validity and have nothing to contribute to cognitive science. Some other foundation must be found.

Cognitive algebra leads to an opposite conclusion. It demonstrates the validity of some concepts and beliefs of folk psychology. Folk psychology can thus contribute to cognitive science, contributions not merely invaluable, but unique.

The working hypothesis of IIT has been that everyday cognition, or folk psychology, is an essential base for construction of cognitive theory. The conceptual terms in the algebraic schemas cited earlier, for example, were taken from everyday cognition. The empirical validation of these schemas demonstrates validity of phenomenology. In this way, phenomenology can be exploited and expanded for rigorous theory.

Of course, understanding folk psychology is not possible solely in its own terms. Folk psychology is sometimes obstinately incorrect, as shown by the persistence of the meaning change hypothesis. Also, folk psychology is essentially incomplete, as shown by the importance of nonconscious sensation and nonconscious emotion. But belaboring the limitations and shortcomings of everyday phenomenology does not demonstrate its uselessness. Physics also has been obstinately incorrect at times, as with the concept of ether. Cognitive algebra has an essential role in assaying and refining folk psychology.

A compendium of philosopher's views, pro and con, on folk psychology is given in Christensen and Turner (1993). The functional view of IIT agrees with the functional view in philosophy (Christensen & Turner, 1993, pp. xxii-xxiv) in considering folk psychology a basis for a rigorous science of mind without requiring reduction to a lower level. IIT does not, however, deny that such reduction is possible in principle. Moreover, IIT makes no appeal to "theory of computation and formal logic." Instead, it lays a foundation with algebraic laws of mind, just as physics employs algebraic laws of matter.

7. Multiple determination is widely recognized throughout psychology, of course, most prominently in the algebraic models conjectured throughout the judgment–decision domain. Similar conjectures appear in additive attitude theories (Chapter 5) and moral algebra (Chapter 7). Multiple determination is also conceptually integral to contextual effects in psychophysics (Chapter 9) and language processing (Chapter 12), to the concept of inconsistency in cognitive consistency theories (Chapter 4), to person–situation interactionism, and to intuitive physics (Chapter 8).

Effective analysis of multiple determination, however, has been lacking in all these areas because they lacked a grounded theory of psychological measurement. The need for measurement theory is well illustrated by the shortcomings of the makeshift measurement methods in judgment–decision theory and in the widespread reliance on magnitude estimation in psychophysics.

Functional measurement theory has provided a foundation for the study of multiple determination. This foundation is grounded in the empirical demonstrations of cognitive algebra presented in the later empirical chapters. Unique to this work is the averaging model, which entails an essentially new outlook on psychological measurement. Because of its emphasis on continuous response, moreover, functional measurement can also be useful with analysis of nonalgebraic integration and configurality.

PREFACE

Cognitive algebra represents a basic mode of cognition. There are equations of mind in psychology just as there are equations of matter in physics. These equations of mind are algebraic rules for information integration.

Addition rules may be diagnosed by a *pattern of parallelism* in a factorial graph. *Multiplication rules* correspond similarly to a *linear fan pattern*. This pattern analysis simultaneously solves the two associated measurement problems, providing veridical scales of the stimulus variables and of the response. The parallelism and linear fan theorems of this chapter thus solve the problem of the three unobservables discussed in relation to Figure 1.1.

The ubiquitous *averaging rule* occupies a special place in cognitive theory. Under the special condition of equal weighting, it obeys the parallelism theorem, thereby allowing easy analyses. In the general case of differential weighting, it yields nonparallelism, thereby accounting for many results discordant with additive theories. Indeed, differential weighted averaging implies an opposite effects, scale-free test between adding and averaging processes.

Aside from the intrinsic interest of algebraic laws of mind, cognitive algebra has quantitative uses. It solves the long-standing problem of true psychological measurement, including both conscious and nonconscious concepts. These measures provide a new window on cognition. Not least important, these measures provide new tools for analysis of nonalgebraic cognition.

Conceptual implications of cognitive algebra are more important than the algebraic precision. Foremost is meaning invariance, strong evidence against entire classes of theories that argue for configurality and interaction, from person cognition to memory and language. Also, cognitive algebra makes affect and emotion integral components of cognition. Other qualitative, conceptual implications may be itemized:

a. Unified approach to social−personality (Chapters 4−7).
b. Assemblage, nonstage view of cognitive development (Chapters 6 and 8).
c. Integration psychophysics founded on psychological law (Chapter 9).
d. Cognitive, not normative, base for judgment−decision (Chapter 10).
e. Shift from reproductive memory to functional memory (Chapter 11).
f. Context and nonverbal informers integral to psycholinguistics (Chapter 12).
h. Fundamental place of value and multiple determination in all areas.

In each of these areas, cognitive algebra has led to a new way of thinking. At bottom, this approach represents a fundamental shift to focus on structure of the internal world. This focus has put the axiom of purposiveness on a scientific base, a foundation for a self-sufficient cognitive theory of everyday life.

Chapter 2

COGNITIVE ALGEBRA

Cognitive algebra represents a basic mode of cognition. There are equations of mind in psychology just as there are equations of matter in physics. And just as in physics, mathematical law provides new tools and leads to new conceptual frameworks. Indeed, cognitive algebra has provided a unified framework with applications in every branch of psychology.

Conceptually foremost in this chapter is the solution to the problem of the three unobservables. This provides a foundation for functional theory, centered on concepts of purposiveness and value. Directly related is the unification of the nomothetic and idiographic orientations, which allows an effective approach to organism–environment interaction. At the human level, moreover, cognitive algebra has provided validational criteria for phenomenology of everyday life. It thus becomes possible to determine whether what people say is a veridical reflection of their cognition. These conceptual implications illustrate the significance of cognitive algebra as a framework for cognitive theory.

The three basic rules of cognitive algebra are addition, multiplication, and averaging. The averaging rule has special interest because it differs qualitatively from the addition rule and because it has broad empirical validity. These three rules are covered in the first three parts of this chapter; some related rules arise in later empirical chapters.

The technical side of cognitive algebra, the main concern of this chapter, rests on a simple logic. If two variables are integrated by some algebraic rule, the *pattern of response* can reveal the form of that rule. A *pattern of parallelism* points to addition or subtraction, illustrated in Figure 2.1; a *linear fan pattern* points to multiplication or division, illustrated in Figure 2.3; and averaging can be distinguished from adding by a *crossover pattern*, illustrated in Figures 2.4 and 2.5. Understanding these figures requires only a modest ability to read factorial graphs, defined in the next section.

Most of this chapter can thus be skipped. With an understanding of how to read the cited figures, the reader can pass on to Chapter 4, which summarizes the foundation experiments on cognitive algebra.

ADDITION RULES

Most problems of cognitive algebra can be made clear with the simplest rule of all, the addition rule. This rule will be considered in some detail, accordingly, and other rules more briefly.

FACTORIAL DESIGN

A basic tool for IIT has been *factorial design*, widely used throughout psychology for joint manipulation of two or more variables. In cognitive algebra, the key idea is to look for patterning in the *factorial graph*.

For two stimulus variables, the factorial design can be represented as a Row × Column matrix. The two variables are denoted by A for rows and B for columns. Each row of the matrix corresponds to one *level* of the row variable, also called the row *factor*. This stimulus level is denoted by S_{Ai} for row i. Similarly, S_{Bj} denotes the stimulus level for column j.

Each cell of the design matrix thus represents one experimental treatment, defined by the corresponding levels of row and column. In cell ij, the experimental treatment is the stimulus pair (S_{Ai}, S_{Bj}); the response to this stimulus pair is denoted by R_{ij}. The R_{ij} constitute a factorial data table, illustrated later in Table 2.1.

A *factorial graph* is obtained from the data table as follows. The vertical axis represents the response. On the horizontal axis, the column stimuli, S_{Bj}, are placed at some convenient spacing, usually at equal intervals. The data points in the first row of the design, namely, R_{1j}, are then plotted above the corresponding column stimuli, S_{Bj}, and connected to form a curve. Each other row yields a similar curve. These row curves constitute the factorial graph. A numerical illustration appears later in Table 2.1 and Figure 2.1; empirical examples are shown in Figures 2.3–2.5.

Factorial graphs are the main tool for data presentation in this book. At the same time, this graph typically summarizes the design of the experiment under consideration. The response is labeled on the vertical axis; the column stimuli on the horizontal axis; and the row stimuli as curve parameter. The pattern in this factorial graph can diagnose the rule by which the two stimulus variables are integrated to form the one response.

PARALLELISM THEOREM

The diagnostic sign of an addition rule is a pattern of parallelism in the factorial graph. This *parallelism theorem* is simple, although not quite as simple as it might seem. Some ramifications are noted in the following sections.

The Three Unobservables. Consider the hypothesis that two stimulus variables are integrated by an addition rule:

$$\rho_{ij} = \psi_{Ai} + \psi_{Bj}. \tag{1}$$

This equation follows the convention of the integration diagram of Figure 1.1 that unobservable, subjective quantities are represented by Greek letters, observable quantities by Latin letters. Thus, ρ_{ij} is the implicit response in cell ij, and ψ_{Ai} and ψ_{Bj} are the subjective values of the row and column stimuli, S_{Ai} and S_{Bj}, respectively.

In this addition rule reappears the problem of the three unobservables from Chapter 1. We do have leverage on two unobservables. We can manipulate the physical stimuli, S_{Ai} and S_{Bj}, thereby manipulating the unobservable stimuli, ψ_{Ai} and ψ_{Bj}. Also, we can measure R_{ij}, a direct link to the unobservable response ρ_{ij}. This can be enough to solve the problem of the three unobservables. The simplest case appears in the following parallelism theorem.

Parallelism Theorem. Two premises are employed in this parallelism theorem:

$$\rho_{ij} = \psi_{Ai} + \psi_{Bj}; \quad \text{(addition)} \tag{2a}$$

$$R_{ij} = c_0 + c_1\rho_{ij}. \quad \text{(linearity)} \tag{2b}$$

The linearity condition says that the observable response, R_{ij}, is a linear function of the implicit response, ρ_{ij} (c_0 and c_1 are zero and unit constants whose values need not be known). Linear scale thus corresponds to, and makes more precise, the common term, equal interval scale. Response linearity is important because it means that the factorial pattern in the observable data will faithfully mirror the pattern in the underlying cognition.

From these two premises follow two conclusions:

Conclusion 1: The factorial graph will be parallel.

Conclusion 2: The row means of the factorial data table will be a linear scale of the ψ_{Ai}; similarly, the column means of the data table will be a linear scale of the ψ_{Bj}.

The proofs of these conclusions require only simple algebra.[1]

The parallelism theorem provides a remarkably simple and precise test of the addition rule. Observed parallelism constitutes strong support for both premises of the theorem taken together. Hence it supports each of them separately.

A cornucopia of benefits thus flows from observed parallelism:

1. support for the addition rule;
2. support for linearity of the response measure;
3. linear scales of each stimulus variable;
4. support for meaning invariance;
5. support for independence of valuation and integration.

The first three benefits correspond to the three unobservables. The first involves the integration rule; the next two involve the two measurement problems, of response and of stimuli. In this way, the parallelism theorem solves the problem of the three unobservables. Each benefit requires brief comment.

Addition Rule. If the factorial graph exhibits parallelism, that obviously supports the premise of additivity. This support is fairly strong (see *A Problem of Evidence* below). Here it may be emphasized that the parallelism test is simplicity itself, being made directly on the raw response. For many applications, no more is needed than visual inspection of the factorial graph.

The value of the parallelism theorem, it should be emphasized, lies in the experimental investigations that demonstrate its empirical reality. Unless addition rules appeared in nature, the theorem would be mainly barren mathematics. The power of parallelism analysis thus rests on the empirical investigations noted under *Parallelism and Nonparallelism* and in later chapters. This section, however, continues with the three unobservables.

Response Measurement. Observed parallelism also supports the linearity of the response scale. The importance of this implication is hard to overemphasize. Response linearity means that the pattern in the observable data is a veridical picture of the pattern in the unobservable cognition. The factorial graph is thus a key to diagnosis of cognitive process.

Response linearity has been a critical issue in psychological measurement theory. Everyone has desired linear response measures, but the validity problem seemed insurmountable: How can we tell whether R is a linear function of ρ when the latter is unobservable? The perplexity of this problem is highlighted by the sharp disagreement between two common methods of obtaining numerical response (see Figure 3.1). This problem has been surmounted by the parallelism theorem, which provides a practicable validity criterion.

Stimulus Measurement. Nothing need be known about the stimulus values to apply the parallelism theorem. The test of parallelism is made directly on the raw response. We manipulate the observable stimuli, S_{Ai} and S_{Bj}, and thereby also manipulate the corresponding unobservable stimuli, ψ_{Ai} and ψ_{Bj}, which may be considered arbitrary functions of the observable stimuli. These unknown stimulus values become manifest in the observed response, from which they can be extracted with the parallelism analysis.

The subjective stimulus values can readily be obtained using the second conclusion of the parallelism theorem. This conclusion asserts that the row (column) means provide a linear scale of the row (column) stimuli of the design. This is called *functional measurement* because it measures the values that functioned in the specific behavior under analysis. Observed parallelism gives validational support to this functional measurement on the stimulus side.

This functional approach to measurement operates in the opposite direction from traditional measurement theories in psychology. The traditional approach begins by attempting to measure the stimulus values to obtain a base for theory construction. This traditional approach began in classical psychophysics (Chapter 9) and has been standard throughout psychology. It appears entirely sensible, but it has not worked. Only by reversing the direction of approach was grounded theory of psychological measurement attained.

Stimulus Independence and Meaning Invariance. The addition rule is a strong premise, for it includes an implicit independence assumption, namely, no interaction between the stimuli. Thus, Equation 2a assumes that S_{Ai} has a fixed value, or meaning, regardless of which S_{Bj} it is combined with. If the stimuli do interact, so that the meanings are not invariant, then the factorial graph will generally be nonparallel. Parallelism in the factorial graph thus implies not simply stimulus additivity, but also the deeper property of meaning invariance.

Meaning invariance may have more interest than the addition rule per se. In the person cognition task of Figure 1.2, for example, meaning interaction was expected from persuasive phenomenological considerations. If phenomenology was correct, the addition rule would have failed. In fact, it succeeded, thereby demonstrating meaning invariance of the adjectives in the person description. The hypothesis of meaning interaction, which would otherwise have been elusive to test, was thus easily and firmly disproved. Meaning invariance, of course, implies a very different conception of the information processing.[2]

V–I Independence. Meaning invariance implies valuation and integration are distinct and independent operations. This independence, which underlies the effectiveness of functional measurement, has been discussed in Chapter 1.

NOMOTHETIC–IDIOGRAPHIC UNITY

A numerical example is useful at this point to illustrate parallelism analysis. It will also illustrate how cognitive algebra can harmoniously combine the nomothetic and idiographic orientations. This example uses hypothetical data, but these data are similar to those in the experimental study of person cognition in the previous chapter.

Two subjects judged how much blame should be assigned to a story child who had thrown a rock that injured another boy. Intention of the harmdoer was varied across three levels: intent to *harm*, intent to *scare*, and *carelessness*.

TABLE 2.1

HPOTHETICAL DATA FOR ADDITIVE MODEL
FACTORIAL DESIGN FOR TWO SUBJECTS

	Person C. H.			Person R. P. McG.		
	Bruised shin	Bloody nose	Black eye	Bruised shin	Bloody nose	Black eye
Harm	14	20	20	18	19	23
Scare	9	15	15	9	10	14
Careless	4	10	10	7	8	12

The damage was also varied across three levels: *bruised shin, bloody nose*, and
black eye. These two variables were combined in a 3 × 3, Intent × Damage factorial design. Each subject thus made blame judgments for 3 × 3 = 9 different
story children.

This factorial design is shown in Table 2.1. The A factor is Intent, with S_{Ai}
= *harm, scare*, and *careless*. The B factor is Damage, with S_{Bj} = *bruised shin,
bloody nose*, and *black eye*. The entries in the two parts of the table represent
blame responses for two hypothetical subjects, C. H. and R. P. McG. Their
corresponding factorial graphs are shown in Figure 2.1.

Nomothetic Generality. The factorial graph for Subject C. H. is shown at the
left of Figure 2.1. The three points on the top curve, labeled *harm*, show the
blame assigned to the three story children who threw the rock with deliberate
intention of harming the other boy. These three points show how assignment of
blame depends on level of damage, which is listed on the horizontal axis. Thus
C. H. considers bloody nose substantially worse than bruised shin, but considers
black eye the same as bloody nose.

The middle curve, labeled *scare*, shows the blame assigned the three story
children who only intended to scare the other boy, not actually hit him with the
rock. This *scare* curve lies considerably below the *harm* curve, considerably
above the *careless* curve. Thus, C. H. considers intent to scare considerably
more blamable than carelessness yet considerably less blamable than intent to
harm. On each curve, nevertheless, the three points exhibit the same relative
effects of damage already seen in the top curve.

The critical feature of the factorial graph for C. H. is the parallelism pattern
of the three curves. By virtue of the parallelism theorem, it appears that C. H.
uses the blame addition schema:

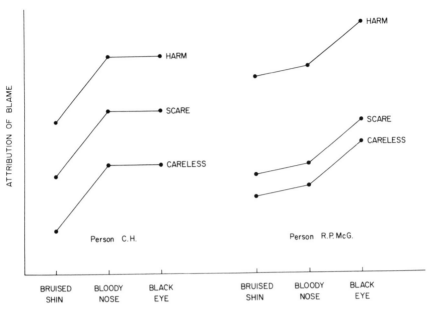

Figure 2.1. Hypothetical data illustrate parallelism analysis. The three curves in each factorial graph represent one person's assignment of blame for bad deeds of each of 9 story children, specified by a 3 × 3, Intent × Damage design. The 3 levels of Intent are listed by the corresponding curve; the 3 levels of Damage are listed on the horizontal axis. The parallelism in each factorial graph shows that both persons followed the same addition schema: Blame = Intent + Damage. The different shapes of the two graphs reflect differences in personal values attached to the same Intent and Damage stimuli. (From N. H. Anderson, 1990, "Personal design in social cognition," *Research Methods in Personality and Social Psychology: Review of Personality and Social Psychology, 11*, 243–278. Copyright 1990 by Sage Publications. Reprinted by permission.)

Blame = Intent + Harm.

Exactly the same applies for Subject R. P. McG., whose factorial graph is shown in the right of Figure 2.1. These three curves are also parallel; R. P. McG. also uses the blame addition schema.

The integration rule is thus the same for both subjects. This is the kind of general law psychologists have long desired. This law represents nomothetic generality. This nomothetic law is verified empirically in Chapter 7, although as an averaging rule rather than an adding rule.

Idiographic Generality. Nevertheless, the factorial graphs for the two subjects look rather different. This difference in appearance reflects their different personal values. To illustrate, compare the shape of the *careless* curve for the two subjects. For C. H., *bloody nose* and *black eye* are equally bad, as reflected in the flat right-hand segment of the curve; and both are much worse than *bruised shin*. If these were real data, one would suspect that C. H. considers head injury much more serious than injury elsewhere on the body. For R. P. McG., on the other hand, the difference between *bruised shin* and *bloody nose* is small, whereas *black eye* is much worse. If these were real data, one might suspect that R. P. McG. thought about possible long-term damage to the eye.

Personal values for intent are also different. These values are shown by the relative elevations of the three curves in Figure 2.1. For R. P. McG., the *scare* curve is close to the *careless* curve and far below the *harm* curve. These relative elevations mean that R. P. McG. considers deliberate intent to harm very blamable, but considers intent to scare only a little worse than carelessness. For C. H., in contrast, the *scare* curve lies midway between the other two; the difference in blame value between *harm* and *scare* equals the difference between *scare* and *careless*.

The personal values just discussed are measurable on true linear (equal interval) scales for each subject separately. This follows from the parallelism theorem. Graphically, the elevations of the three points on each curve are a linear scale of blame values for the damage variable; these elevations mirror the row means of the factorial design. Similarly, the relative elevations among the three curves are a linear scale of blame values for the intent variable.

To sum up, the nomothetic law allows analysis of idiographic value. At the surface level of behavior, the two subjects are rather different. This behavioral difference, however, stems from their personal differences in value. Their cognitive integration obeys the same nomothetic law.

Individual differences have long been a quagmire for attempts to develop a science of psychology. Some have argued that general laws cannot exist because each individual is uniquely different. Cognitive algebra can navigate this quagmire of individual differences. Achieving nomothetic–idiographic unity faces difficulties as yet unmentioned, but it has become a real possibility.

Personal Design. The idiographic capability of cognitive algebra makes possible *personal design*, characterized in ideal form by four properties: experimental manipulation, individual analysis, personal values, and personalized task and/or stimuli. Phobic subjects, for example, may be idiographic in the object of their phobia, yet nomothetic in their reactions. A study of phobia might thus need to preselect stimuli separately for each subject to satisfy specified criteria, such as covering a range from high to low reaction with roughly equal spacing. In marriage satisfaction, similarly, actual incidents from each person's marriage could be used as stimulus levels, as shown later in Figure 2.4.

Personal design aims to embed the experimental task within the knowledge systems of each individual. The first three characterizing properties, including personal values, were illustrated in Figures 1.2 and 2.1. More complete personalization would employ personalized stimuli as well (Figure 2.4).

In most applications, personal design will involve reactions to partly hypothetical situations, as in the marriage study. Of themselves, natural situations would seldom provide a design pattern of experimental conditions with enough constraint for process analysis.. But most of life's decisions are partly hypothetical because of limited information and uncertainty about the future; reliance on partly hypothetical situations is thus not unrealistic.

Personal design can help bring experimental method to all social sciences: anthropology, economics, history, law, political science, psychotherapy, religion, and sociology, unifying them with psychology. The study of social roles, for example, would benefit from this approach, as would the study of the family. Although personal design has obvious limitations, it may be uniquely useful in providing experimental leverage for disciplines traditionally deemed nonexperimental (see further Anderson, 1990b, 1991g; Hommers & Anderson, 1991).

A PROBLEM OF EVIDENCE

Observed parallelism is strong support for the addition rule, but it is not absolute proof. This issue may be clarified with Table 2.2, which relates the two premises of the parallelism theorem to the pattern in the factorial graph. If both premises are true, parallelism is guaranteed by the parallelism theorem. This is case 1 of the table.

If one premise is true and the other false, the observed data will be nonparallel. In case 2, additivity holds, so the factorial graph of the unobservable ρ would exhibit parallelism; but the transformation from ρ to R, being nonlinear, destroys this parallelism. In case 3, nonadditivity holds, so the factorial graph of the unobservable ρ would be nonparallel; since the transformation from ρ to R is linear, the nonparallelism in ρ will be preserved in R.

In the last case in the table, both premises are false. It is tempting to conclude that the data will be nonparallel in this case also. That seems likely in practice, but it is not guaranteed. Logically, nonlinearity in the response might

TABLE 2.2

PARALLELISM AND NONPARALLELISM

Case	Additivity	Linearity	Response Pattern
1	Yes	Yes	Parallelism
2	Yes	No	Nonparallelism
3	No	Yes	Nonparallelism
4	No	No	??

just offset nonadditivity in the integration to yield net parallelism. This may not seem likely, but it is logically possible. Subject to this qualification, however, observed parallelism may be considered good support for both premises of the theorem jointly, and hence for each one separately.

There is a more general parallelism theorem that dispenses with the assumption of response linearity. No more is needed than that R and ρ have the same rank order, that is, that R be a strictly monotone function of ρ. This depends on monotone response transformation discussed in Chapter 3 and illustrated with psychophysical bisection in Chapter 9. At bottom, therefore, no assumption is needed beyond additivity—and that may be tested in the data analysis.

TECHNICAL PROBLEMS

Various problems of data analysis and statistics arise in applying the parallelism theorem. These problems were important in the development of cognitive algebra, and reasonably satisfactory resolutions have been obtained. These problems are discussed in detail in the writer's *Foundations* and *Methods* volumes, and they need consideration in experimental studies of cognitive algebra. In this volume, however, these problems can be largely passed over.

The problem of *goodness of fit*, however, requires discussion. The additive model can always be fitted to the data, but it may fit poorly. It is necessary, accordingly, to evaluate discrepancies between model and data. The simplest approach is with the factorial graph. In Figure 1.2, for example, visual inspection indicates parallelism and hence an adding-type rule. In Figure 2.4 below, the crossovers infirm any addition process.

More formal statistical methods are also available. Any set of data will contain noise, so the observed factorial graph will never be perfectly parallel, even though both premises of the parallelism theorem hold true. Some deviations from parallelism will always be observed, and it is necessary to assess whether they can reasonably be attributed to prevailing noise or whether they reflect real disagreement with the addition rule. Various attempts have been made to establish addition rules, but these generally failed through reliance on invalid methods for testing goodness of fit, illustrated in the following subsection.

How Not to Study Cognitive Algebra: Weak Inference and Linear Models. Experts typically claim their judgments are configural, sensitive to interrelations within given information. In their cogitation, the meaning and implications of any one informer are not fixed, but depend on other informers. If these claims were correct, statistical prediction rules could hardly explain expert judgment.

Strong disagreement with the claims of the experts was voiced by various workers who sought to show that judgments made by experts could be explained by a linear, additive model. Their counterclaim was that experts' judgments were not at all configural, merely a weighted sum of the informer values.

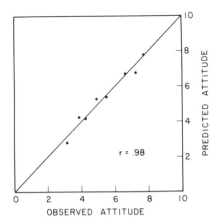

Figure 2.2. Weak inference with linear model. Predictions from linear model plotted on vertical axis as a function of the observed values. Tight scatterplot and high correlation of .98 seem to support the linear model. In fact, the linear model is sharply invalidated by the crossover shown later in Figure 2.5. Correlation and scatterplot are *weak inference* statistics, which seem to test the model but do not really do so.

Unfortunately, the proponents of the linear model relied on invalid method. This invalidity is illustrated in Figure 2.2. These data come from the study of attitudes toward U. S. presidents, presented later in Figure 2.5. An addition rule (linear model) was fitted to the eight data points of Figure 2.5, and the predictions from this linear model are plotted as a function of the observed attitudes in Figure 2.2.

Ideally, the points in Figure 2.2 would lie on the straight diagonal line of perfect fit. Some scatter is inevitable because of natural response variability, of course, even if the linear model is correct. But the scatter seems small; the plotted points cluster closely around the diagonal. Judged by this scatterplot, the linear model might seem to do very well.

Furthermore, the correlation between the observed data and the predictions of the linear model is exceptionally high, .98. Judged by this correlation, the linear model might again seem to do very well.

In fact, the linear model does very ill. It requires all four curves to be parallel in the factorial graph of these same data, shown later in Figure 2.5. Parallelism is sharply violated, however, for Figure 2.5 exhibits an opposite effects crossover. Many other instances have spelled out the same lesson: Correlation–scatterplot statistics obscure and conceal what the factorial graph reveals and makes clear. Correlation and scatterplot only seem to test the rule; they do not really do so. They are *weak inference* statistics.

Weak inference has been prominent in the study of expert judgment. Clinical psychologists, in particular, have claimed to be sensitive to configurality, in which the meaning of each informer in a clinical case depends on its relations with the other informers. Proponents of the linear model claimed otherwise, but their claims were based on weak inference statistics. Whether clinical judgment is sensitive to configurality cannot be answered from these weak inference studies—these statistics are themselves insensitive to configurality, even such gross configurality as the crossover in Figure 2.5. Their claim about expert judgment is a non sequitur (Chapter 10).

Configurality. Configural judgment depends on the pattern, or configuration, of the stimulus information. Configural hypotheses are popular, as just noted with clinical judgment and discussed for cognitive consistency theories in Chapter 4. Demonstrating true configurality can be surprisingly difficult, however, as foreshadowed in the previous subsection on weak inference.

Functional measurement theory can contribute to the study of configurality in two ways. One way is to guard against unjustified configural interpretations. Among these are the change of meaning hypothesis discussed in Chapters 1 and 4, the claim about clinical judgment just noted, and the cases taken up later under *Implicit Additivity*.

Functional measurement can also take a more positive role by helping to demonstrate configurality. This may seem contradictory since the parallelism theorem, in particular, assumes meaning invariance. The parallelism theorem, however, provides a potential means to validate linearity of the response measure. This potential becomes actualized in cognitive algebra. Hence general methodology can be developed that yields linear response scales. This methodology can be applied even when no algebraic rule holds.

With a linear response scale, the pattern in the unobservable cognition will be faithfully reflected in the observable data. With a linear response scale, deviations from parallelism can be considered genuine, deserving substantive interpretation. Cognitive algebra can thus go beyond itself to assist in the study of configural thought and action.

Clinical judgment, in particular, can be studied in this way. Information integration is characteristic of clinical judgment, so parallelism analysis is directly applicable. Parallelism would provide genuine evidence against the claims of configural processing. Nonparallelism could provide evidence for configural processing and—more important—evidence about its nature.

Error Theory and Strong Inference. Actual data will always show some nonparallelism because responses to the very same stimulus vary naturally from one time to another. An *error theory* is needed to assess whether the nonparallelism observed in any experiment is real or merely natural response variability. Let ε denote deviations of individual responses in any cell of the factorial design from the mean for that cell. Because all the deviations in each cell refer to the very same stimulus, their variance, s_ε^2, is a measure of the natural response variability. Hence s_ε^2 provides a yardstick for assessing goodness of fit. If the observed deviations from parallelism are large relative to s_ε^2, they suggest real nonadditivity.

To implement this last sentence requires a suitable index of deviations from parallelism. The addition rule implies that the mean response in each cell equals the sum of the corresponding row and column means minus the grand mean. The difference, or residual, between this predicted mean and the actual mean measures the deviation from parallelism in that cell. The variance of these cell residuals, s^2_{resid}, is a suitable index of deviations from parallelism. If the ratio of s^2_{resid} to s^2_ε is larger than some criterial value, the nonparallelism should be considered reliable.

Standard statistical tools are available to make this approach exact: s^2_{resid} corresponds to the "interaction" term in the analysis of variance; similarly, s^2_ε corresponds to the "error" term. Significant statistical interaction implies that the observed nonparallelism is reliable; nonsignificant interaction supports the addition rule (see discussion of Figure 2.5). In contrast to weak inference, analysis of variance provides a method of strong inference.

This analysis of variance test may be applied at the individual level, as it was in the study of person cognition of Figure 1.2. An analogous test is available for a group of subjects, as in the study of marriage satisfaction of Figure 2.4. The choice between individual and group design is important in research practice, but will not be considered further here.

PARALLELISM AND NONPARALLELISM

It may seem surprising that parallelism analysis was not exploited much earlier, for addition rules have been conjectured in many psychological domains. Two major obstacles had to be overcome: distrust of continuous response measures and prevalence of nonadditive integration rules.

Continuous response measures were distrusted because they are subject to various biases. If bias is present, the observable response, R, is not a veridical measure of the underlying response, ρ. In this event, the pattern in the observable factorial graph is not a veridical reflection of the pattern in the unobservable response. Parallelism and nonparallelism are then both problematic.

Biases were known to be serious, as shown dramatically in Figure 3.1 of the next chapter. Nearly everyone considered the bias problem insolvable.

The second obstacle, the prevalence of nonadditive integration rules, meant that parallelism would frequently be violated in observed data patterns—almost regardless of whether the response measure was linear. Faced with any instance of nonparallelism, therefore, the investigator would be uncertain whether it was real nonadditivity in the integration rule, or nonlinearity in the response measure, or both mixed together. This uncertainty, of course, raised the fear that the instances of observed parallelism were adventitious, and this in turn rendered dubious the notion that observed parallelism could serve as a validational base for the response measure.

These two obstacles seemed insurmountable. Many investigators interested in addition rules accordingly sought alternative methods of measurement. This was a blind alley (see Chapter 3). The path to solving the problem of the three unobservables lay in developing procedures to eliminate the biases in the rating method. This path, however, was complicated by the nonparallelism for the reasons just discussed.

Success lay in the averaging rule. It accounts for much of the nonparallelism that has been observed. Many integration tasks that were expected to obey an addition rule actually obey an averaging rule. The averaging rule, as shown later, yields parallelism under the equal weight condition but nonparallelism under the differential weight condition. Although establishing the averaging rule faced several difficulties (see Chapter 4), this rule provided a unified account of most of the observed parallelism and nonparallelism.

Making the parallelism theorem into a working tool was thus by no means simple. Interpretation of parallelism required understanding of nonparallelism. Understanding nonparallelism involved establishing the averaging rule. Establishing the averaging rule went hand in hand with development of methodology to avoid biases in continuous response measures (see Chapter 3). All three tasks were bound together. In retrospect, it looks straightforward, but in progress it was filled with uncertainties.

MULTIPLICATION RULES

Multiplication rules seem natural in many areas of psychology: Motivation appears to act as an energizer of ability in determining performance; expectancy of success appears to act as a proportionality coefficient on the value of the goal; language quantifiers, such as *slightly*, *fairly*, and *very*, also seem to operate as multipliers. The study of cognitive algebra, accordingly, requires methods for testing and analyzing multiplication rules.

LINEAR FAN ANALYSIS

The basic tool for multiplication rules is the linear fan theorem: A multiplication rule will manifest itself as a linear fan pattern in the factorial graph. The linear fan theorem is similar to the parallelism theorem, but one new obstacle makes its appearance.

Linear Fan Theorem. Two premises are required by the linear fan theorem:

$$\rho_{ij} = \psi_{Ai} \times \psi_{Bj}; \quad \text{(multiplication)} \tag{3a}$$

$$R_{ij} = c_0 + c_1 \rho_{ij}. \quad \text{(linearity)} \tag{3b}$$

The linearity premise is the same as for the parallelism theorem, and it serves the same purpose. From these two premises follow two conclusions:[3]

Conclusion 1: The appropriate factorial graph will be a linear fan;
Conclusion 2: The row means of the factorial data table will be a linear scale of the ψ_{Ai}; similarly, the column means of the data table will be a linear scale of the ψ_{Bj}.

The second conclusion is the same as in the parallelism theorem. The linear fan pattern of the first conclusion, however, will only be obtained if the factorial graph is constructed "appropriately." This requires that the column stimuli be spaced on the horizontal axis in a special way, namely, in proportion to their subjective values.

This requirement for subjective values reflects the algebraic structure of Equation 3a, which implies that the response is a linear function of ψ_{Bj} with slope ψ_{Ai}. Suppose that the S_{Bj} were indeed spaced at their subjective values in the factorial graph. The first row of data, R_{1j}, would then fall on a straight line with slope ψ_{A1}; the second row, R_{2j}, would fall on a straight line with slope ψ_{A2}; and so on. Hence the factorial graph would be a fan of straight lines, if the multiplication rule was true. If the multiplication rule was false, however, then the factorial graph would generally not be a linear fan. This test is simple—but it requires the subjective values.

This requirement might seem insuperable because the subjective values will generally be unknown. Some investigators tried to use objective, physical values instead. This worked poorly, of course, because subjective and objective value generally differ.

Fortunately, a bootstrap operation is possible. If the two premises of the theorem hold, the second conclusion furnishes the required subjective values: They are just the column means of the data table. This factorial graph will yield a linear fan.

In practice, we do not know whether the multiplication rule holds. Provisionally, however, we may use the observed column means in the indicated manner. If both premises of the theorem hold, we will find a linear fan. If we find a linear fan, we are on good ground. This is how it happened.

Implications of Linear Fan Pattern. The linear fan theorem thus provides a simple, precise test of the multiplication rule. An observed linear fan pattern is strong support for both premises of the theorem taken jointly. Hence it supports each of them separately. Just as with parallelism, an observed linear fan yields a cornucopia of benefits:

1. support for the multiplication rule;
2. support for linearity of the response measure;
3. linear scales of each stimulus variable;
4. support for meaning invariance;
5. support for independence of valuation and integration.

The first three benefits correspond to the three unobservables in the integration diagram. The first involves the integration rule; the next two involve the two measurement problems, of response and of stimuli. Each of these unobservables deserves comments similar to those given following the parallelism theorem. In fact, most of that discussion applies directly here and need not be repeated.

The last two conclusions also rest on essentially the same discussion as given with the parallelism theorem. If the value of S_{A1}, say, was not invariant, but depended on which S_{Bj} it was combined with, then the first row of data, R_{1j}, would not in general be a straight line function of the column means of the data table. Without meaning invariance, accordingly, a linear fan would not in general be obtained.

Conversely, obtaining a linear fan provides reasonably strong evidence for meaning invariance and indeed for all five listed benefits. The earlier section, *A Problem of Evidence*, applies in its essentials also to the multiplication rule. Accordingly, although an observed linear fan is not proof, it is heartening support for a multiplication rule.

LINEAR FAN EXAMPLE

A numerical example of linear fan analysis is provided by the hypothetical data of Table 2.3, which lists amounts paid for various drinks as a function of thirst motivation. The idea that motivation acts as a multiplier of incentive value is a long-standing conjecture in behavior theory. This conjecture could not be tested, however, owing to lack of measurement theory.

Table 2.3 shows a Motivation × Incentive factorial design, with three levels of Motivation (slight, moderate, and great thirst) and four levels of Incentive (warm water, cold water, Coke, and beer). The hypothetical integration rule may be written symbolically as:

$$\text{Response} = \text{Motivation} \times \text{Incentive}.$$

TABLE 2.3

AMOUNT PAID FOR DRINK AS FUNCTION OF
MOTIVATION AND INCENTIVE

	Thirst Quencher			
	Water			
Thirstiness	Warm	Cold	Coke	Beer
Slight	13	15	21	17
Moderate	15	21	39	27
Great	20	36	84	52
Mean	16	24	48	32

NOTE: From Anderson (1978a).

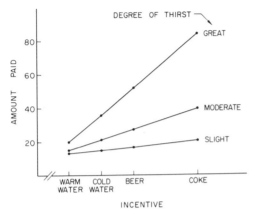

Figure 2.3. Linear fan analysis of multiplication rule, Motivation × Incentive. Response is amount paid for each of four drinks under each of three levels of thirst motivation, listed in Table 2.3. (From Anderson, 1978a.)

The test of this multiplication hypothesis is shown in the factorial graph of Figure 2.3, in which the data points are taken directly from the table. The data points for the three rows form a perfect linear fan. The Motivation × Incentive conjecture becomes testable in this way, and it has received some support.[4]

One unusual feature appears in Figure 2.3: The incentives are unequally spaced on the horizontal axis. In fact, Coke and beer have reversed their order from the table. Only with this spacing is the linear fan revealed.

This spacing of the incentives is prescribed by the linear fan theorem. The spacing was determined by the column means, listed in the last row of the table. If all is well, these column means are the true values, by virtue of the second conclusion of the linear fan theorem. Their actual use is provisional, of course, but justified by the emergence of the linear fan.

The first application of this linear fan analysis provided the first general solution to a classical problem of decision theory, namely, simultaneous measurement of subjective probability and value (see Figure 10.1). Multiplication operations have also been found in many other areas: probability judgment (Figures 10.4 and 10.5), intuitive physics (Figure 8.1), social attribution (Figure 5.5), and language processing (Figure 12.1). These empirical studies demonstrate the psychological reality of the multiplication rule. They add a second dimension to cognitive algebra.

COMPARISON PROCESSES

Comparison processes are ubiquitous in thought and action: Older, younger, prettier, smarter, better paid, and more fortunate are but a few of the comparative judgments of everyday life. One model, suggested by various investigators, assumes that comparison involves a ratio of focal and standard stimuli.

The linear fan theorem provides a simple analysis of this ratio model. Let S_{Ai} and S_{Bj} denote the focal and standard stimuli, respectively. Then the ratio model may be written:

$$\rho_{ij} = \mathbf{V}_A(S_{Ai})/\mathbf{V}_B(S_{Bj}) = \mathbf{V}_A(S_{Ai}) \times [\mathbf{V}_B(S_{Bj})]^{-1}.$$

Here $\mathbf{V}_A$ and $\mathbf{V}_B$ are the valuation functions that yield the psychological values of the stimuli. Nothing need be known about these functions. The linear fan analysis is made directly on the raw response.

In application to comparison processes, a relative ratio model has done considerably better. This relative ratio model may be written:

$$\rho_{ij} = \mathbf{V}_A(S_{Ai})/[\mathbf{V}_A(S_{Ai}) + \mathbf{V}_B(S_{Bj})].$$

This equation has the same form as the decision averaging model of Equation 5b, and may also be analyzed with the AVERAGE program. Applications are given to fairness theory in Chapter 7, psychophysics in Chapter 9, judgment–decision theory in Chapter 10, and psycholinguistics in Chapter 12.

AVERAGING THEORY

The averaging rule is the ugly duckling of cognitive algebra. Its ugliness lies in its nonlinear character, which makes it hard to handle, unlike the easy addition rule. Thought and action, however, have been found to obey the averaging rule across many tasks in which the addition rule has failed. Moreover, the averaging rule turns out to have some swan-like benefits.

OPPOSITE-EFFECTS PARADOX:
SCALE-FREE TEST BETWEEN AVERAGING AND ADDING

To compare the averaging and adding rules was a primary concern in the initial development of cognitive algebra. Addition rules were widely conjectured, in attitude theory, for example, and in judgment–decision theory. Averaging theory, in contrast, predicted an opposite-effects paradox: The same medium positive informer could have incremental or decremental effects, depending on what other informer it was integrated with. This prediction provided a scale-free test between averaging and adding. Because of the importance of this issue, two empirical illustrations are presented here.

Averaging in Marriage Satisfaction. Marriage has its ups and downs, but much of this can be encapsulated in the single dimension of marriage satisfaction. Does marriage satisfaction depend in lawful ways on the incidents associated with the ups and downs?

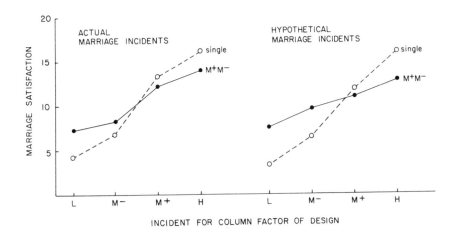

Figure 2.4. Opposite effects test eliminates adding rule, supports averaging. Data are judgments of marriage satisfaction by divorced women. Crossover of dashed curve disagrees with addition process, agrees with averaging process. (L, M^-, M^+, and H denote marriage incidents of low, mildly low, mildly high, and high satisfaction value.) (From Anderson, 1991g.)

To study this, divorced women were interviewed to determine specific incidents in their marriage that had brought them satisfaction or dissatisfaction. Later, they judged overall satisfaction with a hypothetical week of their life characterized by one or by three actual incidents.

Averaging is pitted against adding in Figure 2.4. The critical feature is the crossover in each panel. This crossover eliminates the addition rule; further, the crossover supports the averaging rule. The logic is as follows.

In the left panel, the dashed curve, labeled *single*, represents marriage satisfaction based on the single actual incident from the marriage indicated on the horizontal axis. The solid curve, labeled M^+M^-, represents marriage satisfaction based on three actual incidents, namely, the single incident already specified on the horizontal, together with incidents of mildly positive (M^+) and mildly negative (M^-) value. An addition rule would require that the solid curve lie entirely on one side of the dashed curve.

To see that the addition rule predicts no crossover, suppose the net value of M^+M^- is positive. Adding this positive information will increase the response for all four single incidents listed on the horizontal. Hence the M^+M^- curve would lie above the dashed *single* curve at all four points. On the other hand, suppose the net value of M^+M^- is negative. By similar reasoning, the M^+M^- curve would lie entirely below the *single* curve. The addition rule is thus sharply contradicted by the observed crossover.

The averaging rule, in contrast, predicts the crossover. The M^+M^- information is near neutral in net value, corresponding to the midpoint of the response scale. Averaging in this neutral value will pull up the very negative L information toward the middle of the scale; it will also pull down the very positive H information toward the middle of the scale. The same information can thus have opposite effects. This seeming paradox manifests itself graphically as the crossover shown in both data panels of Figure 2.4.

This crossover test is *scale-free*, holding even under monotone transformation of the response scale. Also, it is almost *rule-free*, or *model-free*, in that it eliminates almost any kind of addition rule. Addition with diminishing returns, for example, would still predict no crossover. The scale-free, crossover test thus provides strong qualitative support for averaging theory. It was a standard tool in the initial work on IIT.

Averaging in Attitude Theory. Attitudes are a central concept in social psychology, and a number of investigators have developed theoretical formulations based on addition rules. These formulations started off on the wrong foot; perhaps without exception, the empirical tests have supported averaging and eliminated adding (see Chapter 5).

One illustrative test with sociopolitical attitudes is shown in Figure 2.5. Subjects judged statesmanship of American presidents described by biographical paragraphs of graded value. The solid curves represent attitudes produced by pairs of paragraphs from a 3×2 design; the parallelism of these three solid curves supports both averaging and adding. The dashed *None* curve represents attitudes produced by the single paragraph listed on the horizontal axis; the crossover of the *None* and *Med* curves eliminates the adding rule and supports the averaging rule. The reasoning is the same as just given for Figure 2.4. In addition to this qualitative support, the averaging rule has passed demanding quantitative tests, further illustrated in Chapters 4, 5, 10, and 12.

AVERAGING EQUATION

Averaging differs qualitatively from adding. This difference appears in the stimulus representation, which requires two parameters, a weight parameter, ω, as well as the value parameter, ψ. Addition rules do not generally allow identification of weight, leaving this concept arbitrary or undefined. The averaging rule can define and measure weight parameters.

Equal Weight Case. In terms of the previous notation, the equation for the equal weight averaging rule may be written:

$$\rho_{ij} = \frac{\omega_A \psi_{Ai} + \omega_B \psi_{Bj} + \omega_0 \psi_0}{\omega_A + \omega_B + \omega_0}. \tag{4a}$$

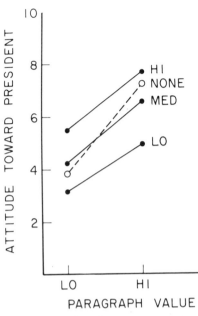

Figure 2.5. Attitudes toward U. S. presidents obey averaging theory. Factorial graph shows judgments about statesmanship of U. S. presidents as a function of given biographical paragraphs. Parallelism of solid curves supports adding-type rule. Crossover of dashed curve eliminates summation rule, supports averaging rule. (From N. H. Anderson, *Methods of Information Integration theory.* Academic Press, 1982.)

The ψs are scale values, as in the addition rule. The ωs are weights, which measure importance of the given information. The equal weight condition means that the S_{Ai} all have equal weight, ω_A, and that the S_{Bj} all have equal weight, ω_B. The zero subscript refers to the initial state, defined later.

The numerator in this equation is just a weighted sum; dividing by the sum of weights in the denominator converts the sum to an average. This is the source of the distinctive properties of the averaging rule.

As it stands, Equation 4a is not distinguishable from the addition rule of Equation 1. The sum of weights in the denominator is constant, the same in every cell of the factorial design, and so may be absorbed into the unit of the response scale. Like the addition rule, therefore, the equal weight averaging rule predicts parallelism for the factorial design.[5]

The averaging rule reveals its nonadditive nature when applied to the single column stimuli, S_{Bj}. Equation 4a then reduces to:

$$\rho_j = \frac{\omega_B \psi_{Bj} + \omega_0 \psi_0}{\omega_B + \omega_0}. \tag{4b}$$

The weight ω_A is absent because the S_{Bj} are given alone. The denominator is thus smaller in Equation 4b than in Equation 4a. Hence the slope of ρ as a function of ψ_{Bj} is greater: $\omega_B/(\omega_B + \omega_0) > \omega_B/(\omega_A + \omega_B + \omega_0)$. This differential weighting is the source of the crossover in Figures 2.4 and 2.5.

The averaging rule also requires the concept of initial state, represented by ω_0 and ψ_0 in Equations 4. This represents pre-experimental belief or attitude. In the presidents experiment of Figure 2.5, for example, subjects already have

prior attitudes from their knowledge of U. S. history. This prior attitude is averaged in with the stimulus information given by the experimenter. It has important functions (see, e.g., *Amount of Information* in Chapter 4).

Differential Weight Case. The general averaging rule allows each stimulus to
have its own weight as well as its own scale value. This rule has the same form
as Equation 4a, except that the equal weight, ω_A, is replaced by the differential
weight, ω_{Ai}. Each S_{Ai} may thus have its own weight as well as its own scale
value. The same holds for the column stimuli. This differential weight averaging rule may be written:

$$\rho_{ij} = \frac{\omega_{Ai}\psi_{Ai} + \omega_{Bj}\psi_{Bj} + \omega_0\psi_0}{\omega_{Ai} + \omega_{Bj} + \omega_0}. \tag{4c}$$

Differential weighting generally produces nonparallelism.

Differential weighting is not infrequent. The negativity effect, for example,
represents greater weighting of more negative informers (see Figure 5.12).
Negativity and other such effects were a serious concern in early work on IIT.
One reason was that differential weighting was at first conceptually unpalatable.
A second reason was that the nonparallelism could instead reflect nonlinear bias
in the rating response, not warranting any psychological interpretation.

Weight can be manipulated experimentally. Weight represents amount,
importance, and reliability of information. Manipulation of these variables has
yielded predictable deviations from parallelism. For example, S_{A1} could be a
single informer, and S_{A2} a pair of informers. Since S_{A2} contains more information, it should have greater weight. This greater weight will cause specifiable
deviations from parallelism.

This manipulation is illustrated in Figure 2.4, in which the *single* curve is
based on less information. The crossover represents the effect of differential
weighting produced by unequal amounts of information, exhibited in Equations
4a and 4b. The averaging rule has done well in accounting for this and other
nonparallelism, qualitatively and quantitatively as well.

Concept of Relative Weight. Differential weighting requires a distinction
between *absolute weight* and *relative weight*. The relative weight of a given
informer in a given combination is its absolute weight divided by the sum of the
absolute weights of all the informers in that combination. In each combination,
therefore, the relative weights sum to unity. Relative weight represents the relative importance of a given informer in a given combination.

With differential weighting, the same informer may have different relative
weights in different combinations. In Equations 4a and 4b, the relative weights
of S_{Bj} differ, being $\omega_B/(\omega_A + \omega_B + \omega_0)$ and $\omega_B/(\omega_B + \omega_0)$, respectively. Relative weights are interdependent, therefore, and this interdependence gives the
averaging rule a configural quality.

The absolute weights have an arbitrary unit, just as inch and centimeter are arbitrary units of length. This unit must be set in the estimation procedure in some arbitrary way, for example, by requiring the sum of all the absolute weights to be 1. If the data obey the averaging rule, it may be used to estimate the absolute weights. Unlike the relative weights, absolute weights are constant across all informer combinations.

Averaging Versus Adding. The qualitative difference between averaging and adding arises from the operation of the weight parameter discussed in the preceding section. Whereas the effective weight of each stimulus informer depends on the other informers, this is not true of the scale value. Weight and value thus have essentially different roles in the averaging model.

In the adding model, in contrast, weight and value have mathematically equivalent roles. They operate together as a product and cannot generally be distinguished (see Note 1). One contribution of averaging theory has been to put this weight–value distinction on solid ground.

Analysis and Estimation for Averaging Model. In the equal weight case, the averaging model is formally equivalent to the addition model. The parallelism theorem thus applies in the same way (see also Note 5).

For the differential weight case, an AVERAGE program for analysis and estimation is available (Zalinski & Anderson, 1991). Weights and values can be estimated separately with uniqueness properties dependent on the structure of the design (see second paragraph of chapter Notes).

DECISION AVERAGING RULE

A relative ratio rule may be derived from averaging theory to represent compromise between two competing responses. In the Bayesian decision study of Figure 10.7, for example, subjects judged probability that a sample had been drawn from one of two specified populations. Attribution tasks, similarly, may involve relative likelihood of two possible causes of some action (Chapter 5) or of two possible interpretations of an ambiguous sound or sentence (Chapter 12). Each alternative is considered to elicit a covert response tendency; the overt response is a compromise between these two tendencies.

Under averaging theory, with the initial state ignored for convenience, this compromise between two competing responses, A and B, would be:

$$\rho = \frac{\omega_{Ai}\psi_{Ai} + \omega_{Bj}\psi_{Bj}}{\omega_{Ai} + \omega_{Bj}}. \tag{5a}$$

The scale values, ψ_{Ai} and ψ_{Bj}, of the two competing responses may be set at 0 and 1, mirroring the dichotomous choice structure of the task. The strengths of the two competing responses are then represented by the weights. This averaging theory analysis thus yields the decision averaging rule:

$$\rho = \frac{\omega_{Bj}}{\omega_{Ai} + \omega_{Bj}}. \tag{5b}$$

The characteristic pattern predicted by this decision averaging rule is a slanted barrel shape, illustrated in Figure 7.5. Quite a few applications of the decision averaging rule have been made in judgment–decision theory (Chapter 10) and language processing (Chapter 12).[6]

SERIAL INTEGRATION

Serial processing is common in everyday life, with relevant information being accumulated over the course of time. This is how we learn about our spouse, our job, social issues, and so forth. This functional learning involves step-by-step integration.

A serial integration rule may be written:

$$\rho_n = \rho_{n-1} + \omega_n(\psi_n - \rho_{n-1}), \tag{6a}$$

where ρ_n and ρ_{n-1} are the responses on trials n and $n - 1$, respectively, and ψ_n and ω_n are the value and weight parameters of the informer at trial n. For a learning task, ψ_n would be the informer (reinforcer) value and ω_n would be the learning rate.

Equation 6a is sometimes called the *proportional-change rule* because the change in response, $(\rho_n - \rho_{n-1})$, is proportional to the distance, $(\psi_n - \rho_{n-1})$, between the present informer and the previous response. This rule may be rewritten:

$$\rho_n = \omega_n \psi_n + (1 - \omega_n)\rho_{n-1}. \tag{6b}$$

Mathematically, this is a weighted average, although it can also represent a process of addition as discussed in a later section.

Only modest processing capacity is required for this serial integration. Once the current informer has been integrated, it need no longer be retained in memory. The functional task memory requires only the two parameters, weight and value, of the cumulative response.

An important case arises when the response is measured only at the end of a sequence of trials. This one response can be fractionated into components, each representing the contribution of the informer on one trial of the sequence. The logic of this analysis is to treat each trial as one factor in a serial-factorial design and apply the parallelism theorem. Often useful is a design with two levels of each factor so chosen that the difference between their values, $(\psi_1 - \psi_2)$, is constant across trials. Then the difference, Δ_n, between the two marginal means at position n is:

$$\Delta_n = \omega_n (\psi_1 - \psi_2). \tag{7}$$

Since the value difference in parentheses is constant, ω_n is proportional to Δ_n, which may be estimated from the data by virtue of Conclusion 2 of the parallelism theorem. The serial curve of weight is thus obtainable. This technique applies both to the adding and the equal weight averaging model.

Serial integration represents a general purpose strategy, applicable in many different areas: learning, adaptation, motivation, belief adjustment, attitude formation, expectancy, and so on. Step-by-step adjustment, with its minimal requirements on memory, suggests a primitive, biological process. Applications are given to attitudes in Chapter 5, to belief adjustment in Chapter 10, and to functional memory in Chapter 11.

LEARNING AND SEQUENTIAL DEPENDENCIES

Learning may be considered information integration, with reinforcing events being treated as *informers*. This informational view seems appropriate for everyday learning, for example, learning of event expectancies or social attitudes. Reinforcement theories seem awkward and strained in attempts to claim that attitudes toward U. S. presidents, for example, or function knowledge in intuitive physics, are learned by reinforcement of responses in the manner of conditioning studies with rats and dogs.

Sequential dependencies arise in learning experiments that present varied informers over a sequence of trials. The response measure will increase and decrease in direct reaction to the informing events on each trial; these increments and decrements are fundamental quantities in learning theory.

The serial integration model of Equation 6a is applied to attitude learning in Figure 5.3. The tree diagram of this figure dramatically portrays the sequential dependence of attitude on information. The model fit well, although the weight parameter of the cumulative attitude increased over trials, contrary to typical learning models.

A partly negative application comes from the task of probability learning, in which subjects predict which of two events will occur next in a sequence of trials. When the two events are presented randomly, optimal strategy is to always predict the more frequent event. Instead, subjects end up *probability matching*: They predict each event in proportion to its frequency, continuing this matching behavior over hundreds of trials.

This nonoptimal behavior became a center of attention in the rise of mathematical learning models in the 1950s, when it was found that simple conditioning assumptions predicted the probability matching. Despite such success with mean learning curves, however, these mathematical learning models were quite unable to account for the sequential dependencies, and so have been largely abandoned. The serial integration model of Equation 6a, however, has done well in a number of tasks of informational learning (see also Chapters 4, 5, and 10).[7]

IMPLICIT ADDITIVITY: LESSONS FOR CONCEPTUAL ANALYSIS

Conceptual analysis sometimes depends on background assumptions that are taken for granted, perhaps without realizing that any assumption has been made. The background assumption of additivity is an instructive case. In the first three following cases, deviations from additivity were interpreted as the operation of some special cognitive process. These interpretations were seen to be invalid, conceptually and empirically, when averaging theory was applied.

Subadditivity. The first example refers to the fact that the second of two informers of equal value often has less effect than the first. This finding seems to implicate some special cognitive process—under the assumption of additivity. If additivity holds, the second of two equal informers should add the same effect as the first; and a third should add the same as the second. The observed subadditivity thus seems to involve some further process.

One suggested process was redundancy: The second informer has some elements in common with the first, and these common elements will have reduced effect in their second appearance. Another suggested process was expectancy–impact: The initial informer sets up an expectancy for more of the same value; being thus expected, the second informer has less impact.

Averaging theory, however, explains the obtained result without bringing in any further process. Subadditive effects follow directly from the theory. This interpretation has been well supported empirically (see *Amount of Information* in Chapter 4 and the related discussion of Figure 5.3).

This outcome has interesting implications for cognitive theory. On the negative side, it rules out a class of semantic feature theories that would predict redundancy in terms of common features of different stimuli. On the positive side, it supports the distinctness and independence of the **V** and **I** operators in the integration diagram of Chapter 1.

Neutral Information. The second example refers to findings that a neutral, uninformative stimulus may decrease the effect of subsequent stimuli. It might seem that some special process, such as crystallization, must be involved that causes subjects to discount the subsequent stimuli—under the assumption of additivity.

But the neutral stimulus, although having a value of zero, may have nonzero weight. Its weight × value effect will still be zero, so it will have zero effect under additivity. Averaging theory, in contrast, accounts for the result without invoking any special process because the nonzero weight appears in the denominator of Equations 4. This prediction from averaging theory has been noted and verified by Sam Himmelfarb in attitude theory and by Jim Shanteau in Bayesian decision theory. In the latter case, Shanteau's *dilution effect* added to previous evidence favoring IIT over the Bayesian approach in judgment–decision theory (see Chapter 10).

Opposite-effects Paradox: Configurality? Averaging? The same informer, as previously noted, may have both positive and negative effects. In Figure 2.4, for example, the medium informer has a positive effect when added to the informer of low value, but a negative effect when added to the informer of high value. Opposite effects seems counterintuitive; some special process seems needed to explain this opposite-effects paradox.

One attractive interpretation is in terms of *contrast*: When the medium informer is paired with an informer of considerably different value, it has been argued, the very contrast between them causes the medium to shift away from the value of the paired stimulus. Contrast is common in sensory psychophysics. A medium gray patch will appear lighter on a dark background, darker on a light background. In the verbal realm, by analogy, the medium informer would become positive when paired with a negative informer, negative when paired with a positive informer. This contrast interpretation not only provides an attractive explanation of the observed results, but points toward uniformity across the verbal and sensory domains.

This contrast interpretation, however, is conceptually problematic and empirically incorrect. Logically, it depends on the background assumption of additivity. Under additivity, it is true, the same stimulus can have opposite effects only if its value changes. But this is not true under the averaging hypothesis, which predicts opposite effects.

The averaging interpretation is not merely an alternative hypothesis. It rests on extensive evidence. The contrast assumption, on the other hand, was disproved by direct test (see *Positive Context Effect* in Chapter 4).

Interactions in Analysis of Variance. Implicit additivity also underlies many interpretations of statistical interaction terms in analysis of variance. In a two-factor design, interactions correspond to nonparallelism in the factorial graph, and such nonparallelism is commonly considered to be meaningful psychological interaction. Such interpretation is not often justified.

One reason is that the operative integration model may be nonadditive. An example with the proportional-change model of Equations 6 is discussed in relation to measurement of forgetting in Chapter 11. A further reason is that the interaction may be an artifact of nonlinearity in the measurement scale, as discussed earlier under *Parallelism and Nonparallelism* (see further Anderson, 1982, Sections 7.10 and 7.11).

MEASUREMENT THEORY

Averaging theory leads to a new outlook on psychological measurement. One sign has already appeared in the two-parameter, $\omega-\psi$ representation of the stimulus. Traditional measurement theory has centered on the concept of scale value; weights have been treated as subsidiary parameters or just ignored. In the averaging rule, however, both parameters, weight and scale value, have equal conceptual status. If anything, weight is more important.[8]

Furthermore, averaging theory makes it possible to identify and estimate weights separately from scale values. This is not generally possible with the addition rule. The weight parameter provides a proper measure of importance, freed from confounding with scale value. Comparing importance of different variables is done frequently but seldom legitimately. Averaging theory can provide legitimate comparisons of importance.

These measures can be in common currency. Qualitatively different factors, such as love and money, or shame and pride, can be measured in the same scale units. Their weight parameters also may be measured in common units. Because of these properties—and because of its empirical validity—averaging theory has a unique role in psychological measurement theory.

INTEGRATION PROCESSES

Thought and action generally require assemblage in operating memory. Much of assemblage involves more molecular levels of processing that are unitized at a molar level in cognitive algebra. The more molecular levels are also interesting and important.

Work to date, however, has been mostly concerned with molar concepts of everyday life, seeking a theory that would be self-sufficient around this level. This molar approach has been effective: Cognitive algebra has been established at its own level without having to await elucidation of lower levels.

The effectiveness of this molar approach is shown in the breadth of empirical applications of later chapters, achieved by a small number of workers. This work now forms a foundation for a functional theory of cognition. Averaging theory, in particular, has many uses and implications that are independent of the nature of the averaging process.

A more pertinent reason for molar analysis appears in the difficulties encountered in establishing cognitive algebra. One group of difficulties arose in understanding nonparallelism, noted earlier in the final section under addition rules. Associated with this was a group of problems of measurement theory, marked by near-total opposition to the rating scale methodology of functional measurement (see next chapter). These difficulties were resolved at the molar level. In retrospect, any other way would evidently have been ineffective.

Once established, however, cognitive algebra can help in analysis of other levels, more molar as well as more molecular. One line of such inquiry concerns various integration processes considered below. Cognitive algebra is not abstract mathematics; each integration rule must have some material embodiment, interestingly illustrated with the various as-if multiplication processes.

Some results and speculations on this matter are given in the following sections for the three algebraic rules.

ADDITION

Addition can be conceptualized as serial, stepwise movement along a response continuum. At each successive step, the last response is adjusted by moving sideward an amount equal to the value of the present stimulus, positive or negative. This integration process requires minimal cognitive capacity. The present stimulus need be kept in operating memory only until evaluated and added in. Longer-term memory is required only for the cumulative response.

A strict addition rule requires that the value of any stimulus informer be independent of the amount of prior information. Strict addition cannot be expected in general, of course, because it requires in principle an unbounded response scale. The more important concern, however, is whether strict addition holds for small numbers of stimuli.

Surprisingly, not much evidence is available. In a study of scale invariance, subjects were instructed to judge total magnitude for pairs of different perceptual dimensions. All pairs showed parallelism, which supports strict addition (Anderson, 1974d). Other instances appear in duty–need integration (Figure 7.2) and in children's belief integration (Schlottmann & Anderson, in press). Most parallelism, however, has represented averaging rather than adding.

Nonstrict addition may appear with various kinds of diminishing returns. A standard example is the subjective worth of an aggregate of goods, or commodity bundle. Although this diminishing returns is termed subadditivity, it usually represents an increasing redundancy of goods. Such diminishing returns would seem appropriately localized in the valuation operation for each successive good. The integration process itself would then be addition.

An ambiguous case may arise when the response scale has definite bounds and values are polarized. A stepwise adding-type rule could then be defined by the proportional-change model of Equation 6b, with ψ_n having only two values, corresponding to the two ends of the response scale. Equation 6b is mathematically an average, and an averaging interpretation would seem justified when, for example, the cumulative response becomes increasingly resistant to change. Alternatively, the mathematical averaging could be localized in the valuation, as with aggregates of positive and negative goods or with redundant information, and the integration accomplished by addition.

An interesting complication appears with the attribution schema for judgments of students' motivation, given information about ability and performance (Figure 5.5). Ordinarily, high (low) motivation is expected to correlate with high (low) ability. When performance is specified, however, this direct correlation may become inverse, so that a student with high ability but low performance is attributed low motivation.

One interpretation is that this attribution task is handled by serial processing. Subjects are assumed to begin with a provisional judgment of motivation based on the given performance information, which has primary salience. To this is added or subtracted an adjustment based on a conditional evaluation of the ability information, relative to performance. This conditional evaluation represents stimulus interaction, and so might be expected to produce deviations from parallelism. However, it can yield parallelism under the plausible assumption that this interaction follows a linear rule (see Note 2).

A rather different kind of addition process would be obtained with feature activation. Added stimulation would activate additional features, with the response governed by total activation. Sensory intensity would be expected to exhibit this kind of integration, with features taken as sensory receptors. Subadditivity would be expected, of course, as progressively fewer receptors or receptors with higher thresholds remain to be activated. A similar process might be expected for certain affects and attitudes.

School arithmetic is notable mainly because it seems rarely used for adding, or for any other integration. Instead, subjects generally appear to use intuitive or analogue processes. It could be interesting, however, to study behavior of subjects instructed to use school arithmetic.

MULTIPLICATION

Multiplication can be performed as an analogue fractionation process. To judge expected value of a single probabilistic outcome, for example, the outcome would be located on the response continuum according to its full value. The probability would then operate as a fractionator of this location (Graesser & Anderson, 1974; Lopes & Ekberg, 1980). This fractionation process is thought to operate in a variety of tasks (e.g., Figure 10.1).

Closely related is the analogue amplification process, thought to apply in certains tasks of intuitive physics. In predictions of travel distance of a ball propelled horizontally off a table, for example, table height amplifies the initial velocity of the ball.[9]

A related multiplication schema is suggested by the lever torque rule, Force × Distance. This schema arises naturally in children's play, and has been studied developmentally with see-saw tasks. Generalized lever schemas may thus arise that could be used in diverse situations.

Interesting complications appear in "as-if" multiplication. Linear fan patterns can appear in the data without any kind of multiplication. Adult judgments of rectangular area exhibit a linear fan, for example, but this pattern is considered to result from a global perception of area, not from any multiplication of height and width. Some kind of addition process seems to operate, not any real multiplication. A quite different kind of as-if multiplication appears in the Adverb × Adjective rule tested in Figures 12.2 and 12.3.

Two other as-if multiplication rules deserve mention. Diane Cuneo asked 3- to 4-year-olds to rate numerosity of rows of beads varied in length and inter-bead spacing. For small numbers of beads, the children made veridical judgments, a counting-type response that perforce mimicked the physical multiplication rule, Length × Spacing (Chapter 8). Friedrich Wilkening asked 5-year-olds to say how far an animal would run along a footbridge in a given time (Chapter 8). These clever children adopted an eye movement strategy, moving their eyes along the footbridge at a rate proportional to the natural fleetness of the animal. This cognitive process is isomorphic to the physical process. Accordingly, it manifests itself as the linear fan pattern produced by the physical multiplication rule, Distance = Speed × Time.

The problem of as-if multiplication complicates the delineation of cognitive units. A multiplication formula implicitly suggests that its terms correspond to cognitive entities. This implication is appropriate in the second of the two examples of the previous paragraph, but not in the first. Analysis of cognitive units thus requires closer study of integration processes.

AVERAGING

Averages can be produced by a variety of processes. One of the simplest is serial integration, analogous to the foregoing stepwise addition process. As noted in an earlier subsection, however, averaging is essentially different from addition because it involves a two-parameter representation of the stimulus: *Scale value* represents the location of the stimulus on the response continuum; *weight* represents its importance in the integrated response. This weight–value representation has a corresponding difference in the stepwise integration.

In stepwise averaging, the first response is at the value of the first stimulus (assuming the initial state has zero weight). The second response moves away from the first response toward the location (scale value) of the second stimulus; the extent of movement is proportional to the relative weight of the second stimulus. This movement may be represented as an average, following the serial integration rule of Equation 6b. This stepwise adjustment may be continued with additional stimuli. On each successive adjustment, the fraction of the distance moved from the last response toward the new stimulus corresponds to the relative weight parameter of that stimulus.

The strict averaging rule requires that the relative weight of any stimulus be independent of the value of the last response. Unlike the addition rule, however, the effect of each stimulus generally depends on amount of prior information; that affects the weight of the last response in the integration rule and hence the relative weight of the stimulus, as in Equation 6b. Also unlike the addition rule, the same stimulus may have opposite effects, depending on whether its scale value is greater or lesser than the present response. This, of course, is the scale-free test between adding and averaging (Figures 2.4 and 2.5).

A fundamental result of the work on cognitive algebra is the empirical evidence for this two-parameter, weight–value representation. This representation is a large part of averaging theory. It is expected to hold fairly generally, even when the integration is not strict averaging. Hence estimation of weights may be justified even when their nonconstancy precludes testing goodness of fit.

This weight–value representation cannot be merely assumed, as indicated with addition processes. Bayesian theory of probability judgment, similarly, allows only a single parameter, corresponding to the weight of the evidence. This makes intuitive sense, for the net effect of each nonnull informer speaks either for truth or for falsity. Such one-parameter representations could be expected generally, a consequence of the approach–avoidance polarity of everyday thought and action (see, e.g., Figure 4.1). The experimental studies, however, have given general credence to the two-parameter representation.[10]

A rather different averaging process appears in the balance scale, used to illustrate the arithmetic mean in statistics. Each of several elements is considered a mass on a massless plank: The location of each mass corresponds to its scale value; its physical mass corresponds to its algebraic weight parameter. The mean is that fulcrum location at which the plank balances horizontally. This kind of balancing process is thought to operate in developmental studies of the balance scale and generally in intuitive statistics (Anderson, 1968b). A mass to represent the initial state may be included.

Mixing will also produce averages; the concentration of a mixture is the weighted average of the separate components. The concentration of each component corresponds to its scale value; the amount of each component corresponds to its weight. Affective or even semantic integration might perhaps be accomplished in this manner. Each informer would activate a sample of affective or meaning elements; the unitized pool of these activated samples from the knowledge system population would represent the integration.

Averaging may also be represented as a normalization process. To illustrate, suppose a given outcome is to be allocated among a group of persons in a just way. One rule of justice is to allocate to each person a proportion of the outcome equal to that person's input divided by the sum of all the inputs. This is a case of the decision averaging rule, in which scale values are 0 and 1 and weights correspond to the inputs (Equation 5b). In any group, the sum of the weights may be viewed as a normalizing factor for the several inputs.

Compromise provides an interesting process for averaging. To continue the moral example, consider obligations to perform two different actions, ρ_1 and ρ_2, with a possible compromise at some intermediate action, ρ. The force exerted by obligation i will depend on its strength, ω_i, and also on the distance between ρ_i and any proposed compromise, ρ:

$$F_i(\rho) = \omega_i(\rho - \rho_i). \qquad i = 1, 2. \qquad (8a)$$

The two forces will balance, having equal and opposite effect, at some point, ρ^*, between ρ_1 and ρ_2. The value of ρ^* can be determined from the equilibrium condition $F_1(\rho^*) = F_2(\rho^*)$:

$$\omega_1(\rho_1 - \rho^*) = \omega_2(\rho^* - \rho_2).$$

Solving yields the weighted average:

$$\rho^* = \frac{\omega_1\rho_1 + \omega_2\rho_2}{\omega_1 + \omega_2}. \tag{8b}$$

The final compromise is thus an average of the two obligations, each weighted by its strength. An empirical example appears in fairness theory in Chapter 7. A related application to group dynamics is given in Chapter 5. The same theoretical rationale leads to the decision averaging rule of Equations 5 above. This decision averaging rule also has applications in judgment–decision and in language processing (Chapters 10 and 12).

VALUATION

Similarity is considered the most important process for valuation. In a common form, similarity represents a relation between a stimulus informer and a referent or standard determined by the task goal. Although the referent may be unitary, as in phoneme identification (Oden & Massaro, 1978; see especially *Configural Feature Integration* in Chapter 12), similarity is assumed usually to involve integration over a distributed memory that includes diverse goal-related aspects or implications of the informer.

Previous work on IIT has suggested that similarity will obey an averaging process. Similarity averaging theory avoids certain difficulties, with asymmetry, for example, that trouble additive feature theories as well as multidimensional theories. No less important, similarity is considered in a functional mode. Hence similarity depends on the task goal, or dimension of response, not just on properties of the stimuli (Anderson, 1974a, p. 256; 1981a, Sections 4.5.4 and 5.6.5; Lopes & Oden, 1980).

Schema inferences constitute a different kind of valuation process. In the performance–motivation–ability schema discussed earlier, for example, valuation of the ability information is constrained by the structure of the schema and the given information. Similar schema-based inferences appear in the problem of imputations about missing information discussed elsewhere in this book.

Both valuation processes just described involve integration. This appears more generally in the view of thought and action as a sequence of **V–I** operations, in which the integrated output at one stage constitutes one input to the following stage (see, e.g., *Molar–Molecular Analysis* at the end of Chapter 12 on language processing).

Valuation applies to all parameters of an integration rule, weight no less than value. In the attitude attribution study of Figure 5.7, the first step was an inference about weight. Weight has interest because it can depend on different factors than scale value, such as reliability and amount of information.

Configural integration may sometimes be localized in the valuation operation rather than the integration itself. One illustration appears in the configural equity rule of Figure 7.5, in which the data patterns differ from those predicted by the nonconfigural decision averaging rule. This difference, however, was accounted for in terms of a configural effect in the weight parameter. With this configural valuation, the nonconfigural integration rule gave a good account of the data patterns, as shown in the figure. The basic integration rule thus remained unchanged. Indeed, it was the means for measuring the configural parameters. This approach may be more generally useful in configural analysis, as in the cited section of Chapter 12 on phoneme identification and in analysis of redundancy and inconsistency (Chapter 11).

The configural equity rule also points up an interrelatedness of valuation and integration. The valuation only became configural by virtue of the integration goal. The algebraic form of the rule remained the same, but the integration constraint impinged on the valuation process.

LEVELS OF ANALYSIS

Cognitive algebra is a self-sufficient theory. It can be established at its own molar level, independent of interpretation in terms of more molecular levels of processing. This is possible because the structure of an algebraic rule provides its own validational constraints in terms of pattern in the observable data. Interpretation of a rule generally refers to constructs manipulated in the experimental design, of course, but these constructs can also receive some validational support through a successful rule.

Meaning invariance is central in the self-sufficiency of cognitive algebra. Meaning invariance implies that $\mathbf{V}$ and $\mathbf{I}$ have independent effects. Both $\mathbf{V}$ and $\mathbf{I}$ can thus be treated at a molar level, without reference to more molecular levels of process.

Cognitive algebra can help in studying lower levels of process. It yields molar boundary conditions that any more molecular theory must obey (Anderson, 1981a, pp. 94, 99; 1982, pp. 303, 341). A lower level theory may thus be tested in terms of its ability to reproduce the molar values and weights derived from the algebraic rule. These molar parameters can be strong quantitative constraints on theory construction at lower levels of process.

Qualitative constraints are even more important. Thus, the finding of meaning invariance eliminated at one stroke an entire class of theories of cognitive consistency (Chapter 4). Similarly, $\mathbf{V}{-}\mathbf{I}$ independence raises doubt about some theories that rely on feature representation.

Integration rules provide other qualitative constraints. The prime example is the averaging rule, which often holds where addition and even multiplication rules had been expected. Examples appear in attitudes (Chapter 5) and in judgment–decision (Chapter 10). Attempts to construct theories around these hypothesized rules do not seem too worthwhile when the rules are false. An additional instructive case appears in equity theory (see *Fairness–Unfairness: Comparison of Two Theories* in Chapter 7).

Cognitive algebra can also cooperate more directly in lower level analysis. One example is the sensory branch of psychophysics, which has largely eschewed direct measures of subjective sensation because of uncertainty about their validity. Cognitive algebra can, under certain conditions, provide validated scales of subjective sensation. This provides a new tool for sensory analysis, with capability for measuring nonconscious sensation (Chapter 9).

Memory is a second area of cooperation between molar and molecular approaches. In this case, cognitive algebra led to a nontraditional conception of memory, together with methods for its analysis (Chapter 11).

Molecular analysis has a clear and present danger. A perennially favorite tack is to postulate sets of features, aspects, or other hypothetical elements, and assume they have properties needed to reproduce known results. Such "derivations" may seem impressive, but they often have little more content than their assumptions. A pertinent warning appears in the failure of once-popular statistical theories of learning, which left little substance behind (Note 7).

There is no doubt, of course, about the fundamental importance of assemblage. Assemblage, however, is in some ways more molar than valuation and integration. This more molar direction of investigation seems richer than concern over molecular structure of valuation and integration and more likely to reward the investigator. For experimental analysis, schemas of intuitive physics discussed in Chapter 8 offer promise.

It deserves reemphasis, however, that cognitive algebra is self-sufficient. It can be validated and applied at its own level. It constitutes a foundation for cognitive theory that treats phenomenology in something like its own terms. This theme will reappear in the final page, *Beyond Cognitive Algebra.*

NOTES

To pursue empirical studies of cognitive algebra requires more extensive background than is given here. Basic references are the writer's *Foundations of Information Integration Theory*, which gives foundation concepts and experiments, and *Methods of Information Integration Theory*, which covers experimental method, design, and statistics, including a general treatment of monotone analysis and a test of goodness of fit for general nonlinear models. Related work is given in Anderson (1974a,b,c, 1978b, and 1991b,c,d).

Analysis of the averaging rule with differential weighting requires iterative estimation procedures and was initially obstructed by statistical difficulties. In addition, uniqueness, or parameter identifiability, presents special problems and special opportunities (Anderson, 1982, Section 2.3). Joint estimation of weights and scale values requires augmenting the regular factorial design with subdesigns to obtain uniqueness of the parameter estimates. Although not recommended for casual use, a user-friendly AVERAGE program (Zalinski & Anderson, 1986, 1991) is available upon request: Norman H. Anderson, Psychology–UCSD, 9500 Gilman Drive, La Jolla, CA 92093-0109 or James Zalinski, 673½ Longfellow Avenue, Hermosa Beach, CA 90254.

Two comments on terminology are in order. *Rule* and *model* are used more or less interchangeably. The former term emphasizes the psychological process, the latter the mathematical form. *Adding-type rule* is a not too satisfactory term to include both adding and averaging rules. Such a term is needed, however, because either rule may be applicable in certain situations, without any way of distinguishing between them or even any interest in doing so (see similarly Note 2.1.1a in Anderson, 1982).

1. To prove the first conclusion of the parallelism theorem, note that Equations 2a and 2b imply that for row i:

$$R_{ij} = c_0 + c_1(\psi_{Ai} + \psi_{Bj}).$$

Similarly, for row h:

$$R_{hj} = c_0 + c_1(\psi_{Ah} + \psi_{Bj}).$$

Subtraction yields:

$$R_{ij} - R_{hj} = c_1(\psi_{Ai} - \psi_{Ah}).$$

In this last equation, the expression on the right is constant, the same for every column, j. This algebraic constancy is equivalent to graphical parallelism.

To prove the second conclusion, note that the mean response $\bar{R}_{.j}$ for column j, averaged over the r rows is:

$$\bar{R}_{.j} = (1/r)\sum_{i=1}^{r} R_{ij}$$

$$= (1/r)\sum [c_0 + c_1(\psi_{Ai} + \psi_{Bj})]$$

$$= c_0 + c_1\bar{\psi}_{A.} + c_1\psi_{Bj}.$$

Since $(c_0 + c_1 \overline{\psi}_{A.})$ is constant, the column mean on the left is a linear function of the column value on the right. Conversely, ψ_{Bj} is a linear function of $\overline{R}_{.j}$, which was to be proved.

Weighting factors may be included in the addition model without essential change in the parallelism theorem. Indeed, differential weighting is allowed, so that each stimulus has its own weight, ω_{Ai} for stimulus S_{Ai} and ω_{Bj} for S_{Bj}. Let $\psi'_{Ai} = \omega_{Ai} \psi_{Ai}$ and $\psi'_{Bj} = \omega_{Bj} \psi_{Bj}$. Then the parallelism theorem applies to ψ'_{Ai} and ψ'_{Bj}, so it is these that are estimated by the marginal means. Mathematically, ω and ψ act as a unit and cannot be separated within the framework of the addition model. Even with differential weighting for each stimulus, therefore, the addition model still predicts parallelism.

A more general parallelism theorem dispenses with response linearity, assuming only additivity and a monotone response measure. Adequate power for testing goodness of fit can be obtained in two ways: with a distribution method for two-variable experiments, illustrated with psychophysical bisection in Chapter 9; and with two-operations models that include two integration operations (see Anderson, 1982, Chapter 5).

For empirical applications, the addition rule is augmented with an additive error term to represent response variability. The same applies to other algebraic rules. Testing goodness of fit relies on standard analysis of variance for the addition and multiplication rules. A replications method has been developed for use with general nonlinear models (Anderson, 1982, Section 4.4).

2. An interaction that is linear in the stimulus values will yield parallelism and so escape detection (Anderson, 1982, p. 71). This qualifies the conclusion about stimulus independence listed in the text. However, if stimulus interaction does occur, it would generally be expected to depend on specific stimulus relations, not merely on value, as with stimulus inconsistency in the person cognition task of Figure 1.2 and Chapter 4.

The question of linear interaction did arise with the positive context effect of Chapter 4, but this possibility was ruled out (Anderson, 1981a, Sections 3.2 and 4.1). An apparent instance appears in the attribution schema discussed in relation to addition processes in a final section of this chapter.

3. To prove the two conclusions of the linear fan theorem, note that Equations 3a and 3b imply:

$$R_{ij} = c_0 + c_1 \psi_{Ai} \times \psi_{Bj}.$$

Hence the entries in row i are a linear function of ψ_{Bj} and hence also a linear function of any linear function of the ψ_{Bj}, in particular, the column means:

$$\overline{R}_{.j} = (1/r)\sum_{i=1}^{r} R_{ij}$$

$$= (1/r)\sum(c_0 + c_1 \psi_{Ai} \times \psi_{Bj})$$

$$= c_0 + c_1 \overline{\psi}_{A.} \times \psi_{Bj}.$$

Hence the column means are a linear function of the ψ_{Bj}. If the rule holds true, therefore, spacing the S_{Bj} on the horizontal axis at the observable column means, $\overline{R}_{.j}$, will yield the linear fan.

To reveal the linear fan pattern requires appropriate spacing on the horizontal axis, as in Figure 2.3, and this spacing is derived from the data themselves. It is a natural concern, therefore, that almost any set of data could be made into a linear fan in this way. An alternative approach would use the first row of data to determine the spacing. This single row can always be made to fall exactly on a straight line with appropriate spacing. But, if the rule is correct, every other row must then also fall on a straight line with the same spacing. This is a strong condition, therefore, and provides a strong test of the multiplication rule.

This alternative approach provides a valid test, but is not statistically optimal. Since each row allows an estimate of the appropriate spacing, it is more efficient to average all these estimates (unless their slopes are too small). Hence the mean row is usually used to determine the spacing, as in Table 2.3. More power to detect real deviations from the linear fan pattern is obtained in this way.

Exact tests of goodness of fit are available from standard analysis of variance. If the multiplication rule holds, the statistical interaction term is nonzero. It should be localized in the Row:Linear × Column:Linear component, however, and the residual interaction term should be nonsignificant.

4. The Motivation × Incentive model has been supported in an experimental study of snake phobics by Klitzner (see Anderson, 1981a, Figure 1.17) and in a six-variable *tour de force* by Klitzner and Anderson (1977):

$$\text{Expectancy}_1 \times \text{Motivation}_1 \times \text{Incentive}_1 \ + \ \text{Expectancy}_2 \times \text{Motivation}_2 \times \text{Incentive}_2,$$

where subscripts 1 and 2 refer to two independent goods, food and drink, respectively.

5. The simplicity of parallelism analysis for the equal weight case of the averaging rule means that this equal-weight condition will often be worth seeking. One advantage of the likableness response used in the person cognition task of Figure 1.2 and Chapter 4 is that a large number of trait adjectives have approximately equal weight on this response dimension. Analogously, the 220 biographical paragraphs used in the presidents experiment of Figure 2.5 were constructed to be roughly equal in amount of information. Normative data on 555 trait adjectives are given in Appendix B and the 220 president paragraphs are reproduced in Appendix C of the cited *Methods* volume.

6. The decision averaging model appears to have been first assessed with a valid test of goodness of fit by Leon and Anderson (1974) with the Bayesian two-urn task (see Figure 10.7 of Chapter 10). A formally identical model was developed independently and tested similarly by Oden (1974, 1987b) for language processing. This latter model has been greatly extended in later work by Oden and by Oden and Massaro (see Chapter 12).

Formally, the decision averaging rule is similar to Luce's (1959a) choice rule. Luce's rule, however, applies only for probabilistic, threshold choice response. The decision averaging rule of IIT, in contrast, also allows continuous response measures. Hence it applies to suprathreshold situations, in which the alternatives have markedly different magnitudes (Anderson, 1981a, Section 1.6.4; see also Chapter 10, Note 3).

The decision averaging rule is also formally similar to the operant matching law, but psychologically different in allowing for—and providing—rigorous treatment of subjective values (see *Matching Law* in Chapter 10).

7. The first systematic theoretical and empirical analyses of sequential dependencies (Anderson, 1959a, 1960) employed linear operator models (Bush & Mosteller, 1955). The key idea of sequential dependency analysis was that the increments and decrements in response produced by varied events over successive trials are direct measures of the psychological effects produced by these events. Hence these sequential dependencies are fundamental quantities in learning theory. This idea was later extended to models with responses measured on a continuous scale, for which sequential dependency analysis is especially powerful (Anderson, 1961, 1964b).

A linear operator-like model, associated with statistical learning theory, was developed by Estes (see 1964), based on then-popular conditioning principles. A notable property of Estes' model was that memory for previous events played no role. This model attracted much attention when it was observed that it predicted the probability matching behavior discovered by Grant and Hake (1949). The cited empirical study of sequential dependencies, however, showed serious shortcomings in Estes' model. These sequential dependency analyses indicated that the success of the theoretical prediction of matching behavior was "fortuitous."

Aside from these inconsistencies between theory and data, this study of sequential dependencies revealed a long-term transfer effect, similar to that later found in the basal–surface representation of attitude structure (Chapter 5; see also Anderson, 1969; Friedman, Carterette, & Anderson, 1968). This long-term effect further supported the claim that the success of the theoretical prediction of matching behavior in probability learning was fortuitous.

Estes (1964) subsequently presented new evidence for his statistical conditioning theory, concluding that "The structure of the choice data can be accounted for quite well on the basis of an elementary learning process" (p. 122). This new evidence, however, involved an artifact (Anderson, 1964a). When this artifact was removed, the long-term sequential dependencies for individual subjects showed that the predictions of the model "disagree with the data in almost every respect" (Friedman, Carterette, & Anderson, 1968, p. 453). An overview is given in Anderson (1982, pp. 150-153).

8. The averaging rule is disordinal, as illustrated with the crossovers of Figures 2.4 and 2.5. With differential weighting, it can be disordinal even in a 2×2 design. Hence it cannot be established with ordinal theories, which have been popular in psychological measurement theory (see Chapter 3). Instead, the empirical success of averaging theory demonstrates the inadequacy of ordinal measurement theory.

9. Applications of functional measurement to intuitive physics are given in Anderson (1983b), Anderson and Wilkening (1991), Dozier and Butzin (1988), Karpp (1994), Karpp and Anderson (in press), Mullet and Montcouquiol (1988), Wilkening (1982), Wilkening and Anderson (1982, 1991), and Wolf (1995).

10. A configural version of the serial averaging rule has been suggested in studies of probability development (Anderson & Schlottmann, 1991, pp. 120*f*; see also Schlottmann & Anderson, in press).

PREFACE

A new theory of psychological measurement is presented in this chapter. It follows a new direction, in which measurement theory is an organic component of substantive theory. Measurement scales are thus derivative from empirical laws. This *functional measurement theory* is not a mathematical promissory note but is solidly grounded in empirical studies across many areas of cognitive algebra.

Measurement of sensory qualities such as loudness and grayness has been controversial since the first proposal in 1860. Even more doubt has attached to measurement of concepts such as expectancy and blame, which lack a correlated physical dimension. Functional measurement theory has been reasonably successful with both kinds of concepts.

Two characteristics distinguish functional measurement. First, it provides a validity criterion for the measurement scales. This validity criterion is given by cognitive algebra, following the logic illustrated with the parallelism theorem of Chapter 2. Previous attempts at psychological measurement have either failed to provide validity criteria or have failed to satisfy them. Cognitive algebra, in contrast, has been empirically grounded.

Second, functional measurement places primary emphasis on continuous response measures. Continuous response measures have been shunned in measurement theory, in part because of biases so dramatically illustrated in Figure 3.1. Most workers, accordingly, sought to construct measurement theory using only choice or rank data. This is possible in principle, as with the monotone analysis method of functional measurement. In practice, however, it is exceptionally difficult and the practical outcome has been meager.

In measurement theory, the averaging rule has a unique role. It is disordinal in general, beyond the scope of other measurement theories. It establishes a two-parameter, weight–value representation as fundamental for psychological measurement. These properties, coupled with its empirical ubiquity, have provided a new foundation for psychological measurement theory.

The key to success lay in developing experimental procedures to eliminate biases in continuous response, thereby obtaining a true linear measure. This was essential for establishing averaging theory.

A primary function of measurement theory, in the present view, is to develop empirical procedures that can yield veridical continuous measures of response. Continuous response measures are essential for studying configurality, interaction, and the many integration tasks that do not follow algebraic rules. They are especially important with behavioral and physiological measures.

Chapter 3

PSYCHOLOGICAL MEASUREMENT THEORY

The search for true measurement of psychological qualities is now well into its second century, yet the main outcome has been disagreement. This disagreement arises even with simple sensory qualities, grayness and loudness, for example, that seem clearly measurable in principle. The different attempts to measure such sensory feelings seem almost to speak different languages.

One argument of this book is that IIT has provided a solution to this measurement controversy. Measurement theory is constructed on a new foundation, namely, algebraic rules of information integration. The validity of this solution will be demonstrated in each of the later empirical chapters.

In this chapter, the first part discusses the general conception of functional measurement. The last part takes up theory and practice of the rating method used in empirical studies of IIT. The middle part presents thumbnail critiques of some alternative attempts at psychological measurement theory.

FUNCTIONAL MEASUREMENT THEORY

Functional measurement theory constitutes a new approach to psychological measurement. In the traditional view, measurement is a preliminary to substantive inquiry. Functional measurement inverts this view to make substantive inquiry the foundation, to which measurement theory is organically related.

The logic of functional measurement has already been discussed in relation to the problem of the three unobservables in Figure 1.1 and in the parallelism theorem of Chapter 2. With the parallelism theorem, diagnosis of a substantive addition rule is bound up with two measurement problems: measurement of the stimulus variables and measurement of the response. The addition rule itself provides the base and frame for resolving both measurement problems. Similar logic holds for multiplication and averaging rules.

The validity of functional measurement appears in the empirical demonstrations of algebraic rules in the following chapters. Functional measurement theory goes hand in hand with this substantive cognitive algebra.

Functional measurement has not been widely accepted in the psychological measurement field. One reason is that it departs from the traditional approach to put measurement on a different foundation, making it an integral component of substantive theory. A second reason lies in its espousal of the rating method, which has been almost universally abjured in measurement theory. Most theories have disallowed continuous response measures, admitting only choice or rank order data. The main other attempt to use continuous response was especially critical of the rating method.

TWO METHODS FOR RESPONSE MEASUREMENT:
RATING AND MAGNITUDE ESTIMATION

At the time of the initial work on IIT, two different methods of obtaining numerical response were in common use. One was the ordinary 1–10-type rating scale. The other was the method of magnitude estimation that had recently been introduced by Stevens (see 1975). With this method, subjects judge stimulus magnitude in proportion to a standard stimulus, which is assigned some convenient value, say, 100. With heaviness, for example, a weight that seems twice as heavy as the standard should thus be called 200; a weight that seems three-fourths as heavy as the standard should be called 75; and so on. In a preferred variant, the first presented stimulus serves as the standard, and subjects are told to call it whatever number they wish.

Rating and magnitude estimation seem very similar. Both methods ask subjects to give numbers in proportion to their felt sensations. Subjects find both methods easy to use. The same subjects may use the two methods in alternate sessions without feeling that they are doing anything essentially different.

In fact, the two methods give radically different results. One outcome is shown in Figure 3.1, taken from experiments in which subjects judged grayness (lightness) of Munsell chips that ranged from white to black. The magnitude estimate of each chip is plotted on the vertical axis as a function of the rating of the same chip on the horizontal axis.

If the two methods were equivalent, the two sets of responses would be linearly related. Hence the curve would be a straight diagonal line. In fact, the curve is far from the straight diagonal; the two methods are far from equivalent. They cannot both provide linear scales of the grayness sensation. At least one must be nonlinear and invalid, not a veridical measure of sensation. This and other such differences led to a rather one-sided controversy, in which the rating method was long and widely condemned.

Figure 3.1. Magnitude estimation differs extremely from rating. Curve gives magnitude estimations of grayness (lightness) of Munsell gray chips, plotted on the vertical, as a function of ratings of same chips, plotted on the horizontal. Equivalence of rating and magnitude estimation would yield a straight diagonal line. Since the ratings satisfy validational criteria for a true linear scale, the deviation of the curve from the straight diagonal reflects bias in magnitude estimation. (After N. H. Anderson, *Methods of Information Integration Theory.* Academic Press, 1982.)

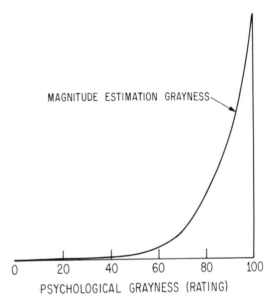

THE PROBLEM OF THE LINEAR SCALE

The controversy between rating and magnitude estimation concerns the *linear scale.* The term *linear* means that the observed response is a linear function of the underlying psychological sensation or feeling (Equation 2b of Chapter 2). Linearity is the essential property of a true measurement scale.

Linearity must refer to psychological quantities. Physical scales will not do. To illustrate, consider an ordinary 3-way light bulb, with settings of 50, 100, and 150 watts. With each successive setting, 50 more watts of light energy strike the retina. If brightness sensation was a linear function of light energy, it would also increase by equal amounts. This is far from true, as you can readily check. The change from 50 to 100 watts produces a substantial increase in brightness, but the change from 100 to 150 watts produces only a feeble increase. As your floor lamp can thus tell you, the psychological sensation of brightness is not a linear function of physical energy.

Most sensory dimensions are like brightness: Equal increments in physical energy yield successively diminishing returns in psychological sensation. This wise provision of nature allows the sensory system to function with weak stimuli without being overloaded by strong stimuli.

But this nonlinear relation between psychological sensation and physical energy highlights the difficulty. Physical scales are inappropriate; psychological laws must be cast in terms of psychological measurement.

MEASUREMENT VALIDITY

How is it possible to decide whether rating or magnitude estimation provides a true linear response measure? Some validity criterion is essential.

Many writers saw no way to obtain a validity criterion for continuous response measures. Neither rating nor magnitude estimation could be trusted, as Figure 3.1 so dramatically demonstrates. A foundation for measurement must be sought elsewhere, they argued, in choice or rank order data, because continuous response measures lack a validity criterion.

Actually, there is a simple validity criterion: the parallelism theorem of Chapter 2. Observed parallelism provides validational support for whatever response measure is used. All methods have the same opportunity to satisfy this validational criterion. In these validational tests, magnitude estimation generally failed, and the rating method generally succeeded (e.g., Figure 9.3).

The actual course of inquiry was complicated by several problems. One was the frequent appearance of nonparallelism. Understanding nonparallelism in terms of averaging processes took some time, as noted in Chapter 2 and discussed further in Chapter 4. An interrelated problem was that experimental procedures had to be developed to remove biases that trouble the rating method.

MONOTONE ANALYSIS

Linear response measures cannot generally be expected, but they are not necessary. Functional measurement theory makes explicit allowance for monotone, or rank order measures. Two issues in monotone analysis deserve mention.

BEHAVIORAL AND PHYSIOLOGICAL MEASURES: MONOTONE PARALLELISM THEOREM

Functional measurement methodology is applicable in infant, animal, physiological, and sensory research, which employ behavioral-type response measures. Infant measures would include looking time and curiosity–play reactions; animal measures would include operant rate and amount consumed; physiological measures would include electrical brain activity and biochemical assays; and sensory measures would include intensity of physical stimuli equated across dimensions. If these measures were linear scales, the parallelism and linear fan theorems would be directly applicable. But of course, linearity cannot be expected to hold for many behavioral-type measures.

Fortunately, linearity is not necessary. A more general parallelism theorem employs only the weak assumption of monotone response. This requires only that the observable and unobservable responses have the same rank order: $R_1 > R_2$ if and only if $\rho_1 > \rho_2$, which seems evident in many tasks. Parallelism analysis is possible even with such monotone response measures.

The idea of the monotone parallelism theorem is simple. The two premises are that the addition rule holds for the underlying response, ρ, and that the observable response, R, is a strictly monotone function of ρ: $R = M(\rho)$. Mathematically, the inverse monotone function, M^{-1}, will then transform R into a true linear scale: $M^{-1}(R) = M^{-1}[M(\rho)] = \rho$. This transformation is determinate, for it is the one that will make the observed data parallel. Monotone analysis is conceptually central to functional measurement theory, illustrated in the bisection experiment of Figure 9.7.

With monotone analysis, only the algebraic structure is at issue. This algebraic structure functions as the base and frame for true measurement. Functional measurement, accordingly, does not require prior measurement beyond a rank ordering of the response. For this reason, functional measurement may be called fundamental measurement.

The parallelism theorem of Chapter 2 may be viewed as special case of monotone analysis. Parallelism in the observed data means that the desired monotone transformation is just the identity transformation. The required transformation, in other words, has been built into the experimental procedure. Such procedure has been developed in functional measurement theory for certain classes of tasks. This greatly simplifies theoretical interpretation.

Three practical difficulties arise with monotone parallelism analysis. The first is how to calculate the transformation; this problem has been solved by workers in numerical analysis, and computer programs are available, at least for addition rules. The second is how to test goodness of fit; this problem can be handled with a replications method developed in functional measurement methodology. The third problem, the most serious, concerns power. The number of cells in an experimental design is seldom large, often no more than 20 or 30. So few data points provide weak constraint on the algebraic rule. Hence data generated by an inherently nonadditive process may be made to seem additive with monotone transformation. In fact, two-factor designs of practical size with a single score per cell generally cannot resist transformation to additivity. Two ways to obtain adequate power are included in the treatment of monotone analysis in Anderson (1982, Chapter 5).

Algebraic rules have interesting potential for behavioral response measures. A basic goal is to develop empirical procedures that can yield linear scales for observable response—then the pattern in the observable data will mirror the pattern in the unobservable response. Operant rate, for example, is often considered a linear response scale but definite evidence is scarce. An algebraic integration rule could allow determination of conditions under which operant rate is indeed linear or establish a monotone transformation that would yield linearity. Analogous integration studies may be possible with such disparate measures as response latency and amplitude, event-related brain potentials, and looking time in infants and animals.

MODEL–SCALE TRADEOFF[1,2]

Monotone transformation involves a tradeoff between model and response scale. A parallelism pattern that supports an addition rule would become a linear fan pattern and support a multiplication rule under an exponential transformation of the response scale. These two model–scale pairs are thus monotonically equivalent; there is a tradeoff, or duality, between the form of the integration model and the form of the response scale. Indeed, there are an infinite number of such equivalent model–scale pairs. From an abstract standpoint, one cannot be considered more correct than another.

At a purely abstract level, the model–scale problem is not resolvable. It applies equally in physics (Ellis, 1966). There is thus an element of convention in cognitive algebra—just as in the laws of physics. No one, however, argues from this ground that the laws of physics are not meaningful. Similar considerations apply to cognitive algebra.

The problem of model–scale tradeoff has long been recognized in functional measurement (e.g., Anderson, 1970, 1974a; see Note 1 below). Multiple lines of evidence support the linearity of the rating method, two of which may be noted here. If subjects are instructed to give an intuitive average of two stimuli, a pattern of parallelism in their factorial graph would argue for averaging. But parallelism would hardly be obtained unless the response was linear. Studies with such prescribed rules in IIT have largely supported the rating method (e.g., Figure 9.3). It could be argued, of course, that subjects multiply, rather than average, but rate logarithmically. Few or none, however, have considered this argument to have empirical substance or likelihood.

In some tasks, the response can be tied to the physical world. Young children's judgments of small numbers, for example, are a linear function of actual number (right panels of Figure 8.4). This would hardly be the case unless they perceived actual number—and their rating was linear. The alternative interpretation that children perceive some nonlinear function of actual number but rate using the inverse function is logically possibility but seems unreal.

The real problem is not model–scale tradeoff, but nonlinear bias. The real problem was to eliminate bias from the rating method. This problem was obscured under misplaced concern with model–scale tradeoff. Functional measurement addressed this problem and, it seems fair to say, found a solution.

Overall, the algebraic models—together with the rating scale—have been supported in a network of evidence (see *Rating Validity* below). It could now be argued that these results are only one of infinitely many model–scale representations, but this argument seems mainly a mathematical curiosity. Certainly, no serious case has been made for any alternative representation. As a matter of working science, model–scale tradeoff no longer seems of much concern with judgmental measures. Nonlinear bias remains a real problem with behavioral and physiological measures, although some progress has been made (Note 9).

OTHER MEASUREMENT THEORIES

Five other approaches to psychological measurement theory are discussed briefly in the following sections (see further Anderson, 1981a, Chapter 5). Three take greater than-less than, choice data as central, not allowing the use of continuous response measures. One has employed continuous response, but in a way quite different from functional measurement.

ADDITIVE UNITS

Strong arguments have been made that true measurement is not possible in psychology. These arguments rest on a conception of measurement in terms of physical operations of additive units. The physical mass of an object may be measured by placing it in one pan of a beam balance and counting how many unit masses must be placed in the other pan to balance it. Physical length may be measured similarly; a meter stick is just an additive concatenation of unit lengths. Additive units, accordingly, is often considered the essential base of measurement in physics.

Psychology, however, lacks such additive units. Addition of the physical stimuli will not do, as shown by the example of the 3-way light bulb. Sensations themselves cannot be placed together, like unit masses in a balance pan, or laid end to end, like centimeter marks on a meter stick. Indeed, the idea of adding sensations hardly seems meaningful.

No possibility of quantitative laws in psychology, at least for psychology of everyday experience, seems allowed under this conception of measurement in terms of additive units. Sensory summation, for example, is hardly testable unless true measurement is possible. The algebraic rules of cognitive decision theory lack meaning if subjective probability and value cannot be measured. Algebraic schemas of causal attribution cannot be established without measurement capability. People cannot be treated fairly, in proportion to their just deserts, unless their just deserts can be measured. Psychologists, accordingly, have been loath to accept the argument of additive units.

Intuitively, moreover, sensations such as loudness and grayness seem clearly measurable in principle. When the physical intensity of a sound is varied, we experience corresponding variations in "loudness." We can readily rank these loudnesses, and they seem to represent a continuous, unitary quality. In principle, therefore, loudness should be measurable on a linear scale.

What we need, accordingly, is a method that assigns numbers to sounds as a linear function of their loudness, and to gray chips as a linear function of their subjective grayness. This method should generalize to nonsensory concepts, expectancy and likableness, for example, that lack a physical correlate. Functional measurement has done this, thereby demonstrating the nonnecessity and insufficiency of the conception of additive units.[3]

FECHNER'S PSYCHO–PHYSICAL LAW

The conceptual analysis of psychological measurement given by Fechner in 1860 was based on the intriguing assumption that the unit of sensation could be taken as the *jnd*, or just noticeable difference. The concept of jnd originated in studies of sensitivity, or resolving power, of sensory systems. The senses differ considerably in sensitivity. The hand is fairly sensitive to changes in heaviness, for example, whereas the tongue is rather insensitive to changes in saltiness. To quantify this sensitivity, one stimulus was considered *just noticeably larger* than another if it was chosen as larger on, say, 75% of choice trials between the two stimuli. A small 2% increase in gram weight may be just noticeable, whereas it takes a 20% increase in salt concentration to be just noticeable.

These studies of resolving power revealed striking uniformity across the stimulus range for any single sense. Let S be one stimulus and $S + \Delta S$ the stimulus that is just noticeably larger. Then the *physical* increment, ΔS, increases in proportion to S. Over the main part of the stimulus range, in other words, relative resolving power is approximately constant:

$$\Delta S / S = c. \tag{1}$$

This is a purely empirical result, known as Weber's law. The constant c is the sensitivity of the sensory system under study.

Fechner's idea was that all jnds are equal *psychologically*. The increase in the *physical* size, ΔS, of the jnd reflects the well-known diminishing returns in sensory systems. But *psychologically*, argued Fechner, each just noticeable increase is an equal increment in sensation. This assumption allowed a simple measure of sensation: The number of jnds between two stimuli is empirically measurable and equals the difference between their sensation values.

Fechner took one notable further step. Of itself, his method of adding jnds would no doubt have remained a minor controversy. But Fechner saw how to couple his assumption of equal jnds with Weber's law, Equation 1, to derive an exact mathematical function. This was Fechner's famous logarithmic law relating psychological sensation ψ to physical intensity S:

$$\psi = c \log S. \tag{2}$$

This equation had extraordinary impact. Fechner's law held the center of attention for a century and more. One attraction is that it provides a reasonable account of the diminishing returns found with sensory dimensions. With sound stimuli, for example, it implies that the logarithmic decibel scale is a linear function of loudness sensation, which seems approximately correct.

What struck psychologists most about Fechner's law, however, was its promise of mathematical relation between the physical world of energy and the psychological world of sensation. This tantalizing hint that the mental realm might be governed by mathematical–physical law gripped the imagination of Fechner's contemporaries and of subsequent generations.[4]

But Fechner's "law" is only a conjecture. It rests entirely on the untested assumption that the jnd can be taken as the unit of sensation. This assumption seemed plausible, but it eluded test. The successive jnds cannot be piled up like unit masses on a balance pan. They cannot be placed side by side to demonstrate their equality. For a long time, no way was found to test Fechner's key assumption. Without a validational criterion, it remained speculation.

Integration psychophysics seeks a foundation fundamentally different from that of Fechner and the Fechnerian branch of psychophysics. The focal concern of integration psychophysics is the *psychological law*, that is, the integration operation of Figure 1.1. In this approach, the *psychophysical* law is derivative from the psychological law. Psychological law can provide a base and frame for quantification both of stimulus and of response, as demonstrated with the parallelism theorem of Chapter 2. This integrationist approach has had some success in the psychophysical realm (Chapter 9).

THURSTONIAN THEORY

The first true theory of psychological measurement is the method of pair comparisons developed by Thurstone (see 1928, 1959). This method requires the data to satisfy certain consistency conditions, and these provide the validational criterion that was lacking with Fechner's method. For the first time, as Thurstone emphasized, it seemed possible to resolve the long argument over Fechner's assumption that all jnds are equal.

Thurstone's approach was simple: Distance between two stimuli was to be measured by their confusability. This idea had already appeared in Fechner's use of the jnd as the unit of sensation. Thurstone, however, saw how to put this idea on a measurement-theoretical basis.

In Thurstone's conception, the effect of each stimulus includes a random component. Hence its operative value will vary from trial to trial, forming a probability distribution. If two stimuli are close together, their distributions will overlap, so the choice between them will be probabilistic. This choice probability will be a function of the sensory distance between the two stimuli, represented as the means of their respective distributions.

Conversely, the sensory distances are determinable from the choice probabilities. If the stimulus distributions are normal with equal variance, the standard normal deviate score will transform choice probability into a linear scale of sensation. Of primary significance, a test of goodness of fit is available: The sensory distance between S_1 and S_2 plus the sensory distance between S_2 and S_3 must add up to the sensory distance between S_1 and S_3. With this consistency condition, Thurstone provided a validational criterion.

Surprisingly, little use was made of Thurstone's method for sensory measurement. One difficulty is uncertainty whether the variances of the stimulus distributions are constant or increase with stimulus magnitude. With the usual assumption of constant variance, for example, subjective length would be a logarithmic function of physical length, which is manifestly incorrect.

With symbolic stimuli, such as attitudinal statements about war or religion, many applications have been made, but these applications have a peculiar meaning. The method of pair comparisons requires imperfect discrimination; choice probabilities of 0 or 1 are ambiguous about degree of preference. Imperfect discrimination is easily obtained with sensory stimuli, which can be taken arbitrarily close on the sensory continuum. Given two statements about religion, however, few subjects will be long in doubt as to which is more favorable. Hence pair comparisons scaling would not be possible with a single subject—or with a group of subjects who all had the same rank order. In practice, scaling is accomplished by pooling data across a group of people who have different rank orders of value. Such group scales could misrepresent the values of every individual in the group. They may exhibit some degree of sociological consensus, but they have little meaning as psychological scales.[5]

Functional measurement theory and Thurstonian scaling theory embody opposite conceptions of psychological measurement. Pair comparisons is intended to be a general purpose scaling method, applicable in all psychological situations. It is considered a methodological preliminary, used to measure stimuli before embarking on substantive investigation.

Functional measurement, in contrast, addresses measurement in concert with substantive investigation. The rules of cognitive algebra are psychological laws. Each serves as the structural base and frame for measurement within its own empirical context.

This conceptual difference is mirrored in a basic technical difference. In functional measurement, the Thurstonian assumption of random stimulus distributions is replaced by algebraic structure. Thurstone's distributions represent random noise, not generally relevant to processes of valuation and integration. The algebraic rules, in contrast, represent psychological structure.

This contrast is underscored by the two fundamental problems of multiple determination and personal value. Both problems are difficult or impossible with pair comparisons (Anderson, 1981a, Section 5.3). Both problems are essential to functional theory, and both are amenable to functional measurement.

Thurstone's work on scaling is nevertheless a signal accomplishment. His papers in the late 1920s are beacons of intellect shining through the murk of argument surrounding Fechner's law. His extension of pair comparisons to categorical response involves an early analytical use of the modern concept of decision criterion. Moreover, Thurstone went beyond psychophysics by seeking to measure attitudes and other concepts of everyday life.[6]

MAGNITUDE ESTIMATION

The method of magnitude estimation propounded by Stevens (see 1975) is simplicity itself: Just ask subjects to give numbers proportional to their sensations. The specific instructions used in this method have already been described in relation to Figure 3.1.

Stevens' idea was not new, for it appears in the common rating method. The rating method had been rejected by Thurstone because he saw no way to eliminate known biases. Magnitude estimation differs from rating, however, in removing the upper bound on the response scale. Whereas rating evaluates the stimulus relative to two end points, magnitude estimation evaluates the stimulus relative to a single standard in the middle of the scale. This seemingly minor difference in method produces radically different results, already illustrated with grayness sensation in Figure 3.1.

Stevens made the strongest claims that magnitude estimation provided a linear (or ratio) scale for sensations such as grayness, loudness, and saltiness. At the same time, Stevens severely criticized the rating method, amplifying the bias problem noted by Thurstone.

Stevens' arguments were remarkably persuasive. This is curious because no real evidence was ever presented. The critical assumption, of course, is that R is a linear (or ratio) scale of ρ when magnitude estimation is used. Stevens' assertions to this effect were gratuitous assumptions (see Chapter 9).

Unlike Thurstone, Stevens did not present a theory of measurement because he failed to provide a validational criterion. Without a validational criterion, Stevens' critical assumption is untestable and his claim is indeterminate.[7]

This issue of validity criterion is also an essential difference between functional measurement and Stevens' approach. Functional measurement provides validity criteria, as illustrated with the parallelism theorem of Chapter 2.

The parallelism theorem is an impartial judge between magnitude estimation and the rating method. If either provides a linear response, it has the opportunity of satisfying the parallelism property.

Magnitude estimation could have succeeded. It would have succeeded, had it been valid. In fact, it failed badly. In the empirical studies, magnitude estimation was found to be biased and invalid. At the same time, the rating method was generally supported (see, e.g., Figure 9.3).

The bias in magnitude estimation is easily understood. It corresponds to a diminishing returns in the use of numbers, as though the difference between 103 and 104 is less than the difference between 3 and 4. This diminishing returns is familiar from everyday life; a dollar price difference seems large for a blank videotape, small for a videotape recorder. The difference between magnitude estimation and rating in Figure 3.1 mirrors this bias of diminishing returns in magnitude estimation.

CONJOINT MEASUREMENT

Functional measurement and conjoint measurement (Krantz, Luce, Suppes, & Tversky, 1971) have several similarities. Both emphasize factorial design with its conjoint manipulation of two or more stimulus variables. Both rest at bottom on monotone, or ordinal analysis. Both focus on algebraic rules. And both recognize the necessity for a validity criterion, specifically, means for testing goodness of fit of the algebraic rule.

The two approaches differ, however, in their foundation. Whereas the functional approach has made measurement theory an organic part of substantive theory, conjoint measurement sought to develop an abstract, axiomatic theory prior to substantive applications. This is inappropriate, in the functional view. In principle, the foundation for measurement resides in substantive, empirical laws, not in the mathematical/statistical techniques used to establish those laws. Conjoint measurement, as is well recognized, has been ineffective at establishing empirical laws.[8]

The starting point for conjoint measurement is eminently sensible: Only monotone or ordinal data are allowed. Two stimuli can be ranked but nothing can be said about the size of the difference between them. This ordinal base, like that of Thurstone, seemed necessary because of uncertainty about continuous response measures, so strikingly illustrated in Figure 3.1. An essential problem, accordingly, is to test goodness of fit for an addition rule using only ordinal information. One ordinal test is the well-known crossover interaction, used to test between addition and averaging rules in Chapter 2. The "independence axiom" of conjoint measurement asserts that there are no real crossovers, which is clearly necessary for an addition rule to hold.

To call the condition of no crossovers an "axiom," however, seems misleading. This condition is statistical rather than substantive. The addition rule itself is substantive—it refers to processes assumed to underly the response to each single stimulus combination. The independence axiom, however, refers to no process, but instead to statistical comparisons among responses to four different stimulus combinations presented on four separate trials; these comparisons are done by the investigator, not the subject. The conjoint "axioms" are thus quite different from axioms of physics or even axioms of Euclidean geometry. In fact, the conjoint axioms seem only ordinal analogues of statistical techniques of monotone analysis in functional measurement.

In practice, however, goodness of fit methods necessary for assessing validity remain undeveloped within axiomatic measurement theory. This has been recognized in the later volume by Suppes, Krantz, Luce, and Tversky (1989, p. xiii), who comment that "the chapter on statistical methods was not written, largely because the development of statistical models for fundamental measurement turned out to be very difficult."

Distrust of continuous response measures is no longer warranted. Numerous experiments have shown parallelism in the raw data. Parallelism demonstrates an additive representation in the simplest possible way. Conjoint measurement cannot do better.

In fact, conjoint measurement cannot do as well. It requires that the data be reduced to rank orders, which jettisons the numerical information plainly visible in the parallelism. This virtually abandons all hope of testing goodness of fit, and hence all hope of establishing algebraic rules.

A fundamental challenge to conjoint measurement appears in the averaging rule. The general averaging rule is disordinal. Hence it is inadmissible within the ordinal framework of conjoint measurement. The averaging rule is a genuine challenge to axiomatic approaches because it has been empirically common, far more so than addition rules. This empirical reality indicates that axiomatic approaches are inherently inadequate to the needs of psychological measurement theory.

Cognitive algebra has passed conjoint measurement by. The parallelism theorem, as noted in Chapter 2, would be largely barren mathematics unless algebraic rules held empirically; the same holds for the theorems of conjoint measurement. The difference is that functional measurement has been effective at finding empirical rules; conjoint measurement has not.

Algebraic psychology has thus been established on a different foundation—not axiomatic, but substantive. These empirical rules constitute a substantive foundation for functional theory of psychological measurement. Moreover, cognitive algebra rises above itself to attack a fundamental measurement problem hardly recognized in previous measurement theories. This problem is considered in the following section.

LINEAR RESPONSE METHODOLOGY

Linear response methodology is essential for general theory. Methods and procedures are needed for continuous response measures that can be considered veridical linear scales—without requiring validation anew in each new experimental situation. Development of such methodology is a primary goal and responsibility of measurement theory. Several considerations indicate the necessity of such methodology.[9]

Linear response methodology makes it possible to go beyond factorial-type design. For strong tests of model–measurement validity, factorial-type design is important. For general use, however, such design is often unwieldy, infeasible, or impossible. If a response methodology has been developed and validated in tasks that do allow factorial-type design, it may then be used with some confidence in tasks that do not. Confidence that the response measure gives a true picture of underlying process can greatly facilitate progress.

A related consideration is that some tasks require considerable time to obtain a single response. It is then impractical to get enough data to validate the response scale within a given study, even when an algebraic rule holds.

The need to go beyond simple algebraic rules is in many ways the most important consideration. Some integrations obey more complex rules, especially when a given stimulus affects two underlying processes. The averaging rule, with its two-process, $\omega-\psi$ representation of the stimulus, required a linear response methodology, especially for parameter estimation. In psychophysics, similarly, the same stimulus may induce both contrast and assimilation processes (Figure 9.11). For configural rules, linear response methodology is uniquely useful because the pattern in the observable data is then a veridical reflection of the pattern in the underlying process.

A final consideration concerns dynamic tasks, in which stimulus parameters may change over time, as in adaptation and learning. Previous integration studies have concentrated on stable state tasks to help assure the independence assumption of parameter constancy, thereby facilitating tests of goodness of fit. A linear response methodology, which allows weaker assumptions about parameter constancy, is needed for analysis of dynamic tasks.

These considerations are especially important with behavioral and physiological response. The use of verbal organisms and verbal-type responses simplifies definition of response quality and facilitates collecting sufficient data. These advantages are often lacking in behavioral and physiological studies, so a proven linear response methodology is all the more useful.

The primary goal of psychological measurement theory should thus be to develop methodology for continuous linear response measures. This issue has not been recognized in other measurement theories. Axiomatic approaches explicitly eschew continuous response measures. This alone makes them inadequate as a foundation for measurement.

Other approaches generally rest on a traditional view that measurement refers to fixed characteristics of stimuli. In Thurstonian theory, as already indicated, the method of pair comparisons is considered a methodological preliminary that will yield stimulus values for general use in subsequent studies. Response scaling hardly enters the picture. Stevens placed similar primacy on single stimuli, claiming that magnitude estimation yielded invariant characteristics of sensory transducers. Both views embody the traditional conception of physical science that measurement refers to invariant properties of objects and events. Neither view is adequate for psychological science, in which values are functional, not fixed properties of external objects and events, but context-dependent constructions of the organism.

In the present view, algebraic rules furnish a priceless base for developing linear response methodology. Substantial progress toward this goal has been made with one class of tasks. This is the subject of the next part of this chapter.

THEORY AND PRACTICE OF RATING

The following sections take up the rating method used in IIT. A theory of the rating process is outlined in the first section. The second section describes the experimental procedures developed to eliminate rating biases and obtain a true linear response scale. The last section summarizes nine lines of evidence for rating linearity.

THEORY OF RATING

Beneath the simplicity of rating lie cognitive abilities that have received little study. Ratings are both comparative and constructive. A rating of sweetness, for example, is not a direct report of the sensory taste experience. Rating involves reference to a dimension and further comparison within that dimension to other experiences stored in memory. Sweetness, moreover, is not the sensory experience itself, but only a partial, one-dimensional representation. This constructive nature of sensory judgments is clear with taste, which may be judged along the distinct dimensions of sour, sweet, bitter, and salt, not to mention hot−cold and pleasantness.

The comparative nature of rating is explicitly embodied in the *end anchor procedure* (see next section). The rating of any given stimulus is considered to depend on similarity comparisons between it and each end anchor. Specifically, let S_L and S_U be the lower and upper end anchors, corresponding to responses R_L and R_U, respectively, usually the two ends of the rating scale. Let S be a given stimulus, and denote its relevant similarity to the lower and upper end anchors by Sim_L and Sim_U. The rating R of S is assumed to be located between R_L and R_U in proportion to these similarities:

$$Sim_L\,(R - R_L) = Sim_U\,(R_U - R).$$

Hence

$$R = \frac{Sim_L R_L + Sim_U R_U}{Sim_L + Sim_U}. \tag{3}$$

The rating is thus a weighted average of the two end responses, with weights equal to the similarities. A simple form of Equation 3 is obtained by setting the two end responses equal to 0 and 1. This merely sets the scale zero and unit, so it involves no loss of generality. In this way, rating is represented as a decision averaging rule (Equation 5b of Chapter 2):

$$R = \frac{Sim_U}{Sim_L + Sim_U}.$$

Strictly speaking, Equation 3 should refer to an implicit judgment, ρ, not to the observable rating, R. It is a further question whether R is a linear scale of ρ, that is, a veridical measure of the unobservable sensation.

The applicability of the rating method across diverse dimensions of judgment is considered to depend on a general metric sense. This same metric sense may underlie ratings of sweetness, expectancy, blame, and other experiential qualities of everyday life.

The linearity of the rating method is thought to derive from motor skills in local space. From infancy onward, well-being depends on accurate movement. The graphical form of the rating scale, which is usual with children, thus embodies a perceptual-motor skill. The numerical format used with adults is considered an extension of this perceptual-motor representation.

EXPERIMENTAL PROCEDURE

Experimental procedure is important for ensuring linear rating measures. Since ratings are comparative, establishing a stable frame of reference is desirable before collecting data. Two or three simple procedures have been generally effective.

The first procedure concerns end anchors. These are stimuli a little more extreme than the regular experimental stimuli, and are given initially to define the ends of the rating scale. If the regular experimental stimuli ranged from 200 to 600 grams in a lifted weight experiment, for example, weights of 100 and 800 grams might be used as end anchors. The 100-gram weight could be given at the very beginning with the instruction: "This is the lightest weight you will ever lift; call it 1." Next, the 800-gram weight could be given with the instruction: "This is the heaviest weight you will ever lift; call it 20."

These two end anchors thus define the range of stimuli and also the range of response. They begin the process of setting up the correspondence between the subject's feelings of heaviness and the external response scale. In addition, they eliminate certain end-effect biases since the response to the regular experimental stimuli come from the interior of the scale (see *Biases* below).

This process is continued with the procedure of practice stimuli. A representative set of stimuli that cover the range is presented, the subject being instructed to "Use numbers between 1 and 20 to signify heaviness of intermediate stimuli in the natural way; just say how heavy it feels to you; it is your own personal feeling that counts." Not much practice is ordinarily needed to establish stable usage of the scale. In some cases, however, repeating the end anchors during the experiment may be desirable to refirm scale usage.

The basic rating format is actually graphic rather than numeric. The graphic format is standard with children, and it is preferred for careful work with adults. The graphic format may be continuous, but is often demarcated into successive steps. With adults, successive steps can conveniently be represented by spacing successive integers along the graphic scale. With children, a correlated dimension is typically used, such as heights of sticks in a row or size of smile of a story child.

Rating methodology is still in process of development. With loudness, the rating method has had some apparent trouble, and any new application must be approached carefully. At best, number or position preferences, for example, will introduce some nonlinear bias. Further refinement and extension are thus of continuing concern (see further Anderson, 1982, Chapter 1).[10]

It is remarkable that subjects can use rating scales in a linear way. This depends in part on the indicated procedures, which largely eliminate the various rating biases. More important, rating linearity depends on cognitive abilities already noted above under *Theory of Rating*. The net result is that simple experimental procedures can yield linear response scales, even with little children (see Chapters 6 and 8).

RESPONSE QUALITY

Although measurement theory is ostensibly concerned with quantity, the problem of quality is more important. Implicit in attempts to construct a measurement scale is the assumption that what is being measured has substantive reality. This assumption seems reasonably secure with sensory concepts such as loudness, grayness, sweetness, and so forth. Concepts of everyday physics, such as time and speed, also present strong claims for psychological reality. It is less clear, however, that expectancy and risk, for example, or likableness, blame, and fairness represent simple qualities.

Theory of measurement cannot ignore experimental procedure; this determines the quality of the response. Instructions and stimulus–response display should be developed carefully to elicit the desired quality of response. One warning was sounded by Jim Shanteau, whose careful work in the Bayesian two-urn task showed that subjects were not judging probability, as the Bayesian studies had assumed, but something qualitatively different (Chapter 10). Such mundane details are an important aspect of measurement theory.

The problem of response quality underscores the role of phenomenology. With sensory concepts, the phenomenal evidence is persuasive in itself and can often be buttressed with physical and physiological considerations. Judgmental, social, and affective concepts are more problematic. Cognitive algebra provides one line of evidence on response quality, on the argument that success of an exact algebraic rule supports the psychological reality of the concepts and terms of the rule.

Interesting examples come from developmental studies of intuitive physics (Chapter 8). Thus, the Area = Height–*plus*–Width rule for young children's judgments of rectangles suggests that they do not perceive the stimulus as integral. Instead, both separate dimensions are operative quantitative concepts.

Similarly, the subtraction rule for uniform motion, Time = Distance − Speed, demonstrates that all three concepts are operational in metric form at 5 years if not earlier. This line of argument for concept reality is not definitive, but it can provide a novel kind of information.

RATING VALIDITY

An extensive, interlocking network of evidence shows that the rating method can, with suitable procedure, provide valid linear measures of psychological quantities. Nine lines of evidence are noted here.

Parallelism and Nonparallelism. The prototypical validity criterion is the parallelism property. As implied by the parallelism theorem of Chapter 2, observed parallelism provides joint support for response linearity together with the addition rule.

This utility of the parallelism property was contingent on explaining the frequent nonparallelism (see Chapter 2). This nonparallelism raised doubt about response linearity. Further, it suggested that what parallelism had been observed might be fortuitous, not trustworthy.

This problem of nonparallelism was largely resolved through discovery of the averaging rule. Averaging theory predicts parallelism with equal weighting, nonparallelism with differential weighting. Experimental manipulation of the weight parameters should thus produce deviations from parallelism with specific, predictable patterns. These predictions were confirmed. Averaging theory thus provided a unified interpretation of a mass of data that were discordant with additive assumptions (see also Chapter 4). And with this support for averaging theory went interlocking support for the rating method.

Fan and Barrel Patterns. Different algebraic rules yield different factorial graphs. Multiplication yields a linear fan pattern, whereas certain ratio rules yield a slanted barrel pattern (e.g., Figure 7.3). The observed rules show fair agreement with expectations based on task structure (see last section of Chapter 2). Finding these rules experimentally adds solidity to the concept of a general cognitive algebra. And with this goes validational support for the rating method used to diagnose these rules.

Of course, these expected patterns are not always found. The default pattern, however, has frequently been parallelism, in agreement with the concept of a purpose adding-type rule (Chapter 8). Subjects are thought to use a simplified mental model of the task. Even in this, algebraic rules predominate.

Scale Invariance. The idea of scale invariance, or stimulus generality, is that different tasks should yield equivalent scales of the stimulus variables. This idea can hardly be utilized, of course, without capability for obtaining linear scales of the subjective stimulus values.

The first demonstration of scale invariance may be that of the two heaviness scales derived from the size–weight illusion and the weight-averaging task shown in Figure 9.2. Scale invariance was also obtained with grayness judgments from three tasks: averaging and differencing, which involved rating, and bisection, which involved the nonverbal response of selecting a physical stimulus (see Figure 9.7).

Scale invariance is not an absolute validity criterion. Scale values are not properties of the stimulus, but constructions of the perceiver. The same stimulus may thus have different values in different tasks. However, demonstration of scale invariance does provide useful joint support for both integration rules—together with the response measures for both tasks.

Threefold Generality. Scale invariance is only one facet of a threefold generality: of stimulus, response, and integration rule. The success of the rating response across diverse domains of human judgment buttresses its validity. This response generality is broader than the stimulus generality of scale invariance, for it applies across measures of different quality.

Rule generality refers to the appearance of similar integration rules across domains as diverse as person cognition, intuitive statistics, and psychophysics. Rule generality is underscored by the many findings of similar rules in young children and adults. This generality of cognitive algebra is strong support for its validity.

These three kinds of generality are interrelated. Each kind of generality refers to one of the three unobservables, indicated in the integration diagram of Figure 1.1. Such interlocking, threefold generality provides stronger theory than could be obtained from any one alone.

Prescribed Rules. Prescribed integration rules have proved useful in measurement theory. Subjects are instructed to give the average, say, or sum, or difference, of two stimuli. Each of these three rules implies parallelism in the factorial graph, and parallelism has typically been observed. This outcome may seem unsurprising, not to say uninteresting, for the appropriate rule is prescribed to the subjects. But parallelism would hardly be obtained unless the response scale was linear. The stronger the prescription to the subjects, the more confidence can be placed in observed parallelism—and in the response measure.

In one such application, Dave Weiss asked subjects to judge average grayness of pairs of Munsell chips. Two response scales were used: rating and magnitude estimation. The rating data exhibited parallelism; the magnitude estimation data exhibited marked nonparallelism (see Figure 9.3). This outcome, incidentally, reflects the fact that subjects do these prescribed tasks intuitively, not by mental arithmetic, for that would yield parallelism with both response measures. The conclusion is clear: Ratings can provide a valid linear scale; magnitude estimation is biased and invalid.

Two-operation Rules. Rules with a second integration operation can provide stronger constraint on the data, and hence stronger constraint on the response measure. One example is the unfairness rule tested in Figure 7.3, which involves both ratio and subtraction operations. The ratio operation predicts a barrel pattern; the subtraction operation predicts parallelism. All six panels of Figure 7.3 agree with these predictions. This agreement provides interlocking support for the two-operation rule—and for the rating method.

This two-operation logic was also used to buttress the finding that 5-year-olds judge area of rectangles by adding height and width. The alternative interpretation that they perceived area veridically but used the rating scale logarithmically would also produce parallel data. This alternative was assessed by asking for area judgments of pairs of rectangles. The logarithmic response interpretation implies nonadditivity of the two rectangles; the linear response interpretation implies parallelism, which was observed.

Agreement with Physical Law. Agreement of cognitive algebra with physical law, although by no means uniform, provides a rather different validity criterion for the rating method. A simple example concerns adults' judgments of area of rectangles, which exhibit a linear fan pattern, in line with the physical rule, Height × Width. The integration process is thought to involve summation of unit areas, but this will mirror the actual area and so produce the fan pattern. This result, prosaic in itself, supports the validity of the rating method. If Thurstone's stimulus distribution bias was operative, for example, systematic deviations from the fan pattern would be expected (see *Biases* below).

This line of evidence may be strengthened with two-operation rules. To continue the example, adults could be asked to judge combined area of two rectangles. The algebraic structure of their judgments would be expected to be isomorphic to the physical rule, Height-1 × Width-1 + Height-2 × Width-2. This two-rectangle study has not been performed with adults, but it seems safe to assume a pattern of data that reflects the physical area, showing a linear fan for each separate rectangle and parallelism for the pair of rectangles. In this thought experiment, the two operations, multiplication and addition, buttress each other—and the response scale.

The worth of this line of evidence may be questioned on the ground that cognitive algebra not infrequently disagrees with physical law. Still, the rating data usually make sense. In the most notable disagreement, already mentioned, 5-year-olds' ratings of rectangle area followed the counterintuitive rule of Height + Width. This, however, appears to be one manifestation of a general purpose adding-type rule already present at 3[+] years of age (see Chapter 8).[11]

Agreement with Physical Metrics. People can be fairly accurate with judgments of a few physical quantities under restricted conditions. Most notable is length, made manifest in the graphic rating response.

A second case is small numbers, up to 6 or 8. A striking application was given by Diane Cuneo, who asked children 3–4 years of age for graphic ratings of numerosity of rows of beads varied in length and interbead spacing. For small numbers of beads, the children could use a counting-type process to make veridical judgments. Hence their judgments should exhibit the fan pattern of the physical rule, Number = Length × Interbead spacing—if they use the rating scale in a linear way. Cuneo did observe the fan pattern; in fact, the ratings were proportional to physical number. These data thus provided cogent support for the rating capability of these young children (Figure 8.4).

Biases. The end-point bias, which refers to an affinity for the end points of the rating scale, has appeared in certain experiments in the form of specific deviations from the prevailing factorial pattern. End-anchor stimuli can eliminate such end-point biases. One empirical example is given in the discussion of Table 4.1.

A second example appeared in work by Friedrich Wilkening on the Height + Width rule in young children's judgments of rectangle area. His initial experiment showed parallelism except for one very deviant response for the largest rectangle. This response was displaced upward from the parallelism pattern toward the end point of the response scale, which suggested an end-point bias. Wilkening accordingly replicated the experiment with the addition of end-anchor stimuli. The deviant point disappeared, leaving a pattern of complete parallelism (for a similar analysis, see Figure 9.2). The ability of end anchors to eliminate such effects testifies to their efficacy in the rating method.

Biases may be notable by their absence as well as by their presence, Absence of known biases provides some degree of support for the response measure. One example appears in the end-effect bias just discussed.

A related example concerns so-called floor–ceiling effects, which would tend to flatten the lowest or highest curve segments in a factorial graph. Initial work on the multiplication rule half-expected to find such flattening at the wide end of the predicted fan pattern. The absence of such flattening (e.g., Figure 10.1) argues against the presence of bias—and for the joint validity of the multiplication rule and the rating response.

Of special importance is the stimulus distribution bias, which refers to the dependence of the response on the entire distribution of stimuli. Subjects have some tendency to spread their responses over the whole rating scale. Hence responses to the same stimuli would be nonlinearly related if these stimuli came from a normal distribution, say, and from a flat, uniform distribution. This stimulus distribution bias caused Thurstone to reject the rating method and most later workers have done the same.

End anchors, together with practice, can largely eliminate the stimulus distribution effect. This effect was a major concern in the initial work on IIT. Factorial design typically yields a normal-like distribution of response values.

Hence the stimulus distribution effect, if operative, would produce systematic deviations from parallelism. When standard precautions of end anchors and practice were used, however, deviations of the predicted form were not observed. Direct tests, moreover, also showed that stimulus distribution effects could be eliminated. Stimulus distribution effects are real and deserve continuing concern. There seems little need to tolerate them, however, when they are not wanted (see Anderson, 1982, Chapter 1).

Cognitive Algebra. The backbone of the foregoing nine lines of evidence is cognitive algebra. Cognitive algebra provided the needed validation for the rating method; and the rating method provided the linear response measure that was needed for effective progress on cognitive algebra. In practice as well as in principle, therefore, measurement theory functions as an organic component of substantive theory.

MEASUREMENT AS SUBSTANTIVE THEORY

Measurement of psychological qualities is interwoven with substantive theory:

> The logic of the present scaling technique consists in using the postulated behavior laws to induce a scaling on the dependent variable. (Anderson, 1962b, p. 410.)

> A guiding idea of functional measurement is that measurement scales are derivative from substantive theory. (Anderson, 1970, p. 153.)

These quotes reflect the functional perspective, in which measurement is an organic part of substantive investigation (see similarly Sjöberg, 1966, 1994).

With cognitive algebra, accordingly, the test of goodness of fit, although essential, is only part of the validational process. Observed parallelism, for example, provides joint support for the addition rule and for response linearity, but alternative interpretations are logically possible, as noted in the discussion of case 4 of Table 2.2. The possibility of alternative interpretations is inherent in empirical science because it rests on an inductive logic of inverse inference, that is, inference from the observations to their hypothesized causes. This character of scientific inference is well-known, and it underlies the accepted principle that theory depends on an interlocking body of evidence.

Cognitive algebra, conjoined with the rating method, constitutes such an interlocking body of knowledge. One view of evidence has been given in the preceding nine-point itemization. More detailed support appears in each of the following empirical chapters. Across these many different substantive domains, the same cognitive algebra appears. Few other theories in psychology have attained comparable breadth and precision. It thus seems fair to say that cognitive algebra, together with the rating method, has a solid claim as a foundation for psychological measurement theory.

PSYCHOLOGICAL MEASUREMENT

Measurement of psychological concepts must be grounded in the nature of the organism and the internal world. The internal world has many characteristics, visual scenes, goal–action sequences, and ambient cogitation, for example, that hardly seem numerical in nature. Measurement theory should consider, therefore, what aspects of the internal world are numerically measurable and why.

This question has not received much attention amid the dominating concern with measurement of psychophysical sensation. Sensations seem clearly real and measurable, and controversy over their scaling absorbed attention to the neglect of more general issues of measurement. The nature of what is being measured is hardly less important than the scales themselves. The following remarks, speculative and incomplete, indicate one approach to this question.

Quantification has survival value. Capabilities for quantification have evolved from interaction of organism and environment. This functional perspective relates to the three operators, valuation, integration, and action, in the integration diagram of Figure 1.1.

Selection pressure to evolve quantification capabilities is clear at a biological level, both on the sensory side of valuation and on the motor side of action. On the sensory side, securing information about the environment is vital in obtaining food, avoiding injury, and perpetuating the genes. Sensory systems have evolved to be sensitive to different forms of physical energy (light, heat, sound, etc.) and to concentrations of different substances (diverse taste and odor qualities, etc.). Selection toward quantification comes from the utility of information about magnitudes of energy and concentration, which may be mediated by frequency of neural impulses.

Quality of sensation is part of measurement. One-dimensionality of saltiness, loudness, and other sensory qualities should not be taken for granted. The sensory experience itself may be complex, as previously noted for taste, in which a number of different qualities may be discerned. Moreover, pain, an important contrary case, often lacks unitary quality.

One source of one-dimensionality lies in the specialization of receptors sensitive to specific forms of physical energy or substance. In addition, there are indications that one-dimensionality may arise at post-receptor stages without specialized receptor cells, as has been argued for the taste senses.

On the action side, quantification is apparent in graded motor behavior, as in locomotion, securing food, and fighting. Motor behavior, moreover, is integrated with sensory monitoring that helps control the temporal development of any action. In such sensory-motor feedback loops, quantification has important functions.

The goal directedness of behavior, which underlies quantification at the biological levels just considered, involves a different kind of quantification in terms of general value. Goal directedness imposes one-dimensional, approach–avoidance constraints (Chapter 1). Values, positive and negative, represent such constraints. A dimensional value representation can thus be meaningful and useful even with complex stimulus fields and goals.

Whereas sensory quantification tends to be specialized in quality, goal-directed valuation tends to be flexible and adaptive. The same capability may subserve diverse domains of action. Thus, the affective senses may integrate specific sensory quantification with a more general affective quantification. The generality of goal directedness could facilitate development of a general metric sense for valuation of diverse qualities.

This conception of goal-directed valuation suggests that the focus on sensory qualities in psychological measurement theory has produced an unfortunate narrowness. One narrowness is the fixation on the concept of psychophysical law, which sees measurement in terms of a sensory function relating physical stimulus and psychological sensation. Laboring under this conception of psychophysical law, traditional psychophysics could not solve its own central problem of sensory measurement. This problem required a broader orientation in the form of integration psychophysics (Chapter 9).

At the same time, narrowness engendered by the concept of psychophysical law caused neglect of quantification in thought and action, especially quantification of goal-defined values. It is certainly more comfortable to talk about measurement of simple sensations than of concepts such as pleasantness, expectancy, and belief, but so narrow a beginning cannot attain the breadth needed for general theory of psychological measurement.

Not less important are social concepts such as attitude, fairness, likableness, blame, and ego defense. General-purpose quantification capabilities developed out of sensory and motor processes are presumably important in such thought and action, as with the general metric sense and the rating capability. At the same time, this top-down approach to sensory-motor systems seems a useful complement to the bottom-up path from the sensory periphery.

The foregoing comments have been mainly concerned with the valuation and action operators. The integration operator is also important in quantification. Indeed, much valuation actually involves integration, as a complex stimulus field is reduced to a single value. More generally, the prevalence of quantification on both the sensory and motor sides entails corresponding quantification in the intervening stages.

Algebraic integration rules would seem to have a central origin. The biological utility of central integration is clear. Signal detection by predator and by prey, for example, will be more effective by integrating signal cues across several senses. Selection pressure toward integration mechanisms arises similarly from the purposiveness of behavior, which imposes a one-dimensional, approach–avoidance representation on function.

The biological base of adding-type rules is indicated by their appearance in children as young as 3 or 4 years, as well as by the animal studies cited in Note 9. These rules would not seem to arise from intrasensory integration, for that is naturally subadditive. Hence they presumably have a central origin, as befits cross-sensory integration.

The evidence for a general purpose adding-type rule with young children (Chapter 8) suggests that much central integration relies on a small number of general purpose mechanisms. Both adding and averaging are at least reasonable approximations to optimality across a variety of situations, and certainly seem economical means to handle the pervasive problem of multiple determination.

Leaving these speculations aside, algebraic rules have the inestimable virtue of providing a base and frame for true psychological measurement. In this way, cognitive algebra can provide help in studying wider problems of quantification, furnishing tools for analysis of nonalgebraic and configural integration and ladders to the study of mental models and assemblage. Cognitive algebra is not just an end in itself; it is also a means for more general analysis of information processing. Truly, as may be said once again, cognitive algebra is a blessing of Nature.

NOTES

The essential ideas of functional measurement theory, including monotone analysis and empirical foundation, appear in Anderson (1962a,b). Summaries of theory and applications are given in Anderson (1979, 1981a, Chapter 5, 1982, 1992a).

1. Model−scale tradeoff has been carefully considered in functional measurement theory (e.g., Anderson, 1974a, Section II.A.6f, pp. 230*f*):

FORMALLY EQUIVALENT SYSTEMS. One final aspect of the [monotone] transformation problem needs a brief discussion. This is the trade-off relation between scale and model . . . The parallelism of the curves in Fig. 1 gives joint validation to the response scale and the integration rule based on the arithmetic mean. Nevertheless, it would still be possible to argue a different interpretation based on an exponential transformation of the data. That would transform the parallel lines to a diverging fan of lines; at the same time, it would transform the arithmetic mean to a geometric mean. Since the exponential transformation is an allowable monotone transformation in functional measurement, it is evident that the arithmetic and the geometric averaging models are formally equivalent interpretations of these data. From a mathematical viewpoint, one model cannot be said to better than the other . . . .

The given indeterminacy is not peculiar to the present approach, but applies equally well to physics. In general, if M is any arbitrary, strictly monotone transformation, then $y = f(x)$ is formally equivalent to $y = fM^{-1}(M(x))$. To say that f is the functional law and x the independent variable is formally equivalent to saying that fM^{-1} is the functional law, and $M(x)$ is the independent variable. In the same way, to say that f is the functional law and y is the dependent variable is formally equivalent to saying that Mf is the functional law and My is the dependent variable. A sensible discussion of these questions from a philosopher's standpoint is given by Ellis (1966), but no ultimate solution is visible. In practice, the well-known criteria of simplicity and unity seem to operate almost silently so that only certain kinds of simple algebraic models are used in most of physics. The data now to be considered give a reasonable basis for expecting the same in a substantial part of psychology.

Luce and Krumhansl (1988, p. 53) criticize functional measurement especially on the ground that it has not recognized the problem of model—scale tradeoff. This is incorrect, as shown in the foregoing quote. Observed parallelism does give joint validational support to the adding-type model as well as whatever response scale is used; this provides a valid representation of the data. It is well known, as Luce and Krumhansl observe, that all measurement representations allow an infinite number of alternative model—scale combinations—but this is explicitly recognized in the foregoing quote. Luce and Krumhansl seem to have relied on Birnbaum's (1982) paper, but this is in error as shown by the foregoing quote (see also following note).

The expectation for algebraic rules expressed in the last sentence of the foregoing quote has been solidly supported in the two decades of subsequent work. Cognitive algebra constitutes a consistent system with valid applications across many psychological domains. Although it might now be argued that the true response system requires some monotone transformation, the primary problem was to establish that consistent system.

2. Misstatements about functional measurement theory cloud the paper by Birnbaum (1982). The positions actually held in functional measurement theory were seldom those criticized by Birnbaum; rather, the positions actually held in functional measurement were very like those adopted by Birnbaum. These include various measurement issues concerning model—scale tradeoff, monotone transformation, parallelism analysis, scale convergence, and context effects. Nearly all the positions advocated by Birnbaum had long been standard in functional measurement theory (Anderson, 1982, p. 350).

Birnbaum's own work has made good use of functional measurement ideas, most notably the principle that algebraic structure is the foundation of measurement. He has made cogent contributions to some issues in averaging theory (see, e.g., *Probability Learning* in Chapter 10).

The paper in question, however, misrepresents the work it criticizes. A number of Birnbaum's positions were well-taken, but nearly all of these were notably similar to previous positions of functional measurement theory. Thus, it was incorrect to say that functional measurement had neglected the problem of model—scale tradeoff, as shown by the quote of Note 1. Similarly, it was incorrect to construe various empirical findings of nonparallelism as criticisms of previous work on functional measurement—nearly all this nonparallelism supported the averaging model with differential weighting previously developed in IIT. Exactly contrary to Birnbaum, therefore, they constituted good support for functional measurement theory (see Anderson, 1982, pp. 257f, 350; see further *Parallelism and Nonparallelism* in Chapter 2, *Understanding Nonparallelism* and Note 4 in Chapter 4).

Monotone transformation, emphasized by Birnbaum, has been an integral part of functional measurement theory in a series of articles beginning in 1962. Moreover, functional measurement theory has developed effective methods to handle the severe data-analytic problems that arise with monotone transformation. These methods could resolve a difficulty that undercuts Birnbaum's approach (e.g., Anderson, 1991e).

3. I suggest that the foundation for measurement in physics has the same logic as functional measurement, namely, that it resides in the algebraic structure of natural laws. This contrasts with a common view of physical measurement in terms of additive units. Indeed, a special committee appointed by the Royal Society in the 1930s to consider the possibility of sensation measurement reached a generally negative conclusion, primarily on the argument that no method of additive units is possible for sensation (Ferguson, 1940). In the present view, additive units is a special case of an algebraic rule, applicable only to some physical quantities that allow physical addition as an integration rule (Anderson, 1981a, Section 5.6.4).

4. The controversies over Fechner's proposal for psychological measurement are reviewed in Boring's (1950, pp. 286*ff*) history. The present term *linear scale* avoids the "quantity objection," which argues that measurement of sensation is impossible because different sensations are not commensurable. As William James put it, our feeling of pink is no part of our feeling of scarlet. Likewise, said Boring, a meter in itself is just as unitary as a scarlet. James' reasoning would imply that the height of this page cannot be measured because it is no part of a meter stick.

Implicit in the quantity objection is a conception of measurement in terms of additive units. The quantity objection has a legitimate point, for sensations themselves are not numerical, but it reflects nonunderstanding of the nature of measurement. What is being measured is not the sensation, which is a phenomenal quality, conceptually different from the one aspect of magnitude. Measurement refers to a linear relation between this aspect of magnitude and the observable response.

5. For symbolic stimuli, Thurstone's method of categorical scaling could in principle be used to linearize ordinary rating scales. This would require application at the individual level, which would be very demanding, and such applications do not seem to have been made. Applications in attitude measurement use pooled group data, which leaves dubious the status of the resulting attitude scales. The functional measurement rating method rests on a stronger foundation, both theoretically and empirically (Anderson, 1981a, Sections 2.4.4 and 5.3; see also *Functional Measurement Attitude Scales* in Chapter 5).

6. The tribute to Thurstone in the text may be amplified by adding that Thurstone was concerned with more "interesting" quantities than psychophysical sensation, an outlook continued in the emphasis on everyday life in IIT. One of Thurstone's papers was thus entitled, "Attitudes can be measured," and he did considerable empirical work in this area. His work on factor analysis attempted to measure complex mental structure with multidimensional representations.

Thurstone also seems the first to do serious work on mathematical learning models based on the idea of conditioning of elements. This idea is carried forward in Estes' statistical theory of learning (Note 7 of Chapter 2) and in current connectionist theory.

7. Actually, validational tests of magnitude estimation were obtained in various studies, but they failed. Stevens claimed that sensation is a power function of the physical stimulus, with the exponent an invariant property of the sensory system. Different standards, therefore, should yield the same exponent—but they do not. This theoretical discrepancy appeared in Stevens' first published empirical application of magnitude estimation. Similarly, the exponent should not depend on the range of stimuli—but it does, very strongly. Stevens, however, either explained away these and other failures of magnitude estimation or just ignored them. This left magnitude estimation free-floating, without a validational base (see reviews by Anderson, 1974a, 1981a, Chapter 5).

Proponents of magnitude estimation have begun to recognize the necessity for validational tests. However, they have hardly addressed the extensive evidence from functional measurement studies that magnitude estimation is biased and invalid.

8. The lack of empirical foundation for conjoint measurement theory was reemphasized by Estes (1975, p. 273):

> One reason for the relative paucity of connections between [conjoint] measurement theory and substantive theory in psychology may arise from the fact that the models for measurement have largely been developed independently as a body of formal abstract theory with empirical applications being left to a later stage. The difficulty with this approach is that the later stage often fails to materialize.

This later stage has failed to materialize in the two subsequent decades.

Others have voiced similar concern over attempts to construct measurement theory on an abstract, mathematical base. Tukey (1969, p. 88) severely criticized the axiomatic approach. Cliff (1992, p. 286), while lauding the axiomatic approach, pointed out that substantive accomplishments of these workers have had little relation to their abstract measurement theory (see also Anderson, 1974a, Section IV, 1981a, Chapter 5). Cliff thus characterizes axiomatic measurement theory as "the revolution that never happened."

9. Any quantitative response measure may be used in functional measurement, including response time, response rate, autonomic reactions, and electrical brain potentials, not to mention magnitude estimation and magnitude production. Indeed, a magnitude production response has been used in a few psychophysical studies, as in the optical illusion of Figure 9.10 and in the number-averaging study of Figure 10.9. Similarly, a functional measurement analysis of reaction time in problem solving has been given by Shanteau (1991). The essential principle is that the algebraic structure of the integration rule is the base and frame for measurement (see also *Matching Law* in Chapter 10).

A notable behavioral application of functional measurement is given by Farley and Fantino (1978) with a bar press response for integration of food reward and shock avoidance. Hawkins, Roll, Puerto, and Yeomans (1983) studied integration of two parameters of a single pulse electrical brain reward using a novel response of the frequency of a comparison paired pulse stimulus chosen by the rat to have reward value equivalent to each given single pulse stimulus. Fundamental work by Gibbon and Fairhurst (1994) on models for integration of reward and time variables with pigeons has used functional measurement as a tool to support a multiplication rule. This work augurs well for the prospects of developing linear response methodology for behavioral response, which would be invaluable.

The emphasis on the rating method in judgment tasks stems from its empirical success. In the initial applications of IIT to integration psychophysics, it was unclear whether rating or magnitude estimation, or either, would succeed. Both had the same opportunity. The rating method has succeeded in many tasks, although not all. Magnitude estimation, in contrast, has failed nearly all validity tests.

Luce and Krumhansl (1988, pp. 52, 64) seem to imply that the extensive use of rating methods, or "partition" procedures, in functional measurement represents some precommitment. Instead, it represents demonstrated empirical utility. Other quantitative response measures may, and have, also been used (see previous note).

10. The third basic experimental procedure for rating method is to use a moderately large number of rating steps. A 20-step scale, usually numerical-graphic, was fairly standard in initial studies of IIT (e.g., Figure 1.2). Although this procedure was adopted on intuitive grounds, it has been justified in work by Parducci (e.g., Parducci & Wedell, 1986), which has shown that increasing the number of rating steps upward from two markedly reduces the *stimulus distribution bias* (through which ratings of the same stimuli from different distributions, uniform, and J-shaped, for example, are nonlinearly related). This bias has been extensively studied by Parducci and his students, who have attempted the tricky task of showing it may partly be a real change in stimulus value, as if some kind of contrast was present. Parducci's range–frequency theory for this bias, based on an averaging model, can be used in conjunction with functional measurement (Anderson, 1975). Since Parducci and his students aim to study this bias, they naturally employ experimental procedures that produce strong bias. For most purposes, however, this bias seems better avoided.

A 0–10 scale, with 11 steps, seems close to the smallest that is really comfortable. Although the two procedures of end anchors and preliminary practice cited in the text also help eliminate bias, scales with only 5 or 6 steps can hardly be trusted unless only a monotone, rank-order scale is needed or unless the purpose is to study the stimulus distribution bias itself, as in the work of Parducci and his students.

11. A striking study of the Height + Width rule by Yuval Wolf (1995) yielded an interesting line of evidence to support the rating method. Wolf hypothesized that a period of handling the stimulus rectangles would induce a shift from the Height + Width rule to the physically correct Height × Width rule. This hypothesis was nicely supported by the data. The same children who showed parallelism (Height + Width) before handling the physical stimuli showed a linear fan (Height × Width) after handling. This same patterning was replicated with triangle stimuli. Wolf's results help elucidate the psychological significance of the Height + Width rule.

Of present relevance, Wolf's study also supports the validity of rating methodology. Although the physically correct Height × Width rule may seem only what should be expected, especially since it appears with adults, it could hardly appear unless the rating scale was veridical. And since the handling should not affect the children's rating usage, the pattern of results has the no less important implication that the Height + Width rule is not a measurement artifact, but cognitive reality.

PREFACE

Information integration theory is a grounded theory of person cognition. Seven basic phenomena can be understood with a single theoretical principle in the following experimental studies. This work led to a new way of thinking, a functional perspective that embodies and actualizes the axiom of purposiveness.

A central issue concerns meaning invariance. Numerous theories of cognitive consistency have been proposed, based on the idea that separate informers in a person description interact to change one another's meanings. A strong test of the hypothesis of meaning interaction was provided by the parallelism theorem of Chapter 2. Meaning interaction implies systematic deviations from parallelism. The experimental studies revealed parallelism, contrary to the hypothesis of meaning interaction. The cognitive consistency theories could not survive the failure of their basic assumption.

Instead, the parallelism supported meaning invariance. Beyond that, it was the harbinger of a general algebra of person cognition.

Altogether, seven basic issues had to be resolved to put this theory of person cognition on good ground. Besides cognitive consistency, other issues also involved the hypothesis of meaning invariance. The much-belabored issue of primacy–recency, for example, was shown to make theoretical sense in terms of attentional factors. The interpretation in terms of meaning interaction, although originally plausible, was thus found also incorrect in the primacy–recency area. Similarly, the positive context effect—that judgment of a part of a whole is influenced by the whole—was shown to reflect a halo integration process. The hypothesis of meaning interaction failed yet again.

The basic integration process of person cognition is one of averaging. The once-popular additive, summation theories were disproved with a paradoxical finding of opposite effects predicted by averaging theory.

The final outcome has been broad, solid support for a cognitive algebra of person cognition. Experimental analysis led to a unified treatment of all seven issues. This chapter thus represents a case history in experimental science.

Person cognition is a prime field for general cognitive theory. The cognitive processes studied in this chapter are basic in many domains, as will be seen in later chapters. A guiding theme is the functional perspective; cognitive algebra gives effectiveness to the axiom of purposiveness. The work summarized here thus constitutes a foundation that goes beyond cognitive algebra toward a unified theory focused on thought and action of everyday life.

Chapter 4

PERSON COGNITION

Person cognition is a fundamental domain of thought and action. This is certainly true in a practical way, for our everyday life continually involves interactions, real and imagined, with other persons. It is true in a personal way, for self-cognition has much in common with our cognition of other persons. And it should be true in a general way, for processes so central to our existence must also operate in other cognitive domains. The study of person cognition thus presents prime opportunities for general cognitive theory.

This chapter shows how information integration theory, IIT, provides a grounded theory of person cognition. Seven phenomena are considered that are basic to any attempt at general theory. All seven are shown to obey a single theoretical principle. This work was the foundation for IIT.

THEORY OF PERSON COGNITION

Person cognition refers to knowledge systems and actions in relation to other persons and to our self. Interpersonal interaction pervades everyday life. Such interaction may be direct, face-to-face, as in family and workplace, but much is indirect. Reports in the news media typically involve actions and opinions of persons. Movies, novels, and comic strips all operate through a remarkable human capability for involvement with imagined persons.

Self-cognition has much in common with other-cognition. Our judgments about our own abilities, for example, rest on success and failure information just as do our judgments of others' abilities. Our self-esteem, similarly, depends on integration of positive and negative informers about our ability and status.

For both self and other, the knowledge–action systems of person cognition are extensively developed through a lifetime of continual use. They constitute a mother lode for general cognitive theory.

FOUNDATION FOR GENERAL THEORY

Starting point and direction are critical throughout science. To develop general theory, starting point and direction must be broad enough to accommodate the phenomena.

The starting point for IIT is the axiom of purposiveness. Although the idea of purposiveness is complex, not to say treacherous, its manifestation in the concept of value allows a priceless simplification of the field of inquiry (Chapter 1). To take advantage of this simplification, however, requires theory for measurement of value.

The direction for IIT is multiple determination, a central fact of behavior, which also must be addressed in any attempt at general theory. Unlike purposiveness, however, multiple determination does not promise simplification. On the contrary, the joint operation of multiple determinants means that thought and action are difficult to predict and difficult to understand.

One natural reaction is to seek mini-theories for single phenomena. This strategy is often useful and informative. But because they must largely avoid the problem of multiple determination, mini-theories frequently run aground, as in the case history of primacy–recency. They are inadequate, moreover, for general theory; that requires capability for handling multiple determination.

As it happened, multiple determination proved theoretically tractable. Indeed, it provided a foundation for general theory through a solution to the problem of personal value. Thereby it transformed the axiom of purposiveness from a tantalizing idea into a working concept of scientific theory.

COGNITIVE CONSISTENCY THEORIES

One other kind of formulation also envisaged unified, general theory. These are the theories of cognitive consistency, which sought some principle of mental harmony as a foundation for general theory of belief and behavior. A consistency theme can be discerned in the first extensive attempt to study how we form impressions of other persons (Asch, 1946). Asch introduced the personality trait adjective task that was adopted and extended in the experiments of this chapter, and he argued strongly for gestalt interaction among the trait adjectives. He tried in several ways to show that the meaning of each trait in a person description was changeable, dependent on its relations to the other traits in the description, as the subject strove to organize the several separate traits into a unified impression. Beyond this claim for interaction, however, Asch had little to say about operative processes.

It was not long, however, before the Zeitgeist spawned a cluster of more or less independent theories with hope and promise of predictive power. The central idea was one of *cognitive consistency*: The mind abhors inconsistency and strives for balance and concord. Imbalance and discord among informers in a person description may be reduced by changing their meanings.

Many writers sought some principle of inconsistency resolution with predictive power: *assimilation, balance, congruity, dissonance,* and other once-popular postulates of cognitive consistency (see the 84 chapters in *Cognitive Consistency: A Sourcebook*, edited by Abelson, Aronson, McGuire, Newcomb, Rosenberg, & Tannenbaum, 1968). They hoped to hit upon a principle that would somehow constitute a base for general deductive theory.

The inadequacy of the consistency theories became apparent with the first integration study of person cognition (Figure 1.2). Functional measurement revealed meaning invariance: Informers did not interact as implied by consistency theory; quite the contrary. Further work, moreover, showed that the mind had substantial tolerance for inconsistency. And further consideration showed that such tolerance had survival value in an uncertain world. General theory, accordingly, could not be erected on any postulate of cognitive consistency. A different conceptual framework was needed.

INFORMATION INTEGRATION THEORY

The difference between IIT and the cognitive consistency theories centers on the **V–I** distinction of the integration diagram (Figure 1.1). Valuation of any informer depends on the goal and so is sensitive to situation and context. Given the goal, however, different informers are typically evaluated independently, without change of meaning. It follows that **V** and **I** are independent cognitive operators. This conclusion undercut the consistency position, which implicitly assumes interdependence of these two operators.

Furthermore, meaning interaction is not generally involved in the integration operation. This conclusion further undercut the consistency position. Both conclusions follow from the averaging rule of person cognition.

To establish the averaging rule was by no means simple. The foremost problem concerned meaning invariance. This problem appeared in several guises, discussed in the first four sections following. Hardly less important was the problem of averaging versus adding, taken up in the next three sections.

Motivation is an underlying theme of the present approach to these two cited problems. Motivation is here particularized as an approach–avoidance dimension of interpersonal likableness, a socially basic response used in all the following experiments. Although the two cited problems may seem narrow, they are a foundation, important in their own right, and essential for general theory. To put them on firm ground was a preliminary to handling more general classes of motivations that arise in later chapters.

SEVEN THEORETICAL ISSUES

Seven theoretical issues in person cognition are discussed in the following sections. Only one or two illustrative studies on each issue will be cited, for the main purpose is to set out the issues and theoretical framework. Some of these issues require close reasoning, but all are essential for general theory.[1]

All these studies used a common task, in which subjects made judgments about a hypothetical person described by a set of personality trait adjectives. This task has many advantages for cognitive analysis, especially that it taps into cognitive processes common in everyday life. It is not surprising, therefore, that the same processes were also found with the more complex stimulus materials of the following chapter.

PARALLELISM ANALYSIS

The parallelism analysis of Chapter 2 has been a basic tool for integration theory. One application is summarized in Figure 4.1. Subjects received pairs of trait adjectives that described a hypothetical person and judged each person on social desirability. The descriptions were constructed according to the 3×10 factorial design that is exhibited in the figure. Thus, the top curve represents judgments of persons described as *earnest* and a second adjective ranging from *unfriendly* at the left to *friendly* at the right.

The parallelism of the three curves in Figure 4.1 is notable. There are some irregularities but no more than would be expected from natural variability in the response. This parallelism pattern solves the problem of the three unobservables of Chapter 1, in accord with the parallelism theorem of Chapter 2.

First, parallelism implies that the trait adjectives are integrated by an averaging rule. It is as though subjects assign a social desirability to each trait and integrate them by a simple arithmetic operation. This issue is pursued further in two later sections, *Averaging Versus Adding* and *Amount of Information*.

Second, the social desirability values of the 10 adjectives spaced along the top curve of the figure are given by the numbers along the horizontal axis. These numbers are the marginal means of the factorial design, which form a linear scale of the social desirability values. That these numbers are true psychological values follows from the second conclusion of the parallelism theorem. These values are averaged over 12 subjects, but similar analyses could be made for each individual subject, as illustrated in Figure 1.2.

Third, the rating response is a veridical measure of the phenomenal impression of social desirability. This solves a fundamental problem of psychological measurement theory: It establishes a methodology in which observable responses are veridical measures of unobservable phenomena.

An interesting implication of response validity concerns the affective bimodality visible in Figure 4.1. All three curves show a jump between *dependent*, which is mildly negative, and *inoffensive*, which is mildly positive. The 10

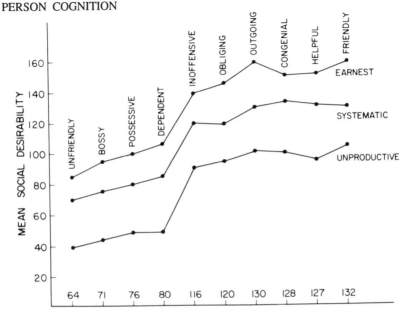

Figure 4.1. Parallelism analysis of social desirability. Each point is the mean of 12 judgments of social desirability of a person described by two trait adjectives, listed in the figure. Data averaged over two different replications of the three row adjectives for each of six subjects. (From Anderson, 1973a. Reprinted by permission.)

adjectives thus form two clusters, 4 negative traits and 6 positive. Similar bimo-dality appears in the complete set of personality trait adjectives.

This bimodal clustering is real. An alternative interpretation is that it is only a bias of avoiding the center region of the response scale. This alternative interpretation is nicely ruled out by the integration design. Comparison of the three curves shows that the jump occurs at different places along the response scale while the curves maintain their parallelism. Hence the clustering is genuine. It is considered to reflect a general bimodality of thought and action that stems from the approach–avoidance purposiveness of behavior.

A more fundamental implication of Figure 4.1 is meaning invariance: Each adjective has a fixed value and meaning. The meaning of *systematic*, for exam-ple, is the same in a *friendly* or *helpful* person as in an *unfriendly* or *bossy* per-son. Many writers have made strong claims to the contrary, arguing that the adjectives interact so that the meaning of each changes, depending on which other adjectives it is combined with.

But such meaning change would produce nonparallelism. Thus, *systematic* and *unproductive* would generally change by different amounts because they would generally have different semantic relations with the other adjective in the description. This would disrupt parallelism. The observed parallelism thus argues against meaning change and for meaning invariance. This issue is pursued further in the following three sections, which take up the positive context effect, meaning invariance, and primacy–recency.

In all, Figure 4.1 supports five conclusions:

- The adjective information is integrated by an averaging rule.
- The subjective values of the adjectives are revealed in the factorial graph.
- The rating response is a veridical measure of the person impression.
- Each adjective has invariant meaning, the same in all person descriptions.
- **V** and **I** are independent operators.

This cornucopia of benefits follows from the parallelism analysis.

This outcome was not a fluke. Similar results have been obtained with other adjectives and other subjects. Similar results have been obtained with other dimensions of response. Similar results have also been obtained with paragraph descriptions in place of single adjectives. Even face-to-face interaction has yielded similar results. The averaging rule is thus a basic process of cognitive functioning.

This outcome cast person cognition in an entirely new light. On one hand, the claims of introspection and phenomenology about the integration process were shown to be incorrect. On the other hand, a form of cognition that had seemed fluid and context dependent, beyond all hope of exact analysis, was found to obey mathematical law.

Simplicity in science arrives in retrospect. Progress at any point is faced with uncertainties that fade away only with the accumulation of further data and theory. In the clear gaze of hindsight, this fog of uncertainty is hardly visible. In the ongoing development, however, this uncertainty is very real. As simple as this parallelism analysis may seem, interpretation of person cognition in terms of cognitive algebra faced serious difficulties. Six of these are taken up in the following sections.

POSITIVE CONTEXT EFFECT

The *positive context effect* refers to an apparent assimilation of single traits in a person description toward the overall impression of the person. Thus, subjects will rate the likableness of the trait *practical* markedly higher in a *warm* person than in a *cold* person. At face value, this positive context effect *is* change of meaning. Subjects are instructed to judge the value of the component trait in context; their judgment ought to be what it purports to be.

But there is an alternative interpretation, namely, as a halo-type process. Teachers, for example, tend to judge docile children as more intelligent than obstreperous children. Their judgment of intelligence is influenced by their overall liking for the child—a halo effect. In work situations, similarly, the more likable subordinate tends to be rated as more intelligent, more industrious, and a better worker, more deserving of a raise.

Such a halo-type process could operate in the personality adjective task because the subject must form some overall impression of the person before judging the single component trait, *practical*. Other traits being equal, the *warm* person will be more likable than the *cold* person; this overall halo will influence the judgment of the component trait without any change in its meaning.

These two interpretations represent quite different cognitive processing. In one, the positive context effect results from interaction among the stimulus traits, as assumed by cognitive consistency theories. In the other interpretation, the stimulus traits do not interact; their meanings do not change; instead the effect results from the action of the overall impression on the judgment of the component stimulus trait.

This important, perhaps subtle, distinction is illustrated in Figure 4.2. The meaning change interpretation is shown in the right panel. The symbols ψ_1 and ψ_2 denote the context-free meanings or values of two adjectives. These are assumed to interact, producing the changed values, ψ_1^* and ψ_2^*, which are integrated to form the person cognition, I. The judgment of the component trait for that person is considered a direct report of the changed value, ψ_2^*.

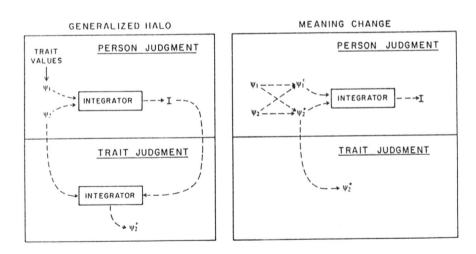

Figure 4.2. Integration diagrams for halo and meaning-change interpretations of positive context effect. Upper panels represent preliminary task: judging likableness of person described by two traits. Lower panels represent focal task: judging likableness of specified single trait of that person. (From N. H. Anderson, *Foundations of Information Integration Theory*. Academic Press, 1981.)

The halo interpretation, shown in the left panel, represents a second integration process. More specifically, the judgment of the component trait in context is considered an average of its context-free value and the overall, integrated impression of the person. Thus,

$$\psi_2^* = \omega\psi_2 + (1-\omega)I.$$

In this generalized halo model, ω is the relative weight of the component trait itself, and $(1 - \omega)$ is the relative weight of the halo process.

This generalized halo model may be tested by manipulating the component trait and the other traits in factorial design. In the experimental task, the subject first forms an overall impression and then judges the specified component trait according to "How much you like that particular trait of that particular person." The halo model implies that the judgment of the component trait will obey the parallelism theorem.[2]

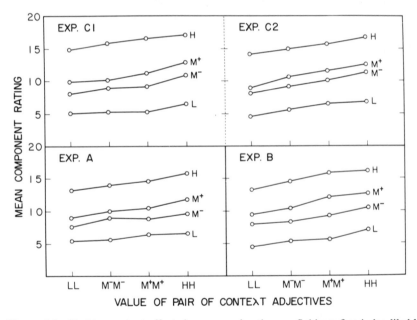

Figure 4.3. Positive context effect obeys averaging theory. Subjects first judge likableness of person described by three trait adjectives, then judge likableness of one specified component trait. Judged likableness of specified trait is plotted as a function of its normative value (curve parameter) and value of remaining two (context) traits in the person description (horizontal axis). Parallelism of curves in all four panels supports the averaging model of the positive context effect as a generalized halo effect. (From N. H. Anderson, *Foundations of Information Integration Theory.* Academic Press, 1981.)

Four experimental tests of this context model are shown in Figure 4.3. All four exhibit near-parallelism, in agreement with the context model. Further support was provided in cogent work by Marty Kaplan, based on experimental manipulation of ω and I in the model equation. This paradigm, it may be noted, allows experimental analysis of halo processes, which have long been presumed important in applied psychology, but almost entirely on the basis of indirect evidence. Indeed, the positive context effect has general interest and importance, and deserves systematic study (see Anderson, 1981a, Sections 3.2 and 4.1).

Consistency theories cannot handle such results. Consistency processes, if present, should depend on semantic and pragmatic relations between particular trait words. The effective meaning of any adjective would thus be variable, depending on which other adjectives it was paired with. Hence consistency theories imply deviations from parallelism. The observed parallelism thus argues against cognitive consistency theories, and more generally, against interaction among the stimulus traits. More important, it argues for a constructive alternative, namely, the averaging theory of the halo effect.

This interpretation of the positive context effect also explains its phenomenology. At face value of the instructions, the positive context effect *is* change of meaning, and subjects understandably interpret it that way. The same explanation no doubt accounts for the general belief in meaning change in various consistency theories. The consistency theories did not look any deeper, which was necessary to elucidate the cognitive processing. The positive context effect thus illustrates once again the necessity for cognitive theory as a base for scientific phenomenology.

MEANING INVARIANCE

Meaning invariance versus meaning change has been the central issue in person cognition. Strong evidence for meaning invariance has appeared in the parallelism patterns discussed in the two preceding sections. Observed parallelism, by the argument just given, infirms the meaning change position—and supports meaning invariance. Two additional lines of evidence are noted in this section.

One objection to the averaging rule is that each subject typically judges a substantial number of person descriptions in the experimental session. This could induce superficial processing, perhaps not representative of everyday person cognition. This objection was not infrequent, although no actual evidence was ever presented to support it. A direct test was made, nevertheless, and this showed the objection to be unfounded.

In the primary experimental condition, subjects first wrote a paragraph describing the person in their own words before rating the person. The control condition used the standard instructions, in which subjects merely read the adjectives in the description, then rated the person. If the superficial processing objection is correct, these two conditions should give different results: Writing the paragraph requires substantially more processing, and so should amplify any tendency toward change. In fact, both conditions yielded equivalent results in two large experiments.

Additional evidence was obtained in this same experiment by asking subjects to make a component judgment of one trait in the description. These component judgments will show the positive context effect described in the previous section. If the positive context effect represents change of meaning, it should be larger in the paragraph condition because subjects must attend more closely to the specific relations among the traits. This test is notable because it applies even if the positive context effect is only partly change of meaning. Here again, the two conditions were equivalent—strong evidence against meaning change and strong support for meaning invariance.

A second line of evidence was obtained from the observation that trait adjectives differ in connotative range. Thus, *able* seems more crisp and well-defined than *nice*. If words do change meaning in context, the amount of change should be greater for words with larger connotative range. This idea was pursued by several investigators, with results almost uniformly against change of meaning and in favor of meaning invariance (see Anderson, 1981a, Section 3.2.3).

Aside from its theoretical importance, the issue of meaning invariance is an interesting case example of progress in science. Intuitively, it seems overwhelmingly clear that words do change meaning as a function of context. Not a few investigators, accordingly, turned their backs on the evidence, taking cognitive illusion for cognitive reality. This issue reappears in later chapters in discussions of stereotypes and of functional memory.

PRIMACY–RECENCY

Information must ordinarily be integrated in a serial manner, one informer after another, for it cannot ordinarily be attended to all at the same time. The same information may thus have different effects, depending on the order in which it is presented or processed. In this widely studied problem of order effects, *primacy* refers to greater influence of the initial information, *recency* to greater influence of the final information.

Substantial primacy is found in the personality adjective task when the subject listens silently while the adjectives are read and then judges the person. For example, the six adjectives

trusting–patient–respectful–stubborn–dominating–egotistical

yielded a likableness judgment of 5.52 on a 1–8 scale. But read in the opposite, unfavorable–favorable order, the judgment was only 4.68. Net primacy is thus .84. This is a surprisingly large effect to get from merely reversing the order of six single words that would fit in short-term memory.

A natural interpretation is that this primacy results from change of meaning. The partial impression produced by the initial adjectives creates a set that selects out those shades of meaning of the later adjectives that fit better with the initial adjectives. In the listed favorable–unfavorable order, the partial impression formed from the initial adjectives would be favorable; hence the less unfavorable shades of the later unfavorable adjectives would be selected, so the overall impression would be more favorable. In the opposite, unfavorable–favorable order, similarly, less favorable shades of the later adjectives would be selected. This interpretation, fairly similar to that of Asch (1946), implies primacy.

An alternative interpretation explains the primacy in terms of attention decrement: The weight of the adjectives decreases steadily across serial position. Each adjective has a fixed, invariant meaning; the reduction in weight is considered to reflect an attentive process that occurs independently of any inconsistency relation between initial and final adjectives.

One class of tests between these two interpretations has a simple logic. Choose some manipulation that would reduce or eliminate primacy under the attention decrement hypothesis but not under the change of meaning hypothesis. One such study asked for casual recall of the adjectives after the judgment; this should reduce the hypothesized decrement in attention to the later adjectives, thereby reducing the primacy. In line with this prediction, primacy was changed to recency, which is awkward to explain as change of meaning. Another study asked for a revised, online judgment after each successive adjective, which again changed primacy to recency. Virtually all other reported studies of this kind have also infirmed the meaning change hypothesis and have supported the attention decrement hypothesis.

Striking support for the attentional interpretation was obtained by Clyde Hendrick, who compared primacy from the adjective description of person P:

trusting–patient–respectful–stubborn–dominating–egotistical,

with the primacy from person Q:

trusting–patient–respectful–withdrawn–silent–helpless.

These two descriptions have the same first three adjectives; they differ in their last three adjectives, which are matched in value. These last three adjectives are semantically inconsistent with the first three adjectives in person P but not in person Q. The primacy effect for person P has already been cited, and that for person Q was measured in the same way (Hendrick & Costantini, 1970).

The theoretical issue is straightforward: If primacy is caused by attention decrement, it should be the same in both persons. But if primacy is caused by the inconsistency, it should be markedly less in person Q. In fact, the observed primacy was a bit larger for Q. Similar results were obtained from the other descriptions in this meticulous experiment (see Anderson, 1981a, Table 3.2).

Hendrick's experimental gem, as it may rightly be called, is cogent evidence against cognitive consistency theory and for the attentional interpretation.

The primacy–recency problem furnishes an interesting case history, with lessons for the conduct of inquiry. The prevailing strategy sought generalizations in terms of surface variables, such as familiarity with the given issue, time interval between successive informers, informer complexity, one- versus two-sided presentation, and so on. This strategy was employed in a mass of primacy–recency studies in social psychology. Unfortunately, simple generalizations did not emerge. Instead, the results became increasingly complicated. The one dependable conclusion was "It all depends."

The integration approach brought conceptual order into the jumble of results that had plagued the primacy–recency area (see Anderson, 1981a, Section 3.3; 1982, Section 7.14). Other approaches had, in effect, focused on valuation rather than integration. Many determinants can affect attention and thereby the valuation process for the weight parameter. Only limited order and regularity could be found at this level of analysis. These valuation processes are important, but they cannot be adequately understood without a foundation in the integration process. Rightly viewed, primacy–recency is a problem of information integration, and it needs to be attacked in this way.

The primacy–recency issue illustrates the difference between ways of thinking discussed in Chapter 1. The integration studies were able to go beyond the attention hypothesis to establish a general averaging model for belief integration. Primacy–recency could then be measured at each serial position in longer sequences of informers.

The old way of thinking appears in the traditional paradigm, which compares effect of presenting the same two informers in opposite orders, AB vs. BA. This paradigm is not only limited to two informers, but cannot even localize the serial position of observed primacy–recency. It is still widely used, although its weakness makes it largely obsolete.

The new way of thinking involved a direct attack on the essential problem, namely, information integration. Moreover, the belief integration model generalized beyond person cognition to judgment–decision theory, as discussed under *Serial Belief Integration: Primacy and Recency* in Chapter 10. This model also plays a key role in functional theory of memory (Chapter 11).

AVERAGING VERSUS ADDING: OPPOSITE EFFECTS TEST

Two different integration rules can account for parallelism: averaging and adding. Despite certain similarities, these two rules have markedly different implications for cognitive theory. Contrary to the adding rule, the averaging rule predicts that the same information can have opposite effects. In one test of this *opposite effects* prediction, subjects judged likableness of persons described by sentences of the form:

The (adjective) man (verbs) people.

Adjective and verb were combined in a 4 × 4 design, shown in Figure 4.4. Since the adjective and verb information have similar semantic character, adding and averaging rules are both plausible. Indeed, both are supported by the near-parallelism of the four solid curves in the figure.

A critical test between averaging and adding is provided by the dashed, *none* curve in Figure 4.4. The points on this curve represent judgments based on the verb information alone, without any adjective. The adding rule implies that this *none* curve should be parallel to the other four curves, which is far from true. The averaging rule, in contrast, accounts for the observed crossover.

The logic of this test is straightforward. The end points on the *none* curve represent judgments of the two descriptions, *The man hates people* and *The man helps people*. If the adding rule is true, addition of the mildly positive information that the man is *moderate* should raise both judgments. The *moderate* curve should thus lie entirely above the *none* curve. Since the *moderate* curve crosses over the *none* curve, the adding rule cannot be correct.

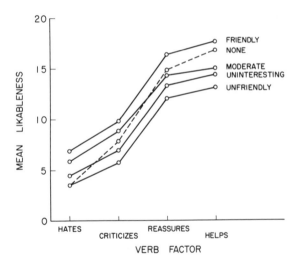

Figure 4.4. Opposite effects crossover eliminates adding rule and supports averaging rule. Subjects judged likableness of persons described by trait adjective (curve parameter) and behavior toward others (verb factor on horizontal axis). Near-parallelism of solid curves supports adding-type rule; crossover of dashed curve is critical evidence against adding but supports averaging process. Some leftward convergence of the four solid curves is visible, reflecting the negativity effect of greater importance weight for more negative verbs. (From N. H. Anderson, *Foundations of Information Integration Theory.* Academic Press, 1981.)

The averaging rule predicts the crossover. Since *moderate* has a mildly positive value, it will average up the very negative *hates people* (the leftmost point on the dashed curve) and average down the very positive *helps people* (the rightmost point on the dashed curve). Hence the two curves will cross over. Similar crossovers may be obtained by comparing effects of one and two adjectives instead of zero and one (see also Anderson, 1965a).

This opposite effects crossover test is scale-free. Unlike the parallelism test, it does not require a linear response scale. By the same token, the crossover test is almost rule-free, for it eliminates almost any variant of the adding rule, such as adding with diminishing returns. Perhaps the only way to account for the crossover with an adding rule would be to assume a contrast effect, in which *moderate* becomes more positive with the negative verb, less positive with the positive verb. But this contrast assumption has been shown incorrect in the foregoing section on the positive context effect.

The crossover test is a qualitative demonstration of an averaging process. Evidence for averaging as an exact rule is provided by the near-parallelism of the solid curves in Figure 4.4. This parallelism gives quantitative support to both rules, averaging and adding; the crossover test then selects the correct rule.

The averaging rule, however, was not yet secure. Two more quantitative problems remain to be treated in the next two sections.

AMOUNT OF INFORMATION

The averaging rule seems counterintuitive: Adding more information of equal value should yield a more extreme response. An *honest, intelligent* woman is better than either an *honest* woman or an *intelligent* woman. Averaging *honest* and *intelligent* cannot account for this.

This problem of amount of information is handled in terms of an initial state in the averaging model. The judgment is an average of the given information— and the initial state. The concept of initial state is clearly necessary when dealing with known persons; it represents prior information or attitude about that person (see Equation 4b in Chapter 2). For hypothetical persons, the initial state may be considered to represent a base rate expectation.

To illustrate how this formulation can account for the effect of added information, consider several High adjectives, all with value 100, and suppose that the initial state has a medium value of 50 on a 0–100 scale. For simplicity, assume unit weights for each H adjective and for the initial state. Then the theoretical responses to one, two, and three H's are:

$$R(H) = (50 + 100)/2 = 75;$$

$$R(HH) = (50 + 200)/3 = 83.3;$$

$$R(HHH) = (50 + 300)/4 = 87.5.$$

In these equations, the numerators are the values of the initial state plus the given adjectives; the denominator is the sum of the weights, here equal to the number of pieces of information. Each additional H thus increases the response, with the amount of increase following an ostensible law of diminishing returns.

The experimental test of this formulation has several points of interest. In an initial experiment, subjects rated likableness of persons described by 1, 2, 3, 4, or 6 adjectives, all of equal value, either High or Low. The rating scale ranged from −20 to +20 (or from −50 to +50). The initial state, accordingly, was assumed to have the neutral, midpoint value, 0. The theoretical response to a description with n adjectives thus simplifies to:

$$R(n) = [n\,\omega/(n\,\omega + \omega_0)]\,\psi,$$

where ω and ψ are the weight and value of a single adjective. The weight of the initial state, ω_0, remains in the denominator even though its value, ψ_0, is zero in the numerator. The unit of the weight scale may be fixed by setting $\omega + \omega_0 = 1$. Solving for ω yields

$$\omega = R(n)/[n\,\psi - (n-1)\,R(n)].$$

The ψ values of the L and H adjectives were set equal to the respective end points of the response scale. All terms on the right of this last equation are thus known, allowing ω to be estimated from the observed response.

Theoretically, ω should be constant, regardless of the number of adjectives in the description. With the given equation, a value of ω may be estimated from the response for each value of n. The constancy of these ω estimates constitutes the test of the averaging model.

The estimated values of ω for the first experiment are shown in the upper four rows of data in Table 4.1. These values are nearly constant, around .45 for $n = 1, 2, 3,$ and 4, in support of the averaging model. For n = 6, however, the values are markedly too large. All four rows show the same pattern.

Two possible explanations of this discrepancy spring to mind. First, redundancy may begin to be important with greater numbers of adjectives; given 4 nonredundant H adjectives, it is hard to find 2 more that do not have some overlap of meaning with the first 4. Second, information overload may cause subjects to partially neglect information in the larger sets of adjectives. But neither of these explanations is viable; both imply that ω would decrease as number of adjectives increases.

An alternative interpretation was in terms of an end effect in the response scale. When the response is near the end of the scale, there may be a tendency to use the scale end point itself as the response. This would affect primarily the response to sets of 6 adjectives because they produced the most extreme responses. The response to the sets of 6 adjectives would thus be biased toward the scale endpoints, and that would cause the estimates of ω to be too large.

TABLE 4.1

WEIGHT PARAMETERS AS A FUNCTION OF SET SIZE

Experiment	Rating scale	Adjective value	Set size					
			1	2	3	4	6	9
1	20	High	.48	.45	.43	.46	.53	
		Low	.44	.43	.44	.47	.65	
	50	High	.49	.44	.44	.44	.48	
		Low	.45	.44	.47	.50	.61	
		mean	**.46**	**.44**	**.44**	**.47**	**.57**	
2	50	High	.44	.37	.36	.36	.37	.49
		Low	.40	.38	.45	.39	.42	.58
		mean	**.42**	**.38**	**.40**	**.38**	**.40**	**.54**

NOTE: After N. H. Anderson, 1967, "Averaging model analysis of set-size effect in impression formation." *Journal of Experimental Psychology, 75*, 158-165. Copyright 1967 by American Psychological Association. Reproduced by permission.

This interpretation created a difficulty. End-bias could presumably be eliminated by including the usual end-anchor descriptions composed of more extreme adjectives. But these anchors had purposely been omitted to allow the simplifying assumption that the values of the L and H adjectives were equal to the endpoints of the response scale. With such anchors present, the effective values would be some unknown value less extreme than the scale endpoints, and these values would have to be estimated, complicating the test of the model.

This difficulty was resolved in a followup experiment by adding 3 adjectives of equal value to the sets of 6 to obtains sets of 9 adjectives. The logic is straightforward. If the discrepancy for the 6-adjective descriptions in the first experiment represents a true defect in the model, it should remain in the followup. But if the end-bias explanation is correct, then the discrepancy should disappear for the 6-adjective sets—and appear for the 9-adjective sets. This follows because the 9-adjective sets now give the most extreme response, and so should absorb the end-bias.

This end-bias interpretation was nicely supported, as can be seen in the lower part of Table 4.1. The discrepancy has indeed disappeared from the 6-adjective sets—and appeared for the 9-adjective sets. The averaging model thus yields an exact account of the effect of amount of information.

This outcome also eliminates a theoretical hybrid, in which averaging and adding processes are both operative. The foregoing crossover test shows that an adding process is inadequate by itself; but that does not show that no adding process is operative. Parallelism could be produced by both processes, with the averaging process responsible for the crossover. The present experiment eliminates the adding model altogether.

This experiment also illustrates the importance of model analysis for conceptual interpretation. The foregoing numerical example exhibits an ostensible diminishing returns, as though each successive H adjective has lesser impact. But all Hs have equal effect within the averaging model. The diminishing returns is merely a surface observable, lacking cognitive reality. Cognitive algebra penetrated below the surface to reveal the underlying process.

This result had further implications for cognitive theory. It argued against popular semantic feature theories of cognitive representation. In these theories, presenting a stimulus word is considered to activate a set of features that represent the word in semantic memory. Integration would be accomplished by set-theoretical union of the activated features of the several adjectives. But this feature interpretation implies a true law of diminishing returns because successive adjectives will become increasingly redundant with features already activated by previous adjectives. The lack of redundancy implied by the averaging model analysis points to a different kind of theoretical representation, one in which valuation and integration are independent operations (see **V–I** independence in Chapter 1).

UNDERSTANDING NONPARALLELISM

Deviations from parallelism are not uncommon, and they must be accounted for in general theory. Two processes that produce nonparallelism are considered in this section.[3,4]

The first process involves inconsistency. If *honest* and *deceitful* are included in the same person description, subjects may be expected to discount one or the other. Most adjectives do not interact in this way—as shown by the obtained findings of parallelism. With strong antonymic inconsistency, however, substantial discounting might be obtained. One of the first followups to the initial study of Figure 1.2, accordingly, was designed for direct assessment of inconsistency discounting (see Anderson, 1981a, Section 3.4.1).

The main result of this study of inconsistency discounting was that even such extreme inconsistencies as *honest–deceitful* had relatively modest effects, about a third of the maximal discounting effect. This tolerance for inconsistency is considered to represent general social adaptation to conflicting information. We often receive conflicting reports about others, especially politicians and other public figures. Many people, moreover, are both friendly and hostile. Wife–husband relations involve more or less affective ambivalence. In general, therefore, people may rightly be untroubled about ostensible inconsistency in given information, for that mirrors their everyday experience. If we could not tolerate inconsistency, life itself would be intolerable.

This interpretation also reemphasizes the two weaknesses in the cognitive consistency theories. Most obvious is that general consistency postulates cannot be valid when people have substantial tolerance for inconsistency.

Less obvious is that the consistency theories could not measure actual inconsistency. Indeed, they could not even separate simple averaging from inconsistency resolution. In short, they had no way to determine whether the process they took as the basis for explanation was actually operative. Hence the consistency theories contributed little to the study of how people actually do handle felt inconsistencies.

In contrast, IIT has contributed effective concepts and methods to study how inconsistencies are resolved. This is by no means easy to do. The cited study is one of the few that have given direct evidence on inconsistency resolution.

A second process that can produce deviations from parallelism is differential weighting. If two informers have unequal importance, or weight, including them as levels of the same design factor will in general produce nonparallelism. This is a basic property of the averaging model.

Differential weighting can be manipulated experimentally, for example, by varying amount of information or source reliability. Theoretically, such manipulations will produce specifiable deviations from parallelism. Such studies have been done by a number of investigators, and they have provided excellent support for averaging theory (Anderson, 1981a, Section 4.4). Indeed, the crossover effect of Figure 4.4 is a special case of differential weighting.

This approach also led to establishing the negativity effect, in which more negative information has greater weight, or importance. Establishing the reality of the negativity effect faces the obstacle of separating importance from value. It is clearly not enough to show that more negative informers have greater effect; that must happen because of their more negative value. Averaging theory made it possible to separate the concepts of importance and value and measure them.[5]

Additive models, it may be noted, predict parallelism even with differential weighting. Predictable deviations from parallelism, noted in the preceding paragraphs, are thus evidence against additive theories and for averaging theory.

The two foregoing processes, *inconsistency discounting* and *differential weighting*, are both configural in that both depend on interrelations among the given informers. They differ, however, in character and locus of configurality. Inconsistency discounting is an active change in effective weight parameter, induced by felt inconsistency among the informers. To reduce inconsistency in the integrated cognition, the effective weight of an informer changes according to meaning interrelations within each set of informers.

Differential weighting, in contrast, refers to natural inequality among the absolute weights (see Chapter 2). These absolute weights operate in the integration. Configurality arises passively in the integration operation because the algebraic form of the averaging rule requires the effective, relative weights of each informer to depend on all others on the context of each judgment.

These two configural processes thus differ in character and locus. The meaning and validity of differential weighting depend on the averaging model, together with **V–I** independence. Without the model analysis, this difference would be hard to understand and harder to establish. This illustrates the usefulness, and necessity, of model analysis in the study of configurality.

THEORY OF PERSON COGNITION

The seven foregoing issues are fundamental for person cognition. They constitute a challenge that must be met by any attempt to develop general theory. At bottom, these seven issues reduce to two: personal value and multiple determination, discussed in the first two following sections.

PURPOSIVENESS AND VALUE

The axiom of purposiveness is manifest in the response dimension of likableness used throughout the foregoing experimental studies. This response embodies approach–avoidance tendencies so prominent in our relations with other persons. It thus embodies affect and motivation, both basic biosocial capabilities, represented as informational knowledge systems in IIT (Chapter 1). The trait adjectives, seemingly simple informational stimuli, tap into complex knowledge systems constructed through social experience.

Effective application of the axiom of purposiveness depends on measurement of value. Functionally, valuation is a constructive process, flexible in reacting to continual changes in the environment—and to ever-changing motivations and goals of the person. Cognitive theory must provide similar flexibility. The capabilities of functional measurement theory for measurement of personal value gives new potential for cognitive theory.

COGNITIVE ALGEBRA

Finding an algebraic rule at the heart of person cognition was unexpected. Judgments of other persons seem far removed from algebraic thought. To introspection, person cognition appears complex and configural, subject to no simple rule, perhaps no rule at all.

The empirical phenomena, moreover, are not simple. Primacy–recency seemed an empirical quagmire. The effect of amount of information, taken at face value, discredited adding and averaging rules alike. Understanding the positive context effect required a nice distinction about processing stages. The parallelism property is simple, of course, but obtaining parallelism depended on development of functional measurement methodology. Most important, interpretation of parallelism depended on understanding nonparallelism.

Yet the averaging rule has done well on all seven issues covered in the preceding sections. Little emendation was needed in the form of supplementary assumptions. The concepts of initial state and differential weighting were essential, but they were part of the basic averaging formulation. A complex and diverse array of results was thus explained, qualitatively and quantitatively, with a single theoretical principle.

Beyond the present experiments, cognitive algebra provides a validational base for cognitive theory of everyday life. Virtually all the integration rules considered in this book involve everyday concepts, even in memory, language, judgment–decision, and intuitive physics. Success of an algebraic rule provides validated measurement scales for these concepts, together with some degree of construct validity. It thus seems possible to develop a scientific phenomenology, in which the primitive terms are among those made familiar by nature and society, revised, purified, and solidified through cognitive algebra.[6]

Scientific phenomenology cannot be developed solely at the level of everyday thinking. This was shown by the finding that the apparent meaning change was a phenomenological illusion. The structure of the integration rules, moreover, is often inaccessible to consciousness. Cognitive algebra goes below the level of phenomenology to provide a foundation for theory that welcomes and uses phenomenology in mutual development.

WHY THE COGNITIVE CONSISTENCY THEORIES FAILED

Cognitive consistency theories are fundamentally inadequate to handle the seven issues of this chapter. These theories begin with a prime assumption that integration is dynamic and interactive, that the meaning or function of each informer depends on the others. This interaction is driven by forces or needs to reinterpret the informers in order to maximize their consistency and harmony in the overall cognition.

Such consistency assumptions cannot handle the facts. Their central failure is the finding of meaning invariance. The informers do not interact as the consistency theories assumed. Hence these theories are incapable of accounting for the seven theoretical issues.

To introspection, the interactive assumption of the theories of cognitive consistency seems self-evident, beyond question, especially in person cognition. Cognition could well have functioned in this way—but it does not. The consistency theories could not survive the loss of their basic explanatory principle. Thus they failed.[7]

The consistency theories did recognize the problem of multiple determination; this is implicit in the concept of consistency. Lacking a theory of psychological measurement, however, they could not resolve their own central premise.

Hoping to light upon some general deductive principle, moreover, most had superficial concern with empirical phenomena. With their failure, therefore, they left little behind.

Cognitive interaction is important, but its nature differs from that assumed in the consistency theories. One primary form of cognitive interaction appears in the valuation operation. Valuation is a constructive process, sensitive to operative goals and dependent on the person's background knowledge. Integration, in contrast, is largely noninteractive in the very task that had seemed so clearly interactive. This independence of the **V** and **I** operators is a key discovery about cognitive processing. This qualitative implication of cognitive algebra is in some ways more important than the quantitative precision.

Consistency can result from information integration alone. Consistency will increase because the average of informers of different value represents a compromise among them. The averaging process thus increases consistency— without invoking any special force or need for consistency. This alternative interpretation of observed tendencies toward consistency in terms of information integration contrasts sharply with the "needs" for consistency hypothesized by the cognitive consistency theories.

The cognitive consistency theories were erected on too narrow a conceptual base. At best confused about the **V–I** distinction, they attributed observed tendencies for consistency to dynamic interaction resulting from attempts to integrate presumptively inconsistent informers. Within the preconceptions of their theoretical framework, the alternative interpretation could hardly arise. IIT furnishes a constructive alternative.

The assumption that the mind abhors inconsistency is rather like the assumption of medieval physics that nature abhors a vacuum. The finding that nature's abhorrence extends only to 30 inches in a mercury column led to a different way of thinking in physics. The finding of meaning invariance leads similarly to a different way of thinking in cognitive theory (Anderson, 1968a, 1981a).

The way of thinking characteristic of consistency theories nevertheless remains common. To postulate some "need" as an explanatory principle is a seductive strategy. This strategy underlies current attitude theory, for example, as noted in the next chapter. It is also common in the recent surge of interest in self-cognition. This strategy is perennially attractive because surplus meaning so readily masquerades as real explanation.[8]

Warnings on this matter go back to Occam's razor and have been stressed by Skinner, who warned that research predicated on such postulates often loses all value when the postulate is found wanting. Skinner's warning is well verified by the work on cognitive consistency theories. Skinner's prescription for this malady, namely, to avoid unobservable concepts, has been helpful, but it forecloses the possibility of cognitive theory. IIT has found a different remedy, one that can endow unobservable concepts with scientific reality.

EVERYDAY PERSON COGNITION

How far will a theory based on the personality trait task generalize to person cognition in everyday life? Everyday flow of information about real persons is complex and uncontrolled, far removed from the task of judging a hypothetical person described by a few trait adjectives. But subjects handle this experimental task by assimilating it to everyday person cognition. The personality trait task taps into processes of everyday thought and action. Hence the processes operative in this trait task must also operate in the information processing of everyday life. The foregoing theory should thus have some generality. This expectation is supported in later chapters.

There are, of course, major differences from the foregoing adjective task. Informers of everyday life are more complicated than single trait words: letters of reference, remarks by others, and face-to-face interaction, including nonverbal informers. Such complex informers, however, can sometimes be treated as simple by virtue of the unitization principle. Hence they can be studied in the same way as the trait adjectives. Integration of such complex informers also obeys averaging theory (see, e.g., Figures 5.1 and 5.12).

Another complication of everyday life is that informers occur in a temporal series, not all together as in most of the foregoing experiments. In extensive work with serial integration, however, averaging theory has done well, as foreshadowed in the cited primacy–recency studies. Indeed, analysis of serial integration led to a new conception of functional memory (see Chapter 11).

Temporal information processing also involves feedback loops between person and environment, notably in family and other interpersonal relationships. Analysis of information processing in such interactive systems is important but still in its infancy. A few experiments that touch on this problem are reported in Chapter 5 (see Figures 5.2, 5.9–5.10, and 5.11).

Affect is central in everyday cognition. The joys of marriage and family life are mingled with their pains. Our interactions with others are suffused with liking and disappointment, admiration and envy, praise and blame. Above all, our self-concerns are heavily affective.

Historically, however, affect has been segregated from cognition, a segregation that has been reinforced in mainstream cognitive psychology. A deaffected conceptual framework cannot accommodate the purposive behavior of everyday life. In IIT, affect is integral to the conceptual framework. With functional measurement, affect becomes a working tool for the study of purposiveness and motivation.[9]

These brief remarks touch only a few of the many complexities of everyday person cognition. IIT is far from a complete theory. It does, however, have substantial generality and power. And it provides concepts and methods that allow progress on real problems of real life.

SELF-COGNITION

The present theory of person cognition also applies to the self. Your self is embedded in a complex of memorial knowledge systems, constructed through previous information integration. Many of your feelings, attitudes, and beliefs have been learned through the averaging process.

This information processing view of the self is harmonious with the sociological schools of symbolic interaction. Sociologists and anthropologists have been sensitive in recognizing that the self is heavily determined by society and culture. Symbolic interactionists accordingly sought to develop a sociology, not from demographic statistics, as in an earlier positivist school, but in terms of social communication, that is, symbolic interaction.

IIT gives precision and generality to this constructivist view of self. The symbolic interaction of the sociologists is treated as information processing, especially valuation and integration. The self is considered constructivist in a double sense: In part, it subsists in knowledge systems of long-term memory, constructed through storage of information integrated on previous occasions; in part, it is a continuously active construction of operating memory, containing William James' stream of consciousness. As noted in an earlier discussion of information integration (Anderson, 1974b, p. 89): "In a very real sense, therefore, people do not know their own minds. Instead, they are continuously making them up."

This information integration view applies readily to your conceptions of your own ability, to take one kind of self-knowledge. Success and failure constitute one class of informers. Others include praise–blame by authority figures and peers, as well as comparisons with others' performances. Past integration of such information determines your background beliefs about your abilities, and these beliefs contribute to your present judgments about goals to pursue and goals to shun. Available evidence points to the averaging rule for these and other self-attributions. Your background belief corresponds to the initial state, ψ_0, which is averaged in with present information.

All your beliefs and attitudes are derived from integration of information. Here again, the averaging rule operates, as illustrated with the experiment on attitudes toward U. S. presidents with which the next chapter begins. Your moral beliefs and attitudes also follow cognitive algebra (Chapters 6 and 7). These beliefs and attitudes are part of the complex of knowledge systems that constitute your self.

Of course, the information field can have a unique nature for self-cognition. We feel our own pleasures and pains, but must infer those of others. The present working hypothesis is that the same principles apply to both kinds of information. Symbolic interaction may thus be unified with affect and motivation. More generally, IIT makes possible some conceptual unification of anthropology, psychology, and sociology, based on experimental analysis.

The role of symbolic interaction may be illustrated with self-esteem. Following James, as well as Adler and Horney among the psychoanalysts, IIT takes self-esteem to be a fundamental biosocial motivation. Self-esteem may be treated in terms of information integration. Success and praise are positive social informers, whose integration into the self-concept raises self-esteem; failure and blame are aversive social informers, and their integration into the self-concept lowers self-esteem. Seeking success and praise and avoiding failure and blame are continual concerns of the person in society. Society, of course, is maintained by regulatory systems of such positive and negative informers developed in cultural evolution.

The motivation to maintain self-esteem is clear in ego defense, epitomized in blame-avoidance and self-pity. Contrary to Freudian doctrine that ego defense is rigidly unconscious, IIT sees much ego defense as conscious. Indeed, excuses and justifications to avoid self-blame and blame from others, are among the most conscious of everyday activities. The same applies to incidents that evoke feelings of social inferiority.

Self-awareness, of course, is limited. Indications of such limits range from Thales' apothegm that the hardest thing is "to know thyself" through Regan's comment on her father, King Lear, that "he hath ever but slenderly known himself" to the failure of the introspectionist school at the beginning of psychological science and to current concerns with the unconscious. A theory of self-cognition must accordingly be able to analyze nonconscious determinants of conscious awareness.[10]

Some capability for nonconscious analysis is available with IIT. With the integration rules, nonconscious sensation, affect, and motivation become measurable. Such capability for analysis of the nonconscious is useful, indeed essential, for developing a theory of conscious thought and action.

MOTIVATION

The axiom of purposiveness implies motivation is the foundation for general theory. The taxonomies of needs common in personality theory illustrate the attractiveness of this direction of inquiry. Similar approaches are standard in attitude theory, as noted in the following chapter, as well as in emotion theory. Without cognizance of motivation, general theory cannot be developed.

The seven theoretical issues may seem surprising, therefore, in their emphasis on information. But motivation *is* information in the present functional perspective—information for purposive thought and action. More particularly, motivation is the source of value, the informational currency of the algebraic integration rules. Motivation is thus fundamental in IIT.

This point is illustrated with likableness, the standard response dimension in the foregoing experiments. Likableness of other persons represents an approach–avoidance motivation that pervades everyday life. Likableness thus embodies a major dimension of social motivation and of everyday knowledge systems. The foregoing experiments have focused on this one motivation to develop a coherent, interrelated body of results and theory. This development is expected to hold good with other motivations.

The theory of information integration seeks a foundation jointly in motivation and in multiple determination. Motivation is embodied in purposiveness and represented in value. Cognitive algebra has made multiple determination tractable in some cases, and thereby provided a base and frame for true measurement of value and motivation. This dual base provides a potential for unified, general theory.

GENERAL THEORY

The work summarized in this chapter proved a foundation for general theory. The same concepts and methods have been effective in other areas, surveyed in the chapters that follow: in social psychology, including attitudes, attribution, group dynamics, and moral cognition; in developmental psychology, including knowledge of the physical world and the social world; and in the areas of judgment–decision theory, psychophysics, memory theory, and language processing. These applications demonstrate a unified, general theory.

The strategy and tactics that underlie these investigations may be of interest. The following points are somewhat idealized, having been in part developed and articulated during the course of this work.

- Basic experimental task.

The personality adjective task has both strategic and practical virtues. On the strategic side, it elicits basic cognitive processes, well-developed in everyday thought and action. On the practical side, it is simple, flexible, and readily generalized to more complex informers, including face-to-face interaction, and to other response dimensions. Behavior in this task is thus expected to be interesting and instructive, almost regardless of the investigator's hypotheses.

- Multiple determination: Analysis and synthesis.

Multiple determination is a prime focus of the present approach. This includes *synthesis*, predicting the response to given informers by virtue of an integration rule, and *analysis*, understanding the response by breaking it down into the separate contributions of these informers, as with the serial curves of belief integration and functional memory. Capability with analysis and synthesis is essential for general theory.

Functional measurement theory furnishes a joint solution to analysis and synthesis through the operations of valuation and integration. By establishing and capitalizing on the algebraic structure of cognition, functional measurement provided a cornerstone for general theory of thought and action.

- Inductive theory.

The two foregoing points agree with the inductive orientation of Chapter 1. In this way of thinking, the traditional strategy of hypothesis testing loses much of the importance that has been attached to it. This issue was illustrated in the foregoing discussion of the cognitive consistency theories, which followed the traditional strategy. With their failure, therefore, these theories left behind little of value.[11]

The inductive strategy is illustrated by the initial integration study of person cognition in Figure 1.2. This study was not predicated on meaning invariance or the averaging rule. Meaning change, had it been operative, would have appeared as meaningful deviations from parallelism. Almost any outcome would have been useful. This larger effectiveness of inductive strategy will appear repeatedly in the chapters that follow.

- Internal world.

The foundation for theory was located in structure of the internal world. Most other conceptual frameworks place essential reliance on structure of the external world. Cognitive algebra, in contrast, focuses on internal structure. This solved the problem of *The Three Unobservables* of Chapter 1, thereby placing the axiom of purposiveness on a scientific foundation.

- Functional perspective.

The functional perspective is particularized in likableness, the basic response dimension in the foregoing experiments. Likableness represents a general approach–avoidance motivation of everyday life. Affect is thus considered goal-relevant information, integral to cognition. With cognitive algebra, the functional approach provides a potentially self-sufficient theory at the level of everyday thought and action.

- Scientific phenomenology.

Feelings and concepts of everyday experience have been a primary concern of IIT. Similar approaches have been long been popular, but everyday experience is not adequate for general theory. Capability with analysis of nonconscious feelings and concepts is essential to assay and refine conscious experience. Cognitive algebra has this capability. Thereby it provides a foundation for developing phenomenology as a core for self-sufficient scientific theory.

- Good fortune.

The discovery of a general cognitive algebra was a blessing of Nature.

Taken all together, this work has evolved into a way of thinking differing from traditional ways in conceptual framework, research strategy, and method. It opens onto a new horizon of investigation.

NOTES

This and following chapters on social cognition summarize contributions by numerous workers. Besides those in the dedication of this book, the following deserve grateful mention: Andrea Abele, Gwendolyn Alexander, Alfred Barrios, Eileen Beier, Donnie Bocko, James Cooper, Susan Fiske, Harry Gollob, Edmund Howe, Jeneva Lane, Rhoda Lindner, John Lynch, Philip Moore, Thomas Ostrom, Dwight Riskey, Milton Rosenbaum, Susumu Takahashi, Dengfeng Wang, Leighton Wong, Rebecca Wong, Robert Wyer, and Chungfang Yang.

1. The experiments summarized in this chapter are discussed in Chapters 2–4 of the writer's *Foundations of Information Integration Theory*, "A case history in experimental science." This book includes detailed references to the literature, which accordingly are omitted here. Normative data on the 555 personality trait adjectives used in these experiments is given in Appendix B of *Methods of Information Integration Theory*.

2. The halo model for the positive context effect predicts parallelism only if the person impression I itself exhibits parallelism. With differential weighting, I would show systematic deviations from parallelism—and the same pattern should appear in the halo judgments. This theoretical prediction has not been directly tested.

3. Nonparallelism might also reflect nonlinearity in the response measure. This was a deep concern in the initial stages of IIT. By now, however, linearity of the rating scale method developed in IIT is supported by an exceptionally solid network of evidence (see last section of Chapter 3).

The averaging model of IIT, it may be reemphasized, has given a good account of most of the nonparallelism that has been observed. Indeed, nonparallelism has provided some of the strongest evidence for averaging theory. This stems from the conceptual identification of weight with amount of information (see also Note 5 of Chapter 2).

4. Birnbaum (1974, 1982) has incorrectly criticized IIT and functional measurement on the ground that it predicts parallelism and does not explain nonparallelism. This criticism is factually incorrect; a number of earlier studies on IIT had already demonstrated real nonparallelism and had interpreted it in terms of differential weighted averaging (e.g., Lampel & Anderson, 1968; Oden & Anderson, 1971).

Similarly, differential weight averaging was a key idea in the integration theory of attitudes (Anderson, 1971). Birnbaum attributes an assumption of constant weighting, whereas differential weighting had already been well established in IIT.

Ironically, Birnbaum's (1974) own evidence for nonadditivity is inconclusive.

As Birnbaum emphasized, the nonparallelism in his first three experiments was ambiguous because it could result from nonadditivity in the integration rule or from nonlinearity in the rating response. Experiment IV, which was claimed to resolve this problem, is subject to the very same ambiguity.

In Experiment IV, subjects judged the difference in likableness between two persons, each described by a pair of adjectives. There is thus a covert integration to obtain the likableness of the two separate persons prior to the overt judgment of the difference between them. Because the two person descriptions were combined in factorial design, the hypothesis that the difference judgments obeyed a subtracting model could be tested directly with the raw data.

> Furthermore, if the subtracting model succeeded, then the design also allowed a test of the hypothesis that the implicit integration to form the person impression obeyed an adding model. . . .
>
> Unfortunately, the subtracting model failed the test of goodness of fit. The difference judgments in Birnbaum's Table 1 show substantial, significant deviations from parallelism. This nonparallelism could result either from an invalid subtracting model or from a nonlinear response scale, but the data provided no way to distinguish between these two possibilities, even with monotone transformation (Anderson, 1981a, p. 126).

Birnbaum's interpretation was thus based entirely on the arbitrary assumption that the subtracting model was correct. Ironically, his experiments failed to disprove even the adding model, and had no bearing on the averaging model of IIT.

Personality impressions are indeed nonadditive, as Birnbaum asserted, but this conclusion did not follow from his data. Rather, this conclusion followed from previous work in IIT, most notably from the opposite effects crossover (e.g., Lampel & Anderson, 1968; Oden & Anderson, 1971; see similarly Anderson, 1965a).

5. The negativity effect—that more negative information has greater importance—presents an interesting theoretical subtlety. How is *importance* to be measured? More negative information will have greater *effect* simply because it is more negative in value. The concept of negativity effect must thus refer to importance weight as distinct from value.

Most attempts to demonstrate negativity effects were inconclusive because they lacked a method to distinguish weight from value. To do this requires a theory of psychological measurement. This separation was first achieved with functional measurement theory (see index entries under *Negativity effect* in Anderson, 1981a, 1982).

Within IIT, negativity is interpreted as greater informational content of more negative information. Negativity thus follows from the axiom of purposiveness; a more negative value is more informative by virtue of being closer to an avoidance goal. Hence it carries more information. An analogous positivity effect is expected on similar grounds.

6. Cognitive algebra in person cognition has been remarked by Christopher Morley in *The Haunted Bookshop* (1934, p. 90). I am indebted for this quote to Laura Martin.

> How quickly a young man's senses assemble and assimilate the data that are really relevant! Without seeming even to look in that direction he had performed the most amazing feat of lightning calculation known to the human faculties. He had added up all the young ladies of his acquaintance, and found the sum total less than the girl before him. He had subtracted the new phenomenon from the universe as he knew it, including the solar system and the advertising business, and found the remainder a minus quantity. He had multiplied the contents of his intellect by a factor he had no reason to assume "constant," and was startled at what teachers call (I believe) the "product." And he had divided what was in the left-hand armchair into his own career, and found no room for a quotient. All of which transpired in the length of time necessary for Roger to push forward another chair.

7. To treat all the cognitive consistency theories briefly as a group involves some oversimplification to bring out the main point. Thus, Festinger's theory of cognitive dissonance produced a coherent series of empirical studies, although with somewhat narrow, artificial tasks. Of historical interest is Osgood and Tannenbaum's congruity theory (see Tannenbaum, 1978), a kind of averaging theory. It ran aground on attempts to average adjective–noun combinations, such as *irresponsible mother*, which is worse than *irresponsible person.* This mistake was avoided in IIT (Anderson & Lopes, 1974; see Chapter 12, Notes 2 and 7). This same point has been made a number of times in the literature, not always recognizing that it had already been predicted and verified in IIT (see Anderson, 1981a, Section 3.5.1, Note 3.5.1a).

8. This critique of cognitive consistency theories remains relevant because their way of thinking remains common. This critique thus serves the further purpose of contributing to a case history of scientific inquiry, a guide to improving payoff of future work.

Skinner's criticism of theory, cited in the text, applies well to cognitive consistency theories. They have indeed left behind little of value. This failure stems from a way of thinking that was fundamentally inadequate to handle the phenomena. This was documented in a detailed scrutiny of the much-cited paper by Asch (1946).

> The main criticism of Asch's formulation is that it failed to clarify the conceptual issues. His basic thesis, that the adjectives in a description interact with one another in forming the impression, is eminently reasonable. Merely to verify the seeming pervasiveness of such interactions, as Asch aimed to do, would have been an important contribution. Asch's evidence did not do that because it rested on inadequate conceptual analysis, which did not make a clear distinction between evaluation of single stimuli and integration of several stimuli or even between stimulus and response.... When the conceptual structure of the problem is made clear, Asch's evidence is seen largely to reach conclusions that are obvious and uninformative.
>
> No one would question that our perceptions of other persons have organization and structure. The same is no doubt true in the personality adjective task. The problem is to develop method and theory that can contribute to the analysis of such organization and structure. Although Asch called attention to an important problem, his phenomenological approach failed to clarify the theoretical issues and his experimental work revealed little about either trait integration or structure in the impression (Anderson, 1981a, pp. 217-218).

Most theories of cognitive consistency exhibited similar lack of cumulative progress. This resulted from a too-narrow framework of strategy and tactics of inquiry.

9. Segregation of affect from cognition began long ago with a quasi-philosophical trichotomy of cognition, affect, and volition. With this trichotomy went the implication that cognition was rational, whereas affect, especially emotion, was subrational or irrational.

This separation was accentuated by various developments in psychology. One was a long allegiance to Schachter's (1964) claim, akin to the James–Lange theory, that all affect and emotion were constituted from a single base of undifferentiated arousal—and that some cognitive cue was necessary to define different emotional qualities, such as anger, fear, and happiness. Schachter's claim rested on two experimental reports, both seriously defective. Indeed, Schachter's claim was actually contradicted by his own results. Support was obtained by selective elimination of about a third of the subjects in one experiment and a smaller number in the other. These two experiments seem rightly labeled as "object lessons in poor science" (Anderson, 1989b, p. 143).

Mainstream cognitive psychology perpetuated the affect–cognition dichotomy by leanings toward artificial intelligence and by focusing on problem solving, memory, attention, reaction time, and other problems in which affect could ostensibly be ignored. This separation is well illustrated in Simon's (1982) remark that cognitive psychology had lived several decades essentially without affect.

Segregationist views similar to Simon's were widely adopted in social psychology (e.g., Berscheid, 1982; Fiske; 1982; Lau & Sears, 1986; Zajonc, 1980), with rare exceptions (e.g., Leventhal, 1982). As Lau and Sears put it (1986, p. 364): "Cognitive psychology, with the problems it has chosen to study, is usually safe in ignoring any purposive influence from the individual over information processing."

Social cognition is heavily affective, so social psychologists could not ignore it, as did cognitive psychologists. It was a mistake, however, to try tacking affect onto concepts borrowed from mainstream cognitive psychology. This point was made in a review of contributions that attempted to do so for social-political cognition:

> The attempts in this volume to utilize poorly understood ideas from another field might have been a useful catalyst were it not that these ideas are ill-suited to the central concerns of socio-political cognition. Much of the problem lies in the very narrow view of information processing that underlies this volume. It either ignores affect, as many of the authors remark, or awkwardly tries to tack it on at the end, whereas affect needs to be incorporated at the beginning. . . .
>
> Social-political cognition requires a more social conception of information processing, one that gives primary place to affect, values, and social goals. . . .
>
> The fact is that cognition has always been central in social psychology. This arises from the focal concern with values and purposes of everyday social life. This historical character of social psychology seems to go unrecognized in the urge to pass as cognitive scientists, which afflicts part of the field. This volume, as a consequence, is largely silent on such basic areas as attitudes, attribution, and group dynamics. . . . By being true to itself, social psychology could be more true to its sister disciplines (Anderson, 1987, pp. 296*ff*).

The need to unify affect and cognition has begun to be recognized, both in social–personality psychology and in cognitive psychology. Progress has been hobbled, however, by persistence of inappropriate conceptual frameworks.

10. The clinical unconscious may be amenable to experimental analysis with IIT, for example, with functional measurement of projection. The present personality task could be extended to combine trait adjectives with the ambiguous figures used in the Thematic Apperception Test or even Rorschach ink blots. Projection should affect the values of the ambiguous figures, as well as the adjectives, and these can be measured at the individual level. Direct judgments of the component stimuli, utilizing the generalized halo model, would seem even simpler. Although speculative, this proposal may yield a rigorous supplement to clinical analysis of the unconscious (see further Conte & Plutchik, 1995).

11. Most consistency theories employed the common hypothetico-deductive strategy, beginning with some general consistency postulate and seeking empirical deductions to be tested. This usually led to artificial experimental tasks, in which the behavior lacked intrinsic interest.

Inductive strategy puts a premium on behavior with intrinsic interest. One such domain in which consistency is important is ego defense. Criticism, blame, and failure, in particular, are informers inconsistent with a positive self-concept. They evoke strong reactions to reduce this inconsistency, as in excuses and rationalization. Had the consistency theories followed inductive strategy, they would have focused on ego defense or other phenomena of comparable interest. Then they would surely have left behind something of value (see further, *Strategy of Theory Construction* in Chapter 1).

PREFACE

Social psychology can be a science. This thesis, begun in the previous chapter on person cognition, is extended to *attitudes, attribution,* and *group dynamics.* A unified theory is shown to be effective across all these areas.

Attitudes, in the functional perspective, are knowledge systems. They function in construction of attitudinal responses in diverse social situations. This function often involves an averaging process, illustrated here with attitudinal judgments about U. S. presidents and with wife–husband interaction. This cognitive algebra has provided a new approach to many problems in the attitude domain, including motivation, measurement, and memory.

A novel contribution is the functional theory of memory, which arose in an early integration study. Attitude cognition could not be understood within a traditional conception of memory. Integration theory led to a functional conception of memory, grounded in the axiom of purposiveness.

Why did she act that way? represents a prototypical question in social attribution, which studies how people attribute causes to explain behavior. Such attributions have been shown to follow causal schemas of exact algebraic form in various situations. Other current theories have attempted rationalist formulations, which are inadequate, conceptually and methodologically, for analysis of attribution processes.

Group dynamics also exhibits cognitive algebra. Bargaining obeys a general social averaging theorem that quantifies compromise. Group cognition obeys rules like those for person cognition in the previous chapter. Of special interest is the family, the most important—and most neglected—social group.

The theory of information integration involves a new way of thinking. Comparisons with prominent theoretical alternatives in each of the three foregoing areas show that all ran aground through attacking multiple determination with makeshift methods. Functional measurement was effective in all three areas.

Fragmentation and compartmentalization are steadily increasing in social–personality psychology. Even within a single area, such as attitudes, numerous mini-theories go their separate ways, with little interaction and little generality of result. This fragmentation stems from old ways of thinking, which cannot handle the basic problems of multiple determination and personal value.

The theory of information integration makes possible a scientific treatment of everyday life in something like its own terms, grounded in the axiom of purposiveness. Although incomplete in many respects, information integration theory provides a unified, general approach in place of the increasing compartmentalization within social–personality psychology.

Chapter 5

UNIFIED SOCIAL COGNITION

The theoretical framework for person cognition in the previous chapter is a core for a unified, general theory of social cognition. This chapter reviews applications to three main social areas: *attitudes*, *attribution*, and *group dynamics*. The same theme, information integration, provides a conceptual and analytical framework for all three areas. The final part discusses research strategy for unified general theory.

ATTITUDES

Attitudes are primary stuff of everyday life. We have attitudes about various other persons, about social, political, and moral issues, about our work, the environment, other nations, and so on. These attitudes are continuously involved in our thought and action. Attitude theory, accordingly, has often been viewed as the conceptual base of social psychology.

Unfortunately, theory and research on attitudes are fragmented. An immense number of studies have been published on attitudes, and many theoretical views have been advanced. Our understanding of attitudes is much broader and deeper than in the 1950s. But this understanding remains unsatisfying to nearly all workers. Indeed, much of this understanding consists of the realization that many variables can operate in complicated, situation-dependent ways, difficult to understand or predict. Conceptually, the attitude domain is fragmented into specific approaches and particular problems, interesting in themselves, but lacking in generality and theoretical unity.

Unified attitude theory has become possible with the discovery that attitudinal judgments obey cognitive algebra. The twin problems of multiple determination and personal value, basic to any general theory, thus became resolvable. The next several sections present empirical illustrations of this cognitive algebra of attitudes. This is followed by discussion of unified attitude theory.

ATTITUDES, HISTORY, AND SOCIETY

United States history is one of the main carriers of our social attitudes. The formation of these attitudes begins in the early grades with stories about Washington and Valley Forge, about Lincoln and the borrowed book. These stories help form attitudes about perseverance and honesty, about dignity and responsibility of the individual, and about our society. They provide standards against which contemporary presidents and other persons are judged. More generally, such attitudes enter into a complex system of sociopolitical cognition that operates throughout the background of everyday life.

The averaging model for person cognition of Chapter 4 applies also in the attitude domain. In the experiment of Figure 5.1, subjects read biographical

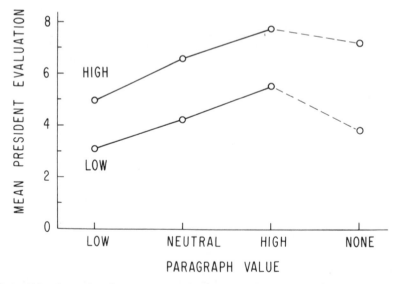

Figure 5.1. Averaging theory governs attitudes toward U. S. presidents. Subjects judge statesmanship of U. S. presidents described by biographical paragraphs. Near-parallelism of the two solid curves implies the biographical information is averaged or added. The two points at the right connected by dashed lines eliminate adding and support averaging theory. (From N. H. Anderson, 1973, "Information integration theory applied to attitudes about U. S. presidents," *Journal of Educational Psychology, 64*, 1-8. Copyright 1973 by the American Psychological Association. Reprinted by permission.)

paragraphs about U. S. presidents and judged each president on statesmanship. These paragraphs were combined in pairs according to a factorial-type design, as indicated in Figure 5.1. Two aspects of this data pattern indicate that these paragraphs were averaged to produce the attitudinal judgment.

First, the two solid curves are nearly parallel. Parallelism supports both averaging and adding rules, and thereby points to a simple algebra of attitudinal judgment. Although the valuation process for each paragraph is complex (see next section), the integration follows a simple rule.

Second, the opposite effects test supports the averaging rule and eliminates the adding rule. The two points at the right, connected by dashed lines, are based on only one paragraph, listed at the left of each curve. The mean attitudinal judgments are 7.23 for the High paragraph and 3.83 for the Low paragraph. The critical question concerns the effects of adding the same neutral paragraph. These effects appear in the middle data points of the solid curves. Adding Neutral to High *decreases* the judgment from 7.23 to 6.61—but adding the same Neutral to Low *increases* the judgment from 3.83 to 4.26. The same added information thus has opposite effects.

Opposite effects obviously disagrees with the sometime popular additive or summation models of attitudes. This finding that the same information can have opposite effects has been verified in virtually every experimental test, including tests by proponents of additive models. The various additive models proposed in attitude theory have accordingly become moribund.

The averaging model, in contrast, predicts such opposite effects, as shown in Chapter 4. Together, the parallelism test and the opposite effects test have repeatedly demonstrated a basic averaging process in attitudinal response.

MOLAR UNITIZATION

Vital to the success of integration attitude theory is *molar unitization*, by virtue of which a complex of information can be treated as a single unit (see also Chapter 1). The importance of molar unitization may be illustrated with one of the president paragraphs[1]:

> President Truman was a strong advocate of Civil Rights, and requested several important reforms be enacted by Congress. Although Congress failed to act, Truman was undaunted. By using his power to issue Executive Orders, Truman achieved major reforms single-handedly. Over the opposition of both admirals and generals, Truman's first order successfully integrated the armed forces. In addition, Truman established a committee to enforce non-discriminatory clauses contained in government contracts. By 1951, Truman's committee had made real progress toward eliminating job discrimination in large sections of the nation's economy.

This paragraph has a nonsimple structure. The main content is that Truman was effective in extending Civil Rights. Three distinct actions are listed, namely, integrating the armed forces, enforcing nondiscrimination in hiring by government contractors, and the unsuccessful request for Congress to act on Civil Rights. Without actually saying so, moreover, the paragraph suggests that Truman was an effective administrator, for he found ways to achieve his aims despite lack of help from Congress. In addition, there is the positive affective tone conveyed by the words *undaunted* and *single-handedly*. Even this short paragraph thus includes multiple items of information.

How any subject processes the paragraph information is not knowable in detail. Subjects may be inattentive to certain words or sentences or fail to draw inferences implicit in the material. Different subjects, moreover, will attach different importance weight and different value to the same item of information. There is no way to determine the valuation processing for any subject, even in principle. Exact theory might thus seem impossible.

But exact theory is possible by virtue of molar unitization and functional measurement. No matter how superficial or intricate the paragraph processing may be, no matter what the subject's valuation processes may be, the net result is a characterization of the paragraph in terms of two parameters: weight and scale value. This characterization is complete and exact; the two parameters summarize all the processing details, however unknown they may be. Exact theory thus becomes possible.

The parallelism theorem illustrates the power of this approach. The parallelism in Figure 5.1 is predicted in terms of the molar values actually operative in this experiment. Nothing need be known of the processing detail; nothing need be known of the past experience of the subjects. The parallelism appears directly in terms of the attitudinal judgments themselves. Functional measurement thus provides tests that are exact—in the functional values.

FAMILY ATTITUDES

The family is a prime locus for attitude research. Attitudes exert continuous control of family interaction, which in turn has continuous formative effects on attitudes of family members. The mutual adjustments of the first months and years of marriage involve development of knowledge systems about spouse and about self, including various changes in one's own attitudes. Parents' attitudes control their parenting, and something of these same attitudes is absorbed by their children. Parental attitudes themselves often change markedly through experience with their first child.

One question for integration attitude theory is whether the averaging process revealed in the foregoing presidents experiment also operates in family interaction. The answer appears to be *yes*, as illustrated in the experimental test of Figure 5.2. Couples received stories about a child who had performed a harmful act with specified intent, using a 2 × 3, Intent × Damage design. They made separate judgments about how much discipline the child deserved.

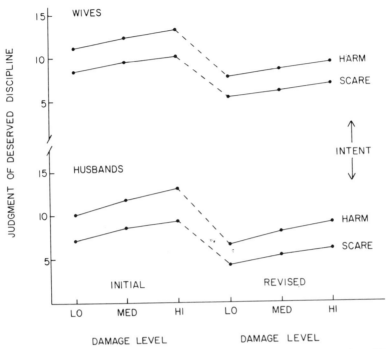

Figure 5.2. Averaging theory governs attitudes in wife–husband interaction. Wife and husband judge deserved discipline for a child who acted with *intent* to Harm or Scare another child (curve parameter), causing Lo, Med, or Hi *damage* (horizontal axis). Initial judgments in left panels show parallelism for intent and damage information given by experimenter. Revised judgments in right panels are made after receiving extenuating information constructed by spouse. Near-parallelism in the right panels implies that spouse-given information is integrated by same averaging rule as experimenter-given information. (After Anderson & Armstrong, 1989; see also Armstrong, 1984.)

The data at the left side of Figure 5.2 exhibit parallelism, both for wives and for husbands. This agrees with the blame schema, Blame = Intent + Damage. This was expected because this blame schema had been supported in previous work with other subject populations (see Chapter 6).

Family interaction, however, was the main concern in this experiment. Following the initial judgment of blame for the child, one spouse composed extenuating information intended to reduce the blame. This information was communicated to the partner, who made a revised judgment. The design was thus *personalized* to the individual couple.

These revised judgments are shown at the right of Figure 5.2. The lower elevation of these revised judgments shows the influence of the extenuating information. The adding model predicts that the revised curves will all differ from the initial curves by a constant. The averaging model, in contrast, predicts that the revised curves will be flatter and closer together, and this prediction was verified. Although these two effects may seem small in the figure, both were highly reliable.

The immediate implication of these data is that the attitudinal judgments of wife and husband each followed a true cognitive equation:

$$\text{Blame} = \text{Intent} + \text{Damage} - \text{Extenuation.}$$

This averaging process applies not only to the intent and damage information given by the experimenter, but also to the extenuating information made up and given by the spouses to each other. Family interaction in everyday life is expected to follow the same processes.

It deserves emphasis that the functional measurement methodology makes exact allowance for the complete wife–husband interaction. This follows from the property of molar unitization already discussed. An alternative approach to marital interaction has used detailed coding of online interaction sequences. This can be invaluable in elucidating the nature of interaction, but much interaction is not observable and much observable interaction is not well codable. Functional measurement methodology finesses these limitations. Paradoxical as it may seem, a method that does not attempt detailed delineation of the interaction can be superior in important respects to methods that do. Both approaches, of course, are needed for complete theory.

Social psychologists have neglected the family, leaving it to sociologists and workers in family studies. This is regrettable; the family is a prime domain for virtually everything of interest to social psychologists, truly an "endless frontier" (Anderson, 1991g).

ATTITUDES AND BEHAVIOR

Attitudes predict contraceptive behavior. A long-standing criticism of attitude theories is that most yield distressingly low correlations with actual behavior. One reason is that most theories assume an adding, or summation, rule for attitudes, which is incorrect. An incorrect rule, of course, will yield lower correlations than the correct rule.

Using the averaging rule of integration attitude theory, Jaccard and Becker (1985) obtained a mean attitude–behavior correlation of .84—at the individual level—for contraceptive preferences of sexually active college students. The data agreed with IIT, but disagreed strongly with summation theories.

This well-done study is also notable for its use of personal design. The experimental design was personalized to take account of the attitudes of each individual subject. Further, the integration rule was testable at the individual level. This application of personal design illustrates a new level of precision in attitude theory.

Such high attitude–behavior correlations as obtained by Jaccard and Becker cannot generally be expected. Behavior generally depends on other determinants than a single attitude, for example, costs and expectations of possible outcomes. Prediction of behavior thus requires unification of attitude theory with judgment–decision theory.

ATTITUDE LEARNING

Learning of attitudes was studied in another experiment with the president paragraphs. Attitudes ordinarily develop over the course of time, as successive informers are received and incorporated into the knowledge system. One question is whether such attitude learning will obey the same averaging process found in the foregoing experiments. A second question concerns relative effect of previous informers on the present attitude. Initial informers may crystallize the attitude, yielding a primacy effect; alternatively, later informers could wash out the earlier, yielding a recency effect.

Attitude learning is portrayed in Figure 5.3. Subjects judged statesmanship of presidents, each described by a sequence of four paragraphs. Judgments were cumulative, being revised after each successive paragraph. Each paragraph could be Hi or Lo in value, and all $2^4 = 16$ Hi–Lo sequences were used.

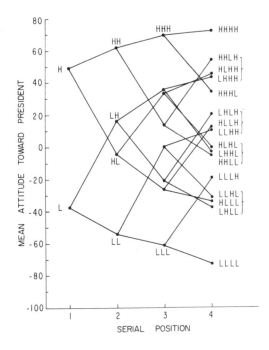

Figure 5.3. Tree diagram of attitude learning. Serial integration of informers about U. S. presidents obeys averaging rule. Subjects receive sequences of four Hi or Lo biographical paragraphs about some U. S. president and make a cumulative judgment of statesmanship after each paragraph. Attitudes rise and fall in direct reaction to information received, showing uniform recency. (From "New light on order effects in attitude change," by N. H. Anderson and A. J. Farkas, 1973, *Journal of Personality and Social Psychology, 28,* 88-93. Copyright 1973 by the American Psychological Association. Reprinted by permission.)

The tree diagram of Figure 5.3 presents the attitudinal judgments at each serial position for each of the 16 presidents. The intertwined branching exactly mirrors the design and exhibits a simple pattern: The attitude toward each president rises and falls in direct reaction to the information received. Analogous graphs with a single time line are common in news media, showing how voter approval of our current president rises and falls as a function of events in his administration.

Recency effects appear throughout Figure 5.3. At serial position 2, recency is indicated by the crossover of the two middle curves. Since these two curves represent the same information in different orders, the difference in response must be due to the order of presentation. And since the LH order yields a more favorable attitude than the opposite HL order, the effect is one of recency: The more recent informer has greater effect. At serial position 3, similarly, LLH is higher than HLL (these are the fourth and second points from the bottom, respectively). Numerous other such comparisons are possible, and every one shows recency at every serial position. This recency is a surface effect, however, as will be seen in Figure 5.4.

Two other aspects of Figure 5.3 deserve consideration. First, the data support the averaging rule, as was shown in the detailed analysis. In the tree format, however, the parallelism pattern is not easy to visualize, and no attempt will be made to explain it here. It deserves emphasis, however, that this outcome helps extend the results of Chapter 4 to more complex informers.

The other aspect of Figure 5.3 concerns resistance to change, a prominent issue in attitude theory. The very top curve shows how attitude develops over a sequence of four High paragraphs. The attitude becomes increasingly favorable as additional H information is added; the shape of this curve agrees with the prediction of the averaging model for amount of information (see Table 4.1). At the same time, the attitude becomes more solid; later information has less overt effect. This may be seen by comparing the three limbs projecting downward from the top curve. Each limb represents the overt effect of one L, and this effect is visibly less at later positions.

This lesser effect of later informers might suggest that they are less important, as though some kind of primacy effect was present. This conclusion would be required by additive or summation theories, but it would be a conceptual mistake. The later paragraphs had no less influence than earlier paragraphs in this experiment. This may be seen by comparing the weight parameters, obtained from the averaging model, across serial position as shown in Figure 5.4. The attitude itself, however, becomes more solid as more information is incorporated. Hence its total weight parameter increases. Relative to this, the apparent, or relative weight, and hence the observed effect of each single later paragraph must decrease, even though all paragraphs make equal contribution. Without the theory, it would be easy to misinterpret the data.

BASAL–SURFACE REPRESENTATION

Integration attitude studies have revealed two components of attitudes: A labile *surface component* that is susceptible to change by incoming information; and a *basal component* that, once formed, is resistant to change. This basal–surface representation is plausible. Most of us have experiences of being swayed by events and persuasion of the moment, only to revert to our previous views once the momentary salience sinks into the past.

But little real evidence is available for distinct basal and surface components. The obvious alternative hypothesis—that there is just a single component—can account for nearly all the data. Thus, well-established attitudes should resist change because they rest on a substantial information base; averaging theory then implies that a new informer will have small effect because its proportionate weight in the whole is small—even though it has just as much effect as any one of the old informers on which the attitude is based (see *Amount of Information*, Chapter 4). Similarly, findings that attitudes decay more slowly after greater time intervals is also expected from averaging theory.

Evidence on this basal–surface representation comes from the president experiment of Figure 5.3. The final response for each informer sequence incorporates the effects of four successive paragraphs. The question concerns the relative effects of these four successive paragraphs. This question can be answered by applying the serial form of the averaging model, Equations 6 of Chapter 2. The final response can thus be fractionated into contributions from the four successive positions—the serial curve of attitude learning.

This serial curve is labeled R4 in Figure 5.4. Each point on the R4 curve represents a weight parameter, that is, the importance of the informer at each serial position in the final attitude. The flatness of the R4 curve over the first three serial positions means that each had equal influence. There is no bowing, as would be expected from the verbal learning hypothesis. However, the upswing at the last point means that the informer at the last serial position had greater weight. The recency effects previously shown at the final attitudinal judgment in Figure 5.3 are thus localized at the last serial position.

Of special significance is the difference between the curves labeled R3 and R4. The R3 curve gives the serial weights for the attitude at the third position. It has the same form as the R4 curve, being flat over the first two serial positions and showing a terminal recency upswing. But this recency in the R3 curve has disappeared in the R4 curve; there the third serial position has no more effect than the first or second. The recency effect is thus short-term, not lasting.

The short-term recency represents the surface component; the flat portion of each curve represents the basal component. These curves show that the basal component builds up uniformly over successive informers. Each serial position has equal weight in the basal component; there is no forgetting of or interference from the earlier information.

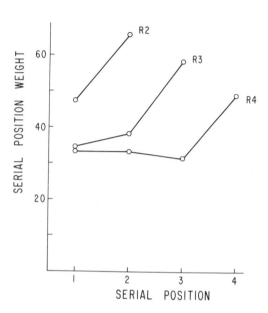

Figure 5.4. Basal—surface representation. Serial position curves for president attitudes of Figure 5.3. Curve labeled R4 shows relative weight of the paragraphs at the four serial positions (see text). (From "New light on order effects in attitude change," by N. H. Anderson and A. J. Farkas, 1973, *Journal of Personality and Social Psychology, 28,* 88-93. Copyright 1973 by the American Psychological Association. Reprinted by permission.)

Current attitude research, without realizing it, seems mainly involved with the surface component. Most studies are limited to one or two communications, with attitude measured shortly afterward. Such attitude measures will likely contain substantial surface component, without lasting significance; the enduring basal component may yield an opposite effect, as in the original study (Anderson, 1959b, see 1991h, pp. 36-40). Some studies do measure attitudes after a delay, but whether delay eliminates the surface component is yet unknown. The elimination of surface component seen in Figure 5.4 may depend on stimulus interference rather than passage of time. The surface component is certainly of interest, but seems to have much less social significance than the basal. This basal—surface distinction may also help explain why field studies seem to find much less attitude change than laboratory studies. As far as social relevance goes, much current attitude research may be hoeing sterile ground.[2]

The basal—surface structure makes ecological sense in terms of limited attentional capacity. Much environmental information is redundant. The brain would thus do well to settle on a judgment or attitude from a few initial observations, thereby freeing processing capacity to deal with other aspects of the environment. This would correspond to the basal component. The surface component, relying on short-term capacity, could still monitor shifts in the environment. This interpretation, admittedly speculative, supports the idea that substantial biological components are woven into the social fabric of attitudes.

ADDITIVE ATTITUDE THEORIES

Algebraic theories of attitudes have been proposed by a number of investigators. Common to all is the idea of representing the attitude issue as a set of features, or attributes, each with a value and a weight. The attributes of a presidential candidate, for example, would include the candidate's stands on various issues, as well as party affiliation, past record, and personality. Although these theories differ among themselves, nearly all employ an addition or summation formula, which may be written in present notation as:

$$A = \sum \omega_i \psi_i,$$

where ψ_i is the value of attribute i, ω_i is its weight, and A is the overall attitude (attitudinal judgment).

This additivity assumption seems almost axiomatic. Adding a favorable attribute should certainly make the overall attitude more favorable.

The additive and summation theories all recognized the need to solve the problem of multiple determination—multiple determination is explicit in the addition formula. They could not solve this problem, however, because they lacked a theory of psychological measurement. As a consequence, they failed to realize that their basic additivity assumption was empirically incorrect.

The failure of the additivity assumption has conceptual ramifications throughout attitude theory. A different conceptual framework emerges from integration attitude theory, as with attitudes and motivation, attitude memory, and other issues discussed under *Unified Attitude Theory*.

COGNITIVE ALGEBRA: FOUNDATION FOR ATTITUDE THEORY

Cognitive algebra has provided a new conceptual base for attitude theory. In case after case, averaging theory leads to different understanding. One case has appeared in the averaging–adding test of Figure 5.1, which showed that the same information could have opposite effects. In additive theories, opposite effects is paradoxical, and seems to require some special explanatory process (see also *Implicit Additivity* in Chapter 2). In averaging theory, in contrast, the result is understandable as straightforward information integration. A second case appeared in the foregoing discussion of resistance to change. In this case, the additive model again took the data at face value to arrive at an incorrect process interpretation. A third case is the demonstration of meaning invariance, which is as important in attitude theory as in person cognition.

Cognitive algebra leads to analogous conceptual restructuring throughout the attitude domain. Attitude memory, for example, stereotype theory, and even the definition of attitude have undergone conceptual transformation through cognitive algebra. Such conceptual implications are the prime end, for which the quantitative model serves as a means. At bottom, this restructuring stems from the capability of cognitive algebra to transform the axiom of purposiveness from teleology to science. This cognitive algebra has provided a foundation for a unified theory of attitudes.

UNIFIED ATTITUDE THEORY

The foregoing results illustrate a solid empirical base for an integration theory of attitudes. Unified theory, however, involves more general considerations, a few of which noted briefly here. Foremost is the functional perspective (Chapter 1).

FUNCTIONAL PERSPECTIVE

Attitudes are useful. They serve purposes. In the present perspective, attitudes function in valuation processing, that is, in the construction of values for stimulus informers in diverse goal-directed behavior.

To illustrate, consider parents raising a female child. Their attitudes about social roles of females continually will influence their decisions, large and small, about her upbringing. Egalitarian attitudes would operate to encourage self-reliance, the feeling *I can do it.* Such attitudes would affect choice of toys, books, and clothes for the child, the tasks assigned the child, and the counsel given when the child becomes discouraged. Such parental attitudes influence every form and aspect of parent–child interaction.

Traditional attitudes, which emphasize female roles as housewives and mothers, would lead to different choices of toys, books, clothes, and tasks. Encouragement, praise, and blame would be dispensed for different activities. The principle remains the same: Parents' attitudes exert strong, often invisible, but continuous influence on child development.

This functional perspective on attitudes is directly related to the axiom of purposiveness (see Chapter 1). Attitudes are adaptive systems. In parental behavior, as just indicated, the same attitude may underlie thought and action in many different situations. Similarly, attitudes about gender roles operate not only in parenting, but also in many aspects of wife–husband interaction and in general social intercourse. A few basic attitudes can be utilized for response in many different social situations. Attitudes are thus general purpose knowledge systems, adaptive and economical in function.

ATTITUDES AS KNOWLEDGE SYSTEMS

The foregoing discussion of attitude function entails a distinction between *attitude* and *attitudinal response.* IIT implies that attitudes, properly speaking, are knowledge systems. They typically have complex structure. Each may function in constructing responses in many situations. These situational responses are the *attitudinal responses* (Anderson, 1976a,b, 1981b).

Definition of the attitude concept, a long-standing issue in attitude theory, depends on this distinction between attitude and attitudinal response. Most theories have adopted a one-dimensional view, defining attitude as an evaluative reaction along a favorable–unfavorable dimension. People thus have liberal–conservative attitudes in politics and pro–anti attitudes on abortion, the environment, and the current president. This one-dimensional view may be seen in the classic definition of attitudes as "readiness to respond." In practice, it is often useful.

As a definition of attitude, however, this one-dimensional view is seriously inadequate. One-dimensional evaluative reactions are just one class of attitudinal responses. Experimental studies of attitudinal responses, including those of the previous section, assess only partial representations of the underlying knowledge system. Such partial, one-dimensional representations are manifestations of the purposiveness of behavior. They embody motivational components of the knowledge system, which underlie the functional values. They can provide information about the structure of the knowledge system. They should not, however, be identified with the knowledge system itself.[3]

Attitudes are thus not a "readiness to respond." Nor are they immediate causes of behavior. Their primary function is to place values on stimulus informers in relation to operative goals. Further prerequisite to behavior is an integration of these values into an overall attitudinal response.

This integration will also contain nonattitudinal components. One class of nonattitudinal components involves reliability and redundancy of informers. A second class includes expectations about various outcomes. A third class includes other forces, including politeness, ulterior motives, or counter obligation, which may compete with the attitudinal component. Understanding attitude function thus depends on understanding the integration that underlies actual behavior. This requires going outside the attitude domain itself. Attitude theory must be developed as part of general cognitive theory.

STEREOTYPES

Stereotypes have much in common with attitudes, which they sometimes combine with roles. Attitudes toward women, for example, involve stereotypes about social and occupational roles suitable and unsuitable for women.

Only one issue in stereotypes will be considered here, one that emphasizes the need for a unified approach. Much current work on stereotypes suffers under a misconception that stereotypes generally bias and distort processing of given information. This misconception is a variant of the change-of-meaning hypothesis, extensively disconfirmed in the studies of person cognition in the previous chapter.

A typical finding in stereotype studies is that the same action is judged differently when performed by members of different social groups. Thus, a successful action may be attributed to skill, when performed by a male, or to luck, when performed by a female. Similarly, violations of the law may receive harder treatment in the justice system for members of a minority group.

The standard interpretation of such results has been that the group stereotype biases and distorts the processing of the given information about the action; the same information takes on different meanings. This interpretation, it might seem, is hardly more than a rephrasing of the observed data. Actually, it rests on a fundamental theoretical assumption. Indeed, this interpretation is just the change-of-meaning hypothesis in a new guise.

An alternative interpretation is indicated by IIT: The stereotype has no effect on the processing of the other given information; instead it is integrated directly into the response. This interpretation follows the meaning invariance hypothesis of person cognition demonstrated in the previous chapter. The cited finding about group stereotypes may thus be an instance of the positive context effect (Figure 4.2).

Other issues may be analyzed similarly. In memory studies, for example, results standardly interpreted to mean that stereotypes affect memory encoding or decoding can often be better understood as direct integration of the stereotype—with no effect on memory for the other informers (Chapter 11). Most results on illusory correlation, similarly, have a unified interpretation in terms of integration theory. Interpretations in the literature generally rest on a confusion between valuation and integration, the **V** and **I** operations of information integration theory.[4]

This theoretical crux, unfortunately, has gone virtually unrecognized in the stereotype literature. As a consequence, few studies have been designed that can distinguish between these two theoretical interpretations. Most interpretations in terms of bias–distortion are thus gratuitous. A notable exception is Petzold (1983), who affirmed stereotype integration theory and also pointed to a general personality factor of context dependence. Also notable is the analysis of stereotype expectations by Heit (Chapter 11).

Unified theory has been handicapped by the fragmentation just indicated between stereotypes and person cognition. Further fragmentation occurs between these two areas and attitude research. These areas have much common content. Moreover, they exhibit commonality in cognitive process, as the foregoing empirical studies have shown.[5]

BIAS

The conception of attitude as knowledge system helps clarify misconceptions about *bias*. Statements such as "Strong attitudes and stereotypes create biases in information processing" are common but often meaningless. They require a standard of correctness relative to which bias can be defined and measured, but often no such standard exists. Dismissing evidence contrary to your well-settled opinion, for example, should not be called a bias for it stems from an efficient, even though imperfect, property of normal information processing.

As knowledge systems, attitudes have a primary function in valuation of stimulus information. Any two persons will have different knowledge systems, so they will construct different values from the same stimulus information and hence make different attitudinal responses. This does not mean that either is incorrect or biased; both could be functioning optimally within their own framework. To consider one or both prejudiced or biased information processors is usually a personal value judgment, lacking scientific validity.

Such bias misconceptions underlie many misinterpretations in the literature, as with certain of the cognitive consistency theories of Chapter 4. Similar bias ideas have long obstructed stereotype theory, as noted in the previous section. They appear again in the primacy–recency issue in judgment–decision theory (Chapter 10). And they have helped perpetuate the artificial separation of motivation and cognition by treating motivational factors as biases (see further Anderson, 1982, Section 1.1.5, Notes 1.1.5b,c).

People certainly do have limitations as information processors. But even when there is an objective standard of correctness, as with limited attention span or with geometrical illusions (e.g., Figure 9.10), the term *bias* adds nothing. And when there is no objective standard, as with attitudinal response, the term *bias* leads toward a mirage. Normal information processing perforce depends on each individual's knowledge systems; recognizing this is an essential step toward general theory of attitudes.

ATTITUDE MEMORY

A novel conception of attitude memory as *functional memory* arose in an early integration experiment (Anderson & Hubert, 1963). At that time, it was taken for granted that attitudes were based on reproductive memory for given information, a view consonant with the reproductive framework of mainstream memory theory, which studies recall and recognition of specified material. This *verbal memory hypothesis* keeps reappearing in various guises even today.[6]

A new conception of attitude memory emerged from the cited experiment. Attitudinal responses are constructed through valuation and integration operations on informer stimuli. This construction is on-line in operating memory, so the current attitudinal response undergoes continual change as new informers are received. This online construction is portrayed in the tree diagram of Figure 5.3. Such attitudinal responses are formed in operating memory and stored in long-term knowledge systems.

In this functional view, attitude memory has a life of its own, qualitatively different from verbal memory of the stimulus informers from which it was constructed. Once the goal-relevant implications of an informer have been evaluated and integrated, the informer may be forgotten. Hence dissociation between verbal memory and attitude memory can be expected, as in the cited experiment (see Figure 11.1).

Analysis of attitude memory requires stronger methods than dissociation, which is a rather limited tool. One such method is functional measurement. With the establishment of the averaging model, it became possible to disintegrate attitude memory into components associated with each separate informer. This capability, illustrated with the serial memory curves of Figure 5.4, provides a powerful new tool for studying attitude memory in terms of informational learning.

This functional view of attitude memory is intimately related to the axiom of purposiveness. In goal-directed thought and action, attitudes have a primary function of placing approach and avoidance values on stimulus informers and goals. This goal-directedness of thought and action is the origin of the evaluative quality generally ascribed to attitudes. By making it possible to measure these values, integration theory breaks out of the teleological circularity of purposiveness to transform it into an explanatory construct.

This functional conception of attitude memory has now been widely accepted in social psychology. Mainstream memory theory, in contrast, remains in the grip of the reproductive conception of memory. Further discussion is given in Chapter 11 on functional memory.[7]

FUNCTIONAL MEASUREMENT ATTITUDE SCALES

Attitude measurement can be simple with functional measurement methodology. In its simplest application, functional measurement utilizes a rating scale defined in terms of the particular attitude issue to be measured. In Figure 5.1, for example, attitude toward a given president was rated on a 0–10 scale. As this example illustrates, functional measurement provides a general purpose method for measuring attitudinal response.

Simplicity is one advantage of functional measurement attitude scales. Most traditional methods of attitude measurement require more or less laborious construction of a set of attitude statements of varied degrees of favorableness about an issue, which the person is to accept or reject. A functional measurement attitude scale may require only a single statement to define the issue, as in Figure 5.1, and a single rating to measure the attitudinal response.

Two related advantages are homogeneity and generality. Traditional attitude scales usually have heterogeneous content. Thus, the set of attitude statements used in a standard scale of "attitude toward women" includes diverse social and occupational roles that are distinct components of a knowledge system. A functional measurement approach would allow each role to be a separate attitude issue. Pooling heterogeneous content is sometimes appropriate, of course, but functional measurement does not require this.

Generality appears in the ready applicability of functional measurement attitude scaling to diverse issues. Most traditional scales are defined narrowly and rigidly by the sets of statements constructed for a given issue. Even for closely related issues, they may be inappropriate and invalid. Hence they are poorly suited for functional theory, which views attitudinal response as goal-directed and dependent on context and situation.

From the present functional perspective, indeed, traditional methods of attitude measurement are conceptually inadequate. They take for granted the traditional conception of attitude as a single evaluative dimension. These methods yield only an attitudinal response, in the present view, or more correctly, some ill-defined average attitudinal response that may not apply to any situation. Such measures may have some practical utility, but they are not a good foundation for attitude theory.

A rather different advantage is that functional measurement attitude scales are true psychological scales. More precisely, they can provide true linear, or equal interval scales of attitudinal response. Certain precautions to avoid rating biases need to be used, as indicated in Chapter 3, but these are usually easy to implement.

Other methods of attitude measurement, except Thurstonian theory, ignore this validity problem. The danger of such ignoral is emphasized by the sharp contrast between functional measurement and the method of magnitude estimation of Figure 3.1. Traditional methods of attitude measurement, for all that is presently known, may be as severely biased as magnitude estimation.

Functional measurement has two additional capabilities, not envisioned in traditional methods of attitude measurement. These concern the other two unobservables in the integration diagram of Figure 1.1, namely, the integration rule and stimulus measurement. In the attitude study of Figure 5.1, for example, the main concern was the integration rule. To test the integration rule, a factorial design was needed. However, when only an attitudinal response is to be measured, as in the traditional methods, factorial design is not needed. Functional measurement of attitude can then be as simple as a rating scale.

The second novel capability of functional measurement concerns stimulus analysis. Traditional methods are generally concerned to measure the response, not the stimuli. Attitudinal response generally depends on multiple stimulus determinants, however, and can hardly be understood except in relation to these determinants. One technique for stimulus measurement is through the parallelism theorem, illustrated in Figure 2.1. A second technique is with self-estimation, illustrated later in the group attitude study of Figure 5.11.

This capability for stimulus measurement extends to nonattitudinal determinants of attitudinal behavior. These include other forces, such as fear, politeness, and ulterior motives, as well as costs, payoffs, and expectancies, that affect expression of attitudes. Such nonattitudinal determinants are outside the purview of traditional methods of attitude measurement, but they are essential for general theory.

At bottom, functional measurement differs from traditional theories of attitude measurement in being grounded in cognitive theory. Unified attitude theory may thus be attainable. Unified theory is not possible with traditional methods because, among other limitations, they do not apply to stimulus measurement nor to integration. This is not a criticism of the traditional methods, which can be useful for certain issues of social action, as in opinion polls, and which have developed many ingenious techniques to handle practical problems. Unified theory of attitudes, however, requires measurement theory with capabilities beyond the reach of traditional methods.

ATTITUDE AND MOTIVATION

Comparisons of IIT with other attitude theories is possible in brief space by reference to McGuire's (1985) second canonical chapter on attitudes. McGuire presents a comprehensive classification and discussion of attitude theories based on four cross-cutting dichotomies, including an affect–cognition dichotomy and a stability–growth dichotomy, the latter referring to processes that promote stability (as in cognitive consistency theories) or growth (as in utilitarian and self-realization theories). Virtually all extant conceptual views are placed into one or another of the 16 cells of this four-fold table, including functional theories other than IIT. McGuire treats all these views as partial truths, and suggests that each should be used where appropriate. This classification is a striking attempt to bring harmony to a congeries of views, with the virtue of seeking the good in all. But McGuire's classification is not a unified theory, the possibility of which it virtually denies.

Unified theory is possible, but it must begin at more basic levels than the views summarized by McGuire. The theme of McGuire's classification is "needs." Most views postulate one or another "need," but these "needs" are largely free-floating, with little empirical anchorage. A prime example concerns "needs" for cognitive consistency, discussed in the previous chapter. Most functional theories of attitudes, similarly, go little beyond armchair classification into utilitarian needs, ego-defensive needs, and so forth. Such appeals to "needs" may point toward important problems, but they are specious as explanations. Often the postulated need is nonoperative; seldom is it studied directly. None of these views begins to provide a theory of social motivation.

IIT places less emphasis on motivation as a cause, more on process. The effectiveness of this tack was shown in the discussion of cognitive consistency theories in Chapter 4. These theories rested on the hope of hitting on some assumption about motivation for consistency that would have general explanatory power. The finding of value invariance in the first integration studies disproved most of these theories in a strong, simple, and general way. Cognitive consistency can be a motivation, but the work on IIT showed that it functions very differently from the cognitive consistency assumptions.

Social psychology has long recognized the centrality of the attitude concept. Indeed, the traditional definition of attitude as an evaluative reaction, or readiness to respond, highlights the motivational aspect of attitudes. This is a functional view, concerned with thought and action of everyday life.

General theory, however, requires extension of the traditional conception of attitude. In seeking such extension, IIT defines attitudes as knowledge systems. This furthers functional analysis because it focuses on the constructive operations of valuation and integration required for attitudinal response. Nonattitudinal determinants, equally essential, have equal status in the theory. The artificial trichotomy of affect–cognition–volition is transformed into functional unity. This approach to attitude theory is effective, as illustrated in the foregoing experiments. Moreover, it unifies attitudes with other areas of social cognition, as shown in the following sections on attribution and group dynamics.

ATTRIBUTION

The term *attribution* refers to judgments in which some property is attributed to another person or the self. Causal attributions have been of central interest, characterized by life's quintessential question, *Why did she act that way?* A cool reaction, for example, might be attributed to indifference, dislike, or to momentary preoccupation. A warm reaction, on the other hand, might be attributed to politeness, warm feelings, or to some ulterior motive. Not only personal affairs, but professional dealings as well, often face uncertainty about motivations underneath surface behavior.

The prototypical attribution, as in the cited question, involves explanation of some observed event. Although important across many areas of psychology, attribution is especially prominent in making sense of personal actions. This area has received considerable attention in social psychology.

The theme of the present discussion is that attribution theory needs reconstruction within a framework of social cognition. Previous work has shown various interesting phenomena. We often overpersonalize causal responsibility, for example, without adequate recognition of extrapersonal causes in the environment. Again, base rate is often undervalued. Interesting developmental trends have also been obtained.

Theory, however, has made little progress. Most social attribution theories, as is widely recognized, are stalled almost where they started. Their failure is a consequence of their attempts to build on a rationalist base, thereby obscuring cognitive process. Associated with this has been a narrowness that has largely ignored the rest of social psychology and even much of attribution itself.

An alternative conceptual framework has been provided by IIT. This approach is effective in the central problem of analyzing attribution schemas. Furthermore, it unifies attribution with other domains of social psychology.

SCHEMA THEORY OF ATTRIBUTION

To explain some observed behavior depends on assemblage of a mental model that represents the dynamics of the action. Essential elements of the mental model include possible causes of the behavior, together with an integration operation that leads from the causes to the behavior—and/or from the behavior back to the causes. Also needed are valuation operations that relate the strength of each cause to situational specifics. The cognitive organization involved in these operations justifies using the term, attribution *schema*.

One classic attribution has the form:

$$\text{Behavior} = \text{Person} \circledast \text{Environment}.$$

One cause of the Behavior is the Person, who seeks some goal, often facing obstacles from the other cause, the Environment. The symbol $\circledast$ denotes the dynamic component of the mental schema used by the attributor to integrate the two causes into observed behavior. Excuse schemas are one common example, in which failure to achieve a specified goal is attributed to obstacles in the Environment, not to shortcomings in the Person. Another application appears in evaluating praise or promises, which may owe more to momentary forces to satisfy the recipient than to sincerity of the actor.

Two kinds of attribution schemas must be distinguished. In *forward inference*, we predict some future behavior from present information. Symbolically, let F and G denote two possible causes underlying some behavior, B. The causal schema may then be written:

$$B = F \circledast G,$$

where $\circledast$ is a generalized integration operator. Forward inference involves predicting B, given F and G.

In *inverse inference*, we postdict some cause for present behavior. Inverse inference thus involves postdicting F, say, given B and G. This symbolic schema may be written:

$$F = B \circledast' G,$$

where $\circledast'$ is an inverse integration operator. The forward inference is not generally constrained, for the two causes are often independent. But the inverse inference may be constrained by the forward inference, for F and G together should suffice to produce the given B. An example is given in the next section.

Some attributions obey cognitive algebra. These algebraic rules are proper schemas, embodying cognitive organization (Chapter 1). The multiplication schema of the next section, for example, reflects the subject's conception of the dynamics of behavior. Schema algebra provides a fitting tool for development of attribution theory.

BEHAVIOR–MOTIVATION–ABILITY SCHEMAS

Expectations about behavior, of our self as well as of others, pervade everyday life. Present commitments are often predicated on expectations about future behavior of others, for example, that our friend will be willing and able to do her share. Setting personal goals, similarly, depends on expectations about our own abilities and feelings at future times.

Two obvious determinants of such expectations are beliefs about ability and motivation. Belief of high ability gives rise to high expectations, but behavior level may be low if motivation is weak. Attributions about ability and motivation, as well as behavior, are woven into our judgments about our children, our spouse, our students, and, most important, our self.

A more specific conjecture is that expectations about behavior follow the multiplication schema:

$$\text{Behavior} = \text{Motivation} \times \text{Ability}.$$

To test this schema requires allowance for personal values of the Motivation and Ability terms because different persons will construct different values from the same given stimulus informers. Also required is a method for testing the algebraic structure in the judgments of Behavior. Both capabilities became available with the linear fan theorem of functional measurement theory presented in Chapter 2.[8]

In the first empirical test, subjects role-played a coach judging tryouts for college track. Judgments of expected behavior, given information about motivation and ability, are shown in the left panel of Figure 5.5. The linear fan pattern in these data may be better appreciated by noting that the vertical distance between the top and bottom curves increases by 60% from left to right. This linear fan is strong evidence for the hypothesized schema, in this case a schema of forward inference.

Subjects also made two other judgments: of motivation, given behavior and ability; and of ability, given behavior and motivation. These two judgments require inverse inference, from behavior back to cause. Rationally, both should follow the division rules implied by the forward schema for prediction of behavior: Motivation = Behavior ÷ Ability; Ability = Behavior ÷ Motivation. These causal schemas also imply linear fan patterns.

Instead, both causal attributions followed subtraction rules. This is manifest in the near-parallelism in the center and right panels of Figure 5.5. There is thus an exact cognitive algebra:

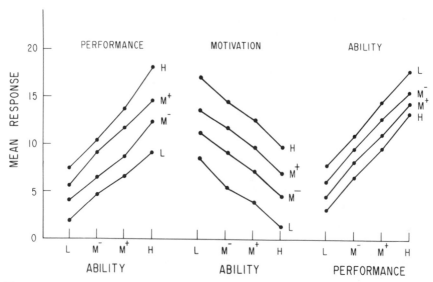

Figure 5.5. First exact attribution schema in social psychology. Subjects role-play coaches to judge tryouts for college track. They judge each of three dimensions, Performance, Motivation, and Ability, given information about the other two. Linear fan pattern in left panel reveals multiplication rule: Performance = Motivation × Ability. Parallelism patterns in center and right panels reveal subtraction rules: Motivation = Performance − Ability and Ability = Performance − Motivation, respectively. Attribution obeys cognitive algebra but not mathematical algebra. (From N. H. Anderson and C. A. Butzin, 1974, "Performance = Motivation × Ability: An integration-theoretical analysis," *Journal of Personality and Social Psychology, 30,* 598-604. Copyright 1974 by the American Psychological Association. Reprinted by permission.)

$$\text{Behavior} = \text{Motivation} \times \text{Ability};$$

$$\text{Motivation} = \text{Behavior} - \text{Ability};$$

$$\text{Ability} = \text{Behavior} - \text{Motivation}.$$

This cognitive algebra clearly differs from the rational mathematical algebra.

These algebraic schemas support the implicit assumption that the Motivation and Ability terms reflect cognitive reality. The exactness of the integration rules implies that they themselves are true cognitive operations—and that the concepts of Motivation and Ability are also cognitively real. Cognitive algebra thus aids the process of transforming and purifying the terms of common language into true scientific concepts. This is one of the qualitative implications of cognitive algebra, which are in many ways more important than quantitative precision per se (see *Beyond Cognitive Algebra* in Chapter 13).

This was the first test of an algebraic schema for causal attribution in social psychology. Later work has supported this initial study, especially by Ramadhar Singh and by Colleen Surber. The main qualification is that an averaging rule sometimes appears instead of the multiplication rule for prediction of behavior. In either case, the attributions follow algebraic schemas.[9]

SCHEMA DEVELOPMENT

Evidence on the nature of schemas comes from studying their development in children, the most interesting area of recent attribution research. In Cliff Butzin's Ph. D. thesis, subjects were told how much money their mothers had promised to story children for helping with housework and how much they had actually helped. Subjects judged goodness of the story children.

The pattern of results, in Figure 5.6, shows a notable developmental trend. Judged goodness is a direct function of the promised money for the 5-year-olds, a null function for the 7-year-olds, and an inverse function for the 9-year-olds. Analogous results have been obtained with other tasks by other investigators. Each age group presents an interpretational problem.

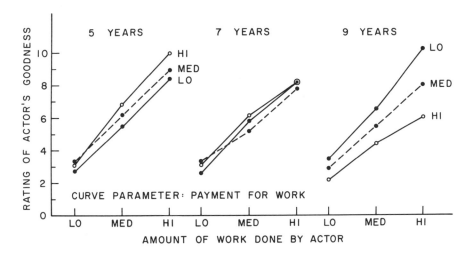

Figure 5.6. Development of causal attribution schema from 5 to 9. Children of three age groups judge goodness of story child as a function of how much he helped his mother (horizontal axis) and how much money his mother had promised him for helping (curve parameter). (From Butzin, 1978; see Butzin & Dozier, 1986.)

Judgments by the 5-year-olds are considered to result from the general purpose integration rule described in Chapter 8. At this age, children understand
that both informers are relevant, but, lacking adult appreciation of inverse inference, they fall back on the general purpose adding-type rule. The direct relation
between goodness and money, although odd by adult standards, has a straightforward interpretation. The reinforcement relation between goodness and
reward, which is salient for children, is direct: Those who do more get more;
reversely, those who get more have done more. Analogous thinking in adults is
not uncommon.

The inverse relation between goodness and money of the 9-year-olds
depends on understanding the causal schema. Two forces determine the action
of the story child, personal goodness and amount of promised reward:

$$\text{Helping} = \text{Goodness} \oplus \text{Money}.$$

Prediction of Helping, given Goodness and Money, would be simple forward
inference, expected to obey an adding-type schema. The inverse inference in
the actual task, namely, judging Goodness, given Helping and Money, is constrained by this forward inference, which implies that Goodness and Money
vary inversely for given Helping.

This inverse constraint is assembled into the operating memory for making
the judgments. This constraint is considered a general purpose operator that can
be applied across diverse tasks. Its developmental origin is unknown, however,
and presents something of a puzzle. The puzzle arises because the adding-type
schema does not reflect social necessity. The promised money does not necessarily reduce goodness, logically or even psychologically. Either Goodness or
Money alone could produce the Helping; the two together need not produce
anything more.

This puzzle may perhaps be illuminated by considering analogous schemas
from intuitive physics. In Area = Height × Width, for example, Area and Width
uniquely determine Height. A decrease in Width requires an increase in Height
if Area is to stay constant. The social schema may develop from such physical
schemas. This hypothesis could be assessed by training on physical tasks and
testing for transfer on social tasks.

The null relation for the 7-year-olds also presents a puzzle. One interpretation is that they have unlearned the direct relation of the 5-year-olds but have
not yet developed the inverse relation of the 9-year-olds. Another interpretation
is that both relations are operative and nullify each other. The first interpretation
leaves open the explanation of the unlearning; the second requires joint operation of two different processes. Single-subject analysis across a battery of tasks
of graded difficulty would be desirable to explore this problem. Such developmental studies are a useful domain for understanding assemblage processes and
operating memory in causal attribution.

TWO-STEP PROCESS MODEL FOR ATTRIBUTION OF ATTITUDES

One typical form of attribution involves a two-step process, an initial inverse inference followed by a forward inference. The inverse inference determines weight–value parameters for given single informers. The forward inference then integrates these single informers into an overall attribution. If the averaging model applies to the forward inference, it can be used to measure the outcome of the inverse inference.

In the attitude attribution experiment of Figure 5.7, subjects received three statements, one pacifistic and two militaristic, said to have been written by one student in high school essays about war and peace. These statements were combined in the 3 × 3 design shown in the figure. The label by each curve represents how militaristic the pair of militaristic statements was; the horizontal axis shows the pacifistic value of the single pacifistic statement. The design thus

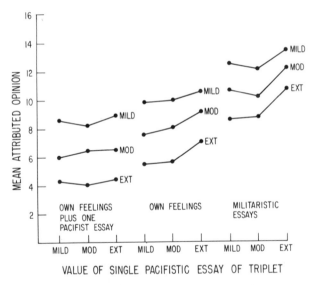

Figure 5.7. Attribution of attitude obeys averaging model of information integration theory. Subjects judged attitude of persons characterized by three essays they had written about militarism and pacifism under three different constraints listed under each panel. Curve parameter indicates value of the pair of militaristic essays in each set of three; horizontal axis indicates value of single pacifistic essay in each set. Near-parallelism reveals operation of averaging rule. Elevation, slope, and vertical range in each panel are predictable in terms of weight parameter of averaging theory. (From S. Himmelfarb and N. H. Anderson, 1975, "Integration theory applied to opinion attribution," *Journal of Personality and Social Psychology, 31,* 1064–1072. Copyright 1975 by the American Psychological Association. Reprinted by permission.)

defines nine stimulus persons. Subjects judged true attitude of each stimulus person, lower numbers corresponding to more militaristic attitudes.

A further experimental manipulation concerned the situational pressure on the stimulus person. The baseline was the Own Feelings condition, in which stimulus persons were said to be under instructions to express their own feelings. These data yielded a pattern of parallelism, shown in the center panel of Figure 5.7. This parallelism pattern indicates that subjects averaged the given informers to arrive at their attribution.

In a second condition, subjects were told that stimulus persons had been required to include one pacifistic essay regardless of their own feelings. This single pacifistic essay should be partly attributed to the situational constraint— and so receive lower weight in the attitude attribution. This is verified by the lower (more militaristic) judgments in the left panel of Figure 5.7.

In the third condition, subjects were told that the stimulus person had been required to write all militaristic essays. The single pacifistic essay then defies the situational constraint, and so should receive higher weight. This is verified by the higher (more pacifistic) judgments in the right panel of Figure 5.7.

The importance of this experiment resides in comparison of the data patterns across the three panels of Figure 5.7. All three panels are approximately parallel, but they differ in three properties: From left to right, successive panels are at a higher elevation, they show greater slopes, and they have lesser vertical separation. Within the averaging model, all three properties can be shown to result from the weight parameter attributed to the single pacifistic essay. A complex pattern of data is thus explained in a uniform theoretical way.

Two successive attributions, as already noted, are involved in this task. The first attribution determines the weight parameter: The single pacifistic statement is attributed with more or less confidence as the true attitude of the stimulus person in light of the given situational constraint; this confidence determines the weight. The second attribution integrates the given informers (the single pacifistic essay and the pair of militaristic essays) to arrive at the overt attribution. The first attribution represents inverse causal inference; the second attribution represents forward causal inference. With the averaging model, the forward inference can be analyzed to measure both the weight and the scale value of the inverse inference. This constitutes a general and fundamental advance on other attribution theories.[10]

THE ANOVA CUBE

The most prominent alternative approach to social attribution is Kelley's (1972) ANOVA cube. Kelley sought to conceptualize attribution in terms of schemas, but he provided no method for schema analysis. Lacking method for cognitive analysis, he attempted a rational, normative approach. This misrepresented the cognitive concept of schema.

Kelley began with J. S. Mill's rules, which attempt to define causality in terms of covariation: Causes of an event must covary with the event. In Kelley's theory, attribution thus became a huge mental table for recording observed frequencies of event covariation. This huge mental table does not constitute psychological theory; for that some psychological structure is needed.

Kelley claimed to see psychological structure in this mental frequency table in the form of three specific dimensions:

Consistency: past reactions of the given person in the same situation;
Consensus: past reactions of other persons in the same situation;
Distinctiveness: past reactions of the given person in similar situations.

This presumed three-dimensional table of frequencies was Kelley's idea of causal schema. The table itself was called the ANOVA cube, by loose analogy with the statistical technique of analysis of variance.

As a definition of causal schema, the ANOVA cube was a conceptual mistake. Contrary to Kelley's theory, the ANOVA cube is not a schema. Instead, it misrepresents the operative schema.

To make the issue concrete, suppose we see a person flee from a snake. Everyday psychology sees two obvious causal factors, namely, a trait of fearfulness in the person and a property of dangerousness in the snake. If the snake is small and in a cage, for example, we evaluate its dangerousness as low and attribute high fearfulness or snake phobia to the person.

A causal schema should refer to cognitive entities, to the causal forces operative in the attributor's mental model of the situation. This is what everyday psychology aims at in the snake example. IIT would begin with everyday psychology by studying the indicated schema:

$$\text{Fleeing Behavior} = \text{Fearfulness} \circledast \text{Dangerousness}.$$

Kelley's formulation, in contrast, has no capability for schema analysis. Consistency–consensus–distinctiveness are not causal forces; they are only three—among many—informers about the two causal forces. Although Kelley and others sometimes refer to operative causal forces, these are obscured and misrepresented in the ANOVA cube. Indeed, the term, ANOVA cube, is itself misleading; no analysis of variance is involved, nor any other quantitative method for schema analysis. Experimental applications go no further than showing that information about consistency–consensus–distinctiveness can affect judgment. In all the literature, not even one application seems to have assessed exact structure of any attribution schema. Even within its own framework, the ANOVA cube is ineffectual. As rationalist theory, the Bayesian formulation of causal inference (Chapter 10) is conceptually much superior.

Adherents of the ANOVA cube recognize that people are not rational as postulated. People often give less weight to consensus information, for example, than rationality seems to prescribe. Other rationalist theories of attribution suffer similar troubles. Nonrationality in human behavior has been demonstrated repeatedly in the history of psychology, so the failure of these rationalist attribution theories could have been foreseen (see Chapter 10). Despite such failures, the rationalist approaches have not been abandoned. The formulations introduced in the 1960s have continued to this day with little change.

A different orientation is needed. People should be studied as they are, not in terms of rationalist assumptions of what they ought to be. Cognitive process, terra infirma to the rationalist approaches, should be the foundation for theory development. The segregation of attribution from other domains of psychology, so marked in the rationalist approaches, should be replaced by integration.

PSYCHODYNAMICS OF EVERYDAY LIFE

Attribution is often involved in the psychodynamics of everyday life, as in praise, blame, excuses, and self-esteem. Praise and blame are primary mechanisms for social organization, which needs continual regeneration from newborn infants. They deserve analysis as devices for social control.

Praise and blame are also of interest because they combine affective evaluation with social responsibility. One instance of an algebraic blame schema has already appeared in the study of wife–husband interaction of Figure 5.2. This is part of a general algebra of blame, studied further in Chapters 6 and 7. Attribution of praise, by contrast, has been slighted, a reflection of corresponding asymmetry in their everyday frequency. This is unfortunate, for society would improve with less blame and more praise.

Excuses have inestimable functions in defense and maintenance of the ego. Feelings of personal worth and self-confidence are essential components of well-being. They are under continual attrition, however, from common failures and ubiquitous blame. Although excuses are usually viewed pejoratively, they are in fact a positive mechanism of personal adjustment.

The attribution schema for excuses may be written:

$$\text{Action} = \text{Self} \circledast \text{Circumstances}.$$

Here a bad Action is given, and the Self seeks to direct as much responsibility as possible to Circumstances. This helps avoid blame, self-blame no less than other-blame, for the bad action. Several compilations and typologies of excuses have been given, but all rest mainly on armchair analysis. The field of excuses, and related concepts, is wide open for experimental analysis.[11]

FOUNDATIONS OF SOCIAL ATTRIBUTION THEORY

The nature of social attribution theory can be seen in the classic schema:

$$\text{Behavior} = \text{Person} \circledast \text{Environment}.$$

This symbolic B–P–E schema makes intuitive sense, for we feel that our actions stem in part from our desires, in part from external forces, and similarly for the actions of others. To predict behavior, we make a forward inference from information about Person and Environment. To explain a given behavior, we make an inverse inference about Person and/or Environment from information about Environment and/or Person. Both forms of attribution are common in everyday thought and action.

The symbolic B–P–E schema lacks analytical power. It points toward a problem, but goes no further. Theory development requires concepts and methods that can transform this symbolic schema into cognitive reality.

The symbolic schema does, however, make explicit the problem of multiple determination. But previous attempts to handle multiple determination in the attribution domain have failed. Behavior–Motivation–Ability schemas were conjectured by Heider, but he lacked capability to test them (see Note 8). Subsequent attempts by Kelley were ineffectual. This lack of capability to handle multiple determination is a primary reason that attribution theories have been "stunted," to use a term applied by one of their proponents. When IIT was applied, these schemas were found to obey algebraic rules, although not generally the rules conjectured by Heider.

Much work on attribution can be viewed as concerned with valuation rather than integration. Some qualitative aspects of valuation can be studied by varying one variable at a time. Thus, work of Jones (see Jones & McGillis, 1976) can be considered primarily concerned with valuation processes that govern the importance weights assigned various informers in the integrated attribution (Anderson, 1974b, pp. 5–6).

Valuation and integration are both essential to development of general theory of attribution. IIT has been mainly concerned with integration processes of forward and inverse inference. This provides a measurement solution to valuation, but leaves open problems of valuation processes that relate the weight–value parameters to situational determinants.

GENERAL ATTRIBUTION THEORY

Attribution processes occur everywhere in psychology, most notably in person cognition. Attributions about traits such as honesty, intelligence, sociability, and so on, are expected to follow the theory developed in Chapter 4, at least for forward inference. This theory is also expected to apply to attributions about other characteristics, such as mood states, abilities, skills, and especially knowledge.

Many self-attributions may be treated the same as attributions about others. Your judgments of your abilities depend on integration of success–failure experiences and on comparisons with others, just as do your judgments about abilities of others. Self-judgment may also be influenced by desire and by biosocial confidence, not ordinarily present in other-judgment, but such determinants are allowed in integration theory. Similar attributional processes may be expected with ego-maintenance mechanisms, such as blame-avoidance. IIT thus leads naturally to a constructionist view of the self, in harmony with other views, especially symbolic interactionism in sociology.

Attribution is no less important outside social–personality. The rise of pragmatics in language processing reflects growing recognition of the ubiquity of attributions about intentions and knowledge of others in everyday communication (Chapter 12). Attributions about external reality are primary processes in psychophysics and perception (Chapter 9). The same holds for intuitive physics (Chapter 8). In judgment–decision theory (Chapter 10), attributions range from imputations about missing information to the canonical problem of inverse causal inference, as from symptom to disease.

Common to all these domains is the problem of multiple determination. This is a foundation for development of unified theory. Other attribution theories could not solve this problem because they lacked a theory of measurement. IIT has made some progress in all these domains. Despite the manifold limitations of this work, it provides a solid beginning.

SOCIAL GROUPS

Much behavior takes place in groups: family groups, school groups, friendships, dates, work groups, teams, committees, and so on. These groups have a conceptual existence beyond the individual members, as loci of social interaction and as carriers of social knowledge systems. Many consider groups the heart of social psychology. Attempts to develop group theory, however, have been sporadic and inconclusive. One reason is a failure to integrate group theory with the rest of social–personality psychology.

In IIT, group processes are considered informational, including transmission, valuation, and integration of information. This informational approach is illustrated in applications to several issues of group dynamics in the following sections. Related applications to fairness–equity theory are given in Chapter 7. These applications also illustrate how group dynamics can be unified with general social–personality psychology.

SOCIAL AVERAGING THEOREM

Groups must often reach a common decision. Newlyweds must work out innumerable adjustments of living together. Faculty must agree on whom to hire and whether to promote. Different group members will have different preferences, so the group decision will ordinarily require compromise. Under certain reasonable and general conditions, this group compromise will obey a social averaging theorem.

Since group members have individual preferences, any proposed decision will cause some dissatisfaction. A dissatisfied member may exert various forces: rational arguments, emotional pleas, complaining, wheedling and cajolery, recrimination, and threats, in seeking a more satisfactory decision. The final decision of the group will be where the forces exerted by the several members balance out.

To formalize this group dynamics, consider a one-dimensional decision axis, Ψ, on which each member has a unimodal preference function, with the most preferred position for member i denoted by ψ_i. For any proposed decision, ψ, the force, $F_i(\psi)$, exerted by member i is assumed proportional to the discrepancy between the preferred and proposed decisions:

$$F_i(\psi) = \omega_i (\psi_i - \psi).$$

The final decision of the group members, ψ^*, will be that point at which the $F_i(\psi^*)$ of the members sum to zero net force:

$$\sum F_i(\psi^*) = 0 = \sum \omega_i(\psi_i - \psi^*).$$

Solving for ψ^* yields the social averaging theorem:

$$\psi^* = \sum \omega_i \psi_i / \sum \omega_i.$$

This theorem states that the final group decision is a weighted average of the members' preferred decisions. The ω_i are the members' social weights, which depend on individual differences as well as experimental task factors.

Social weights are molar parameters. They encapsulate each and all detail of the group interaction. This follows from the unitization principle discussed in connection with Figure 5.1. If the social averaging theorem applies, the social weights are a complete and valid summary of all process details. If the social averaging theorem can be established empirically, it will confer the inestimable advantage of finessing questions of detail to allow exact analysis at a molar level of group decision.

This theorem is expected to apply generally to conflict resolution. The present derivation has referred to conflict between individuals. A similar derivation applies to within-individual conflict, to conflict among roles, for example, or among moral obligations.

TESTS OF THE SOCIAL AVERAGING THEOREM

The social averaging theorem did quite well in a series of incisive experiments in Cheryl Graesser's Ph. D. thesis on group bargaining. In the first experiment, a preference function was assigned to each member of two-person groups. These preference functions specified the profit for each member as a function of

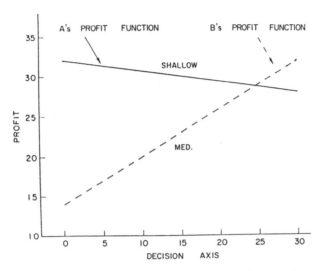

Figure 5.8. Illustrative preference functions. Elevations of curves give payoff or profit for each of two group members as a function of the decision alternative (horizontal axis) chosen by the group. (From Graesser, 1978, 1991.)

the group decision. A gain for one member was a loss for the other, which contributed to a lively and absorbing bargaining process.

Figure 5.8 illustrates one condition: Member A has a shallow preference function (solid line); member B has a preference function with medium slope (dashed line). The horizontal axis is the decision axis; the vertical axis represents the profit for each member. A decision at 10, for example, would yield a profit of about 20 for A, 31 for B. To gain one unit, A must force B to give up more than four units. With these preference functions, therefore, B is expected to have higher social weight than A.

In the experiment, A and B were instructed to reach a joint decision by making a series of offers, beginning with their most preferred points, 0 and 30 on the decision axis. Neither saw the other's preference function until after the final decision was reached.

Results are shown in Figure 5.9, in which the vertical axis is now the final decision; higher values represent decisions more favorable to B. The spread among the three curves represents the effect of B's preference function. With a steep function, B negotiates harder and obtains a more favorable decision. The slopes of the curves show the analogous effect for A.

One curious implication of these data deserves mention. A fair decision, it can be argued, would give each member equal payoff; this decision would be at the intersection point of the two preference functions. When the preference functions for A and B had unequal slope, however, the final decision was far away from the equal-profit point, in the direction of the midpoint compromise.

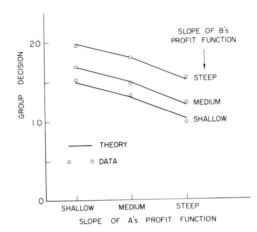

Figure 5.9. Social averaging theorem accounts for group bargaining. Circles give mean group decision as a function of slopes of profit functions for member A (horizontal axis) and member B (curve parameter). Solid lines show the predictions from the social averaging theorem. (From Graesser, 1978, 1991.)

The member with the steeper profit function does negotiate harder, it is true, but not hard enough to compensate for the relative loss entailed by the steeper slope. For the condition of Figure 5.8, the group decision was about 17 (see Figure 5.9). Hence A's profit was around 30, whereas B's profit was only about 24. Group bargaining thus seems to work against the member with more to lose.

This result may have societal counterparts. Each dollar means more to the poor than to the rich. The poor thus have, in effect, steeper preference functions. Figure 5.9 thus suggests that social distribution achieved through standard bargaining procedures is biased against the poor.

Of more immediate importance is the success of the social averaging theorem, shown in Figure 5.9. The curves are theoretical, and provide a good fit to the actual data, denoted by the open circles. Mean magnitude deviation was only 0.2. This deviation from theoretical prediction was statistically nonsignificant, using a valid test of goodness of fit. Graesser extended the social averaging theorem in a second experiment to study coalitions, a traditional problem in group dynamics, with equally good results.

SOCIAL AVERAGING THEORY
VERSUS SOCIAL DECISION SCHEMES

One other theory has attempted a quantitative treatment of group bargaining, namely, the social decision schemes of Davis, which have generated a considerable literature (see Stasser, Kerr, & Davis, 1989). These schemes prescribe how the initial distribution of member preferences is resolved into a group consensus.

TABLE 5.1

THEORETICAL PREDICTIONS OF MEAN DECISIONS

Dyad Graphs	Decisions	Social Averaging Theorem		Social Decision Scheme	
		Predictions	Discrepancy	Predictions	Discrepancy
Steep, Steep	53.4	53.8	0.4	54.2	0.8
Steep, Medium	45.2	44.3	0.9	50.0	4.8*
Steep, Shallow	35.0	35.7	0.7	47.8	12.8*
Medium, Steep	63.0	63.6	0.6	58.3	4.7*
Medium, Medium	54.3	54.2	0.1	54.2	0.1
Medium, Shallow	45.1	44.6	0.5	51.9	6.9*
Shallow, Steep	73.4	72.3	1.1	60.6	12.8*
Shallow, Medium	62.8	63.8	1.0	56.4	6.2*
Shallow, Shallow	54.3	54.3	0.0	54.2	0.1
Mean Discrepancy			0.6		5.5

* Discrepancy significant (.05) by two-tail t test. (From Graesser, 1978, 1991.)

The equal-distance compromise model, for example, postulates equal compromise by both members.

To compare Davis' scheme theory with social averaging theory, Graesser ran a third experiment, with an experimental task that had previously been used in scheme theory with seemingly favorable results. Groups of two subjects were asked to play the role of district representatives to a county committee. Each received a histogram that portrayed the number of voters in their district who advocated different decisions about such issues as what percentage of the budget should go for road repair. These constituency histograms mimicked the preference functions that had been used in the previous work on scheme theory, and were somewhat similar to the preference functions of Figure 5.8. Method and procedure were also similar to the original experiment on scheme theory. Both members were instructed to bargain so as to obtain the best deal for the voters of their district.

Social averaging theory was markedly superior to the social decision schemes. The observed mean decisions are shown in the leftmost data column of Table 5.1; they show a pattern similar to that of Figure 5.9. Adjacent to this are the means predicted by social averaging theory, together with the discrepancies between observed and predicted. These discrepancies have a mean of 0.6 points on the 100-point response scale; none approached statistical significance. Equally good support for social averaging theory was obtained in other tests and in a fourth experiment.

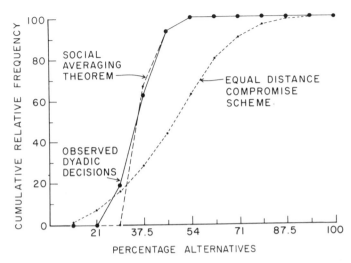

Figure 5.10. Social averaging theory is superior to social decision schemes. Solid curve gives observed cumulative frequency of group decisions along horizontal decision axis. Long-dash curve gives predictions from social averaging theorem; short-dash curve gives predictions from social decision scheme. The other eight conditions in this experiment showed equally good predictions by social averaging theory but even larger mispredictions by scheme theory; see Table 5.1. (From Graesser, 1978, 1991.)

Social decision scheme theory did very poorly: The two rightmost columns list the theoretical predictions and discrepancies. The mean discrepancy is 5.5 points, and the individual discrepancies were significant in six cases. The other three cases are nondiscriminative because both members had equal slope and the mean decision is necessarily at the midpoint. On all six discriminative tests, therefore, the social decision schemes were far off.

The failure of the scheme formulation is shown graphically in Figure 5.10. The cumulative frequency (solid curve) of observed group decisions is plotted as a function of the value of the decision on the horizontal axis. Also shown are the predictions from the social decision scheme (short-dash curve) and social averaging theory (long-dash curve). The scheme formulation is far from the data whereas social averaging theory is close. Similar graphs were obtained in all nine experimental conditions; Figure 5.10 represents the condition most favorable to the scheme formulation. Very similar results were obtained in Graesser's fourth experiment. Tested on its own ground and in its own terms, Davis' scheme theory failed badly.

Graesser's work was incisive and definitive. The failure of the social decision schemes resulted from basic conceptual inadequacies exposed in Graesser's work. Social decision schemes have been applied in numerous studies in the literature, but nearly all these studies are now seen to be uninterpretable because of these conceptual flaws. Graesser's work is impressive for its quantitative support for social averaging theory, but its greater value lies in its conceptual framework for group dynamics.[12]

GROUP ATTITUDES

Interaction with other persons is a common source of our attitudes. Attitudes formed in social interaction should exhibit the same processes found in the attitude studies cited in the first part of this chapter. Group discussion exposes the group members to various informational influences, and their attitudes are changed through integration of such information. The term, information, is used broadly to include verbal arguments, prestige suggestion, nonverbal stimuli, social pressure, and other forms of social influence.

Averaging theory provided a good account of attitudes formed in group discussion in the following experiment. Present concern, however, is with two general problems that arose in planning the experiment. The first problem concerns information flow in the group discussion:

> The informational flow in the group is complex and largely uncontrolled. The impact of any group member on the others is spread out in time, conditioned by his (her) motivations to influence and to conform, interlinked with the others' comments and silences, dependent on prior knowledge and on expressive factors from clarity of thought to eye contact and personal attractiveness. Thus, the attitude of each group member reflects an ongoing, time-dependent process in which the informational components seem close to unknowable. (Anderson & Graesser, 1976, p. 210)

The unknown nature of the operative information seems to preclude the possibility of exact theory. All approaches must face this problem.

In IIT, this problem of unknowable interaction detail can be handled with principle of molar unitization, discussed earlier in relation to the Truman paragraph. Molar unitization also applies to group discussion. Although the informational flow is partly unknown and indeed partly unknowable, it can be treated as a molar unit in an exact and complete manner. In this way, exact theory becomes possible.

The second problem concerned *self-estimation*. The factorial designs used in the attitude studies of the first part of this chapter are often impracticable in group experiments. To extend the scope of IIT, accordingly, it was decided to try a method of self-estimation. Subjects were asked directly for the weights and scale values of each informer, and these self-estimated parameters were used in the analysis.

Each subject in a group of three received a different paragraph about the same U. S. president and made an initial judgment of statesmanship based on their own paragraph. Following group discussion, in which the members exchanged their information, each subject again judged the president. Also,

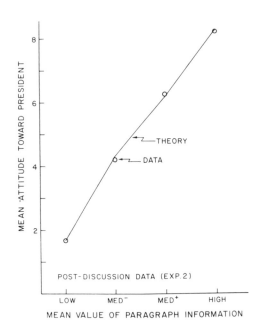

Figure 5.11. Attitudes in group discussion obey averaging model. Open circles are observed attitudes after group discussion; curve shows predictions from averaging model. (After N. H. Anderson and C. C. Graesser, 1976, "An information integration analysis of attitude change in group discussion," *Journal of Personality and Social Psychology, 34*, 210-222. Copyright 1976 by the American Psychological Association. Reprinted by permission.)

each subject estimated the scale value and importance weight of their own paragraph—and of the discussions of each other group member. By hypothesis, the final judgment was a weighted average of the three informers just specified. The self-estimated parameters were used to test the averaging model.

Averaging theory did well—see Figure 5.11. The four circles denote mean group attitudes for each of the four information conditions indicated on the horizontal axis; the solid curve represents the theoretical predictions. Mean discrepancy between observed and predicted was nonsignificant, only .06 on a 10-cm graphic attitude scale. Two other experimental conditions yielded comparable support for the theoretical model.

The implications of this experiment deserve emphasis. Both cited problems are vital for group theory, and both were successfully resolved. By virtue of the principle of molar unitization, the discussion of each group member could be treated as a unit that contained the effect of all interaction. Regardless of the nature and complexity of the group dynamics, it is all represented in the parameters of the integration model. Coupled with the self-estimation method, this unitization allowed an exact test of the model for group attitudes, a rare feat in group dynamics. At the same time, development of attitudes in group discussion is unified with the attitude theory presented initially in this chapter.

GROUP ATTRACTIVENESS

The existence and functioning of many social groups depend on their ability to attract new members and to retain present members. They do this by appealing to various needs. A straightforward conceptualization would represent the group as a set of attributes, each with a value and an importance dependent on the need structure of an individual member or potential member. These are integrated to determine the attractiveness of the group to that individual.

Just as person likableness is a weighted average of person attributes, so group attractiveness should be a weighted average of group attributes. The few experiments on this question have supported averaging theory. The main discrepancy was a curious configurality for ad hoc groups of criminals; a substantial minority of subjects judged badness of the group solely in terms of the single baddest member. This work is regrettably limited, however, in that group attributes other than group members have not yet been considered.[13]

Group attractiveness often involves formation of semi-independent subgroups. Such subgrouping may involve complex, often implicit, acquaintanceship, bargaining, and affect. How far the foregoing results can be usefully applied to such complexity is an open question. In principle, however, these processes seem amenable to conceptualization as information integration.

ATTRIBUTION IN CLOSE RELATIONSHIPS

Our interactions with another person involve a continual sequence of attributions: about the other's status, abilities, knowledge, traits, attitudes, moods, motivations, and intentions. The concepts and methods previously discussed apply to these classes of interpersonal attributions.

The basic principle is valuation–integration of multiple informers. Inverse inference will often be required for valuation of single informers. Forward inference will almost always be required to integrate multiple single informers into an overall attribution. Such two-step processing, illustrated with attitude attribution in Figure 5.7, holds quite generally.

The theory developed for person cognition in Chapter 4, together with its extensions to cover attitude and attribution in this chapter, are thus expected to apply generally to attribution in close relationships. The seven problems of Chapter 4 remain basic. The averaging rule appears to be a common process of person cognition. The work on marriage illustrated in the next section supports this view. This is not surprising, of course, because behavior in typical experiments is embedded within everyday knowledge systems.[14]

Close relationships involve other phenomena, two of which deserve comment. One is affect, often intense. Although not properly an attribution to another person, affect is a major facet of interpersonal relationships, a consequence of the fact that our goals and values often involve others, as in family, in friendship, and in work. The averaging rule has had some success with mild affects of likableness and blame, but generalization to strong affects is untested. Some optimism comes from the expectation that strong affects will operate at the valuation stage, with an invariant integration rule. Hence functional measurement can be applied to assess the affective values.

The second phenomenon is person memory, an integral part of close relationships. Attributions have a dual memory function, indicated in the earlier section, *Attitude Memory*. One function occurs in operating memory, which governs the momentary attributions of online interaction. The other function relates to long-term memory, as online attributions are stored in knowledge systems about the other person. Common cases are attributions about reactions to success–failure, criticism, and compliments. Such attributions are continually made in relation to particular incidents, these online attributions then being integrated into the knowledge system about the other.

To study close relationships, experimental analysis is desirable but limited in scope. Wife–husband relationships, for example, could hardly be studied by providing female volunteers with experimental husbands tailored to the hypotheses of the experimental design because of the well-known recalcitrance of this class of stimulus materials. Even the modest goal of studying marital quarrels can hardly be approached by experimental manipulation of quarrels.

With *personal design*, however, some advantages of experimental analysis can be obtained, even with close relationships. The idea is to design an experiment around some personalized situation, chosen to be meaningful within the relationship. Data analysis could be at the individual level, as in Figures 1.2 and 2.1, or with pooled data, as in Figures 5.2 and 5.12. A real blame episode from the subject's life could be chosen, for example, with hypothetical but realistic levels of determinants of blame, such as intention and extenuation. Marital dissatisfaction and causal attribution for hypothetical actions of spouse or friend could be studied in the same way. Such personal design might also be beneficial in counseling and therapy (Anderson, 1990b).

THE FAMILY

The most important social group is the family. Two problems in family interaction are considered here: marriage satisfaction and spouse influence. Both illustrate the methodology of personal design.

Family interaction is manifestly complex, but it does exhibit one functional simplicity: Much of it is focused on the single dimension of satisfaction. Sources of satisfaction and dissatisfaction are many and diverse, of course, but a significant part of their content can be captured in this quantitative form. Satisfaction–dissatisfaction thus offers an important simplicity for experimental analysis of marriage and family.

In the experiment of Figure 5.12, divorced women judged unfairness of marital living arrangements. In this personal design, each woman identified areas of

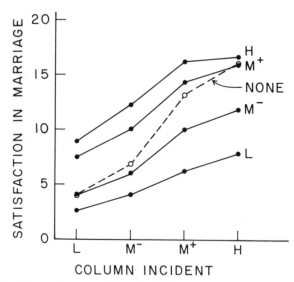

Figure 5.12. Divorced women follow averaging rule in judgments of marriage unfairness based on actual incidents from their marriages. Steeper slope of dashed curve indicates averaging process. Solid curves are somewhat nonparallel, indicating differential weighting—more negative incidents have greater weight. Hence greater unfairness cannot be represented merely by a more extreme unfairness *value*; greater unfairness also has greater importance, or *weight*. This negativity effect, first definitely demonstrated in integration studies of person cognition, would be hard to pin down without averaging theory to separate weight from value. (After N. H. Anderson, *Foundations of Information Integration Theory*. Academic Press, 1981.)

unfairness from her own marriage (e.g., division of household chores, division of child care, degree to which she was allowed to work, and freedom to go out with her friends). Two such areas were selected that could be varied over four graded levels to form a 4 × 4 design. The women judged unfairness for each of the single stimulus informers as well as for the 16 pairs. The design was personalized through this individual selection of actual marriage issues.

These unfairness judgments obeyed an averaging rule. The dashed curve in Figure 5.12 shows judgments based on the single informer listed on the horizontal axis. This dashed curve is steeper than and crosses over the solid curves, which represent judgments based on pairs of stimuli. This curve comparison is a critical test between averaging and adding; the crossover supports averaging according to the logic given with Figure 2.4 (see also legend of Figure 5.12).

One curious footnote to this experiment deserves mention. Personal design could not be implemented for males as planned; the concept of unfairness in marriage seemed foreign to most males in this off-the-street sample. These divorced men expressed plenty of dissatisfaction with their marriages, but it did not have the phenomenal quality of unfairness. This outcome emphasizes the importance of studying phenomenology of close relationships, in family, in friendship, and in work.

A second issue concerns how attitudes develop and function in family interaction. The spouse influence study of Figure 5.2 illustrated an averaging process, an outcome extended in related work. Intra-couple influence can also be measured with such design, and a substantial wife–husband similarity in moral value was revealed in this way. This methodology has also revealed a striking mother–son similarity in moral judgment (Chapter 6).

The family has great social importance. It contains almost everything of interest to social psychologists, a prime field for growth of unified theory. This opportunity has been terribly neglected. IIT seeks to integrate family psychology with the rest of social psychology. The family should become a crucible for development of social–personality theory.

GENERAL THEORY OF SOCIAL GROUPS

Future work on social groups should go hand in hand with the rest of social psychology. Previous work has uncovered interesting and important phenomena, very dramatically in studies of conformity and bystander apathy, in which group pressures induce people to violate their moral norms. Such phenomena have been revealing about social motivation, but they have remained isolated phenomena, with little relation to general theory.[15]

Multiple motivation is a fundamental issue, underlying much group interaction. In group attractiveness, motivations correspond to needs subserved by the group, together with the associated costs. Family life involves a spectrum of everyday motivations. And in the conformity and bystander studies, of course, the conflict is constituted of multiple motivations.

Lacking capability to analyze multiple determination, group theory has been severely limited. Given two conflicting motivations, no more can be said than that the greater should predominate, which does not even handle compromise. Given three conflicting motivations, even less can be said.

The conformity studies are instructive in this regard. They show that conformity–obedience motivation is, under certain conditions, surprisingly strong. This is an important finding, but it is an empirical result, not a strand of theory. It contributes little to general analysis of multiple social motivations.

Capability for analysis of multiple motivations underlies all the foregoing studies. In this conceptual framework, motivations function to place values on stimulus informers. Where averaging theory is applicable, therefore, it provides an analysis of multiple motivations. For group attractiveness, the motivations include tendencies to approach and avoid other group members. In group bargaining, the motivational forces correspond to different persons. This approach also showed promise in studies of the family, much neglected in the social psychology of groups. Group phenomena are complex, but IIT has shown real albeit modest progress. This information integration approach also unifies group dynamics with attitudes, attribution, and person cognition.

UNIFIED SOCIAL COGNITION

Unification of social cognition requires an appropriate conceptual framework. Prevailing frameworks produce increasing fragmentation. This fragmentation results from ways of thinking, useful in themselves, but too narrow to permit unified theory. Instead, they work in the opposite direction. To reverse this fragmentation and work toward unification requires a conceptual shift.[16]

PROMISE AND DISILLUSION

Experimental method came late to social psychology, beginning in earnest only after World War II. Its initial impact was exhilarating. It brought clean experiments, testable hypotheses, and definite answers to replace vague generalities. It promised systematic progress on important social problems.

Continued experiments, however, became increasingly enmired in increasingly complicated results. More and more variables were found to influence even simple tasks. The influence of each variable varied across situations and depended on other variables. Clean generalizations rarely emerged; literature reviews typically concluded "It all depends." Amid the proliferating compartmentalization that has ensued, the possibility of a unified approach has been lost to sight.

> Fired at first sight with what the Muse imparts,
> In fearless youth we tempt the heights of Arts,
> While from the bounded level of our mind
> Short views we take, nor see the lengths behind;
> But more advanced, behold with strange surprise
> New distant scenes of endless science rise!
>
> ... we tremble to survey
> The growing labors of the lengthened way,
> The increasing prospects tire our wandering eyes,
> Hills peep o'er hills, and Alps on Alps arise!
> (From Pope, *An Essay on Criticism.*)

This disintegration of faith in the experimental method in social psychology produced several reactions. One was to criticize laboratory experiments on lack of social relevance and argue for the study of natural social situations, such as medical and legal systems. This put healthy emphasis on phenomena that had been avoided in most laboratory studies. It broadened conceptual horizons. Most attractive, it promised ecological validity—societal meaningfulness and generality not attainable in laboratory tasks.

But the critics of laboratory experiments are even more vulnerable to their own criticism. Real-life behavior is situation-dependent, not easily generalizable to other situations. The operative variables are often not known, moreover, which further hobbles generalization. Hence ecological validity has been more elusive than experimental validity. Ironically, the attempts to transcend experimental analysis have reemphasized its importance.

A second, rather broad reaction is interactionist, or contextualist. Its theme is that behavior can be understood only in terms of interaction between person and social situation; *social–personality* is an essential union. This was a dual reaction: Against the experimentalist preoccupation with stimulus variables as determinants of behavior; and against personality theories that reified personality traits as causes of behavior. Interactionist views are well-taken, as far as they go, but they have not gone far. Although they insist on the need to study interaction of person and situation, they have done little to develop effective concepts or methods for this purpose.[17]

It is hardly one step beyond the interactionist position to argue that social psychology cannot be science. General laws, it is said, such as are found in physics and chemistry, do not exist in social psychology. Instead, social psychology should be treated as history. This extremist position may have been useful in emphasizing the two previous reactions, but it has little intrinsic merit. Cognitive algebra is living proof that social psychology is a science.

A rather different reaction appears in attempts to transpose mainstream cognitive psychology to the social domain, as in discussions of social cognition, social schemas, social prototypes, social memory, and so on. Much of this is cognitive cosmetics. The bulk of what is currently called social cognition is old ideas in new words, just a change from the suddenly old-fashioned term *behavioral* to the sparkling modern term *cognitive*.

Some studies, it is true, have made earnest attempts to utilize mainstream cognitive psychology, but with meager benefits. Benefits have been meager because mainstream cognitive psychology is ill-suited for social cognition. It is dominated by the reproductive conception of memory, for example, whereas social memory is primarily functional memory; it has eschewed affect and motivation, which are central for social behavior; it has largely ignored problems of value and value measurement; and it has remarkably little to say about information integration. Prominent problems in mainstream cognitive psychology include reproductive memory, pattern recognition, categorization, speech perception, reaction time, and attention. These are important problems on which significant progress is being made. These problems, however, are far removed from social psychology.

Social psychology is truly cognitive. It always has been. This is evident in its basic concepts: attitude, attribution, person cognition, self, morality, roles, friendship, family, and diverse social affects and motivations. Mainstream cognitive psychology says little about these concepts. Indeed, it is inimical to them. Social psychology needs to develop its own cognitive theory.[18]

RESEARCH STRATEGY

The need for unification is apparent throughout the social–personality domain. Study of social groups has been scattered over disconnected issues, with signal neglect of the family, by far the most important social group. Analysis of social attribution has been handicapped by rationalist formulations that obstructed cognitive analysis and obscured affect and motivation. Person cognition has been led astray by seductive but erroneous assumptions about cognitive consistency and bias–distortion. Attitude research might seem an exception, for numerous theories have been advanced, centered on one or another postulate of need or motivation. But effective analysis of motivation has been lacking. Indeed, the very multiplicity of these theories exhibits their conceptual disarray.

Unified theory requires capability for handling the fundamental problem of multiple determination. Various attempts have been made, but nearly all have done poorly. The root cause has been lack of measurement theory for psychological values. This point was dramatically demonstrated with the failure of the consistency theories noted in the previous chapter—the first application of functional measurement theory showed invariant meaning, contrary to the various consistency postulates.

This same point reappears in comparisons between IIT and major theoretical alternatives in the three areas covered in this chapter. These alternative theories made some attempt to handle multiple determination, but with makeshift methods that largely confused the problem.

Many previous workers selected problems for which measurement theory was not essential. This way of thinking has produced many important results. It has certainly made us wiser about the diversity and complexity of social behavior. But it has led to severe compartmentalization, reflecting the absence of a unifying conceptual framework armed with effective methodology.

IIT has developed a unified approach. The same concepts and methods developed in person cognition in the previous chapter have here been applied to the three areas of attitudes, attribution, and group dynamics. The next two chapters extend this approach to social development and moral judgment. Multiple determination, largely beyond the scope of previous approaches, has been transformed into a foundation for general theory. This conceptual framework is effective and productive, with applications across every branch of social psychology. These studies have revealed a uniform order within the social–personality domain and beyond.

Research strategy in IIT emphasizes the inductive mode of inquiry discussed in the last part of Chapter 1. The inductive mode often seems strange to those accustomed to the mini-theory strategy that has characterized most work in social–personality. Mini-theories have many attractions: They typically involve concepts with face meaningfulness; they address specific issues of interest and importance; they seek definite, testable hypotheses; they follow the seeming scientific ideal of hypothetico-deductive inquiry; and many bypass or seem to bypass the roadblock of psychological measurement.

Because of these advantages, and because this approach is so popular, it has come to be considered an ideal of research strategy. This has been a strategic misdirection. The standard strategy cannot lead to unified theory because it does not handle psychological measurement and hence is ineffective with multiple determination. This argument is echoed in the increasing fragmentation in the social–personality field. And in practice, as various writers have remarked, cumulative progress has been severely disappointing.

Unified theory can be achieved following the inductive strategy used in IIT. Multiple determination becomes tractable under certain conditions, together with the measurement problem. The axiom of purposiveness is thereby established as a core for functional theory. This claim is grounded in the cumulative progress illustrated in this and the other chapters of this book.

How general this approach will prove remains to be seen. It should be useful and effective with various issues of current concern. More significant, however, are issues raised in previous integration studies whose analysis is by no means clear.

One major class of such issues concerns cognitive organization. Integration is an organizing process, of course, as is valuation, reflecting their goal-directed character. However, additional forms of organization also need consideration. One group of these involves functional memory. Organizational functions of memory appear with redundancy and inconsistency, for example, vital cognitive processes about which surprisingly little is known (Chapter 11). Organization in long-term memory is also important for understanding attitudes, motivations, and other knowledge systems.

Perhaps the most interesting problems of functional memory, and potentially the most fruitful, concern operating memory. The importance of operating memory has been foreshadowed in the discussion of attribution schemas, and will appear more strongly in the treatment of assemblage theory in Chapter 8. Cognitive algebra can help study these forms of organization, but new concepts and methods are needed.

A second group of problems of cognitive organization concerns interpersonal interaction. Such organization may appear on-line, as with the studies of Figures 5.2, 5.9, and 5.11, and more generally in family, friendship, and work, or as memorial knowledge systems, as with interpersonal attitudes and with various attribution schemas, including those that appear in pragmatics of language communication (Chapter 12). The work to date has provided a toehold on some of these problems of cognitive organization. The two following chapters extend this approach to morality, a form of cognitive organization with joint psychological and sociological significance.

NOTES

Entries into the literatures of social psychology are given in many excellent chapters in the second and third editions of *The Handbook of Social Psychology* (Lindzey & Aronson, 1969, 1985) as well as in occasional chapters in the *Annual Review of Psychology*. Comprehensive surveys of attitude theory are given by Eagly and Chaiken (1993) and in two canonical chapters by McGuire (1969, 1985). These writers also cover traditional functional approaches in attitude theory, antecedents of the present functional theory. A useful overview of attribution is given by contributors to Jaspars, Fincham, and Hewstone (1983). Group processes are considered in Hendrick (1987a,b).

1. Reliability and power can be much increased by using within-subject, repeated measures design, but this has been rare in attitude research. The reason is confounding. If two attitude messages on the same issue are given to one subject, the change produced by the second is confounded with effects of the first. Hence between-subject design has been standard, which yields markedly less reliability.

To allow within-subject design, 220 "president paragraphs" of graded value were constructed for 17 U. S. presidents (reprinted in Anderson, 1982, Appendix C). Each president represents a comparable, independent issue. Hence the same subject may be used with different message conditions for different presidents. In the experiment of Figure 5.1, each of 48 subjects judged each of 8 presidents. To obtain equal power with between-subject design would have required 510 subjects.

2. Definite evidence for the basal−surface, two-component representation of attitudes was first obtained in a study of attitude formation with legal case material (Anderson, 1959b). The serial branching structure of the design revealed three effects: a surface recency; a basal recency; and a hidden basal primacy at successive branch points (see Anderson, 1991h, pp. 36-40). Basal−surface effects in learning studies are given in Anderson (1960, 1969) and Friedman, Carterette, and Anderson (1968).

The serial curves of Figure 5.4 have been replicated by Dreben, Fiske, and Hastie (1979) and in part with children by Schlottmann and Anderson (in press). These results raise the possibility that the surface component can be largely eliminated by appending a neutral informer at the end of the sequence, which would be a welcome simplicity.

The basal–surface representation is fundamental for attitude research and theory. Most attitude research appears to be concerned or confounded with the surface effect, which seems of relatively minor significance. Unfortunately, even establishing the existence of these two distinct components of attitude is difficult, as noted in the text. Clear evidence arose in the cited studies because of the branching structure of the serial-factor design, but this was serendipitously dependent on the actual locus of the basal buildup. Serial curves remain attractive for further work, but alternative approaches may be more effective. A direct approach, studying attitude retention as a function of the separate and joint effects of time delay and near-neutral informers, might find how to eliminate the surface effect. This would facilitate further analysis.

3. The inadequacy of the one-dimensional conception of attitudes is well illustrated with attitudes toward women, which include innumerable aspects of interpersonal interaction, from dress and appearance to roles in work, family, and parties. Attitudinal responses include goal-directed plans to approach or avoid, rationalizations for dubious actions, arguing and ego defense to protect threatened attitudes and goals, and conceptions of appropriate and inappropriate role actions. Much such attitudinal response is essentially qualitative, even when quantified into approach–avoidance.

Other writers have also criticized the one-dimensional view, beginning with reactions to Thurstone's original 1928 article, "Attitudes can be measured." The one-dimensional view, however, has maintained its grip, in part through encapsulation in previous theories of attitude measurement. Functional measurement theory provides a new approach that recognizes and unifies qualitative and quantitative aspects of attitudes.

4. A notable integrationist treatment of illusory correlation is given by Busemeyer (1991), who also handles more general problems of cause–effect covariation. Busemeyer shows that the averaging model includes most previous models as special cases. Analytically, moreover, the averaging model is at once simpler and more powerful (see *Covariation* in Chapter 10).

5. The adaptive functions of stereotypes in everyday thought and action are a focus of IIT (Anderson, 1991m). This follows the pioneering analysis of Lippmann (1922), who recognized the advantages as well as the disadvantages of the simplified pictures that stereotypes provide. Later work on racial prejudice led to a negative view of stereotypes as irrational and pernicious, losing sight of their functional nature. Recent workers have attempted to develop information processing approaches, but remain hobbled by the bias–distortion outlook, as in a current guise of schemas.

The root issue in understanding stereotypes lies in the distinction between **V** and **I** processing modes (Figure 1.1), already set out in the contrast between the hypotheses of meaning invariance and change of meaning. Much interpretation in terms of bias–distortion lacks meaning because it has not recognized this distinction (see *Meaning Constancy Revisited* in Anderson, 1991m, pp. 187, 201).

A new tool for stereotype research comes from the capability of functional measurement to assess relative importance of stereotypes and other kinds of informers. Many studies eliminate all other information, in order to maximize the stereotype effect. This tactic, unfortunately, says little about how stereotypes operate in practice—in conjunction with other informers. A stereotype informer that has a big effect by itself may well have a tiny effect when paired with other informers. Studies that include only the stereotype informer may thus lack social relevance.

6. The verbal memory hypothesis was a major theme of the group around Carl Hovland in the 1950s, which aspired to utilize the near-century of research on verbal learning and memory as a foundation for attitude theory. A governing idea was that the change in a person's attitude produced by a message would depend directly on what was remembered from that message. Strong tests of this hypothesis seemed unavailable, but correlations of attitude change with message recall were obtained. These correlations were disappointingly modest, but modest correlations could readily be explained in several ways, for example, by unreliability of the measures of recall and attitude across subjects. No one was happy with these modest correlations, but the verbal memory hypothesis remained without any real alternative.

The first real alternative to the verbal memory hypothesis was given by Anderson and Hubert (1963; see Figure 11.1). This study gave the first definite evidence against the verbal memory hypothesis—and for a functional attitude memory.

A major problem in pursuing functional memory was to establish the integration model as a base for measurement of this kind of memory. This model was established following the initial study (see, e.g., Figure 5.3). Using this model, strong support for the functional conception of memory has been obtained (Dreben, Fiske, & Hastie, 1979; Riskey, 1979; see also Zajonc, 1980, discussed in Note 4 of Chapter 11).

This new conception of attitude memory entails a similar conception of attitude learning and indeed of learning itself. Traditional learning and memory theories are conceptually akin; both are too narrow for unified theory of cognition (Anderson, 1973b, 1981a).

7. The attitude memory hypothesis of Anderson and Hubert (1963) has been widely adopted in social psychology. Their distinction between memory for given verbal materials and memory for attitude based on those materials was utilized as a major theme in every chapter contributed to *Person Memory* (Hastie, Ostrom, Ebbesen, Wyer, Hamilton, & Carlston, 1980; see Anderson, 1989a, pp. 175, 179, 190, 192, 194, 205, and 209).

Similarly, the distinction between "on-line" and "memory-based" popularized by Hastie and Park (1986) is essentially the same as the original distinction of Anderson and Hubert (1963). "Memory-based" corresponds directly to the original verbal memory hypothesis of the Hovland group (see previous note); the alternative model presented by Anderson and Hubert is a prototypical "on-line" model.

8. The multiplication rule, Behavior = Motivation × Ability, was proposed by Heider (1958) on the argument that an addition rule could not hold because zero Motivation would yield zero Behavior even with nonzero Ability. The weakness of this argument mirrors Heider's lack of capability for assessing his conjecture. Functional measurement analysis has shown that the multiplication rule holds in some situations, the averaging rule in others (Anderson, 1974b, 1978b).

9. Other work on attribution algebra is given in Anderson (1991l), Singh (1991), and Surber (1985a,b). The multiplication rule, Behavior = Motivation × Ability, obtained by Anderson and Butzin (1974), has been replicated under conditions that rule out the possibility that the linear fan pattern is caused by averaging with differential weighting (Anderson, 1983d, pp. 73−76; see similarly Singh, 1991).

An interesting application of schema algebra concerns imputations about unspecified, or "missing" information. This issue, also important outside the social domain, is reviewed in Anderson (1991l, pp. 73–84).

The decision averaging model of Chapter 10 is expected to have considerable application in social attribution because it deals with inverse inference. Applications in Chapter 10 show it to be superior to the normative Bayesian model for inverse inference. Related applications to language processing are given in Chapter 12. As yet, however, applications in social attribution seem lacking.

Of special interest is attribution of knowledge, a ubiquitous social process, but one that has received relatively little attention. In the social domain, knowledge attribution often underlies status attribution, as in patient–doctor and student–teacher relations. Similarly, everyday communication depends intimately on knowledge attributions to others, as strongly emphasized in language pragmatics (Chapter 12).

10. Forward inference has been oddly neglected in social attribution, which has centrated on inverse inference. Inverse inference applies to single informers with ambiguous causal interpretation, as with the pacificistic statement in the attitude attribution study of Figure 5.7. Multiple informers are generally operative, however, requiring integration as forward inference, also illustrated in this study of attitude attribution.

When there is no causal ambiguity, as is often the case, inverse inference may not be needed for single informers. Instead, the valuation operation may assign it weight and value parameters directly, following which it may be integrated with other informers or with the initial state to arrive at an overall attribution.

11. Blame and excuses are covered in Anderson (1983c,1991k), which include references to literature in psychology and sociology. A complementary schema may be used for praise and credit. The importance of praise and credit for social cognition mirrors their importance for society, yet they are much less studied than blame and excuses.

12. One direction for further work on social averaging theory of group dynamics concerns deeper study of individual differences. Some individuals in Graesser's study were effective bargainers, others were ineffectual. The same seems true of everyday life, in which some people find bargaining aversive. Explicit or implicit, bargaining pervades everyday interpersonal interaction, so its quality and function in personality dynamics and everyday life deserve systematic study.

A second direction concerns multiple decision axes. Unions, for example, bargain not only over pay rate, but also over fringe benefits to arrive at a package deal. Wife and husband bargain, often implicitly, over multiple interwoven decisions. To extend social averaging theory to study such multiple decisions requires tradeoff parameters to represent bargaining interaction between the decision axes.

Subsequent to Graesser's (1978) test between social averaging theory and Davis' theory of social decision schemes, a more integrationist approach has been considered by Stasser, Kerr, and Davis (1989). Regrettably, they fail to consider that Graesser's work had rendered uninterpretable the bulk of their published papers on social decision schemes, as illustrated in the discussion of Figure 5.10 and Table 5.1 (see also Graesser, 1991, Notes 3 and 4, Editor's Note 1, and p. 38). This seems surprising since a prominent proponent of social decision schemes was on Graesser's Ph. D. committee.

13. Applications of averaging theory to group attractiveness are cited in Editor's Note 2 in Graesser (1991, pp. 36*ff*). The configurality in judgments of criminal groups was found by Leon, Oden, and Anderson (1973).

14. Of special interest for interpersonal perception is the attempt by Kenny (1994, pp. 65*ff*) to extend averaging theory to such questions as consensus (Are you perceived similarly by different others?) and meta-accuracy (Do you know how others perceive you?). Kenny thus addresses a class of neglected questions that are important for social interaction. In this development, Kenny departs from the common reliance on vignettes about hypothetical people to stress social interaction, as in the foregoing group studies.

Kenny's extension of averaging theory has interesting differences from previous work in IIT. One difference relates to Kenny's use of correlation as his basic measure. Consensus, for example, is defined as a between-subject correlation of ratings of target persons (p. 68). This correlational definition loses the ratings of the individual target persons, which have been the usual focus in IIT. The relative advantages and disadvantages of these two kinds of measures are not clear.

Two minor corrections of Kenny's discussion of averaging theory may be added. First, the initial impression in IIT refers to all prior information about the target person. Kenny's (p. 66) statement that the initial impression is based on a lack of information applies only to the special case of persons about whom no prior information is available. Contrary examples include the presidents experiments of Figures 5.1 and 5.3 and the marriage studies of Figures 5.2 and 5.12.

Second, contrary to Kenny (p. 211), the person perceiver in IIT is conceptualized as an active processor of information. Valuation, in particular, is goal-directed operation of knowledge systems. Integration may involve configural effects, as in the original 1965 study of inconsistency discounting cited in Chapter 4. More generally, integration is itself an active, goal-directed process.

15. Future work on social groups should also go hand in hand with sociology, which has expended much more effort on the family than has psychology. Group interaction, however, is interaction between individuals. Psychology of groups must thus rest squarely on psychology of individuals. Sociological theory, for the same reason, must be grounded in psychological theory.

Sociologists suffer from an aversion to psychological concepts that cripples their field (see Anderson, 1991k, Note 2, 1991g, pp. 225–229). The *Handbook of Sociology* (Smelser, 1988) contains no chapter on attitudes or personality, and barely a single chapter on group dynamics. The one chapter that would seem familiar to psychologists, "Gender and Sex Roles," deals mainly with large-scale sociological aspects, with minimal concern for individual cognition. The orientation of the symbolic interactionists would seem to push them into cognition, but they often seem the most articulately averse of all sociologists. Because of this neglect of individual cognition, the conceptual framework of sociology seems entirely inadequate for the study of individual–society relations. Joint psychological–sociological investigation is thus desirable, especially in the conceptual domain of social roles and in the central empirical domain of marriage and family life.

16. It seems appropriate to quote two evaluations made by persons not personally involved in IIT. Hastie (1983, p. 513) commented:

> Information Integration Theory is the most complete and coherent theoretical position in social psychology, and it is also the most firmly grounded in empirical research. The basic psychological mechanisms are stated concisely as general algebraic equations that can be clearly related to other models expressed in the same "language," as well as to more informal theoretical analyses. The general framework of the theory includes the molar processing stages that must be part of any cognitive model. Thus, the theoretical and methodological solutions presented by Information Integration Theory define questions that must be addressed by any adequate cognitive theory. This is a very sobering implication for social psychologists who do not acknowledge measurement, stimulus valuation, identifiability, and process model sufficiency problems, much less propose solutions to them.

In a review of Volume II (Social) of *Contributions to Information Integration Theory*, Pratkanis (1994, p. 445) itemized five contributions of IIT. The second says:

> Serves as a tutorial on how to develop a successful theory. The reason for the success of this theory lies in three essential ingredients that set information integration theory apart from most social psychological theories. First, it is a theory about a general process (information integration) and not a specific phenomenon (say, equity, innuendos, or the sleeper effect) as is the case with many social psychological theories.... Second, the theory is straightforward and has stimulated considerable empirical research.... Finally, information integration theory is one of the few social psychological theories that incorporates a measurement theory—a particularly difficult issue in social psychology. It is functional measurement that ensures that information integration theory will be a dynamic and developing theory.

17. Person–situation interaction has frequently been identified with the statistical interactions from analysis of variance of a Person × Situation factorial design. This identification rests on two strong, unrecognized assumptions. First, the interactions are artifacts unless the response is measured on a true linear scale. This linearity assumption can be satisfied with functional measurement, but this has rarely been applied. Second, the interactions are artifacts unless the response scale has a common unit across persons. How such interpersonal comparability of units may be established, or even tested, seems entirely unknown. Psychologically, therefore, these statistical interaction terms seem meaningless (Anderson, 1982, Chapter 7).

In IIT, person–situation interaction occurs especially in valuation. Because persons differ in their knowledge systems, they will construct different values for the same situational informers. Functional measurement provides leverage through its capability with single-person design and analysis (see, e.g., Figure 1.2; Lopes, 1976a).

18. Cooperation between social cognition and mainstream cognitive psychology is desirable, but not straightforward. The two have addressed different classes of issues, reflecting different conceptual frameworks. In particular, social–personality psychology has an abiding concern with everyday life, which is too much outside the mainstream cognitive framework. This difference in conceptual framework is well illustrated by the reproductive–functional memory distinction of Chapter 11. Theory of social cognition must be constructed around the primary concerns of social–personality psychology, a brave new world for cognitive psychology (Anderson, 1987).

PREFACE

Two very different views of moral development are contrasted in this chapter: developmental integration theory and stage theory.

The influential stage formulations see moral development as a succession of stages, discrete and discontinuous, each with a distinctive moral character. Within each stage, moral thinking is controlled by a single organizing principle. Four or five such principles are claimed to explain all moral thinking. Study of moral development thus becomes a search for these principles; they promise great simplification in theory construction.

Developmental integration theory adopts a functional view: Morality is a class of biosocial knowledge systems. These knowledge systems have adaptive functions in assemblage of moral judgments and decisions in the diverse situations of everyday life. No precommitment is required regarding discrete stages, which indeed seem unlikely. Instead, it is suggested that moral ideas of early years remain functional in later life. Adult moral cognition thus involves assemblage of moral motivations and values from all periods of development.

With this difference in conceptual framework goes a difference in methodology. Stage formulations place primary emphasis on verbal protocols obtained in structured interviews. Developmental integration theory employs functional measurement, with simple judgments that require minimal verbal ability.

These two approaches yield very different results in studies of blame and fairness. Developmental integration theory reveals that young children have advanced, flexible capabilities for moral judgment—capabilities that have been denied by the interview methodology. The interview method is insensitive to moral cognition. Indeed, it presents false claims with great confidence in their truth, failing to see what functional measurement reveals.

Functional measurement reveals a moral algebra. For blame, in particular, the modal integration rule is averaging, invariant from 4 to 20 years. This rule invariance allows cross-age comparisons through measurement of idiographic moral values, which is essential for general moral theory.

A unified approach is needed, treating moral development as part of general social–cognitive development. Stage formulations, imprisoned in their conceptual precommitment, have shunned social cognition and judgment–decision theory. A cooperative approach is suggested, in which moral algebra provides a touchstone for developing valid interview methods—a needed methodological tool for cognitive theory of everyday life.

Chapter 6

SOCIAL DEVELOPMENT

The most prominent approach in current work on moral-social development has two primary characteristics, one of method and one of theory. The *method* involves structured interviews. People are presented with hypothetical moral dilemmas, make a moral choice, and are then questioned systematically about their reasons for their choice. This interview method looks for the structure of people's moral conceptions in their stated reasons.

The *theory* begins with the assumption that development follows a progression of moral *stages*: Each successive stage involves complete reorganization of moral principles and reasoning. This method and this theory underlie the dominant contemporary approaches to moral development.

The interview method, however, has produced a fundamental misrepresentation of moral cognition. When concepts and methods of developmental integration theory are applied to the same situations that have been studied with interview methods, children's moral cognition appears very different.

This integration theory of moral development is illustrated in the first two parts of this chapter, first for blame and then for fairness. In both domains, the interview method failed to discern developmental structure of moral cognition. Instead, it confidently presented false conclusions as true.

Stage conceptualizations, moreover, are subject to grave reservations. Much of the evidence presented for stages is vitiated by artifacts of method. At best, the evidence for true stages is very weak. The integration studies, in contrast, suggest continuity in moral-social development, with even the earliest moral ideas persisting in adult life.

A unified approach to moral development is outlined in the last part of the chapter, which compares developmental integration theory with three stage-type formulations. Moral development is conceptualized as an integral part of general social development. Moral judgment needs to be studied by combining the interview method used in the stage approaches and the moral algebra discovered in developmental integration theory.

BLAME SCHEMA: MOTIVE ⊛ DAMAGE

Two main determinants of blame, as everyday knowledge indicates, are the motive or intention of the actor and the damage produced by the action. This motive–damage question has been extensively investigated. Early work by Piaget led him to conclude that children under 10 years old do not integrate these two determinants. Instead, they "center," making their judgments on the basis of motive alone or damage alone. This concept of centration became a central tenet of Piagetian theory (see further Chapter 8).

Centration, however, is an artifact of Piagetian methodology. Applications of developmental integration theory have shown that children as young as 4 years of age can integrate motive and damage. Not only do they integrate, but their integration often follows algebraic rules.

MORAL ALGEBRA OF BLAME

The reference study of motive–damage integration is the thoughtful, meticulous thesis by Manuel Leon (1976, 1980). Subjects rated badness of a story child, given information about motive and damage of some action by the child, for example, bruising another child by throwing a rock with harmful intent. Motive and damage were varied in a 3×4 factorial design. Each subject thus judged 12 motive–damage stories, together with the 7 stories that presented only the motive or only the damage information.

Two sets of stories were used. In the standard stories, based on Piaget, motives were implicit or even undefined. These standard stories, however, were found to be unusable below third grade (8 years old) because motives were not well understood. To extend the integration task down to first grade, Leon added simple stories in which motive was stated explicitly. First- and second-graders received only the simple stories; third-, fifth-, seventh-, and college-grade subjects received both the simple and standard stories.

Leon's results are summarized under the following 11 points. This itemization illustrates how much information can be obtained from a single developmental integration study.

1. Algebraic Blame Schema. The most prominent outcome of Leon's work was the evidence for the averaging rule:

$$\text{Blame} = \text{Motive} + \text{Damage}.$$

The blame schema thus has an exact algebraic structure. For the standard stories, the averaging rule was uniform across all age groups; from third grade to college grade, the factorial graphs exhibited parallelism, of the form previously illustrated in Figure 2.1. For the simple stories, averaging was the modal rule, but alternative rules were also found, as noted next.

2. Accident-configural Schema. A substantial minority of subjects used an accident-configural rule for the simple stories: Blame was independent of damage when it was accidental; otherwise the averaging rule applied. This accident-configural schema appears as a characteristic factorial pattern: a flat horizontal line for accident and two nonflat parallel curves for the two non-zero levels of motive. This rule was more frequent with younger children, although still found in an occasional adult.

That younger children should exhibit a more complex rule may seem odd but has a developmental rationale. Younger children have less foresight and so get into more "accidents"; they have personal interest in evaluating absence of specific intent as nonculpable. Older children, through socialization of foresight, may be readier to attribute accidents to culpable lack of foresight. This interpretation, incidentally, suggests that adults who exhibit the accident-configural rule may be deficient in foresight and prudence.

3. One-dimensional Schemas. A small number of subjects, mainly in first and second grades, judged on the basis of only one variable, following a motive-only or damage-only rule. One-dimensional schemas are also diagnosed by a simple factorial pattern. With the damage-only rule, for example, the curves for the three levels of motive are essentially identical.

These same children, however, made normal judgments when the variable ignored in the combination was presented alone. The damage-only subjects thus attributed greater blame for greater motive when only motive information was presented. They thus appreciated the motive information even though they gave it zero weight in judging the combination.

One-dimensional rules have various possible explanations, but little evidence is available. One possibility, of considerable developmental interest, is that some children are generally deficient in integrational capacity. Further work could select such children with a screening test and study them more extensively with a battery of tests designed to assess integrational capacity.

4. Centration Versus Integration. Piaget's centration hypothesis failed badly. The integration methodology provides a strong test because centration implies one-dimensional rules. In fact, most of Leon's children not only integrated, but followed an algebraic rule. The few exceptions noted in the preceding item do not warrant Piaget's claim that centration is a general characteristic of young children's thought.

5. Age Invariance. A fairly general age invariance in moral algebra made its first appearance in Leon's results. Most subjects of all ages used the same integration rule. This is presumably a general purpose rule, not essentially moral, but applicable across different judgment domains. Even stronger evidence for age invariance was obtained in the study of the extended blame schema cited below. Age invariance can be expected only in simple tasks, of course, because integrational capacity does increase markedly with age.

A happy consequence of age invariance is a unique opportunity for developmental comparison of moral value. Success of the rule allows true measurement of value, and these value patterns may be legitimately compared across ages. Similar comparisons may be possible across different cultural groups.

6. Experimental Paradigm. The foregoing evidence for integration rather than centration stems from a basic difference in experimental paradigm. Leon used a standard integration paradigm: Subjects judged degree of badness of a single story child, based on information about motive and about damage. The Piagetian studies used Piaget's basic choice paradigm: Children made a discrete choice of the naughtier of two story children, one with bad motive who caused little damage, the other with near-neutral motive who caused substantial damage. But such choice data say nothing about the relative effects of motive and damage. The question of relative effects refers to the conceptual variables of motive and damage per se. The data, however, represent the specific stimulus levels of the two variables, which are arbitrary and noncomparable. Further consideration shows that Piaget's choice paradigm is incapable of distinguishing centration from integration.

Piaget apparently based his centration interpretation on the verbal justifications, but this involves an artifact. The only sensible justification perforce refers to the more negative variable for the story child chosen as naughtier. When this artifact is removed, as Leon showed, the seeming centration disappears. This flaw in Piaget's basic methodology ramifies through all his work.

7. Stimulus Methodology. Leon included the Piagetian stories and choice task, and these data generally replicated previous results. In particular, they replicated the main result from previous work, namely, an apparent increase in relative effect of motive with age. Leon's procedure was thus comparable with that used in the Piagetian studies.

The main implication, however, was to expose numerous shortcomings of the Piagetian method, first noted and itemized by Leon. In particular, the Piagetian stories are sometimes unclear about the harmful motive. Hence they are invalid for assessing development of sensitivity to the motive variable. The apparent increase in sensitivity to motive may be merely an artifact, a consequence of careless construction of stimulus stories.

8. Imputations. Some older children and adults made imputations about missing information. When information was presented only about motive (or damage), the data showed that some subjects imputed an implicit value to the other, unspecified variable and averaged that imputed value with the given informer. These results were the first substantial evidence on the now popular topic of imputations. The power of integration theory to uncover this hidden aspect of cognitive processing deserves emphasis. These and related results infirm the concept of default value as a defining property of schemas (Chapter 1).

9. Averaging Versus Adding. The pattern of parallelism observed in the factorial graph supports adding and averaging equally. These two rules can be distinguished with scale-free crossover tests based on the single-variable stories (see, e.g., Figure 2.4). These scale-free tests ruled out adding and supported averaging for younger children on the simple stories. This generality of the averaging rule found in the two previous chapters indicates a basic commonality of cognitive process across the moral and social domains.

10. Measurement Theory. Success of the averaging rule has several implications for psychological measurement. Most important, it provides evidence that the rating *response* was a veridical, linear psychological scale. This implication agrees with parallel results in many other domains. One contribution of functional measurement has been this evidence that the rating method can, with appropriate experimental precautions, yield veridical measures of feelings such as blame and fairness in young children.[1]

A second measurement issue concerns the *stimulus* variables. Functional measurement methodology provides psychological scales of both stimulus variables, motive and damage. The blame schema is thus assessed in terms of the personal values of each individual child. A third measurement issue appears in the popular question about relative importance of motive and damage, which is discussed in the next section.

11. Individual Analysis. The capability of diagnosing integration rules for individuals, employed in Leon's work, deserves emphasis. This allows for personal values of each child and makes it possible to measure those values (see Figure 2.1). These are the functional values, which will depend on the prevailing motivation of the child and on the social situation. This capability for person—situation measurement is useful, perhaps essential, for the study of moral development.

Individual diagnosis is also useful for developmental comparisons across age. The parallelism *pattern* is comparable across age regardless of differences in values. The same holds for other patterns. Cross-cultural comparisons may also be made in this way. Such pattern analysis provides useful potential for moral-social theory, nicely illustrated below in Leon's study of social learning.

RELATED STUDIES OF MOTIVE ⊛ DAMAGE

Extended Blame Schema. Further evidence for moral algebra was obtained by extending the blame schema to include the third variable of recompense, or reparation for the damage by the harmdoer (Hommers & Anderson, 1985, 1991). To make the task meaningful across age, a stamp collector scenario was used, in which one child damaged some stamps belonging to another child. The data revealed an averaging rule invariant from age 4 to 20:

Deserved Punishment = Motive + Damage − Recompense.

Paradoxically, the recompense variable had greater effect than the damage for which the recompense was made. Moreover, this paradoxical effect was strongest at the youngest ages. A suggested interpretation is that recompense has two components: an objective component of material reparation and a subjective component referring to the moral character of the harmdoer. The latter component could augment the former, thereby accounting for the paradoxically large effect of recompense.

Relative Importance. The most studied question about the motive–damage task cannot be answered with the methods that have been used. This question involves the plausible speculation that damage, which is objective and observable, will be more important for younger children than motive, which is subjective and unobservable.

This question involves a perhaps subtle distinction between importance of a variable per se and the arbitrary stimulus levels of that variable used in the task. The observed effect of a variable depends both on its importance and on the value difference between its levels. In a 2 × 2, Motive–Damage design, the motive variable will have very small effect if its two levels are very close in value, even if its importance is high. Value differences cannot be equated without measurement theory; no merely empirical procedure can unconfound importance from value difference. Virtually all reported results on this question are thus uninterpretable (Anderson, 1982, Chapter 6).

Colleen Surber (1982) showed how averaging theory could be used to determine relative importance of motive and damage. Importance of a variable corresponds to the weight parameter, ω, in the averaging rule; value of each stimulus level corresponds to its scale value, ψ. Averaging theory makes it possible to estimate weight separately from value, thereby unconfounding importance and value. Surber's results indicated that damage was more important than motive for first graders, less important for fifth graders. This appears to be the first and still the only published study of this question that rests on valid method. Surber's approach makes possible more analytical studies of determinants of importance across age and subculture.

This finding of developmental changes in relative importance rests on a developmental invariance—in the integration rule. Surber's results, like those of Leon, generally supported the averaging rule from 5 to 20 years of age. Surber also gives a wide-ranging, cogent discussion of implications of IIT for other developmental problems.

Social Learning of Sons and Mothers. Moral-social development depends jointly on social learning and cognitive maturation. These two themes have a standing antagonism, which often assumes an ideological cast that obstructs the need for cooperative inquiry. The mother–son similarity in the following experiment shows how integration theory can study learning and maturation together.

Sons follow the same Motive ⊕ Damage schemas as their mothers (Leon, 1984). The simple motive–damage stories mentioned previously were given to 32 mothers and their 7-year-old sons. Integration schemas for individual mothers were diagnosed from the patterns in their factorial graphs. Eighteen mothers exhibited the parallelism pattern characteristic of the averaging rule; their sons showed the same pattern. Ten mothers exhibited the pattern characteristic of the foregoing accident-configural rule; their sons showed the same pattern. Four mothers exhibited the pattern characteristic of a damage-only rule; their sons showed a similar, although less regular, damage-only pattern.

There is thus a remarkable correspondence between the schemas used by the mothers to organize their moral judgments and those used by their sons. This similarity was observable despite differences in values. For example, all three groups of mothers considered a broken window substantially more serious than a broken pot, whereas all three groups of children considered the two about equally serious. Functional measurement allowed assessment of the schema similarity at the same time that it established the value dissimilarity.[2]

Theoretically, the averaging rule is a general purpose integration schema that may be applied to many judgments, moral and nonmoral. This schema is considered to develop maturationally, without specific reinforcement either from society or from the environment. Indeed, it may develop despite being incongruent with environmental contingencies, as illustrated in Chapter 8. The accident-configural and damage-only rules, on the other hand, would seem to be a product of social learning. Leon's results thus argue for the joint operation and joint importance of social learning and cognitive maturation.

Further Work on Social Learning and Development. Social learning is hard to study because its effects generally accumulate gradually over long periods. Standard correlational studies are notoriously difficult to interpret; short-term experiments generally have small effects that disappear beneath the massive, continuing action of the social surround; long-term experiments are costly and risky. It is desirable, therefore, to have methods that can reveal long-term effects using short-term observation.

Some leverage on this problem may be obtainable with IIT through the use of collateral knowledge about causal influence. In itself, the foregoing mother–son similarity is correlational, for the form of the mothers' integration rule was observed as individual differences. The averaging rule itself may be a general purpose rule, primarily maturational, and so not causally informative about parental influence. However, the mother–son similarity of the accident-configural and damage-only rules does argue for causal influence. Greater analytical power would seem attainable by selecting a battery of tasks of moral judgment, chosen to elicit causally diagnostic rules, such as the damage-only rule. At the same time, developmental changes in moral value could also be informative about social influence.

DESERVING AND FAIRNESS

People are not born fair and just. Quite the contrary; children's internalization of moral-social standards is as notable for its rough effectiveness in the continual re-creation of society as for its fitful coexistence with self-interest. Relatively few studies, however, have studied development of knowledge about deserving and fairness.

MORAL ALGEBRA OF FAIRNESS

An adumbration of moral algebra appears in the idea of fairness: What we get should be in proportion to what we deserve. This idea of just proportion, however, might be little more than a philosophical verbalism, lacking cognitive reality. Empirical test is needed. Empirical test is possible because functional measurement allows for individual values. The following 10-point itemization shows how much information can be obtained from a single developmental integration study of deserving–fairness.

The children's task was to assign "fair shares" to one or two story children, given information about their deserving (Anderson & Butzin, 1978). A Santa Claus scenario was adopted with two purposes in mind: to embed the task within the children's everyday sense of deserving, and to allow inclusion of information about *need* as well as *deed*. The deed information was specified verbally and pictorially, in terms of how much the story children had helped their mothers with cleaning up the dishes. The need information was specified verbally and pictorially, in terms of how many toys the story children already had, a manipulation that has a natural relation to the Santa Claus scenario. The subject children, from 4 to 8 years of age, were told to play Santa Claus and give a "fair share" of toys to a single story child or to divide fairly between two story children. Each response involved integration of two or four pieces of information in different experiments.

The results showed that the children followed algebraic schemas, even at the youngest age of 4 years. These schemas, moreover, were generally similar to those obtained with adults (see following chapter).

1. Deserving Schema. Judgments of deserving of single story children followed an adding-type rule. The operation of this adding-type rule was diagnosed from the pattern of parallelism for both deed–deed integration and for need–deed integration. Similar parallelism was observed in a third experiment, which involved need–deed integration of deserving for each of two story children prior to fair shares division.

2. Fairness Schema. Division of toys or candies between two story children was expected to follow a decision averaging rule: Fair shares for both children proportional to the relative ratio of their deserving. This rule, previously found with adults (see following chapter), was supported for the children. In this division task also, children's moral schemas had an algebraic form.

3. Social Comparison: Fairness Integration Versus Input Integration. An interesting question about social comparison arises when deserving is specified along both of two dimensions, such as need and deed. A natural hypothesis is that both are integrated to obtain a single input value of deserving for each story child; the fair-shares division is then based on these unitary input values.

This hypothesis of *input integration* had been taken for granted in fairness theory until functional measurement provided a way to test it. It was then found false; instead the data supported an alternative hypothesis of *fairness integration*: Children made two implicit fairness divisions, one for need and one for deed. These two implicit fairness judgments were integrated to determine the actual division.

Input integration and fairness integration represent different processes of social comparison. This difference in social comparison is discussed in relation to Equations 2 and 3 of the following chapter. There it is shown that adults also typically handle heterogeneous inputs in terms of fairness integration. A significant cognitive process of adult sharing behavior is thus present at early ages and can be diagnosed with integration theory.

4. Configural Integration. The rule of fairness integration was found to involve a configural effect. Less weight was placed on the need (or deed) dimension when the two story children were equal on that dimension. A dimension of difference, in other words, had more effect than a dimension of no difference. Here again, children's cognitions are like adults.'

5. Proportional Thinking. A notable outcome was that even 4-year-olds were capable of proportional thinking. One form of proportional thinking appears in the ratio prescription of the fairness schema: Children divided the toys in proportion to deserving.

A second form of proportional thinking appears in the rating response itself. Success of the integration rule implies that the response was a true linear scale, in accord with the logic of the parallelism theorem (Chapter 2). The observable judgment of deserving for single story children was thus proportional to the implicit feeling of deserving.

Both forms of proportional thinking represent impressive quantification capabilities. Both also disagree notably with Piagetian theory, which asserts that proportional thinking requires formal operations—and cannot possibly be present in the preoperational stage. This major failure of Piagetian method and theory is not peculiar to moral judgment. It appears again in knowledge about the external world, taken up in Chapter 8.

6. Personal Values. Functional measurement methodology tests the integration rules in terms of each child's personal values for the need and deed information. No assumption about these personal values is needed, nor any assumption about relative importance of need and deed. This measurement capability is vital because moral values may differ sharply across individuals.

7. Need Versus Deed. Previous work had been taken to mean that objective factors, such as deed, had more effect at young ages than subjective factors, such as need. The present study, in contrast, found somewhat greater effect of need. But this particular comparison, like nearly all others in the literature, confounds each variable with the specific stimulus levels used to exemplify that variable in the experiment. Need might have greater effect because its levels were farther apart, not because need per se had greater importance than deed. The main value of the present result is to reemphasize that the methods commonly used for assessing relative importance are logically incapable of doing so. When the averaging model applies, however, valid comparisons of relative importance become attainable (Chapter 2).

8. Centration Versus Integration. Piagetian theory claims that younger children cannot integrate stimulus information. Instead, they center on one or another piece of information and base their judgment on that one alone.

The present results show that children can integrate, reaffirming results of other integration studies. Analysis of individual children showed that the result was not an artifact of averaging over children, some of whom centered on need, some on deed (see similarly Height + Width rule in Chapter 8).

9. Integrational Capacity. Integrational capacity showed strong dependence on age. In Experiment 3, individual child analyses showed that every 8-year-old integrated all four pieces of information, with a regular decline at younger ages. Many 4-year-olds, however, turned in creditable performances.

The strong dependence of integrational capacity on age indicates its importance as a developmental variable, one that has been little studied. The present methodology provides a useful tool for further analysis. The greater response variability at younger ages, however, causes some statistical problems discussed in the original article.

10. Age Invariance. No age trends were found, except as just noted for integrational capacity. The statistical interactions of age with each stimulus variable were generally nonsignificant, evidence that moral values for this task are well developed by 4 years of age and constant thereafter. The patterns of data, moreover, were similar across ages. In the moral domain, some adult integration schemas are thus operative at 4 years of age (see also Bogartz, 1994).

FURTHER WORK ON DESERVING AND FAIRNESS

Replication and extension of the foregoing study is needed. A single study allows only provisional conclusions. Integration schemas, it should be emphasized, are usually less firmly establishable with children than adults because less data can be obtained. Indeed, adults use a subtraction rule rather than the ratio rule for fair shares division under some conditions, so the same would be expected with children. To pursue this issue developmentally would require extensive data for single children, obtained over multiple sessions.

Extension to other social situations is also desirable. The Santa Claus scenario has a useful function, but it involves an ideal standard not usually operative in everyday life. Sharing situations from everyday experience, however, may follow similar schemas. Such everyday scenarios could be useful for studying the development of values associated with groups based on kinship, friendship, work, and other forms of social interaction.

Unfairness is more important and interesting than fairness. Unfairness is the everyday reality; fairness is only one point on the continuum of unfairness, an ideal, often not attained. Unfairness is a strong motivation, serving also as an ego defense, which is woven into the fabric that constitutes society.

With adults, unfairness judgments have had special significance in moral algebra (see next chapter). With children, however, unfairness remains virtually unexplored. Experimentally, an obvious attack would be to transpose the unfairness tasks used with adults to the child's frame of cognition. Of special interest would be developmental analysis of the determinants of phenomenological unfairness, and indeed of the origin of unfairness feeling itself.

First-party scenarios have special social significance. The foregoing study asked for third-party divisions, in which the child has no personal interest. Third-party scenarios can reveal development of knowledge of social standards, but everyday morality usually involves an additional factor of self-interest. How self-interest may be integrated with obligations to others is an important social-moral question, little explored even with adults.[3]

STAGE THEORIES

The elementary facts of cognitive development lead naturally to stage-like conceptions. All facets of cognition, whether moral, social, linguistic, or other, exhibit long-term developmental changes that appear qualitative rather than merely quantitative, that involve changes in structure rather than mere accumulation of amount. Description of development almost inevitably divides the developmental sequence into discrete categories or stages. At a descriptive level, stage language and stage conceptions are both natural and convenient.

Stage *theories*, however, are fundamentally different from convenience descriptions. Stage *theories* claim that each successive stage constitutes a unified system that is qualitatively different from and requires general reorganization of the preceding stage. In the moral domain, moreover, each stage is claimed to be characterized by a single organizing principle. The central problem of developmental analysis, accordingly, is to elucidate the structure and operation of each stage—in terms of the single organizing principle.

Developmental integration theory is not incompatible with stage theories, but it builds on a different conceptual foundation. It does not prejudge the reality of stages. Instead, the foundation for analysis is sought in problems of integration and valuation. Stage principles, if real, would reveal themselves in these integration–valuation analyses.

The following discussion aims to bring out the potential of cooperative inquiry based jointly on the stage approaches and the theory of information integration. To such cooperative effort, IIT can contribute effective methods of cognitive analysis, including a validity criterion for verbal reports. It also entails a broader conception of moral cognition. The following comparisons with three stage formulations, although brief, indicate the potential, and the need, for cooperative inquiry.

PIAGET'S INTERVIEW METHOD

Only one issue concerning Piaget's theory of moral judgment is considered here. This concerns the interview method, *la méthode clinique*, which Piaget used almost exclusively. This method led to incorrect representations of children's cognition. One such failure of the interview method appears clearly with the problem of integration.

The concept of *centration*, which asserts that young children cannot integrate, is basic in Piagetian theory. Given two pieces of information that bear on some judgment, these children base their judgment on one or the other, for they are incapable of integrating the two. In his original work, Piaget asked children to say which of two story children was naughtier, one who accidentally did a lot of damage or one who had bad motives but did only a little damage.

We obtained the following result. Up to the age of 10, two types of answer exist side by side. In one type actions are evaluated in terms of the material result and independently of motives; according to the other type of answer motives alone are what counts. (Piaget, 1932/1965, pp. 123–124.)

This striking conclusion denies that children under 10 years integrate the motive and damage information. Instead, there are two distinct moral "attitudes," objective, or damage-centered, and subjective, or motive-centered. Only one of these moral attitudes may act at any time. Piaget thus concludes that young children cannot integrate in the moral realm.

But this striking conclusion is invalidated by the facts. Children can integrate very nicely, as shown in the moral realm by the foregoing studies. Indeed, integration is found with children much younger than studied by Piaget. Even in this simple case, Piaget's method reached a seriously incorrect conclusion. It not only missed the facts, but claimed to see something quite different, something that was not there.

This failure of Piaget's methodology is not an isolated mishap. His later work did not correct this initial mistake, but amplified it. Centration became a general principle of the theory, a prime characteristic of the preoperational stage. It has done just as badly, however, in nonmoral domains.

This failure is serious for Piaget's entire theory because his theory was built on this interview method. That his primary method failed in so simple a case undercuts other conclusions obtained with the same method.

The root problem is that Piaget's basic methodology yields systematically invalid results—and that his theory is constructed from these invalid results. Indeed, invalid results were similarly obtained in Piaget's studies of development of knowledge about the external world (Chapter 8).

In moral judgment, it should be noted, Piaget did not hold to a stage theory in the strict sense, as he did in knowledge about the external world. His two stages of heteronomy (morality of constraint) and autonomy (morality of cooperation), however, have generally been recognized to be inadequate. But later workers, instead of seeking a new foundation, attempted to revise Piaget's approach. Nowhere has this been more fateful than in the subsequent work on stage theories of moral judgment.

FAIRNESS STUDIED WITH INTERVIEWS

Functional measurement method yields results entirely different from the interview method commonly used in stage theories of moral development. The work of Damon (1977) provides a good reference example of the interview method because of his careful, thoughtful concern with methodology (see Damon's Chapter 2) and because of its application over the same age range from 4 to 8 years as in the study of fairness itemized above.

Damon developed a standard list of questions about a hypothetical situation in which a class of boys and girls were to divide a whole lot of money they had gotten from making and selling pictures. Illustrative questions asked whether kids should get more money if they made more pictures, or better pictures, or were better-behaved, or were poor, and so forth. These questions were to be asked in a flexible, probing manner that constitutes a main attraction of the interview technique. Answers to these questions from one group of children were used to develop a classification of morality levels, with each level characterized by a single organizing principle. The associated scoring system for the interview protocols had high reliability and high correlation with age, the primary evidence given for the psychological reality of the moral stage levels.

Damon's results disagree totally with the foregoing integration study of fairness. His level 1-A, found predominantly at age 5, is characterized by equal shares for everyone and is "so overridingly consistent that 1-A reasoning often takes on a quality of inflexibility and absolutism. . . . and no mitigating circumstances or reasons are allowed or recognized" (pp. 81–82). In sharp contrast, the 5-year-olds in the integration study shared unequally, with good regard to the need and deed information about each story child.

Again, a main characteristic of Damon's level 2 is that the "new notion of need" (p. 84) first enters the sharing at 8 years of age, whereas 4- to 5-year-olds, at level 0, base their reasoning on personal desires. This developmental picture again differs from the integration study, which showed that 4- to 5-year-olds were quite sensitive to need. At every age, the two methods present entirely different pictures of moral development.

Damon's method evidently failed to assess the children's understanding of fairness. Damon's theory requires the 5-year-olds, for example, to ignore both deed and need and to allot equal shares in the foregoing integration study. These children were free to allot equal shares, but they did not. Instead, they took sensible account of both deed and need and made proportionate allotments. Damon's interview method thus failed to see what integration methodology revealed and made clear.

The integration study of fairness is consistent with many related studies, especially the foregoing studies of blame. Thus, Leon's subjects allotted blame with proportionate consideration of motive as well as damage. Young children are also sensitive to the third variable of recompense by the harmdoer, even to mere apology. All these studies show that young children have moral understanding qualitatively different from that claimed by Damon's method.

The fairness of comparing these two methods, or rather these applications of these two methods, deserves emphasis. Both can be used over the 4- to 8-year age range, and both seek to study the child's world in the child's own terms. Both use hypothetical situations, which allow systematic variation of conditions for each child. Both obtain extensive data from each child and both seek for meaning in patterns of response. Yet the interview method went wrong in just that respect that purports to be its primary value.

The interview method, evidently, is doubly dangerous. Not only did it fail to see what was readily revealed by the integration method, but it claimed to see something quite different. The fault lies in the interview method itself, for Damon's application was exceptionally thoughtful and careful.

This failure of the interview method reflects the treacherousness of verbal reports for cognitive analysis. The problem is not that verbal reports sometimes fail, for that can be said of any method. The problem is that verbal reports are so prone to "false successes," presenting false pictures as truth.

Adding to this validity problem is that applications of interview methods in moral development have generally rested on some prejudged assumption of stages, each having a distinctive organization. Damon cautiously uses the term level, rather than stage, but the same presupposition appears in his classification of the verbal protocols. Without a validational base in cognitive methodology, the interview method is not fail-safe. Its propensity for false successes is catalyzed by prior theoretical assumption.

The integration method, in contrast, is fail-safe. It has prior theoretical assumptions, but it does not impose them on the data. Indeed, it does not even assume that children integrate, but tests whether they do and how. It thus provides a needed corrective and, it may be hoped, a useful companion to the interview method.

KOHLBERG'S STAGE APPROACH

The influential work of Kohlberg (e.g., Colby, Kohlberg, Gibbs, & Lieberman, 1983; see Modgil & Modgil, 1986) focuses on verbal reasoning subjects use in talking about certain moral dilemmas. Five moral stages are currently assumed, ranging from the morality of obedience through the morality of law and duty to the morality of rational, egalitarian cooperation. Each stage is governed by a single moral principle. Each successive stage develops through qualitative reorganization of the previous stage, as a new moral principle replaces the old. Each stage is thus a structured whole that governs all moral judgment.

In Kohlberg's best-known dilemma, a local druggist has invented a new radium treatment that might save Heinz's wife, who is dying from a special kind of cancer. Heinz can raise only half the price demanded by the druggist, and must decide whether to steal the drug. Subjects respond orally to a series of probing questions that branch out from the two initial questions: *Should Heinz steal the drug?* followed by *Why?* or *Why not?* These verbal protocols are broken down into scoring units, and each unit is categorized by a stage level of reasoning. Stage theory rests essentially on the face validity of these levels of reasoning, coupled with evidence that the interview reasoning of a given individual lies within a single stage or at a transition between two adjacent stages.

Objections to Kohlberg's theory will be mentioned only briefly here (see Anderson, 1991i; Modgil & Modgil, 1986). Of prime concern, as various writers have pointed out, is that evidence for the basic stage assumption is very weak. Moreover, the total reliance on the interview method and the scoring system for verbal reasoning is not only questionable but lacks a validity criterion. Verbal reasoning can be seriously invalid, as noted in the two previous sections, even in much simpler situations. Verbal reasoning surely reflects something about moral cognition, but what is veridical in this reflection seems undecidable within Kohlberg's methodology. Indeed, the methods of the stage theories seem incapable of ruling out even the extreme hypothesis that the verbalization is nothing more than rationalization induced by the interview.

A second set of objections concerns the narrowness of Kohlberg's theory. As several writers have noted, moral judgment is virtually equated with justice, to the neglect of the moral domain of benevolence. Again, Kohlberg's method can hardly be applied below 10 or 12 years of age, whereas moral development begins much earlier, as already seen with blame and fairness.

Moreover, Kohlberg's stage approach has had virtually no contact with social cognition. Ideas from person cognition, attitudes, attribution, and family psychology are notable by their absence. This neglect of the rest of social psychology is deliberate, stemming from strong preconception that the moral and social-cognitive domains are fundamentally different. The work on developmental integration theory, however, has shown substantial similarities between the two domains. This outcome suggests that the stage approach has been misguided.

A deeper limitation is that Kohlberg's theory says nothing about how conflicting considerations in a moral dilemma are actually resolved. This central moral-social issue involves the twin problems of multiple determination and personal values, that is, of integration and valuation. Conflict *is* multiple determination; and each determinant must be evaluated within the moral system of the individual.

Neither problem is addressed by Kohlberg's theory. Kohlberg recognizes the importance of integration, for he speaks of justice as fairness in "balancing or weighing of conflicting claims" (Colby, et al, p. 7). The theory, however, includes no process whereby such balancing or weighing of conflicting claims may be accomplished.

Valuation could be accomplished by means of the stage principles. Thus, obeying an order commanding action contrary to law would be evaluated positively under the obedience principle, negatively under the law principle. But quantification of these values is necessary, and the theory says nothing about quantification. To speak of "balancing or weighing" says little in the absence of capability for measurement of moral values.

COOPERATIVE APPROACH

The cooperation advocated here is between analyses of information integration and of verbal reasoning, setting stage theory itself aside. Verbal reasoning, despite its cited failures, can be a valuable source of information. Kohlberg's system for classifying verbal reasoning may be useful in such cooperative work. Despite and because of their qualitative differences in method and data, combining the two approaches seems potentially fruitful.

Stage theory itself, in contrast to verbal reasoning, is probably a barren blind alley. The stage formulation is closed and bounded by a priori identification of moral judgment with verbal reasoning in terms of presumed principles of justice. This preconception has been welded into the conceptual framework and into the stage scoring system. If the stage assumption is false, little of this work will remain meaningful.

A great attraction of stage theory is its promise of conceptual simplification—the few basic stage principles would constitute the foundation of theory. Establishing such principles would be a major accomplishment. If they are not true, however, they cannot well be established.

Moral algebra cannot be established by verbal reasoning; subjects' explanations of their integrations typically have little relation to the rules revealed in the pattern of their integrated judgments. The sharpest example is the twofold failure in the work of Piaget and of Damon: Failing to find integration—and claiming to find nonintegration.

Cooperation could employ concatenation of the two methodologies. Subjects would begin by making a moral judgment in accord with usual procedure in IIT, following which an interview–reasoning method would be applied. Functional measurement could reveal the true effects of each stimulus informer. These measurements could serve as a validity criterion to assess the reasoning, as illustrated qualitatively here with Damon's study. Ideally, valid procedures for obtaining verbal protocols could be developed in this way.

Cooperative work requires development of tasks that allow both quantitative response and verbal response. Some revision of the interview questions and procedure would thus be needed. The methods could be combined directly by using a standard list of reasons and asking subjects to rate goodness of each, analogous to the procedure used by Rest (1983). This could also largely eliminate the confounding with verbal ability that troubles the interview method.

Problems of moral conflict resolution, that is, "balancing or weighing of conflicting claims," are amenable to moral algebra, as with fair shares distribution (see also Chapter 7). Tests of this rule with more severe dilemmas would be desirable. Success of the rule would allow functional measurement of the strengths of the competing claims. These measures could then provide validity criteria for self-reports of conflict dynamics.

The focus on moral dilemmas has obscured much of moral psychology, which is much broader than dilemmas. Indeed, morality is also much broader than moral judgment, which has been virtually the sole concern of the approaches of Piaget and of Kohlberg. In particular, moral algebra applies to moral feelings, or sentiments, which are prominent among the multitude of moral concepts noted below under *Everyday Morality*. Also, moral algebra applies to moral behavior, as in the foregoing study of fair shares division. In both respects, developmental integration theory goes beyond Piaget and Kohlberg. In addition, developmental integration theory is founded on experimental analysis, whereas Kohlberg's approach is founded on the interview method. In these three ways, an integration perspective can remove the straitjacket of stage theory, welcoming the rich diversity of the moral realm.

FUTURE WORK ON MORAL DEVELOPMENT

Two directions for future work on moral development are noted briefly here. The first concerns moral thought and action of everyday life. Despite scattered efforts by many workers, this domain has been relatively neglected amid the attempts to impose a stage conception on the phenomena. The search for a general conception of morality and moral development should begin by striking up an open-hearted acquaintance with moral thought and action in family, playground, work, sports, organizations, politics, and law.

The second direction looks to unification of moral cognition with general cognitive theory. Moral thought and action are inseparable from social thought and action, especially person cognition. Also inseparable are nonsocial concepts from judgment–decision theory, including probability, tradeoff, and cost–benefit analysis. In this respect, IIT differs from Kohlberg's theory, in particular, which sees moral judgment as qualitatively different from the rest of psychology. In the present view, the moral realm can be understood only through incorporation in a broader realm of cognition.

EVERYDAY MORALITY

Moral development takes place in everyday life, which furnishes a multitude of moral concepts that deserve investigation. Among the diverse determinants of moral thought and action are obligation, duty, need, motivation, intention, carelessness, foresight, culpa, extenuation, recompense, apology, remorse, penitence, and so on. These are not merely stimulus determinants; they represent moral-social concepts whose developmental course and cognitive structure require study. Some determinants, obligation and culpa, for example, figure among the moral judgments themselves, together with blame, responsibility, deserving, fair play, unfairness, punishment, reparation, justice, forgiveness, benevolence, and altruism, among others. Various moral motivations and affects, from shame and guilt to blaming and getting even, deserve similar analysis. These moral-social concepts operate as part of general social knowledge. One unifying theme is motivation, especially motivations involving ego maintenance and ego enhancement.

Contact with everyday life is tenuous in the stage approach to moral judgment. Many writers have complained that the standard moral dilemmas are artificial and unreal. These artificial dilemmas would no doubt reveal the underlying principles of moral reasoning—if the foundation stage assumption was correct. If a person's moral judgments were all organized by a single justice principle, as Kohlberg insists, this principle would manifest itself in almost any moral dilemma. But if this foundation assumption is not valid, reasoning about artificial dilemmas may have little relevance to moral cognition.

From the standpoint of developmental integration theory, children begin early to develop attitudes about right and wrong. This view seems consistent with many schools of developmental thought. These moral-social attitudes are knowledge systems that subserve thought and action within diverse situations and in relation to diverse goals. These attitudes contain primitive components from childhood that remain active in adult life. More abstract principles of justice are adjoined to these early attitudes, but they are not thereby wholly reorganized and restructured as stage theories require.

Moral education may also profit from focusing on everyday morality. An admirable aspect of Kohlberg's work was his active dedication to moral education, based on reflection about moral dilemmas. But reflection on the dilemma of Heinz and the drug seems largely meaningless and irrelevant for children and perhaps even for adults. Moral questions from family and peer group seem more appropriate. When is it right to ''tattle''? When is it OK to lie? When lying is wrong, how wrong is it under the circumstances? Why not take advantage of your siblings if you can? How honest should you be with your spouse? How can one recognize and deal with the many temptations to commit shabby acts, such as being mean or unfair, lying to save face, failing to give due credit, or shorting your obligation? These are the moral questions that children—and adults—face in everyday life. These everyday moral questions should form a base of moral education.

MORAL COGNITION

Moral cognition is an organic part of social cognition in the theory of information integration. Moral attitudes, considered as knowledge systems, are a primary locus of moral cognition. Honesty and fairness, for example, are not moral-personality traits, but knowledge systems that include major situation-specific components. This situational flexibility reflects a functional view, which sees moral development as learning–adaptation to the social world.

Person cognition is similarly interwoven with moral cognition. Judgment of right and wrong action ordinarily involves some judgment about an actor, whether another person, the gods, or one's self. Attribution of blame is just one example, and this typically involves a prior attribution of motive or intention.

Morality, it is true, consists substantially of obligations and prohibitions, enforced by such motivations as sense of duty, self-respect, feelings of right and wrong, fear, shame, guilt, and pride. But these motivations are not uniquely moral, nor do they seem essentially different from other social motivations. Rather, they point up a functional conception of morality as social motivation.

GENERAL MORAL THEORY

Information integration is central to moral theory. Conflict between obligations is conflict between informers; resolving such conflict requires information integration. The same applies to conflict between obligation and self-interest. Estimating the overall moral value of any proposed course of action also requires information integration.

Previous workers, philosophers as well as psychologists, have lacked a theoretical framework for analyzing information integration. This lack contrasts with the general reliance on moral dilemmas, which are perforce matters of information integration. As a consequence, the central issue of balancing conflicting claims could not be addressed in any serious way.

The importance of information integration has been recognized in occasional conjectures about moral algebra. The algebraic rule for fair shares suggested by Aristotle is a formula for balancing conflicting claims (see next chapter). This and other such conjectures remained conjectures, however, because of lack of theory and method for analysis of information integration.

Effective analysis of moral information integration has been illustrated with the blame schema and the fairness schema discussed in this chapter. The same approach applies to other problems in moral judgment. An early look at moral development is thus possible, at least as early as 4 years of age. Moral algebra also facilitates cross-age comparisons, as illustrated with the age-invariance of the fairness schema. It is thus useful for studying moral development, which is the foundation for moral psychology.

The present approach also unifies the moral realm with the general social realm. The results on moral cognition of this chapter are similar to those of the two preceding chapters on person cognition and social cognition, and they were obtained using the same concepts and methods. The issue of social comparison becomes central in fairness theory, which is elaborated in the next chapter. This extension is carried beyond the social realm in Chapter 10 on judgment–decision concepts, which are basic to evaluating net moral worth of alternative courses of action.[4]

Moral algebra is a beachhead on moral theory, with many opportunities. Moral dilemmas, for example, often require all-or-none choice, rather than graded compromise, which may elicit indecision processes not yet represented in algebraic models. Algebraic thinking may still be expected, however, in calculating the balance of good over evil in each choice alternative.

Moral theory is integral to general social theory. Morality is a great social evolution, ever continuing, which structures and shapes society and self in mutual interaction. Focus on individual cognition must take explicit account of society, especially family, school, and peer group, as carriers of morality. The present work, a very small step, is dedicated to this grand goal.

NOTES

This chapter is revised and shortened from Anderson (1991i), which includes extensive references and more detailed documentation of the conclusions.

1. The rating response has exceptional value for developmental analysis because it requires little verbal ability. Cross-age comparisons are thus largely unconfounded with verbal abilities, avoiding a severe problem with verbal protocols. This advantage is amplified by reliance on patterns of response as a basis for comparison. Pattern analysis made it possible to establish age-invariance of the cited rules of moral integration. Age-invariance, in turn, allows meaningful cross-age comparison of values. For the same reasons, this methodology should be useful for cross-cultural comparisons.

2. Rule similarity of mother and child has not been replicated in the careful thesis of Arlene Young (1990). Young's method was similar to Leon's, although using mildly different stories and children 4 years older.

Relative effect of damage and intent variables yielded wife−husband correlations of .5 in a study of marital communication (see Anderson, 1991g, pp. 214−218), This index of relative effect may be a more useful measure of parent−child similarity, for it applies even when all subjects follow the same integration rule.

3. Of special interest is conflict between self-interest and other-obligation. In principle, this could be handled in the same way as conflict between two other-obligations. Such conflict, however, underscores the issue of valuation, specifically, deciding how strong the other-obligation really is. Thus, the conflict may be reduced by conveniently deciding the other-obligation is not so strong after all.

4. Only a few applications of IIT have been made to social development outside the moral realm (see, e.g., Butzin & Dozier, 1986; Dixon & Moore, 1990; Dozier & Butzin, 1988; Singh, Sidana, & Srivastava, 1978). Developmental integration analyses of person cognition, attitudes, stereotypes, attributions, and roles present many opportunities.

PREFACE

The idea of moral algebra goes back to Aristotle's rule for fair shares, and was made a cornerstone of the utilitarian philosophy of Bentham and Mill. Everyday language, similarly, often refers to moral obligation in accounting terms. But moral algebra has been merely conjecture. Without capabilities for handling two basic problems of moral theory—multiple determination and measurement of personal value—moral algebra was untestable.

Moral algebra becomes testable with functional measurement theory. Moral algebra has received considerable empirical support in applications to blame and punishment, duty, and fairness–unfairness. This provides a base for unified theory of moral cognition.

Fairness–unfairness, the main concern of this chapter, is notable for its multiplicity of comparison processes. Even simple fairness judgments involve three different comparisons: between deserving of two persons; between their rewards; and between the two persons themselves. These comparison processes follow exact algebraic rules.

Aristotle's rule of fairness is psychologically correct in its comparison structure although incorrect in algebraic form. The most popular modern rule is incorrect in both respects. The decision averaging rule of the theory of information integration is correct in both respects.

Comparison structure is studied further in three extensions: to multiple dimensions of deserving; to multiple dimensions of reward; and to multiple comparison persons. These extensions also follow a moral algebra, although in unexpected ways. Beyond its moral significance, fairness–unfairness may be a useful area for general cognitive analysis of comparison processes.

Moral algebra brings science into ethics. Moral thought and action depend entirely on moral values. Ethical philosophy, barring prescriptive views of value, has a certain hollowness because it has lacked capability for value measurement. Moral algebra makes values measurable, thereby providing a new line of attack on ethics. Also, moral algebra can go beyond measurement of values to confer some measure of scientific substance on concepts of the good and the bad, such as duty, obligation, temptation, sin, shame, blame, punishment, atonement, and forgiveness.

Chapter 7

MORAL ALGEBRA

Moral cognition pervades everyday life: right and wrong, fairness and unfairness, blame, guilt, duty, and obligation. These and other moral concepts are woven into the structure of society and into the nature of the individual in society. Despite their importance, moral concepts have received relatively little experimental attention.

The utilitarian philosophers in the last century proposed moral arithmetic as a foundation for social and political theory. Two independent theses were involved. First, the morally best action is that which brings into being the greatest balance of good over evil. Second, good is defined in nonmoral terms of happiness or pleasure.

These two theses promised a simple, rational framework for a problematic domain. The first thesis implies that moral conflict and choice are in principle decidable by arithmetical calculation. The second thesis defines good in observable terms that all can appreciate—passing by interminable arguments about the nature of duty and right. Moreover, the utilitarian view seems more or less correct in many situations. Despite continued attacks for nearly two centuries, therefore, the utilitarian view has remained at the center of ethical theory. Currently, in fact, it enjoys renewed prosperity.

The main alternative to the utilitarian view revises the second thesis to define good in terms of duty and obligation, or similar moral concepts. Something like the first thesis is usually retained, however, so moral choice involves moral arithmetic. To give up the first thesis altogether would allow moral choices to be undecidable in principle, a view few philosophers have wished to accept.

The idea of moral arithmetic is very old. It appears in everyday language and action, as in obligations to repay social "debts," making the punishment "fit" the crime, getting "even," and so forth. An exact algebraic rule was suggested as early as Aristotle:

$$\frac{\text{Your Reward}}{\text{My Reward}} = \frac{\text{Your Work}}{\text{My Work}}. \qquad \text{(Aristotle's Fairness Formula)}$$

Do people actually think in this way? Is moral algebra psychologically real? The answer to both questions appears to be substantially *yes*. This chapter illustrates the operation of cognitive algebra in three moral domains. First, however, it is desirable to consider why empirical analysis of moral algebra has seldom been taken seriously.

OBJECTIONS TO MORAL ALGEBRA

One objection to moral algebra is that morality is in principle not quantifiable. This partial truth overlooks the ubiquity of quantitative judgments in everyday morality. Deserving and blame, for example, are commonly proportioned to the circumstances. Obligations vary in degree, as when we justify breaking a promise by adducing a greater obligation. No number captures the phenomenal feeling, to be sure, but that should not be expected with moral concepts any more than with other social concepts such as likableness or even with psychophysical concepts such as loudness or sweetness.

A second objection is that moral algebra is untestable speculation. This objection is correct—without capability for measurement of personal values. Suppose you and I are members of the same academic department, and I wish to test whether your mind obeys Aristotle's formula for fairness in the matter of promotion. I must put your personal values into Aristotle's formula. The values you place on *your work* and *my work*, especially our research, will surely differ from mine; but my values cannot explain your feelings. If I wish to test whether your mind follows Aristotle's formula, I should not be concerned whether your values are reasonable or justified. To test Aristotle's hypothesis, I must measure your personal values.

This measurement problem is fundamental. Unless it can be solved, moral algebra must remain verbal analogy, lacking analytical power.

This measurement problem can be solved. The solution lies in moral algebra itself. These moral equations provide the base and frame for measurement of moral values. This is just functional measurement. The validity of this approach in the moral realm has already been demonstrated with the blame and fairness schemas of the previous chapter. Buttressing evidence is given here, most notably an interlocking group of experiments on fairness–unfairness.

The third objection is based on the observation that values are not constant, but variable, being affected by temporary states of motivation or stress. Rightly appreciated, this nonconstancy of values is not an objection, but rather a strong argument for the importance of moral algebra.

Nonconstancy of values is a basic fact of human nature. A child is more likely to swipe a candy bar when hungry than when full. Deception and lying are more likely when one is liable to shame or blame. An extramarital affair is more likely at age 40 than 60. Moral theory cannot ignore temptation, in particular, which involves temporary motivational states.

How to handle nonconstant values is a central problem in cognitive analysis. This problem can be handled under certain conditions with IIT. A key to value analysis lies in the finding of independence of valuation and integration discussed in Chapter 1. Because of this independence, nonconstancy of values has no necessary connection to integration. It is no criticism of the averaging rule, therefore, to say that values vary with motivation or that weights depend on attention. On the contrary, the averaging rule provides a means for determining such functional values and weights.

HARM AND RECOMPENSE

The nature of right action has been much discussed, as has the problem of punishment for wrong actions. Relatively neglected is the issue of amelioration of harmful actions. Yet recompense and atonement are basic to social morality. This issue of recompense has been a major concern of Wilfried Hommers.

> The moral rule not to do harm has a corollary moral rule to undo harm that is done. This moral rule of undoing harm is well recognized in everyday life. A child who dirties some object may be required to clean it. A person who insults another may be required to apologize. In married couples, recompense in the forms of gifts or soft words is often part of "making up" for distressful acts. So ubiquitous is this moral rule of recompense that at least one philosopher has elevated it to a prima facie duty.
>
> In law, too, recompense has a basic role. In civil law, the court may impose some form of reparation for breach of contract or for certain classes of property damage or personal injury. In criminal law, the judge may impose reparation as part of the sentence. A more general outlook on reparation appears in the social doctrine that offenders must "pay their debt to society."
>
> Despite its moral importance, recompense has received little attention from psychologists. One difficulty in studying recompense is that it usually involves other moral variables. Recompense ordinarily involves reference to the harm for which recompense is made, and evaluation of harm may require taking culpability into account. Various kinds of mitigating circumstances may also be relevant. Hence the study of recompense cannot get very far without capability for handling multiple determination. (Hommers & Anderson, 1991, p. 101.)

EXTENDED BLAME SCHEMA

The purpose of the experiments considered here was to extend the blame schema of Chapter 6 to include the variable of recompense. This extended blame schema may be written:

Punishment = Culpa + Damage − Recompense.

Adult subjects were told stories about two stamp collectors, one of whom ruined some stamps belonging to the other. They were told to imagine they were the victim and to say how much the offender should be punished. The main set of stories specified three informers: culpa (motive), damage, and recompense. Auxiliary stories specified only two of the three informers.

In the left panel of Figure 7.1, the two dashed curves show the culpa–damage integration pattern for stories that specified only these two informers; the parallelism supports the blame schema:

Punishment = Culpa + Damage.

The two solid curves show the culpa–damage integration pattern for the stories that specified all three informers; these data are averaged over the third variable

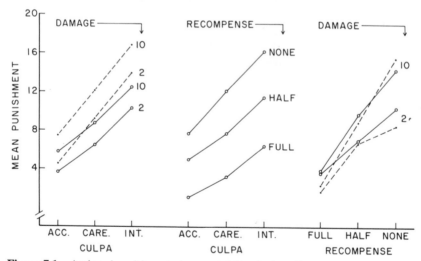

Figure 7.1. Assigned punishment obeys cognitive algebra. Three determinants—culpa, damage, and recompense—are integrated by the averaging rule of IIT. Each panel gives factorial graph for one pair of the moral variables, listed as curve parameter and on horizontal axis. Solid curves for three-factor design; dashed curves for two-factor designs. (ACC. = accidental; CARE. = careless; INT. = intentional; None, Half, and Full mean that none, half, and all of the 2 or 10 damaged stamps were replaced. (From Hommers & Anderson, 1991, Experiment 1.)

of recompense. These solid curves are lower than the dashed curves because recompense lowers judged punishment. The main point, however, is that these solid curves are also parallel.

By virtue of the parallelism theorem, these two sets of parallel curves support the averaging rule for culpa and damage. This confirms and extends the blame schema of Chapter 6, showing that it continues to hold when the third variable of recompense is included.

The integration of recompense and culpa is shown in the center panel of Figure 7.1. These curves are nonparallel. They exhibit a divergence pattern that is expected from an averaging rule in which full recompense has greater weight than half or no recompense. Analogous divergence can be seen for the recompense–damage integration in the right panel. Both integrations are thus consistent with averaging theory with differential weighting of recompense.

An alternative interpretation must also be considered. This divergence pattern could be produced if recompense had a multiplication effect, reducing the assigned punishment in proportion to the amount of recompense.

Averaging is supported over multiplication by comparison of the dashed and solid curves of the right panel. Whereas the dashed curves represent judgments based on only the two informers, damage and recompense, the solid curves are averaged over the third variable of culpa. The multiplication rule requires that the solid curves, having lesser slope, should also have lower elevation, whereas the opposite is true. The multiplication rule also has difficulty in accounting for the crossover of the solid curves by the dashed curve. The averaging rule, in contrast, agrees with all aspects of the data.

In short, the results confirm and extend the basic blame schema. All three moral variables are integrated by averaging. The recompense variable, however, has a greater weight parameter for higher levels of recompense. Similar results have been obtained with children; the integration rule appears to be age-invariant down to 4 years.

PARADOXICAL EFFECT OF RECOMPENSE

Recompense had a paradoxically large effect, much larger than the damage for which the recompense was given. The main effect of damage is shown by the vertical separation between the paired curves in the left panel of Figure 7.1; the main effect of recompense is shown by the vertical separation of the curves in the center panel. As can be seen, the recompense effect is several times larger than the effect of the damage for which the recompense was given.

The paradoxical effect of recompense may derive from a biological base of submission reactions, common in mammalian interaction. Mere apology can have substantial effects, even without any actual reparation, as though it betokened a submission reaction. Even when the apology is only formal courtesy, it still reflects deference to the other person. This interpretation seems consistent with developmental studies, in which young children have shown even larger effects of recompense than adults.[1]

CONCEPT OF SCHEMA

The present results extend the schema formulation of the previous chapter. However, they argue against the standard conception of schemas in terms of slot-and-default value discussed in Chapter 1. The evidence comes from a further experiment, which included stories that specified only recompense. Logically, recompense cannot occur in the absence of damage. On a rational basis, therefore, subjects could not make a judgment without some imputation about the unspecified damage variable. The damage variable corresponds to a slot and it should have a default value, to be used as the imputation.

The data, however, showed little or no such imputation; damage did not have a default value, even though one was readily available from the experimental context. Instead, it appeared that subjects attached a moral value to recompense, and made a judgment on that basis.

Moral schemas are important in everyday life, as illustrated with the blame and fairness schemas of the previous chapter. These moral schemas help organize possibly complex stimulus fields to provide ready action. The present results support and extend the conception of a general algebra of moral schemas.

DUTY

Concepts of duty and obligation are common in moral thinking, but they have been little studied experimentally. This section presents a preliminary study of duty–need integration done in collaboration with John Verdi. In addition, a theoretical model is presented for conflict of obligation.

DUTY–NEED SCHEMA

The operation of duty depends on need. With kinship relations, duties may be *latent*, only activated by need. Our duty to help a parent entails no action unless help is needed. Keeping promises, on the other hand, is a *self-sufficient duty*, being operative regardless of need. Yet breaking the promise may be somewhat excusable, even warranted, if the actor's need is pressing and the other's need is not. In both cases, other's need seems to amplify the duty. Actor's need, in contrast, represents a counter force.

How duty and need are integrated is thus a basic issue in moral conflict. The present experiments concern an actor who fails a duty to another person; subjects judged badness of this failure of duty. Two specific integration problems are of concern, which may be symbolized thus:

Blame = Other's Need ⊛ Actor's Need;

Blame = Other's Need ⊛ Actor's Duty;

where ⊛ represents a general integration rule.

A subtraction rule is plausible for the first, need–need integration: Actor's need extenuates the failure of duty. High actor's need might even overbalance duty to yield a net goodness for failing a weak duty. It was a theoretical question, however, whether extenuation would obey a strict subtraction rule, a subtractive-averaging rule, or no exact rule at all.

A multiplication rule is plausible for the second, duty–need integration, at least with latent duties such as kinship. Not helping your mother is not blamable if she is not in need; zero need would multiply a nonzero duty to produce zero blame. Subjects, however, sometimes exhibit adding-type rules in analogous tasks, as in judgments of gratitude. Thus, the theoretical question was whether this duty–need integration obeyed a multiplication rule, an adding-type rule, or no exact rule at all.

To study these two integration questions, subjects were given brief paragraphs about an actor who was under some specified duty to help another, but failed to do so. They judged the badness of this failure of duty. Three variables were manipulated in factorial design: two levels of duty; three levels of other's need; and three levels of actor's need. To define duty and need in pure form, the instructions emphasized that the duty was undertaken willingly, that it was failed intentionally, and that both parties were aware of each other's need at the time of the failure of duty.

The first experiment studied the duty of fidelity: Under high duty, the actor had borrowed money from the other with a promise to repay it at a specified time; under low duty, the actor had promised to lend money to the other at a specified time. The second experiment replicated this fidelity condition and included similar designs with two additional duties: kinship and gratitude for past help. All conditions yielded similar patterns of results, so the pooled data are presented here.

The main results may be summarized simply. Actor's need and other's need are averaged to determine the moral judgment. Actor's duty, in contrast, is added to other's need. Moreover, actor's need, which may be considered a form of extenuation, has disproportionately large effects.

This disproportionate effect of extenuation may be seen in the left panel of Figure 7.2. The response scale on the vertical axis is oriented so that 0 is most bad, higher numbers indicating less bad actions. Thus, the upward sweep of the curves shows that the action is judged less bad when the actor's need is higher (horizontal axis). The vertical separation among the curves shows that the action is rated as less bad for lower levels of other's need (curve parameter). The main concern, however, is with the patterns in the data.

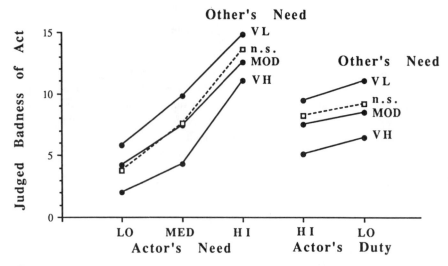

Figure 7.2. Judged badness of failure of duty obeys cognitive algebra. (0 = most bad; higher numbers indicate less badness. Levels of Other's Need denoted by VL (Very Low), MOD (Medium), and VH (Very High); n.s. denotes need not specified.) Similar results were obtained across two experiments and three duty conditions; overall mean data are presented here. (From Verdi, 1979; Anderson & Verdi, 1984.)

In magnitude, the upward sweep is about twice the vertical separation. Thus, actor's need has a little over twice the effect of other's need. This is surprising because the ostensible range for actor's need was less than for other's need (Low to High versus Very Low to Very High). Moreover, the actor was always at fault, so it seems hardly just that his need should be more important than the need of the other. This result, however, seems consistent with the paradoxical effect of recompense noted in the discussion of Figure 7.1.

An averaging rule is used to integrate the two needs, of actor and other. The pattern in the factorial graph in the left panel of Figure 7.2 allows an easy diagnosis. First, the near-parallelism of the three solid curves implies that actor's need and other's need are integrated by an adding-type rule. Second, this adding-type rule is actually averaging, not adding. This rule diagnosis is given by the crossover of the dashed curve (other's need not specified) and the middle solid curve. Such crossover is the sign of an averaging process, in accord with the logic of Figure 2.4.

Duty–need integration, in contrast, follows an addition rule, as indicated in the right panel of Figure 7.2. The hypothesized multiplication rule implies that the data should exhibit the pattern of a linear fan, diverging to the right. In fact, the pattern is one of near-parallelism, which infirms the multiplication rule.

The near-parallelism of the solid curves in this panel is consistent with both adding and averaging. The dashed curve corresponds to cases in which no duty information was specified; it also falls into the parallelism pattern; the crossover in the left panel does not reappear in the right panel. Essentially the same pattern appeared in each separate duty condition. This result suggests, therefore, that other's need is added to actor's duty. This finding has special interest since addition rules have been infrequent; most adding-type rules have turned out to involve averaging rather than adding per se.

CONFLICT OF OBLIGATION

One prototypical moral dilemma involves conflict between two obligations. Compromise is possible in some cases, and this compromise may obey a general averaging theorem.

To illustrate, consider a working mother in conflict between spending time with her infant child and with an older stepchild. For simplicity, it is assumed that she has a fixed amount of time to allocate between them and that each child needs the full time. Her felt obligation to child i, denoted by O_i, will depend the child's age, health, personal appeal, and so forth. According to the decision averaging rule of Equation 5b of Chapter 2, the proportion of time allocated to child i will be the relative ratio:

$$\frac{O_i}{O_1 + O_2}.$$

In words, time is allocated in proportion to the felt obligations.

This decision averaging rule has done well with fair division of pay, discussed in the following sections. No tests have been made of compromise in moral dilemmas. Intuitively, proportional allocation seems reasonable, if not rational, but experimental analysis is needed.

Some moral dilemmas do not allow compromise. If one duty is fulfilled, the other must be failed. Rationally, the choice seems straightforward. Fulfilling one given duty entails good consequences while failing the other entails bad consequences. The moral sum of these two consequences is the net moral value of fulfilling the given duty. The rational choice is then the greater good or lesser evil. This prescription is just the first utilitarian thesis mentioned earlier. Whether people do evaluate moral choices in this way, however, remains unknown.[2]

Temptation must also be considered in any moral theory, philosophical as well as psychological. Duty–temptation compromise may be expected to follow a similar relative ratio rule: Temptation/(Temptation + Duty). The badness of yielding to temptation, on the other hand, might be expected to follow a subtraction rule involving the moral value of the duty and any extenuating value of the temptation. Here again, nothing seems known about moral algebra.

FAIRNESS AND SOCIAL COMPARISON

Fairness is relative. Adverse conditions may be endured cheerfully if others are treated the same. But strong feelings of unfairness and resentment may accompany even substantial rewards if another is seen as getting more for less.

Comparison processes are thus central to fairness theory. Actually, three different comparison processes require consideration. One is personal: comparison between two or more persons, or between person and some social standard. The other two refer to *input*, what each person contributes, and to *outcome*, what each person receives. The structure of fairness judgments resides in these three kinds of comparisons, studied impressively by Arthur Farkas.

THREE MODELS OF FAIRNESS

Consider two persons, A and B, in a social situation to which a fairness constraint applies. The symbols I and O will denote input and outcome, respectively, with A and B as personal subscripts. By far the most popular current model of fairness has been that of Adams (1965), which defines the state of fairness by the formula:

$$\frac{O_A}{I_A} = \frac{O_B}{I_B}. \qquad \text{(Adams' Model)} \qquad (1a)$$

The O/I ratio may be viewed as a rate of pay, either hourly or piece-rate. Persons A and B are fairly treated, other things being equal, when both have the same rate of pay. Work that requires greater skill or involves greater risk represents higher input, and so deserves higher outcome. The ratio should stay the same, however, to maintain fairness. This rate of pay conception reflects Adams' concern with industrial applications.[3]

Another fairness model had been formalized more than two thousand years earlier. According to Aristotle, the fair state of affairs is defined by the following formula:

$$\frac{O_A}{O_B} = \frac{I_A}{I_B}. \qquad \text{(Aristotle's Model)} \qquad (1b)$$

In words, the ratio of outcomes for the two persons should equal the ratio of their inputs.

These two models differ in their comparison structure. Adams requires initial within-person comparisons of O to I separately for person A and person B; these within-person comparisons are followed by a between-person comparison of the two ratios. Aristotle prescribes the reverse order: two initial between-person comparisons—one for O, one for I—followed by comparison of these two ratios.

Which model seems more plausible? Adams' model makes good sense when O/I is a rate of pay. But suppose that I is seniority and O is number of weeks vacation. These two hardly seem comparable; it is unclear how one could quantify vacation time and seniority in the comparable terms needed to take their ratio. Aristotle's model avoids this difficulty since both ratios in Equation 1b involve comparable terms.

Actually, the two models are algebraically equivalent. If Aristotle's model is cross multiplied by O_B/I_A, it becomes Adams' model. Despite the difference in their psychological comparison structure, the two models are not empirically distinguishable.

The third and final model was obtained from decision averaging theory, Equation 5b of Chapter 2. This model defines the fair state of affairs according to the formula:

$$\frac{O_A}{O_A + O_B} = \frac{I_A}{I_A + I_B}. \qquad \text{(Averaging Model)} \qquad (1c)$$

The comparison structure of this model is like that of Aristotle's: Initial between-person comparisons are required for both ratios, of outcome on the left and of input on the right. These two ratios are relative, however, rather than direct as in Aristotle's model. Both denominators in Equation 1c are group totals. This feature of the averaging model makes explicit that the idea of fairness rests on a social constraint of group belongingness.

It is easy to see, however, that this averaging model itself is algebraically equivalent to the other two models. Some new approach is needed to diagnose the comparison structure of fairness. This new approach involves a conceptual shift—from fairness to unfairness.

THREE MODELS OF UNFAIRNESS

Fairness refers to an ideal state that is seldom attained. Most situations contain more or less unfairness, which is a primary motivation of everyday life. Moral theory thus needs to shift away from previous focus on fairness to give first place to analysis of unfairness.

An unfairness model may be generated from each fairness model by taking the difference between the two ratios. The larger this difference, the greater the unfairness. Provisionally, unfairness is taken proportional to the difference, an assumption justified by the empirical results.

In this way, each fairness model may be transformed into an unfairness model. These three unfairness models are listed in the following table, together with their predictions about which factorial graphs will exhibit nonparallelism. As written, a positive difference represents unfairness to person A. The decision averaging model for unfairness yields a positive difference when A's relative outcome, $O_A/(O_A + O_B)$, is less than A's relative input, $I_A/(I_A + I_B)$.

TABLE 7.1

THREE MODELS OF INTERPERSONAL UNFAIRNESS

Model	Algebraic form	Nonparallel graphs	Shape
2a	$\dfrac{O_B}{I_B} - \dfrac{O_A}{I_A}$	$I_B \times O_B,\ I_A \times O_A$	Fan
2b	$\dfrac{I_A}{I_B} - \dfrac{O_A}{O_B}$	$I_A \times I_B,\ O_A \times O_B$	Fan
2c	$\dfrac{I_A}{I_A + I_B} - \dfrac{O_A}{O_A + O_B}$	$I_A \times I_B,\ O_A \times O_B$	Barrel

NOTE: From N. H. Anderson and A. J. Farkas, 1975, "Integration theory applied to models of inequity," *Personaliy and Social Psychology Bulletin*, 1, 588-591. Copyright 1975 by Sage Publications. Reprinted by permission.

These three unfairness models, in contrast to the fairness models, are not algebraically equivalent. They predict different data patterns. To illustrate, consider the factorial graph for O_A and O_B. These two variables are separated by a minus sign in Model 2a, which corresponds to an additive integration. By the parallelism theorem, therefore, their factorial graph should be a set of parallel curves.

In Model 2b, however, O_A and O_B are separated by a division sign, which corresponds to a ratio rule of integration. By the linear fan theorem, their factorial graph should have the pattern of a linear fan. In Model 2c, O_A and O_B are integrated by a relative ratio rule. This relative ratio rule generates a barrel-shaped factorial graph.

Altogether there are six pairs of variables, and each pair may be analyzed in the same way as just illustrated with O_A and O_B. Each model thus predicts the patterns for six two-way factorial graphs. Four of these graphs are parallel for each model and two are nonparallel, as listed in Table 7.1. These predictions about data patterns provide strong tests between the three unfairness models. Hardly more is needed than to do the experiment and plot the graphs—they will speak out and say which, if any, of the three models is correct.

One empirical comparison of the unfairness models is summarized in Figure 7.3. Each panel shows the factorial graph for one pair of variables. Model 2a does badly. It predicts that the two left panels will be parallel, whereas they exhibit a pronounced barrel shape. It also predicts that the two right panels will be linear fans, diverging toward the right. These two panels do show a small divergence, but in the wrong direction.

Model 2b, derived from Aristotle's model for fairness, does reasonably well. It predicts parallelism in the two center and two right panels, all of which show near-parallelism. It also predicts nonparallelism in the two left panels. These

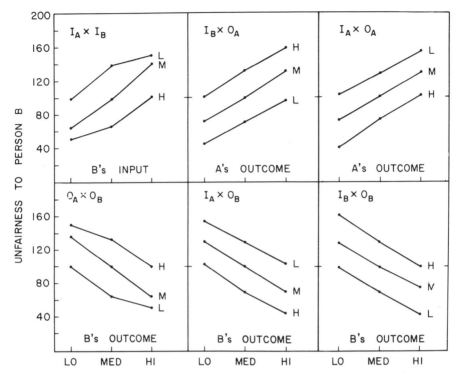

Figure 7.3. Judgments of unfairness obey cognitive algebra. Factorial data patterns support decision averaging rule of IIT, disagree with rules proposed by Aristotle and by Adams (see discussion of Table 7.1). (From Anderson & Farkas, 1975.)

do show nonparallelism, although the observed barrel pattern disagrees with the predicted linear fan.

Model 2c, derived from IIT, provides a complete account of the pattern of Figure 7.3. Like Aristotle's model, it predicts parallelism in the four panels that show parallelism, Like Aristotle's model, it predicts nonparallelism in the two panels that show nonparallelism. Unlike Aristotle's model, it correctly predicts the pattern of nonparallelism that was actually obtained. Virtually identical results were obtained in a second experiment, using alcoholic patients in a VA hospital as subjects.

Three different comparison operations are required in fairness–unfairness theory, as already indicated. The foregoing experiment was the first to determine their structure. Despite its popularity, Adams' model was qualitatively wrong in its psychological comparison structure. Aristotle was the better psychologist, for he was qualitatively correct about the comparison structure. The averaging model improved on Aristotle in its mathematical form.

It is remarkable, of course, that any algebraic model holds. The models suggested by Aristotle and Adams were armchair models, lacking serious empirical foundation. Empirical assessment was not possible without capability for psychological measurement. All three models could well have failed the present functional measurement tests. Even this negative outcome would have been a significant advance over previous conjecture. The positive outcome is not only good in itself, but it provided a new foundation for analysis of moral cognition. Indeed, it provided a general method for studying comparison processes, a method applicable also outside the moral domain.

This success of decision averaging theory was extended in a trenchant sequence of experiments by Farkas (1977, 1991), who considered several other aspects of social comparison. Farkas' experiments, discussed in the next several sections, provide impressive support for a general cognitive algebra of fairness–unfairness. In these experiments, as it happened, virtually all previous conjectures turned out to be wrong.

COMPARISON STRUCTURE OF INPUT PROCESSING: FAIRNESS INTEGRATION VERSUS INPUT INTEGRATION

The problem considered in this section arises from the multidimensional character of input. In the preceding models, input was taken as one-dimensional, denoted by I. Often, however, a person's input has more than one dimension. Students, for example, may be graded not only on their exam performance, but also on how hard they tried. Faculty members may be evaluated for promotion not only on research, but also on teaching. Wives and husbands have multiple roles: companion, sex-partner, parent, money functions, and so on, each of which can be considered a dimension of input to their spouse. In general, as in these examples, fairness will depend on several dimensions of input.

A new comparison problem is raised by this multidimensional nature of input. The precept of fairness states that outcome should be proportional to input. But how can a one-dimensional outcome be proportional to a multidimensional input?

A natural answer is to assume a one-dimensional mediator: All relevant input dimensions are integrated to obtain a single overall value of input. Under this hypothesis of *input integration*, the multiple stimulus field is reduced to a single value on an overall input dimension.

Input integration, however, requires that all determinants be reduced to common currency. The different input dimensions have to be compared and expressed in common units. But some input dimensions seem hard to compare. Research and teaching, for example, are rather different in quality. The same holds for sex, parenting, and money in marriage. Without some means to handle the comparison problem, integrating these disparate dimensions seems like adding apples and soup.

An alternative hypothesis of *fairness integration* is also possible: Each input dimension is processed separately to determine a partial value of fairness. These partial fairness values are then integrated to determine overall fairness. In this mode of processing, both steps involve only comparable qualities.

Input integration and fairness integration involve different comparison processes. These comparison processes appear in the algebraic structure of the fairness models. To illustrate, consider the two input dimensions of performance and effort. Let P_A and P_B denote performance for A and B, and let E_A and E_B denote effort for A and B. Under the hypothesis of input integration, the first processing operation consists of integrating performance and effort to get a single overall input: $I_A = P_A + E_A$ and $I_B = P_B + E_B$. With a total amount T to be divided, therefore, the rule of input integration implies that the fair share for A will be:

$$O_A = \frac{I_A}{I_A + I_B} T = \frac{P_A + E_A}{(P_A + E_A) + (P_B + E_B)} T. \tag{2}$$

Under the alternative hypothesis of fairness integration, separate fairness ratios are calculated for P and E and these are weighted and added:

$$O_A = \omega_P \left[\frac{P_A}{P_A + P_B} \right] T + \omega_E \left[\frac{E_A}{E_A + E_B} \right] T. \tag{3}$$

Quite different data patterns are implied by these two hypotheses. Fairness integration, Equation 3, implies that P_A and E_A combine additively because they are separated by a plus sign. Input integration, Equation 2, in contrast, implies nonadditive combination. Hence the factorial $P_A \times E_A$ graph should be parallel if the hypothesis of fairness integration is correct, nonparallel if the hypothesis of input integration is correct. In fact, input integration implies nonparallelism in all six two-factor graphs. Fairness integration, in contrast, predicts data patterns like those already seen in the six panels of Figure 7.3.

The hypothesis of fairness integration received excellent support, visible in the upper layer of Figure 7.4. The two left panels show barrel shapes, as predicted by the hypothesis of fairness integration. The remaining four panels show near-parallelism, again as predicted. Very similar patterns were obtained in a second experiment, shown in the lower layer of the figure. The hypothesis of input integration thus failed, whereas the hypothesis of fairness integration gave a remarkably precise account of the data patterns.

The hypothesis of input integration had generally been taken for granted in social and industrial psychology, as well as in utilitarian philosophy. It is rational, to be sure, but it is not psychologically correct. There is a moral algebra, but it has a different structure.

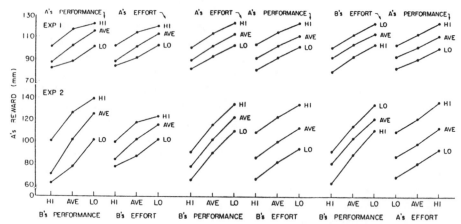

Figure 7.4. Social comparison for fair reward obeys cognitive algebra. Factorial data patterns support decision averaging rule, with separate calculation of fair reward for each of two input dimensions, Performance and Effort. Barrel shape of the two left panels and parallelism of four right panels agree exactly with theoretical prediction. (From A. J. Farkas & N. H. Anderson, 1979, "Multidimensional input in equity theory," *Journal of Personality and Social Psychology, 37,* 879-896. Copyright 1979 by the American Psychological Association. Reprinted by permission.)

The rule of fairness integration may only hold when the dimensions of input are qualitatively heterogeneous, as with effort and performance. In another experimental condition, the two input dimensions were qualitatively homogeneous (performance at two different times). The rule of input integration was anticipated, since two homogeneous dimensions seem readily integrable. These data did not agree with input integration, however, and also showed small but worrisome discrepancies from fairness integration. In fact, a four-factor addition–subtraction model described these data fairly well. This may reflect the operation of the general purpose addition process.[4]

CONFIGURAL EFFECT IN INPUT PROCESSING

One interesting complication also deserves mention, for it illustrates the analytical power of cognitive algebra. A configural effect was found in the foregoing study: Each input dimension had less influence when A and B were equal on that dimension. In terms of Equation 3, the weight parameter, ω_P, had two values, the lower applying when $P_A = P_B$, the higher applying when $P_A \neq P_B$. Similarly, ω_E would be lower when $E_A = E_B$, higher when $E_A \neq E_B$.

This configural effect cancels out in the two-factor graphs of Figure 7.4 because of the symmetry in the design. Instead, it appears in the three-factor graphs, one of which is presented in the upper half of Figure 7.5. All three

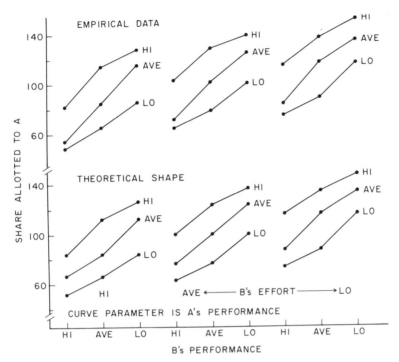

Figure 7.5. Judgments of fair shares obey decision averaging model of IIT. Theoretical patterns (lower panels) are exactly mirrored in observed judgments (upper panels). Every nuance in the theoretical patterns is visible in the data. (From A. J. Farkas & N. H. Anderson, 1979, "Multidimensional input in equity theory," *Journal of Personality and Social Psychology*, *37*, 879-896. Copyright 1979 by the American Psychological Association. Reprinted by permission.)

panels show the same basic shape: a slanted barrel with a middle curve of greater slope. This is the pattern of the basic ratio model. But closer inspection shows systematic differences among the three panels. In the left panel, the top curve is bowed, whereas the bottom curve is nearly straight. The right panel shows the complementary pattern; the top curve is nearly straight, whereas the bottom curve is bowed. Although these differences among the three panels are not large, they are reliable—and meaningful.

This configurality interpretation was assessed by estimating separate values for the weight parameters according as A and B were equal or unequal. The theoretical predictions are shown in the bottom half of Figure 7.5. Each theoretical panel is virtually identical to the empirical panel just above. This configural model fits the data remarkably well.

The configural effect reflects greater effect for a dimension of difference, as though the subject was partly cancelling the dimension of no difference. Early development of this configural effect with children was noted in the previous chapter, and a similar configural effect was found in the unfairness study of Figure 7.3 (see Anderson, 1991e). This configurality thus seems fairly general.

These results also illustrate how meaning can be drawn from relatively minor features of the data with functional measurement. This methodology may help study analogous configural effects conjectured in other domains.

UNFAIRNESS PARADOX IN OUTCOME PROCESSING

Outcomes typically have multiple dimensions: Job performance is rewarded not only with money, but also with job security, vacation time, fringe benefits, working conditions, and status symbols. Job satisfaction will accordingly depend on how individual workers evaluate and integrate diverse outcome dimensions. The same principle applies to satisfaction in other social roles, such as marriage and friendship, which also have multiple determinants.

An unfairness paradox will illustrate the social importance of outcome processing: Two persons may both feel unfairly treated by what both would consider objectively fair treatment. Suppose that 10 units of each of two outcome dimensions, X and Y, are to be shared between A and B, who are assumed to have equal input and identical personal values. Each would, accordingly, feel fairly treated with a $5X:5Y$ distribution on the two outcome dimensions.

It is also assumed, for simplicity, that A and B place equal value on each unit of X and Y. Thus, A will be just as happy with 8 units of X and 2 units of Y as with 5 units of each, and similarly for B.

Suppose then that A receives an $8X:2Y$ distribution, with B receiving the complementary $2X:8Y$ distribution. By assumption, A considers the $8X:2Y$ distribution just as good as the equitable $5X:5Y$ distribution, and similarly for B. Hence it would seem that A and B will both feel fairly treated.

But this conclusion depends on an implicit assumption, namely, that A and B integrate the two outcome dimensions to obtain a unitary value of outcome. The conclusion depends entirely on this assumption of *outcome integration*.

The alternative assumption, *unfairness integration*, is that A calculates a value of unfairness separately for each outcome dimension and integrates these two unfairness values. Since A's overpayment of 3 units of X equals the underpayment of 3 units of Y, they might be expected to cancel. But over- and underpayment differ psychologically. The feeling of resentment engendered by underpayment has no counterpart with overpayment. Accordingly, overpayment and underpayment should not be expected to cancel. Hence A will feel unfairly treated—and so will B. Under this alternative assumption about social comparison processing, therefore, a situation that is objectively fair, even in the values of the two persons themselves, can generate strong feelings of unfairness.

This theoretical implication has not been tested directly, but it is in line with the results of the next section.

COMPARISON STRUCTURE OF OUTCOME PROCESSING: UNFAIRNESS INTEGRATION VERSUS OUTCOME INTEGRATION

The two foregoing hypotheses, outcome integration and unfairness integration, differ in their comparison structure. They can be distinguished, accordingly, by applying the same functional measurement analysis that was illustrated in the previous section on input processing.

For Farkas' experimental study, let D and V denote the outcome dimensions of dollars pay and vacation time, respectively. Also, let U_A denote unfairness to person A, represented by positive numbers. With a single input dimension, I, the model for *outcome integration* may be written:

$$U_A = \frac{I_A}{I_A + I_B} - \frac{(D_A + V_A)}{(D_A + V_A) + (D_B + V_B)}. \qquad (4)$$

Unfairness to A is thus the difference between the relative input and the relative outcome of A, which are given by the two respective terms on the right side of this equation.

According to the alternative model of *unfairness integration*, a separate value of unfairness is calculated for each outcome dimension. Total unfairness is then the sum of these two partial unfairness values:

$$U_A = \left[\frac{I_A}{I_A + I_B} - \frac{D_A}{D_A + D_B} \right] + \left[\frac{I_A}{I_A + I_B} - \frac{V_A}{V_A + V_B} \right]. \qquad (5)$$

These two models of outcome processing may be distinguished through their additivity structure. Unfairness integration predicts additivity of D_A and V_A, for example, whereas outcome integration predicts nonadditivity.

Farkas' experimental data eliminated the hypothesis of outcome integration and showed excellent agreement with the hypothesis of unfairness integration. Subjects made separate comparisons on each outcome dimension, in line with the foregoing result on input processing.

Outcome integration has commonly been assumed in industrial applications. It is also a frequent assumption in judgment–decision theory and in utilitarian ethics. It rests, however, on the assumption that disparate quantities can be and are added together.

Outcome integration is reasonable and rational, but it seems to be false. This is unfortunate because it implies that the foregoing unfairness paradox is socially real. Social cognition appears to have a built-in bias toward feelings of unfairness in society.

INPUT–OUTCOME LINKAGE

Still another comparison problem arises when input and outcome are both multidimensional: Specific input and outcome dimensions may be linked. In the study of Figure 7.6, subjects made separate divisions of money and praise between two persons, characterized by performance and effort on a common task. Money division was expected to be more strongly linked to performance, praise division to effort.

These expectations about input–outcome linkage were confirmed. In the left panel of the figure, the curves labeled M and P represent money and praise assigned to person A as a function of A's performance. The steeper slope of curve M shows that performance had greater weight in the division of money than praise. The complementary pattern appears in the right panel; here the steeper slope for curve P shows that effort had greater weight in the division of praise.

Input–outcome linkage can be quantified. In fact, the weights are proportional to the slopes of the curves. From Figure 7.6, it can thus be seen that performance was almost five times more important than effort in money division, whereas effort was almost three times more important than performance in praise division. Such linkage quantification can be important in general theory of social reinforcement.

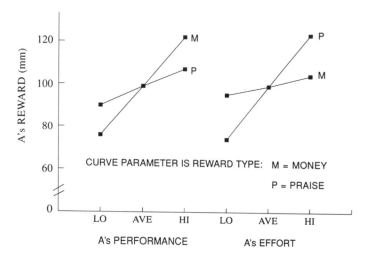

Figure 7.6. Input-outcome linkage in fair shares judgment. Reward for person A is either money (curves labeled M) or praise (curves labeled P). Left panel shows that performance is rewarded more with money than praise; right panel shows that effort is rewarded more with praise than money. (After Farkas, 1991.)

In addition, detailed analysis of the complete design showed excellent support for the hypothesis of fairness integration. For this design, fairness integration predicts a set of curve patterns similar to that of Figure 7.3. This predicted pattern was obtained.

Input–outcome linkage is an important social mechanism for increasing the general level of satisfaction. The person who tries hard but accomplishes little can still feel compensated with a greater share of praise. This principle extends far beyond the variable of praise itself. The present experiment, of course, only shows a social norm for this kind of division. This social norm needs to be translated into social action. Some translation can be seen in child rearing practices, with children being praised for trying, and in "employee-of-the-month" programs in business. More effective translation would be desirable, for example, by teaching habits of praising others in school and at home. More praise and less blame is a recipe for improving society.

Related social mechanisms concern weighting and valuation of outcomes. In team dynamics, one function of the coach is to weight less glamorous jobs upward by showing how they are essential for team functioning. Dynamic weighting may also occur at a personal level. In the foregoing example, persons who tried hard but accomplished little could amplify their satisfaction by raising the weight for praise and effort in their own mind. Such weighting may be expected generally from ego support processes, of which the "sour grapes" and "sweet lemon" reactions are classic if extreme examples. This ego support mechanism can be pushed further by favorable personal valuation of one's own contributions and/or corresponding denigration of others'. The measurement problems involved in verifying these mechanisms are complex, however, and little definite is known.

MULTIPLE COMPARISON PERSONS

Only two persons have been considered in the foregoing comparisons. Social fairness, however, often involves comparisons with more than two persons. Two modes of comparison need consideration: *individual* and *group*. These two comparison modes may be illustrated with the case of two other comparison persons, B and C.

Under the *individual comparison hypothesis*, separate comparisons are made between A and B and between A and C. This yields the same additivity structure as Equation 5 for unfairness integration. In particular, the B × C factorial graph should exhibit parallelism.

Under the *group comparison hypothesis*, B and C are integrated to provide a single standard of comparison, which may be envisaged as their average. This yields a different additivity structure, and implies, in particular, that the B × C factorial graph will not be parallel.

Surprisingly, the results clearly supported the group comparison hypothesis. Individual comparison was expected from the foregoing results, which showed separate comparisons for input dimensions and for outcome dimensions. Furthermore, the two comparison persons in this experiment were unrelated individuals, not forming any natural group. Nevertheless, the data patterns showed that comparisons were made to a group norm, not to the separate individuals. This result, accordingly, suggests the importance of groups as a general standard of comparison in social judgment.

In general, of course, comparison structure will depend on the situation. Indeed, the general rule for everyday life would involve comparisons both with a group norm and with specific other persons. The present methods can be used as an analytical tool for studying such comparison processes.

Social comparisons are not limited to fairness–unfairness, but include other moral qualities and varied personal characteristics. With multiple possible comparison standards, it becomes a tricky problem to determine which standards a subject relies on and how strongly on each. This problem becomes amenable to attack with IIT.

FAIRNESS–UNFAIRNESS: COMPARISON OF TWO THEORIES

The effectiveness of IIT with issues of fairness and unfairness may be indicated by the following summary comparison with Adams' theory, which has been the most popular alternative.

- The algebraic form of Adams' model is incorrect. Not one study has supported Adams' model over the integration theory model.

- Adams' assumption of input summation is incorrect. Input variables of different quality are not generally summed, averaged, or otherwise integrated to form a single overall input. Instead, each input dimension is often processed separately to yield a relative input value for each separate dimension. These separate input values are then combined by a rule of fairness integration.

- Adams' assumption of outcome summation is incorrect. Outcome variables of different quality are not generally summed, averaged, or otherwise integrated. Instead, each outcome dimension is often processed separately in a manner analogous to that for input processing.

- No support has been found for Adams' assumption of a threshold for overpayment unfairness. If overpayment unfairness is real, it appears to involve salience weighting rather than a threshold.[5]

- The comparison structure of Adams' model is qualitatively incorrect. Social comparisons of fairness and unfairness follow a different flow of information processing.

In short, as Farkas (1991, pp. 72–73) points out, nearly every definite assumption in Adams' theory is incorrect. This failure should not be taken as a criticism of Adams, who focused attention on an important aspect of social interaction, with special concern for smooth functioning of social organizations. His assumptions were entirely plausible, and his main theoretical article was written before effective concepts and methods capable of testing these assumptions had been well established. It is a virtue of Adams' assumptions that they could be put to definitive test, as they were with functional measurement theory. Given their plausibility, their failure is a form of progress. Farkas' cogent studies also made a more positive contribution by establishing alternative assumptions in their place.[6]

UNIFIED THEORY OF MORAL COGNITION

Cognitive algebra provides a foundation for unified theory of moral cognition. The potential of this moral algebra has been illustrated with the concepts of blame and fairness in the previous chapter, and in this chapter with the concepts of recompense, duty, and fairness. These moral judgments appear to follow algebraic rules found with other classes of judgment. To some extent, moreover, this moral algebra seems age-invariant.

CONFLICT, VALUE, AND MORAL ALGEBRA

Conflict is endemic in moral thought and action. Much of morality represents socialization to control self-interest in the interest of society. When duty does not conflict with self-interest, it often conflicts with some other duty. Other forms of conflict involve extenuating circumstances for harmful actions and ego-defense reactions to one's own dubious deeds. Conflict resolution is thus central to moral thought and action.

Conflict resolution brings in the two basic themes of IIT: multiple determination and personal value. Conflict *is* multiple determination. But multiple determination is more extensive. The strength of any duty itself usually depends on multiple determinants. Our duty to help a relative, for example, depends on the degree of kinship, the relative's need and character, as well as cultural factors beyond awareness in our moral knowledge systems. Analysis of moral cognition presents two seemingly formidable difficulties: first, for measuring personal moral values, second, for analyzing multiple determination.

Two unifying ideas, however, run through the moral realm. One is moral value: *good–bad* or *right–wrong*. This familiar idea of moral value provides a general motivational representation that transcends particular issues. A good part of the complexity of moral judgment is reducible to this summary dimension of moral value. This moral value representation is a key to analysis.

The concept of moral value, however, only becomes sharp and effective when values can be measured. The need for measurement is illustrated by the foregoing five-point comparison between two fairness theories. To implement his theory, Adams had to make arbitrary assumptions about multiple determination, as with his assumptions of input summation and outcome summation. His assumptions were reasonable, and they might have been correct. Adams recognized the need to measure personal values, but he had no way to do so. His assumptions, accordingly, remained arbitrary. Nearly every one, as it happened, turned out to be incorrect.

The second unifying idea is moral algebra. The multiple determinants of moral thought and action are integrated by algebraic rules in many situations. Here again, measurement is essential. Moral algebra can be set on solid ground only when the operative determinants can be measured. Both ideas thus depend on measurement, the Gordian knot of moral theory.

This Gordian knot can be untied and put to use. The solution lies in moral algebra itself. By virtue of functional measurement, moral algebra provides a base and frame for measurement of moral value. Thereby, it also provides a base and frame for moral psychology.[7]

COMPARISON PROCESSES

Comparison is a recurrent theme in thought and action, especially in the moral field. This field, accordingly, may provide a useful developmental ground for general theory of comparison processes.

Comparison processes were operative in all three moral concepts considered in this chapter, most prominently in fairness theory. Each fairness–unfairness model involved three comparisons: between inputs, between outcomes, and between persons. Each of these three comparisons, moreover, could involve multiple subcomparisons, between dimensions of input and outcome and between multiple persons. Still further comparison processing appeared in the analysis of input–outcome linkage given in Figure 7.6. Nearly all these fairness–unfairness comparisons followed algebraic rules.

For general cognitive theory, accordingly, fairness–unfairness may be a fruitful task area for studying comparison processes. Fairness–unfairness is a pervasive axis of social morality. It seems reasonable to expect that comparison processes found in this task will apply generally. A sign of such generality may be seen in the analysis of multiple comparison standards in the optical illusion of Figure 9.10, which has the same comparison structure as the test between fairness integration and input integration of Figure 7.4. The multiplicity of comparison processes of fairness–unfairness just noted, their ready experimental manipulation, the meaningfulness of this class of judgments, and the prevalence of algebraic rules all suggest the potential for further study.

MORAL KNOWLEDGE SYSTEMS

There is an exact parallel between moral judgment and attitudinal judgment. Moral attitudes, in the present view, are primary components of moral knowledge. Moral judgments are thus derivative from moral attitudes, which are considered knowledge systems in the sense of Chapter 5.

Also important in moral knowledge systems are situational determinants. Honesty, for example, is not absolute. Children often consider that their lies to authority figures are warranted by the social relationship. Something of this remains in adult knowledge systems. Similarly, a person who would consider it repellently wrong to take something belonging to another person may feel even a touch of virtue in taking something that belongs to the government. A different class of examples appears in the well-known conformity studies, in which social pressure induces extreme violations of moral standards. This importance of situational determinants in the domain of moral prohibitions is amplified in the moral domain of beneficence. Being helpful or kind, in particular, are less moral obligations than personal virtues.

In this functional view, much of moral knowledge relates to applicability in various social situations. General principles are only part of moral knowledge. Construction of moral values depends in essential ways on situational specifics as mediated by moral knowledge system. Moral algebra, with its capability for value measurement, can help delineate moral–social knowledge systems.

UTILITARIANISM

Moral arithmetic was a cornerstone of utilitarian ethics. The experimental moral algebra presented here seems in harmony with the utilitarian view.

Utilitarianism has certain assumptions, however, which disagree with the facts of moral algebra. One assumption is that each moral alternative is reducible to a single sum of values; this corresponds to input summation in the foregoing fairness experiments. Input summation failed in these experiments, however, which supported the alternative hypothesis of fairness integration.

Averaging processes, through which the addition of a good can decrease the total good, are also inconsistent with utilitarian theory (see also *Sure-thing Axiom* in Chapter 10). The unfairness paradox for outcome processing also seems incompatible with utilitarian theory. To the extent that utilitarian approaches aim at psychological reality, they need reconsideration in the light of experimental moral algebra.

Utilitarianism can be, and perhaps usually is construed differently, as an ideal, rational theory of morally optimal action. It could thus be argued, for example, that the rule of input summation is rationally desirable and that not using it is a shortcoming of moral cognition. From this standpoint, the study of moral cognition would be propaedeutic to development of moral education.

There is, however, a second aspect of ethical theory, more basic and less rational. This concerns moral value. Some moral values can be rationally grounded, being determinable by moral arithmetic from more elementary values. Other moral values, however, are not and cannot be rationally grounded. The concept of equality of persons, for example, so central in modern ethical theories, is a recent development in civilization. A hierarchical, class society is not less rational and might be more stable in the long run. Moral values would differ in these two forms of society.

This nonrational quality of value sets limits to any rationalist utilitarian approach. Rationally, a moral dilemma may be decidable by applying the utilitarian summation rule to calculate which alternative has the highest net sum of values. This rational prescription has little force, however, without knowledge of the values to be used in the calculation.

Bentham resolved the value problem with simplicity. He declared that the good was pleasure and the bad was pain, thereby doing good to subsequent writers by giving them a standing target. Bentham's universal arithmetic of pleasure–pain seems inadequate to handle the various forms of social motivation that have existed historically. The subtle variations among philosophical positions often obscure the reality that moral values differ across social groups, individuals, and even within the same individual at different times. Philosophers mostly pass by the value problem with appeals to the ideals of their culture and/or recognition that values may be extrarational. The lack of progress in moral philosophy stems from this inability to handle the value problem.

All moral philosophy must face the two fundamental issues of multiple determination and moral value. The utilitarian ideal of the greatest balance of good over evil assumes a summation rule, together with the possibility of measuring goods and evils in comparable units. This ideal has rightly been criticized, but it clearly recognized the two basic problems. Bentham himself gave explicit consideration to the measurement problem.[8]

Later writers have made little progress on these two problems, beyond criticizing Bentham, and have mainly sidestepped them. Their theories have a certain emptiness, therefore, even as attempts to prescribe moral behavior. At the same time, later writers have neglected much of the moral domain, including envy, temptation, and atonement. For substance and vitality, moral philosophy needs grounding in moral psychology.

Concepts of the good can be put on a scientific basis with functional measurement. Bentham's solution was objective only at a verbal level, for he could not measure pain and pleasure. Moral algebra, however, can provide true measurement of moral concepts such as right, duty, fairness, temptation, and blame. Measurement endows these concepts with scientific reality. Moral algebra can thus provide a new base for moral psychology and, to some extent, for moral philosophy as well.

NOTES

This chapter is greatly indebted to seminal work by Arthur Farkas. Contributions by Wilfried Hommers, Manuel Leon, and Yuval Wolf were also significant. A special debt of gratitude is owed to John Verdi.

1. The general problem of mitigation deserves systematic study, including recompense, apology, atonement, extenuation, fault-finding, and fault-denial. Three judgment perspectives are those of the putative harmdoer, the injured person, and a generalized social third party, of which the first two have have been neglected. Study of the harmdoer's perspective may be facilitated with personal design (Anderson, 1990b), constructed around real incidents in which the person was subject to moral criticism. An interesting comparison of college students and circuit court judges is given by Howe (1991).

2. The difference between dilemmas that do and do not allow compromise is significant for experimental analysis. Compromise can allow the use of continuous response measures and applications of functional measurement methodology. If no compromise is possible, the all-or-none choice provides minimal information about the relative strengths of the conflicting forces, making analysis difficult. Even with discrete choice data, therefore, it would seem advisable to develop continuous response measures, for example, measures of the overall moral value of the action or of the separate moral values of fulfilling and failing the two obligations.

3. Models for fairness, or equity, as it was usually called, generated a flurry of publications when it was observed that Adams' formula is ambiguous with negative input. For suppose that person A has positive input and negative outcome in Equation 1a. If person B has the same input and outcome, the situation will evidently be fair. But the equation remains true mathematically if the signs of B's input and outcome are reversed, although this situation would be manifestly unfair. None of these publications actually attempted empirical analysis, although the needed methodology was by then available. Instead, they sought armchair alternatives, a tactic that generally led to even more serious contradictions. Their approach seems misconceived, moreover, because negative input, harmdoing in particular, has no necessary conceptual relation to fairness−unfairness (Anderson, 1991f; Farkas, 1991, Note 1).

4. An alternative approach to fairness theory by Mellers (1982, 1985) has been undercut by internal contradictions. The subtraction rule obtained by Farkas and Anderson (1979) was interpreted to result from tendencies for task simplification. Their interpretation was supported by work of Singh (1985) in India, who reported a subtraction rule for students but a ratio rule for professional managers with industrial experience.

This subtraction rule was also pursued by Mellers (1982, 1985), who made strong claims that fairness−unfairness should follow subtraction rules in general, contrary to the ratio rules in the text. Subtraction rules require parallelism, however, contrary to the frequent finding of barrel shapes predicted by the ratio rules (e.g., Figures 7.3 and 7.4). Accordingly, Mellers attempted to force the data of Figure 7.3 to be parallel using monotone transformation and claimed to succeed.

Mellers' claim, however, cannot be correct. The data in question contained large crossover interactions. To make them parallel by monotone transformation is mathematically impossible. Mellers' claim to do the mathematically impossible stems from an invalid methodology that obscured these clear, scale-free violations of parallelism (Anderson, 1991e, pp. 90–94).

5. As an attempt to handle asymmetry of over- and underpayment, Adams claimed that an overpaid person felt unfairness only if the amount of overpayment exceeded some threshold. This generated a number of studies, the net outcome of which gave little support to Adams' claim. Tests by Farkas (1991, Figures 5 and 6), not cited in the text, clearly disproved Adams' claim. These tests also extended IIT to the important problem of interpersonal salience.

Adams' primary assumption was that overpayment and underpayment generated unfairness feelings of similar quality. This seems contrary to phenomenology. Underpayment generates resentment and envy; overpayment generates delight and perhaps anxiety over being a target of envy.

6. Adams' (1965) article on equity theory was important for its emphasis on the multiplicity of factors that can influence feelings of satisfaction and fairness in industrial situations—and the realization that these factors generally had to be represented as subjective, individual values. His anecdotal examples in this article retain their interest.

7. Other work on moral judgment includes Howe's (1991) study of the important issue of mitigation, using Circuit Court judges as subjects, and Przygotski and Mullet's (1993) study of blame judgments by incarcerated persons. A curious configural effect in judgments of criminal groups was found by Leon, Oden, and Anderson (1973). Developmental studies are covered in Chapter 6.

8. Bentham (1823/1907, p. 30) observed that "the value of a pleasure or pain . . . will be greater or less according to seven circumstances," including intensity, duration, certainty or uncertainty, and propinquity or remoteness. Although this does not address the several measurement issues, especially establishing common units within and between individuals, it seems in advance of its time. Bentham was a practical philosopher, concerned with legislation and the penal system. His writings had extensive influence in his day.

PREFACE

Two developmental theories are compared in this chapter with respect to commonsense knowledge about the external world: developmental integration theory and Piagetian theory. The problem of stimulus integration is central to both theories, as shown in their basic experimental paradigms. Direct comparison of the two theories is thus straightforward.

Piagetian theory makes several interrelated claims: that children up to age 5 or 6 years cannot integrate two variables into a single judgment; that knowledge develops by discrete stages, each qualitatively different from its precursor; that algebraic rules are not possible until the final stage of formal operations, in the midteen years; and that stimulus integration in the final stage is reversible and mirrors physical law.

All these Piagetian claims are seriously incorrect. This is shown by experiments in developmental integration theory. Children even younger than 4 years can integrate very well, and their judgments often exhibit algebraic rules. In some tasks, indeed, young children exhibit true operational thought. Adult judgment, on the other hand, often disagrees with physical law.

Experimental applications of the functional measurement paradigm are given in four areas: time–speed, conservation, number, and probability. In all four areas, functional measurement has led to a picture of knowledge development radically different from that of Piaget. Children are not merely more advanced than Piaget claimed, but qualitatively different.

Isomorphism is the linchpin for Piagetian theory—isomorphism between the physical world and the final stage of development. This assumption also provided a framework for understanding the course of development, which must be interpreting as tending toward final isomorphism. But developmental integration studies show that Piaget's isomorphism assumption is fundamentally incorrect. Cognition differs qualitatively from Piagetian claims at every age. Piagetian theory is incorrect in its basic assumptions and needs to be replaced by assemblage theory.

Assemblage theory is a genuine alternative to Piagetian stage theory because it allows joint action of processes and abilities from all periods of development. Whereas stage theory requires all thinking within each stage to have one homogeneous quality, assemblage theory envisages thinking as generally heterogeneous, with components from all levels of development. Assemblage theory differs from stage theory already in Piaget's preoperational stage, and this difference becomes greater with further development.

Chapter 8

COGNITIVE DEVELOPMENT

A unique historical figure in psychology is that of Jean Piaget. His monumental empirical contributions are matched by monumental theoretical confusion. Although mainly influential in developmental psychology, Piaget aimed at nothing less than a general epistemology, which he sought to approach through developmental analysis. His main focus, accordingly, was on development of knowledge of the external world. He did extensive, pioneering work on many problems of commonsense physics, that is, everyday knowledge of the external world, opening up a broad field of inquiry with innumerable fascinating observations and discoveries.

The best-known of Piaget's discoveries is *nonconservation*: that young children, up to 5–6 years old, do not conserve quantity. If liquid is poured from a narrow glass into a wide glass, thereby decreasing the height of the liquid, the children really think the amount of liquid has decreased. Adults are incredulous at reports of this behavior. To adults, conservation of quantity seems virtually self-evident. Yet many skeptical replications have found that nonconservation is genuine, not an experimental artifact.

No longer so well-known is Piaget's discovery of *centration*: that young children cannot integrate two stimulus variables. Instead, claimed Piaget, they *center* on one or the other variable and act on that one alone. Centration is not mere inattention or task simplification, but an essential incapability of coordinating two variables to form an integrated response. Centration was considered a general characteristic of thinking up to age 6 or even 10 (Chapter 6).

Centration made a fine explanation of nonconservation. Suppose children center on the height of the liquid, unable to integrate diameter with height. Then they will indeed think the amount has changed when the height changes. The nonconservation found with other quantities may be explained similarly, and this harmonized with the claim that centration was a general characteristic of thinking in young children.

But centration is invalid. Numerous studies have shown that young children find it easy and natural to integrate information. Contrary to Piaget, centration is not a general characteristic of young children's thinking. Instead, centration is an artifact of Piaget's basic methodology.

This contrast between the empirical study of conservation and its theoretical interpretation in terms of centration is a fitting commentary on Piaget's work. Although he opened up many issues with ground-breaking empirical observations about children's thinking, his theory is pervaded with internal inconsistencies, question begging, and non sequiturs. When its treatments of specific problems are scrutinized, they repeatedly fall apart from internal contradictions and logical incoherence. In its claims about the nature of cognitive development, moreover, Piaget's theory is seriously incorrect.[1]

This chapter compares developmental integration theory and Piagetian theory in four knowledge domains. In each, developmental integration theory has led to a very different outlook from that given by Piaget. The nature of cognition and its development differ markedly from that envisaged in Piagetian theory. It is not simply that young children are more capable than Piaget recognized—they think in a different way. To understand cognitive development requires a different conceptual framework.

TWO PARADIGMS FOR DEVELOPMENTAL ANALYSIS

Stimulus integration is a prime concern of both the theory of information integration and of Piagetian theory. Stimulus integration is an essential property of Piaget's basic choice paradigm, which he applied with minor variations in every domain. In this choice paradigm, the child is presented two objects, each defined on two dimensions, and asked to choose which is greater in some specified respect. Good performance requires integration of the two dimensions for each object, followed by a choice of the one with the greater integrated value.

Piaget's choice paradigm has now been shown to misrepresent the nature of children's thinking, sometimes in an extreme manner. In the next two sections, accordingly, the choice paradigm is contrasted with an alternative paradigm of functional measurement.

These two paradigms are comparable because both deal with the problem of stimulus integration. This similarity is discussed further in the final part, following experimental comparisons in four domains of commonsense physics.

PIAGET'S CHOICE PARADIGM

In Piaget's choice paradigm, the child is shown two stimuli and asked to choose which is greater in some specified respect. Among the examples considered here are: Which of two glasses contains more liquid? Which of two rows of beads has more beads? Which of two toy trains runs the longer time?

The main use of the choice task is when the two choice alternatives differ in opposite ways on the two dimensions. One glass might have a higher water level but smaller diameter, so it could be hard to decide which actually contained more liquid. One row of beads, similarly, might be longer but spaced farther apart, again a possibly difficult choice for young children. Optimal performance, of course, requires integration of the two dimensions according to the actual physical rule. Piaget made a basic assumption of isomorphism, by which this physical rule was the final stage of development.

But, said Piaget, young children cannot integrate two dimensions, even in such simple tasks as just described. They choose perforce on the basis of one dimension alone, that is, they *center*. Piaget, it should be recognized, did not rely solely on the choices, but also on directed questioning about the reasons for the choice. Illustrative answers to such questions were actually the main data he presented. In such questioning, however, a serious artifact appears. When questioned about the reason for the choice, a child who chose the glass with the higher water level will naturally refer to its higher level. Its smaller diameter is contrary to the choice, so it will hardly be cited as justification even if it did figure in the choice. Hence the failure of the child to refer to the contrary dimension is hardly evidence that it was ignored.

Centration is only one failure of the choice paradigm. More serious failures appear in Piaget's claims about the development of concepts of time, speed, number, probability, and so forth. These failures undercut Piaget's basic theoretical assumptions, including isomorphism and the theory of stages.

FUNCTIONAL MEASUREMENT PARADIGM

The typical integration experiment presents a single stimulus and obtains a judgment on a continuous scale, as with a graphic rating. The single stimuli are varied along two or more dimensions according to a factorial design. For example, a row of beads might be varied in length and density, with the child asked to judge numerosity of each row. The factorial graph of these judgments can reveal the child's integration rule (see Figure 8.4).

This functional measurement paradigm seems ideal for studying centration. Centration on one dimension would yield an especially simple factorial graph, for only that one dimension would have an effect (see Figure 8.3). The continuous response measure, moreover, is sensitive to small effects of the second dimension and so would give a quantitative measure of development.

Furthermore, the functional measurement paradigm is simpler than the choice paradigm in an important respect: Performance requires integration only for the one given stimulus. With the choice paradigm, in contrast, correct performance requires correct integration for both given stimuli to allow their comparison. Also required is an ability to keep the result of one integration in mind while the other is being performed.

On the response side, however, the functional measurement paradigm is more demanding. Substantial quantitative capabilities are needed to use a continuous response in a sensible way. Not only must the child evaluate and integrate the dimensions of each single stimulus, but these integrations must be placed in relative order on the usually arbitrary rating scale. It was notable, therefore, to find that children as young as 4 years could rate with little trouble.

Indeed, these young children can actually use the rating scale as a true linear measure. This is considered to reflect a general purpose metric sense for response quantification. Methodologically, this result is priceless, for it means that the pattern visible in the factorial graph exactly mirrors the pattern of cognition. For developmental psychology, this result bespeaks notable cognitive capabilities. First, it shows true metric quantification in cognition. Second, it implicitly demonstrates proportional thinking. Both capabilities are allowed by Piaget only at the stage of formal operations, at 12 or more years of age. Both capabilities are actually present in children under 4 years of age, as shown by the functional measurement paradigm. This stark age contrast highlights an essentially new outlook on cognitive development.

TIME AND SPEED

Developmental integration theory and Piagetian theory are nicely contrasted in Friedrich Wilkening's striking studies of time and speed. Concepts of time and speed are basic to cognition of the external world. The two paradigms, however, yield radically different conclusions.

EINSTEIN'S QUESTION AND PIAGET'S ANSWER

In his foreword to *The Child's Conception of Time*, Piaget (1969) records that his interest in time was sparked by a question of Einstein about the nature and origin of commonsense notions of time. Following an extended program of research, Piaget arrived at the answer that the concept of time was not itself primitive, but was derived from concepts of speed and distance.

To understand Piaget's answer, it is necessary to understand his experimental paradigm. In his prototypical time task, two toy trains run on parallel tracks, covering the same or different distances with the same or different speeds. Children are asked which train ran for the longer time or if the times were equal.

Similar questions may be asked about speed and distance run. Following their choice, the children are asked a series of probing questions intended to elicit their understanding. This choice paradigm is a standard method throughout Piaget's work.

In Piaget's choice paradigm, correct judgments develop later for time than for speed or distance. At 5–6 years, children appear to judge on the basis of distance cues alone; they say the train that stopped farther ahead took more time, even when it took less time by virtue of greater speed. Later, speed may also affect judgment, although perhaps erroneously, for children may judge one of two equal times greater if the train went slower. Only around 8–9 years do children become moderately proficient at time judgments, even when the correct choice is clear to an adult eye.

From many such interrelated experiments, Piaget concluded that speed and distance are the primary concepts and that time is derived from them. Such late development of the concept of time may seem surprising, but Piaget's conclusion was well supported in followup work by others. Most notable was the study of Siegler and Richards (1979), which employed a revised choice paradigm that did not rely on verbal protocols. Their only major departure from Piaget was that the concept of time seemed to be mastered only at 10–12 years of age, even later than Piaget had thought (see Note 10).

WILKENING'S INTEGRATION STUDIES

An entirely different picture of the development of time understanding was obtained when Wilkening (1982) applied a functional measurement paradigm. Instead of choosing between two events, children made a quantitative judgment about a single event.

In the experimental situation, the children saw a fierce dog pictured in a cave on one side of a foot bridge. They were shown pictures of seven animals, graded in running speed from snail to horse, and were told that all the animals were afraid of the dog and would flee over the foot bridge for as long as the dog kept barking.

Three variables were explained to the children: *time* (how long the dog barked); *distance* (how far the animal fled); and *speed* (the natural running speed of the pictured animal). Three separate conditions were run. In each condition, two variables were manipulated in a factorial design, and the children judged the third variable.

The most important result, for present purposes, is that 5-year-olds followed a subtraction rule for judgments of time. In this time task, they were given the identity of the animal and shown how far it had run. They were instructed to press a button to make the dog bark for as long as it would have taken the given animal to run the given distance. These actual time responses are plotted in Figure 8.1.

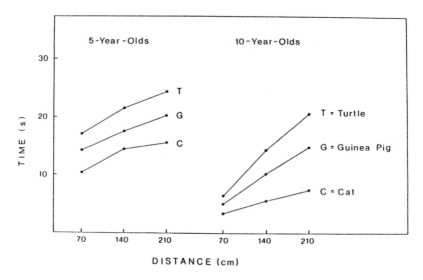

Figure 8.1. Judgments of time required by turtle, guinea pig, and cat to run 70, 140, or 210 cm. Judgments made by producing an actual duration of a barking dog record. Parallelism in left panel shows that 5-year-olds follow the subtraction rule, Time = Distance − Speed. Linear fan in right panel shows that 10-year-olds follow the normative division rule, Time = Distance ÷ Speed. (After Wilkening, 1982.)

The left panel in Figure 8.1 shows near-parallelism for the 5-year-olds. This parallelism indicates the operation of *Wilkening's integration rule*:

Time = Distance − Speed.

This remarkable result demonstrates functional understanding of all three concepts at 5 years of age. A more radical transformation of previous ideas about development of time–speed concepts is hard to imagine. The implications of Wilkening's rule deserve itemization.

First, the children had conceptual understanding of each of the three separate variables. This understanding is explicit in the integration rule. A time concept is already present at 5 years, therefore, far earlier than had been indicated with the choice paradigm. The speed concept, moreover, is explicitly symbolic, for it is specified by the picture of the animal.

Second, all three concepts are metric, mirrored in the cognitive algebra. The subjective metric for each concept is operative in the children's cognitions and can be assessed with functional measurement. According to Piaget, metric concepts can only appear in the late stage of formal operations, some 6 or more years later. Wilkening's study, in contrast, revealed metric concepts even in the so-called preoperational years.

Third, Wilkening's rule shows that the three concepts are interrelated according to a sensible, although nonphysical algebraic relation. All three concepts are thus operational in a practical sense, and indeed in a formal sense as well. In short, developmental integration theory reveals a knowledge system entirely different from that envisaged in Piagetian theory.

A fourth implication, less direct, also points to operational concepts of time and speed. The data imply that the children operate under an assumption of uniform speed: The *Speed* term in the foregoing equation is a functional unit. But uniform speed is unnatural; everyday objects are continually speeding up or slowing down. A concept of uniform speed must operate at an abstract, symbolic level in the task assemblage. This view of uniform speed as an operating idea, present at early ages, is quite different from Piaget's explanation of the concept of speed (see Note 1). This view is consistent with the view that the integration operation itself is abstract and symbolic.

The last implication is qualitative. The algebraic rule shows that the children are proficient at assemblage, which embodies qualitative understanding of the task. The time task just described involves notable feats of mental assemblage, in which an imagined animal with an appropriate imagined speed runs an imagined distance in fear of an imagined dog, all neatly scaled down to the small dimensions of the stimulus display. The algebraic rule, remarkable in itself, is not less remarkable as an indicator of this qualitative assemblage that underlies task performance. The study of such qualitative assemblage is a general and fundamental problem in cognitive theory. Cognitive algebra thus has important potential for analysis of nonalgebraic assemblage processes (see *Assemblage Theory* in Anderson & Wilkening, 1991, pp. 20–24).

NONREVERSIBILITY

In Piaget's theory, adult thinking is governed by abstract, formal operations and has the basic property of reversibility. Reversibility implies that the time–speed–distance trinity must be mathematically consistent and indeed should mirror the physical relations. With the functional measurement paradigm, Wilkening showed that reversibility does not hold. Adults exhibited the following trinity of integration rules:

$$\text{Distance} = \text{Speed} \times \text{Time};$$

$$\text{Time} = \text{Distance} \div \text{Speed};$$

$$\text{Speed} = \text{Distance} - \text{Time}.$$

The subtraction rule for speed is inconsistent with the multiplication rule for distance and with the division rule for time. This nonreversible cognitive algebra disagrees with Piagetian theory. This disagreement is accentuated by Piaget's treatment of time as the prototype of reversible thought.[2]

Similar inconsistency in cognitive algebra is fairly common (see, e.g., Figure 5.5). Cognitive algebra must be understood in cognitive terms, not in the physicalist terms that Piaget assumes are the final stage of development.

This point may be emphasized by interpreting the foregoing time–speed asymmetry in terms of assemblage theory. Part of the assemblage for each judgment is a mental model of an object traveling the specified distance. When speed is specified, it is easy to visualize the object in actual travel along the given distance. To judge time, given distance and speed, subjects could construct a mental model of the object moving the given distance with the given speed and judge the experiential time of the mental movement. But to judge speed, given distance and time, the same mental model would require trial and error to decide what speed would be required to complete the specified distance in the specified time. Faced with this more demanding task, even adults apparently revert to the general purpose addition rule. This interpretation, as yet speculative, implies that complicating an experimental task will generally produce shifts from multiplication–division rules to addition–subtraction rules.

CONSERVATION

Young children judge area of rectangles as though they added height and width. This result hardly seems credible; the child need merely look to see how much is there. Direct, perceptual apprehension of size would lead to some semblance of the physical rule, Height × Width, without any arithmetic calculation. Older children and adults did show the Height × Width rule under the same conditions. For the 5-year-olds to add height and width seems not only needlessly complicated, but lacking rhyme or reason.

The initial observation of the Height + Width rule thus seemed untrustworthy, but an extended sequence of experiments done in collaboration with Diane Cuneo showed it to be valid. It was interpreted as a manifestation of a general purpose adding-type rule present as early as 3^+ years of age. The following sections discuss this rule and its implications. Associated work that bears on the interpretation of conservation will also be considered.

HEIGHT + WIDTH RULE FOR AREA

The Height + Width rule was found serendipitously in an experiment in which children were told about a hungry story child and judged how happy that child would be with rectangular cookies of various sizes. Cookies were presented according to a 3 × 3, Height × Width design, and each child judged all 9 cookies on a sad–happy face rating scale.

Centration was notably absent in the results of the 5-year-olds, shown in the factorial graph of Figure 8.2. The slope of the curves shows that height has a

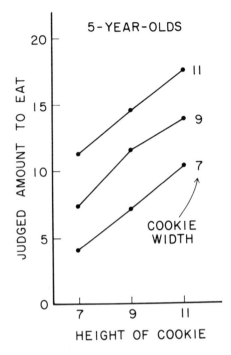

Figure 8.2. Mean judgment of amount for rectangular cookies. Parallelism implies 5-year-olds add Height and Width in judging area. (After N. H. Anderson & D. O. Cuneo, 1978, "The Height + Width rule in children's judgments of quantity," *Journal of Experimental Psychology: General, 107,* 335-378. Copyright 1978 by the American Psychological Association. Reprinted by permission.)

substantial effect; the separation of the curves shows that width also has a substantial effect. Height and Width both affect the response, a result verified in analyses for the individual children.

More striking, the three curves are essentially parallel. By virtue of the parallelism theorem, the 5-year-olds appear to judge the area of rectangles by adding height and width. This outcome is contrary to the centration hypothesis of Piaget, which disallows integration at this preoperational age.

HEIGHT + WIDTH RULE VERIFIED

The natural reaction to the Height + Width rule is that something is wrong, for it seems to make no sense. An estimate of size seems available simply by looking. Such a global perceptual judgment should reflect the physical area, that is, a Height–*times*–Width rule. These judgments need not be exact, but they should surely show systematic deviation from parallelism. The Height + Width rule, moreover, is cognitively more complicated that the perceptual judgment. Why should the children do something cognitively complicated when a simpler perceptual strategy is available?

Several alternative explanations had to be considered. Only after a sequence of eight experiments did the Height + Width rule rest on solid ground. The main alternative explanations may be enumerated as follows.

1. The outcome may stem from some peculiarity of the stimulus display.
In the initial experiment, the rectangles were placed flat on the table near the child. It was thought that placing them upright, or at a greater distance, might elicit a global perceptual response. However, several variations of this kind all yielded the Height + Width pattern of parallelism.

2. The observed parallelism may reflect low power.
This might be a reasonable objection to the one initial experiment, but the Height + Width pattern was observed uniformly across all six relevant experiments in this study. No sign of the physical multiplication rule was obtained. Hence the power objection can be dismissed.

3. The 5-year-olds may use the response scale logarithmically.
The virtue of this interpretation is that it is consistent with a global perception of size. This global percept would obey the Height *times* Width rule, but the logarithmic response function would make the observed data appear parallel, or additive. However, there is not the slightest evidence for this interpretation. On the contrary, several lines of evidence indicate that the rating method is veridical. Much of this evidence is summarized in Chapter 3, and a collateral line of evidence is noted in the later section on number concepts.

4. Centration may be valid; the parallelism pattern may be an artifact.
This alternative explanation argues that some children center on height, others on width. Any numerical example will quickly reveal that mean data, averaged over both classes of children, would exhibit parallelism. This alternative explanation was readily ruled out by doing the analyses for each individual child; all showed substantial effects for each variable.

A more subtle attempt to save the centration hypothesis assumes that the same child centers on height on some trials, on width on the other trials. This response strategy will also produce parallelism in the mean data, as may be shown in the same way. This interpretation can also be ruled out, although a more subtle argument is required. This interpretation implies that the 7×11 rectangle will yield bimodal data, with one mode produced by responses to the 7-cm height, the other mode produced by responses to the 11-cm width. In contrast, the 9×9 square will yield unimodal responding because height and width are equal and elicit equal response. This interpretation implies, therefore, that within-child variability will be greater for rectangles than for squares. No such difference was obtained, which rules out this centration explanation. This analysis, it may be added, also illustrates some of the power obtainable with continuous response methodology.

To sum up, the four cited alternative interpretations of the parallelism pattern could all be rejected. The Height + Width rule seemed real. Its meaning is taken up next.[3]

GENERAL PURPOSE INTEGRATION OPERATOR

Because the addition rule was counterphysical in this task, its appearance suggested that some compelling reason must underlie its operation. In line with this reasoning, the Height + Width rule was interpreted as a manifestation of a general purpose integration operator. In the judgment task, the child understands that some quantitative judgment is wanted, but does not possess adult understanding of the concept. The child does, however, understand the relevance of one-dimensional cues to the quantity judgment. The judgment is made, accordingly, by applying the general purpose operator to integrate these one-dimensional cues.

If this interpretation is correct, addition rules should also be found in other tasks of commonsense physics in which the physical rule is multiplication. Notable support for this implication was obtained by Cuneo, who showed that young children judged numerosity of a row of equally-spaced beads by a Length + Density rule (see following). Further support was given by the time–speed studies already discussed in Figure 8.1.[4, 5]

The general purpose addition rule is considered a biological capability. This conclusion is based in part on the appearance of adding-type rules in diverse integration tasks. Foremost among these are other tasks of commonsense physics in which the physically correct rule is also multiplication. Also significant is the prevalence of addition rules in moral–social tasks that lack an objectively correct rule (Chapter 6). This biological interpretation is consistent with later work by Cuneo, who found the Height + Width rule already present at 3[+] years of age (see below).

A general purpose integration operator makes biological sense. Capability for integration of information is a survival characteristic selected for throughout evolution. There are, of course, sense-specific integration mechanisms, but there is also a role for general purpose mechanisms, especially for integration of higher-level informers. The addition rule, moreover, makes ecological sense, for it can give moderately accurate results even when the physical integration rule is nonadditive.

HEIGHT–ONLY RULE: A CONTRADICTION

The path of scientific inquiry is seldom straight. Ideally, truth would reveal itself to the careful observer, as Bacon thought. In reality, as every empirical investigator will attest, truth is typically elusive and clouded, hidden behind uncertainties, confoundings, and apparent contradictions.

So it was with the Height + Width rule, for it was contradicted by a Height-only rule that appeared in another condition of the same initial experiment. This other condition employed a functional measurement paradigm to test Piaget's interpretation that nonconservation of liquids in glasses stems from centration.

In a standard test of conservation, using Piaget's choice paradigm, the child is shown two identical glasses filled equally high with liquid, and affirms that both contain equal amounts. While the child watches, the experimenter pours the contents of one glass into another of different diameter and asks whether both contain equal amounts or if one contains more. Children up to age 6 or 7 typically reply that the glass with the higher level contains more liquid; they seem noncomprehending that simply pouring the water has not changed its amount. In short, they fail to conserve.

In Piaget's interpretation, nonconservation occurs because children *center* on height of the liquid; they are unable at the same time to take account of the diameter. Centration thus provides an explanation for nonconservation, not only for liquids in glasses, but also for other quantities. Centration is widely cited as an explanatory concept in developmental psychology.

A direct test of Piaget's concept of centration seemed easily obtainable by applying a functional measurement paradigm. To implement this, the children were told about a thirsty story child and judged how happy the child would be with different amounts of Kool–Aid to drink. The Kool–Aid was shown in glasses with three diameters and three heights of Kool–Aid using a factorial design similar to that for the cookies.

It was expected that 5-year-olds would integrate height and diameter because integration had previously been demonstrated in the moral–social and judgment–decision domains. This expectation was sharply disconfirmed; the 5-year-olds followed a Height-only rule, shown in Figure 8.3. The upward trend of the three curves shows that liquid height has strong effects. But the three curves, one for each glass diameter, are essentially identical; glass diameter has negligible effect. The pattern in the factorial graph thus points clearly to the one-variable, Height-only rule.

Had only this liquid-in-glasses condition been used, the outcome would have seemed striking support for Piagetian theory. The functional measurement paradigm is sensitive to even small effects of glass diameter, yet no hint of such effect was obtained. At face value, Figure 8.3 seems exceptionally strong evidence for Piagetian centration.

But the centration hypothesis failed in the parallel task using rectangular cookies; there the same children added height and width. If centration was a general characteristic of young children's thinking, as Piaget claimed, it should appear with cookies as well as glasses. The pair of results thus disagrees with the centration hypothesis. This pair of results is reliable, for Cuneo (1980) replicated it with 3- and 4-year-olds in subsequent work.

Nevertheless, the two results disagree between themselves. The glass, considered in two-dimensional cross-section, is similar to the cookie. Both should reveal similar integration rules. If cookies exhibit a Height + Width rule, glasses should exhibit a Height + Diameter rule.

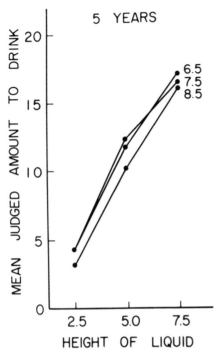

Figure 8.3. Mean judgment of amount for glasses of liquid. Near-identity of curves implies 5-year-olds ignore glass diameter, judging on the basis of liquid height alone. (After N. H. Anderson & D. O. Cuneo, 1978, "The Height + Width rule in children's judgments of quantity," *Journal of Experimental Psychology: General, 107,* 335-378. Copyright 1978 by the American Psychological Association. Reprinted by permission.)

The disagreement between the two results in this initial experiment thus led to two questions that took a sequence of seven further experiments to resolve satisfactorily. The first question concerned the validity of the Height + Width rule, already considered in the two previous sections. The second question concerned the meaning of the Height-only rule, which is considered next.

WHAT DOES THE HEIGHT–ONLY RULE MEAN?

The Height-only rule cannot be centration in the sense of Piaget, for the reasons already given. Instead, the Height-only rule seems peculiar to liquids in glasses. A further experiment showed the same result with various solids in glasses, which implicated the glass container itself.

A clue to the interpretation of the Height-only rule came from the reflection that the height of liquids in glasses and cups has everyday importance for young children. Liquid height is a controlling cue in drinking from a glass or cup, a messy motor skill for young children. Since glasses and cups mostly have similar diameter, moreover, liquid height is the primary cue for judging how much there is to drink. On this interpretation, the Height-only rule observed in Figure 8.3 would be a manifestation of a learned response from everyday life.

This interpretation may be tested by separating the liquid from the glass. Inside the glass, the liquid should be judged by the Height-only rule. Standing alone, the liquid should be judged by the Height + Width rule.

This predicted pattern of results was verified in two further experiments. The experimental requirement of separating the liquid from the glass was met by using a frozen liquid in the form of wax cylinders. The same child judged the same wax cylinder by the Height + Diameter rule when it stood alone, by the Height-only rule when it was placed inside the glass. The Height-only rule thus appears to be an experiential response heavily overlearned from breakfast, lunch, and dinner on many, many days.

TWO THEORIES OF CONSERVATION

Where does conservation come from? This is a basic question raised by Piaget's finding of nonconservation at younger ages. One might think conservation could be made quickly evident by pouring the water back and forth between glasses of different diameter and telling the child: "Look! It's the same water!" But this has surprisingly little effect. Recognition that it's the same water does not imply that its *quantity* is the same, and this is what is at issue. What the child does see is that the height changes, and height is a primary cue to quantity.

Piaget's answer to this question also illustrates the fundamental role of quantification in his general theory. Piaget claimed that older children arrive at understanding of conservation of quantity only by virtue of capabilities for actually calculating the quantity, thereby recognizing that it does not change. More specifically, Piaget explained conservation in terms of *compensation* and *extensive quantification*. Compensation refers to a qualitative understanding that an increase in height can be compensated by a decrease in width. But compensation is not sufficient, Piaget emphasized, because an increase in height and a decrease in width could yield a larger, smaller, or equal total quantity. Hence quantification is also necessary.

Quantification played a central role in Piaget's theory. Quantification was a concomitant of his basic, guiding assumption that thought at the adult stage of formal operations mirrors the physical world. Piaget required, in other words, that adults understand that Area = Height × Width, and that Speed = Distance ÷ Time, in the same sense as these laws are taught in schoolbook physics.

Moreover, Piaget assumed that quantification developed in the form of additive units, just as measurement is commonly understood in physics. For a rectangle, in particular, area is conceived as addition of small unit squares that cover the rectangle. Only with such quantification capability can the child understand conservation. In Piaget's view, therefore, conservation can develop only after prior development of a sophisticated repertoire of operations.

By one of those non sequiturs common in Piaget's theory, the gap between these premises and the conclusion is left empty. Piaget never shows that children actually apply quantification to derive conservation, even for rectangle area. Moreover, liquids in glasses, the showpiece case of conservation, he treats only in two-dimensional cross-section. Piaget's theory, however, requires a three-dimensional quantification of liquid volume, so Piaget's explanation is inconsistent with Piaget's theory. Accordingly, his explanation of conservation makes no sense.

At the same time, conservation of liquids in glasses is well developed by age 7–8, considerably earlier than extensive quantification in Piaget's theory. In short, Piaget's attempts to explain the development of conservation is logically fallacious and empirically invalid.

An alternative interpretation (Anderson & Cuneo, 1978a,b) is that conservation develops in part from conditioning of a primitive concept of object constancy to specific object properties of amount, and in part from specific experiences, whose importance has been seen in the analysis of the Height-only rule. One such experience is that things can be used up, that there is only so much, a suggestive indicator toward conservation, one that is continuously important to young children.

At a later stage, conservation may become an operating idea, now virtually "self-evident." This concept of operating idea differs from Piaget's because it does not require quantification. On the contrary, it implies that conservation responses can appear when quantities are not conserved. One such case is the area of a rectangle enclosed by a string of fixed length, but varied in height and width. Adults often say that area is conserved, which disagrees with Piaget's theory and agrees with the present interpretation.

JUDGMENT OF NUMBER

The hypothesis that a general purpose addition rule underlies the Height + Width rule has a strong implication. If this hypothesis is correct, addition rules should be found in other tasks, including tasks in which the correct physical rule is multiplication.

This was Diane Cuneo's reasoning in her Ph. D. thesis on number judgment. The child's task was to judge numerosity of rows of beads, varied in length and density (spacing between beads). The correct physical rule, of course, is Length *times* Density. But, if the hypothesis of a general purpose integration operator is correct, the experimental data should reveal a Length *plus* Density rule.

CUNEO'S LENGTH + DENSITY RULE

The Length + Density rule was verified in two extensive, meticulous experiments (Cuneo, 1978, 1982), of which one has special interest for its individual analyses of 3- and 4-year-old children. Each stimulus consisted of a 30-cm strip of white styrofoam on which was centered a row of equally-spaced small blue beads. Children rated numerosity on a graphic rating scale.

The main condition used numbers of beads ranging from 7 to 15, beyond these children's counting capability. These results are shown in the two left panels of Figure 8.4 for the two age groups. Both panels exhibit parallelism, clear evidence that the children added length and density in judging numerosity of the row of beads.

This agrees with the concept of a general purpose addition rule. The children understand that length and density are both cues to numerosity but lack

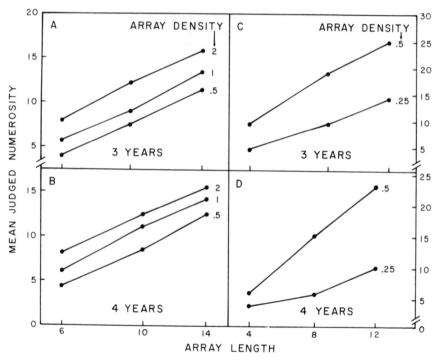

Figure 8.4. Left panels show judged numerosity of rows of 7 to 15 beads varied in length (horizontal axis) and interbead spacing (curve parameter). Parallelism supports the addition rule, Length + Density, length having about four times the effect of density.

Right panels show judged numerosity of rows of 2 to 7 beads. Linear fan pattern supports (as-if) Length × Density rule—and hence the linearity of the rating method.

Individual analyses demonstrated rule validity at individual level. For the left panel, all children showed nonsignificant interaction terms, with one marginal exception. For the right panel, all children showed significant bilinear and nonsignificant residual interaction terms, with the same one exception.

Twelve children in each age group served in 10 experimental sessions, 5 sessions at each array density, with 2 replications of the factorial design per session. Very similar results were obtained in a related experiment. (From Cuneo, 1978, 1982, Experiment 3.)

adult capability for integrating them. They exhibit adaptive thinking, however, for they take account of density in a sensible although suboptimal way.

Cuneo's Length + Density rule extends the addition rule observed with rectangles to a new domain. Thereby it provides cogent support for the hypothesis that this rule represents a general purpose integration operator. The numerosity task also avoids a peculiarity of rectangles, for which height and width are similar. It could thus be argued that the Height + Width rule is not true addition, but that the child merely estimates the one-dimensional perimeter (see Note 3). With rows of beads, no analogous alternative exists. Length and density are qualitatively different cues. Hence the parallelism pattern must reflect true conceptual addition.

The functional measurement paradigm thus revealed a new outlook on numerosity. Previous work had shown that length is a potent cue; young children may actually choose the less numerous array of beads if it is spaced out longer. Density, or close-togetherness, also seems a reasonable cue, but the previous work, which had relied on Piaget's choice paradigm, had not established an effect of density. This agreed with Piagetian theory, of course, which implied that children would center on the length cue. Cuneo not only demonstrated integration, but went beyond to reveal an exact algebra of integration and to trace out its developmental trend from addition to multiplication at older ages.

INDIVIDUAL ANALYSIS

Completely satisfactory evidence for integration rules requires analysis at the individual level. Group means could mask deviations from the rule if such deviation were in opposite directions for different children. Individual analysis usually requires substantial data for each child. Accordingly, Cuneo tested each child in the foregoing experiment in 10 replications of the 3 × 3 design over 5 successive days, yielding a total of 90 observations from each child.

All 24 children followed the Length + Density rule except one 3-year-old. The analysis of variance showed highly significant main effects of density as well as length for every child, further evidence against the Piagetian concept of centration. All individual graphs showed parallelism, with the one exception, and these graphical tests were supported by the statistical tests (see legend of Figure 8.4). Cuneo's devoted labor of data collection thus reached a definitive theoretical conclusion.

The appearance of an addition rule at such young ages suggests it is built-in, having an essentially biological base. Certainly an addition rule was never learned by these children from society. Nor was it learned from nature, which ministers a multiplication rule. It thus seems appropriate to think that a perceptual–cognitive addition operator matures early in life and underlies much of adult judgment–decision.

RESPONSE SCALE VALIDITY

Cuneo provided unique validation of the rating response in an extension of the foregoing experiment. With small numbers, children can give veridical reports. This may relate to the subitizing–counting distinction with adults, who immediately apprehend number of objects up to about 7 or 8, but must adopt some more systematic counting process with higher numbers.

Cuneo saw that this veridical capability with small numbers could assess whether 3- to 4-year-olds use the rating scale in a true linear way. The same 24 children were run 5 additional sessions using rows of 2 to 7 beads. The children were encouraged to count, although they did not overtly do so. The rows were constructed from a 2 × 3, Density × Length design indicated in the right panels of Figure 8.4. As before, the children rated numerosity on a graphic scale.

The key feature of the right panels of Figure 8.4 is that the curves are not parallel, but form a linear fan for both the 3- and 4-year-olds. This linear fan mirrors the physical rule, Density × Length, and was supported in the individual analyses (see figure legend). Closer inspection shows that the response is approximately proportional to the actual number. Since the children perceive these small numbers veridically, their response mirrors the physical rule and hence forms a linear fan.

The crucial point, of course, is that the rating response must also be veridical. Otherwise, the fan pattern would not be obtained. With this ingenious, arduous study, Cuneo provided invaluable support for the rating methodology of developmental integration theory.

DEVELOPMENT OF QUANTIFICATION

Cuneo's work on early quantification has special significance because it goes down to 3^+ years of age, long before the end of the so-called preoperational period. Her work puts early quantification in an entirely different light from Piagetian theory. Several aspects of this different outlook on quantification deserve comment.

Foremost, of course, is the integration capability. Integration is a quantification capability in that it operates on metric stimulus values to yield a metric response. The Length + Density rule itself, moreover, is also quantitative in its algebraic form.

It may be objected that the addition operator may not be conceptual, on the ground that the general purpose integration operator may be a primitive biological capability. The task assemblage, however, is conceptual, both in stimulus valuation and in quality of response. Integration would not occur except for the goal-directed task assemblage. Considering the integration operator as a primitive capability does not detract from treating the Length + Density rule as conceptual quantification.

Second is the quantification of the two stimulus variables. Density, in particular, is treated by the children as a metric variable—as demonstrated by the Length + Density rule. These young children not only understand that density is relevant, but they evaluate it in a sensible metric way and they integrate this metric value with the other variable of length.

Third is the response, itself directly on a quantitative scale. It deserves emphasis, as in Chapter 3, that the rating method involves a sophisticated repertoire of quantification and assemblage capabilities. Most notable is that it represents true proportional thinking: The subjective feeling of numerosity is mapped into the objective graphic response in proportion to its magnitude. By virtue of functional measurement theory, therefore, the response is not merely ordinal, or rank order, but truly metric. This relationship, denoted by the action function, **A**, in the functional measurement diagram of Figure 1.1, demonstrates true quantification—and true proportional thinking—at 3^+ years.

This interpretation of the response is solidified by joint implication from the Length × Density and Length + Density rules of Figure 8.4. Although the former rule is considered to represent counting, not true multiplication, it nevertheless serves the inestimable function of validating the overt response measure as a true metric of the implicit feeling of numerosity. This in turn buttresses the treatment of the latter rule as conceptual addition.

A further implication, which follows from the judgments of small numbers, is that counting may be considered true quantification. The alternative hypothesis is that counting is merely a rote verbal response, devoid of quantitative content. The judgments of small number, however, were truly metric in quality, as demonstrated by the appearance of the linear fan pattern in the right panel of Figure 8.4. The functional measurement paradigm thus showed that counting yielded metric understanding of number.

This point may need emphasis. Metric understanding of number is generally either taken for granted or ignored. In fact, numbers are verbal symbols; to attribute metric meaning to number responses requires embedding them within a larger conceptual system. The necessity for such embedding is clear in the sharp difference between two common methods for obtaining numerical response shown in Figure 3.1. Most studies of number and counting with children show at most ordinal, or rank order understanding.

Cuneo's work thus has double value for number understanding. First, it demonstrates that counting can be truly metric in quality as early as 3^+ years. Second, it shows a way to supplement traditional approaches to development of number understanding.

Cuneo's results require a new way of thinking. Her results can be neither assimilated to nor accommodated within the Piagetian framework. Cuneo's work is constructive, however, for it exhibits an effective way to study early quantification.

PROBABILITY

To developmental psychology, the concept of probability presents an interesting puzzle because it is not an observable property of single events. Whereas time and number can be made concrete in a single event, typical probability tasks involve thinking in terms of classes of events. This difference is highlighted by the consideration that a correct judgment can be actually incorrect—when an unlikely event occurs—and similarly that an incorrect judgment can be actually correct.

TWO CONCEPTIONS OF PSYCHOLOGICAL PROBABILITY

In a traditional conceptualization, probability is defined in terms of long-run frequencies. This frequentist view is familiar from standard problems with dice, coin tosses, and cards. It gives an objective definition of probability in terms of objective frequencies of observable events. Frequentist conceptualization is adopted by one major class of mathematical probability theories.

An analogous frequentist approach could also be used with psychological probability. Probability would be taken as conceptually defined in terms of relative frequency. Development of probability cognition would be the development of this conceptual understanding. This frequentist approach treats the essential aspects of probability cognition as capabilities with relative frequencies, much as in standard problems about tossing dice and coins.

Just this approach was adopted by Piaget, who treated the psychological concept of probability as essentially identical with an understanding of schoolbook probability. Thus, Piaget and Inhelder (1951/1975) devote nearly a third of their book to experiments with permutations and combinations, which they consider prerequisite to development of the concept of probability. Their conception of probability also requires capability with numerical ratios, which is necessary to calculate probability as relative frequency of favorable and unfavorable cases. Capabilities with permutations and combinations and with numerical ratios appear only in the stage of formal operations, in early teen years. Younger children, accordingly, could not have a concept of probability.

Piaget's frequentist view dovetailed with his general physicalist position. Probability was considered an observable property of classes of physical events. The near-literal identification of psychological probability with schoolbook probability reflected an epistemological principle that development tends toward isomorphism with the external, physical world. This frequentist view was developed in many ingenious experiments, the results of which were taken to imply that young children possessed no conception of probability.

A quite different conceptual framework is adopted in developmental integration theory. Psychological probability is treated as belief or expectancy, not as relative frequency. Two properties are considered essential: *Variability of outcomes* refers to an understanding that more than one outcome can occur in a given situation; *graded expectancy* refers to uncertainty about the occurrence of some particular outcome. These two properties seem sufficient to define a reasonable understanding of the probabilistic nature of events. Whereas Piaget virtually identifies probability understanding with capabilities for actually calculating probabilities, the expectancy conception focuses on what seem to be the essential aspects of the cognition.

Under the expectancy conception, probability is interwoven with everyday thought and action. Young children are thus expected to possess some understanding of probability. Indeed, an expectancy conception presumably has a biological base. The present view of probability is thus consistent with expectancy theories of learning and motivation.

This expectancy conception is also akin to subjectivist views of mathematical probability theory. It avoids the well-known objection that the frequentist view has difficulty with probabilities of unique events, for example, the probability that your grant proposal will be funded. Piaget, however, strongly rejected subjectivist views, both for mathematical probability theory and for the psychological concept of probability.[6]

COGNITIVE ALGEBRA OF PROBABILITY

Good evidence for a cognitive algebra of probability has been found in developmental integration studies. Young children appear to have reasonable understanding of probability in the form of expectancy. Although probability judgment seems harder than time, quantity, and number, similar cognitive processing is involved.

Basic to these results on the development of probability concepts is the shift from the Piagetian choice paradigm to a functional measurement paradigm. In a typical Piagetian task, the child is shown two plates, each containing some red and some blue marbles, and asked which plate is preferable for a blind draw of a single red marble. Correct choice requires calculation and comparison of two red/(red + blue) proportions, for example, $2/(2 + 3)$ and $3/(3 + 5)$. Such ratio calculations, however, involve capabilities quite distinct from probability understanding. Adults may make mistakes from arithmetical incompetence, despite clear understanding of probability. Children could be correct, moreover, even though they applied other rules, in this example, choosing the plate with the smaller difference between red and blue marbles ($3 - 2 = 1$ and $5 - 3 = 2$). Piaget's choice paradigm harmonizes with his frequentist conception of probability, but it seems even less appropriate here than with time, quantity, and number in previous sections. A number of previous investigators had attempted to demonstrate understanding of probability at younger ages, but they were unable to resolve the difficulties and confoundings of Piaget's choice paradigm, which everyone relied on.

In a standard functional measurement paradigm, the children see only one plate of marbles. They judge how easy or hard it is to get a red marble in a blind draw. This paradigm provides a simpler stimulus field and task, as noted in the discussion of time. The continuous response, of course, is more informative than an all-or-none choice. Indeed, the continuous response is attuned to the approach–avoidance axis of purposiveness from everyday life.

Work in collaboration with Anne Schlottmann using the functional measurement paradigm indicates that even 4-year-olds take sensible account of both the number of winner marbles and the number of loser marbles. The integration is thought to involve serial processing. The child first identifies the more numerous color and makes an initial implicit adjustment toward the corresponding end of the response scale, graded in accord with the number of the more numerous color. A second adjustment is then made toward the opposite end of the response scale, graded in accord with the less numerous color.

This serial integration process seems a fine example of adaptive thinking. It embodies the essential task demands, but requires less cognitive capability than the ratio rule, red/(red + blue). It is conjectured to represent a general purpose strategy of serial integration that should be found in other tasks (Anderson & Schlottmann, 1991; see also Schlottmann & Anderson, in press).

In the present probability task, the relative weight of the more numerous color is a developmental parameter that decreases toward the physically correct value at older ages. Younger children exhibit strong response polarization in this task, whereas older children exhibit more graded expectancy. The polarization is thought to reflect a confidence-in-action operator, a general biological capability related to the approach–avoidance polarization associated with purposiveness. A similar tendency may perhaps be seen in findings of over-confidence by adults in various judgment–decision tasks.

EXPECTED VALUE

In everyday life, probability does not usually function alone, but in relation to goals. The primary mode of probability functioning is in *subjective expected value*, that is, the value of the goal integrated with the probability of attaining it. This reflects the axiom of purposiveness and fits nicely with the expectancy conception of probability. Adults judge expected value according to the multiplication rule, Probability × Value, as in Figure 10.1.

Nearly all developmental studies, however, have centered on pure probability tasks, described in the previous section. Expected value has received little attention. To study development of expected value, a prize is placed beside the red sector of a red–blue circular disc. A puppet, Hilda-the-Hippo, spins an arrow spinner and wins the prize if the arrow stops on the red sector. The child judges how happy Hilda will be to play such games, varied in size of red sector and number of crayons in the prize (Schlottmann & Anderson, 1994).

The 5- and 6-year-olds followed an addition rule. This rule shows understanding that the probability variable, although not of value in itself, does affect the worth of the event. This represents qualitative understanding of expected value because the two physical variables, red sector and prize, are physically independent, related only through the task scenario. Also implied by the addition rule, of course, is a functional metric of the probability concept.[7]

The multiplication rule shown by the three older age groups requires more advanced understanding of how probability operates. How this understanding develops is an important question about which little is known. Hardly of less importance is the sophisticated assemblage process needed to construct the operating memory for task performance.

These results provide further evidence that young children possess rather good understanding of probability. Indeed, children at all ages showed understanding of *probability dependence* (that the probabilities of the two separate outcomes are inversely related) in a second task in which this dependence was not physically built in, but only conceptual. Overall, the results exhibit probability understanding in the functional mode of expected value.[8]

FURTHER WORK ON PROBABILITY DEVELOPMENT

Two directions for future work on probability understanding are suggested by assemblage theory. One is toward biosocial expectancy, a direction that will require construction of experimental tasks more closely related to everyday life. Previous work, following the Piagetian conception of probability as relative frequency, has used abstract probability tasks almost exclusively. The biosocial view adopted here points instead to an origin of probability in primitive expectancies, together with development through operation of expectancy in everyday thought and action.

Expected value is a primary mode of probability cognition. Expected value, however, has been almost entirely neglected in developmental studies, perhaps because it involves the nonprobabilistic concept of value. Even the foregoing task of expected value, however, requires unfamiliar assemblage to represent the task demands. Tasks more closely related to everyday affairs would tap more directly into development of probability cognition.

The other direction is toward older children, in whom probability understanding and assemblage operation are both better developed. Although Piaget investigated across the age range, most subsequent work has been with younger children, in part a reaction to Piaget's claim that younger children had no concept of probability, in part a consequence of the prevailing research tactic of studying times at which concepts first emerge. Later development is conceptually more robust and less problematic to interpret. It is structurally richer, moreover, and has greater significance, both cognitively and educationally.

TWO THEORIES OF COGNITIVE DEVELOPMENT

Developmental integration theory is readily compared with Piagetian theory because stimulus integration is central to both. This integration theme has been the basis for the between-theory comparisons in each of the four knowledge domains considered in this chapter.

At no age, however, has Piagetian theory solved this problem of stimulus integration. Instead, it has presented false solutions. When concepts and methods of developmental integration theory were applied, Piagetian theory was seen to be radically incorrect. At every age above 3 years, the structure of knowledge differs sharply from the claims of Piagetian theory.

STIMULUS INTEGRATION AND QUANTIFICATION

Stimulus integration is a central concern of Piagetian theory. This issue generally has not been appreciated. It deserves comment, accordingly, because it is prerequisite to understanding Piagetian theory.

The problem of integration is imposed by the external world. Amount of liquid, probability, and many other physical concepts, have two or more determinants. Knowledge of the external world should reflect this multiple determination. Piaget's focal concern with knowledge of the external world led naturally to his concern with multiple determination.

The choice paradigm explicitly embodies this multiple determination; it was Piaget's diagnostic tool for studying knowledge of the external world. This paradigm requires a choice between two alternatives, each varied on two dimensions. In the conservation task, for example, the two glasses may differ in diameter and also height of liquid. In the probability task, the two plates may differ in number of winner marbles and also in number of loser marbles. Piaget also used this paradigm to study moral development (Chapter 6).

Integration is involved because the net value of each alternative depends jointly on both dimensions. One choice alternative may be better on one dimension, worse on the other. A simple tactic would be to ignore one dimension, choosing whichever was larger on the other dimension. This tactic could do fairly well, but it could often be wrong. For good performance, it is desirable to take account of both dimensions, ideally following the physical rule. The problem facing the investigator is to ascertain how subjects actually do handle these choice integration problems.

To solve this problem, Piaget made an assumption of isomorphism. Thus, a conservation response, in Piaget's view, requires integration of diameter and height in an actual calculation of liquid quantity. Probability judgment, similarly, requires calculation of ratios of winners and losers. These operations, characteristic of the final stage of development, are assumed to be isomorphic to physical reality.

Isomorphism has two aspects integration, just discussed, and quantification of the one-dimensional concepts. Metric concepts, the final stage of development, are also assumed to mirror physical reality. This measurement isomorphism is implicit in Piaget's theory of conservation, which entails calculation of physical quantity, and explicit in his treatment of time–speed–distance (Note 1) and of probability (see next section). This *measurement isomorphism* goes hand in hand with the *integration isomorphism* just considered.

Isomorphism between the final stage of cognition and physical reality was the linchpin for Piaget's genetic epistemology. Isomorphism defines and specifies the final stage of development—and the direction of earlier development. Isomorphism thus requires more detailed consideration.

PIAGETIAN THEORY: TWO FUNDAMENTAL ASSUMPTIONS

Piaget's goal of genetic epistemology led naturally to his predominant concern with commonsense physics of time, speed, quantity, and other aspects of the physical world. These knowledge domains refer to objective, physical concepts and simple algebraic laws—physical standards of correctness that are open to observation. In principle, therefore, children can learn these concepts and laws through their own action in the physical environment. Commonsense physics was the primary ground for Piaget's work, and his treatment rests on two fundamental assumptions.

First is the well-known assumption that development proceeds through distinct stages. The stage assumption promises notable theoretical simplification because all thought within any stage is required to have similar quality, governed by a single mode of cognitive organization. Developmental theory would thus reduce to determining the few modes of cognitive organization, for these would be uniform across knowledge domains.

Transition from one stage to the next involves qualitative discontinuity in mode of thinking. Each successive stage requires complete reorganization as new structures replace the old. Piaget's four stages (sensory–motor, preoperational, concrete operational, and formal operational) are not descriptions of the obvious trends in cognitive development. Instead, they embody strong theoretical assumptions about cognition—and equally strong constraints on interpretation of empirical results.[9]

The second fundamental assumption is isomorphism. Development is assumed to follow a course for which the final stage of knowledge is isomorphic to physical reality, as already discussed. Isomorphism is clear in Piaget's application of formal operations in each knowledge domain considered in this chapter. Conservation is claimed to depend on extensive quantification of the physical quantity. With time–speed–distance, formal operations are assumed to mirror the physical operations. In the probability domain, formal operations are assumed to involve permutations, combinations, and ratio thinking, exactly as in schoolbook probability formulas. These integration operations mirror the actual physical laws.

Isomorphism was taken more or less for granted by Piaget. Isomorphism assumes that the final developmental stage of knowledge is the same as schoolbook formulas. This schoolbook view of knowledge is explicitly developed in Piaget's treatment of probability, and it underlies his treatment of time–speed–distance and other domains of commonsense physics.

Subsequent workers have not appreciated the force of this assumption, in part because they have been more concerned with earlier development. Isomorphism is a guiding principle throughout Piagetian theory. Without this assumption, the end stage of development would be indeterminate in the theory. No less significant, isomorphism imposes a direction and framework on development, which must be construed as tending toward the presumed final stage.

But isomorphism often fails with integration operations. As already seen, Wilkening found that adults use the isomorphic rule, Time = Distance ÷ Speed, but the nonisomorphic rule, Speed = Distance − Time. In adult probability judgment, similarly, nonisomorphic rules are frequent (Chapter 10), and the same holds for causal attribution (Figure 5.5).

Isomorphism applies not only to integration but also to measurement, or valuation. Quantification is essential in knowledge of the external world, and Piaget saw that it required explicit theoretical consideration. But Piaget's measurement theory recognizes only isomorphic, objective measures of physical quantities. Thus, Piaget's treatments of conservation and probability understanding, as already indicated, explicitly assume measurement isomorphism.

When functional measurement theory was applied, isomorphism was quickly seen to be false. The integration rules used by subjects are not generally isomorphic, even with adults. Their measurement scales are seldom isomorphic. Functional measurement thus has a unique capability in analysis of commonsense physics, for it can determine integration rules and psychological measures without reliance on structure of the external world.

The stage assumption also is discordant with the foregoing integration studies. Contrary to the centration hypothesis, preoperational children have notable capabilities for integration. Centration is an artifact of Piagetian methodology. Furthermore, preoperational children have advanced quantitative capabilities, including capability for proportionate quantification, again contrary to Piagetian theory. In short, so-called preoperational children have notable capability for operational thinking. The developmental discontinuity between preoperational and operational stages claimed by Piaget does not exist.

The issue of centration deserves reflection. Piaget took centration to be a basic characteristic of preoperational thought. Centration is woven into the fabric of his conceptual framework. With the failure of the centration hypothesis, the concept of preoperational stage begins to fall apart. It is not merely that young children are more capable than Piaget recognized; their knowledge systems are qualitatively different.

The failure of centration has a deeper implication. It reveals fatal inadequacy of Piaget's basic methodology. The ease with which centration is found wrong with the functional measurement paradigm underscores the obtuseness of Piaget's choice paradigm—including the associated methodology of verbal questioning. Since the choice paradigm misrepresented development so seriously in so simple a matter, no less serious failures must be expected in matters less simple. Failure of centration thus brings a pall to the general Piagetian framework, for it rests almost completely on this methodology.

At the stage of concrete operations, thought is required to be reversible. Reversibility requires mathematical consistency among different forms of the same physical relation. But in fact, operational thought is not generally reversible, as illustrated in the initial sections on time and speed (see also Note 2). Nonreversible thought also appears outside the domain of commonsense physics, as in social cognition (e.g., Figure 5.5).

At the stage of formal operations, Piagetian theory is also askew. Reversibility fails in this stage much as it did in the stage of concrete operations. At this stage, moreover, thought is required to mirror physical reality. But this isomorphism assumption also fails, as already noted, both for the form of the integration rules and for quantification.

Knowledge of the external world is certainly correlated with the external world, for survival would not otherwise be possible, and this correlation shows marked developmental trends. Correlation, however, is not isomorphism. The Height + Width rule, for example, gives a very high correlation with area, but it is qualitatively different from the physical rule of Height × Width. Contrary to Piagetian isomorphism, knowledge of the external world generally has different structure from the external world itself.

A different conceptual foundation is needed. Everyone recognizes the obvious facts of development, that later thinking is more advanced, more organized, and in various respects qualitatively different from earlier thinking. Piaget attempted to rise above these facts of development to provide a general theory. This attempt failed because his two fundamental assumptions were invalid. Efforts to emend Piagetian theory are misguided because its fundamental assumptions are cross-grain to the structure of cognition.

DEVELOPMENTAL INTEGRATION THEORY

A theory of cognitive development must solve the problem of stimulus integration. Piaget saw that this problem was central, but his solution has failed. This failure arises in substantial part from his choice paradigm, which has a strong propensity for false successes. It claims to see things that are not there.[10]

The functional measurement paradigm is a constructive alternative. It shows that Piagetian methodology is systematically invalid in each of the four physical knowledge domains reviewed in this chapter. It does this constructively, by revealing cognitive structures essentially different from those claimed in Piagetian theory. It achieves this by focusing on structure of the internal world, without recourse to structure in the external world, isomorphism in particular.

Counterparts to Piaget's two fundamental assumptions appear in developmental integration theory. The stage assumption is replaced by an assemblage assumption. Heterogeneity, not homogeneity, is thus an essential quality of thinking, as with conjoint operation of intuitive and symbolic thought.

The isomorphism assumption is replaced in a different way, namely, with functional measurement methodology. Assumption is thus replaced by diagnostic method. Structure of the external world is replaced by structure of the internal world. In this way, integration rules used by children can be assessed directly, almost as empirical matters of fact. This has every advantage over the assumption of isomorphism.

Quantification, central in both theories, is also viewed differently in developmental integration theory. This difference begins with empirical demonstration of true metric concepts even before age 4, long before they are allowed in Piagetian theory.

In their origin, metric concepts are thought to be assembled from biologically grounded capabilities of general metric sense, proportionate action, and general purpose integration rule. Assemblage theory thus fuses intuitive and conceptual quantification.

Developmental integration theory gives a unified approach across different knowledge domains. To Piaget, the physical and moral domains were essentially different. Piaget looked for operational stages in the moral domain, but concluded they were not there, perhaps because isomorphism was inapplicable. Other workers, it is true, have argued for moral stages, but these are different from the Piagetian stages (Chapter 6). The difference in Piaget's treatment of these two domains seems almost an internal contradiction in his stage framework, for the problem of stimulus integration appears in both domains. In developmental integration theory, indeed, the basic processes of valuation, integration, and assemblage are similar in both domains. Psychological quantification is similarly feasible in both domains. Moreover, specific structural similarity across domains appears in the form of cognitive algebra.

In adult cognition, furthermore, the same concepts and methods have yielded a unified approach across many domains. This has already been illustrated in previous chapters on person cognition and general social cognition. It is further illustrated in the following chapters on psychophysics, decision theory, memory, and language processing. Developmental studies in these areas may reasonably be expected to exhibit similar generality.

THREE DEVELOPMENTAL ISSUES

Three loci of development have special importance for developmental integration theory. One concerns developmental course of integration rules, for example, whether transition from addition to multiplication is gradual or all-or-none. Synchrony of rule development across different tasks is also of interest, as is development of integrational capacity. These questions may require extended study of individual children using a battery of tasks.

A related question concerns cognitive processes that underlie integration rules. Primary concern to date has been to establish cognitive algebra empirically. Further questions of process have accordingly received relatively little experimental attention (see last part of Chapter 2). Training–transfer schedules would seem useful for process analysis. For example, children could be explicitly trained on the analogue fractionation process for multiplication in one task, with transfer tests in other task domains. Also of interest would be explicit training with the stepwise, serial integration strategy.

Integration rules have educational interest. What little attention school curricula give to integration mainly concerns formulas for rectangular area and other physical quantities. These formulas make little contact with the more intuitive integration processes that underlie everyday thought and action. This latter form of integration needs to be incorporated in the curriculum and interrelated with the schoolbook formulas. In this way, training–transfer studies could also have educational benefit as a means for unifying intuitive and symbolic thought.

A second locus of development concerns value. Stimulus valuation generally has been much simplified in previous studies in order to focus on the integration operation. Values, however, represent important aspects of the structure of knowledge. Values would thus be expected to exhibit significant developmental trends in every knowledge domain.

Functional measurement methodology has several advantages for value analysis. It is relatively simple. It can be applied to individual children. It makes minimal demands for verbal skills, which facilitates cross-age comparisons. In principle, it applies to nonverbal behavior. Although only applicable under certain conditions, it can give unique power.

The most important locus of developmental trends concerns assemblage. All the foregoing experiments have required rather complex assemblage for task performance. The probability task, for example, rests on a goal-directed set toward winning the prize, animistically attributed to the puppet. A mental model of the task must be assembled, with an action role based on the idea of a blind draw, coupled with understanding that shaking the marbles around on the plate makes the blind draw uncertain. Central to this mental model, of course, is a subassemblage for the integration operation. Also required are subassemblages dealing with stimulus valuation and with the response quantification required in the rating method (see Chapter 3). Such assemblage processes are in many ways more interesting than the focal concept in the task. Assemblage is a qualitative form of integration, and the study of its developmental trends and structure has fundamental importance (Bogartz, 1994).

ASSEMBLAGE THEORY VERSUS STAGE THEORY

Assemblage theory provides a genuine alternative to Piaget's stage theory because it embodies an essentially different structure of cognition. In particular, assemblage theory allows for joint action of different kinds of processes and abilities. Whereas stage theory requires all thinking within a stage to be homogeneous in quality, assemblage theory envisages thinking as generally heterogeneous. Whereas *décalage*, the fact that the same process appears at different times in different tasks, is a theoretical embarrassment in Piagetian theory, it is a theoretical expectation in developmental integration theory. Different kinds of thinking, perceptual and operational, concrete and abstract, intuitive and symbolic, may be assembled for thought and action in the task at hand.

Assemblage theory allows for qualitative development in cognition, as with changes from concrete to abstract thinking. It does not, however, require concrete and abstract thinking to correspond to distinct stages, as in Piaget's conception of concrete and formal operations. Quite the contrary; concrete and abstract thinking are expected to go hand in hand in assemblage.

Development is essentially continuous in developmental integration theory. Sudden changes in understanding may occur with particular problems, but even these take time and practice to become general characteristics of cognition. Development may be nonhomogeneous, moreover, with much higher levels in one or two tasks and skills than in others.

Assemblage theory leads to an array of tactics of investigation that have been discussed elsewhere (Anderson, 1983b, 1991j; Anderson & Schlottmann, 1991; Anderson & Wilkening, 1991). Among these are the ergodic heuristic, which suggests that longitudinal information can be obtained from cross-sectional behavior on a battery of tasks of varied difficulty (e.g., Dozier & Butzin, 1988); a treatment of memory as functional rather than reproductive (Chapter 11); the tactic of task complication to counterpoise the predominant tactic of task simplification; and reversal of the dominating concern with times at which concepts first emerge to study concept functioning at older ages, when concepts are more robust.

The tactics just cited all relate to the nonunitary view of concepts incorporated in assemblage theory. In the standard view, concepts are unitary and elemental—building blocks of cognition. The standard simplification tactic is intended to eliminate auxiliary abilities to reveal the naked concept. The heavy emphasis in developmental psychology on ages at which concepts first emerge flows directly from the standard view that concepts are unitary and autonomous, and, once developed, ready to act when needed.

In assemblage theory, in contrast, concepts typically begin as part of various skills and abilities, from which they may never become completely distinct. Especially at early ages, concepts may be far from autonomous, existing largely within the separate abilities in which they manifest themselves. An important part of the theory of any concept, accordingly, is understanding how it is assembled into operating memories for performance on various tasks. The complication tactic and the emphasis on older ages both aim at developmental study of assemblage capabilities.

Assemblage always requires knowledge and abilities distinct from the concept under study. Such heterogeneity of concepts was illustrated in the foregoing partial description of assemblage in the probability task and in similar comments earlier on the time–speed–distance task. The need to study assemblage has been obscured by the standard view of concepts as autonomous. This conceptual heterogeneity of assemblage is one form of adaptiveness in everyday purposiveness. It is important for study in its own right and, in the present view, as the normal mode of concept functioning.

Assemblage theory bears directly on issues of instruction and transfer. Instruction based on the idea of unitary, autonomous concepts is likely to be counterproductive, a view in line with the long history of difficulties in obtaining transfer in educational psychology. Instead, concepts should be taught as part of assemblage, for this represents their natural mode of functioning. Instruction will be more effective in obtaining transfer when it incorporates an assemblage conception of the relations between knowledge and action.

HOMAGE TO PIAGET

Piaget made numerous fascinating discoveries about children's understanding of the external world. His wide-ranging work has restructured this facet of developmental psychology. Thereby it has led to deeper understanding of adult cognition. Taking his positive contributions to psychological science all together, Piaget must rank among the great psychologists of all time.

It is not ungrateful, however, to criticize both Piaget's method and his theory. Although Piaget recognized the central problem of stimulus integration, his methodology and his theory were mutually inadequate to resolve it. His choice paradigm has been fruitful and still has usefulness; the criticism is warranted by the demonstrated artifacts and misconceptions it has also produced.

The inadequacies of Piaget's theory are well illustrated by the contrast at the beginning of this chapter between the empirical discovery of nonconservation and its theoretical interpretation in terms of centration. These criticisms are intended to help clear the way for continuation of the trail-blazing empirical discoveries of Jean Piaget.

NOTES

This chapter owes much to contributions by Clifford Butzin, Diane Cuneo, Edward Karpp, Manuel Leon, Anne Schlottmann, Friedrich Wilkening, and Yuval Wolf, as well as Richard Bogartz, Mary Dozier, Colleen (Surber) Moore, and Etienne Mullet. Related material, including references to the literature, is given in Volume III of *Contributions to Information Integration Theory* (Anderson, 1991d, reviewed by Bogartz, 1994).

1. The logical incoherence in Piaget's writings is recurrent in his attempts to explain how quantitative, metric understanding develops from qualitative, greater than–less than understanding. This qualitative-to-quantitative thesis is central to Piaget's genetic epistemology. Piaget claims to present explanations, but repeatedly begs the question.

This issue may be illustrated with the concept of speed, which Piaget claims begins as a qualitative understanding of overtaking of one [slower] object by another [faster] object, which may be considered a reversal of order. Extensive development is needed to get from this beginning merely to reach a stage of formal operations that enable qualitative comparison of speed of successive movements over equal distances with unequal times, or over unequal distances with equal times. Thus, for two objects traveling equal distances, the lesser time corresponds directly to the greater speed. When one variable is constant for both objects, it can be ignored and a qualitative, rank-order comparison made on the other variable. Qualitative, greater than–less than reasoning thus suffices—when one variable is constant.

The situation is quite different when the two objects travel unequal distances in unequal times. Suppose, for example, that one object travels 4 cm in 2 sec, the other 5 cm in 3 sec. Qualitative reasoning no longer suffices. Metric understanding is necessary to determine which has greater speed.

In discussing this numerical example, Piaget (1970) assumes without remark and without justification that the child possesses veridical metric understanding of time and indeed of time differences. Thus, he asserts that the child compares the difference in time (1 sec) with the time taken by the first object (2 sec); and he compares the difference in distance (1 cm) with the distance covered by the first object (4 cm). "Comparing these two he then arrives at the idea that 1 cm's difference is less in relation to 4 cms, than one second in relation to two seconds, and thus he concludes that in the first example the second object moves slower than the first" (p. 304).

But how the child "arrives at the idea" that this comparison solves the problem is what was to be explained. Piaget begs the essential question. He further begs the question in that the stipulated comparison implicitly assumes that the movements occur at uniform speed, whereas Piaget explicitly asserts that the concept of uniform speed is dependent on prior metric understanding. Moreover, this explanation makes development of a metric speed concept depend on prior development of a metric time concept—which contradicts the grand conclusion of Piaget's theory of the time concept, namely, that time is derivative from speed (see further Anderson & Wilkening, 1991, pp. 37*ff*).

Metric understanding, both intuitive and symbolic, is a remarkable human capability, and a special problem for developmental psychology. This issue arose naturally for Piaget because of his focus on the external world, and it was essential to his basic assumption of isomorphism. As Piaget saw it, he needed to explain how metric understanding developed from nonmetric, qualitative understanding of greater than–less than. Piaget claimed to have accomplished this, but he only begged the question. He slips in what needs to be proved at critical junctures. Similar question begging appears in his attempt to explain the development of conservation, as noted later in the text.

Everyone agrees that Piaget's writings are difficult to understand. One reason is that they often make no sense.

2. The Piagetian concept of reversibility requires that any operation must develop conjointly with its inverse operation. Reversibility is considered a fundamental characteristic of thinking even at Piaget's stage of concrete operations (roughly 7 to 11 years of age). At this stage, however, lack of mathematical consistency among integration operations is even more pronounced than at the stage of formal operations (see also Surber, 1987). These failures of reversibility in integration tasks are not surprising; the concept had done poorly in earlier tests by other investigators using different experimental paradigms.

Reversibility, it may be noted, can be considered a form of isomorphism, but isomorphism with logical form of thought rather than with physical reality. Piaget's strong emphasis on reversibility may thus arise from a preconception that isomorphism will characterize knowledge structure.

3. Actually, there was one more explanation of the Height + Width rule, namely, that children judged the perimeter. Height and Width need not be cognitive units in this interpretation, so it could be misleading to speak of their integration. Some evidence against this perimeter interpretation may be seen in the finding of parallelism for right and isosceles triangles (Anderson & Cuneo, 1978a, Experiment 4). For these figures, the perimeter is not additive in height and width. Much stronger, however, was Cuneo's demonstration of the Length + Density addition rule for numerosity discussed later. In this task, the perimeter interpretation has no analogue.

4. The Height + Width rule for rectangular area led to some controversy, mainly of interest as a case lesson about tactics of science. The most important implication of the Height + Width rule was the hypothesis of a general purpose integration operator. The rectangle task, however, was ill-suited to follow up this implication. Instead, a shift to other tasks was indicated.

Most followup studies, nevertheless, centered on the area task and on objections to the Height + Width rule. Overall, these studies show that Height + Width is the modal rule for 5-year-olds, but that other rules may be used as well, for example, the rule of maximal one-dimensional extent (Leon, 1982). Among these studies, careful methodological work by Silverman and Paskewitz (1988) suggested that better results might be obtained with a unipolar version of the bipolar, sad–happy face rating scale used in the original study. Mullet (e.g., Mullet & Montcouquiol, 1988) has presented an instructive approach to analysis of individual differences in rule usage. A striking extension to three dimensions with the rule, Volume = Height + Width + Depth was found by Wolf and Algom (1987; see Figure 9.12). Even more striking is Wolf's (1995) finding that a short period of handling the stimulus rectangles produced a shift in rule from Height + Width to Height × Width.

The Height + Width rule had two important implications. One was the hypothesis of a general purpose adding-type operator. The area task, however, was chosen as a properly two-dimensional comparison for the Piagetian task of liquids in glasses, which was the main initial concern in the original study (Anderson & Cuneo, 1978a). The Height + Width pattern was unexpected, and the five followup experiments on area judgment in the original report had the primary purpose of establishing that this pattern was valid, not a consequence of some peculiarity of stimulus materials or procedure. These followup experiments led to the interpretation as a general purpose adding-type operator.

These followup experiments also made clear that the area task was not well-suited to pursue the hypothesis of a general purpose operator. In particular, the perimeter interpretation discussed in the preceding note cannot be definitely eliminated. Also, area can be judged on a perceptual basis, as a global judgment of amount, which could confound certain developmental questions. The adult linear fan pattern presumably results in this way, not from conceptual development of a true multiplication rule.

The other implication of the Height + Width rule is that it represents a conceptual integration in a task in which perceptual integration seems overwhelmingly natural. This conceptual–perceptual contrast is notable at 5 years of age, especially since adults presumably use the perceptual mode. The slow appearance of the linear fan pattern with older children suggests perseverance of the conceptual integration. This implication has not been pursued, although it seems important. Other than this, however, the area task lost its main usefulness once it had performed its serendipitous function of suggesting the idea of a general purpose integration operator.

As a matter of research tactics, therefore, shifts to other physical tasks would surely have been more productive than the centration on the Height + Width rule. Just such shifts were made with Cuneo's work on numerosity and with Wilkening's work on time–speed–distance, as well in work on mass–volume–density relations by Mullet and Vidal (1986) and on the ergodic heuristic by Dozier and Butzin (1988).

The numerosity and time–speed–distance studies discussed in the text were not only more convincing evidence for the general purpose rule, but also yielded important results in their own right. That other rules may also be used for area is not really an objection to the Height + Width rule; the rule is not in the task, but in the mental model assembled for the task. This mental model may depend on details of task–procedure and on individual differences. Hence the integration rules are of interest both in themselves and as tools for analysis of mental models and assemblage.

The cited articles on area were useful, but except for the two signal studies by Wolf, the total outcome of subsequent studies of area judgment is not impressive. A more positive outlook, with a shift to study one of the two main implications of the original finding, would have been more rewarding. Although it seems partly ungracious to say so, the bulk of these studies provide a case history of how the need for replication in science can lead to an adversarial stance that shortchanges itself.

5. Criticism of developmental integration theory and cognitive algebra by Gigerenzer and Murray (1987, pp. 91*ff*) suffers many misconceptions and errors.

Gigerenzer and Murray are seriously incorrect in their repeated assertions that cognitive algebra is limited to hypotheses that can be expressed in terms of analysis of variance. The ubiquitous averaging model, in particular, cannot be expressed in these terms. With differential weighting, the averaging model is inherently nonadditive (Chapter 2). The major premise of Gigerenzer and Murray, that "Out of all the possible cognitive algebra hypotheses, only those that fit the linear, additive structure of the analysis of variance are even considered," is contrary to fact.

Other assertions by Gigerenzer and Murray are also in error. (a) Their statement that IIT localizes cognitive development in the integration rule is wrong, for it overlooks the central importance of valuation and assemblage in developmental integration theory. (b) Their question about power neglects to note that this question had been asked by Bogartz (1978) and answered quite satisfactorily by Anderson and Cuneo (1978b). (c) Their criticism of the rating method neglects the directly relevant study of Cuneo (1982) discussed with Figure 8.4 and seems unaware of the multiple lines of evidence for response linearity summarized in Chapter 3. (d) Their concern about model–scale trade-off fails to recognize that this issue had been carefully considered in functional measurement theory (see Chapter 3, Notes 1 and 2). (e) Their discussion of relative centration has no relevance to Piaget's concept of centration as inability to integrate two stimulus cues. This latter concept of centration was considered by Piaget to be characteristic of preoperational thought, as well as an explanation of nonconservation. This latter concept of centration was at issue in the integration studies criticized by Gigerenzer and Murray. (f) Their reiterated assertion to the effect that only those algebraic rules that fit the linear, additive structure of the analysis of variance are considered in cognitive algebra is far from truth, as already noted with the averaging model and as shown also by the various configural rules found with cognitive algebra. Indeed, a notable advantage of functional measurement lies in linear response methodology, a unique tool for analysis of nonalgebraic rules (see *Linear Response Methodology* in Chapter 3).

6. Discussions of subjectivist probability theory are given in Fishburn (1986) and Shafer (1987), both of which include commentaries and reply that indicate the diversity of views on the foundations of mathematical theory of probability. The present contrast between subjective and frequentist theories of psychological probability is amplified in Anderson (1991j) and Anderson and Schlottmann (1991).

7. Attention should be called to failure to replicate an earlier study of developmental integration theory, which showed the linear fan pattern of a multiplication rule for judgments of expected value by 5-year-olds (Anderson, 1980). The experiments cited in the text did not verify the fan pattern at this age, but indicated an adding-type rule instead. Work with other tasks since the earlier study of expected value has found little evidence for true multiplication rules even as young as 6 years. The observed linear fan should thus probably be considered a statistical false alarm.

8. Probability dependence refers to the understanding that the separate probabilities for the two outcomes are inversely related. This dependence is built into the circular disc because the two sectors have a constant sum of 360°. This physical dependence was eliminated by replacing the disc with a tube with two independent lengths of colored paper to represent the two probabilities. The children readily understand that if one outcome occurs, the other will not, but this does not automatically translate into understanding that the two probabilities are inversely related. Hence it was expected that younger children would exhibit a "more-is-better" strategy. All ages, however, showed clear qualitative understanding of probability dependence.

9. The concept of "stage" has been much discussed, and other workers have disagreed with Piaget's stage formulation on other grounds. Recent views on the stage issue are given in Levin (1986).

10. False successes also invalidate Siegler's (e.g., 1981) rule-assessment methodology, as shown in conjoint theoretical and empirical analyses by Wilkening and Anderson (1982, 1991) and Wilkening (1988). Siegler attempted to improve Piaget's choice methodology by using a battery of choice items, selected to winnow out alternative interpretations of the underlying rule. This rule-assessment methodology was applied in many tasks of commonsense physics, and it showed excellent agreement with Piaget, in harmony with its reliance on Piaget's choice paradigm. Unfortunately, Siegler's methodology has a strong propensity for false success, not merely failing to see the rules that are there, but claiming to see rules that are not there.

This propensity for false successes was documented by applying Siegler's method to hypothetical data constructed from an addition rule. Since Siegler's method did not allow the addition rule, it ought to have diagnosed these data as unclassifiable. Instead, it generally diagnosed various nonintegration rules, contrary to fact.

One empirical false success from Siegler's methodology appeared in the study of development of the time concept by Siegler and Richards (1979), cited in the text. Siegler's methodology diagnosed nonintegration rules up to age 10–12, leading to the claim that development of the time concept was equally late. In sharpest contrast, Wilkening's functional measurement study (Figure 8.1) showed an integration rule—and a true concept of time—at age 5. Siegler's rule assessment methodology is ineffectual, because it fails to find the correct rules, and invalid, because it presents false rules as true.

PREFACE

Integration psychophysics involves a fundamental conceptual shift. The venerable concept of *psychophysical law* has been a historic misdirection, influential but barren. A shift is needed to *psychological law.*

The senses are fundamental to thought and action, means whereby the brain constructs its remarkable internal representation of the external world. In the traditional conception of psychophysical law, this external–internal relation was assumed to rest on a single, simple mathematical function, the same for all senses. This assumption became taken for granted; the controversy was over *which* function was correct.

But this conceptual framework of psychophysical law never resolved its own central problem, namely, measurement of experienced sensation. For this, the psychophysical framework was inherently too narrow.

Adherents of psychophysical law assumed that Nature's order and law would be found in the sensory interface between the external and internal worlds. Integration psychophysics, in contrast, seeks order and law in the structure of the internal world itself. Of special significance is the algebraic structure of integration rules, or *psychological laws.*

Integration psychophysics was thus able to resolve the central problem of traditional psychophysics, namely, measuring experienced sensation. This can be done simply, as illustrated with the parallelism theorem of Chapter 2.

This resolution is not a mathematical hope but an experimental reality. This reality is demonstrated here with empirical applications to nine classical problems of psychophysics and perception.

Integration psychophysics has a broader horizon than traditional psychophysics. Multisensory integration, which is hardly amenable to representation in terms of psychophysical functions, is handled straightforwardly in two of the empirical illustrations. Context effects, often considered sow's ears in traditional psychophysics, can be made into silk purses in integration psychophysics. Nonconscious sensation, a neglected concept in psychophysics, can be defined and measured with functional measurement methodology.

Integration psychophysics can cooperate with sensory psychophysics, the other main branch of traditional psychophysics. Whereas sensory psychophysics follows a periphery-inward path, integration psychophysics follows a center-outward path. Sensory psychophysics, largely eschewing the psychophysical law, has made striking progress. It has difficulty with multisensory integration, however, and tends to ignore more cognitive processes. Functional measurement provides a grounded methodology for cooperative inquiry.

Chapter 9

INTEGRATION PSYCHOPHYSICS

We live in two worlds together. One is the external physical world, in which our bodies move and function. Within our bodies is a very different world, a world of everyday sights, sounds, and other sensory–perceptual experience. We take for granted that this internal psychological world mirrors the physical world. We are only surprised when this correspondence fails, as with geometric illusions (see, e.g., Figure 9.10).

Everyday theory of perception assumes we have direct contact with the external world. We think, without really thinking, that the eye somehow transmits little images of the external world to our conscious apprehension. The reason we see objects and motions is simple: That's what's there. The force of this direct perception theory is illustrated in the consternation caused among some early investigators (and some rather recent) by the realization that the lens in the eye produces an inverted image on the retina: Why don't we see the world upside down?!

This naive theory of direct perception has persuasive arguments in its favor. Perception seems effortless and immediate. Simple arithmetic and memory tasks often give us trouble, but perceiving complex scenes does not. Everyday experience gives little reason to suspect that perception involves complex processing, especially in the dominant visual sense.

A different argument comes from perceptual constancies. If perception were based on the retinal image, nearby people would change size dramatically as they moved about; doubling their distance would halve their size. The phenomenal fact of size constancy argues that we are in direct contact with our environment.

Of course, this commonsense theory of direct perception is not correct. This became clear when systematic study of the sensory systems was begun. The sensory nerves do not transmit little images. Instead, they transmit neuroelectrical impulses, a biological computer code. Everyday consciousness is totally unaware of nature's engineering marvels by which our sensory systems convert physical energy, such as light, into neuroelectrical impulses—and from this computer code of the nerves construct this fantastic internal world of three-dimensional shapes, motions, and chromatic magnificence.

This relation between the two worlds was a prime concern of the early psychophysicists, a concern manifest in the very term, *psycho–physics*. Without sense organs to provide information about the external world, the newborn infant could not survive. What is so remarkable is that the sense organs allow newborns, as you yourself once were, to make sense of the external world, perceiving it so closely as it really is. How is this possible? What engineering capabilities has Nature evolved that allow small-brained organisms to drive cars at high speed, to appreciate baseball and Mozart, and, indeed, even to invent cars, manage a baseball team, and compose a symphony?

Two perspectives on the relation between the two worlds are considered in this chapter: *traditional psychophysics* and *integration psychophysics*. Traditional psychophysics assumes that the search for Nature's laws should focus on the sensory interface between the two worlds. Integration psychophysics, in contrast, searches for Nature's laws within the internal world itself.

PSYCHOPHYSICAL LAW AND PSYCHOLOGICAL LAW

Some mathematical law connects the internal world of psychological sensation with the external world of physical stimuli: This has been a central idea of one main branch of traditional psychophysics. Just as there are mathematical laws of the physical world, it was thought, so should there be mathematical laws governing the dependence of sensation on the physical world.

That such *psychophysical laws* exist has been taken more or less for granted for well over a century; the controversy has been about which law is correct. This belief in psychophysical law reflects the focus on the interface between the two worlds. Nature's engineering marvels must be located in this interface. The psychophysical law was thus seen as a foundation and key for the study of sensation. Sensation, in turn, was seen as the foundation for knowledge of the external world, and indeed for all psychological science.[1]

Two main contenders have fought for the title of *the* psychophysical law. These are taken up in the next two sections. An alternative perspective—a shift away from the very concept of psychophysical law—is then presented.

LOGARITHMIC FUNCTION

The simplest psychophysical law would be the linear law: sensation proportional to the intensity of the physical stimulus. But proportionality is infrequent in sensory systems. Nature evolved systems with diminishing returns, sensitive to faint stimuli, yet not overloaded with stimuli millions of times more intense. The owl can hear the mouse rustle in the leaves, yet not have its eardrum blasted by the thunder. You and I, similarly, can see both by moonlight and in the noonday sun.

This consideration shows that sensation is not veridical perception of physical reality; instead, some nonlinear relation is involved. However, the thought that this nonlinear relation might have a simple form, the same across different sense modalities, hardly crossed anyone's mind until the work of Fechner.

In 1860, Fechner proposed his psychophysical law, which asserts that psychological sensation, ψ, is linearly related to the logarithm of the physical stimulus, S. In simple form:

$$\psi = c \log S. \qquad \text{(logarithmic function)}$$

This log law is at least roughly true, reflecting the diminishing returns built into sensory systems. Sound intensity, for example, is usually measured in decibels, which is a logarithmic scale of the physical energy.

The enduring impact of this simple equation would be hard to overestimate. It pointed to a unity across diverse sensory systems, all obeying the same law. It bypassed physiological problems, claiming a direct link between the physical stimulus, S, and the conscious sensation, ψ. Indeed, it claimed an exact mathematical relation between the physical and mental worlds. It thus promised uniform, mathematical order in the mental realm, which had previously seemed almost outside the scope of science.

But Fechner's logic has a missing link. Fechner gave a rational derivation of his logarithmic formula, based on the assumption that all *just noticeable differences* (jnds) in sensation represented equal units of sensation (see Chapter 3). Were this assumption true, sensation would indeed be proportional to the logarithm of the physical stimulus energy, truly a psycho–physical law. But neither Fechner nor later workers provided validational tests to support this critical assumption. Fechner's "law" was attractive, but it was not really a law, only a conjecture, resting on a missing link.

POWER FUNCTION

Only in recent times has Fechner's logarithmic function, despite recurrent criticism, had any serious competitor. This is the power function proclaimed so strenuously by Stevens (see 1975). The essential part of Stevens' claim was that the method of magnitude estimation, described in Chapter 3, provided a veridical measure of subjective sensation. Empirically, the magnitude estimation response, R, is often an approximate power function of physical stimulus intensity, S:

$$R = cS^n. \qquad \text{(power function)}$$

This power function, claimed Stevens, was the long-sought psychophysical law. The exponent, n, moreover, was claimed to be an invariant characteristic of each sensory system.

Stevens' claims were remarkably effective. Innumerable applications of magnitude estimation have been published, covering dozens of psychophysical dimensions, from loudness and heaviness to odor of coffee and roughness of sandpaper. Innumerable exponents have been presented, each claiming to represent some invariant sensory truth. Whereas the reaction to Fechner had been generally critical, the main reaction to Stevens was one of almost unquestioning acceptance.

Yet the critical link in Stevens' claim was never supplied. This issue is not subtle, but it does ask for a careful distinction. The issue is whether magnitude estimation gives a veridical measure of sensation. The observable power function just cited means little, for it only deals with the observed response, R. The real issue, pointed out by various investigators from the beginning, concerns the unobservable sensation, ψ. What Stevens claimed was that ψ was a power function of S—but at most he showed that R was a power function of S. The critical link between R and ψ was missing.

Stevens' missing link can be spotlighted by comparing magnitude estimation with an alternative method of obtaining numerical judgments, namely, the rating method. Figure 9.1 plots magnitude estimates of Munsell gray chips as a function of ratings of these same chips. If the two measures were equivalent, the curve would be a straight diagonal line. The curve is far from straight; at least one of the two measures is biased and invalid. Without a validity criterion, neither method can be trusted.[2]

Stevens never supplied a validity criterion. This is his missing link. He merely assumed that $R = \psi$; he merely assumed that magnitude estimation provides a veridical measure of unobservable sensation. Although some attempts were made to validate this assumption, they did unusually poorly.

Stevens' power "law" thus remained merely conjecture, just as Fechner's logarithmic law. A new approach was needed to resolve the issue of validity.

PSYCHOLOGICAL LAW: A NEW FOUNDATION[3]

Integration psychophysics is primarily concerned with dynamics of the internal world. This entails a conceptual shift—away from the *psychophysical law* to the *psychological law*. This shift in law entails a corresponding shift in conceptual framework and focus of inquiry.

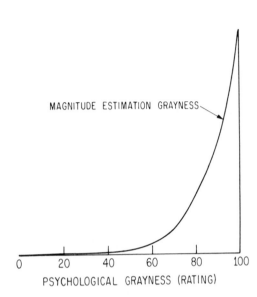

MAGNITUDE ESTIMATION GRAYNESS

PSYCHOLOGICAL GRAYNESS (RATING)

Figure 9.1. Magnitude estimation differs radically from rating. The curve represents magnitude estimations of grayness (lightness) of Munsell gray chips, plotted on the vertical, as a function of ratings of same chips, plotted on the horizontal. Equivalence of the two response measures would appear as a straight diagonal curve. The curve is far from the straight diagonal, which means that the two response measures are far from equivalent. Since the ratings satisfy validational criteria for a true linear scale, the deviation of the curve from the straight diagonal must reflect bias in magnitude estimation. See also discussion of Figure 3.1. (After N. H. Anderson, *Methods of Information Integration Theory.* Academic Press, 1982.)

The focus on psychophysical law rested on the belief that Nature's law and order would be found at the interface between the external and internal worlds. In contrast, the focus on psychological law rests on the belief that law and order can be found within the internal world itself. In terms of the integration diagram of Figure 1.1, the conceptual shift is from the valuation operator, **V**, to the integration operator, **I**.

Major reorganization of the conceptual framework of psychophysics is entailed in this shift from **V** to **I**. Multiple stimulus cues are the norm in psychophysical tasks. Hence *synthesis*, determining the integrated response to multiple determinants, is a primary theoretical problem. Equally important is *analysis*, that is, dis-integrating such response into its operative components.

These two problems, analysis and synthesis, are the heart of integration psychophysics. The traditional framework of psychophysical law gives little help with either analysis or synthesis. Instead, it actively discourages their study because it refers only to a single stimulus determinant. An integration perspective thus opens onto a quite different foundation for psychophysical investigation (see also McBride, 1993; Sjöberg, 1994).

Furthermore, the missing link in the traditional approaches to the psychophysical law can be forged. This link is a validity criterion, lacking in the work of Fechner and Stevens both. One form of this validity criterion is the parallelism theorem of Chapter 2, illustrated empirically in the later experiments. Magnitude estimation and rating have equal opportunity to satisfy the parallelism theorem. The parallelism property can—and has—forged the missing link.

Integration psychophysics can thus solve the problem of the psychophysical law. Given the success of the addition rule, the marginal means of the factorial data table are validated functional scales of sensation. The graph of these sensation values as a function of the physical stimulus values thus constitutes a determination of the psychophysical law, as with grayness in Figure 9.8. The long controversy initiated by Fechner can thus be brought to an end.

More important, however, is the shift in conceptual framework. The psychophysical law loses much of its interest and presumed value from an integrationist perspective. The concepts and methods developed to study psychological law contribute to a different class of issues, issues concerned with both sensory and cognitive aspects of psychophysics.

STUDIES OF INTEGRATION PSYCHOPHYSICS

Nine experimental studies of integration psychophysics are considered in the following sections. Most address classical problems, but in a new conceptual framework and with new methodology. Nine studies may seem overkill, since the first one alone demonstrates nine advantages of the integration-theoretical approach. In view of the foregoing criticisms of traditional psychophysics, however, it seems advisable to show that integration psychophysics is not conjecture, but working reality.

SIZE–WEIGHT ILLUSION

A pound of lead is heavier than a pound of feathers. This strong contrast illusion makes a surefire classroom demonstration (actually better done with an ounce of each). The effect is caused by the visual appearance; a larger object (feathers) feels lighter than a smaller object (lead) of the same gram weight. Although long considered a minor curiosity, this size–weight illusion presents some basic problems in psychophysical analysis. The following itemization shows how much information can be obtained from a single study with integration methodology.

In the left panel of Figure 9.2, subjects lifted a single, visible gray cylinder and judged its apparent heaviness on a numerical scale. There were 25 cylinders, ranging from 200 to 600 grams in weight (curve parameter) and from 15 to 3 centimeters in height (horizontal axis). The top curve shows the heaviness judgments for the five 600-gram cylinders; the upward slope of the curve shows that the smaller cylinders feel heavier. This is the size–weight illusion.

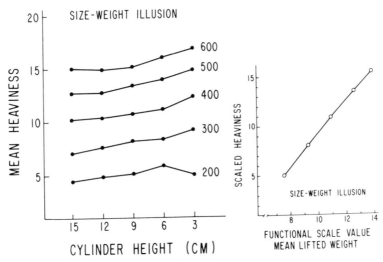

Figure 9.2. Size–weight illusion obeys addition rule, exhibits scale invariance. Left panel shows mean judgments of heaviness for 25 cylindrical weights, varied in height (horizontal axis) and gram weight (curve parameter). Parallelism supports addition rule: Heaviness = "Size" + "Weight." Right panel exhibits scale invariance for heaviness: Data points plot psychophysical function from left panel against psychophysical function obtained from collateral task of weight averaging. Observed linearity indicates scale invariance across the two tasks. (After Anderson, 1972a.)

1. Size–Weight Additivity. The primary feature of the left panel is the near-parallelism of the five curves. This argues for an adding-type rule:

Heaviness Sensation = "Weight" + "Size,"

where quotes are used to denote subjective stimulus values. The most popular explanation of the illusion had been that subjects were really judging density. Without capability for psychological measurement, the density hypothesis remained conjectural. The density hypothesis involves a division rule, however, which would yield a linear fan pattern, not parallelism. Functional measurement thus provided a simple diagnosis of the integration rule, making it visible in the factorial graph.

2. Psychophysical Law for Weight. The psychophysical function for heaviness as a function of gram weight may be obtained from the factorial graph. The curves are closer together toward the top; each additional 100 grams adds less heaviness sensation. By virtue of the second conclusion of the parallelism theorem (Chapter 2), the vertical elevations of the five curves are a linear scale of the heaviness values of the physical gram weight stimuli. Plotting these elevations as a function of gram weight gives a determination of the psychophysical function.

The unique advantage of functional measurement is that it includes a validational base for the psychophysical function. More than five points would be desired for curve fitting (see Figure 9.8). In principle, however, the missing link in determining the psychophysical law can at last be forged.

3. Cross-modal Psychophysical Law for Size. A second psychophysical function is also available—for heaviness as a function of size. This is portrayed in the shape of the curves; the upward slope reflects the influence of the size cue on the heaviness response. The biggest effect is produced by the change from 3 to 6 cm in height, with diminishing returns thereafter.

This psychophysical function is novel, for it is cross-modal. It could not be obtained directly by asking subjects how much heaviness would be produced by a given size. Instead, it is derived from the functional measurement analysis of the psychological law.

In similar way, it may be added, psychophysical functions may be derived for stimulus variables that do not possess a physical metric. This is one way in which the confines of traditional psychophysics are enlarged in integration psychophysics.

4. Scale Invariance: Cross-task Response Validation. In another condition, subjects lifted two unseen weights in succession and judged their average heaviness. If subjects do average, then the factorial graph should exhibit parallelism, as indeed it did. This parallelism is not surprising, of course, because the instructions prescribe additivity. But granted an additive integration, parallelism will be obtained only if the numerical response measure is a valid measure of sensation. As prosaic as it is, this weight-averaging task has an important function. In particular, the parallelism in the weight-averaging task provides cross-task validity, or response scale invariance, for the rating method.

5. Scale Invariance: Cross-task Stimulus Validation. More information is available. The psychophysical function can be determined for the weight-averaging task in the same way as just indicated for the size–weight task. The question is whether these two psychophysical functions agree. The answer is *yes.* The five points in the right panel of Figure 9.2 plot one psychophysical function against the other. The linearity of this curve means that both experiments yield the same psychophysical function. This is cross-task validity, or scale invariance, on the stimulus side, perhaps the first such demonstration.

6. Magnitude Estimation Is Invalid. Invalidity of the method of magnitude estimation is implied by the cited results. These results show that the rating method is a true linear measure of sensation. But rating and magnitude estimation are nonlinearly related, as seen in Figure 9.1. The conclusion follows that

"Since the rating data satisfy both internal and external consistency, they constitute the true measure of sensation. Magnitude estimation, in contrast, must be biased and invalid." (Anderson, 1972a, p. 389).

This conclusion has stood the test of time. As noted in a commentary (Anderson, 1989c, pp. 268–269) on a review article by Krueger (1989), a one-time proponent of magnitude estimation: "This conclusion was viewed as near-heresy at the time, but, in light of Krueger's discussion, it may now be near-orthodoxy" (see also review by Sjöberg, 1994).[4]

7. One-point Discrepancy. One point in Figure 9.2 deviates from the prevailing parallelism. This represents the response to the shortest, lightest cylinder, and it is interpreted as an end-point bias in the rating scale. Ordinarily, special end-anchor stimuli are used to tie down the end points of the response scale, so the regular experimental data come from the interior of the scale (Chapter 3). In this experiment, as it happened, a low end anchor was not included. The stimulus cylinder in question was thus itself at the low extreme of the given stimuli, thereby causing subjects to shift their response toward the end point of "1" (see similarly Table 4.1). This one-point discrepancy is not considered to reflect adversely on the overall pattern of parallelism, but it does provide a warning about experimental procedure in using the rating method.

It also deserves mention that this one-point discrepancy was enough to cause statistical significance of the deviations from parallelism. This illustrates the great statistical power of the analysis of variance methods used in IIT.

8. Context Effects: Silk Purses from Sow's Ears. Context effects are often considered a nuisance in psychophysics. The psychophysical law does not recognize them because it is a one-variable function of the focal stimulus. It has no place for a second, context variable. Context effects would constitute bias. Lifted weights are usually presented behind a screen, therefore, to eliminate bias from the visual appearance.

Integration psychophysics, however, provides a psychophysics of context. In the size–weight study, the context effect served as the validational base for the psychophysical law. It is not of less interest, of course, to study context effects for their own sake (see later sections).

9. Nonconscious and Conscious Sensation. Psychophysical theory requires methods for measuring nonconscious sensation. The conscious sensation of heaviness in the size–weight task is an integrated resultant of the two stimulus cues. Their separate effects, however, remain preconscious, inaccessible to introspection. Functional measurement makes it possible to measure both of these preconscious sensations. One of these is the psychophysical function for gram weight; the other is the corresponding psychophysical function for visual appearance. Consciousness is thus fractionated into preconscious components.

The issue of consciousness can be pursued further to assess equivalence of nonconscious and conscious sensation. In the weight averaging task, the heaviness sensations of the two stimulus weights are conscious, for the subject lifts each separately. These heaviness sensations need not agree with the sensation of the weight stimuli in the size–weight task, for the latter is preconscious. In fact, they do agree, for they yield equivalent psychophysical functions as already indicated in the right panel of Figure 9.2. This agreement suggests that a common information source is utilized in both tasks. This line of inquiry may provide new clues about the flow of information processing.

RATING VERSUS MAGNITUDE ESTIMATION: GRAYNESS JUDGMENTS

Rating and magnitude estimation were compared by Dave Weiss, who asked subjects to judge average grayness of pairs of Munsell chips. Since an averaging operation is prescribed, the factorial plot would be expected to exhibit parallelism—if the response measure is a linear scale. This task thus provides a validity criterion to adjudicate between the two response measures, rating and magnitude estimation. The missing link in Stevens' logic can thus be found.

The results are shown in Figure 9.3. The rating data in the left panel show near-parallelism, which supports the validity of the rating method. In contrast, the magnitude estimation data in the right panel show extreme nonparallelism, highlighted by the equal-length vertical bars at the left and right. This nonparallelism implies that magnitude estimation is biased and invalid. The bias appears to reflect diminishing returns in the use of numbers, noted in Chapter 3. The curves diverge at higher intensities because increasingly larger number differences are needed to express equal subjective differences.

ADDITIVITY OF COLOR CONTRAST

In color contrast, one hue induces its complementary hue. Thus, a gray field adjacent to a red field will appear tinged with green, the complementary hue to red. In the same way, a green field adjacent to a red field will seem to become greener. Such contrast effects provide important information on the operation of the visual system.

Leo Stefurak hypothesized that color contrast should obey an addition rule: The apparent hue of a test field should be the sum of its own hue when alone plus the contrast effect from an adjacent inducing field.

To test this addition rule, Stefurak applied functional measurement. The visual display included two adjacent color fields, each variable from red to green. A symmetrical two-factor design, Inducing Field × Test Field, was used. The five hue levels of the Test Field are indicated on the horizontal axis of Figure 9.4. The same five hue levels were used for the Inducing Field, each

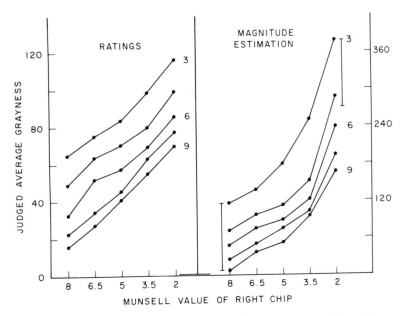

Figure 9.3. Rating passes validity test; magnitude estimation fails. Subjects judge average grayness of two gray chips, with Munsell grayness values of the right and left chips indicated on horizontal axis and as curve parameter, respectively. Parallelism in left panel supports validity of rating method; extreme nonparallelism in right panel infirms magnitude estimation. Same subjects served in both response conditions on alternating days. (Note optical illusion in right panel, indicated by the two equal-length vertical bars, which makes the curves seem more parallel than they really are; see Anderson 1982, Note 1.1.7a.) (After Weiss, 1972.)

represented as a connected curve in the figure. Subjects were told to attend to the Test Field, and to rate it on a continuous scale from "red 9" to "green 9."

Contrast is demonstrated by the vertical separation among the curves. The middle, dashed curve represents a neutral, white inducing field; it acts on a test field that varies from red to green on the horizontal axis. Relative to this neutral baseline, the top curve, which represents a red inducing field, causes the test field to look greener. Similarly, the bottom curve, which represents a green inducing field, causes the test field to look redder.

Color contrast is additive. The parallelism shows that the inducing field has a constant effect. Regardless of whether the test field is red or green, the inducing field adds the same amount of redness or greenness.

The linearity of the curves in Figure 9.4 implies that the physical hue scale on the horizontal is a true scale of hue sensation. This hue scale has a sensory basis, in terms of relative activation of red and green cones, and was developed

Figure 9.4. Additivity of red–green contrast. Hue judgments plotted as a function of hue of judged test field (horizontal axis) and hue of contrast-inducing field (curve parameter). Parallelism of solid curves implies that the apparent hue of the test field is the sum of its own proper hue and the contrast hue from the inducing field. Dotted curve represents baseline response to test field by itself and provides evidence for secondary induction (see text). Each point is the mean of 10 judgments of Subject K.F.P. Scale on horizontal is relative activation of red cones, with total (red + green) luminance held constant. Data from Stefurak (1987), who includes useful tips on rating methodology. Presented with kind permission of Leo Stefurak.

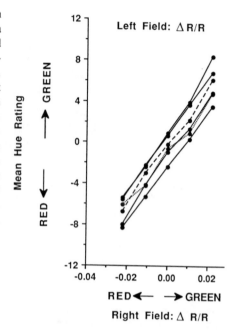

for general use in color vision with the hope that it would be a true linear scale. The linear relation between the sensory and judgment scales provides mutual support for both. Stefurak's work is thus a nice illustration of cooperative use of integration psychophysics and sensory psychophysics.

Finally, the dotted curve demonstrates the interesting phenomenon of secondary induction. This dotted curve represents judgments of the test field by itself, without any inducing field; it is flatter than the other curves, for which an inducing field is present. Stefurak's interpretation may be illustrated by comparing the dotted curve with the dashed curve for the neutral, white inducing field. The test field induces a complementary hue in the neutral inducing field; this induced hue elicits a reciprocal, secondary induction in the test field—which increases its saturation. Hence the dashed curve is steeper than the dotted curve. Furthermore, this secondary induction occurs in the same degree even when the inducing field is not neutral but red or green, a striking conclusion that follows from the parallelism. Overall, Stefurak's work provides new analytical power on the much-studied phenomenon of color contrast.

THE CHEMICAL SENSES: TASTE AND SMELL

Taste and smell are important in everyday life, especially at the dinner table. The importance of smell in food perception becomes clear when we have a cold; coffee tastes dull and flat, for example, because our olfactory sense is not functioning normally. What we "taste" thus depends on integrated action of both sensory systems, taste and smell.

In fact, what we ordinarily call taste is complex. Within the taste modality alone, sensations of sweet, sour, salty, and bitter may operate. The aroma, similarly, may consist of several qualities. Even the appearance of food and its textural quality may contribute to our "taste." Food perception is thus a prime field for analysis of stimulus integration.

Taste–Odor Integration. Cogent, dedicated work by Bob McBride has revealed a fruitful role for IIT in the chemical senses. One example is taste–odor integration, illustrated in Figure 9.5. Subjects sipped liquid mixtures varied in sucrose concentration and in orange odor. They judged overall intensity of each mixture.

The factorial graph of Figure 9.5 shows that both variables influenced the intensity judgment. The upward slope of the curves represent the effects of increasing sucrose concentration; the vertical separation among the curves represents the effect of the orange odor. The important feature of these data is the parallelism, which implies that the two variables are integrated by an adding-type rule:

$$\rho = \Psi_{taste} + \Psi_{smell}.$$

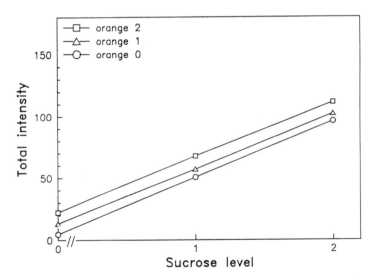

Figure 9.5. Taste–odor additivity. Subjects judge total intensity of a drink with varied sweetness and odor. Parallelism signifies an additive integration. (From McBride & Anderson, 1991.)

Without functional measurement methodology, this addition rule would be hard to establish. Although addition rules have often been conjectured in the chemical senses, these conjectures are not testable without solving the double problem of measurement of stimulus variables and measurement of response. In fact, the foregoing equation reemphasizes the problem of the three unobservables discussed in Chapter 1. The parallelism theorem allows a simple, simultaneous solution to all three unobservables.

Non-integration Rule. In studies of heterogeneous mixtures, McBride found evidence for a *dominant component model*. In this model, perceived intensity is determined by the stronger component alone; there is no integration. Aside from its importance in taste psychophysics, this result poses an interesting puzzle for cognitive theory.

The response pattern implied by a dominant component model is shown in the factorial graph of Figure 9.6. In this study, subjects tasted sweet–sour solutions and judged their overall intensity. The top curve shows the mean judgment for the highest acid concentration. This curve is essentially flat; total intensity is the same for the acid alone (leftmost point) as for acid combined with the very sweet (.80M) sucrose concentration (rightmost point). A similar pattern appears in the second curve from the top. It seems that the judgment is determined solely by the acid component.

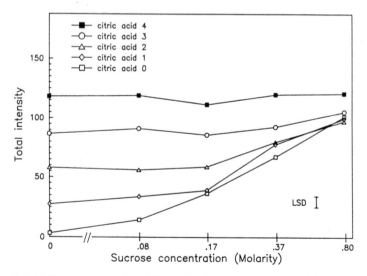

Figure 9.6. Mixture suppression follows dominant component model (see text). The factorial plot gives total intensity judgments of sucrose–acid mixtures. (After McBride, 1989.)

The two bottom curves show the complementary pattern. The lowest curve is for sucrose alone, so the upward trend of the points shows the intensity of the sucrose component per se. The next lowest curve is essentially identical over the three largest sucrose concentrations; the level of acid has no effect. This comparison indicates that the judgment is determined solely by the dominant sucrose component.

Thus, it seems that the sweet and sour components of a mixture are not integrated into the perception of total intensity. The interest in this effect is accentuated by the previous study, which showed integration of sweetness and odor. This pair of results suggests the possibility of some inhibitory process among the senses of the tongue that does not extend to odor.

Also of interest is that judgments of the sweetness or sourness of the mixture, as distinct from its overall intensity, do obey an integration rule, namely, a subtraction rule. In other data from this same study, the level of acidity caused a constant decrease in perceived sweetness (above threshold); similarly, the level of sugar caused a constant decrease in perceived sourness. This mixture suppression rule for these two quality judgments contrasts sharply with the non-integration rule for overall intensity. Although their implications are still uncertain, such results can provide penetrating information on process models of the chemical senses.[5]

Everyday Psychophysics. These results are important in everyday psychophysics. As McBride explains, the universal appeal of soft drinks depends on joint action of sugar and acid. Sweet drinks alone are no more than mildly pleasant. The acid component provides high intensity, the ''hit'' of the drink. But acid at the needed concentration is distinctly unpalatable. The sugar has a strong suppressant effect on the perceived acidity, whereas the acid has substantially less suppressant effect on perceived sweetness. Hence the sweet and sour qualities of the drink are both desirable and so is the ''hit.'' McBride's analysis thus explains the international prosperity of the cola companies.

PSYCHOPHYSICAL BISECTION

Functional measurement does not require a linear response scale. Hence it is potentially applicable with behavioral, physiological, and sensory measures, which will not generally be linear scales. This requires monotone analysis, illustrated here with the classical problem of psychophysical bisection.

The century-old problem of bisection arose as an alternative to Fechner's proposal for adding jnds. In grayness bisection, patterned after the original task used by Plateau, the subject is told to select a response chip that lies midway in grayness between two given stimulus chips. One advantage of this task is that it deals with suprathreshold response measures. This avoids the uncertainty of Fechner's assumption of equal jnds. Another advantage is that the response is not verbal but perceptual. This avoids uncertainty whether number-words can be taken at face value as true numbers.

Bisection Model. The analysis rests solely on the algebraic structure of the bisection model. A standard hypothesis is that the subject is equating two sense distances:

$$\psi_1 - \rho = \rho - \psi_2.$$

Here ψ_1 and ψ_2 are the sensation values of the two given stimuli and ρ is the sensation value of the response. Solving for ρ yields the average:

$$\rho = \tfrac{1}{2}(\psi_1 + \psi_2).$$

But bisection need not be at the midpoint. Subjects could be instructed, say, to form a 60:40 division, and they might be doing something like that even when instructed to form a 50:50 division. A more general model is required, accordingly, which includes a weight parameter, ω, to represent proportionate division:

$$\rho = \omega\psi_1 + (1-\omega)\psi_2.$$

This equation involves the problem of the three unobservables, already discussed in Chapter 1. The terms, ρ, ψ_1, and ψ_2, are unobservable sensations. That is as it should be, for the bisection occurs in the subjective metric. The investigator, however, can observe only the physical reflectances, that is, R, S_1, and S_2, not the grayness sensations themselves. This is why the bisection problem has resisted analysis.

Data Analysis. The data analysis is based on the monotone parallelism theorem, noted in Chapter 3. Subjective grayness is some monotone function of the physical reflectance, which is observable. If the bisection model holds, therefore, the observable R can be made additive by a monotone transformation. Indeed, this transformation is just the psychophysical law.

This approach was applied to the bisection experiment summarized in Figure 9.7. The observable reflectance values of the bisection response are plotted in the left panel of the figure; these curves are not parallel, of course, because the physical metric of reflectance is not the psychological metric of grayness. After monotone transformation, however, the data appear parallel, as shown in the right panel.

All that is at issue in this analysis is the structure of the bisection model. The response need only be monotone, or rank-order. No other assumption is needed. Furthermore, the additivity assumption of the bisection model is only pro tem; it is tested in the data analysis.

Psychophysical Function. The psychophysical function may be derived from these data by virtue of the second conclusion of the parallelism theorem. Each parallel curve gives the relative sensation value of the Munsell chips listed on

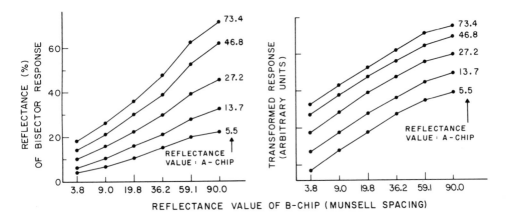

Figure 9.7. Monotone analysis for grayness bisection. Subject chooses response chip to lie midway in grayness between two stimulus chips. Left panel plots physical reflectance of response chip; right panel plots reflectance response after monotone transformation. Parallelism in right panel supports bisection model and reveals the psychophysical function; see also next two figures. This monotone analysis used a distribution method to obtain adequate power to detect nonadditivity, together with a replication method to allow valid test of deviations from additivity (see Anderson, 1982, pp. 236*ff*; Carterette & Anderson, 1979, p. 276). (From N. H. Anderson, *Foundations of Information Integration Theory.* Academic Press, 1981.)

the horizontal axis. Since the Munsell chips are spaced on the horizontal at equal intervals in the Munsell scale of grayness (or lightness), the curvature toward the right shows that the Munsell values differ from the true sensation values at higher reflectances. Although the Munsell grayness scale was intended to be a linear, equal interval scale, it is not. Nonlinear bias begins to appear in the middle of the stimulus range. This bias, curiously, is readily visible when the Munsell chips are spread out in a row.

A more complete portrayal of the psychophysical function is obtainable by interleaving the row and column means of the right panel of Figure 9.7. The result in Figure 9.8 plots grayness sensation as a function of physical reflectance. The curve in Figure 9.8 is a fitted power function, with an exponent of .14. This is the psychophysical function for grayness.

Figure 9.8 provides a validated psychophysical function. It is supported by scale invariance in three tasks in Figure 9.9. These results thus have some claim to be the first validated psychophysical law in the history of psychophysics.

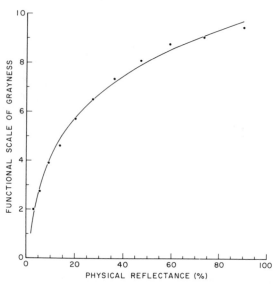

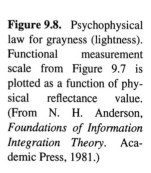

Figure 9.8. Psychophysical law for grayness (lightness). Functional measurement scale from Figure 9.7 is plotted as a function of physical reflectance value. (From N. H. Anderson, *Foundations of Information Integration Theory*. Academic Press, 1981.)

The severe bias in magnitude estimation, previously seen in Figure 9.3, reappears in Stevens' value of 1.2 for the exponent of the psychophysical function for grayness. Stevens' claimed psychophysical law is thus convex upward. This is a law of increasing returns; equal increments in light energy add larger and larger increments in sensation magnitude. In contrast, the convex downward function validated by functional measurement represents diminishing returns, more in line with biological considerations.

SCALE INVARIANCE

The subjects in the foregoing bisection experiment also served in two other conditions. The factorial stimulus design was the same, presenting 5 × 6 pairs of gray chips. The task, however, was changed. In one condition, subjects were instructed to rate the average grayness of the two chips. In the other, they were instructed to rate the grayness difference between the two chips.

Both instruction conditions prescribe an additive integration, so parallelism would be expected—if the response measure is a true linear scale. Near-parallelism was observed with both conditions. By virtue of the parallelism theorem, this provides joint support for the prescribed rule of integration and for the rating response. It should be noted, in this regard, that subjects do this task on an intuitive basis, not by arithmetic calculation.

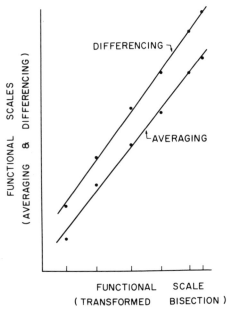

Figure 9.9. Cross-task scale invariance for grayness (lightness). Points on horizontal axis are functional scale values from Bisection task. Right curve plots functional grayness values for same stimuli obtained from Averaging task; the linearity implies that Averaging and Bisection yield equivalent sensation values. Same argument applies to left curve for Differencing task. Physical stimuli equally spaced on Munsell scale; hence unequal spacing on horizontal axis implies Munsell scale is not truly linear, with equal intervals. Instead, it exaggerates differences toward white end of continuum. (From N. H. Anderson, *Methods of Information Integration Theory.* Academic Press, 1982.)

Scale invariance was the main concern: Do the stimulus scales from these two verbal response tasks agree with those from the nonverbal bisection response? The answer is *yes*. All three tasks yield virtually identical psychophysical functions. This may be seen in Figure 9.9, which plots the functional scale of grayness sensation from the averaging and differencing tasks as a function of the grayness scale from bisection. The two curves are essentially linear and parallel. All three tasks thus yield equivalent psychophysical functions, another instance of cross-task scale invariance. The verbal and nonverbal tasks buttress one another through this scale invariance.

INTEGRATION PSYCHOPHYSICS
VERSUS ADAPTATION-LEVEL THEORY

Look at the two line segments in the left panel of Figure 9.10. The two large boxes seem to make the centerline look shorter; the two small boxes seem to make the centerline look longer. The size contrast between boxes and lines appears to affect the length of the lines, even though they are aligned vertically. This is one of a number of geometrical illusions that have attracted scientific and popular interest for over a century. Despite continued attention by many workers, however, little is known even today about illusion processes.

A natural interpretation of Figure 9.10 is in terms of a context effect of comparative judgment. The centerline is not judged absolutely, but in part by comparison with the context boxes. Compared to the large boxes, the line looks small; compared to the small boxes, it looks large.

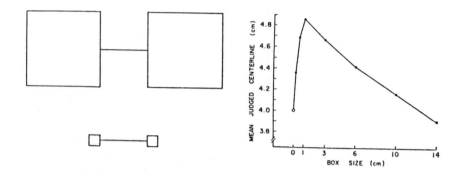

Figure 9.10. Line–box illusion, shown in left panel. Right panel shows magnitude of illusion as a function of box size. (After J. E. Clavadetscher & N. H. Anderson, 1977, "Comparative judgment: Tests of two theories using the Baldwin figure," *Journal of Experimental Psychology: Human Perception and Performance, 3,* 119-135. Copyright 1977 by the American Psychological Association. Reprinted by permission.)

Two theories have attempted mathematical analysis of this line–box illusion. Helson's (1964) theory of adaptation-level asserts that perceived magnitude of a focal stimulus is determined by comparing it with the *adaptation-level*, which is postulated to be a geometric mean that includes prevailing contextual stimuli. Symbolically, apparent size would be proportional to:

$$\text{Line}/(\text{Left Box} \times \text{Right Box}),$$

in which the denominator represents the geometric mean.

A simple test of adaptation-level theory is available through functional measurement. Just vary the sizes of the left and right boxes in factorial design and plot the data. In this design, it may be emphasized, the subject sees only a single line–box figure and judges line length. The symbolic equation just listed implies that the factorial graph will have the pattern of a diverging fan.

An alternative model from IIT includes separate comparisons with each box. Symbolically, apparent size is proportional to the sum or mean of the two separate comparisons:

$$\text{Line}/\text{Left Box} + \text{Line}/\text{Right Box}.$$

This model predicts Left Box–Right Box additivity. This additivity prediction was verified in the experimental tests. Adaptation-level theory thus failed; IIT seemed to succeed.

But an unexpected outcome upset this model from IIT. The contrast interpretation of the line–box illusion had been universally accepted, and it was also employed in the model of comparative judgment from IIT. Unexpectedly, the data showed complete absence of contrast.

This absence of contrast is shown in the right panel of Figure 9.10, which plots perceived length of a 4-cm line as a function of the size of the flanking context boxes. The critical result is for the no-box control, that is, the line judged alone, with no context boxes. This is represented by the open circle at the left end of the box-size curve. Relative to this control, nearly every box makes the line look longer.

The curve in the right panel thus shows that the small and large boxes produce not contrast, but assimilation. Both make the line look longer. The presumed contrast effect is only the difference between the greater assimilation for the small box and the lesser assimilation for the large box.

In a full century, no one seems to have included the control condition. The contrast interpretation was so obvious, there seemed no need. Contrast had been anticipated in the present experiment also; the control condition was included as part of a parametric variation of box size. The cited outcome, of course, indicated that the comparative judgment model from IIT was inadequate. A model based on assimilation processes gave a rather good account of the data, but it too left some results unexplained. This matter was brought to a successful conclusion with functional measurement analysis of a two process theory.

TWO PROCESS THEORY OF ILLUSIONS: CONTRAST AND ASSIMILATION

Geometrical illusions attracted much attention at the beginning of scientific psychology. Such dramatic misfunction of the visual system was expected to provide clues to its nature and operation. This hope has been disappointed. Despite continued attention, not much has been learned. The prevailing outlook today is that many illusion processes are operative and that general theory is unlikely. John Clavadetscher's two process theory has led to new hope.

The two concepts of *contrast* and *assimilation* had been suggested early in the study of geometric illusions. Contrast was typically thought to operate by a process of comparative judgment like that already discussed for the line–box illusion. Assimilation was often thought to operate by a melding of the focal and contextual components. In the line–box figure, assimilation would reflect judgment of a composite figure, consisting of the line itself and the proximal box field.

The big problem is that assimilation and contrast typically work in opposite directions. Allowing two such processes to act together carried the dual danger of being able to explain almost anything and to predict almost nothing. The natural reaction was to seek for pure illusions, in which only one or the other process was operative. Many such attempts were made, and each generally explained most of the data. Without exception, however, all quickly ran into trouble as other investigators found results that could not be accommodated by the theory. As a pertinent example, adaptation-level theory had seemed to give

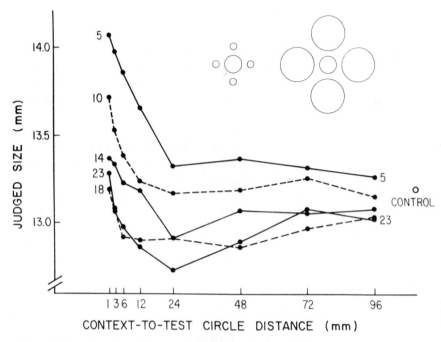

Figure 9.11. Clavadetscher two process model. Joint action of assimilation and contrast shown by U-shaped curves for circles illusion. Judged size of 14-mm center circle plotted as a function of size of context circle (listed as curve parameter) and distance between center and context circles. Control data point represents apparent size of center circle with no surrounding context circles. (After Clavadetscher, 1977, 1991.)

an excellent quantitative account of the line–box illusion until the cited discovery of box–box additivity.

A new approach was initiated by Clavadetscher, who applied integration psychophysics to the Ebbinghaus–Titchener circles of Figure 9.11. Clavadetscher aimed to prove that contrast and assimilation effects were jointly operative. To do this, he began with the hypothesis that contrast would be effective at much greater distances than assimilation. This hypothesis seemed reasonable, on the argument that the visual comparative judgment thought to produce contrast would be effective at greater distances than the perceptual melding of center and surrounding context circles.

The key result is the U-shaped curves for the larger context circles, shown as the 18- and 23-mm curves in Figure 9.11. For these large context circles, contrast and assimilation have opposite effects: Contrast makes the center circle look smaller; assimilation makes the center circle look larger. At close distances, both effects are about equal and cancel, so the center circle has the same apparent size as the control. As distance increases, assimilation decays rapidly but contrast decays slowly. In the middle distance, therefore, assimilation is negligible but contrast is still strong. Hence the curves dip below the control. As distance increases still further, contrast decreases still more, so the curves slowly rise to meet the control. Even at the largest distance of 96 mm, however, contrast is still visible in the ordering of the curves.

Clavadetscher's U-shaped curves thus provide a unique demonstration of the joint operation of assimilation and contrast. More important, they open a way to two process theory of illusions. Indeed, a more quantitative analysis can be obtained by fitting an integration model to the data, assuming exponential decay of the two processes. Rough estimates indicate decay rates of .10 and .01 for assimilation and contrast, respectively. This analysis suggests a new analytical approach to illusion theory because it allows quantification of the two basic processes, acting jointly.[6]

MEMORY PSYCHOPHYSICS

Although the senses have a primary function of guiding ongoing thought and action, they are also important in memory function. One question in memory psychophysics is whether the same processes are utilized in judgments based on remembered scenes as on actual scenes.

A notable study of this question by Wolf and Algom (1987) asked children to judge volume of three-dimensional objects. In an initial training session, children learned to associate circles of different hues with each of eight parallelopipeds. In the following test session, the *perceptual group* judged volume of the actual objects; the *memory group*, in contrast, was presented only the colored circle; they were asked to remember the object and to judge its volume.

Both groups, memory and perceptual, followed the addition rule:

$$\text{Volume} = \text{Height} + \text{Width} + \text{Depth}.$$

This addition rule may be seen in the form of the three-dimensional parallelism of Figure 9.12.

This addition rule may seem surprising, for the physical rule is multiplication. However, a similar addition rule, Area = Height + Width, had been established for 5-year-old's judgments of rectangle area (see Figure 8.2). These area judgments followed a multiplication rule for 10-year-olds, and this was confirmed in an auxiliary condition by Wolf and Algom. The volume judgment is more difficult, of course, and the addition rule for 10-year-olds in Figure 9.12 may result from task simplification. This addition rule is considered a manifestation of the general purpose addition operator of Chapter 8.

For memory psychophysics, of course, the specific form of the integration rule is less important than its similarity across the perceptual and memory conditions. This rule similarity, as Wolf and Algom point out, is evidence for common process in the two conditions.

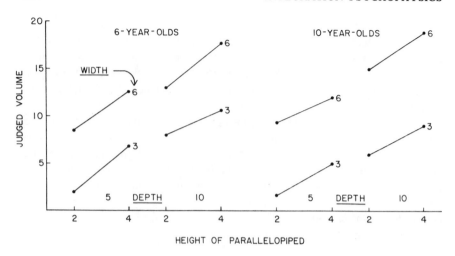

Figure 9.12. Children judge volume of 3-dimensional parallelopipeds by addition rule, Volume = Height + Width + Depth. Addition rule obtained for both perceptual and memory conditions. (After Y. Wolf & D. Algom, 1987, "Perceptual and memorial constraints in children's judgments of quantity: A law of across-representation invariance," *Journal of Experimental Psychology: General, 116,* 381-397. Copyright 1987 by the American Psychological Association. Reprinted by permission.)

    Over time, memory values may fade in many tasks, and so depart systematically from the original perceptual values. The same integration processes, nevertheless, may still hold in both realms. Functional measurement can establish rule similarity at the same time that it assesses value dissimilarity. This provides a tool for quantifying temporal evolution of memory.

    Sensory memories are important in everyday life, not only in such premier senses as vision, but also with food and sex. Multiple determination is prominent in all of these, as previously emphasized in the discussion of food perception. Sex, similarly, should be a whole-body experience. To these fascinating problems, IIT can make useful contributions.

FOUNDATIONS OF PSYCHOPHYSICS

From an integrationist perspective, the concept of psychophysical law has been a historic misdirection. All psychophysics aims to get from the physical stimuli at the sense receptors to the conscious, central sensation. The psychophysical law sought to do this in one bold leap. One simple mathematical law, the same across all sense modalities, was assumed to hold between objective stimulus and subjective sensation, truly a *psycho–physical law.*

This idea that sensation must be some simple function of the physical stimulus is a strong presumption, originating with Fechner's logarithmic function and enduring to this day. This idea has been a major formative influence in one main branch of psychophysics.

But this idea of psychophysical law failed to solve its primary problem: measurement of sensation. This failure was inherent in the conceptual framework. The psychophysical law was defined as a function of a single variable, but a single variable does not provide constraint to validate the response measure. To solve this problem required a conceptual shift to psychophysical integration. This allowed two or more variables, which can give sufficient constraint to validate the response measure. As pointed out in an exposition of functional measurement applied to psychophysical analysis:

> The experimental base of traditional psychophysical scaling with direct, numerical response methods is inherently too narrow to support a solution to its problems. Tasks based on psychophysical information integration provide a broader and potentially simpler approach. (Anderson, 1970, p. 153.)

This integration psychophysics has done well in the subsequent empirical work, illustrated in this chapter. The long controversy over which psychophysical law is correct seems largely misdirected, and indeed singularly barren.

The narrowness of this branch of traditional psychophysics has had further harmful effects. Phenomena that did not fit into the framework of the psychophysical law were avoided or attacked awkwardly. Integration psychophysics has a liberating, fruitful influence.

PSYCHOLOGICAL LAW AND PSYCHOPHYSICAL LAW

Integration psychophysics is based on a conception of *psychological law*. Psychological law differs from psychophysical law in two primary ways: multiple determination and subjective stimulus values.

The prototypical psychological law is a function of two or more variables, whereas the psychophysical law is a function of a single variable. Thus, the psychological law explicitly recognizes the fundamental problem of multiple determination, whereas the psychophysical law does not. This broader framework incorporates context effects and hedonics, among other phenomena, which are largely outside the narrow framework of psychophysical law.

This one variable–many variable distinction appears in the integration diagram of Figure 1.1. The psychophysical law corresponds to the V operator for a single sensory variable; the psychological law corresponds to the I operator, which takes account of many variables.

The second difference is that the psychophysical law is a function of a physical variable, whereas the psychological law is a function of psychological variables. This difference is as important as the first. It would not suffice to admit multiple physical variables in the psychophysical law because most integration is in terms of psychological values, as indicated in Figure 1.1.[7]

A priori, the psychophysical law seems inviting because it involves only one unobservable. This one-variable simplicity was reified into the conception of psychophysical law, which sought for order and law at the interface between the external world and the internal world. This intellectual enterprise has been sustained for over a century by this belief that the two worlds are related by a simple, general mathematical function of a single variable.[8]

But this one-variable approach is inherently too narrow to solve its own primary problem, as observed in the foregoing quote. The missing link, lack of a validity criterion, is built into the one-variable formulation. With more than one variable, a validity criterion becomes possible in the form of integration rules.

This issue of validity criterion is illustrated with the parallelism theorem of Chapter 2. Whereas the psychophysical law is concerned with the values of each separate variable, the psychological law is concerned with the pattern of response to the combined variables. A pattern of parallelism is a validational test for an addition rule; an addition rule brings with it measures of the stimulus variables, and of the response. Such validity criteria are not absolute, as noted in the discussion of Table 2.2 and in Note 1 of Chapter 3, but empirical science does not allow absolute validity.

The psychological law is much less inviting. Instead of a single unobservable, there are three (Figure 1.1). The psychophysical law promises a simpler, divide-and-conquer approach, one reason for its endurance.

With its greater difficulty, however, the psychological law brings greater opportunity. One opportunity is to establish a validity criterion, the missing link in previous quests for the psychophysical law. This opportunity has been realized with some sensory dimensions, as with heaviness in Figure 9.2 and grayness in Figures 9.3, 9.7, and 9.8.

More important opportunities arise from broadening the field of inquiry. Some of these opportunities are indicated in the following sections.

CONTEXT EFFECTS

Context effects are one orphan of the psychophysical law. Being a function of a single variable, namely, the focal stimulus, the psychophysical law has no place for a second, context variable. Context effects are ubiquitous and have been widely studied, but in a fragmented manner, lacking general theory.

Context effects are as welcome in the psychological law as they are unwelcome in the psychophysical law. In the size–weight study of Figure 9.2, for example, the contextual size cue was at once the focus of interest and a tool for analysis. Demonstration of an adding-type integration rule—the psychological law—yielded the cornucopia of benefits already itemized.

Context effects have general interest; they represent natural modes of sensory-perceptual function. Algebraic rules provide an effective approach with some generality across stimulus domains. General theory of context effects thus becomes possible.

> Functional measurement provides a general perspective on the role of context effects in judgment theory. Instead of being treated as undesirable biases, context effects can be incorporated into substantive theory and thereby made a base and frame for measurement. . . . In contrast to . . . magnitude estimation, functional measurement (a) allows context effects to be treated as substantive phenomena, interesting in themselves, useful in scaling, not just undesirable biases; (b) provides a clear conceptual definition of interval [linear] scale; (c) does not require sensation to be conscious; and (d) derives the psychophysical law from the more basic psychological law. (Anderson, 1975, p. 462.)

SIGNAL DETECTION THEORY WITH FUNCTIONAL MEASUREMENT

An integration decision model may be obtained by combining signal detection theory (SDT) with functional measurement (Anderson, 1974a, pp. 246ff). Thus, the SDT prediction of constancy of d', the well-known measure of signal sensitivity, appears in IIT as the parallelism property of a linear model for integration of signal and criterion.[9]

Two extensions deserve consideration. One is to use algebraic structure of the integration rule as the base for analysis, thereby avoiding the normality assumption of SDT. The other is to focus directly on continuous response measures rather than on discrete choice tasks. Thus, the rating method commonly used in IIT is a magnitude response, whereas the rating method in SDT is confidence in a choice response (see Macmillan & Creelman, 1991).

Magnitude measures raise the possibility of suprathreshold response. Suprathreshold response measures may not seem appropriate, considering that detection theory is formulated in terms of probabilistic response. The two seem to represent different domains. Stimuli close in magnitude may be perfectly discriminable and hence infinitely far apart in the d' metric. But although discriminability differs from magnitude, the two should be related in some lawful way. Unified theory must include magnitude response, which may be useful, perhaps necessary, for understanding discriminative response.

Moreover, certain concepts such as familiarity judgments in recognition memory to which SDT is currently applied, seem inadequately represented in probabilistic terms. To be uncertain whether one has seen a stimulus previously, or whether a radiograph signifies liver cancer, does not mean that one's yes–no judgments will be probabilistic. A continuous response can extract additional metric information from individual stimuli. One approach is with functional measurement, which can factor out various context effects that are outside the purview of SDT.

COMPOUND STIMULI

Context effects are special cases of the general class of compound stimuli. Taste and odor are common examples, as in Figure 9.5. Pure stimuli are rare outside the laboratory, yet they are almost all that are allowed within the framework of psychophysical law. Hence the psychophysical law, even were it at hand, could tell us little about everyday psychophysics or about general perception. Instead, the conceptual framework of psychophysical law has obstructed the study of compound stimuli.[10]

NONMETRIC STIMULI

The concept of psychophysical law imposes further narrowness through its requirement of a physical metric of the stimulus. Of course, nonmetric stimuli are common in psychophysics. Compound stimuli, in particular, generally lack a one-dimensional representation. This plain fact has been obscured in preoccupation with the psychophysical law. Psychophysical analysis is fundamentally incomplete without capability for handling nonmetric stimuli.

The psychophysical law for grayness of Figure 9.8, for example, refers to a focal stimulus of uniform reflectance under uniform illumination. This says little about stimuli with nonuniform reflectance and/or nonuniform illumination. Such stimuli lack a definite physical metric and so lie outside the scope of psychophysical law.

Nonmetric stimuli are at home in functional measurement. The parallelism and linear fan theorems need only nominal definition of the stimulus.

These theorems, furthermore, can measure the functional stimulus values. Functional measurement can thus confer psychological metrication on stimuli that lack any physical metric. This capability, which rests on the internal world, is a useful extension of traditional conceptions of psychophysics.

HEDONICS

The functional nature of psychophysics is prominent in affective senses, such as taste, temperature, and sex. The concept of psychophysical law, however, has little place for affect. It is concerned with intensity.

This affect−intensity distinction is clear with saltiness. Too much salt may be even less desirable than too little. The psychophysical law only concerns itself with the intensity of the salt taste as a function of concentration. This says nothing about affective preference, which is clearly not a monotone function of concentration.

Affect is one biological function of the affective senses, which have evolved for approach−avoidance survival value. Psychophysics of intensity, however important in receptor analysis, ignores the primary purpose and function of the affective senses. To understand affective senses requires a functional view.

Functional measurement provides a direct approach to hedonics (Anderson, 1989b; McBride, 1993; McBride & Anderson, 1991). Moreover, nonsensory determinants, such as visual appearance and learned symbolic cues, can be studied together with psychophysical cues. Integration psychophysics thus embodies a functional perspective on affective senses in everyday purposiveness.

NONCONSCIOUS SENSATION

Nonconscious sensation is hardly recognized within the psychophysical law. Indeed, it is not uncommon to read that consciousness is a defining property of sensation. Some such view, perhaps skirting the word consciousness itself, appears in the concept of psychophysical law, which assumes a direct relation between physical stimulus and experienced sensation.

In an integrationist view, nonconscious sensation can be meaningfully defined and measured under certain conditions. In the size–weight illusion, the proper effect of gram weight, processed through the kinesthetic receptors, is preconscious. What reaches the peephole of consciousness is the integrated resultant of this preconscious sensation and the no less preconscious sensation resulting from the visual size cue. Within the straitjacket of psychophysical law, nonconscious sensations are more or less nonthinkable. Within the framework of psychological law, rigorous analysis is possible.

PSYCHOPHYSICAL LAW

Integration psychophysics can forge the link missing from traditional attempts to establish psychophysical law. Validated measures of sensation become available. The psychophysical law corresponds to the graph of these sensation measures as a function of the physical stimulus. The controversy between Fechner, Stevens, and other claimants can thus be resolved. Several aspects of this controversy deserve consideration.

First, Stevens' method of magnitude estimation is subject to extreme bias. The magnitude of this bias, shown in Figure 9.1, reappears in the discussion of the psychophysical law for grayness of Figure 9.8. Whereas Stevens claimed an exponent of 1.2 in a power function for grayness, functional measurement yielded a validated exponent of .14. This functional measurement exponent was supported in tests of within-task validity (Figures 9.3 and 9.7) and between-task validity (Figure 9.9). The table of exponents for various senses published repeatedly by Stevens seems devoid of scientific significance.

The invalidity of magnitude estimation was indicated long ago with the initial studies of cognitive algebra in the judgment–decision domain. With this discovery of algebraic rules went the validity of the rating method of functional measurement used to establish them. But rating and magnitude estimation are nonlinearly related, as emphasized so strongly by Stevens and reemphasized so clearly in Figure 9.1. That magnitude estimation is biased and invalid is thus a direct implication of this work on cognitive algebra, verified in Figure 9.3.

There is some evidence that Fechner's assumption of equality of jnds is approximately correct. This assumption is testable by comparing the cumulated jnd scale with scales derived from functional measurement. Existing evidence is limited because cumulated jnd scales are laborious to construct and subject to unreliability from cumulation of error.

Curiously, the power function may prove preferable to the logarithmic function. This is a convenience in descriptive statistics, however, not reflecting any basic psychophysical process. Stevens' exponents are seriously invalid, as illustrated in the foregoing studies of grayness. If a power function is to have psychophysical meaning, most of his exponents would have to be replaced by functional measurement exponents. How far these would be invariants of each sensory system is an open question.

Ironically, one main consequence of putting the psychophysical law on a solid base has been the realization that it is not very important after all. One reason is its lack of usefulness in studying integration processes. A deeper reason is growing realization that many processing stages may lie between physical stimulus and conscious sensation. The psychophysical "law" is a composite of multiple successive transformations. This composite may have predictive utility, but general theoretical significance seems unlikely (Anderson, 1975).

Most important is the broadening of psychophysics. Each of the foregoing sections—context effects, compound stimuli, nonmetric stimuli, hedonics, and nonconscious sensation—has pointed up basic areas of psychophysics that lie outside the conceptual horizon of psychophysical law.

These areas lie within the conceptual horizon of integration psychophysics. Some are amenable to present methodology. Functional measurement theory is not an easy road to truth, but it opens the road rather than closing it off. And it has made some progress on all these problems.

ALGEBRAIC PSYCHOPHYSICS

Algebraic laws for psychophysical integration have been conjectured by many investigators (see Anderson, 1970, 1974a; see also Note 3). One of the earliest appears in Plateau's attempt to use grayness bisection as a validity criterion for Fechner's logarithmic function.

Satisfactory analysis of algebraic integration rules is difficult, however, because of the problem of the three unobservables. Lacking a solution to this problem, the many previous conjectures about algebraic psychophysics remained conjectural. The problem itself was confused and obscured, moreover, by the fixation on the one-variable conception of psychophysical law.

Functional measurement theory has provided a solution to the problem of the three unobservables. The conjectures about algebraic rules become testable. Psychophysical measurement thus becomes an organic component of substantive psychophysical theory.

Algebraic integration rules have been found with some frequency, as illustrated in this chapter. These psychological laws have, almost as a byproduct, put the psychophysical law on a determinate base. More important, they go beyond the psychophysical law to broader and deeper domains of psychophysical inquiry.[11]

The functional perspective of IIT is manifest in integration psychophysics. Sensory systems embody the axiom of purposiveness, notably in affective senses and in many context effects. Algebraic rules, moreover, go beyond themselves to help develop veridical continuous response measures. These provide unique leverage for analysis of nonalgebraic rules and configurality.

SENSORY PSYCHOPHYSICS AND INTEGRATION PSYCHOPHYSICS

Traditional psychophysics has two main branches. The foregoing critique of the branch associated with the psychophysical law does not apply to the other branch, sensory psychophysics, which has been notably productive.

Sensory psychophysics emphasizes receptor and peripheral processes of sensory systems. This branch has generally eschewed the psychological law and indeed subjective measures of sensation. It thus avoided the controversy initiated by Fechner, and it has developed alternative methods that allow effective progress. In the matching method, for example, people and animals can be instructed, in effect, to match some quality, such as hue or brightness of two color patches. Measurement is thus in terms of physical stimulus parameters. The power and versatility of this approach are well illustrated in the impressive volume on human color vision by Boynton (1979; Kaiser & Boynton, in press).

Sensory psychophysics seeks to work from the periphery to the center. Notable progress has been made. Yet the path to the center remains shrouded in darkness. Multisensory perception tends to be neglected, moreover, partly because of the peripheral focus, partly because each sensory system constitutes an increasingly intricate speciality, thereby inhibiting interaction among workers on different sensory systems.

Integration psychophysics seeks to work from the center to the periphery. It provides a complement to sensory psychophysics that rests on a grounded base of psychological law at the center. Under certain conditions, functional measurement can establish valid scales of conscious sensation and fractionate such sensation into multisensory, preconscious components. Integration analysis of multisensory perception can thus provide a common language for different sensory systems. An ideal goal is to cooperate and link up with the periphery-inward approach of sensory psychophysics.

NOTES

The development of integration psychophysics owes much to work by Daniel Algom, William Cain, Edward Carterette, John Clavadetscher, Jan Frijters, Hans-Georg Geissler, Larry Marks, Sergio Masin, Bob McBride, William McGill, Anne Schlottmann, Lennart Sjöberg, Leo Stefurak, David Weiss, and Yuval Wolf.

1. The history of psychophysics and the perplexities caused by the concept of psychophysical law are well portrayed in the learned volume by Boring (1950). More extensive treatments of integration psychophysics are in Anderson (1970, 1974a, 1990a, 1992a; see also commentaries 1989c,d, 1992b, 1993).

2. Ratings also follow power functions (Marks, 1968). Since both methods yield power functions, the question becomes which, if either, is correct. Proponents of magnitude estimation have failed to answer the question satisfactorily. The main apparent reason for the uncritical acceptance of Stevens' claims, namely, the ubiquity of power functions obtained with magnitude estimation, thus loses its evidential power. This ubiquity merely reflects statistical flexibility of the power function in fitting laws of diminishing returns—as shown by its fit to two sets of data that differ as greatly as in Figure 9.1.

Ratings, of course, yield different exponents from magnitude estimation. Stevens' exponents, far from being invariants of the sensory system, suffer severe biases from Stevens' method of magnitude estimation (see, e.g., discussions of Figures 9.3 and 9.8). Whether the rating exponents are sensory invariants is an open question.

Magnitude estimation furnishes a curious case history of psychological science. The dominant concern has been to determine exponents for diverse sensory dimensions in the belief that these exponents were valid, invariant characteristics of each sensory system. With the invalidation of the method of magnitude estimation, this work loses all value.

This was foreseeable. The issue of validity was raised by several writers at an early stage, and some validity tests were actually made. These were generally unfavorable to magnitude estimation, but they were explained away or ignored. Only after some 30-odd years is it beginning to be generally recognized that magnitude estimation is biased and invalid on most sensory dimensions (e.g., Krueger, 1991). In its initial stage, magnitude estimation was a legitimate hope, but something went wrong. How this happened deserves historical inquiry to help keep future science on more productive tracks.

3. Integration studies in psychophysics have been done by many investigators. As noted in Anderson (1974a, p. 215), "There is a long tradition of viewing perception as integration of stimulus information. The organism resides in a multitudinous stimulus field, and the job of the perceptual apparatus is to combine or integrate the varied stimulus cues into some more-or-less unified percept." Many interesting integration phenomena, especially relating to context effects, have been studied by numerous workers. But this work has remained fragmented, lacking general theory. What is new in IIT is the extended research program that has put algebraic psychophysics on a solid theoretical and empirical base.

4. Proponents of magnitude estimation, with two or three notable exceptions, have been loath to recognize the mass of evidence on invalidity of this method (see summaries in Anderson 1974a and 1981a, Section 5.4; see also Note 7 in Chapter 3 and "Plea for tolerance" in McBride & Anderson, 1991, p. 317).

Functional measurement, it should be reemphasized, is neutral in the controversy between rating and magnitude estimation. It lies at a higher level; it provides a validity criterion that applies equally to both methods (see similarly Sjöberg, 1966, 1994). Had magnitude estimation satisfied these validational tests, it would have been gratefully adopted. As it happened, magnitude estimation generally failed. The rating method itself only succeeded through the development of certain procedures noted in Chapter 3.

5. Cross-modal intensity comparison may become possible with the dominant component model. In this sweet−sour application, the intensities of sweet and sour are equal when an increase/decrease in sweet concentration causes a shift in which component is dominant. This allows only an equating of the physical scales, but this might be extendable to the corresponding functional scales, as by direct rating of the intensities of concentrations of the separate components. A common unit for the two scales, sweet and sour, may thus be obtainable.

6. The circles remain circles; the illusion affects size but not shape. This constancy of shape suggests an independence of perception of form and size and/or a central process. The perceptual melding assumed to produce assimilation might have been expected to deform perceived shape, depending on the point-by-point distance between the two figures. That such deformation does not occur suggests that the assimilation process acts more centrally, on unitized representations of the two figures.

7. Gibson's (1966) information-based theory of perception differs from information integration theory in a fundamental way: Whereas Gibson's theory is based on correct perception of structure in the external world, IIT is based on structure of the internal world.

This difference may be illustrated with illusions. IIT treats illusions as normal information processing, as with the four illusions studied in Figures 9.2, 9.4, 9.10, and 9.11. Gibson's approach, in contrast, is founded entirely on correct perception of the external world, and "must explain incorrect perception by supplementary assumptions" (p. 287). Support for the present approach appears in the generality of the same few algebraic integration rules elsewhere in perception as in illusions, and also in judgment−decision, social cognition, and language processing.

Structure of the internal world has close relations with structure of the external world, but it is not essentially isomorphic thereto as Gibson's theory requires. Gibson's tack of supplementary assumptions to explain illusions is inadequate because perception has varied nonveridical elements. IIT, in contrast, offers a unified approach based on structure of the internal world (see further *Internal World and External World* in Chapter 1 and related discussions under *Cognitive Theory* in Chapter 13).

8. The ultimate expression of the conceptual framework of psychophysical law would seem to be that of Luce (1959b), who attempted a mathematical demonstration that the psychophysical law necessarily had one of a very few mathematical forms. Thus, if the physical variable was a ratio scale and the psychological variable an interval scale, then the relation between them would necessarily be either a log function or a power function. This theorem seems remarkable for it claims to show, on essentially mathematical grounds, that the psychophysical law exists and that it necessarily has only one of two forms for common sensory dimensions (but see Rozeboom, 1962; also Luce, 1962).

On physiological grounds, it seems clear that the relation between physical energy and psychological sensation cannot be determined by abstract axioms. The physiological mechanisms that mediate this relation may be expected to follow a law of diminishing returns, but in principle such mechanisms could be constructed to exhibit any of a great many mathematical forms of diminishing returns.

Luce's argument seems to rest on an implicit assumption that scales can be characterized as ratio or interval in their own right, prior to establishment of empirical laws. In functional measurement, in contrast, the character of the scales depends on invariance properties derivative from whatever empirical laws may be established. These invariance properties may also depend on the design, as with the averaging model (Chapter 2).

9. To illustrate the integration–decision model (Anderson, 1974a) within the SDT framework, consider a stimulus field of N sources, each of which can be in various states. Each source–state combination is assumed to correspond to an independent normal distribution of information value with equal variance, x_{ij} for Source i in State j. Let $I(A)$ be the integrated information value for a given array A of source–state combinations. With a weighted sum rule,

$$I(A) = \sum_A w_i x_{ij}$$

has a normal distribution with constant variance across arrays. In a yes–no task, the response is decided by comparing $I(A)$ with a criterion k. Hence the observed proportion of *yes* responses corresponds to the normal deviate

$$z_{yes}(A) = I(A) - k = -k + \sum_A w_i \psi_{ij}.$$

where ψ_{ij} is the mean of x_{ij}. Thus, $I(A)$ is a linear function of the observable $z_{yes}(A)$, which is itself a linear function of the source values and the criterion. Accordingly, $z_{yes}(A)$ will obey the parallelism theorem of functional measurement.

A special case yields the classic result of constancy of d', the sensitivity index in SDT. In a two-source design, let *Signal* and *Noise* be the states of the first source, and let the states of the second source be different criterion values. From the foregoing equation, it follows that $z_{yes}(\text{Signal})$ and $z_{yes}(\text{Noise})$ will plot as two parallel curves; the parallelism property of functional measurement thus corresponds to the prediction of constant d' in SDT. The data would also provide a linear scale of the criterion values.

More interestingly, the functional measurement approach suggests the potential of analysis of the raw information variable, $I(A)$. In SDT, as the foregoing equations indicate, the continuous variable $I(A)$ is transformed into a discrete choice by reference to the criterion; these discrete choices are converted into a continuous proportion by pooling over repeated trials; and this proportion is retransformed by the assumed normal distribution. A direct attack using a continuous response measure, possibly with a linearizing transformation, to bypass the choice discreteness has several potential advantages.

The d' metric refers to discriminability, not to sensory magnitude, as noted in the text. Magnitude measures are also important, and in some ways more appropriate for recognition memory and other concepts that, although uncertain, are not really probabilistic. In such cases, magnitude measures may be more informative.

Functional measurement can fractionate observed response into contributions from sensory factors and contextual factors, such as expectancy and bias. Contextual effects can thus provide a base for theory construction. The usefulness of this approach was illustrated with the nine-point itemization of implications for the size–weight illusion of Figure 9.2. This measurement-theoretical approach is in the same spirit as SDT. It has a requirement of an algebraic model stronger than that of SDT, but with wider applicability. Serial integration tasks seem empirically likely to provide integration rules with simple structure.

Since the original presentation of this approach, considerable evidence has developed for the decision averaging model of Chapter 2 (see discussion of Figure 10.7, Note 10 of Chapter 11, and the second half of Chapter 12)). The decision averaging rule has the same form as Luce's choice rule, but is not limited to response probability. The non-parallelism predicted by the decision averaging rule may be able to account for the frequent situations in which d' is not constant.

10. The difficulties of applying traditional psychophysics to compound stimuli are illustrated in a comparison of adaptation-level theory and functional measurement for variegated gray figures in Anderson (1992a, p. 58).

11. Schlottmann has suggested that functional measurement theory can be useful for studying direct perception, especially in analyzing joint effects of environmental structure and experiential learning (Gibson, 1966, Chapter 13). Interesting evidence comes from Schlottmann's application of averaging theory to an integration study of Michotte's theory of phenomenal causality (Schlottmann, 1987; Schlottmann & Anderson, 1993). Weight estimates revealed "good–bad" strategies in reliance on given cues, strategies that were evidently more cognitive than perceptual in nature, not well in accord with Michotte's theory. In Schlottmann's view, this outcome argues against Michotte's thesis of innate perception, although not against the more general thesis of direct perception. Further work in this direction seems attractive because such algebraic rules have novel power in assessing perceptual structure and function.

A reservation about Schlottmann's suggestion is that similar algebraic rules have appeared in social cognition as in perception–psychophysics. Direct perception cannot apply generally to social cognition because there is often no objective reality to perceive. If similar processes underlie the rules in both domains, that would seem awkward for direct perception. Of course, the similar algebraic form may stem from different underlying processes, about which little is yet definite (see last section of Chapter 2).

Leaving this theoretical issue aside, Schlottmann's insightful analysis exhibits the power of averaging theory to penetrate below the unrevealing surface level of behavior and uncover the operative processes of valuation and integration. Schlottmann's analysis is also notable in transforming individual differences, which had been a source of confusion to Michotte's critics, into a crucible for theory construction.

PREFACE

Cognitive algebra is a foundation for cognitive theory of judgment–decision. Algebraic models have often been conjectured, but they remained untestable conjectures due to lack of capability for psychological measurement. Functional measurement theory made it possible to demonstrate the reality of cognitive algebra in the judgment–decision domain.

The linear fan theorem of functional measurement provided the first general method for testing the elusive multiplication model for Subjective Expected Value. Similar multiplication models have done well in further studies. Sometimes these models agree with normative algebra, sometimes not.

The normative Bayesian framework was shown to be conceptually inappropriate to describe human judgment—by establishing the alternative decision averaging model of information integration theory. Averaging theory also furnishes nonprobabilistic disproof of the sure-thing axiom, once considered a cornerstone for judgment–decision theory.

A cognitive–normative antinomy troubles the judgment–decision field. The dominant normative approach prescribes algebraic models for optimal behavior in various tasks, and many hoped that these models would describe actual behavior. This hope has been repeatedly disappointed; cognitive algebra is real but it differs from normative algebra, mathematically and conceptually.

The normative models, however, were not really given up. Instead, deviations from the normative models were reified as "biases" and treated as psychological phenomena that needed explanation. This is misguided logic; the bias exists only by reference to a normative model—whose invalidity the bias demonstrates. This invalidity can hardly endow the bias with cognitive reality.

Information integration theory takes a positive approach to biases, in strong contrast to the negativism of the normative view. This point may be extended by noting that information integration studies had yielded basic evidence against three popular heuristics (representativeness, anchoring and adjustment, and availability) before they were first propounded.

Cognitive–normative cooperation is desirable, especially as regards values. The cognitive–normative antinomy is well illustrated by the makeshift character of value measurement in normative analysis. Normative models can be useful as prescriptions for optimal behavior, but these prescriptions typically depend on subjective values, outside the normative domain. Without values, the normative approach is hollow. Cognitive algebra can be a companion and aide because it can operate in this transnormative realm of values.

Chapter 10

COGNITIVE THEORY
OF JUDGMENT-DECISION

Cognitive algebra seems ideally mated to judgment–decision theory, for the operations of valuation and integration are central to both. Decision embodies purposiveness, and purposiveness defines value. Multiple values are typically relevant and must be integrated in making any single decision.

Furthermore, algebraic rules arise naturally in judgment and decision. Overall value of a bundle of commodities should be additive; probability and value should multiply to determine expected value; estimation of central tendencies involves averaging; cost–benefit calculations should obey addition–subtraction rules; fair reward involves ratio comparisons. In short, cognitive algebra seems a prime order of business in the judgment–decision domain.

Judgment–decision researchers, accordingly, should have been in the vanguard of cognitive algebra. With a few significant exceptions, however, cognitive algebra has been of slight concern. One main reason has been an underlying cognitive–normative antinomy. The dominating concern has been with optimal, or normative behavior—what people rationally should do. But what people do do often differs from what they should do. *Cognitive algebra*, in particular, often differs from *normative algebra*.

Had this cognitive–normative antinomy been better appreciated, it could have led to beneficial accommodation between the two perspectives, both of which are important. Instead, the normative perspective has dominated the field. Theoretical preconceptions, focal issues, choice of tasks and response measures, all have been heavily constrained by the normative framework. Many workers have attempted to consider cognitive process, to be sure, but they have been hobbled and misdirected by the normative framework.

This chapter has two themes. The first is that cognitive algebra provides a cornerstone for a cognitive theory of judgment–decision. The main concern of the chapter, accordingly, is to demonstrate the reality of cognitive algebra in classical problems in the judgment–decision domain: subjective expected value, probability integration, the Bayesian approach, formation and revision of beliefs, multiattribute analysis, and biases.

The second theme is cognitive–normative cooperation. The normative emphasis on biases and shortcomings of human thought and action is mainly negative. A positive approach requires a functional perspective, focusing on accomplishments and processes of human cognition. Through understanding cognitive processes that underlie the shortcomings, better progress can be made toward alleviating them.

Moreover, implementing normative prescriptions for optimal behavior generally requires subjective values—outside the normative boundaries. For cash value, therefore, normative theory depends on psychological measurement. Cognitive algebra has provided a foundation for psychological measurement theory, a helpmate and companion for normative analysis.

SUBJECTIVE EXPECTED VALUE THEORY

The concept of expected value is central to normative theory of judgment–decision, for expected value determines rational behavior in an uncertain environment. Expected value for a single probabilistic outcome may be written in terms of objective probabilities and values as:

$$\text{Expected Value} = \text{Probability} \times \text{Value};$$

$$E V = P \times V.$$

Multiple independent outcomes may be handled by adding expected values of the separate outcomes. This EV model provides a rational way to handle uncertainty, exemplified in the actuarial calculations used by insurance companies. Its usefulness, however, is limited by the need for measurement scales of Probability and Value.

SUBJECTIVE EXPECTED VALUE

The EV model cannot represent human thought and action because it does not allow for subjective measures. Value is personal, as is probability. The same goal may be attractive to you, unattractive to your departmental colleagues, say, or your spouse. You may consider some undesirable consequence unlikely, whereas others may consider it likely. The EV model is normative, requiring objective measures. Cognitive theory requires subjective measures.

Many writers, accordingly, have speculated about a cognitive isomorph. Each term in the EV model would be replaced by a cognitive counterpart:

Subjective Expected Value = Subjective Probability × Subjective Value;

$$SEV = SP \times SV. \tag{1}$$

This SEV model has been a central concern in modern decision theory.

As it stands, this SEV model is only a conjectural verbalism. It has no force or substance without measures of subjective probability and subjective value, which are essential to testing the SEV model. In the absence of grounded theory of psychological measurement, satisfactory analysis of the SEV model was not possible. Some writers, indeed, concluded the SEV model was not testable.

FUNCTIONAL MEASUREMENT: FOUNDATION FOR SEV THEORY

A simple resolution of the SEV model was provided by functional measurement theory. The linear fan theorem of Chapter 2 was originally developed for just this purpose. This theorem provided the first general method for joint, simultaneous measurement of subjective probability and subjective value, which is essential to testing the SEV model.

The first application of the linear fan theorem is shown in Figure 10.1. Subjects made intuitive judgments of personal worth of lottery tickets:

You have _____ chance to win _____.

Chance to win was defined by a die throw, indicated on the horizontal axis of the figure. Amount to win was defined by coins, listed as curve parameter.

Figure 10.1. Subjective expected value obeys multiplication rule. Subjects judged personal worth of lottery tickets with specified chance to win (horizontal axis) and amount to be won (curve parameter). Linear fan pattern implies multiplication rule. Note nonlinear spacing of subjective probabilities on horizontal axis. (After N. H. Anderson and J. C. Shanteau, 1970, "Information integration in risky decision making," *Journal of Experimental Psychology, 84,* 441–451. Copyright 1970 by the American Psychological Association. Reprinted by permission.)

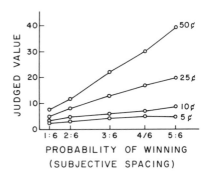

The data of Figure 10.1 exhibit a clear fan pattern. This solves the SEV problem in a simple, general way. The fan pattern implies that the two stimulus variables, subjective probability and subjective value, are integrated by the hypothesized multiplication rule. The linear fan theorem, moreover, provides measurement scales for both stimulus variables at the same time that it validates the measurement scale for the SEV response itself.

The probability values are spaced on the horizontal axis according to their subjective values, obtained with the linear fan theorem. The unequal spacing reflects the difference between objective and subjective probability. Thus, the subjective difference between 3/6 and 2/6 is twice that between 2/6 and 1/6. The subjective values of the coins, similarly, are given by the slopes of the curves. The linear fan theorem provides validated subjective measurement of both stimulus variables at the same time that it reveals the integration operation.

This positive outcome is pleasant and useful. A different outcome would not have been surprising; the multiplication rule seems too good to be true. Deviations from the linear fan pattern would be expected, therefore, but even such negative outcome would have been an advance on previous conjecture. This initial verification of the SEV rule has been supported in later work.

SUBADDITIVITY

The SEV rule has a direct extension to more than a single event, and this was also studied in the foregoing experiment. This rule is again isomorphic to the normative rule. Given two independent outcomes, for example, tickets in two different lotteries, with values SV_1 and SV_2 and probabilities SP_1 and SP_2, the extended rule would be written:

$$SEV = SP_1 \times SV_1 + SP_2 \times SV_2.$$

A linear fan is predicted for both indicated products. A parallelism pattern is predicted for each of the other four pairs of variables, such as SP_1 and SP_2, because they are separated by an addition sign. Such factorial graphs assess algebraic structure of this compound integration process.

Surprisingly, the addition rule failed even while the multiplication rule succeeded. The two linear fans were obtained, but systematic deviations from the predicted parallelism were also found in the very same judgments. The addition rule is implicit in the instructions to judge total worth, and addition seems easier than multiplication. Nevertheless, the data patterns in this and subsequent experiments pointed to a real subadditivity effect.[1]

Also surprising is the absence of followup work on subadditivity. Subadditivity seems fundamental for judgment–decision theory, yet it has been passed by in the spate of concern with other judgment–decision biases. The most obvious explanation would be in terms of diminishing returns. Against this explanation is the fact that subadditivity is found with ostensibly nonredundant outcomes of low value. An alternative possibility is that an averaging process with differential weighting is overlaid on an adding process.

MEASURING FUZZY PROBABILITIES

The need for subjective measurement of probabilities is underscored by the unequal horizontal spacing already discussed in Figure 10.1. Even though these probabilities were specified objectively by the throw of a die, the subjective and objective values differed substantially.

In everyday life, of course, probabilities are typically specified in fuzzy terms. A frequent form of specification is with fuzzy phrases, such as *almost certain, likely, not too likely*, and so on. These fuzzy phrases can be measured in the same way as in the study of Figure 10.1.

Measurement of fuzzy probability phrases was first accomplished by Jim Shanteau in his Ph. D. thesis using the linear fan analysis. Subjects judged value of lottery tickets of the form already indicated. Chances to win, however, were specified by the probability phrases of Table 12.1. The objects to be won, such as *sandals*, were also in nonquantitative form.

The data formed a linear fan, rather neater than that seen in Figure 10.1. This allowed functional scales of the probabilities and values, which are listed in Table 12.1. These scales represent only a central tendency of the fuzzy distribution. With such validation of the response measure, however, it becomes possible to measure degree of fuzziness. One such extension was made by Shu-Hong Zhu, also discussed in Chapter 12.

COGNITIVE AND NORMATIVE

The dominant view treats the SEV model as normative, essentially similar to the EV model. Use of subjective rather than objective values is not considered to change the epistemological character of the SEV model itself. This normative perspective is common in judgment–decision theory and reappears in other areas, as with the Bayesian model discussed later.

In the theory of information integration, however, the EV and SEV models are fundamentally different. The SEV model is embedded in substantive, empirical theory. It is not just the EV model with objective measures replaced by subjective measures. The SEV model resides in cognitive processes of valuation and integration that have no counterpart in normative theory.

The multiplication operation, in particular, must have cognitive reality. The present hypothesis is that the multiplication process is analogue fractionation. The prize is represented as some distance along a mental representation of the response scale; the probability term acts as a fractionator of that distance (see Chapter 2). This multiplication process is essentially different from the multiplication operation in normative EV or SEV theory.

The present formulation is also more general than the standard SEV model, for it uses weights rather than probabilities. For two outcomes, the general integration model would be written:

$$\omega_1 \times \psi_1 \;+\; \omega_2 \times \psi_2,$$

where ω and ψ denote weight and value, respectively. These weights may depend on other factors than probability. In particular, "A potential loss, e.g., might have greater felt importance than an equivalent gain" (Anderson & Shanteau, 1970, p. 450). A similar conception of decision weights was adopted in the prospect theory of Kahneman and Tversky (1979).

Cognitive algebra constitutes a foundation for psychological measurement theory. The linear fan pattern of Figure 10.1 provides the base and frame for measurement of both the response and the stimulus variables, following the linear fan theorem of Chapter 2. This measurement capability extends to multi-outcome models and even to measurement of subadditivity. This functional measurement approach employs the continuous response methodology developed in IIT (Chapter 3).

The normative view treats the SEV model as a putative universal truth; the normative view cannot cope when the model fails empirically. The cognitive view considers the SEV model as a limited truth, whose domain of validity requires empirical determination. The subadditivity, moreover, is not merely a bias, but a form of cognitive functioning. And the success of the multiplication operation provides a tool for studying the subadditivity.

The cognitive view is epistemologically different from the normative view. It requires a different way of thinking. This epistemological difference is underscored by the many cases in which subjects fail to use SEV-type rules when normative theory prescribes them—and by the many cases in which subjects continue to use SEV-type rules when normative theory prescribes otherwise (see *Lopes Effect* and *Information Purchase* below).

SURE–THING AXIOM

Averaging theory disagrees with the *sure-thing axiom*, a cornerstone in Savage's (1954) attempt to establish an axiomatic foundation for a subjectivist theory of probability. If A is preferred to B, the sure-thing axiom asserts that $A + C$ will be preferred to $B + C$. If $B = 0$, so that A is positive, $A + C$ will be preferred to C. This seems self-evident, regardless of whether C is positive or negative, and so deserves the status of an axiom.

Averaging theory, however, disproves the sure-thing axiom: $A + C$ may be less preferred than C. This violation of the sure-thing axiom is demonstrated in the following four experiments.

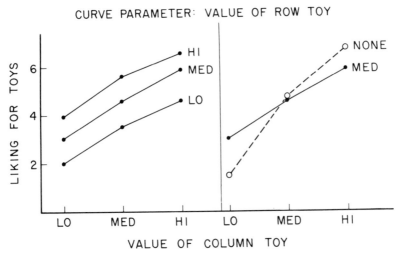

Figure 10.2. Failure of sure-thing axiom. Children judge worth of pairs of toys (solid curves) or single toys (dashed curve). Parallelism in left factorial graph supports adding-type rule. Crossover of dashed and solid curves in right graph shows that the same medium toy has opposite effects: It increases total worth with a low toy, but decreases total worth with a high toy. Similar results obtained for younger and older children from 5 to 13 years. (From N. H. Anderson, *Foundations of Information Integration Theory.* Academic Press, 1981.)

Averaging theory applies to children's judgments of toys, shown in Figure 10.2. In the left panel, the parallelism indicates an adding-type rule for judged worth of pairs of toys. Primary concern, however, is with the right panel. There the dashed curve gives the judged worth of the single column toy, listed on the horizontal axis. The solid curve gives the judgments of these same toys paired with an added toy of medium (positive) value. Hence the sure-thing axiom requires the solid curve to lie entirely above the dashed curve. The crossover disagrees with the sure-thing axiom—but agrees with averaging theory. This opposite effects paradox has been discussed in relation to Figures 2.4 and 2.5.

Similar violation of the sure-thing axiom was found in a choice test of the averaging hypothesis. Subjects saw a pair of person descriptions and chose the more preferred person. Adding mildly favorable adjectives to very favorable adjectives *decreased* the choice frequency; adding mildly unfavorable adjectives to very unfavorable adjectives *increased* the choice frequency (see Anderson, 1981a, Table 2.4). Both results are as predicted by averaging theory; both results disagree with the sure-thing axiom.

The third illustration is found in the common marketing strategy of *product bundling*, in which a tie-in product of small value is sold together with a primary product of larger value for a single price. A long-lived example appears in

Crackerjack, children's boxes of caramel popcorn that include small prizes. Similar examples are often seen in advertisements. Standard economic theory assumes that the value of a product bundle equals the sum of the values of the component products.

Averaging theory, as already illustrated, implies that the tie-in product can actually have a negative effect. A low quality tie-in, even though positive in itself, will have a low scale value, and hence can average down the perceived value of the product bundle. This prediction was made and verified by Gaeth, Levin, Chakraborty, and Levin (1990).

Striking support for the product bundling strategy was also found: A high quality tie-in could produce *superadditivity*, making the perceived value of the bundle greater than the sum of the component values. The salience of the tie-in presumably makes its decision weight greater than its proportionate dollar value. Superadditivity can then result from adding conjoined with averaging or from averaging alone if the tie-in has a higher quality scale value than the primary product. This ingenious study demonstrates failure of the sure-thing axiom in a realistic consumer situation at the same time that it shows the potential of IIT.

In the final example, by Anne Schlottmann, children judged worth of low, medium, and high chances to win a skip rope, or of low, medium, and high chances to win a box of marbles, or of the nine combinations of these two. Chance to win each object was manipulated by adjusting angular size of a colored sector of a disc, beside which the object was placed.

These judgments, as predicted by averaging theory, violated the sure-thing axiom. The near-parallelism of the three solid curves in each panel of Figure 10.3 supports both adding and averaging rules. The crossover of the dashed curve shows that adding a second object may increase or decrease subjective worth. Such opposite effects of the same stimulus are sharply contrary to the sure-thing axiom. Similar results were obtained for 5- to 8-year-olds in the left panel and for 8- to 11-year-olds in the right panel. Schlottmann's striking results disprove the sure-thing axiom and give cogent support to IIT.

Only the second example involves a discrete, either–or choice. The other three compare continuous worth judgments of the separate alternatives. These worth judgments, however, are implicitly comparative within the frame of reference for the judgment scale (see Chapter 3). Such judgments of single alternatives are often the basis for decision in everyday life, and they avoid certain biases that trouble choice tasks. Previous theory has been dominated by discrete choice conceptions, in part owing to lack of a theory of psychological measurement. Functional measurement furnishes a more powerful approach.

The first three foregoing failures of the sure-thing axiom are unique in that no chance element is involved. Other counterexamples to the sure-thing axiom involve probabilistic peculiarities that limit their relevance and even validity. In the well-known Allais paradox, for example, people choose a lower expected

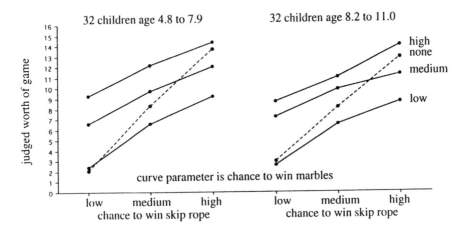

Figure 10.3. Failure of sure-thing axiom. Children judge worth of pairs of chances (solid curves) or single chances (dashed curves) to win skip rope and/or marbles, listed respectively on horizontal axis and as curve parameter. Near-parallelism of solid curves supports adding-type rule. Crossover of dashed and *Med* solid curve shows that adding the same Medium chance to win marbles has opposite effects: It increases (decreases) total worth with low (high) chance to win skip rope. The complementary dashed curve for chances to win marbles alone was very similar to the dashed curve shown for skip rope alone. (From A. Schlottmann, unpublished experiment, October, 1993.)

value to avoid a small chance of losing a large prize. Many people do not consider this irrational, however, but rather rational insurance against the small chance of bitter regret. The foregoing results point to a deeper difficulty: The sure-thing axiom assumes qualitative addition whereas averaging processes are pervasive in cognition.

COGNITIVE PROBABILITY RULES

Mathematical probabilities of certain compound events obey addition and multiplication rules. That human judgment obeys analogous rules has often been speculated. These speculations became testable with functional measurement.

COMPOUND PROBABILITY MODEL

In this experiment, subjects saw two urns, each with a specified proportion of red and white beads. One urn was to be picked with specified probability, and one bead drawn randomly from that urn. Subjects estimated the probability that the bead would be white.

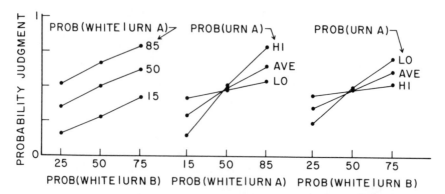

Figure 10.4. Subjective probability obeys three-factor, multiplication–addition rule isomorphic to objective probability rule. Urn A has 15, 50, or 85 white beads in 100; Urn B
has 25, 50, or 75 white beads in 100; Urn A is to be chosen with Hi, Ave, or Lo probability, and a single bead drawn randomly from it. Subjects judged probability that this bead
would be white. (N. H. Anderson, unpublished study, 1975.)

Mathematical probability theory suggests a multiplication–addition model:

$$\text{Prob(White)} = \text{Prob(Urn A)} \times \text{Prob(White | Urn A)}$$
$$+ \text{Prob(Urn B)} \times \text{Prob(White | Urn B)}. \qquad (2)$$

Functional measurement makes it possible to test this two-operation model in
terms of subjective probabilities. This test is straightforward using the parallelism and linear fan theorems of Chapter 2.

The test of this model is shown in the three factorial graphs in Figure 10.4.
The left panel plots the graph for the two conditional probability factors,
Prob(White | UrnA) and Prob(White | UrnB). Since these are separated by a
plus sign in the model, the curves should be parallel, as indeed they are.

The center panel shows the graph for Prob(Urn A) and Prob(White | UrnA).
The hypothesized multiplication operation of Equation 2 implies the data should
form a linear fan, as indeed they do. In the same way, a fan pattern is predicted
and verified in the right panel.

These three graphs furnish notable support for the model, especially from the
interlocking of the two algebraic operations. In this case, the normative model
has a cognitive counterpart. Such cognitive–normative correspondence is not
too surprising, for cognition must have some correspondence with physical reality. Still, an exact cognitive rule could hardly have been expected. This algebra
of probability cognition has some generality, as shown by the multiplication
rules in the following two studies, which used rather different tasks.

LOPES EFFECT: INTUITIVE BETTING

People act in proportion to their confidence. This rule of proportionate behavior may seem obvious and sensible. In fact, it may be nonrational, as shown in the Ph. D. thesis of Lola Lopes.

Subjects had to pass a poker screening test to serve in Lopes' five-day experiment, which employed a simple, computerized version of five-card stud. On each play, the computer showed the single male subject all five of his cards, as well as the four upcards and the bet of each of two computerized opponents, A and B, who followed conservative and average playing styles, respectively. The subject rated his probability of winning and/or made an even-money side bet with the computer, between 1¢ and 30¢, that he could beat both opponents. The computer then turned over the down card of each opponent and paid off or collected from the subject. Subjects were given an initial stake to begin play, and could keep it plus their winnings.

Lopes' theoretical hypothesis was the cognitive analogue of the multiplication rule for independent probabilities:

$$\text{Prob(Beating A and B)} = \text{Prob(Beating A)} \times \text{Prob(Beating B)}. \qquad (3)$$

This multiplication rule implies a linear fan pattern, verified in Figure 10.5. Each curve represents one hand strength for opponent A, indicated by the specified array of High and Low upcards and the specified bet. The points on the horizontal axis represent hand strengths for opponent B, spaced according to their functional measurement values.

Linear fans were obtained for both responses, rated likelihood of winning and amount of the even-money side bet. Subjects do follow the hypothesized multiplication rule—both for the verbal rating and for the behavioral bet shown in the figure. Subjects thus bet in proportion to their confidence in winning.

For the bet response, however, the multiplication rule is suboptimal. Rationally, the subject should bet the minimum (of 1¢) when his subjective probability of winning is less than .5; similarly, he should bet the maximum (of 30¢) when his subjective probability of winning is greater than .5. Each curve in Figure 10.5 should thus be a step function. Although the linear fan pattern has some normative warrant for the rating response, it is counternormative for the bet response. This *Lopes effect* reflects the epistemological difference between cognitive algebra and normative algebra. Normative algebra may give useful hints about cognitive algebra, but it has only heuristic status.

INFORMATION PURCHASE

Seeking additional information to reduce uncertainty is common in decision making. However, information search involves two often perplexing problems: Assessing actual informational content and determining how much to pay for it.

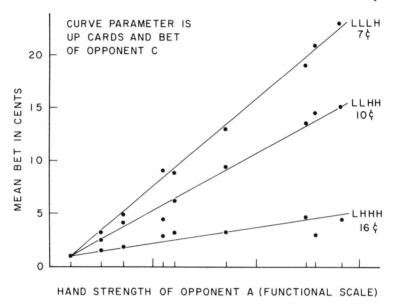

Figure 10.5. Poker betting follows probability multiplication rule. Subject makes even money bet that he can beat both of two computerized opponents at five-card stud, given 4 upcards and amount bet for each opponent; H and L denote high and low upcards. Factorial design based on 3 hand strengths of opponent A, listed by the curves, and 8 hand strengths for opponent B, spaced on the horizontal axis at their functional values (high numbers mean low hand strength). Linear fan pattern implies that amount bet is proportional to product of subjective probability of beating A times subjective probability of beating B. (From L. L. Lopes, 1976, "Model-based decision and inference in stud poker," *Journal of Experimental Psychology: General, 105,* 217-239. Copyright 1976 by the American Psychological Association. Reprinted by permission.)

The following application of cognitive algebra revealed an interesting contrast between cognitive and normative theory.

Subjects judged how much to pay for extra information in a binary decision task, which was to guess the color of a random bead drawn from an urn with known proportions of white and red beads, ranging from 50:50 to 100:0 in five even steps. The closer this proportion is to 50:50, the greater the uncertainty about the bead color and the more valuable the additional information. In the *Truth-or-Lie* condition, this additional information was provided by a die throw, which told the truth about the bead color with probabilities of 3/6, 4/6, 5/6, or 6/6, and otherwise lied.

A multiplication rule was expected. The known white:red proportion determines the need for additional information. The greater the need, the more useful is the additional information. Hence the need should act as a multiplier on the informativeness of the die information. This hypothesized multiplication rule is

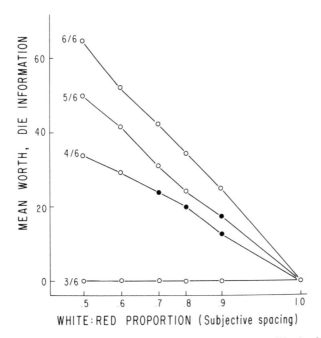

Figure 10.6. Cognitive algebra disagrees with normative algebra. Worth of information follows a multiplication rule: Need × Informativeness. Normative statistical theory implies that the four filled circles represent worthless information. Hence these four points should lie down on the horizontal, 3/6 line, whereas they lie up on the linear fan pattern. This linear fan implies subjects obey uniform multiplication rule. (From J. Shanteau & N. H. Anderson, 1972, "Integration theory applied to judgments of the value of information," *Journal of Experimental Psychology, 92*, 266-275. Copyright 1972 by the American Psychological Association. Reprinted by permission.)

nicely supported by the linear fan pattern of Figure 10.6. This rule is considered to result from the analogue fractionation process previously discussed in relation to the SEV multiplication rule of Figure 10.1.

Nonnormative behavior appears in the four filled circles in Figure 10.6. The additional information is worthless unless the die probability exceeds the known prior probability of the urn. With a known urn ratio of 90:10, for example, the 4/6–2/6, *Truth-or-Lie* information is less informative than the urn ratio and cannot augment it. Hence all four filled circles should lie on the horizontal line defined by the clearly worthless 3/6 die information. Even in this relatively simple task, subjects treat worthless information as beneficial. The proliferation of stock information letters, not to mention mutual funds, is thus not surprising.[2]

The cognitive–normative distinction is further emphasized in this result. Subjects understand the objective task structure well enough to adopt a multiplication rule; to this degree their behavior mirrors the normative. It may also be optimal, in a functional sense, by providing an economical approximation to the normative standard over a range of task conditions.

It would be a mistake, however, to construe the behavior in normative terms. This fails to account for the four nonnormative points in Figure 10.6. More seriously, these four nonnormative points reflect a deeper normative incapacity to recognize the cognitive character of the multiplication operation itself.

MATCHING LAW

The behavioral matching law of operant psychology can be generalized to allow subjective values with functional measurement theory. According to the matching law, an organism will distribute responses between two alternatives in proportion to their respective rates of reinforcement:

$$\frac{R_1}{R_1 + R_2} = \frac{r_1}{r_1 + r_2}. \qquad \text{(behavioral matching law)} \qquad \text{(4a)}$$

where R_i is the observed response rate for alternative i and r_i is the corresponding rate of reinforcement (Herrnstein, 1970).

A notable property of this matching law is that all four terms are observable. No parameters need be estimated; an exact test on the raw data is possible. However, the ratio on the right involves an implicit assumption that the reinforcement has equivalent quality for the two response alternatives. This will not generally be true, as a number of writers have pointed out.

To take account of quality of reinforcement, the observable r_i need to be replaced by psychological values, ψ_i. Using R to denote the relative response ratio on the right, a psychological form of matching law can be written:

$$R = \frac{\psi_1}{\psi_1 + \psi_2}. \qquad \text{(psychological matching law)} \qquad \text{(4b)}$$

This psychological matching law has the same form as the decision averaging rule, Equation 5b of Chapter 2.

This psychological matching law differs essentially from the behavioral matching law because it involves unobservable quantities, namely, the ψ values. Some writers have argued that any psychological matching law must be tautological, that is, that ψ values could always be found to make it true. This argument is not correct (Anderson, 1974c, 1978a). Functional measurement theory can provide rigorous tests of the psychological matching law, since it is formally identical with the decision averaging rule of Figure 10.7. If it succeeds, moreover, it provides validated measures of the unobservable stimulus values. A related application is given by Farley and Fantino (1978). Unobservable constructs can thus be incorporated in rigorous scientific theory.

COGNITIVE AND NORMATIVE

Probability judgment does follow algebraic rules in many tasks. The studies of Figures 10.4–10.6 illustrate multiplication rules, and a decision averaging rule appears in the later sections on Bayesian theory. Also pertinent is the serial integration rule observed in probability judgments by children (Chapter 8).

Functional measurement theory was essential to test this cognitive algebra. Without capability for measuring personal probability, these rules could not have been established.

Hardly less important than the algebraic rules is the validational support for the continuous response methodology. The pattern in the observable response thus mirrors the pattern in the unobservable cognition. This response methodology furnishes a powerful tool for studying the many tasks that do not follow simple algebraic rules.

Cognitive algebra succeeded where normative algebra failed. Normative algebra had heuristic value, it is true, for it suggested the multiplication rules tested in the foregoing experiments. Indeed, judged by the data patterns of Figure 10.4, cognitive algebra might seem normative algebra with subjective values. This seeming would be mistaken. The studies of Figures 10.5 and 10.6 showed multiplication rules even though normative theory called for step functions. These results underscore the epistemological difference between cognitive algebra and normative algebra.

COGNITIVE ALTERNATIVE TO BAYESIAN THEORY

Bayesian theory is one of the class of subjectivist theories that seek to legitimize probability statements about unique events, for example, the probability that the reviewers will praise your submitted paper or that your grant application will be funded. The Bayesian emphasis on subjective probability makes it attractive to psychologists. Moreover, it focuses on inverse inference and revision of belief, both basic problems in judgment–decision.

Although the Bayesian model is normative statistical theory, its subjectivist character suggested it might also serve as a model of cognitive process. In fact, an initial surge of interest in psychological decision theory stemmed from this view of Bayesian models. That these normative models would also be cognitive models was the main claim.

Functional measurement theory made it possible to test the Bayesian models as true cognitive models. This work, however, infirmed the Bayesian approach. What limited success the Bayesian models have had reflects occasional coincidence of cognitive and normative algebra. This work was constructive, moreover, for it demonstrated the usefulness of cognitive algebra in this subdomain of judgment–decision.

DECISION AVERAGING RULE FOR INVERSE INFERENCE

Inverse inference, backwards from events to their causes, is characteristic of science. A canonical form of inverse inference appears in a two-urn task used for experimental studies of the Bayesian model. In this task, subjects see two urns, each with a specified ratio of red and white beads. One urn is chosen secretly, and the subject is shown a random sample of beads from that urn. The task is to judge the likelihood that the sample came from one or the other urn.

A ratio model derived from averaging theory was applied to this two-urn task. The sample is considered to activate two competing response tendencies, corresponding to the subjective likelihoods that the sample came from urn A or urn B separately. The overt response represents a compromise between these two competing response tendencies, and this compromise is assumed to be a weighted average. This yields the decision averaging rule of Chapter 2:[3, 4]

$$R = (\omega_{Ai}\psi_{Ai} + \omega_{Bj}\psi_{Bj})/(\omega_{Ai} + \omega_{Bj}). \tag{5a}$$

In this two-alternative task, the scale values correspond to the end points of the decision axis. Their values may thus be specified as $\psi_{Ai} = 0$ and $\psi_{Bj} = 1$. The decision averaging rule then reduces to the ratio of the likelihood weights:

$$R = \omega_{Bj}/(\omega_{Ai} + \omega_{Bj}). \tag{5b}$$

This decision averaging rule provided a good fit to the data. One test is shown in Figure 10.7, in which the solid curves show the theoretical predictions. These theoretical curves lie close to the actual data, indicated by the open circles; the discrepancies were not significant in the test of goodness of fit.

Three other aspects of this study deserve mention. First, the estimated likelihood weights for the more likely urn were strongly dependent on the composition of that urn, being roughly twice as large for the 90:10 as for the 60:40 urn. This likelihood weight was also sensitive to sample size, but only 1½ times as large for the 4-red sample as for the 1-red sample. Contrary to expectation, moreover, weights were not any simple function of sample composition. For the less likely urn, indeed, weights were nearly constant, with a small effect of urn composition and negligible effect of sample size. The model-estimated weights thus reveal aspects of decision processing not otherwise obtainable.[5]

Second, the Bayesian model disagrees sharply with the data. One disagreement is the asymmetry of weights for the less and more likely urns just noted. A second disagreement comes from the three cases of complementary, or symmetric urns (e.g., 90:10 and 10:90). For such symmetric urns, a R:W pairing is uninformative because it could come equally well from either urn. Only the excess of red over white in the sample carries information. Normative theory accordingly makes the strong prediction that the judgment will depend only on the (red − white) difference in the sample, regardless of total sample size.

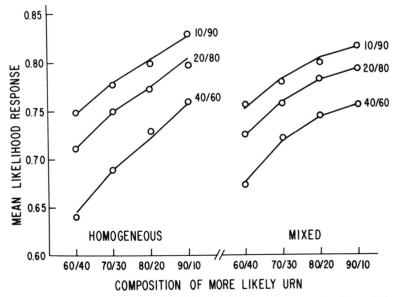

Figure 10.7. Decision averaging rule holds for Bayesian two-urn task. Open circles are data; curves are theoretical. Subject sees sample of beads drawn at random from one of two urns, each with specified numbers of red and white beads (listed on horizontal axis and as curve parameter, respectively.) Data points are mean judged probabilities that the sample comes from the more likely urn. Left panel averaged over four homogeneous samples (1, 2, 3, and 4 red beads); right panel averaged over four mixed samples (3:2, 3:1, 4:1, and 6:2 red:white ratios); see also horizontal axis of Figure 10.8. (From M. Leon & N. H. Anderson, 1974, "A ratio rule from integration theory applied to inference judgments," *Journal of Experimental Psychology*, *102*, 27-36. Copyright 1974 by the American Psychological Association. Reprinted by permission.)

In Figure 10.8, therefore, the two top curves, labeled 90:10, should be identical in the left and right panels because the (red − white) differences are equal, point by point, on the horizontal axis. These curves are clearly not identical, either in elevation or in shape. The two bottom curves, labeled 60:40, are also not identical. Similar failures had been observed in isolated instances in previous work, but this seems to have been the first systematic study. These data are contrary to the Bayesian formulation, and no proponent of the Bayesian view has attempted to account for them.

Third, the data disprove the representativeness heuristic of Kahneman and Tversky (1972), which asserts that judgments are independent of the base rate. In this Bayesian two-urn task, the base rate is determined by the urn proportions. Figures 10.7 and 10.8, however, both show large effects of urn proportions. Such base rate effects had been observed with sequential sampling in the

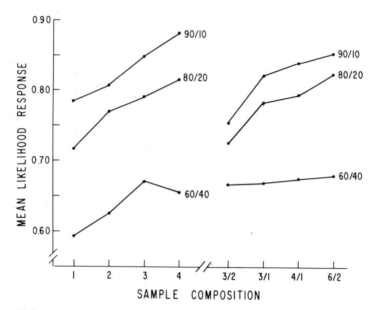

Figure 10.8. Judgments in Bayesian two-urn task disobey Bayesian model. Each curve represents data for complementary urn pairs, e.g., 90:10 and 10:90, for which Bayesian theory implies that the probability depends only on the (red − white) difference in the sample. Hence the set of three curves at the left must be identical with the set of three curves at the right, according to Bayesian theory, because the net number of red beads in the sample (listed on horizontal axis) is the same, point by point, across both panels. (From M. Leon & N. H. Anderson, 1974, "A ratio rule from integration theory applied to inference judgments," *Journal of Experimental Psychology, 102*, 27-36. Copyright 1974 by the American Psychological Association. Reprinted by permission.)

Bayesian studies, but Kahneman and Tversky dismissed these as demand artifacts of sequential responding. Simultaneous presentation was used in this study, however, so this base rate effect does disconfirm the representativeness heuristic, the first of many such failures. More important, these results supported the decision averaging model, which has done well in subsequent work.

SHANTEAU DILUTION EFFECT

Irrelevant or nondiagnostic information can influence judgment and decision. This nonrational effect is clearest in Shanteau's (1975) study of the Bayesian two-urn task just considered. The two urns had complementary red:white proportions, and subjects received a sequence of samples coming from an unknown one of the urns. Following each successive sample, subjects revised their judged probability that the samples were coming from a specified urn.

In this task, a sample of 2 red and 2 white (2R:2W) is nondiagnostic. Such a sample is as likely to come from the 80:20 urn as from the complementary 20:80 urn. Before receiving any sample, subjects judge that each urn is equally likely; this judgment is unchanged when the first sample is 2R:2W. Subjects thus understand the nondiagnostic nature of this sample.

But suppose the first sample is 2R and the second is 2R:2W. The judgment following 2R moves away from equally likely, of course—but it moves part way back following 2R:2W. This seems irrational because the 2R:2W is nondiagnostic, and the subjects understand this. Shanteau called this the *water down effect*, renamed the *dilution effect* by subsequent investigators. It obviously disagrees with rational theory, Bayesian theory in particular.

Averaging theory can accommodate Shanteau's dilution effect in terms of the two-parameter, weight–value representation. The scale value of 2R:2W is at the neutral zero point, which corresponds to the equally likely point on the probability response scale. However, the weight of 2R:2W is not zero. With an addition rule, its weighted value remains zero, so it would have no effect. With the averaging rule, however, the weight appears in the denominator, so it does have an effect. A similar result was predicted and obtained by Himmelfarb with social attitudes.

This interpretation also illustrates a qualitative difference between the two-parameter, weight–value representation of averaging theory and the one-parameter, diagnosticity representation of Bayesian theory. Here again, normative algebra differs from cognitive algebra.[6]

SERIAL INTEGRATION

Serial integration is the norm in everyday thought and action. Information is usually received at successive points in time and is normally integrated as it is received. Such accumulative integration has been considered in the serial integration model of Chapter 2. This model was compared with the Bayesian model by Shanteau (1970; see also 1972), who presented successive samples from a single urn that contained an unknown proportion of white to red beads. Under *inference* instructions, subjects were to judge the probability that the urn had more white than red beads; under *estimation* instructions, subjects were to judge the proportion of white beads in the urn.

The serial integration model of IIT proved superior to the Bayesian model for the inference task in several respects. In particular, the data showed substantial recency effects, which could be accounted for in terms of the weight parameter of averaging theory. The Bayesian formulation, in contrast, disallows recency because that is nonnormative in the given task.

A more serious difficulty for the Bayesian approach was that subjects appeared to be doing something qualitatively different from the Bayesian task instructions. In the inference task, which mimics the standard Bayesian two-urn inference, judgments should obviously approach 0 or 1 as sample size increases. In fact, they approached the cumulative sample proportion, being indistinguishable from the estimation judgments. This behavior, which persisted with carefully revised instructions, called into question the meaningfulness of much previous work in the Bayesian framework. Shanteau's careful work indicated that subjects are not "conservative" Bayesians; they are not Bayesians at all.

PROBABILITY LEARNING

Contingencies in everyday life are seldom all-or-none. Probabilistic outcomes are the rule. Much attention, accordingly, has been given to judgment under uncertainty. The Bayesian two-urn task embodies such uncertain outcomes, and it can be used to study how people learn contingencies.

Such a probability learning task was studied by Birnbaum (1976), who reconceptualized a task employed by Lichtenstein, Earle, and Slovic (1975) in terms of the averaging model of IIT. Subjects were initially trained with probabilistic feedback to predict a numerical criterion separately from each of two probabilistic numerical cues, whose correlations (cue validities) with the criterion were .45 and .89. They were then tested without feedback on pairs of cues, as well as on the single cues themselves.

The normative Bayesian model for this task is the ordinary regression model, with regression weights equal to the standardized cue validities. The Bayesian formulation, accordingly, requires that adding a medium-value cue will have a constant effect, regardless of the value of the other cue. In fact, Lichtenstein et al. found this effect to be nonconstant, inversely related to the value of the other cue. This was a well-established finding in averaging theory (e.g., Figure 10.2).

Lichtenstein et al. accordingly switched to a counternormative averaging rule. They remained within the normative framework, however, assuming that subjects "regressed" the separate cues (a normative correction for unreliability) and averaged these regressed values. This averaging-of-regressed-cues model was also disproved in Birnbaum's cogent study.

The averaging model from IIT, in contrast, gave a near-perfect account of the data. In particular, since the weights sum to unity in the averaging model, it implies that the effect of one cue is inversely related to the validity of the other cue. This disagrees with the averaging-of-regressed-cues model, as Birnbaum pointed out, but was confirmed by the data.

Averaging theory also explains how adding information of equal value can yield a more extreme response (see *Amount of Information* in Chapter 4), a result also disallowed by the averaging-of-regressed-cues model. The normative formulation required multiple ad hoc assumptions to explain the data. The averaging model of IIT, as Birnbaum emphasized, provided a unified theoretical interpretation.

COVARIATION

Ability to detect covariation or contingency among events in the environment is important in adaptive behavior. Animals need to be responsive to signal–food contingencies, physicians to symptom–disease correlations, and each of us to promise–fulfillment contingencies. Judgments of covariation have accordingly been studied in many psychological domains, including learning theory and causal inference, as well as clinical diagnosis. Virtually all this work, however, has been concerned with special cases and with normative issues.

A new perspective on covariation was developed by Jerry Busemeyer, who showed that averaging theory provided a more powerful and more general analysis than previously possible. A popular version of the covariation task uses a 2 × 2 decision table, illustrated with the symptom–disease contingency table of Table 10.1. The cell entries represent frequencies or proportions of the four possible event pairings. Subjects judge degree of covariation of symptom and disease, more specifically, how well the symptom predicts the disease.

What rule do subjects use in judging covariation? Many conjectures have been made. The simplest rule is to base the judgment solely on cell a, the proportion of positive confirming cases. The confirmation–disconfirmation rule adds confirming cases, $(a + d)$, and subtracts disconfirming cases, $(b + c)$. One conditional probability rule takes the difference between the conditional probabilities of correct prediction for the two rows. None of these rules has received serious test, however, due to primitive methods of analysis.

Busemeyer (1991) showed that IIT allows an exact, general treatment of nearly all the rules that have been conjectured—with due allowance for subjective weighting. The informer in each cell is considered to have two parameters, scale value and weight. Since there are just two outcome events, it is no restriction to set the scale values equal to 1 or −1 for the informers in each cell. The subjective weights, however, will depend on the cell proportions and may be denoted $\omega(a)$, and so on.

TABLE 10.1
2 × 2 CONTINGENCY TABLE FOR INTUITIVE STATISTICS

Disease

		yes	no
Symptom	yes	a	b
	no	c	d

NOTE: a, b, c, and d are cell frequencies.

To illustrate, consider the cited conditional probability rule. This may be written as the difference of two weighted averages:

$$R = \frac{\omega(a)}{\omega(a) + \omega(b)} - \frac{\omega(d)}{\omega(c) + \omega(d)}. \tag{6}$$

Since $\omega(a)$ and $\omega(d)$ are separated by a minus sign, variation of the two corresponding cell entries should yield parallelism in the factorial graph. A complete family of such tests is available, identical to those of Equation 7.3 and Figure 7.3. Such tests, however, have not yet been made.

This functional measurement analysis requires no assumption about the subjective weights in Equation 6. The most common alternative analysis has equated the subjective weights with the objective frequencies. Even if this was correct, it would only apply when the frequency information was given in numerical form. Moreover, it makes no allowance for weighting effects of attention and serial position. Busemeyer's functional measurement analysis is thus more general.

Busemeyer presents a general discussion of the covariation problem, including applications to illusory correlation, that is, belief in contingencies that do not actually obtain, as in stereotypes. His analysis is also an interesting illustration of the power of mathematical thinking. It requires fewer assumptions than previous approaches, so it provides a more general analysis—one that is also more powerful. A notable application is given by Kao and Wasserman (1993).

COGNITIVE AND NORMATIVE

IIT proved superior to the Bayesian formulation in all the foregoing experimental tests. These tests seem to have been convincing, for proponents of the Bayesian approach have made little attempt to offer alternative interpretations. These tests have been constructive, at the same time, contributing to unified cognitive theory of judgment–decision.

Furthermore, IIT provides methods for subjective measurement, which is outside the normative domain. The weight parameters in serial integration, for example, are nonnormative and require a nonnormative framework. These weights can be determined with functional measurement, thereby providing information on attention and memory functioning.

IIT is also more general than Bayesian theory. The Bayesian model deals only with probability, but much inverse inference and much serial integration deal with other concepts. In attribution, for example, we often judge degree of some quality rather than probability of some all-or-none cause (see Anderson, 1991m, p. 208). In listening to a job talk, for example, we make attributions about the degree of the candidate's knowledge, intellect, and sense of problem. Cognitive theory thus leads to a more unified, general approach.

SERIAL BELIEF INTEGRATION: PRIMACY AND RECENCY

Beliefs form and change as new informers are received and assimilated. Such serial integration is fundamental in the study of belief.

> In everyday life, information integration is a sequential process. Information is received a piece at a time and integrated into a continuously evolving impression. Each such impression, be it of a theoretical issue, another person, or a social organization, grows and changes over the course of time. At any point in time, therefore, the current impression looks both forward and back. In one perspective, the current impression is the cumulated resultant of all past information. In the other perspective, it is the initial impression into which future information will be integrated. (Anderson, 1981a, p. 144.)

How does belief at any stage depend on previous informers? Answering this question requires a theory of information integration.

Previous workers did not possess an integration theory. They focused, accordingly, on a problem that seemed to lie within their grasp, namely, primacy–recency, which dates back at least to 1925 in social judgment. This problem, unfortunately, led into a morass (see Chapter 4). To bypass this morass required a new paradigm.

TWO PARADIGMS FOR STUDYING SERIAL INTEGRATION

The traditional method for studying serial belief integration employs an order effect paradigm. Two informers, A and B, are presented in both the AB and BA orders. Although both orders contain the same information, they often yield different beliefs. The key traditional measure is the difference between the beliefs produced by the two orders of presentation. This difference is called primacy or recency, according as it favors the first or last informer. Primacy might be expected on the hypothesis that the first informer crystallizes the belief; recency might be expected on the hypothesis that the first informer fades in memory, thus having less memory strength than the last informer.

Many studies have used this traditional order effect paradigm, but the theoretical implications have remained confused (Chapter 4). One reason is that the AB–BA paradigm confounds the two serial positions. Thus, primacy might result from a decreased effect of B in the AB order, from a decreased effect of A in the BA order, or from some unknown combination of these two. The traditional paradigm, as this example shows, is inherently inadequate to analyze serial integration.

A more effective paradigm has been provided by IIT. This integration paradigm is not limited to two informers, as is the traditional paradigm. The influence of each successive informer on the final belief can be determined. A complete serial curve of belief formation can thus be obtained.

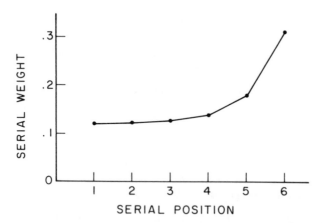

Figure 10.9. Serial position curve for weight parameter in number averaging task. Subjects give intuitive average of sequence of six two-digit numbers. Judgment is fractionated into six components, each representing the importance of the number at a given serial position. (After Anderson, 1964c.)

BELIEF INTEGRATION MODEL

In a prototypical task of belief formation, subjects gave intuitive averages for sequences of six two-digit numbers. Their judgment is to be fractionated into six parts, each part representing the contribution of one serial position. This fractionation was accomplished using functional measurement together with appropriate experimental design. Parallelism analysis supported the hypothesis that the intuitive average was a weighted arithmetic mean of the six (subjective) numbers. The weight at each serial position could thus be measured, using Equations 6 of Chapter 2. These weights constitute the serial curve of informer importance.

This serial importance curve is shown in Figure 10.9. Normative theory would require equal weighting for each number, a flat serial curve. The observed curve is not flat, but shows strong recency. Indeed, the last number in the sequence carries almost a third of the total weight.

The recency effect of Figure 10.9 is considered to be fairly general. Everyday illustrations appear in political attitudes (see Figure 5.3), which are reactive to the latest events, taking attentional salience for appropriate statistical weight. Although such recency may seem a mistaken bias, it can have biosocial advantages. It suggests, in particular, that family quarrels and national wars can be smoothed over with subsequent peaceful behavior. It may also be expected in animal behavior, as in adaptation and expectancy formation, a reflection of the basal–surface representation noted in the next section.

This number averaging study bears on the cognitive–normative antinomy. The normative approach to this and similar tasks has focused on bias, or inaccuracy; the cognitive approach focused on structure in the behavior, without special regard to accuracy. The difference may seem merely one of emphasis in this simple task, in which the inaccuracy is logically equivalent to the behavior. The normative studies, however, could not even test whether the response was an arithmetic mean or some other measure of central tendency. The cognitive approach uncovered the processes underlying the observed behavior.[7]

This was the first study to yield a complete serial curve of belief formation. The functional measurement methodology allowed subjective values for the number stimuli, without assuming that they equaled their objective values. This same approach is applicable to serial integration of verbal and other stimuli that do not have objective values (e.g., Figures 5.4 and 11.1).

GENERAL THEORY OF PRIMACY–RECENCY

A general theory of primacy–recency effects has evolved from work on serial integration in IIT. Two main explanatory processes are attention and the basal–surface representation.

The importance of attention in primacy–recency first appeared in assessing the claim that a certain primacy effect in beliefs about persons was caused by meaning interaction among the informers. Instead, this primacy was found to result from a steady decrement in attention to later informers (see *Primacy–Recency* in Chapter 4 and Figure 11.1). The ubiquitous recency effects can usually be understood analogously in terms of attentional factors. In general, attentional factors affect the weights given the separate informers.

In the basal–surface representation, belief has a surface component elicited by each new informer that largely disappears when the next informer is received. Belief also has a basal component that, once formed, is quite durable. In Figure 5.4, as previously discussed, the surface component is manifest as the marked recency at the last position on each serial curve. The near-flatness at the earlier positions indicates that the basal component increased by nearly equal amounts at each serial position.

With these two processes for the weight parameter, IIT has accounted for most observed order effects in serial integration of meaningful informers. More important, however, is the qualitative shift in paradigm—from the traditional AB–BA paradigm to the functional measurement paradigm. Of equal associated importance is that serial integration has obeyed an algebraic model in numerous studies. This model constitutes a new tool for cognitive analysis.

Nearly all other work on primacy–recency has used the traditional AB–BA paradigm. This paradigm confounds the effects of the two serial positions, and this confounding is amplified with more than two. With the development of the integration paradigm, the traditional paradigm became largely obsolete.

COGNITIVE AND NORMATIVE

Primacy and recency are both biases—according to the standard normative view. The information is the same, regardless of its order of presentation, so it should yield the same response. The bias approach, however, foundered in the disorder of the empirical determinants of primacy and recency. Only by focusing on a deeper level of process was a unified framework obtained.[8]

The biosocial heuristic of Chapter 1 interrelates the basal–surface representation and attention. The basal component represents a durable belief that can be built up from the first several informers, thereby allowing attention to be shifted to other aspects of the environment. The surface component, which represents attentional salience of the present informer, allows monitoring for systematic changes in the environment. This provides an efficient memory system for utilizing limited processing resources.

MULTIATTRIBUTE ANALYSIS

Multiattribute analysis promises a simple solution to the often difficult problem of choosing among several alternatives, and it has been extensively applied in power plant siting, school desegregation plans, health status, and so on. Conceptually, the overall value of each alternative is obtained by information integration. Each alternative is represented by its location, or value, on each of several attributes, or dimensions. Also, each dimension is assigned a weight to represent its importance. The net value of any alternative, A, is the weighted sum of its values on the several attribute dimensions; this is the multiattribute formula:

$$V(A) = \sum \omega_i \psi_i. \tag{7}$$

The choice decision rule is simplicity itself: Choose the alternative with the highest value.

MEASUREMENT THEORY

Application of this multiattribute formula depends critically on measurement of the weights and values. Unless these are valid measures, the choice prescribed by the formula may be far from optimal. In fact, the multiattribute formula requires unusually strong measurement assumptions, and it is sensitive to violations of these assumptions. Values and weights must be on linear scales, the weights having a known zero. Even more stringent is the assumption of common unit for these scales, which is essential to adding up the attribute values. Under likely violations of these measurement assumptions, the multiattribute formula can erroneously assign highest value to a less preferred alternative.

Current practice in multiattribute analysis relies on makeshift measurement of dubious validity (see Anderson, 1982; Anderson & Zalinski, 1988; Zalinski & Anderson, 1989, 1991). One prominent method for obtaining weights uses the method of magnitude estimation. Magnitude estimation, however, has long been known to suffer extreme bias, illustrated in Figure 3.1.

A second common method is point allocation, in which 100 points are distributed among the attributes to indicate their relative importance. Point allocation, however, exhibited biases up to 50% when assessed with functional measurement in judgments of job satisfaction (Zhu & Anderson, 1991).

Perhaps the most common method involves tradeoff: Subjects judge how much of one dimension should be given up (traded off) to get a unit increase in another dimension. Tradeoffs, however, exhibited inconsistencies in the cited study of job satisfaction. In particular, tradeoffs were larger for the dimension on which the response was made.

Still other work relies on weights obtained from regression analysis. These weights, however, are nearly always confounded with the unit of the value scales. As measures of psychological importance, therefore, they are usually uninterpretable.

SELF-ESTIMATION METHODOLOGY

Resolution of the measurement issue requires development of *self-estimation methodology*, in which judges estimate directly the weights and values of the several separate attributes. Self-estimation is essential because multiattribute analysis typically deals with natural situations in which factorial-type design is impracticable or impossible. Self-estimation by experts has often been used in applied multiattribute analysis, but the validity of these self-estimates remains unknown. It is known, however, that different methods yield different results, which indicates that invalidity is a serious issue.

Self-estimation methodology can be put on a solid foundation with functional measurement. The functional measures constitute a validity criterion for the self-estimated measures. With a validity criterion, current methods of self-estimation can be improved or discarded. This is the goal: To develop methods for self-estimation that can be used generally, for there are many situations in which no validity criterion will be available.

To implement this approach, tasks would be selected for which algebraic rules have been established using factorial-type design. Two kinds of response would be obtained: the overall integrated judgment of each combination of stimulus attributes; and self-estimates of the weight–value parameters of each separate attribute. The overall integrated judgment would be analyzed to derive the functional measurement weight–value parameters. These constitute a validity criterion for the self-estimates (see also Sjöberg, 1994).

Just this approach was used in the cited study of job satisfaction, a task known to obey an averaging rule. Functional measurement analysis could thus be applied to measure weight parameters on a ratio scale with common unit across the separate attributes. This constitutes the validity criterion for the self-estimated weights, which were obtained using a variety of methods. Point allocation suffered severe bias, as already noted. The rating method, however, agreed well with the functional weights.

Although this one study needs replication, it suggests that the rating method can provide valid self-estimates of weight. The point allocation and tradeoff methods, moreover, could perhaps be revised to remove the biases. Building from this foundation in cognitive algebra, it seems possible to develop self-estimation methodology for valid measurement in multiattribute analysis. Although much remains uncertain, the work to date has shown promise.

COGNITIVE–NORMATIVE COOPERATION

The cognitive–normative antinomy should be a harmony in multiattribute analysis. For many practical decisions, the normative addition formula seems exactly what is wanted.

It is generally understood, moreover, that values are extranormative and must usually be measured empirically. The shortcomings of the makeshift measurement methods in current use have long been known. In particular, as already noted, different methods are known to yield different estimates of the multiattribute parameters.

It is astonishing, therefore, the virtually all applications of multiattribute analysis continue to rely on such makeshift measurement. Self-estimation methodology is a prime area for cognitive–normative cooperation.[9]

BIASES

One idea has dominated judgment–decision theory: Human judgment should be rational and optimal. Much research, accordingly, has revolved around normative models, which claim to prescribe rational–optimal behavior. A recurrent hope has been that normative models would not only prescribe but also describe behavior—the laws of logic should be the laws of thought. This hope has repeatedly, often grudgingly, bowed under the evidence. People often seem far from rational and optimal.

This outcome is hardly surprising; biases have a long history in psychology. Primacy–recency in social psychology, halo effects in industrial psychology, the atmosphere effect in syllogistic reasoning, and stereotypes in general thought and action are venerable examples from early in this century.

In judgment–decision, however, the normative view was not really given up in the face of such nonnormative behavior. Instead, the deviations of behavior from normative prescription were reified as psychological phenomena and given special names, such as conservatism. Once named, these biases assumed an air of reality and became the object of explanatory study.

Reification of biases is strange science. If the normative model is cognitively invalid, deviations from that model cannot generally have cognitive significance. Such deviations may have practical importance, of course, but they are not prima facie psychological phenomena. The normative focus on bias has thus misdirected the course of inquiry.

BIASES

One of the more-studied biases was *conservatism*, which arose in attempts to treat Bayesian decision theory as descriptive of human judgment. In the Bayesian two-urn task described previously, human judgments are generally less extreme than the statistically correct response. With 70:30 and 30:70 urns, the probability that a sample of three red beads comes from the 70:30 urn is .93, substantially higher than most people think. This bias was reified by calling it conservatism, as though people were somehow *holding back* on following the dictates of the sample evidence. Conservatism became the focal issue of the Bayesian approach; many attempts were made to "explain" it.[10]

This normative focus obscured the psychological processes. Instead of seeing the behavior, it was distorted in the Bayesian model. One symptom of this distortion is that many reports presented, not the actual data, but mean accuracy ratios or inferred log likelihood ratios derived through the Bayesian model. Identical behavior with different urns would thus yield different derived ratios. The actual behavior was irretrievably lost in these Bayesian ratios. These reports are now largely uninterpretable.

Treating conservatism as a psychological phenomenon was a mistake. The behavior called conservatism invalidates the Bayesian model as a description of human cognition. But conservatism only exists by reference to this Bayesian standard. Once that standard is seen to be invalid, conservatism loses claim to psychological reality. Conservatism is not a cognitive illusion; it is a cognitive noneffect.

The normative misdirection appears even in so simple a task as number averaging (Figure 10.9). Here the normative focus on inaccuracy might seem unobjectionable, for the task virtually prescribes an accuracy criterion. For studying behavior, however, inaccuracy and conservatism have similar faults. The important questions are how the stimulus numbers are evaluated and integrated. For this process analysis, inaccuracy is irrelevant and misleading. The essential datum is the subject's integrated judgment, which is to be disintegrated to determine the information processing.

This dis-integration was possible with cognitive analysis, which gave a simple answer. The information processing could be represented as serial averaging, quantified with the serial curve of weight. This representation lies outside the normative capability. As noted in a related integration study, previous reports "consider high accuracy to be the most important result that had been obtained. Such results . . . can obscure the basic theoretical problem" (Anderson, 1968b, p. 392). The normative approach had missed the main issue.

Ironically, the inaccuracy only became comprehensible in terms of cognitive analysis. A similar moral appeared in the foregoing discussion of Birnbaum's application of IIT to probabilistic number averaging. Here again, the positive approach of cognitive theory proved superior to the negative emphasis on inaccuracy and bias.

The general issue of biases is important; the problem is how to define bias and how to study it. Kahneman and Tversky (see Kahneman, Slovic, & Tversky, 1982) made signal contributions, presenting clever demonstrations of many previously known biases and adding some new phenomena, such as the conjunction fallacy. In part because of its importance, however, the concept of bias has been and remains a treacherous guide for inquiry. Much current work suffers from opportunistic compromises of normative and cognitive concepts that cannot attain conceptual clarity or even practical generality.

Further normative limitation is also suggested by the serial number averaging task, a prototype of the ubiquitous serial integration of everyday life. In general, the stimuli will not be crisply numerical, as in this experiment, but fuzzy verbalisms, without definite objective values. The accuracy criterion then fades away, and with it the foundation for normative analysis. General theory requires a different way of thinking.

This different way of thinking appears in the serial curve of Figure 10.9. This serial curve is far more powerful than the traditional index of primacy–recency. Such serial curves may also be obtained for purely verbal stimuli, as in Figure 11.1. In the latter case, moreover, the serial curve relates integration to memory processes.

A more general illustration appears in averaging theory. The averaging rule not only violates the sure-thing axiom, as previously discussed, but also the consistency theories noted in Chapters 4 and 5. Indeed, if there is any one basic normative principle, it is consistency. These and various other instances of nonnormative bias have received a unified interpretation within the conceptual framework of averaging theory.

The normative approach is negative, emphasizing human shortcomings. The cognitive approach is positive, seeking to understand human judgment in its own framework. Even for the normative goal of improving human judgment, the cognitive approach is useful, if not essential. This positive approach has been the guiding theme of IIT in the judgment–decision domain.

HEURISTICS

One of the fads that sweep across psychology appears in the "heuristics" proclaimed by Kahneman and Tversky in a series of papers in the early 1970s (see Kahneman, Slovic, & Tversky, 1982). Three heuristics were presented as attempts to explain assorted biases. All three, however, were inconsistent with substantial pre-existing evidence. Subsequent work has extensively confirmed this inadequacy of the three heuristics.

The *availability* heuristic asserts that judgments about event frequency or probability are determined by those instances that can be recalled. This is an instance memory hypothesis, a special case of the verbal memory hypothesis of traditional reproductive memory. This memory representation had already failed, however, in a direct experimental test (see later section on *Functional Memory*).

Moreover, as pointed out by Fiedler (1983), the availability heuristic rested almost entirely on anecdotal demonstration, with little effort at experimental scrutiny. Fiedler used a typical decision task, but his experimental results disconfirmed the availability heuristic. Indeed, Fiedler arrived at an interpretation similar to the two-memory representation of functional memory theory.

The *anchoring and adjustment* heuristic is a special case of serial integration. To integrate two informers, subjects make an initial response based on one (the anchor) and revise this response to take account of the second (the adjustment). The phrase, anchoring and adjustment, is just metaphorical reexpression of serial integration, without further substantive content. In one respect, however, the statement of the heuristic went beyond this metaphor to make a substantive assertion, namely, an empirical generalization that adjustments are "typically insufficient." The first informer is overly effective, in other words, as though it held back or anchored the adjustment.

This substantive assertion, however, disagreed with then-known facts. Adjustments are not "typically insufficient." Quite the opposite; insufficient adjustment corresponds to a primacy effect; but recency, which corresponds to *over*sufficient adjustment, has been far more common, especially in judgment–decision. Examples of recency appear in the number averaging study of Figure 10.9 and in Shanteau's (1970) study of serial integration in the Bayesian task considered earlier. The anchor metaphor, with its claim of insufficient adjustment, disagreed with the previous literature.

In social psychology, primacy–recency effects had been studied since early in the century. Both primacy and recency had been obtained under certain conditions, and several process interpretations had been considered (see *Primacy–Recency* in Chapter 4). None of these process interpretations was considered in the anchoring and adjustment heuristic; the claim of insufficient adjustment was presented as an empirical generalization. As an empirical generalization, however, this heuristic was more false than true.

A more effective approach to serial integration had previously been obtained in IIT. Consider two informers with values ψ_1 and ψ_2 and weights ω_1 and ω_2, and let R_1 and R_2 denote the response following the first and second informers. The averaging rule may then be written in the proportional-change form, similar to Equation 6a of Chapter 2:

$$R_2 = R_1 + \omega_2(\psi_2 - R_1). \tag{8}$$

Metaphorically, the first response, R_1, anchors the judgment at the first informer. The proportional change, $\omega_2(\psi_2 - R_1)$, may similarly be called an adjustment. This proportional adjustment moves the response only part way toward the second informer, as though it was held back, or anchored, by the first informer. This, of course, merely reflects serial integration of information, that both past and present informers affect present judgment. Aside from the erroneous empirical claim of insufficient adjustment, the anchoring and adjustment heuristic is only a catchy metaphor for serial integration.[11]

This serial integration rule has every advantage over the heuristic. It is rigorously testable, and it has been successfully tested many times. It allows both primacy and recency effects, even within a single sequence. It allows construction of a complete serial curve of weight (e.g., Figure 10.9). And it has had some success in analyzing deeper levels of process.

The *representativeness* heuristic asserts that people judge probabilities solely by reference to similarity between sample and target population. In the Bayesian two-urn task, in particular, the controlling variable is thus the red:white proportion in the sample; urn proportions and sample size will be ignored. These are strong claims; both were strongly disconfirmed in Figure 10.8. The large effects of urn proportion are visible in the figure as the vertical separation among the curves; the effect of sample size is clear in the substantial difference between results for the 3:1 and 6:2 samples, which have the same red:white proportion. This initial failure of the representativeness heuristic has been extensively corroborated in subsequent work.[12]

The representativeness heuristic was also applied to person cognition by Kahneman and Tversky. Pertinent here is its claim that size of information sample (keeping value constant) will have no effect. This claim had previously been shown incorrect (see *Amount of Information* in Chapter 4).

The representativeness heuristic made a third strong claim: Subjects will ignore reliability of information, for this is external to the sample itself. Here again, contrary evidence had already been found in several integration studies that manipulated information reliability.

No one doubts that sample–target similarity is important; this has long been known. What was novel about the representativeness heuristic was the strong claim that this similarity is all-important, that nothing else matters. This claim has failed, and with it the representativeness heuristic.

All three heuristics contained grains of truth. Much of this truth, however, was not novel; much of what was novel was untrue. In fact, all three heuristics disagreed with substantial prior evidence, and this disagreement has been accentuated in subsequent work (Anderson, 1991a). The popularity of these heuristics mirrors a general lack of cognitive theory in judgment–decision.

EXPERT JUDGMENT, LINEAR MODEL, AND WEAK INFERENCE

Decisions in any business, government agency, or public institution generally depend on experts for evaluation and integration of pertinent information. Empirical studies, however, have suggested that expert judgment has many faults and biases. One aspect of this complex issue is considered here: What concepts and methods are necessary for cognitive analysis of expert judgment? This question will be considered in relation to the controversy whether expert judgment is configural, as experts claim, or nonconfigural, as has been claimed by many proponents of linear, additive models.

The linear–additive argument asserts that expert judgment is well described by linear, additive models. These models are nonconfigural. Contrary to the expert judges, it was therefore argued, expert judgment is not configural.

The linear–additive argument is inconclusive. It rests on *weak inference*, methods that seem to test a model but do not really do so. Weak inference and strong inference are contrasted in Figure 10.10. In the left panel, predictions from a linear, additive model are plotted as a function of observed judgments of a consumer product. With perfectly reliable data, the linear model predicts the points will all lie on the straight diagonal line. In practice, data are not perfectly reliable, so some scatter around the straight diagonal will be found. The scatter in Figure 10.10 seems small, however, and the correlation of .98 between predicted and observed seems impressively high. If it is judged by these correlation–scatterplot statistics, the linear model seems to do very well.

In fact, the linear model does poorly: It predicts parallel curves in the factorial graph of the data. This graph is definitely not parallel, as shown in the right panel of Figure 10.10. The curves cross over, and the statistical interaction is highly significant. The linear, additive model is seriously incorrect.

How can a model that is so bad seem so good? The answer is weak inference: Correlation and scatterplot obscure and hide serious discrepancies from the model. Strong inference, in the form of factorial design and analysis of variance, is much more effective at uncovering discrepancies from the model. In SEV theory, to take another example, similar weak inference had led to claims for an addition rule, Subjective Probability *plus* Subjective Value, whereas Figure 10.1 clearly reveals a multiplication rule.[13]

Weak inference was the foundation for the linear–additive argument that expert judgment is not configural. Experts claim to think configurally. Whether in clinical diagnosis, personnel selection, or what have you, experts say they

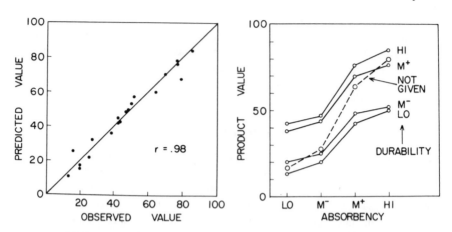

Figure 10.10. Weak inference versus strong inference. Subjects judged product value as a function of absorbency and durability. Left panel plots values predicted from a linear model as function of the observed judgments, with a predicted–observed correlation of .98. This weak inference analysis seems to give good support to the linear model. Right panel plots same observed judgments as factorial graph. Crossover of dashed curve disproves linear model. (After N. H. Anderson & J. Shanteau, 1977, "Weak inference with linear models," *Psychological Bulletin, 84,* 1155-1170. Copyright 1977 by the American Psychological Association. Reprinted by permission.)

evaluate and integrate each informer in contingent relation to other informers. If the linear–additive model is correct, however, the experts' claim of configural processing is incorrect. And indeed, expert judgment did seem to obey the linear–additive model—when analyzed with weak inference. This argument was widely accepted in the judgment–decision domain.

But weak inference does not warrant any conclusion about the nature of expert judgment. Look back at Figure 10.10. Weak inference fails to detect the crossover. This crossover represents configurality in which the same information has opposite effects. When weak inference is blind to such blatant nonadditivity, it cannot possibly detect more subtle forms of configural thinking. Expert judgment may or may not be configural; weak inference cannot say.

The issue of configural thinking had previously appeared in person cognition, specifically as claims that meaning changes across context. These claims had previously been found incorrect; establishing the averaging model supported meaning invariance (e.g., Figure 1.2). At the same time, however, the effective weights are relative, so weighting is configural. Such configural weighting might justify some self-reports of expert judgment.

Two loci of expert judgment need to be distinguished: valuation and integration. Configurality can occur in either of these two operations. Indeed, the former may be more important, as indicated in the earlier section on multiattribute analysis. Studies with linear models, however, mostly used ordinary linear regression with makeshift measurement for the predictor variables. Hence the role of expert judgment in valuation could not be assessed. Without valid subjective values, moreover, the operative integration rule is not determinable. Weak inference methods, although still common, are thus doubly inadequate for analysis of expert judgment.

Functional measurement can, under certain conditions, solve the valuation and integration problems. When the integration is configural, some progress is still possible with a linear response measure. In these ways, and conceptually as well, IIT has provided useful tools for analysis of expert judgment.[14]

COGNITIVE AND NORMATIVE

The cognitive approach to biases is positive, whereas the normative approach is negative. The normative view faults and condemns human judgment for its shortcomings and limitations. There is ample to fault and condemn, to be sure, but faulting, condemning, and holding up an optimal standard is often suboptimal for improving human judgment. Unless biases are understood within their functional framework, they will generally be hard to ameliorate.

The normative negativism has been accentuated by simplistic views of organism and environment. In particular, the very definition of bias presupposes a normative standard that is more or less arbitrary, a point also made in various forms by other writers. Primacy and recency, to take one pertinent illustration, are biases by presupposition that the sequence of informers arises from a stationary process, without systematic temporal trend.

But life is nonstationary. Once the stationarity assumption is given up, the definition of bias becomes problematic because it depends on the real trend in the environment. Real trend is generally difficult to determine. Unless the real trend is known, however, bias may be indeterminate.

The biosocial heuristic suggests that bias is not merely inevitable, but in some degree not really bias. More recent informers, in particular, may be expected to be more valid. The biosocial heuristic thus suggests that the recency effect of Figure 10.9 stems from a functional mode adapted to the everyday world, a mode that allows for a changing environment. People cannot preface every serial integration with an assessment of the operative environmental trend; they need online answers. People can cope, as various writers have pointed out, because they have general purpose capabilities that provide ready online answers for many situations, even though they may be suboptimal in particular situations. What is remarkable is that answers are given at all and that they have substantial survival value. Understanding these biosocial capabilities is important for developing social instruction for more effective behavior. Such understanding is no less important for general theory.

FUNCTIONAL MEMORY

Memory processes are important in judgment–decision, but they have been taken for granted and neglected. One reason is that the traditional conception of memory as reproductive is ill-suited to the operations of valuation and integration. Instead, a functional conception of memory is needed.

A functional view of memory suggests three principles relevant to the judgment–decision domain (Anderson, 1982, Section 7.17). First, judgment and action are constructive processes for which memory is a reservoir of information. Value construction, in particular, relies heavily on similarity operators that compare present stimuli with knowledge systems in semantic memory.

Second, an operating memory is required that constitutes the ongoing judgment and action. Foremost in operating memory is a mental model of the task, assembled from interaction between schemas in semantic memory and perceived characteristics of the present stimulus situation. This is also part of the constructive process, involving interaction among the environment, an active operating memory, and a more passive semantic memory.

Third, contents of operating memory may be stored in semantic memory for future use. Belief revision is a prime example, as in the belief integration model of IIT. The revised belief updates prior belief with present informers. Storing this revised belief has a double advantage. It preserves relevant aspects of the present informers, so future judgment is not dependent on their separate retention. And since this preservation is in processed form, future judgment can economically utilize the present valuation–integration. Functional measurement theory gives effectiveness to this functional conception of memory.

> Judgment research has taken memory for granted despite its importance for valuation processes, which are immersed in background knowledge. . . . At the same time, memory research has tended to pass by judgment theory. . . . Not only does judgment theory require coordination of memory to a superstructure of operations, it may also require more complex representations than have been characteristic of memory theories. These interrelationships between judgment and memory reflect the many opportunities for cooperative inquiry. (Anderson, 1981a, p. 311.)

> Integration theory embodies a functional approach that considers memory as an aid to judgment and action. Whereas traditional approaches to memory focus on reproduction of given stimuli, the functional approach is more concerned with how memory is utilized for attaining goals. The person's prevailing goal affects the processing of prior memory; it also affects the storage of new memory. (Anderson, 1982, p. 345.)

This interdependence of judgment and memory is well illustrated in the integration model for belief revision developed in IIT. This was the origin of the functional conception of memory taken up in the next chapter.

COGNITIVE THEORY OF JUDGMENT–DECISION

The two fundamental problems in judgment–decision are valuation and integration. Values represent the purposiveness of thought and action. Multiple values typically operate, as in expected value, cost–benefit analysis, and belief revision, and these values must be integrated into a judgment–decision. These two problems are the core of many issues in the judgment–decision domain.

Cognitive algebra and functional measurement have yielded an effective attack on both problems. The usefulness of this approach has appeared across the array of long-standing issues covered in the foregoing empirical sections. Cognitive algebra and functional measurement have thus provided a cornerstone for cognitive theory of judgment–decision.

COGNITIVE ALGEBRA

Cognitive algebra has done fairly well in demanding tests in the experimental studies surveyed in this chapter. These studies cover a range of long-standing problems and indicate substantial generality of algebraic cognition.

To establish cognitive algebra required a conceptual shift away from the prevailing normative framework. Normative conjectures about algebraic models have been common, but they remained conjectures, largely untestable. With functional measurement theory, the normative models became testable. In the experimental tests, however, they did not fare well.

Multiplication rules, for example, sometimes agree with normative prescription, sometimes not. Striking agreement appears in the SEV rule of Figure 10.1 and the compound probability model of Figure 10.4. But the probability rule of Figure 10.5 is nonnormative, as is the multiplication rule of Figure 10.6.

A deeper inadequacy of normative algebra appears in the averaging rule. This rule implies that the same stimulus informer can have both positive and negative effects, contrary to the sure-thing axiom, and contrary to virtually any normative rule. This and related results became explicable with the shift to a cognitive framework.

Cognitive algebra represents a mode of cognition. It is more than a set of algebraic rules, for these rules represent cognitive processes. An algebraic rule is only a surface manifestation of an assemblage in operating memory. Beyond its intrinsic interest, therefore, cognitive algebra ramifies into study of functional memory, mental models, and assemblage processes.

MEASUREMENT THEORY

Measurement is central in the judgment–decision domain. This is clear with probability and value, two all-pervasive concepts in judgment and decision. Without measurement capability, theory development cannot get very far.

Because of normative preoccupation, however, measurement theory has been largely neglected in judgment–decision.

Measurement requires cognitive theory. Normative theory is inherently inadequate because values are generally personal. This fact was recognized in the postulation of the multiplication model for subjective expected value. Traditional measurement theories were unable to solve the measurement problem, however, so this model remained untestable.

Only by inverting the traditional approach—by taking the algebraic structure itself as the base and frame for measurement—did the measurement problem become solvable. Thus, the linear fan pattern of Figure 10.1 supported the multiplication rule for subjective expected value at the same time that it provided true psychological measures of probability and value. With the averaging rule, to take a second example, the concept of weight was placed on a solid base.

A second conceptual shift—from *choice* to *preference*—appears in functional measurement. Other approaches have taken choice data as basic, in part because they could not handle continuous response measures. This has given rise to a view that judgment–decision is choice theory in its essential nature. In functional measurement, in contrast, preference, or worth, responses for single alternatives are basic. These preference responses may be implicitly comparative, of course, but they provide greater power and flexibility than discrete choices. In the present view, preference is more general and basic than choice. This view is affirmed by the applications illustrated in this chapter, which have provided a foundation for psychological theory of measurement.

COGNITIVE–NORMATIVE COOPERATION

In the judgment–decision domain, cognitive and normative approaches both have prime importance. They should cooperate, but effective cooperation is by no means straightforward. Although the two operations of valuation and integration are fundamental in both approaches, their natures differ. The normative focus is on accuracy, comparing behavior to some optimal standard prescribed by a rational integration model. The cognitive focus is on the behavior itself, with primary concern for psychological process. Effective cooperation must recognize and coordinate the different aims and purposes of the two approaches.

Current issues and tasks, however, are generally derivative from the normative framework. Many are thus already misstructured for cognitive analysis, as has appeared with every issue covered in this chapter. Many workers proceed, in effect, by trying to blend cognitive concepts into the normative framework. The normative misstructuring may not be recognized. As noted in the discussion of bias, for example, the very term *bias* tends to reify a deviation from a normative standard. Such attempts at cognitive–normative blending accentuate the strategic mistake of seeking to transplant normative models into cognitive ground. Although some local progress can be made this way, it hinders emergence of a general conceptual framework. Such hindrance ranges from so simple a task as number averaging to the inverse inference of Bayesian theory.[15]

One locus for cooperation lies in value, a representation of purposiveness. Normative theory is hollow without values, but values lie generally outside the normative realm. Through value measurement, cognitive theory can contribute to normative applications. One such contribution appeared in the discussion of multiattribute analysis, which has almost entirely depended on makeshift measurement. Functional measurement theory has shown how to put multiattribute measurement on a solid foundation.

Another locus for cooperation lies in reducing normative biases. Although the biosocial heuristic indicates that the concept of bias is far less well-defined than normative approaches have assumed, it still has some of the importance that has been attached to it, especially in practical applications. The biosocial heuristic also suggests that so-called biases often have deep-seated origins and will not be easy to change, a suggestion that accords with the long history of difficulties in changing behavior. Understanding behavior is generally prerequisite to improving it, but understanding requires a cognitive framework (see also Levin, Louviere, Schepanski, & Norman, 1983; Lopes, 1987a,b).[16]

A third locus of cooperation lies in applying cognitive theory to realistic problems, especially field problems of business and government. Cognitive approaches tend to simplify experimental tasks, a tendency that often feeds on itself, with increasing loss of generality and relevance to everyday life. Normative approaches stand out for their concern with real problems of society. They can have a vitalizing influence on cognitive approaches.

UNIFIED THEORY

Cognitive algebra is a cornerstone for unified theory of judgment–decision. Unity appears in the applicability of the same concepts and methods across the diverse applications surveyed in this chapter. Generality also begins to appear in these applications, which cover many classical problems of this field. Unity and generality appear further in applications to other domains as different as memory, attitudes, and ethics, which are considered in other chapters.

Judgment–decision may be considered a unifying framework for psychology. The kinds of problems considered in this chapter underlie thought and action in every domain. No domain theory can go far without resolving these judgment–decision problems in its particular context. Despite the many differences between such domains as social–personality, psychophysics, and language processing, for example, similar processes of judgment–decision are common to all. In this framework, therefore, may lie the best hope for unification of psychological science.

NOTES

The work summarized in this chapter owes much to contributions by Eileen Beier, Michael Birnbaum, Jerome Busemeyer, Clifford Butzin, Joseph Farley, Robert Hawkins, Ann Norman Jacobson, Martin Kaplan, Eileen Karsh, Michael Klitzner, Manuel Leon, Irwin Levin, Lola Lopes, Jordan Louviere, Dominic Massaro, Kent Norman, Gregg Oden, Allen Parducci, Anne Schlottmann, James Shanteau, Ming Shen Wang, David Weiss, Richard Whalen, William Wright, James Zalinski, and Shu-Hong Zhu. Further discussion of cognitive decision theory is given in Anderson (1974c, 1986, 1991a).

1. The subadditivity interpretation rested in large part on the success of the multiplication rule. This supports the linearity of the rating response, by virtue of the linear fan theorem. Without evidence for response linearity, the subadditivity could be merely response bias. This interpretation pushes these data to their limit, following two-operation logic, but response linearity is supported by multiple lines of evidence (see last part of Chapter 3). Subadditivity has been replicated by Shanteau (1974), who used a similar task but with the stimuli of Table 12.1, and was also obtained in certain conditions of Gaeth et al. (1990). In contrast, Klitzner and Anderson (1977) and Schlottmann (Figure 10.3) found joint support for multiplication and addition.

2. That worthless information will often have an effect may be expected from the general propensity to integrate whatever is in the stimulus field. In the information purchase experiment of Figure 10.6, the face value of the extra information is positive, and some understanding of probability theory is needed to realize how the actual value depends on the given information. Even when the information is clearly worthless, however, it may still have an effect through an averaging process (see *Shanteau Dilution Effect* below).

3. The fuzzy logical model of perception (FLMP) considered by Massaro and Friedman (1990) may be a special case of the decision averaging model of IIT, studied by Leon and Anderson (1974; see also Anderson, 1981a, pp. 66*f*, 77*ff*). Massaro and Friedman give an incorrect and misleading comparison of their model with IIT. The decision averaging model of IIT fits the data of Figures 10–11 of Massaro and Friedman exactly as well as their FLMP. Indeed, the "American-football-shaped curves" taken to support the Massaro–Friedman model had appeared long ago as a "slanted barrel" pattern in averaging theory (e.g., Equations 5 of Chapter 2, Figures 7.3–7.5 of Chapter 7).

Contrary to Massaro and Friedman, therefore, their data actually support IIT. IIT does not predict parallelism, as they claim, but nonparallelism of the form shown in their data. This is no surprise, since their Equation 6, which they use to fit the data of their Figures 10–12, is mathematically equivalent to Equation 5b, a special case of the general averaging model of Equation 5a.

Massaro and Friedman wrongly restrict IIT to linear integration: "Integration involves a linear combination of scale values made available by valuation." (p. 236; p. 242). But analysis of (nonlinear) multiplication models was first put on an effective base with the functional measurement analysis of IIT in the study of Figure 10.1. The same applies to the averaging model with differential weights, which is inherently nonlinear. This capability with nonlinear models was essential in establishing the general cognitive algebra presented in this book.

In view of the extensive work on nonlinear models in IIT, it is not easy to understand why Massaro and Friedman recognize only the linear model. Ironically, as evidence for the linear model, they cite the study of judgments of rectangle area by 5-year-olds (Chapter 8). Adults, however, judge area by a multiplication rule, a rule that is essential at a corresponding point in the Massaro–Friedman formulation.

To avoid confusion, it should be noted that Massaro and Friedman consider a task that involves two successive operations for its complete analysis. In their application of IIT, they assume the decision averaging rule for one operation, and a linear integration rule for the other. This analysis is inappropriate because it fails to recognize the extensive work on nonlinear models in IIT. Moreover, the data analyses of their Figures 10–12 involve only the one operation to which the decision averaging model would rightly apply (see similar application to covariation, pp. 337f). Since the decision averaging model has the same form as their FLMP, it would fit these data exactly the same.

The same situation of two successive operations had appeared in the Bayesian urn task studied by Leon and Anderson (1974; see also Anderson, 1974a, Section II.B.11, 1981a, Sections 1.6.4 and 1.7.4). One operation concerned the integration of evidence from the given sample to determine two covert responses corresponding to the choice polarity of the task. The other operation concerned the integration of the two covert responses to determine the overt response. The decision averaging model was successfully applied to the second operation. Hence functional measurement yielded the value parameters produced by the first operation. These showed configural effects in relation to sample evidence (see discussion of Figure 10.7, p. 332). Whether the Massaro–Friedman approach can account for such configural effects is questionable.

Massaro's book (1987, pp. 23, 51) adopted an integrationist approach together with functional measurement, and made notable contributions to categorical–continuous perception and to general language processing (see Chapter 12; Massaro, 1991). The error in Massaro and Friedman should not obscure the essential commonality with IIT.

There is, however, an important difference between the decision averaging model of IIT and the model of Massaro and Friedman. They consider their model to be equivalent to the Bayesian model, at least observationally. The Bayesian model failed in Leon and Anderson (1974), however, and in other studies in IIT (see Note 14 below).

4. Formally, the Bayesian model also has a ratio form, analogous to the decision averaging rule of Equations 5 (see Note 10). It would be a conceptual misdirection, however, to consider the decision averaging rule as a Bayesian rule with subjective values. The temptation to do so seems to stem from reverence for the normative framework, as though it had some higher psychoepistemological standing that compensated for its empirical failures and for its lack of theory of psychological measurement.

5. Inverse inference with more than two alternatives is important, but little studied. The decision averaging rule has a direct generalization to N alternatives with an interesting potential for $N - 1$ independent responses. Point allocation, for example, would involve allocating 100 points among the N alternatives, although the bias problem noted under *Self-estimation Methodology* would require consideration.

Different operations of serial processing and discounting seem not unlikely with even a third alternative. Theory development based on the special case of two alternatives may thus find itself too narrow to handle the general case.

6. A hidden flaw in a standard argument for Bayesian theory is also pointed up in this two-parameter, weight–value representation. This standard argument is that sufficient evidence will force everyone to converge to the same final belief, regardless of differences in their initial beliefs. Hidden in this argument is a normative assumption that everyone will evaluate evidence in the same direction, pro or con. Although this normative assumption holds in standard statistical examples, it is not true in general. Different persons may interpret the same objective evidence in opposite directions for social, political, and ethical issues. Additional evidence may thus amplify initial differences, contrary to the Bayesian presumption, but in accord with history.

7. The number averaging task of Figure 10.9 is a prototype of one process for serial integration (Chapter 2). The two-parameter, weight–value representation of the stimulus seems almost imposed by the nature of the task. The task similarly imposes a demand to adjust the last cumulative response in the direction of the present stimulus. Of course, instructing subjects to average does not mean that their judgments will follow an arithmetic average or show any other regularity.

Functional measurement did reveal a notable regularity: The stepwise adjustment was proportional to the difference between the past response and the present stimulus; the proportionality coefficient was independent of the present stimulus. In short, the judgments followed an exact arithmetic averaging rule. As in this number task, exact averaging processes have appeared everywhere in judgment–decision.

Some tasks will surely not obey an exact averaging rule, even though they may exhibit similar stepwise adjustment. Such behavior, by generalization from the exact averaging rule, might be considered qualitative averaging. The weight parameter could thus be evaluated for each trial and used as a descriptive statistic.

8. Hogarth and Einhorn (1992) present a belief-adjustment model with many similarities to the belief integration model developed in IIT over the last three decades. They make two major changes, however, one technical, one conceptual.

The technical change concerns the definition of the weight parameter. With the Hogarth–Einhorn definition, serial curves of weight lose their meaning.

The conceptual change involves a reversion from the integration paradigm to the traditional primacy–recency paradigm. Although the Hogarth–Einhorn model is ostensibly an integration model, their analysis is essentially limited to the traditional problem of primacy–recency. In the present view, this paradigm and problem no longer have much efficacy or value.

SERIAL WEIGHT CURVES. Serial weight curves appear to lack meaning in the Hogarth–Einhorn model. In the IIT model for belief integration, the weight of an informer depends on its serial position, but is normally independent of the current level of belief. The serial curve of weight is thus meaningful in IIT. It represents fundamental properties of the serial processing.

In contrast, weight depends on current level of belief in Hogarth and Einhorn's model (their Equations 6a and 6b). Hence the same informer at the same serial position may have a high or low weight, depending on the current level of belief. Since the current level of belief depends on the previous informers, so does the weight of the current informer. In their formulation, therefore, weight cannot be a simple function of serial position. Hence the serial curve of weight lacks meaningfulness in their model.

A critical challenge is thus presented by the serial curve of Figure 10.9. This curve is fundamental in the IIT analysis of belief integration. It represents the influence of the informer at each serial position on the final response. Many such curves have been presented (e.g., Figures 5.4 and 11.1). Although Hogarth and Einhorn do not discuss this issue, the inability of their model to handle serial curves of belief integration seems a serious shortcoming (Anderson & Schlottmann, 1995; Schlottmann & Anderson, 1995).

PRIMACY AND RECENCY. Primacy–recency effects are extremely sensitive to details of procedure, as emphasized by Anderson (1981a, p. 153, 1982, Section 7.14) and reemphasized by Hogarth and Einhorn (1992, p. 41). This suggests that order and law will not be found at the surface level of empirical determinants of primacy and recency. Instead, process analysis is needed.

Three process explanations of a certain primacy effect in person cognition had been considered in previous integration studies. The first, change of meaning, was ruled out fairly early (see Chapter 4). The second, weight discounting, was first suggested from the results of one integration study, but was soon shown incorrect (see *A False Step* in Anderson, 1981a, p. 187). The third, attention decrement, also hypothesized in the integration studies, successfully accounted for the cited primacy effect.

Simultaneously, attentional factors were also found to be important determinants of recency. Much of the disorder in observed primacy–recency thus became comprehensible. Attentional processes, together with the basal–surface representation, provide a general framework for understanding primacy and recency, as noted in the text.

MODEL ANALYSIS. The belief integration model of IIT has done well in exact, quantitative tests in numerous experiments. Hogarth and Einhorn do not discuss this issue. Neither do they indicate why their model might be preferable.

The IIT model may be considered an anchoring and adjustment process, as noted in Anderson (1986, pp. 77-79); anchoring and adjustment is merely serial integration. Unlike the anchoring and adjustment heuristic, however, IIT does not claim that primacy is typical (see also *Heuristics* in the text).

Moreover, IIT provides a unified treatment of both models considered by Hogarth and Einhorn. Their model for *estimation* tasks is identical to the IIT model, except for their redefinition of the weight parameter. Their *evaluation* task, called *inference* in previous studies in IIT, has been handled by taking scale values at the end points of the response scale (e.g., Shanteau, 1970; Lopes, 1976b; see similarly Equation 5b of the text). With this unified treatment, serial curves may be obtained similarly for both tasks.

ADDING AND AVERAGING. The claim by Hogarth and Einhorn that estimation tasks obey an averaging process and that evaluation, or inference, tasks obey an adding process is incorrect, both in principle and in fact. Their claim rests on the mathematical form of their models, but this form is only assumed. Mere assumption cannot imply this substantive conclusion. In any case, mathematical form is in principle insufficient to diagnose process (see ''as-if'' models in Chapter 2).

In fact, some evaluation tasks obey an averaging process. The decision averaging rule of Equation 5b and Figure 10.7 is one case. Again, the estimation task of Figure 7.2 shows averaging for one variable and adding for another. An adding process also appears in an estimation task under certain conditions in Schlottmann and Anderson (1995).

STRATEGY OF INQUIRY. A new way of thinking about serial belief integration has been developed in IIT. Serial weight curves obtainable with functional measurement are far more revealing than the traditional primacy–recency paradigm.

Hogarth and Einhorn, in contrast, rely on the traditional primacy–recency paradigm. This traditional paradigm is weak. It is inherently inadequate to handle the general problem of order effects in serial belief integration. This traditional paradigm has not found order and law, but instead has misdirected the course of inquiry.

9. Reflecting the cognitive–normative antinomy, psychological measurement theory has been largely neglected in the judgment–decision field. Optimal scaling, in particular, relies on weak inference and ignores the need for testing goodness of fit to validate measurement scales (see Figure 10.10). A notable exception is Louviere (1988), who adopted functional measurement theory because it does allow tests of goodness of fit.

Relevant studies of self-estimation from IIT are summarized in Anderson (1982, Chapter 6) with updates in Anderson and Zalinski (1988), Zalinski and Anderson (1989), and Zhu and Anderson (1991). A notable application of self-estimation to multiattribute analysis has been given by Wang and Yang (1994). Within the context of an actual environmental issue on Taiwan, Wang and Yang showed how functional measurement could provide a validational criterion for several methods of self-estimation.

10. The Bayesian formula for the probability that a given sample, S, was drawn from urn A may be written in the ratio form, $X/(X + Y)$, as:

$$\text{Prob(urn A} \mid S) = \frac{\text{Prob}(S \mid \text{urn A}) \times \text{Prob(urn A)}}{\text{Prob}(S \mid \text{urn A}) \times \text{Prob(urn A)} + \text{Prob}(S \mid \text{urn B}) \times \text{Prob(urn B)}},$$

where Prob(urn A) and Prob(urn A $\mid S$) are the prior and posterior probabilities of urn A, and Prob($S \mid$ urn A) is the probability of drawing S from urn A. With 70:30 and 30:70 urns, the probability of a 3-red sample is $.7^3$ from A and $.3^3$ from B. With equal prior probabilities of A and B, the posterior probability of A is $.7^3/(.7^3 + .3^3) = .927$. Typical judgments are considerably less, a normative inaccuracy labeled "conservatism." This result shows that human judgment does not obey normative Bayesian theory. It does not follow, however, that conservatism is a phenomenon to be explained. From a cognitive standpoint, conservatism is a noneffect.

11. The anchoring and adjustment heuristic is a prime example of how surplus meaning can masquerade as explanation. The phrase, *anchoring and adjustment*, has been popular because it seems to implicate some dynamic process as explanation. It says no more, of course, than that belief is revised when new informers are received. "Anchoring and adjustment" sounds so fine, however, that it has been used to "explain" recency effects even though this heuristic asserts that primacy is typical.

12. The failure of Kahneman and Tversky (1972) to find an effect of base rate (urn proportion) was attributed to poor experimental procedure by Leon and Anderson (1974, p. 34). The review by Slovic, Fischhoff, and Lichtenstein (1977) took issue with Leon and Anderson and favored the representativeness heuristic. In their own later experiment, however, Fischhoff, Slovic, and Lichtenstein (1979) silently corroborated Leon and Anderson. A review of base rate studies is given by Koehler (in press), with a commentary by Anderson (in press).

13. It may be surprising that correlations as high as .95 or even .99 are not generally good evidence for a model, as shown in the discussion of weak inference. One reason is that the predictor variables are typically chosen to cover a large range; this practically guarantees high correlation, almost regardless of the form of the model.

A deeper reason is that the correlation tests the wrong thing, namely, the degree of agreement between the model and the data. That this is the wrong thing is illustrated in Figure 10.10 of the text. What needs to be tested are the *deviations* from the model predictions, a point also illustrated in Figure 10.10.

This inadequacy of correlation for model analysis was pointed out in the first empirical paper using functional measurement (Anderson, 1962a) and discussed in relation to configural judgment in Anderson (1972b). General discussion of weak inference is given in Anderson (1982, Chapters 4 and 7). Reference papers for the linear–additive argument are Goldberg (1968) and Dawes and Corrigan (1974).

The linear model, despite its shortcomings for cognitive analysis, can be useful for practical prediction. Even with the disordinal data of Figure 10.10, the linear model comes close to most of the data points. It is a mistake, however, to confuse this practical predictive value with psychological meaningfulness.

14. Apparent configurality appeared with the estimated likelihood weights in the study of Figure 10.7, which showed no simple dependence on sample composition. This disagreed with Bayesian theory. With the failure of this prediction, Bayesian theory has no place to go (Anderson, 1991l, p. 67f).

IIT can go further because the configural sample weights can be estimated from the decision averaging rule and used to study the configurality. The advantage of IIT over the Bayesian model is not simply better performance in the foregoing tasks, but also potential for studying nonnormative process.

15. Normative perspectives are no less attractive—and no less treacherous—outside the judgment–decision domain. One example is social stereotypes, long condemned as pernicious biases, a tack that actively hindered understanding and had little social benefit. Recent attempts to treat stereotypes as normal information processing continue to be handicapped by the conceptual heritage of "bias" and "distortion" (see Anderson, 1981a, 1991m). A different example appears in memory theory, with its monolithic emphasis on reproductive accuracy, which failed even to recognize the very different functional conception of memory. A rather different example appears in Gibson's (1966) theory of direct perception (see Chapter 9, Note 7).

16. Lopes (1987a) criticizes mainstream judgment–decision theory of risk because it ignores most concepts of everyday experience: "Here are some words that are not to be found in the theoretical vocabulary: fear, hope, safety, danger, fun, plan, conflict, time, duty, custom" (Lopes, 1987a, p. 286). These words represent important aspects of functional cognition of everyday judgment and decision. They should be a primary concern of theory construction, in accord with Lopes.

PREFACE

Memory looks very different from a functional perspective. Traditional memory research is focused on accuracy—reproduction of specified material. The prototypical task is remembering a list of words. Functional memory, in contrast, is concerned with judgment and decision—assemblage of past experience and present stimuli to pursue present goals. The prototypical task of functional memory involves valuation of present stimuli by means of memorial knowledge systems, together with integration of informers.

This functional–reproductive distinction arose serendipitously in a 1963 study of memory in person cognition. Subjects received a serial list of trait adjectives that described a person; they judged likableness of the person and also recalled the adjectives. According to then-unquestioned conceptions of memory, the judgment of the person should have been determined by the recalled adjectives. The results showed otherwise; the functional memory of the person had storage different from that for the adjectives themselves.

Functional measurement theory can analyze memory. Under certain conditions, an integrated response can be dis-integrated to reveal its memorial structure. In the cited task, the recall curve shows recency, whereas the functional memory curve shows uniform primacy (see Figure 11.1). This contrast implies that the functional memory is distinct from the recall memory. Further, this measurement capability provides a basis for studying functional memory.

The functional–reproductive distinction is underscored by the concepts of redundancy and inconsistency. These have peripheral importance in traditional reproductive memory, but they are central in memory function. Much information we get in everyday life is repetitious; some of it disagrees with what we already believe. Valuation of incoming information thus requires reference to memory knowledge systems to assess redundancy and inconsistency.

Affect is basic in functional memory, as in our knowledge systems about our family, our colleagues, and our research. Affect is also basic in our beliefs and attitudes. Information integration theory provides a useful approach to this and other problems of memory function in everyday thought and action. Affect, attitude, belief, redundancy, and inconsistency are among the many issues that come to life in a functional approach to memory.

Functional memory is congruent to the axiom of purposiveness; the function of memory is to subserve goal-oriented thought and action. Functional memory is constructive and active, as recognized in the conception of an operating memory for online control of thought and action. Functional memory is thus unified with judgment–decision and other fields considered in previous chapters.

Chapter 11

FUNCTIONAL MEMORY

The function of memory is to bring past experience to bear on present action. This function is manifest in our everyday judgments and decisions of family and work and in our personal mental life. Memory in everyday life may accordingly be called *functional memory*.

Functional memory is barely recognized in the traditional perspective of *reproductive memory*. More experiments have been done on memory than perhaps any other domain in psychology, yet nearly all have been concerned with reproduction of specified material. The prototypical memory experiment consists of a list of words the subject is required to memorize. This mirrors the standard stereotype of memory as remembering and forgetting.

The hallmark of reproductive memory is *accuracy*. The material is specified; the subject's task is to get it right. This accuracy standard applies not only to traditional memory experiments on verbal recall and recognition, but also to recently popular issues of face recognition, eyewitnessing, autobiographical memory, and even memory for gist. This accuracy standard is narrow, barely relevant to much memory function.

Much memory function is bound up with two basic operations: valuation and integration. Valuation of stimulus informers is a constructive process relative to some goal. With external informers, valuation often involves similarity to memorial material. Similarity is different from recall, of course, in its dependence on interaction among the informer, the memorial material, and the goal. Even when the informers come from memory, they still generally require valuation relative to the operative goal.

Memory thus has a central function in valuation of informers. In most valuation, however, there is no objectively correct answer. Concepts and methods of memory research developed under the accuracy standard of reproductive memory have limited relevance for valuation.

Integration also is central in memory function. Thought and action typically depend on multiple memories that need to be evaluated and integrated to arrive at a unified, goal-directed response. What is stored in memory, moreover, is often an integrated resultant that embodies goal-relevant aspects of external informers. These integration problems, largely unrecognized in traditional memory theory, are a main concern of functional memory.

The purpose of this chapter is to discuss this functional conception of memory. The first part presents the original evidence that led to the functional–reproductive distinction, followed by some conceptual implications. The second part takes up some issues in functional memory.

ASPECTS OF FUNCTIONAL MEMORY

The present conception of functional memory arose serendipitously in a study of person cognition. This study is presented first to indicate how the traditional verbal memory hypothesis failed and how the data pointed to a new conception. Following this, some general properties of functional memory are discussed.

PROTOTYPICAL TASK OF FUNCTIONAL MEMORY

The functional–reproductive distinction arose from a study of person memory that combined a recall task with an integration judgment task. Subjects heard a serial list of trait adjectives that described a person. After hearing the list, they had two tasks: to judge how much they would like that person and to recall the adjectives. The aim was to compare primacy–recency in the person judgment with primacy–recency in the adjective recall.

Verbal Memory Hypothesis. The natural hypothesis—from a reproductive perspective—is that judgment depends directly on memory of the given stimulus materials. Hence the person judgment would be based on those adjectives that could be recalled. This *verbal memory hypothesis* was long taken for granted, and it keeps reappearing in various guises. In social–personality psychology, it held out the great promise that social attitudes could be related to the mass of results on verbal learning and memory (Notes 6 and 7 of Chapter 5).

One such result is the serial curve of verbal recall. The *recall curve* in Figure 11.1 is the serial curve for recall of the words in the list; it shows the well-known bowed shape. There is a mild initial primacy effect, with higher recall for the first adjective than for the next two or three. There is also a strong

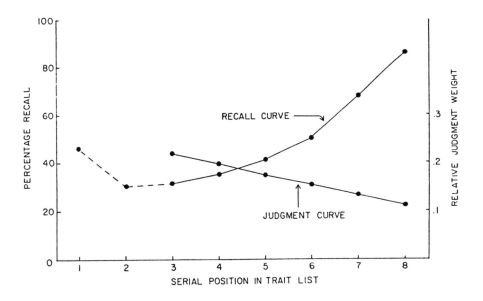

Figure 11.1. Evidence for two memories. *Recall curve* for adjectives in person description shows strong recency over last six serial positions. *Judgment curve* for effect of these same adjectives in person impression shows uniform primacy, with lesser effects at later serial positions. Contrast between recall recency and judgment primacy implies that person memory differs from verbal memory. (Recall curve from Anderson and Hubert, 1963; judgment curve slightly idealized from results of Anderson, 1965b, 1973c.)

terminal recency effect, with much higher recall of the last adjectives. Many such recall curves have been published, but the study of Figure 11.1 seems the first in which a judgment task was also included.

The verbal memory hypothesis makes a simple prediction: The later adjectives, being better recalled, should have greater effect on the judgment of the person. This effect is given by the *judgment curve* in Figure 11.1. This judgment curve, accordingly, should also show a strong recency effect, reflecting the recency in the recall curve. To avoid complications, the initial primacy component of the recall was factored out of the judgment by using filler adjectives in the first two positions. As far as the judgment is concerned, therefore, the recall exhibits pure, strong recency. Hence the judgment should do the same—if the verbal memory hypothesis is correct.

In fact, the judgment showed weak recency or primacy. The verbal memory hypothesis thus appeared to be wrong. Person memory cannot be understood within a reproductive framework.

Two-memory Representation. The two-memory hypothesis, which was suggested by the foregoing experiment, assumes a second memory distinct from the verbal memory for the stimulus adjectives. In a simple form of two-memory representation, a person memory is considered to develop through step-wise integration. As each successive adjective is given, the subject evaluates it and integrates this valuation into the accumulative judgment memory of the person. Once its meaning has been extracted and integrated, the adjective itself is no longer necessary. It may be stored separately or forgotten. The main functional memory is the integrated memory about the person.

Cognitive economy is one advantage of this functional memory. The subject need keep only two things in mind: the present adjective and the integrated memory developed from the previous adjectives. And once the person memory has been updated to take account of the present adjective, it too may be dispensed with.

Further economy appears in the storage of the person memory for later use. In everyday life, information about another person is not presented in one short sequence, as in this adjective experiment, but is scattered over longer time periods. The stepwise valuation–integration processing, however, is even more useful in this case. At each step, the subject may store the integrated memory as it has developed up to that point. This memory encapsulates all the previous information in a processed form. At the next step, accordingly, it is not necessary to retrieve and reprocess the separate informers, as the verbal memory hypothesis would require. Instead, the previously processed judgment memory may be retrieved for present use.

Judgment Memory Curve. A key theoretical problem was to determine the *judgment memory curve*, that is, the curve measuring the effect of the adjective at each serial position on the overall judgment. In the foregoing experiment, primacy–recency in judgment was assessed by comparing the overall effects of the first and last halves of the adjective list in the manner discussed in Chapter 4. This crude index of primacy–recency sufficed to show that the judgment curve differed from the recall curve. But this index, all that was then available, falls far short of a complete curve of the judgment memory (Chapter 10, Note 8).

The curve of judgment memory, however, is not observable. It is qualitatively different from the recall curve. The recall memory curve is observable, obtained by plotting the recall frequency of the adjective at each serial position, as in Figure 11.1. But there is only a single judgment, at the the end of the list. How can a complete serial curve for all six serial positions be constructed from the single judgment at the last serial position?

Conceptually, the judgment memory curve should show the effect of the word at each serial position on the overall judgment. Whereas the subject's task is to integrate the separate individual words into a unified whole, our task is to dis-integrate this unified whole into its constituent parts. In the present case, we must disintegrate the final judgment into six parts, one for the word at each serial position.

This disintegration must mirror the subject's integration. We should not just assume, say, that the effect of each word is proportional to its probability of recall. Even if this was true, it would require proof. To perform the disintegration requires a theoretical model of the integration process.

This theoretical model is now known. The studies of person cognition summarized in Chapter 4 have put the averaging model on a solid foundation. Hence functional measurement methodology may be applied to disintegrate the final, overall judgment into its constituent parts.

This judgment curve, slightly idealized, shows a downward slope in Figure 11.1. Although the words are equivalent at every position, each later word has lesser effect. This primacy effect is considered to result from attention decrement, one theoretical issue in the foundation studies of Chapter 4. Present concern, however, is with the contrast between the up-slope of the recall curve and the down-slope of the judgment memory curve. This contrast demonstrates the inadequacy of the verbal memory hypothesis.

Underlying this theoretical analysis is the capability for inferring the judgment memory curve of Figure 11.1. This capability did not exist at the time of the original experiment, which had to make do with the crude standard index of primacy–recency. To measure the judgment curve depended jointly on the theoretical development of the integration model and on resolving certain associated statistical problems. These developments provided a needed tool for analysis of functional memory.

Both curves, recall and judgment, were obtained by Dreben, Fiske, and Hastie (1979), who replaced the adjectives with sentences describing various behaviors of a person, such as a helpful action. Similar results were obtained: Recall showed a strong recency effect, whereas the judgment showed a small recency effect or even primacy. Of special interest was the similarity of the judgment curves obtained with and without recall. Since the recall instruction markedly increases recall (Anderson & Hubert, 1963), its failure to affect judgment provides collateral support for the functional memory hypothesis.

Person Memory. The judgment curve of Figure 11.1 is actually a memory curve. It represents a functional memory of the stimulus words. The words themselves have largely vanished, as emphasized by the collateral finding that only two of eight words were recalled when recall was requested without warning. Each word, nevertheless, left its impress in memory, an impress quantified by the serial curve.

The judgment curve also represents the main functional memory of the person in this task. The words have served their main function and are no longer primary memory elements. This point is emphasized by Riskey's (1979) finding that following the list with a standard task of counting backwards markedly reduced subsequent recall but left the judgment curve essentially unchanged. This finding, together with the cited recall result of Dreben et al. indicates that the verbal memory has little role in the person judgment in this task.

This separation into two distinct memories will not hold in general, of course. Even in this simple task, a subject requested for some unexpected judgment, about the person's intelligence, for example, would no doubt utilize any remembered adjectives. In everyday life, moreover, our memories for familiar entities, family members, say, or theoretical controversies, are knowledge systems that contain a diversity of integrated judgments and episodic material. What components are activated in any task will depend on operative goals. The integration model provides one tool for analysis of such memory function.[1]

FUNCTIONAL MEMORY

The person memory task is a prototype of functional memory. It embodies the serial, accumulative nature of much everyday memory. It brings out the importance of valuation–integration processes, both in online memory function and in long-term storage. Integration theory and functional memory thus go together, hand in hand.

This particular task actually favors the operation of verbal memory. The adjectives are few in number, within the span of short-term memory, and they are all the given information. The verbal memory hypothesis that the judgment is based on the retained adjectives is thus eminently reasonable. Even under these favorable conditions, however, the verbal memory hypothesis did poorly. The major role of judgment memory in this task thus argues for its general importance.

The person memory task also exhibits a prototypical form of organization: The stimulus informers refer to a single entity, in this case a person. Organization in the entity schema will influence the memory processing, which may thus differ in many ways from the memory processing of the arbitrarily organized word lists commonly studied in reproductive memory research. This organization appears in the task processing, especially in the valuation and integration operations involved in entity construction.

Associated forms of organization reflect structure in the entity. Redundancy among given informers, for example, must be defined in contextual relation to the entity and the operative goal. Redundancy is just one of various forms of organization that spring to life in the study of memory about persons, objects, events, issues, or other entities.

The "person" in this person memory task is hypothetical, it is true, but the task elicits operation of long-term knowledge systems about real people. This is the source of the organizational processes just noted, and a source of much of the interest of this task. At the same time, the hypothetical nature of the task has its own interest. Subjects adopt the task set so readily that we may fail to appreciate the complex assemblage processes involved. This very conjunction of hypothetical and real reflects the flexibility of functional memory, which is important in pursuing the ever-changing goals of everyday life.

A further class of problems arises with familiar persons or other entities. These knowledge systems include products of past valuation–integration processing relative to a variety of goals as well as diverse incidents and interactions, both particular and generic. Such memories are expected to be distributed and to include affect and other nonreproducible components. The term, knowledge system, recognizes this memorial complexity. It also emphasizes the functional role of memory in online, goal-directed thought and action.

This class of knowledge systems presents numerous problems for memory theory. One problem concerns longer-term retention, one aspect of which appears in the basal–surface representation found with attitudes and with expectancy learning (Chapter 5). A potentially useful task would be to study how personalized, hypothetical information is integrated into knowledge systems about specific well-known persons or other entities.

Organization in knowledge systems is a fundamental issue. It has received much attention, but progress has been limited. Attempts to apply multidimensional scaling, for example, have mainly shown that multidimensional representations are inappropriate for most knowledge systems. Misconceptions about memory processing, discussed later, have also been a hindrance. Present methods can help elucidate how knowledge systems operate in valuation of incoming information, and this could help delineate their structure.

Also of interest is the function of particular memories. Our memories of familiar persons seem rich with particular incidents and interactions. These instance memories might be expected to have prominent informational functions. On the other hand, previous valuation–integration processing will be strongly developed for familiar persons and may dominate the knowledge system. Particular memories may thus have even less importance than in the personality adjective task, being perhaps little more than epiphenomenal foci for the actual determinants. On this question, little is known.

CONSTRUCTION PRINCIPLE

Functional memory is constructive memory. One kind of construction appears in the valuation operation. In the personality adjective task, the adjective values must generally be constructed because they depend on the operative dimension of judgment. A *happy-go-lucky* graduate student, for example, may be likable at the departmental picnic, unlikable for data analysis. For a few basic judgment dimensions, values may have already been stored with the words, but most will require constructive inferences. Constructive evaluation is even more apparent with sentence/paragraph material, as with the biographical paragraphs about U. S. presidents of Figure 5.1.

The output of the valuation operation may be very different from the input. Indeed, the same stimulus input may yield very different values, depending on the operative goal. Valuation does rely on long-term memory, but in a constructive rather than a reproductive way.

A second kind of construction appears in the integration operation. The output of the valuation processing for individual incoming stimuli must be integrated into the current operating memory.

Moreover, the contents of operating memory may be stored in long-term memory, as already illustrated with the serial integration model. Much long-term memory content is thus constructed memory, memory already organized in terms of goal-directed function.

The construction principle is derivative from the axiom of purposiveness and the problem of multiple determination (Chapter 1). These are embodied in the valuation–integration operations. Cognitive algebra provides a tool for studying these two operations in memory theory.

Constructive aspects of memory function have been considered by many investigators, but this work has been dominated by the reproductive framework. A long sequence of studies of eyewitness reports, for example, has shown that errors may readily be induced by leading questions and by prior expectations. Such construction, however, has typically been interpreted in reproductive terms, as memory bias or *dys*function (see *Misconceptions about Memory Processing* below). This interpretation is literally correct in the eyewitness studies, it is true, in which the accuracy standard has specified validity. Unfortunately, this reproductive perspective has obscured recognition of the broader importance of constructive memory.[2]

Our memory system is biosocially derived. Ability to make inferences from limited information, about food and danger, for example, has survival value. No less valuable are abilities to store this processing and retrieve it in future assemblage. In society, these abilities take on new importance, notably in language. They can lead one astray, as the eyewitness studies show, and societal instruction needs improvement. Effective improvement, however, requires an approach that treats these abilities less as bias and dysfunction, more as natural modes of processing.

In everyday life, people continually make judgments and decisions that incorporate plausible but fallible inferences. Utilizing prior belief in construction of present judgment is reasonable and adaptive, even though it leads to error on occasion or in certain kinds of tasks. In this functional view, memory has a proper constructive role, one that cannot be understood in terms of the standard and measure of reproductive memory. New methods of analysis are needed, including methods that can measure functional values, as illustrated with the judgment memory curve of Figure 11.1, and assess inferences (see *Schemas and Imputations* below).

OPERATING MEMORY

A concept of operating memory arises as a corollary of the construction principle. Operating memory on any occasion is considered an assemblage, organized under direction of the prevailing goal. This goal focuses attention on particular features of the present stimulus field. It activates associated information from long-term memory together with schemas and operators, such as stereotypes and roles in person cognition or causal schemas in intuitive physics.

The term *operating memory* is appropriate in two senses. First, it is the active assemblage that operates in goal-directed behavior. Second, operators are among its components, especially operators of valuation and integration.

A simple example of operating memory appears in the foregoing study of person cognition. At each step in the list, operating memory includes the present adjective, together with valuation operators utilized in constructing the goal-directed value of that adjective. Also included are the cumulative memory developed from the previous adjectives, together with an integration operator for incorporating the present adjective. Operating memory can be more complex, of course, including judgments about the person's sex or intelligence, for example, in addition to the specified goal dimension of likableness. Qualitative structure of person cognition may also be included.

This conception of operating memory may be contrasted with a traditional view, in which stimuli activate features or meaning elements in semantic memory. Integration then occurs automatically as the aggregation of features activated by the several stimuli. This traditional view appears in the verbal memory hypothesis and even in the gestalt theory of memory. It is implicit, if not explicit, in various theories based on feature and network representations. It disagrees, however, with the present view of operating memory.

The present conception of operating memory stems in substantial part from the independence of the valuation and integration operators established in the early studies of meaning invariance (Chapters 1 and 4). Valuation is sensitive to specifics of task and situation, as is desirable for flexible, goal-directed thought and action. In integration, however, the separate informers are insensitive to one another. This contrast implies a cognitive independence of these two operations, a structural difference from the traditional view.[3]

AFFECT AND VALUE

Affect and value are fundamental to functional theory. They embody the one-dimensionalization imposed by the goal-directed nature of thought and action (Chapter 1). Much affect seems primarily biological, one of nature's tools for survival. The heavy socialization of affect may be seen in interpersonal relations, for example, as well as in preferences and aversions involving food and sex.

Value is more general than affect, for it includes symbolic evaluation, more or less abstract in nature. Such symbolic evaluations arise, for example, in weighing the pros and cons of alternative courses of action (Chapter 10), in schemas of causal attribution (Chapter 5), and in mental models of intuitive physics (Chapter 8).

Affect and value reemphasize the prototypical nature of the personality adjective task and its relevance to memory theory. Present affect and value may be stored for future use, as already indicated in the comment on cognitive economy. No less important is the function of long-term memory in affective valuation of present stimuli. Affect and value are essential in a functional theory of memory—and in a functional theory of cognition.[4]

OTHER APPROACHES TO MEMORY

Diverse commonalities between IIT and other approaches to memory deserve consideration. The present constructionist view, for example, is in the same spirit as that of Bartlett (1932), who strongly criticized the Ebbinghaus rote memory tradition and treated memory as active reconstruction of meaningful material. Reconstruction remains within the reproductive framework, however, and the biases and distortions reported by Bartlett are defined with respect to an accuracy criterion. In the present view, biases and distortions often reflect sensible cognitive processes, emphasized in the cognitive–normative distinction in judgment–decision theory (Chapter 10). To a considerable extent, indeed, memory functioning is more judgment–decision than memory.

Other commonalities concern schema theory, everyday memory, working memory, long-term memory, recognition memory, and affective memory. Some comments on these issues are given in other sections. More detailed discussion would be desirable but is outside the scope of this chapter. Three general points, however, may be noted here.

First, as already emphasized, other approaches remain largely within a reproductive framework. In part, this represents a conception of the nature of memory, in part a reliance on methodology based on accuracy. Accuracy is a splendid tool, of course, as shown by numerous applications in current memory research. Accuracy is insufficient, however, often hardly relevant to functional memory. Valuation, a primary function of memory, differs qualitatively from retrieval.

The second point, related to the first, is that issues focal in other approaches are often peripheral in IIT. Episodic and semantic memory information, for example, function jointly and presumably equivalently in functional memory. The episodic–semantic distinction may thus have limited relevance for memory function. Similarly, IIT is largely independent of network–feature representations, although such findings as $V-I$ independence may be helpful in the study of these more molecular representations.

The last point concerns level of analysis. IIT aims foremost at molar, or macroanalysis, seeking theory at the level of concepts of everyday experience. Other approaches to memory, especially in recent times, have aimed at molecular, microanalysis, as with feature and network representations. This difference, however, makes the macro–micro interface a potential locus of cooperation. Thus, micro values must obey the $V-I$ independence established with macroanalysis. Also, functional measurement of macro values provides boundary conditions that micro theories must satisfy (Chapter 13).

ISSUES IN FUNCTIONAL MEMORY

The following issues in functional memory seem important, but most present problems that have been little studied. The following comments, accordingly, are mainly intended to suggest the potential of this direction of inquiry.

MEASUREMENT OF MEMORY

The accuracy standard has dominated traditional research on memory. The two primary dependent variables, recall and recognition, are both accuracy measures, assessing the response as correct or incorrect. Accuracy measures have notable advantages. They are simple, especially with lists of unrelated words or visual forms; they are objective and well defined; they possess an evident kind of validity; and they are essentially theory-free. Reflecting these advantages, the very definition of memory often seems tied to an accuracy standard—and thereby to a reproductive conceptualization.

Accuracy measures, however, are not sufficient for functional memory. This limitation was seen in the contrast between the recall memory curve and the judgment memory curve of Figure 11.1. To obtain the judgment curve required a different kind of memory measure.

Analysis of functional memory, unfortunately, is not in general theory free. To obtain the judgment curve of Figure 11.1 required establishing the serial integration rule as a base for functional measurement. More direct evidence may be available in some tasks, but in general some theoretical model seems necessary to handle the twin problems of valuation and integration.

Even within traditional reproductive memory, integration is important. Thus, recognition memory may involve cue integration to obtain a judgment of familiarity, qualitatively similar to judgments studied in IIT. Algebraic models of familiarity integration thus offer promise for analysis of traditional memory (Anderson, 1982, Section 7.17; see also Note 9 of Chapter 9 and *Recognition Memory and Expectations* below). Nonmemory variables, such as expectation and decision criteria, can thus be unified with memory variables. This approach may apply more generally, as with judgments of frequency.[5]

A special form of recognition memory involves identification of given stimuli as letters, words, and so forth. Reading and listening thus depend on a continuous stream of identifications of given stimuli by reference to prototypes in long-term memory. These identifications often, if not typically, depend on stimulus integration, illustrated with the contextual influences emphasized by many writers. Numerous experimental applications of the decision averaging model to identification problems in language have been made by Oden and Massaro, and are considered in the next chapter.

More general problems of memory measurement are illustrated in the following sections. Measurement of effective redundancy and inconsistency is important for understanding how people process information about natural entities; certain misconceptions about memory revolve around measurement problems; schema analysis involves measuring inferences about missing information; finally, analysis of affective memory requires capability for measuring nonconscious affects.

REDUNDANCY

Redundancy is not dull, as it may seem, but full of interest and importance for cognitive analysis. Although of minor concern in traditional memory research, redundancy becomes a major issue in functional theory. If a list contains both *dependable* and *reliable*, it would be an error to omit either one in a standard memory task. If the list describes a person, however, the error may be in failure to allow for the redundancy. This problem is prominent in everyday life, in which much information that we receive has substantial redundancy.

How to conceptualize redundancy is a basic problem for functional theory. This leads into the problem of measuring redundancy effects, which is closely related to theoretical models for redundancy. Related problems concern the processes whereby redundancy—and the associated nonredundancy—are recognized and evaluated. These problems arise in processing present stimuli both for present thought and action and for memory storage. The following remarks, brief and incomplete, are intended to point up the interest of redundancy.

A functional concept of redundancy must be broader than the ordinary, context-free sense of commonality of meaning. In the first place, semantic aspects of redundancy must take account of the dimension of judgment. Two informers might be redundant in components of meaning that are irrelevant to the dimension of judgment, but nonredundant in relevant components. For example, consider the two informers, {*youthful, quick-witted*} and {*young, dependable*}, each pair of adjectives presented as descriptions of the same person by a different acquaintance. *Youthful* and *young* are redundant with respect to judgment of the person's age, but irrelevant to judgments of, say, honesty. Although this example may seem artificial, the issue it illustrates is real with textual materials.

Pragmatic aspects must also be considered. Thus, an informer that would be redundant if repeated by the same source may be nonredundant if repeated by a different source. Most sources being more or less unreliable, an independent source adds credence to the informer stimulus. This problem has been pursued in experimental studies of information reliability by Martin Kaplan, Michael Birnbaum, Colleen Surber, Ramadhar Singh, and Shu-Hong Zhu, all of whom have verified the theoretical expectation that information reliability can be incorporated as a weighting factor in the averaging model of IIT. This theoretical representation as a weight indicates that reliability is conceptually independent from semantic content, which is represented in the scale value. Here again, commonality of meaning is too narrow for conceptualization of redundancy.

Measurement of redundancy could be approached directly with self-estimation. Subjects could be asked, for example, to judge functional similarity of two given informers. Functional similarity differs from the usual concept of similarity, for it refers to goal-relevant content, as illustrated in the second previous paragraph. Alternatively, conditional judgments could be used, that is, how much new relevant information a second informer adds to a first. Conditional judgments would allow for asymmetry; S_A could be completely redundant with S_B, yet S_B largely nonredundant with S_A. Such self-estimates have intrinsic interest, although their relation to the operative redundancy in the given integration task cannot be taken for granted.

Indeed, the concept and definition of redundancy depend on theory, as the following argument illustrates. Much integration shows diminishing returns, with steadily decreasing effects of added stimulus informers. Those who assumed additive theory interpreted such diminishing returns to reflect some redundancy process. But in fact, averaging theory applies, and it produces diminishing returns without any special redundancy process (see discussions of Table 4.1 and Figure 5.3). In general, as in this example, redundancy must be defined and measured through substantive theory.

Averaging theory provides a base for definition and analysis of redundancy. It makes definite that a primary locus of redundancy is in the weight parameter and provides a theoretical basis for measurement. In this way, redundancy can be a tool for analysis of knowledge systems. As an important form of cognition in everyday life, redundancy should repay systematic study.[6]

INCONSISTENCY

Integration of inconsistent information has attracted widespread attention, but little more is known than for redundant information. One result established in IIT is that people are often untroubled by ostensible inconsistencies (Chapter 4). This accords with the biosocial heuristic in two ways. First, informers are often more or less uncertain and unreliable, at least in their implications relative to operative goals. Personal and social conflicts typically evoke a welter of conflicting claims, a state of affairs to which people adapt fairly readily. Second, the averaging rule may be considered a biological adaptation process that resolves disagreements among informers by simple compromise, without requiring any higher process of inconsistency resolution.

The averaging rule points up a distinction between nominal and effective inconsistency. Two informers with different scale values may be said to be nominally inconsistent. Effective inconsistency, however, means that the two informers interact in the valuation operation. Nominal inconsistency need not produce such interaction, for it may be handled automatically by simple averaging. Effective inconsistency, in contrast, corresponds to some interactive process in the valuation. One such process is discounting, with a reduced weight for one informer or even both. Another interactive process is change of meaning or value.

This nominal–effective distinction relates to various theories of cognitive consistency studied in social–personality psychology. These theories were generally concerned with effective inconsistency, but took it for granted; they manipulated nominal inconsistency and assumed it was effective without providing evidence. This was a mistake, as shown by the meaning invariance established with cognitive algebra. This mistake was underscored by the finding that affective inconsistency (e.g., *sociable* and *unreliable*) had as much effect as affective plus semantic inconsistency (e.g., *dependable* and *unreliable*). In this same study, even gross nominal inconsistencies had relatively modest effects. The cognitive consistency theories, which had been postulated on the hope of one or another general principle of cognitive consistency, were thus seen to be generally incorrect (Chapters 4 and 5).

Inconsistency resolution is an important process, but fruitful study has two requirements seldom satisfied in work on the cognitive consistency theories. The first involves a tricky measurement problem. To demonstrate effective inconsistency of an informer depends on showing that the informer has an effect different from its effect had there been no inconsistency. But if the hypothesized effect is indeed present, the control condition of no inconsistency effect, which is needed for the demonstration, may not exist (see further Anderson, 1981a, Section 3.4; 1982, Chapter 7).

The second requirement is to choose an experimental domain in which consistency processes have strong effects. One such domain is self-esteem. Failure experiences and blame, inconsistent with positive self-concept, are aversive informers. Integrating such experiences into the self-concept will lower self-esteem. Everyday mechanisms of ego defense have the function of minimizing such aversive effects, especially by discounting of the weight parameter. People are generally conscious and articulate in employing these ego defense mechanisms, which makes them open to study, in sharp contrast to the unconscious elusiveness of Freudian defense mechanisms. In addition to their interest for cognitive consistency theory, these everyday ego defenses are an important form of social motivation.

MISCONCEPTIONS ABOUT MEMORY PROCESSING

One class of misconceptions about memory processing has already appeared in the discussion of the verbal memory hypothesis. Some others are discussed here that help indicate the nature of functional memory.

Memory for Inconsistent Information. The strong grip of the reproductive conception of memory appears in the much-discussed finding that inconsistent adjectives in a person description may be remembered better than consistent adjectives (see review by Hastie, Park, & Weber, 1984; see also Stangor & McMillan, 1992). This seemed puzzling because the consistent adjectives were considered more important in the person cognition. By implicit appeal to the verbal memory hypothesis, these more important adjectives should be better remembered. The opposite finding thus presented a conceptual puzzle.

This puzzle vanishes in the light of the foregoing two-memory representation. Whereas recall is determined by the verbal memory, the judgment of the person depends on a separate functional memory. The cited finding may thus be reinterpreted as novel support for the foregoing two-memory representation.

Instance Memory. The strong grip of reproductive memory also appears in the availability heuristic of Tversky and Kahneman (1973), which asserts that judgments of event frequency are determined by availability of memory instances. The popularity of the availability heuristic reflects the grip of traditional thinking about memory, for it has rested almost entirely on anecdotal evidence, not on experimental tests. Indeed, the availability heuristic is a special case of the verbal memory hypothesis, previously disproved by Anderson and Hubert (1963; see further Chapter 10).

Nonmemory Judgment Processes. Another class of misconceptions arises from failure to appreciate information integration. In a typical example from social stereotype research, subjects first saw sentences of the form:

Sue, a [*waitress, librarian,* or *stewardess*], is [*attractive* and *loud*].

Eight such sentences were used to describe each of the three listed occupations, with various trait adjectives being paired equally often with each occupation. Subsequently, when asked to estimate the frequency of each occupation–trait pairing, subjects made higher judgments for stereotype traits than for nonstereotype traits.

What does this result mean? The interpretation in the stereotype literature was that the occupation stereotype biased the memory processing of the trait information. The only question was the locus of this bias in memory processing.

Two possibilities were considered: First, that the stereotype influenced initial memory processing to yield better initial memory storage for stereotype than nonstereotype traits; second, that the stereotype caused better subsequent memory retrieval of stereotype traits.

Overlooked was a third possibility—identical memory processing for stereotype and nonstereotype traits. The observed result could instead be obtained by integration of the stereotype directly into the judgments of frequency. *Attractive–loud* is part of the stereotype for *waitress*, but not for *librarian* or *stewardess*; subjects have greater expectation that a *waitress* will be *attractive–loud* than a *librarian* or *stewardess*. This expectation corresponds to the initial state variable in averaging theory; theoretically, it will be integrated into the judgment of frequency. The result will thus be obtained even with identical memory processing for stereotype and nonstereotype traits. The given memory interpretations are gratuitous on such evidence (Anderson, 1983a, 1991m). Indeed, the memory bias hypothesis mirrors the change-of-meaning hypothesis previously disproved in person cognition.[7]

A similar issue has arisen independently in the study of eyewitness testimony. Subjects who view an auto accident at an intersection with a YIELD sign may answer *yes* to the misleading question, *Did you see the STOP sign?* From an integration standpoint, the misleading question is indeed misleading because it presents ostensibly correct information. This information will naturally tend to be integrated into the answer, especially for subjects with weak visual memory. This answer, of course, may itself be stored in memory and influence later judgments. Both effects follow directly from integration memory theory.

Loftus (1979) has pursued a deeper argument, namely, that the verbal information can change the real visual memory of the yield sign into a new, unitary memory of a stop sign: "The way a question is phrased and the assumptions it makes have a subtle, yet profound effect on the stored information" and "Stored information is highly malleable and subject to change and distortion by events (such as misleading questions . . . .)" (pp. xiif). This argument has been criticized by McCloskey and Zaragoza (1985) on grounds similar to the foregoing integration analysis, and this has occasioned some controversy (see Loftus, Donders, Hoffman, & Schooler, 1989, and references therein). Evidence against distortion and for integration appears in Heit (1993), discussed below.

IIT allows for more than one memory store, as with the original two-memory hypothesis of Figure 11.1. Functional memory allows for assemblage across multiple, distributed memories. Hence the verbal information can be stored in a separate memory and influence judgment without any effect on the original visual memory itself. Such assemblages may themselves be stored, so a composite memory may develop as a cognitive unit.

IIT also suggests a new way to study this problem of memory structure. A task would be employed that used a continuous response as a compromise between the original and misleading information. If this compromise obeyed an averaging rule, functional measurement could separate and measure the contributions of the two sources of information. If the memory is indeed unitary, both contributions should show similar forgetting curves (see following). If the memory is not unitary, similar forgetting curves would not be expected.

Measurement of Forgetting: Shape Function Model. A recurrent question in memory theory is whether forgetting is faster in some conditions than others. Does degree of initial learning, for example, affect rate of forgetting? Plausibility arguments can be made either way: The more that is learned initially, the more there is to forget and the faster it will be forgotten; or that higher initial learning is more solid and hence more resistant to forgetting.

The question requires comparing two or more forgetting curves, each measured in terms of amount retained as a function of time or trials since initial learning. This comparison depends on how rate of forgetting is to be measured. A still-common approach is to interpret a significant statistical interaction between different learning conditions and time or trials as signifying different rates of forgetting. This use of interaction seems conceptually incorrect (Anderson, 1963). Consider two forgetting curves that decrease halfway from different initial levels to the same final level in each unit of time. In percentage terms, they have the same forgetting rate. The interaction test, however, will imply that they have different forgetting rates. The percentage conception of forgetting rate seems preferable in principle, even if too simple in practice.

Rate of forgetting is a conceptual matter. It cannot generally be defined except within some theoretical model. *Amount* of forgetting may be definable in purely empirical terms, but not *rate*. This has been recognized by most who have worked on the problem, but attempts to define and measure rate have not been generally satisfactory.[8]

The *shape function model* (Anderson, 1963, 1982, Section 3.9) provides a fairly general approach to this problem. The key idea is separability: The shape of the forgetting function is assumed to be separable from its initial and final levels. Formally, let $R(t)$ be the amount retained at trial or time t and let $f(t)$ denote the shape function, normalized so that $f(0) = 0$ and $f(\infty) = 1$. Then the shape function model can be written:

$$R(t) = a + (b - a)f(t),$$

where a and b represent the initial and final levels of response, respectively. This model includes the foregoing percentage concept of rate as a special case. It applies more generally to learning, growth, and other forms of change.

To illustrate, suppose b is the same for all conditions. Under the null hypothesis that all conditions have the same shape function, the foregoing equation becomes a multiplication rule, and the linear fan theorem may be applied. This functional measurement analysis holds regardless of the form of $f(t)$.

Insightful and significant developments of this functional measurement logic have been given by Bogartz (1990) and Paul (1994). Paul's careful analysis avoids limitations and objections to various previous articles and makes available a computer program for the general case of unequal initial and final levels and truncated forgetting curves. Paul also shows that the shape function method has reasonable statistical power.

It is a platitude in memory theory that time per se does not cause forgetting, but rather something that occurs in time. What this something is has proved elusive. Bogartz notes that the shape function $f(t)$ may be considered a linear scale of what causes forgetting. Manipulated schedules of intervening interference may thereby become measurable on functional scales. Bogartz' proposal may thus provide a unique tool for memory analysis.[9]

RECOGNITION MEMORY AND EXPECTATIONS

Expectations influence performance in recognition memory, as in social stereotypes and eyewitness testimony (see earlier subsection on *Nonmemory Judgment Processes*). An important theoretical analysis by Evan Heit (1993) tested three competing theories of expectation effects and found good support for information integration theory. The expectation does not distort or otherwise affect the memory processing. Instead, the expectation is evaluated independently and then integrated with memory trace information.

In the empirical studies at issue, a social stereotype expectation was induced, following which subjects studied person descriptions, lists including items both congruent and incongruent with the stereotype expectation. The subsequent recognition memory test included "old" items from the studied list and "new" items not seen before, both congruent and incongruent. Subjects were to say which items they thought had been in the descriptions they had studied.

A review of three dozen such published papers (Stangor & McMillan, 1992) showed two general findings: *Probability of recognition* was higher for congruent items; *discriminability*, measured as d', was higher for incongruent items. Both differences increased with stronger expectations.

Only the conclusions of Heit's analysis will be presented here. He employed a feature-type representation of memory traces, coupled with a ratio rule for response probability, a rule formally the same as the decision averaging rule of the preceding and following chapters. His conclusions, however, do not seem sensitive to these two theoretical assumptions.[10]

Integration theory assumes that recognition familiarity of a test item is an average of two similarities: one between that test item and memory traces for items in the studied list; the other between that test item and expectation. The former similarity is theoretically independent of expectation and hence equivalent for congruent and incongruent test items; the latter similarity is high for congruent test items and low for incongruent test items.

The relative weight of the latter similarity increases as expectancy increases. In parallel, therefore, recognition probability changes little for congruent test items, because both similarities are high, but decreases substantially for incongruent items, because the latter similarity is low and its relative weight increases. In this way, the first empirical finding is accounted for.

For discriminability, integration theory implies that increased expectation will markedly decrease discriminability between old and new congruent items. As expectation increases, the relative effect of the (discriminative) memory trace information between old and new shows a corresponding decrease. At the same time, apparent familiarity increases for both old and new congruent items because both are similar to expectation. Hence discriminability decreases markedly between old and new congruent items. For incongruent items, on the other hand, discriminability stays roughly constant. Although not intuitively obvious, this happens because both old and new items have low similarity to expectation, so familiarity decreases for both as expectation increases. In this way, the second empirical finding is accounted for.

Furthermore, as Heit shows, information integration theory provides a unified account of the effects of several experimental manipulations: retention interval, memory load, expectancy strength, and study time, not to mention ratio of congruent and incongruent items in the original memory list. Of course, Heit's approach goes far beyond social stereotypes to expectations generally.

Weighting theory assumes that memory traces are weighted upward or downward according to whether they are congruent or incongruent with expectation. This can account for the finding on recognition probability, but not for discriminability. This failure arises because weighting affects old and new test items in similar ways. Hence it fails to predict the decrease in discriminability between old and new congruent items when expectation strength increases.

Distortion theory assumes that memory traces themselves are changed in the direction of the stereotype, a change-of-meaning theory. Distortion is also predicted by the slot-and-default value conception of schema, discussed in the next section. This can account for one or the other of the two effects, but not for both together. For example, distortion of incongruent memory traces incorrectly predicts poorer discriminability for incongruent than congruent items. This analysis, it may be added, appears to infirm Loftus' (1979) hypothesis of memory distortion discussed above.

Heit's comparison of these three theories for recognition memory provides an interesting parallel to the primacy–recency studies of Chapter 4. There three essentially similar theories were at issue, and information integration theory proved superior to weighting theory and change-of-meaning theory in a variety of directed tests. Recognition memory is very different from primacy–recency, of course, but this very difference suggests the potential power of simple integration principles.[11]

SCHEMAS AND IMPUTATIONS

Although memory makes past experience available for present use, such use typically requires construction. Inferences and imputations from given information need to be constructed with the aid of memory to meet the demands of the present task.

The concept of *schema*, considered as an organized memory package, was thought to solve certain problems of memory-based inference. Whenever a schema is retrieved from memory, according to one popular proposal, "All the information within it is made available at once." Schemas were assumed to have slots, corresponding to variables, with default values to be used in case available information did not specify the value of the variable. This idea of slot-and-default value was an attractive promise to endow the schema concept with substance and predictive power.

Algebraic rules are schemas par excellence. The stimulus variables of a rule correspond to the slots, and the success of a rule supports its psychological reality. Hence the operative default values should be revealed by functional measurement.

The slot-and-default value conception has failed in empirical studies of cognitive algebra. Subjects frequently do not employ default values. This issue arose with force in the first studies of the blame schema: Blame = Intent + Damage. When only the intention behind a harmful action was specified, some subjects did impute a default value to the missing damage information, but others did not. Even more striking, when the third variable of recompense or reparation was specified, subjects generally did not impute a default value to unspecified damage information, even though damage is logically implied by the recompense (Chapter 7).

·Imputations about unspecified information were studied in a *tour de force* by Ramadhar Singh (1991). The initial study of the schema, Gift size = Generosity × Income, had yielded a linear fan pattern of data, which had been taken to support the hypothesized multiplication rule. However, the fan pattern could also be produced by averaging with differential weighting. Indeed, Singh began by showing that omitting information about Income yielded the crossover pattern used to support the averaging rule (see Figures 2.4 and 4.4). This interpretation, however, assumes no imputation about the missing Income information. If imputations are operating, as seems plausible in this task, the multiplication rule could also account for the crossover. The further analysis became more complex, but Singh persevered to reach a definitive conclusion: The multiplication rule did hold; missing Generosity information was imputed a single fixed value; missing Income information was imputed a variable value, correlated with the value of the given Generosity information. Singh's chapter is a fine example of the power of cognitive algebra for schema analysis.

These studies of cognitive algebra show that schemas are not self-contained memory packages. A more flexible, constructivist approach is needed. The operative schema in any task results from assemblage processes, jointly determined by long-term knowledge systems and by present goals and informers. This is illustrated by Singh's finding of variable imputations for the Income variable. The imputation was not a default value included in the schema, but was inferred indirectly from other information given in the task.

Underneath the algebraic form lies a second kind of schema. This is a mental model of the task. Tasks of intuitive physics, for example, involve construction of a mental model containing objects, forces, motions, times, and so forth (Chapter 8). Attribution of causes to explain a person's behavior involves similar mental models, but containing social rather than physical representations (Chapter 5). Such mental models are part of the assemblage process, and reflect the subject's attempt to understand the task and goal. In some cases, a mental model may already be present in the subject's knowledge system, requiring only light processing to be activated into operating memory. In other cases, extensive construction may be required.

AFFECTIVE MEMORY

Affective memory is basic in a functional perspective. Pain and pleasure are information that control behavior. Biologically, pain and pleasure have been incorporated in various motivational systems, involving food, sex, dominance–submission, and so forth. Society has developed similar control systems, including various achievement motivations as well as self-esteem and morality. Even where the biological base is strongest, the knowledge system will be heavily influenced by experience. This pervasiveness of affect is embedded in the nature and functional role of memory in purposive behavior.

A prime locus of affect is in attitudinal knowledge systems. Thus, our memory systems of other persons, especially parents and spouse, have complex affective components. The common definition of attitude as evaluative reaction reflects this affective character of attitude. Although this one-dimensional definition misses the deeper nature of the attitude concept, it does point up the function of attitudes in assemblage of thought and action. It also emphasizes the importance of attitudes as a basic form of functional memory.

Despite its importance, not much is known about affective memory. Mood effects have been studied by a number of investigators, but the results have typically been interpreted in traditional terms. The mood effects are assumed to depend on some mediating process, for example, serving as a retrieval cue for memories of similar affective tone. Integration theory, in contrast, allows present mood to be integrated directly into the present response. No mediating process of memory is necessary (see similarly *Misconceptions about Memory Processing* above and Notes 7 and 12 below).

Affective experiences are not generally reproducible in the manner of words or even visual forms. Indeed, the function of affective memory is not generally to reproduce past experience, but to help in constructive thought and action—true functional memory. Standard memory tasks and methods, based on accuracy criteria, are not readily applicable and may have only distant relevance to affective memory. New tasks and methods need to be developed. One example is the person memory task of Figure 11.1, in which the operative memory is substantially affective.

The concept of nonconscious affect underscores the nature of the integration approach. Conscious awareness is usually treated as a defining characteristic of affect, as in most current emotion theories. This accords with the common notion that affect is something we feel. Nonconscious feeling might almost seem a contradiction in terms.

In an integration perspective, however, nonconscious affect is one determinant of conscious affect. The principle is the same as with nonconscious sensation in psychophysics (Chapter 9). Functional measurement can fractionate conscious affect into components that include nonconscious affect, thus endowing the concept of nonconscious affect with genuine explanatory power.

FUTURE WORK ON MEMORY

Dissatisfaction with traditional memory research has sharpened in recent years. One cause has been the failure to develop general principles and theory—even for the standard memory tasks of paired associates and serial lists. As asserted by Tulving (1979, p. 27): "After a hundred years of laboratory-based study of memory, we still do not seem to possess any concepts that the majority of workers would consider important or necessary." No other area of psychology has been this disappointing.

One reaction to this dissatisfaction has been a shift toward natural memory, memory in everyday affairs. Commending this line of inquiry, Neisser (1982, p. xii) deepened Tulving's criticism with the assertion that mainstream memory theory has been and still is "accumulating the wrong *kind* of knowledge." This reaction has led to work on such diverse topics as eyewitnessing, face recognition, autobiographical memory, remembering to do things, memory for gist, and so forth. This turn toward everyday life is well-taken, but this work is still hobbled by the reproductive conception of memory, as indicated by the continuing reliance on accuracy measures.[13]

Natural memory is not primarily reproductive, but functional. The disappointment with traditional memory research results from centering on reproduction, to the neglect of function. The function of memory is to subserve goal-directed thought and action. Memory theory needs a functional foundation.

A functional foundation requires unification of memory with general theory of thought and action. As stated in previous treatments of IIT:

> Few areas of psychology have received as intensive study as verbal learning and memory. From the viewpoint of judgment theory, however, this body of work seems strangely incomplete, largely untouched by concern with the use and function of memory. Verbal learning is seldom an end in itself; memory is typically in the service of judgment and decision. Memory retrieval, for example, can hardly be understood without reference to the immediate goals of the person, as reflected in the valuation operation. (Anderson, 1981a, p. 96)

> Integration theory embodies a functional approach that considers memory as an aid to judgment and action. Whereas traditional approaches to memory focus on reproduction of given stimuli, the functional approach is more concerned with how memory is utilized for attaining goals. The person's prevailing goal orientation affects the processing of prior memory; it also affects the storage of new memory. Accordingly, this functional approach is a useful supplement to a narrow concern with reproductive memory. (Anderson, 1982, p. 345)

Memory for belief is a prime example of functional memory. Belief memory cannot be understood within the reproductive framework, as shown in the study of Figure 11.1. Affect, which represents goal directedness of everyday memory function, is likewise largely outside the reproductive framework. Functional analysis requires different concepts and different methods.

Some problems of affect and belief can be effectively studied with functional measurement theory, as also shown in Figure 11.1. Thereby IIT helps unify memory with social–personality and judgment–decision, two primary domains of natural memory (see *Functional Memory* in Chapter 10).

A further cluster of issues concerns organization. Memory is typically about organized entities, such as persons and research issues. Such organization brings in new problems, as indicated in the discussions of redundancy and inconsistency. Redundancy, for example, is conceptually different in a functional approach, and takes on dimensions not apprehended in the reproductive approach.

More general forms of organization appear in the concepts of knowledge system, assemblage, and operating memory. On such problems of organization, IIT has made hardly a beginning. New developments are needed to study qualitative aspects of organization.[14]

To education also, memory research has contributed little, again a consequence of the reproductive framework. The study of what we learn and retain from our school work—and what we should learn and retain—have great importance. Yet these problems are largely ignored in work on verbal learning and memory, as can be seen by glancing over current texts and treatises. Educational psychologists have recognized the problem, but their attacks on it have been more misguided than aided by mainstream learning–memory theory.

This point may be illustrated with American history, which is a carrier of social attitudes. The stories of Washington and the cherry tree, of Lincoln and the borrowed book, of Nixon and Watergate, serve to develop attitudes toward personal integrity and social ideals that play a role in individual memory parallel to their role in societal memory. In educational psychology, however, attitude is virtually synonymous with motivation to be a good pupil. In psychology itself, traditional memory theory has little place for attitudes because they are knowledge systems, containing affect, not amenable to a reproductive view.

In other areas of educational psychology, learning–memory theory has done little better. The reproductive perspective reappears in the conditioning and reinforcement principles of classical learning theories. However important, these principles are subsidiary to the problem of what should be learned. The cognitive approach is more open, but its centerpiece of schemas has been disappointing, as already noted, and has yet to take cognizance of cognitive algebra. In science education, for example, algebraic schemas provide an ideal ground for unifying everyday intuition with the algebraic formulas of science textbooks. Chapter 8, in particular, indicates the prevalence of intuitive schemas in everyday thought about the physical world. Cognitive algebra is thus a base for cognitive analysis that is directly relevant to science education.

A functional conception of memory is not new. It appears in the longstanding concern with transfer of learning, as well as in certain approaches to problem solving. The essential issue has been how past experience functions in present thought and action. Indeed, a functional conception of knowledge has been widely accepted as a principle for education. It has become commonplace that factual knowledge changes rapidly and that teaching should develop adaptive capabilities for ever-changing environments. But this educational principle, despite significant exceptions, has had little recognition in memory theory, which is not badly caricatured by the century-old nonsense syllable and rote learning tasks of Ebbinghaus.

Unfortunately, this educational principle lacks body. It provides little guidance on any of the foregoing problems of functional memory. It is silent on the basic problems of valuation and integration. Even at a general level, it does not say what should be taught or how. The near-total lack of training to teach for those who will become college teachers is paralleled by the near-total lack of research on what it is that should be taught. What should be taught can hardly begin to be understood without analysis of knowledge systems and their functioning in the years after college graduation.

All academic disciplines have a social-moral responsibility to give their students a worthwhile product, relevant and functional in life after school. Psychology has a higher responsibility than other disciplines because its domain includes cognitive processes and memory. This chapter, with keen awareness of its many limitations, is dedicated to this goal.

NOTES

This chapter is based on material in Anderson (1981a, 1989a, 1991h,l). The nature of current work and views on memory can be seen in overviews in Klatzky (1980), Eysenck and Keane (1990), and at a more advanced level by contributors to Posner (1989). I wish to thank Shu-Hong Zhu for helpful comments on earlier drafts.

1. The two-memory hypothesis makes an essential distinction between reproductive memory and memory for integrated resultants of previous valuations. These typically differ in a qualitative way. The case considered in the text contrasts memory for given verbal stimuli and memory for a judgment constructed from these verbal stimuli. This contrast is not peculiar to verbal material, of course, but applies generally to instance memory. The instance memory hypothesis claims that the latter memory is derived from the former. This claim is contradicted by the cited evidence, which instead supports the two-memory hypothesis (see also Notes 6 and 7 of Chapter 5).

This reproductive–functional distinction should not be confused with current controversies whether episodic and semantic memory, for example, or implicit and explicit memory represent different memory systems (see, e.g., Roediger & Craik, 1989; Schacter, Chiu, & Ochsner, 1993). Semantic and implicit memory have some similarity to functional memory, but they have remained within the reproductive framework.

The present functional conception of memory allows that the instance memory and the integrated resultant are both components of a larger, distributed memory system, as with memories for known persons. In part, at least, this must be true (Anderson, 1981a, 1989a). The proposal of Weber, Goldstein, and Busemeyer (1991) that both kinds of memory information may be integrated in making judgments thus reaffirms the position developed in IIT. Their concern to unify memory theory and judgment–decision theory agrees similarly with a long-standing concern of IIT, illustrated in the extended program of work to develop a theory for uncovering the judgment memory curve of Figure 11.1 and in the two quotes toward the end of this chapter.

2. Views of memory as reconstruction rather than mere retrieval have been advocated by writers from Münsterberg (1909) and Bartlett (1932) to the present. The constructionist approach of IIT has a natural affinity with reconstructionist views of memory. Construction and *re*construction are different, however, for the latter remains grounded in the reproductive framework (Anderson, 1991h).

More pertinent here are studies of meaning integration, as in Bransford and Franks (1971), in which subjects showed greater recognition confidence for four-element sentences that had never been presented than for the elements themselves, which had been presented. In part, this result may be a natural consequence of an averaging process for familiarity (see *Amount of Information* in Chapter 4). In part, presumably, this result also depends on the fact that the four elements together formed a connected story. Such qualitative integration is important and as yet hardly studied in the present approach.

3. William James' distinction between self-as-knower, or "I," and self-as-known, or "me," has some correspondence with the present distinction between operating memory and long-term memory. The present concept of operating memory also has some similarities to that of working memory (Baddeley, 1986). The two have different applications, however, and rest on different kinds of evidence. Baddeley has sought to demonstrate two short-term systems, roughly auditory and visual in nature, in terms of performance decrements produced by using up limited processing capability in auxiliary tasks.

Primary evidence for operating memory, in contrast, comes from such evidence as **V–I** independence. Operating memory might be considered to correspond to Baddeley's concept of central executive, but this concept remains unelucidated, "the area of residual ignorance within the working memory system," as Baddeley terms it.

4. The attitude toward affect in cognitive psychology may be illustrated with Simon's (1982, pp. 337*ff*) comment and query that "Cognitive psychology has lived for several decades essentially without affect" and "How can two languages [of affect and cognition] that are so radically different, not only in vocabulary and syntax, but in their units of meaning, communicate with each other?"

This is in large part a false question, stemming from a narrow view that sunders affect and cognition (see also Anderson, 1987). In IIT, affect is an integral part of cognition. Cognitive algebra provides a vocabulary that can accommodate both discrete and continuous representations (see also Chapter 12).

The artificial sundering of affect and cognition appears throughout psychology (e.g., Note 7 of Chapter 4). A pertinent example appears in Zajonc's (1980) interpretation that Anderson and Hubert's (1963) two-memory representation implies independence of affect and cognition. This seems inappropriate. In particular, the two-memory hypothesis is not limited to affective judgments, but applies to continuous judgments of "cognitive" quantities such as age, size, and probability (Anderson, 1989b, p. 144).

There is a real distinction between discrete and continuous representations, or between qualitative and quantitative representations. This distinction, however, has no necessary connection with any distinction between "affective" and "cognitive." Indeed, continuous response tasks may be useful as tracers to study structure of discrete or qualitative representations.

5. Judgments of event frequency present an interesting problem in memory theory. Like familiarity judgments, they require something more than reproduction. To illustrate a functional measurement attack, suppose a subject is presented an extended sequence of several kinds of stimuli, with their frequencies systematically varied across serial position. At the end of the sequence, one kind of stimulus is specified, and the subject judges its frequency. By using factorial design to construct the sequences, a serial position curve can be obtained that represents the memory strength at each serial position.

Hasher and Zacks (1984) have argued that event frequency is encoded automatically, independent of such usually powerful memory variables as individual ability, practice, and experience. Their argument appears to imply that the serial curve of frequency judgment will be flat. For, if primacy–recency effects were observed, their magnitudes would presumably be moderated by the cited variables. Regardless of outcome, the shape of the serial curve of frequency judgments would be informative about memory storage and how it is processed for judgment.

This functional measurement approach seems more powerful than previous methods, and more informative, especially with within-subject design. This approach may apply to other kinds of judgments as well. Frequency judgments of composite classes, for example, might shed light on the nature of memory storage and processing. Moreover, a unified treatment can be given of memory and nonmemory variables, such as decision criteria and prior expectation.

6. The study of redundancy is complicated by the distinction between operating memory and long-term memory, as may be illustrated with the $V-I$ independence of Chapter 1. Valuation of given informers is sensitive to the dimension of judgment, so substantial redundancy effects may be expected between given informers and what is already known. The independence of valuation and integration, on the other hand, argues against redundancy interactions between given informers, an argument supported by the study of amount of information of Table 4.1. Although this argument is limited to tasks in which a dimension of judgment is explicitly given, it indicates the need to allow for the two different loci of redundancy. This issue also arises in relation to long-term storage, which may include storage of specific given informers and also integrated resultants from operating memory. Factual material may allow easier definition and measurement of redundancy.

The importance of redundancy suggests looking for a biological base. One may perhaps be seen in adaptation, which appears at low phylogenetic levels. Repetition of an informer stimulus produces progressively less effect, which is suggestive of a redundancy process. In some cases, adaptation could be produced automatically by an averaging process, as noted in the text, without requiring any further redundancy process.

7. The change-of-meaning interpretation is perennially attractive (see, e.g., index entries under *Meaning change* in Anderson, 1981a). Other examples include the study of text comprehension by Tyler and Voss (1982) who presented a flow diagram to portray their claim that prior attitude influenced processing of text passages attributed to *Pravda*. They failed to realize that their chief finding, namely, positive correlation between prior attitude and judgment of the text passage could result equally well from direct integration of prior attitude without any effect on the processing of the given material (Anderson, 1991h, pp. 42*f*).

Stein and Trabasso (1982), in a study of children's story comprehension, similarly claimed that following a story about a child's motivation with added information about a subsequent action by the story child caused the subject children to reinterpret the story child's motivation in the original story. They failed to realize that their data could result equally well from direct integration of the added information—without any effect on the meaning of the original information (Anderson, 1991l, pp. 75*f*).

The theoretical fallacy in all these studies had already been exposed in the work on meaning invariance in IIT (see Chapters 1 and 4). The change-of-meaning interpretation may be true in some of these studies, but demonstrating this requires experimental design that can cope with a somewhat subtle theoretical problem (see similarly Note 12).

8. Wixted (1990) has presented a clear, thorough, and illuminating classification and discussion of definitions and measures of forgetting. Forgetting may be defined in terms of four different properties of forgetting curves, each of which may refer to the observed data or to some assumed underlying scale of memory. Wixted notes that some controversy over forgetting issues has arisen because different investigators have defined and measured forgetting in different ways. Wixted also emphasizes the neglected importance of joint study of multiple measures of memory performance.

9. Standard forgetting curves may not be very sensitive or informative. Nearly all have the same general shape, as various writers have remarked, with a rapid initial decline and steadily slowing later decline. Mathematical description of their shape seems unlikely to tell much about forgetting processes, all the more because shape is biased when averaging across subjects and/or items with different forgetting rates.

Essentially this point arose in the development of mathematical learning theory, where it was found that mean learning curves were insensitive for testing learning models. More sensitive descriptive statistics were required (see *Learning and Sequential Dependencies* and Note 7 in Chapter 2). Similarly, experimental manipulation of forgetting, together with Bogartz' proposal for functional measurement of what causes forgetting, may be useful.

10. Heit's ratio model may be written mnemonically as:

$$\text{Recognition probability} = \text{old} / (\text{old} + \text{new}),$$

where *old* and *new* denote similarity of the given test item to the "old" and "new" response categories the subject is told to use. Heit's analysis is notable in capitalizing on the joint pattern in two distinct response measures.

A similar stimulus identification model has been used by others, cited by Heit, and it is also similar to Oden's fuzzy logic model discussed in Chapter 12. Further, it is also similar to the decision averaging model of IIT, which has the advantage that it applies to continuous response measures, such as ratings of familiarity, as well as probability of discrete choice categories (see also Note 9 of Chapter 9, Notes 3 and 4 of Chapter 10, and Anderson, 1974a, pp. 246*ff*).

In Heit's application, the "new" category is not explicitly defined and Heit assumes that all items have equal similarity to this category, that is, that the "new" term in the ratio rule is constant. This usage is similar to the initial state in IIT (see Chapter 2).

Heit's analysis reemphasizes the importance of simple concepts of information integration for research strategy. The many studies of memory for expectancy–congruent and expectancy–incongruent information cited by Stangor and McMillan (1992) overlooked the direct informational role of expectancy cited under *Nonmemory Judgment Processes*. Also overlooked was the relevance of the two-memory representation of functional memory theory cited under *Memory for Inconsistent Information*.

11. IIT recognizes the importance of weighting, distortion, and other configural effects (see, e.g., following section on *Schemas and Imputations*; also Figure 7.5 and Anderson, 1981a, pp. 192–196, 289–290). Such effects can hardly be studied, however, without taking account of simple operations of information integration. Moreover, IIT can provide useful tools for analysis of such effects. One such tool is functional measurement methodology for establishing true linear response scales. With response linearity, the pattern in the observable data is a veridical picture of the pattern in the unobservable cognition (see *Linear Response Methodology* in Chapter 3).

12. Mood effects can be obtained by direct integration, according to IIT. In one typical study, subjects who received a small, unrelated gift thought better of their cars and TV sets (Isen, Shalker, Clark & Karp, 1978). This was interpreted to mean that the good mood induced by the gift served as a retrieval cue for positive affective memories from long-term memory.

A simpler interpretation is that the good mood induced by the gift is integrated directly into the judgments of the cars and TV sets. This interpretation is consistent with previous work on IIT (see Anderson, 1989b, p. 169).

In other studies, present judgments about pain or emotional intensity of past diary incidents are shown to be correlated with present pain or emotion, findings interpreted by Bower (1981) and Eich, Reeves, Jaeger, and Graff-Radford (1985) in terms of effects of mood on memory. A simpler interpretation appeals to the positive context effect of Chapter 4: Present pain or emotion may be integrated directly into the present judgment. Present pain or emotion are part of present operating memory, which governs present judgments. The valuation process for the past incident itself must make reference to long-term memory, but this dependence need have no relation to present pain or emotion, which may produce the observed effect through direct integration. These two interpretations are portrayed graphically in Figure 4.2.

The theoretical issue in these studies had already been exposed in the work on meaning invariance in IIT (Chapters 1 and 4). The cited mood studies do not allow a distinction between these two interpretations, and the evidence from the integration studies is only suggestive in this experimental context. The integration studies do, however, illustrate how distinguishing tests can be obtained. Beyond that, they suggest a new approach to mood and memory.

Abele and Petzold (1994) have reported that mood is integrated into the overall judgment, but not into the scale values for the individual informers. This latter result is not required by IIT, and may depend on procedural relations between the informers and the response dimension in the valuation operation (e.g., Anderson, 1982, Section 2.3.4). Where this result holds, however, it can provide useful simplification.

13. Everyday memory is considered by Cohen (1989) and by contributors to Gruneberg, Morris, and Sykes (1988) and Neisser and Winograd (1988). A major concern in this work has been to liberate the study of memory from traditional experimental tasks, and interesting phenomena have been addressed. Virtually all this work, however, remains bound by the traditional conception of reproductive memory. The same applies to Bruce's (1989) explicit concern with functional explanations of memory.

14. An interesting example of the functional perspective on memory appears in the Ph. D. thesis of William Wright (1995), who sought to pin down the attractive but elusive idea that people have personal knowledge of the causes of their own behavior. The contrary view of Nisbett and Wilson (1977) claimed that any accuracy of self-report of causes of behavior depends on shared cultural norms. Hence an observer exposed to the same stimulus field as the subject would be as accurate as the subject in judging the separate causal effects of each field element on the subject's reaction to the whole stimulus field. This issue of veridicality of self-report is concerned with the contents of operating memory and its relation to long-term memory.

Nisbett and Wilson cite studies of self-estimates of importance as the only area in which they found even meager accuracy of self-report. But they denied that even this accuracy stemmed from private, introspective knowledge. As Nisbett and Bellows (1977, p. 615) said in their experimental assessment of self-estimates of importance:

> The present analysis also leads to the expectation that observer predictions should be as
> accurate as subject reports. . . . Subjects gain little or nothing through private access to

the operations of their own judgmental processes and base their reports exclusively on causal theories that are shared by observers.

Evidence congenial to Nisbett's position comes from the studies of person cognition in Chapter 4. The change-of-meaning hypothesis rested mainly on conscious introspection, but was found to be in error. This outcome adds to the mass of evidence on the severe limitations of conscious report. Nisbett and Wilson, however, made a far stronger claim, namely, that people never have privileged access to the causes of their behavior.

Wright studied self-report accuracy in date judgments, a task directly analogous to that used by Nisbett and Bellows. Subjects judged persons described by a photograph and one or two personality traits on a scale of date attractiveness. For each description, they also judged the relative importance of the photo in their overall judgment of attractiveness, and similarly for the traits.

Wright's central finding was that subject's self-reports of importance were more accurate than those of another subject given the same person description. Contrary to Nisbett and Wilson, importance estimates of the other subject were less accurate. Wright concluded that people do have unique personal knowledge of the causes of their own behavior. The failure of Nisbett and Bellows to obtain this result stems in part from shortcomings in their experiment (Anderson, 1982, Section 6.2.6).

Wright's careful work seems conclusive, for it resolved two serious difficulties that had troubled previous attempts. One difficulty is that considerable accuracy would appear merely as a correlational consequence of common cultural norms. Although this accuracy could represent self-knowledge, it must be factored out to get conclusive evidence. Wright solved this difficulty with a double yoking procedure, in which person descriptions were constructed for pairs of subjects to include photographs with opposite polarity for the members of the pair.

The second difficulty was to obtain a valid measure of self-report accuracy. How can valid scales of the relative importance of photo and traits, unconfounded from their scale value, be obtained? Wright accomplished this with functional measurement methodology based on averaging theory of person cognition. With this well-designed, well-executed experiment, Wright reached a conclusive result that eluded previous workers.

Wright's investigation helps elucidate the functional conception of memory. Thus, the issue of veridicality raised by Nisbett and Wilson can be understood as asking whether subjects rely on long-term memory of cultural stereotypes or whether they assemble their judgment from personal knowledge and have access to their operating memory of this assemblage. The subject's behavior in this task involved memory processes at every stage, but these are beyond the purview of traditional reproductive memory. Wright's work thus demonstrates a novel way to study the nature of these memory processes and their mode of operation.

PREFACE

Cognitive algebra has many applications in language processing. The work of Gregg Oden, Dominic Massaro, and Shu-Hong Zhu, which underlies much of this chapter, ranges from phoneme perception through adjective quantifiers and prototype analysis to sentence understanding.

Meaning invariance is one major implication of cognitive algebra. Quantifiers have the same linguistic meaning in different contexts, as shown by the success of multiplication and averaging models. A quantifier will elicit different behaviors in different contexts, it is true, but it is a misconception to conclude that its meaning depends on context. The different behaviors can result from integration of an invariant meaning with the variable context.

Continuous language concepts have a natural home in functional measurement theory. True psychological measurement becomes possible for "fuzzy" concepts, such as class membership, ambiguity, and quantifiers. The theory of information integration provides a cognitive alternative to the normative approach of fuzzy logic, an alternative with greater generality.

Language parameters derived from cognitive algebra have many uses. Context becomes measurable, including nonverbal context; affect and value become integral to language analysis; qualitatively different language cues can be measured with a common unit; language parameters can be compared across subcultures and languages; prototypes can be shown to have cognitive reality; the thought–word relation becomes determinable.

Functional theory emphasizes communication functions of language. It focuses on reader/listener construction of meaning. Part of this construction is at psycholinguistic levels of syntax, semantics, and pragmatics. A further part depends on inferences from world knowledge systems outside the psycholinguistic domain. Cognitive algebra provides a unified approach that can address all aspects of this construction of meaning.

Pragmatics falls naturally within a functional theory. Of special interest are social knowledge systems for context-dependent inferences that help fill in what is unsaid and reduce ambiguity. Linguistic pragmatics can be extended to social pragmatics; attribution schemas and general person cognition become integral components of language processing.

Cognitive algebra may constitute a *language universal*. All language users face the same two basic problems of valuation and integration. The algebraic rules found here for language processing have appeared in most other areas of psychology. These rules appear to arise naturally, not induced by culture. Cognitive algebra may thus be a universal characteristic of language processing.

Chapter 12

ALGEBRAIC LANGUAGE PROCESSING

THREE THEMES OF LANGUAGE PROCESSING

Three themes from previous chapters reappear in the study of language processing. First is the axiom of purposiveness and the associated functional perspective on thought and action. This appears in the construction principle, in particular, that the reader/listener is continuously engaged in constructing meaning. Online processes of judgment–decision, involving operations of valuation and integration, are thus basic in reading/listening.

Meaning invariance, the second theme, is a key to study language theory. Meaning invariance is a prime finding from integration studies of language. Also, meaning invariance underlies further usefulness of algebraic analysis.

Continuous language concepts is the third theme. Continuous concepts have been central in cognitive algebra, and this development has made useful contributions across a spectrum of language processing tasks. With functional measurement, true psychological scales of language parameters become attainable. This resolves a crux in language theory, making determinable the relation between thought and word.

FUNCTIONAL PERSPECTIVE

From a functional perspective, language is less important for what is said than for what is inferred—this is the effective communication. Linguistics, and psycholinguistics, originally proceeded in the belief that the study of language could be self-contained in terms of syntax and truth-conditional semantics, the former referring to the rules that define well-formed expressions, the latter to linguistic conditions that determine truth or falsity of such expressions.

In the last two or three decades, however, it has been increasingly realized that language usage involves person cognition. Understanding a sentence generally depends on some attribution about the speaker's intentions, which must be inferred through interpersonal knowledge systems. The sentence, *She did it*, is ambiguous in all three terms, as with whom specifically *she* refers to. Communication with this sentence depends on situation and context, including the listener's knowledge system of the speaker and vice versa, to infer who whated what. For example, the listener's inferences will utilize the conversational principle that the speaker intended the sentence to be unambiguous and would have added disambiguating information had that been thought necessary. This line of thought indicates that language processing depends on a domain of *pragmatics*, as it is called, not reducible to syntax and semantics.[1]

Beyond linguistic pragmatics lies a second level of inference, more concerned with reader/listener goals. Linguistic pragmatics, like syntax and semantics, has been focused on accuracy of communication. The writer/speaker is assumed to have some definite meaning in mind; the problem is how the reader/listener extracts, or fails to extract, that intended meaning. The second level of inference goes further to consider meanings for which external accuracy criteria are often not available and may not even exist, such as personal likableness or intention. This second level of inference is a primary business of everyday communication and a primary concern of this chapter.

This functional perspective on language echoes the functional perspective on memory in the previous chapter. There the distinction was drawn between traditional reproductive memory and the functional memory of everyday life. In psycholinguistics, a reproductive tradition has also been dominant, also characterized by external standards of accuracy. Syntax and semantics have focused on the problems of determining truth value of sentences and correctness of communication; pragmatics has largely followed suit. These problems are incomplete. General theory of language processing must go beyond language to include social cognition and judgment–decision theory.

MEANING INVARIANCE AND CONTEXT

A fundamental finding of IIT concerns invariance of meaning. The same word may evoke different reactions in different contexts, as has been shown in many studies. This fact has often been interpreted at face value to conclude that the context interacts with the word to change its meaning. This interpretation confuses a surface phenomenon with underlying process. Moreover, this interpretation is often false. Underneath such contextual variability, language parameters may be invariant.

This issue arose in the initial studies of person cognition (see *Meaning Invariance* in Chapters 1 and 4). The averaging rule implied that the meaning of each trait adjective in the person description was invariant, independent of what other traits it was combined with. Meaning invariance has repeatedly been found with language stimuli, beginning with Figure 1.2 of Chapter 1. Similar invariance appeared with the quantifiers of Table 12.1 and Figure 12.1 below.

Meaning invariance provides a base for language parameters. Most algebraic rules assume independence: That the value for each stimulus is independent of the other stimuli being integrated. Success of the algebraic rule thus argues for value independence. Value independence, in turn, argues for meaning independence; for if meaning changed, so in general would value. And meaning independence helps confer reality on the language parameters of the integration rule.[2]

The fallacy of the argument for meaning interaction becomes clear in an integration perspective. The context may be integrated directly into the response, with no effect on the meaning of the given stimulus, as diagramed in Figure 4.2. The fallacy stems from failing to distinguish between valuation and integration.

In IIT, the outlook on context changes by 180°. Instead of being a source of irregularity and flux, context becomes a locus of regularity and order—a base and frame for linguistic analysis. Language and nonlanguage stimuli can be treated in a unified way, moreover, as is necessary for general theory of communication.

CONTINUOUS, DIRECT LANGUAGE CONCEPTS

The functional measurement methodology of IIT has unique value for language analysis because it can provide validated measures of continuous concepts. The response measure may thus be established as a veridical measure of underlying thought. The functional stimulus scales, furthermore, are veridical measures of language parameters.

Traditional approaches, lacking a theory of measurement, perforce rely on other methods. Intuition has been favored by linguists, who seek ideal examples to illuminate issues ranging from grammatical categories and sentence parsing to what is presupposed in such statements as *Did she do it?* But intuition, although invaluable, has substantial limitations. It may be invalid, as in its argument against meaning invariance. It lacks power for analysis of multiple linguistic constraints. It lacks penetration for analysis of nonconscious levels. And it lacks capability for analysis of continuous concepts.

Experimental studies of language have generally relied on choice data, especially *yes–no* responses whether a given stimulus belongs to some category. This method seeks to avoid the uncertainty of intuition, but it suffers some of the same limitations. Also, it has typically confounded individual differences with the stimulus variable (see discussion of Figure 12.6 below). Moreover, discrete choice data are weak tools for studying continuous language concepts (see, e.g., Note 3).

The typical response measures of cognitive algebra are not only continuous, but direct. The subject is asked to judge some specified concept, such as probability, or some semantic quality, such as personal likableness. This measured concept is the focus of inquiry. Reaction time, in contrast, is ordinarily an indirect measure of some qualitatively different concept.

Functional measurement can measure subjective meaning—at the level of the individual subject and even the individual language stimulus. It can fractionate the response into contributions from each of multiple determinants; this yields language parameters. Functional measurement attains its power through continuous language concepts. Although only applicable under certain conditions, functional measurement provides novel capability for language analysis.

These capabilities for language analysis are illustrated in the experimental studies of this chapter. The first part considers quantifiers. A central problem was to develop and validate a measurement theory that can provide true quantification, that is, a theory in which observable judgments are veridical measures of underlying thought. The multiplication and averaging rules of cognitive algebra have yielded promising results.

The work on quantifiers leads on to more general analysis of continuous language concepts, discussed in the second part of this chapter. These studies show how cognitive algebra provides effective theory that applies across many levels of language processing, from phoneme perception to sentence/paragraph understanding. These studies also provide a psychological basis for conceptualizing and studying "fuzzy" concepts.

QUANTIFIERS

The study of quantifiers highlights a basic problem in language theory: What is the relation between our thoughts and words? An identity relation is often taken for granted, a useful tactic, but one that passes over an important and difficult question. Even pragmatics, which goes beyond words to their contexts, typically identifies the words of writers/speakers with their thoughts.

Word and thought, of course, stand in the relation of observable to unobservable. This relation is represented by the action operator, **A**, corresponding to the last of the three unobservables in the integration diagram of Figure 1.1. The term *action* here refers to cognitive construction that embeds the thought in words. A simple identity relation cannot be merely assumed. The observable words are only clues to the unobservable thoughts, which are the main concern in language and communication.

This thought–word problem may be illustrated with quantifiers such as *three*. At first glance, the meaning of *three* might seem simple enough in terms of truth conditions about cardinality of a set. This approach could be extended to say that the density of an object is 3, even though density is not a set cardinality, and indeed is a continuous variable. Physical measurement is thus meaningful in terms of observable truth conditions.

This is not enough for psycholinguistics. Language quantifies sensation, expectancy, and affect, but these are not definable in terms of observable truth conditions in any direct manner, certainly not in the manner of physical measurement (see Chapter 3). Some other way must be found to determine the meaning of the quantifiers in such expressions as *I'm pretty sure her thesis research will secure some essentially new results.*

Functional theory of quantifiers thus requires a theory of psychological measurement. This is essential to determining the thought–word relation. This measurement approach has multiple benefits, as the following studies show.

MEASUREMENT OF PROBABILITY WORDS

Language analysis requires a concept of subjective probability. We use *unlikely* and *probable* readily enough, but what do we mean by them? This question cannot be answered by counting event frequencies; some method of cognitive analysis is essential. Number-words such as .05 and .50 present the same question. Measurement of functional values of such words is essential to understanding their role in language.

Multiplication Rule. Measurement of probability words became possible through establishing the multiplication rule for subjective expected value, Equation 1 of Chapter 10. The linear fan pattern of Figure 10.1 supported the multiplication rule, in accord with the linear fan theorem of Chapter 2. By virtue of the independence property, the success of the multiplication rule implied that the probability words had invariant values in the experiment. These language parameters were determinable with functional measurement.

Subjective values for a set of common number-words have already been portrayed in Figure 10.1, and they are reproduced here in the left part of Table 12.1. Most notable is the large discrepancy between objective and subjective probabilities, highlighted by normalizing the first two subjective values to be 1 and 2, proportional to the objective values. The third subjective value, 3.9, is then much larger than its objective counterpart of 3.

Subjective values for a set of common probability phrases, also obtained with the multiplication rule, are shown in the right part of Table 12.1. In this case, objective values are nonexistent, reemphasizing that cognitive theory is essential for measurement.

Invariance and Interaction. Many writers have argued that quantifiers change meaning across context. The evidence they present, however, typically rests on the same fallacy already noted with respect to meaning invariance at the beginning of this chapter. The in-context meaning may be an integrated resultant of the context and an invariant, context-free meaning. The fallacy resides in confounding these two meanings and concluding that variable in-context meaning vitiates the concept of context-free meaning.

TABLE 12.1

SUBJECTIVE VALUES OF PROBABILITY TERMS
ETABLISHED WITH FUNCTIONAL MEASUREMENT

Stimulus number	Subjective probability	Stimulus phrase	Subjective probability
1/6	1.	No chance	0.
2/6	2.	Unlikely	.18
3/6	3.9	Somewhat unlikely	.27
4/6	5.6	Not quite even	.50
5/6	7.2	Tossup	.54
		Better than even	.66
		Fairly likely	.69
		Highly probable	.84
		Sure thing	1.

NOTES: Entries lacking decimal digits set arbitrarily to fix zero and unit of scale. Data at left after Anderson and Shanteau (1970); data at right after Shanteau (1974).

The point at issue concerns the concepts of independence and interaction. Both should be defined with respect to language parameters in an integration rule, not with respect to the observable effects. Indeed, the observable effect of each quantifier in Table 12.1 is not constant; it depends on the prize, as shown by the linear fan pattern of Figure 10.1. Success of the multiplication rule implies that quantifier and prize both have invariant value and meaning.

These studies defined a new potential for the study of language quantifiers. Vague quantifier words can have exact functional meanings. These meanings can be exactly determined with cognitive algebra.

INVARIANCE OF VERBAL QUANTIFIERS

In the experiment of Figure 12.1, subjects were instructed to

Take (*some, many, lots,* etc.) of the marbles from this box,
and put them into this box.

It might seem that *some,* for example, should refer to a fixed number of marbles, regardless of the number in the first box. Pilot work quickly showed this hypothesis to be incorrect. By analogy with the studies of Table 12.1, accordingly, a multiplication rule was hypothesized: Each quantifier should correspond to a constant proportion of the given marbles.

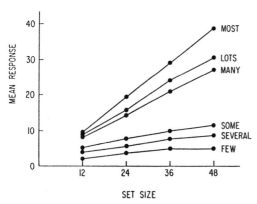

Figure 12.1. Linear fan supports multiplication rule for number quantifiers. Vertical axis plots number of marbles taken as a function of instructions to take (*most of the, lots of, . . .*) marbles from box containing 12 to 48 marbles. (From M. A. Borges & B. K. Sawyers, 1974, "Common verbal quantifiers: Usage and interpretation," *Journal of Experimental Psychology, 102,* 335-338. Copyright 1974 by the American Psychological Association. Reprinted by permission.)

The success of the multiplication rule is clear in the linear fan pattern of Figure 12.1. The number of marbles in the first box varied from 12 to 48, as listed on the horizontal axis. Six verbal quantifiers were used, indicated with labels by the six curves. Although some leveling off appears at the lower right, the six curves form a clear linear fan. Thus, the in-context effects of the quantifiers follow a regular rule:

$$R = Q \times N, \tag{1}$$

where R is the response, Q is the value of the quantifier, and N is the number of marbles in the first box. The success of this rule implies that Q is constant, independent of context. This constancy justifies Q as a context-free language parameter.

The number term N in this equation is a subjective concept. In this particular experiment, subjective N was proportional to the objective N, as shown by the equal spacing on the horizontal axis of Figure 12.1. This subjective–objective equivalence will not hold in general, of course, but it is not needed to apply functional measurement analysis.

This experiment has additional interest in that the response is behavioral; the subject actually reached into the first box and withdrew marbles. A followup experiment used a verbal response: *If you were to take (some, many, etc.) marbles from (12, 36, . . . , 108) marbles, you would take* ____ *marbles,* with subjects writing in a number. These judgments revealed a curious bimodal usage of several, with *low-several* and *high-several* subjects righteously convinced of their own usage. More important, these verbal judgments also showed a linear fan, just as did the behavioral response. This pair of experiments reinforces the congruence of word and action noted with the poker bets of Figure 10.5.

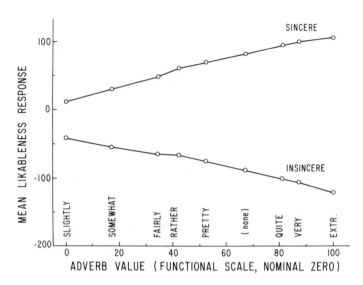

Figure 12.2. Linear fan pattern supports *as-if* multiplication rule for adverb—adjective combinations. Adverbs spaced on horizontal axis according to their functional scale values as prescribed by linear fan theorem. The label *none* represents the adjective alone, with no adverb; the location of *none* on the horizontal represents the prototypical value of the adjective. Thus, *sincere* and *insincere* have equivalent prototypical value. (From Anderson, 1974c.)

ADVERB–ADJECTIVE AS-IF MULTIPLICATION

Adverbial quantifiers have been hypothesized to act as multipliers on the adjectives they qualify. Seeming support for this multiplication rule appears in the linear fan of Figure 12.2. The adjectives *sincere* and *insincere* were prefixed by the adverbs listed on the horizontal. Subjects judged likableness of a person described by each adverb—adjective combination. Spacing the adverbs at their functional scale values, as prescribed by the linear fan theorem of Chapter 2, does yield a linear fan.

Closer consideration, however, suggests a two-step alternative to the multiplication rule. The first step is to evaluate quantity for the adjective as specified by the adverb, for example, how much sincerity is represented by *fairly sincere*. The adverbs are assumed to have fixed locations on a general quantity dimension. These quantifier locations are mapped linearly onto the specified adjective dimension. Hence adverbs will have proportionate locations along different adjective dimensions.

A second processing step is needed, however, to get from the adjective dimension to the actual dimension of judgment. The subject's task is not to say how sincere the person is, but how likable. Underlying this valuation operation is assumed to be an ideal point, which represents maximum desirability on the adjective dimension. For simplicity, the valuation function may be assumed to fall off linearly on either side of this ideal.

For *sincere* and *insincere*, the ideal points are assumed to lie outside the range of the given adverbs. Within this range, greater sincerity is better, and so is less insincerity. Hence the judgment curves are straight lines in the functional adverb metric.

On this interpretation, the multiplication rule has only as-if status. The adverbs do not multiply the adjectives in any psychological sense. Instead, the adverbs define proportionate locations on each adjective dimension. The psychological processes appear in this proportionate quantification, together with the valuation function from adjective dimension to judgment dimension.

This alternative interpretation may be tested with "golden mean" adjectives such as *cautious*. Ideally, a person should be fairly cautious; slightly cautious and extremely cautious are both less desirable. Such golden mean adjectives have their ideal points interior to the adverb range. Hence the judgment curve for a golden mean adjective should exhibit a sawtooth shape, not a linear fan. This prediction is supported in Figure 12.3 for *cautious* and perhaps also for *neat*. Further study at the individual level is desirable, since averaging across subjects smears out a sawtooth shape.[3]

The multiplication rule is thus seen to be incorrect, for it disagrees with the sawtooth shape for the golden mean adjective, *cautious*. Where it seems to apply, as in Figure 12.2, the cognitive processes are rather different from multiplication. Even for the first processing step, which quantifies the adjective dimension, what might seem to be multiplication instead appears to be a linear constancy of quantifier location across different adjectives.

The present analysis thus yields a view of the information processing rather different from multiplication. The quantifier constancy just noted is interpreted to mean that the quantifiers embody a general metric that may be applied to diverse particular tasks. This constancy is here exhibited in a functional task, one that goes beyond quantification of the adjective to one of its implications, specifically, the judgment about the person. Such functional quantification extends linguistic quantification to concerns more typical of everyday language processing. This further illustrates the usefulness of person cognition as a domain for analysis of language function.

Also of interest is the opportunity for quantifying the prototypical value of the adjective proper, unqualified by any explicit adverb. The prototypical value of *sincere* corresponds to *sincere* with no adverb. This is obtained by placing *none* on the horizontal so that the response to *sincere* unqualified by any explicit adverb lies on the given curve. The same may be independently repeated for *insincere*. Both adjectives appear to have equivalent prototypical values, midway between *pretty* and *quite*.[4]

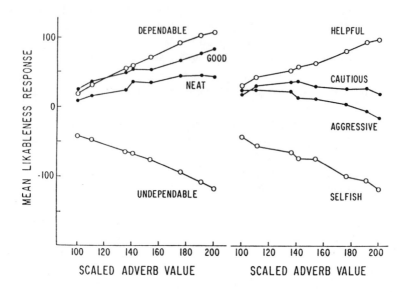

Figure 12.3. Test of processing hypothesis for judgments of adverb–adjective combinations. Adverbs spaced on horizontal as in Figure 12.2 according to their functional values defined by the two polar pairs, *dependent–independent* and *helpful–selfish*. Theoretically, the *cautious* curve should be a sawtooth, peaking at an ideal point; individual differences in the ideal location will round down the tooth. (From N. H. Anderson, unpublished study, 1970; see Anderson, 1974b, pp. 18*f*, 1974c, pp. 280*ff*.)

ADJECTIVE–NOUN MULTIPLICATION

One class of quantifier adjectives involves relative judgment. *Hot* and *small*, for example, signify physically different quantities when applied to different nouns. A *hot day* is hotter than a *hot night*; a *small car* is larger than a *large cat*. The useful flexibility of such relative quantifiers depends on their obeying some rule by virtue of which they can be encoded by the writer/speaker and decoded by the reader/listener. Such quantifiers are evidently relative to an implicit, prototypical location of the noun on the dimension specified by the adjective. However, little is known about the structure of such judgments.

One possible analysis is suggested by the first processing step for the adverbial quantifiers considered in the preceding section. The unquantified noun would correspond to a standard, comparison level on the adjective dimension. A general metric is assumed for the adjective dimension, on which the quantifiers occupy equivalent locations relative to the comparison standard for the noun. Thus, *big car* and *big cat* would bear the same size relation to *car* and *cat*, respectively. Different nouns would have different comparison standards on the physical dimension, but the quantifier locations would be proportionate across nouns, with units corresponding to the ranges within noun classes. Hence judgments along the physical dimension, of size, for example, would exhibit a linear fan with an adjective–noun factorial design.[5]

An extension to actor–verb–adjective–noun integration suggests itself, in which the actor–verb–noun configuration defines the comparison standard. Thus, *many* would imply different numbers in these six sentences:

The man eats many grapes.	The man eats many apples.
The man carries many grapes.	The man carries many apples.
The child carries many grapes.	The child carries many apples.

Number judgments for two quantifiers, *many* and *some*, for example, should then form a linear fan like that of Figures 12.1 and 12.2, if the multiplication rule holds. The functional value of each actor–verb–noun configuration would then be given by the marginal means of the data table, by virtue of the second conclusion of the linear fan theorem. This quantifies the configuration. This approach is speculative, and no evidence seems available, but it may be useful for configural analysis.

SUBJECT–PREDICATE AVERAGING

To judge likableness of the man in the sentence

The (*adjective*) man (*n-verbs*) people

requires integration of the subject and predicate information; both are relevant informers. In the present study, the adjectives were polar pairs, such as *interesting–uninteresting*. The verb *likes* was quantified at one of five *n*-levels from *dislike* to *like*; the subject saw a line labeled *dislike* and *like* at the ends, with an arrow at one of five equally spaced levels along the scale.

The parallelism of the two solid curves in Figure 12.4 supports an adding-type rule, by virtue of the parallelism theorem of Chapter 2. The upper and lower solid curves correspond to positive and negative adjectives in the person description. The points on the horizontal axis represent the specified verb quantification, in this case, degree of liking other people.

An opposite effects test between adding and averaging appears in the dashed curve. This curve denotes judgments of five sentences in which no adjective was given. The crossover of the dashed curve contradicts the adding rule and supports averaging, according to the logic illustrated in Figure 4.4 of Chapter 4. The subject–predicate integration rule may thus be written:

$$\frac{(\omega_S \psi_S + \omega_P \psi_P)}{(\omega_S + \omega_P)}, \tag{2}$$

Figure 12.4. Adjective–predicate integration obeys averaging rule. Parallelism of solid curves supports both adding and averaging rules. Crossover of dashed curve eliminates adding rule, supports averaging rule. Levels of verb quantification spaced at equal intervals on the horizontal; decrease in slope at either end of the curves thus signifies diminishing returns for verb quantification. Curves labeled *positive* and *negative* are averaged over four single adjectives (*efficient, broad-minded, interesting, educated*) and (*inefficient, narrow-minded, uninteresting, uneducated*). For dashed curve labeled *none*, no adjective was given. (From N. H. Anderson, unpublished study, 1973.)

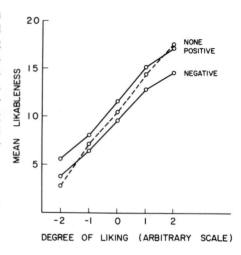

where ω and ψ represent weight and value, with subscripts S and P for subject and predicate. The prior belief term of the theory is here implicitly included in the subject term.

A quantified verb was used in this experiment to obtain a homogeneous predicate term. In the earlier experiment of Figure 4.4, different predicate levels were obtained by using verbs of different quality. In the present experiment, in contrast, different predicate levels were obtained by quantifying one verb at different levels. Both experiments support averaging theory for subject–predicate integration.

Relative to their vertical range, the curves lie fairly close together. It may thus be tempting to think that the adjective was less important than the verb. But this conclusion holds only for the arbitrary levels of adjective and verb used in this experiment and hence means little. Averaging theory, however, makes possible a valid comparison of importance of adjective and verb per se, independent of the arbitrary levels of each (Chapter 2).

Verb quantification may deserve incorporation into the language, requiring only minor extension of the increasingly common 1–10 rating schema of everyday life. To begin saying "I 7-like this book" or "I .8-expect her to finish on time" may seem affected, but it would be more efficient than the word system in current use and conducive to more careful thinking.[6]

VERB–OBJECT MULTIPLICATION

The preceding integration rule was extended to study verb–object integration in sentences of the form:

The man (*n-verbs*) (*objects*).

The verb was quantified at five *n*-levels by arrows equally spaced on a graphic scale ranging, for example, from *criticize* to *praise*, as in the previous section. The objects were *people*, *physicians*, and *sales clerks*. As before, the subject's task was to judge the likableness of the man.

In this experiment, the subject term, *The man*, is constant across all sentences. In the subject–predicate integration rule of Equation 2, accordingly, ω_S and ψ_S are both constant, as is their product, which may be denoted by c. The integration rule may thus be written:

$$\left[\frac{c}{\omega_S + \omega_P} \right] + \left[\frac{\omega_P}{\omega_S + \omega_P} \right] \times \psi_P. \tag{3}$$

The verb term in the specified sentences determines the value of the action per se and so is identified with ψ_P. The object term determines the importance of the action and so is identified with ω_P.

Equation 3 is an addition–multiplication rule: the function of ω_P in the first bracket plus the function of ω_P in the second bracket times ψ_p. The factorial graph will thus form a semilinear fan, that is, a fan of straight lines with a slightly shifting point of intersection.

This fan prediction is verified in Figure 12.5, in which both axes are plotted in terms of the observable response. To get the theoretical fan pattern requires spacing the verb degree on the horizontal axis in the same way as for the linear fan theorem. The shorter intervals at either end signify diminishing returns, already noted in the legend of Figure 12.4.

The conceptual structure of this verb–object multiplication derives from averaging theory and differs from naive expectation. Since *physicians* is more positive than *people*, a naive multiplication rule would imply that the *physician* curve should lie above the *people* curve for positive verbs, below for negative verbs. Under averaging theory, however, verb and object correspond to qualitatively different terms, value and weight, respectively. The weight, which governs the curve slope in Figure 12.5, is determined in part by diagnosticity: *People* is a more comprehensive class than *physicians*, so liking *people* is more diagnostic than liking *physicians*. Hence the *people* curve has greater slope than the *physician* curve. The lesser slope for *sales clerks*, on the other hand, presumably reflects lesser occupational prestige than physicians.[7]

The invariance property reappears in this study. Verb and object are represented by separate parameters, and each is constant, independent of the value of the other. The observed effect of the verb, it is true, does depend on the object, but this is accounted for by the multiplication rule. It would be a conceptual mistake to conclude that the meaning of the verb depended on the object context (see similarly Anderson, 1981a, Section 3.6).

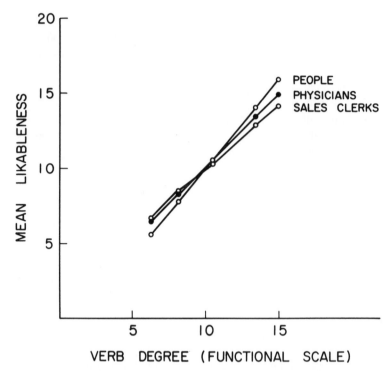

Figure 12.5. Fan pattern supports addition—multiplication rule for verb—object integration. Verb levels plotted on the horizontal at their functional scale values. Data averaged over four verb dimensions: (*criticize-praise, hinder-help, dislike-like, distrust-trust*), each quantified at five levels by equally-spaced arrows along a graphic scale labeled at the two ends by the verbs of each listed polar pair. Objects were the three classes of people listed as curve parameter. (From N. H. Anderson, unpublished study, 1974.)

QUANTIFIER ALGEBRA

The study of quantifier algebra faces an apparently formidable difficulty: The functional metrics of the quantifier variables are necessary to assess algebraic rules. These metrics, however, are unknown and might even seem unknowable. Even if well-defined metrics exist for probability words such as *unlikely* and *probable* or for number words such as *several* and *many*, they may not be determinable. Moreover, given knowledge of stimulus metrics for each separate variable says nothing about integration of two variables.

This difficulty was declared insoluble in principle by Hörmann (1983), in one of the few psycholinguistically-oriented discussions of this issue. Hörmann showed, for example, that *a few* (in German) elicited different numbers when applied to *crumbs* and to *cookies*. This implies, as Hörmann says, that the listener calculates the effective value of *a few* as a function of context. This implication agrees with the construction principle of IIT. Also, it underscores the functional perspective, especially as regards the second level of pragmatic inference noted in the introduction.

But Hörmann emphatically denied that there was any fixed rule of calculation, evidently unaware of previous work on quantifier algebra. The study of Figure 12.1 demonstrates a fixed rule for the class of quantifiers considered by Hörmann. Indeed, this rule has an exact algebraic form, which shows that Hörmann's interpretation is not correct. This is shown constructively, by giving method and theory to establish quantifier algebra.[8]

All three themes of this chapter are manifest in this example. The functional perspective appears in the focus on context-based inference. Context is treated as integral to language processing. Indeed, context provides a means to demonstrate meaning invariance of the focal stimulus. Thereby it supports the cognitive reality of the language parameters derived from the model. These analyses manifest the theoretical power of continuous, direct language concepts.

THOUGHT AND WORD

Problems of thought–word relations have appeared in various forms in the foregoing experiments. Prominent is the problem of thought–word linearity: Under what circumstances are quantity words veridical measures of quantity thought?

This linearity question has hardly been considered in psycholinguistics, even by those concerned with quantifiers. Linearity, however, is a simple form of a central issue in language use. Unless the thought–word relation can be pinned down in this simple case, functional theory of language will be seriously limited.

The linearity question has a long history in psychophysics, specifically in measurement of sensations such as loudness and grayness. The perplexity of this question has been seen in Figure 3.1, which shows that two plausible number "languages" yield very different results. Corresponding number-words in the two languages thus represent very nonequivalent thoughts.

Which language—if either—is correct? In which language—if either—is the word a veridical measure of the thought?

These questions have been answered with functional measurement theory. The parallelism and linear fan theorems provide a validational frame for the response measure. This frame was grounded empirically through the experimental investigations. In this way, observable number-words were established as veridical measures of unobservable sensation in psychophysics. These theorems have also been successful with language processing, as has been shown in the foregoing experiments.

A related aspect of the thought–word relation appears in the stimulus values, or language parameters, illustrated in Table 12.1. The values of these number-words were not directly observed, as was the response, but were derived using the parallelism and linear fan theorems. By virtue of these theorems, however, they may be considered veridical metrics of the number-thoughts. These number-thoughts may be nonconscious, not otherwise measurable.

Quantification, it may be added, has a qualitative implication: It argues for cognitive reality of the dimension quantified and of the quantifiers themselves. This qualitative implication is only suggestive, but it may be as important as quantification per se. This argument goes beyond quantifiers to more general concepts in language processing, illustrated in the next part of this chapter.

QUANTIFICATION AS FUNCTION

An important generalization of the quantifier domain appears in those foregoing studies that used a task of person cognition. The quantifiers in these tasks typically differ in kind from the probability and numerosity words, which are nominally quantitative per se. The studies with person cognition, in contrast, employed a response dimension of different quality from the stimulus dimension. Thus, a *happy-go-lucky* person could be judged on distinct dimensions of likableness, honesty, and so forth, even though *happy-go-lucky* does not lie directly on these dimensions and is not nominally quantitative.

Such indirect quantification pervades thought and action. Indirect quantification embodies the axiom of purposiveness of Chapter 1; goal-oriented thought and action lead naturally to dimensional value representations. The foregoing results thus point to a central role of quantifier algebra in functional language theory.

CONTINUOUS LANGUAGE CONCEPTS

The importance of continuous concepts in language processing goes far beyond the quantifiers considered in the foregoing sections. Ambiguity and fuzziness are ubiquitous in understanding language, with different interpretations being less or more sensible or likely. Class membership may be continuously graded. More generally, many concepts of everyday communication, such as expectancy, sensation, affect, and diverse interpersonal feelings, attitudes, and attributions, are continuous quantities.

Information integration theory provides a natural framework for language analysis because it has developed theory and methods for analysis of continuous concepts. Information integration is at once a fundamental problem of language processing and a foundation for language theory. Cogent applications have been made by Gregg Oden, Dom Massaro, and Shu-Hong Zhu, some of which are reviewed here. Their work has established a new beachhead for analysis of language processing.

CONTINUOUS SEMANTIC CONSTRAINTS

Any proposition derives its coherence and meaning from the constraints it embodies. In *A socializes with R*, for example, the verb constrains both the agent A and the recipient R. Hence A and R should not only be animate but stand in some social relationship. Such constraints are essential in construction of a meaningful interpretation from what would otherwise be a disconnected sequence of words.

How multiple constraints are integrated is thus a basic question in language processing. To study integration of continuous semantic constraints, Oden and Anderson (1974) asked subjects to judge 25 propositions based on the sentence:

> Mr. A is *(adverb)* sociable; how likely is it
> that he will socialize with *(adverb)* sociable people?

Each adverb was varied over five graded levels, from *very un-* to *very*, as indicated in Figure 12.6.

The likelihood judgment was hypothesized to be the product of the two constraints in the given sentence:

$$\text{Likelihood} = \text{Verb–agent constraint} \times \text{Verb–recipient constraint.} \quad (4)$$

This multiplication rule is well supported by the linear fan pattern shown in Figure 12.6. Supportive results were obtained in other conditions in this experiment. However, some sign of an addition process appeared when distinct adjectives were used in place of the quantified adjective *sociable* in the above example (Oden & Anderson, 1974, Figure 2).

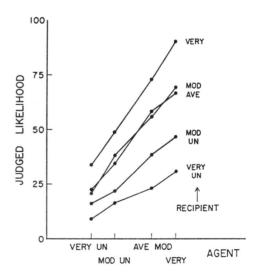

Figure 12.6. Multiplication rule for integration of semantic constraints. Horizontal axis indicates adverbial level of agent sociableness for the sentence displayed in the text; curve parameter indicates level of recipient sociableness; (*average* and *moderate* yielded nearly identical results and have been combined on the horizontal). (After Oden & Anderson, 1974.)

The implications of this experiment deserve itemized emphasis.

1. Constraint Integration. Some semantic constraints obey an algebraic integration rule. In psycholinguistics, semantics is considered *compositional*: The meaning of an expression is a determinate function of its parts. This assumption is grounded here by empirical demonstration of an algebraic composition function. Capability for analyzing algebraic composition rules is a new tool for language analysis.

2. Language Judgment Measures. The judgment response is a direct language measure, that is, a direct measure of language understanding. In earlier experimental work on language, judgment measures had generally been avoided, for they seem subjective and poorly defined. Reaction times and error indexes, in contrast, seem objective and definite. Judgment measures can, however, be placed on firm ground with functional measurement.

Direct language measures of comprehension have important advantages over such indirect measures as reaction time and error indexes. As noted in the original report (Oden & Anderson, 1974, p. 147): "In syntactic analysis . . . indirect methods are often equivocal because they may reflect extraneous processes, such as retrieval in a memory task. The same conclusion applies to semantic analysis . . . This ability to obtain validated, interval [linear] measures of meaning provides a powerful new tool for the study of the language."

3. Intuition and Theory. Intuition and theory can be integrated. Intuition is the base for selecting direct judgment measures, of course, and is also important in selecting the language stimuli. Success in the search for algebraic rules is thus heavily dependent on intuition.

In return, success of an algebraic rule helps validate intuition. Intuition has been a primary method for language analysis, and it can be invaluable. It is insufficient for nonconscious processing, however, and it can go astray at the conscious level, as it did over meaning invariance.

In the present case, the multiplication rule supports the veridicality of the response scale. The linear fan theorem implies that the response is a true measure of underlying thought. The multiplication rule goes further, however, to suggest that the conceptual quality of the response has cognitive reality. The cognitive reality of the stimulus constraints also receive some measure of validational support.

Much linguistic analysis depends on carefully simplified examples that will command general intuitive agreement. When intuitions begin to differ, progress falters. The present approach provides a way to unify intuition and experimental analysis.

4. Individual Analysis. Continuous measures facilitate language analysis at the individual level. Each individual may be asked to judge a patterned set of related propositions, as was done in the present experiment. The data for each individual may be graphed exactly as in Figure 12.6; the pattern in this graph mirrors that individual's processing. Figure 12.6 is actually pooled over subjects, but each subject could be treated in the same way. Functional measurement methodology provides a needed means to allow for individual differences at many levels of language processing.

5. Single Propositions. Analysis for single linguistic propositions is facilitated with direct language measures. The present design was a "single proposition design" in that the 25 propositions were variations on a single underlying proposition, with graded degrees of each adverbial modifier. In alternative designs, single propositions could be used as component stimuli, and their meanings obtained through stimulus quantification. Response quantification, analogously, allows direct judgments of complex linguistic stimuli.

> Too often, psycholinguistic data are gross, qualitative differences, averaged over groups of propositions, and over groups of subjects as well. . . . Linguistic stimuli are complex and notoriously susceptible to confounding. Averages over groups of propositions may conceal important differences. Furthermore, since the same word often means different things to different people, averages over groups of subjects must also be treated with caution.
>
> Psycholinguistic theory must be capable of handling the individual linguistic unit, at the level of the individual person. . . . The methods of integration theory and functional measurement have this capability. (Oden & Anderson, 1974, p. 147.)

6. Stimulus Quantification. True psychological scales of stimulus parameters can be obtained. By the linear fan theorem of Chapter 2, the functional values of the agent constraint are represented by the spacing of the adverbial modifiers on the horizontal axis of Figure 12.6. The slopes of the curves give a similar scale of the recipient constraint. The two scales appear equivalent, a reflection of the interpersonal symmetry in the judgment task.

This stimulus quantification is applicable at the individual level. Each subject's data could be treated similarly. Functional measurement theory thus provides a tool for measuring language stimulus parameters.

7. Response Quantification. The likelihood response may also be considered a true psychological scale. Establishing the integration rule simultaneously validates the response measure, following the logic of the linear fan theorem. The judgment response thus becomes more meaningful theoretically than reaction time and error measures, which will in general be no more than monotone, or ordinal, scales.

Response quantification is important because it can transcend the immediate task. Stimulus values are in principle goal-specific, and hence have limited generality across tasks. The same response methodology, however, may be applied across diverse tasks, even though response quality varies (see *Threefold Generality* in Chapter 3).

A trustworthy method for response quantification has another advantage: It can be applied even when no algebraic rule holds. Although the evidence of this chapter shows that algebraic language rules are frequent, many tasks will not obey any simple rule. With a veridical response, however, patterning in the observed data will exactly mirror patterning in underlying process. This approach can be useful in studying stimulus interaction and configurality.

8. Language Parameters. The foregoing points may be combined under the single heading of language parameters. The stimulus parameters represent functional meaning of the language components of the proposition. The response has a similar relation to the whole proposition. These stimulus and response parameters constitute basic data for language theory.

Nonverbal components of communication may be represented as language parameters. Of special interest are nonverbal aspects of speech and gesture, as well as social–physical context. Functional measurement theory thus provides a general approach to language parameters.

9. Continuous Language Variables. Continuous language variables find a natural representation within IIT. As noted in the original report (Oden & Anderson, 1974, p. 143):

> In the present theoretical approach, semantic constraints are allowed to be continuous, numerical variables. . . . This point requires comment since it departs from the typical all-or-none view of semantic relations.
>
> Linguistic semantics has usually employed the "convenient fiction" (Lakoff, 1972) that semantic variables have only two allowable values, truth and falsity, or sense and nonsense. . . . In psychology, similarly, current models of semantic memory (for example, Rumelhart & Norman, 1973) have been primarily propositional and discrete; something either is a bird or it is not.
>
> Sociableness, however, is a matter of degree. Indeed, *sociable* refers to some moderate degree of sociableness, and that degree is a proper part of the meaning of the word itself. . . . Lakoff (1972) suggests that the all-or-none propositional fiction reflects the lack of an adequate alternative that can handle continuous semantic variables. He discusses possible applications of Zadeh's (1965) fuzzy set theory in which set belongingness may be a matter of degree. Integration theory provides another alternative, one that has certain advantages in empirical power and in generality. . . . Further, it applies to a wider range of problems than could be handled in set-theoretical terms.

DECISION AVERAGING MODEL FOR DISAMBIGUATION

Nearly all expressions have some degree of uncertainty or ambiguity of meaning. We are usually unaware of this because constraints within the expression or from the external context allow quick, automatic narrowing down of intended meaning. That *spring comes* refers to a noun seems clear, but the evidence indicates that the verb meaning, as in *spring up*, has also been briefly activated and discarded in the processing. Such constraints must be incorporated in language theory, but attempts to do so have done more to uncover difficulties than to resolve them. Fundamental work by Gregg Oden, summarized in this and following sections, has provided a cogent attack on disambiguation.

In his Ph. D. thesis, Oden (1974, 1978b) postulated a language decision model with two processes: absolute and relative. The absolute embodies a threshold criterion that serves to eliminate potential meanings of low sensibleness at early stages of processing, thereby avoiding overload from having to consider the often enormous number of possible meanings (see Oden, 1974, p. 10). The relative pertains to competing meanings that are not rejected by the absolute criterion, but retain some acceptable degree of sensibleness. This two process conception, Oden showed, could harmonize the conflicting evidence on whether ambiguity slows or otherwise interferes with online processing.

Oden aimed to test whether the relative decision process for competing meanings obeys cognitive algebra. If ψ_A and ψ_B are the sensibleness values of two interpretations of given stimulus material, Oden's model assumed that subjective likelihood, $L(A)$ of interpretation A, was the decision ratio:

$$L(A) = \frac{\psi_A}{\psi_A + \psi_B}. \tag{5}$$

If both interpretations are equally sensible, $L(A) = .5$, regardless of their absolute strengths. Similarly, if B is complete nonsensible, with $\psi_B = 0$, then $L(A) = 1$. A somewhat different theoretical rationale for Oden's model can be given in terms of averaging theory (Equations 5 of Chapter 2).

Oden developed a useful device of manipulating sensibleness values using informers external to the ambiguous sentence itself. This allows experimental separation of two kinds of disambiguating information, which is needed to test the integration model. In one condition, subjects received stimuli like:

> A girl was looking out of her window toward
> (*the park across the street*)
> where there were a bunch of
> (*boy scouts who were bird watching*).
> She was looking for a boy with a pair of binoculars.

The ambiguity in the final sentence refers to who had the binoculars, the boy or the girl. Paraphrases of these two interpretations of the ambiguous sentence, one of which is listed Figure 12.7, were presented to the subjects. They judged relative likelihood of the listed interpretation on a 0–100 scale. The quoted stimulus is represented by the middle right data point in Figure 12.7; the judged likelihood that the boy had the binoculars is about .65.

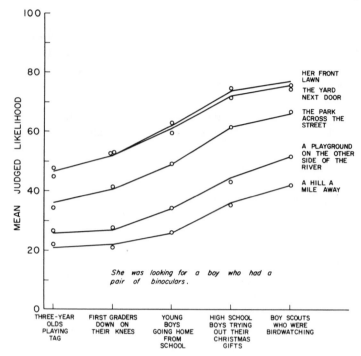

Figure 12.7. Data points and theoretical curves from Oden's model for competing interpretations of ambiguous sentences. Vertical axis plots relative likelihood of the interpretation listed in the figure. Model analysis was done individually for each of 30 subjects; curves give mean model predictions, averaged across subjects. Deviations from prediction were statistically nonsignificant. (After Oden, 1974, 1978b.)

The upward slope of the curves represents the effect of the five informers listed on the horizontal axis. This informer variable affects the sensibleness of the interpretation listed in the figure. Thus, possessing binoculars is more sensible for a boy scout who is bird watching than a three-year-old boy playing tag. The other informer variable represents the distance between the girl and the boy, listed by the row curves. It affects the sensibleness of the other interpretation, namely, that the girl was looking through the binoculars.

Oden's theory of ambiguity resolution did quite well. The curves in Figure 12.7 are theoretical and lie close to the observed data points. Similar results were obtained with other conditions, using lexical, surface-structural, and deep-structural ambiguities, and two different methods for manipulating the sensibleness values. Language parameters can be derived, and these are listed in Table 12.2. By the uniqueness properties of the decision averaging model (Chapter 2), the sensibleness values for the agent and recipient factors are directly comparable, being on a linear scale with known zero and common unit.

TABLE 12.2

SENSIBLENESS VALUES FOR LANGUAGE CONSTRAINTS

Agent factor		Recipient factor	
hill a mile away	1.47	Boy Scouts	1.00*
playground	.87	high school boys	.70
park across street	.36	young boys	.38
yard next door	.18	first graders	.23
her front lawn	.17	three-year-olds	.19

NOTE: Sensibleness values on common scale for both factors. Entry marked * normalized at unity. (From Oden, 1974, 1978b.)

The agent and recipient informers act independently, according to the integration analysis. Thus, the distance between the girl and the boy affects only the sensibleness value of the interpretation that the girl was looking through the binoculars, with no effect on the sensibleness of the alternative interpretation that the boy had the binoculars. This independence property may seem counterintuitive, but intuition refers to the relative ratio rule of Equation 5. Underneath this relative judgment, valuation operations for the two informers are independent, as demonstrated by Oden's functional measurement analysis.

Special importance attaches to Oden's use of a direct language measure. The usual approach in psycholinguistics would have been to present each stimulus to a large group of subjects and measure the proportion who spontaneously gave one or the other interpretation. But this proportion can hardly be expected to be a true linear response scale. With sensibleness values in a ratio of 9 to 1, for example, hardly any subject could be expected to give the less sensible interpretation. Moreover, the group proportion will be affected by individual differences, adulterating its purity as a language measure. Validity of Oden's judgment measure, of course, is supported by the success of his model.

Treating sensibleness as a continuous language variable has several advantages. Foremost is that is it realistic. Although the writer/speaker may have just a single intended meaning, the reader/listener must cope with degrees of uncertainty. Also, continuous variables allow analysis at the level of the individual subject and even at the level of the individual proposition, as in Oden's design. The success of Oden's model supported not only the validity of the response measure, but also the cognitive reality—and cognitive independence—of the constraints hypothesized in the intuitive linguistic analysis. Oden's work thus contributes also to semantic memory theory, which has been fixated on discrete, propositional representation.

DECISION AVERAGING MODEL FOR TRUTH VALUE

Although class membership has traditionally been treated as all-or-none, class boundaries have generally been recognized to be uncertain, ill-defined, or "fuzzy." This applies not only to categories such as young–old or gray, which impose cutoffs on a continuous underlying variable, but also to discrete categories such as birds and vegetables.

The prime requisite for studying fuzzy class membership is a theory of psychological measurement. This is needed to treat class membership as a continuous variable. In the following experiments, Oden (1977a) showed how his theoretical model, together with functional measurement methodology, could be applied to study fuzzy classes and continuous truth values. In a typical experimental condition, subjects were asked: Which of the following two statements is truer, and how much more true is it?

> An eagle is a bird.
> A pelican is a bird.

Subjects judged "how much more true" on a continuous scale. This format can be extended to compare truth value across distinct classes, for example, the class of birds and the class of vegetables:

> A robin is a bird.
> A tomato is a vegetable.

For this task, Oden's cognitive algebra was essentially the same as he used for ambiguity resolution in the previous section. Each statement is assumed to have a truth value, ψ, and the judgment is assumed to equal the relative ratio of the two competing truth values:

$$\frac{\psi_A}{\psi_A + \psi_B}, \tag{6}$$

where A and B index the two paired statements. This relative ratio model fit the data quite well.

Functional measurement yielded truth values for each statement, and some of these parameter values are presented in Table 12.3. *A robin is a bird* was judged most true, so its truth value was normalized to unity. Sparrow and eagle are also considered good exemplars of the class of birds. Penguin is neither a good bird nor a good animal, the latter presumably because college students consider animals to be mammals. Lamp is not considered a good object, which suggests a similar, everyday, nondictionary parlance of categories.

Oden's study was the first to provide validated measurement of continuous truth value. Also important, it extended the validity of the rating method to judgments of class membership.

TABLE 12.3

Continuous Class Membership Values

Birds		Birds		Other	
robin	1.00	pelican	.42	tuna (fish)	.67
sparrow	1.00	ostrich	.34	tomato (vegetable)	.55
eagle	.84	penguin	.23	penguin (animal)	.25
hawk	.77	bat	.12	lamp (object)	.21
buzzard	.49	butterfly	.02	pickle (vegetable)	.20
				whale (fish)	.20

NOTES: All entries on common scale. Parameters normalized by setting value for robin to unity. In the "Other" column, *tomato (vegetable)* denotes the degree to which tomato is considered a vegetable, etc. (After G. C. Oden, 1977, "Integration of fuzzy logical information," *Journal of Experimental Psychology: Human Perception and Performance, 3,* 565-575. Copyright 1977 by the American Psychological Association. Reprinted by permission.)

The most popular hypothesis about class membership has been in terms of similarity to a class prototype. Oden noted that his results raised doubt about this hypothesis. Eagle and sparrow, for example, have marked dissimilarities, yet both are considered good birds. Oden's favored interpretation was in terms of multiple prototypes, in this example, separate prototypes for birds of daily life and birds of prey. Pursuing this line of thought suggests a deeper level of fuzziness, in which definition and membership of classes is not stable, but dependent on context and situation. General fuzziness is not simply a continuous class membership; the class itself becomes ambiguous.

MULTIPLICATION RULE FOR FUZZY LOGICAL OPERATIONS

Formal development of fuzzy logic (Zadeh, Fu, Tanaka, & Shimura, 1975) requires fuzzy analogs of standard logical operations of *and* and *or*, conjunction and disjunction, respectively. This development also raised the hope that human thinking, which is well known to deviate from formal all-or-none logic, might still obey formal fuzzy logic. As Oden (1977b) showed, this hypothesis becomes testable with functional measurement theory.

Two rules have been suggested for fuzzy conjunction. The minimum rule is:

$$\text{truth}(A \text{ and } B) = \min[\text{truth}(A), \text{truth}(B)].$$

The multiplication rule is:

$$\text{truth}(A \text{ and } B) = \text{truth}(A) \times \text{truth}(B). \tag{7}$$

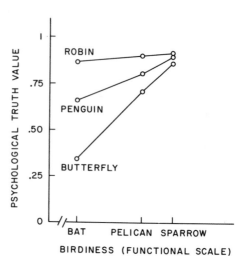

Figure 12.8. Fuzzy logical disjunction obeys multiplication rule as shown by linear fan pattern. (After G. C. Oden, 1977, "Integration of fuzzy logical information," *Journal of Experimental Psychology: Human Perception and Performance, 3,* 565-575. Copyright 1977 by the American Psychological Association. Reprinted by permission.)

Fuzzy disjunction may be treated by taking truth(not A) = 1 − truth(A) to define negation. The two rules just listed thus yield two complementary rules. The maximum rule is:

$$\text{truth(A or B)} = \max[\text{truth(A)}, \text{truth(B)}].$$

The falsity multiplication rule is:

$$1 - \text{truth(A or B)} = [1 - \text{truth(A)}] \times [1 - \text{truth(B)}]. \tag{8}$$

One experimental test of the two fuzzy disjunction rules is shown in Figure 12.8. Subjects judged statements of the form: "How true is it that a sparrow is a bird *or* a penguin is a bird?" The converging linear fan pattern in the figure eliminates the maximum rule and supports the falsity multiplication rule. Analogous results for the conjunction test eliminated the minimum rule and supported the multiplication rule, although with some suggestion of a compound addition–multiplication rule.

The conceptual structure of information integration theory is well suited to the study of subjective logic, as this and the preceding experiments show. Fundamental to analysis of subjective logic is capability for psychological measurement. Oden's studies were the first to resolve the problem of psychological measurement of continuous logical conjunction and disjunction.

FUZZY LOGICAL MODEL FOR PHONEME IDENTIFICATION

A notable extension to a deeper level of processing was made by Oden (1978a) in a study of phoneme identification. By combining the two integration rules considered in the two previous sections, a theoretical account could be given of two successive integration stages in phoneme identification: The multiplication rule was applied to feature conjunction in the first stage of phoneme evaluation; the decision averaging rule was applied to the response competition among phonemes in the second stage to determine the overt response. This key development formed the basis for numerous later applications by Oden and Massaro of Oden's fuzzy logical model.

Identification of a speech sound as one of the phonemes, /da/, /ta/, /ba/, or /pa/, depends on conjunction of two features: place of articulation and voicing.

/da/:	*alveolar*	and	*voiced.*
/ta/:	*alveolar*	and	*not-voiced.*
/ba/:	*not-alveolar*	and	*voiced.*
/pa/:	*not-alveolar*	and	*not-voiced.*

Each phoneme is considered to be represented by a "cognitive prototype" in long-term memory, which corresponds to the listed conjunction of features.

The first stage of integration governs the valuation for each separate phoneme. This involves conjunction of the two listed features, and this conjunction is assumed to follow the multiplication rule of the previous section. Presentation of a given stimulus is assumed to elicit two values, one for each separate feature, obtained by similarity matching to the cognitive prototype in long-term memory. The complement rule for negation is also assumed to hold, so the response strength of each phoneme can be written in normalized form as:

$$\psi_{/da/} = \psi_{al} \times \psi_{vo};$$

$$\psi_{/ta/} = \psi_{al} \times (1 - \psi_{vo});$$

$$\psi_{/ba/} = (1 - \psi_{al}) \times \psi_{vo};$$

$$\psi_{/pa/} = (1 - \psi_{al}) \times (1 - \psi_{vo}). \tag{9}$$

Here the subscripts correspond mnemonically to the above phoneme array.

The second stage of integration is one of competition among the four phonemes. This was assumed to follow the foregoing decision averaging rule in terms of response probability. Thus, the probability of responding with /da/ would be its relative response strength, that is, $\psi_{/da/}$ divided by the sum of the four response strengths. Since some response was required, the four response probabilities must sum to unity. Hence the normalized response strengths of Equations 9 equal the response probabilities.

This model gave a good fit to data of Sawusch and Pisoni (1974), who had covaried the two cues in synthetic speech consonants. Tests by Oden and Massaro (1978) and by Massaro and Cohen (1976, p. 713) with factorial designs have provided even stronger support for Oden's fuzzy logical model.

Feature multiplication makes phonemic sense in terms of the stimulus manipulation. The two extremes of voicing completely dominated the choice between voiced and non-voiced, regardless of place of articulation. An addition rule obviously cannot account for such a data pattern; a multiplication rule can, by assigning values near 0 and 1 to the two extremes of voicing.[9]

Feature independence was one implication of Oden's analysis. The success of the model implies that valuation proceeds independently for the two features with no interaction between them. This conclusion differs from that of Sawusch and Pisoni, who argued for feature interaction. An additive model did not fit their data, but including a nonadditive term improved the fit. This they interpreted as reflecting an interaction between the acoustic features. Nonadditivity, however, does not imply interaction in any psychological sense (see concluding section on *Meaning Invariance*). Oden's model is nonadditive, yet provided an even better fit—with no feature interaction.

Oden entitled his model a "fuzzy logical model" because it treats feature evaluation as continuous, in contrast to the then-predominant all-or-none perspective. It deserves emphasis that continuousness is not assumed but demonstrated. The model allows the operative feature values to be only 0 and 1, but they were not. Any given speech sound may thus be considered as less or more similar to a prototype phoneme stored in memory. If similarity is treated as a measure of truth value in this case, it is then less or more true that the given speech sound is an instance of the prototype. Oden suggested further that phoneme perception itself was continuous rather than categorical. This approach was put on effective ground with cognitive algebra and functional measurement (see also Figure 12.9 below).

CONFIGURAL FEATURE INTEGRATION

In a *tour de force*, Oden and Massaro (1978) extended Oden's fuzzy logical model to incorporate configural phoneme structure. The same phoneme identification task was employed, but with the two acoustic features, voicing and place of articulation, varied in factorial design. The multiplication rule for feature conjunction then implies that the data should plot as a linear fan. This linear fan pattern was verified to a good approximation for each of the four phonemes.

Hardly of less interest were some small but systematic deviations from the linear fan pattern. These were considered to reflect nonorthogonal structure of the memory prototypes for the four phonemes. In natural speech, voicing actually differs somewhat for different phonemes, depending on place of articulation. The memory prototypes will embody this nonorthogonal structure. This will appear in the data, of course, because the memory prototypes determine the valuation of each feature. Hence deviations from the linear fan will be expected, for it assumes orthogonal structure of the experimental design.

Oden and Massaro went farther to measure the configurality. This was represented in the model by adding exponential weights to the features in Equations 9. Functional measurement theory was applied to scale the feature values and exponents, thereby allowing graphical depiction of the psychological parameter space. The configurality appeared as a phoneme boundary shift along the dimension of alveolarity: The medium level of alveolarity is more likely to be identified as alveolar, /da/ rather than /ba/, for higher levels of voicing, and more likely to be identified as nonalveolar (labial), /pa/ rather than /ta/, for lower levels of voicing.

Analogous evidence for nonorthogonality had been observed in a few previous studies, but had been taken to represent interaction between the stimulus features. In the Oden–Massaro fuzzy logical model, however, feature evaluation is not interactive. What appears as interaction in the data reflects configural structure of the natural phoneme prototypes in long-term memory.

This is a remarkable result. Natural stimuli, ranging from phonemes to sentences, must often be expected to exhibit configural structure. Configurality is generally difficult to analyze. The Oden–Massaro approach illustrates one potential use of cognitive algebra for configural analysis. Indeed, whereas previous work had argued for configurality in the integration process, Oden and Massaro showed that the configurality lay in the representation structure of memory.

FUZZY LOGICAL MODEL
FOR VISUAL LANGUAGE IDENTIFICATION

Visual language perception may be approached in the same way as just indicated for auditory phoneme perception. In a study of letter identification, Oden (1979) and Massaro and Hary (1986) varied two visual features in factorial design to obtain artificial letters with graded degrees of similarity to the letters G and Q. As with phoneme identification, the first integration stage consists of matching the given stimulus to letter prototypes in memory to determine the strengths of the two response alternatives. These then compete in the second stage of integration to determine the actual response.

The formal model was the same as just discussed for phoneme identification. The first stage was assumed to obey the multiplication rule, the second stage to obey the decision averaging rule. Both cited studies provided good support for this two-stage model.

An interesting difference between the two studies is that Oden used a rating judgment of relative similarity, whereas Massaro and Hary used probability of choice response. To get a probabilistic choice response required short, tachistoscopic presentation of the stimuli. The rating response, in contrast, was obtained using presentation times of a second or so. The processing seems different in these two tasks, deliberate with the judgment response, automatic with the recognition response. It would be of great interest to determine whether these two procedures yield the same parameter values. Unfortunately, the stimulus displays differed in minor ways, so the parameters from these two studies are not properly comparable. A positive answer, that the automatic and deliberate processing tasks yield equivalent language parameters, would point to an important invariance in language processing.

DECISION AVERAGING MODEL FOR CATEGORICAL PERCEPTION

Categorical perception has been an important issue because it implies top-down processing, in which a learned category imposes itself on a lower level of sensory–perceptual processing. Compelling phenomenological evidence for categorical perception appears with phonemes. If sound frequency parameters are varied continuously between the phonemes /ba/ and /da/, the conscious percept of the listener does not undergo corresponding continuous variation. Instead, there is a clear, sudden shift between hearing one phoneme and hearing the other. This discontinuous perception seems almost to mandate categorical perception, in which the learned phoneme categories impose themselves on the perceptual processing. Categorical perception thus seems a clear example of the influence of higher cognitive process on perception.

A new approach to categorical perception was employed by Massaro (1987), who transformed the issue into an information integration paradigm by adding an independent visual cue to the auditory cue. Subjects heard sounds that varied smoothly in nine steps between the acoustic parameters characteristic of /ba/ and /da/. They also saw a synchronized video of a person exhibiting lip movements characteristic of /ba/, /da/, or nothing. These three lip cues are quite different visually, and had substantial effects on the auditory perception, shown by the differences among the three sets of data points in Figure 12.9.

The curves in Figure 12.9 are theoretical. The left panel shows predictions from the decision averaging model discussed in preceding sections; the right panel shows predictions from the categorical perception model. Although the categorical model ideally predicts abrupt, all-or-none transition between /ba/ and /da/, variability in the decision criterion across trials acts to smooth out an abrupt transition, in agreement with the data. Nevertheless, the categorical model does poorly for the middle curve for no lip movement. The continuous model, in contrast, comes very close to the data points. The superiority of this continuous, noncategorical view was supported in an extensive program of research by Massaro, making systematic use of integration tasks and functional measurement (Massaro, 1987, pp. 23, 51).

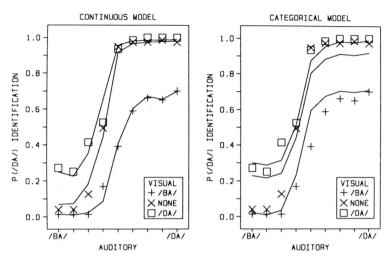

Figure 12.9. Continuous versus categorical theory of speech perception. Data points represent identifications of artificial phonemes such as /da/ as a function of two stimulus cues, visual and verbal. Same data points in both panels. Theoretical curves from continuous model in left panel are generally close to the data points; theoretical curves from categorical model in right panel show substantial discrepancies. (After Massaro, 1987.)

DECISION AVERAGING MODEL FOR SENTENCE CONTEXT IN WORD RECOGNITION

That syntactic and semantic constraints can influence word recognition has been demonstrated in many studies of reading. Few, however, have gone further to analyze underlying process. One major question concerns interaction among the stimulus informers. Independence among informers is parsimonious but seems too simple. Interaction hypotheses are attractive, all the more because they can explain almost any pattern of data.

An interactive interpretation was adopted in a pioneering attempt by Tulving, Mandler, and Baumal (1964), who rejected independence and concluded that the stimulus informers interacted. Their analysis, however, rested on an implicit assumption that recognition is all-or-none; partial information was not allowed. Massaro (1991) showed that the assumption of continuous information supported the hypothesis of independence.

In the Tulving et al. study, subjects read the last 0, 2, 4, or 8 words of sentences like "Her closest relative was appointed as her legal ... "; they then received a very brief visual presentation of the test word, in this case, *guardian*, for times ranging in 8 equal steps from 0 to 140 msec. They were instructed to write down the test word, making use of the context and guessing if they were not sure.

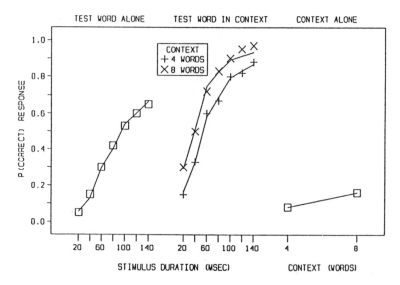

Figure 12.10. Identification of word in sentence context follows fuzzy logical model. Data points after Tulving, Mandler, and Baumal (1964); theoretical curves from Oden–Massaro fuzzy logical model. (From Massaro, 1991.)

The separation between the two curves in the center panel of Figure 12.10 shows that the sentence context had substantial effects on probability of correct recognition. The upper curve for 8-word context shows over 10% better recognition than the lower curve for 4-word context. The theoretical question concerns the rule by which the sentence context is integrated with the brief presentation of the test word.

Probability theory provides an algebraic rule for conjunction of two independent events, and this rule was tested by Tulving et al. If w and c denote the probabilities of recognition based on the word alone and the sentence context alone, then the probability of recognition based on word and context together would be $w + c - wc$. Accordingly, estimates of w and c were obtained from the single-cue data in the left and right panels of Figure 12.10 and used to predict the data of the center panel. This probability model did poorly. Accordingly, Tulving et al. rejected the assumption of independence and concluded there was interaction among the stimulus informers.

But implicit in their probability analysis is the assumption that recognition is all-or-none: Presentation of a stimulus either produces recognition or it does not; continuous, partial information is not allowed. In contrast, the decision averaging model used by Massaro allows continuous information from both informers that is integrated to determine probability of response.[10]

Predictions from Massaro's model are given by the solid curves in Figure 12.10. These are very close to the data points. This indicates that the two information sources do not interact, but are processed independently. More important, of course, is that the informer integration obeys an algebraic rule, a rule that may be used for functional measurement of language parameters.

DECISION AVERAGING MODEL FOR
CROSS-LANGUAGE PARAMETER COMPARISON

Only one step to understanding comes with the identification of words from the auditory and visual information that we receive. The more important problem is to interpret the propositions they form. In the proposition, *the horse the man kicked*, for example, the problem is to decide whether the man or the horse did the kicking. Among the relevant informers are syntactic cues, such as word order, semantic informers, such as animacy, and prosodic informers, such as stress. A cross-linguistic study of these three informers by Bates, McNew, MacWhinney, Devescovi, and Smith (1982) was used by Massaro to illustrate the integration analysis. Subjects received phrases with two nouns and a verb, and selected the subject of the sentence, that is, the one who did the action. Three word orders (NVN, VNN, and NNV), three levels of animacy (both nouns animate, first noun only animate, and second noun only animate), and three levels of stress (no stress, stress on first noun, and stress on second noun) were varied in a three-factor design.

The model analysis requires two integration stages, the first to evaluate each single informer, the second to integrate these informer values to determine the response. As in preceding sections, the first stage was assumed to obey a multiplication rule, the second stage a decision averaging rule. This fuzzy logical model fit the data reasonably well, both for English and for Italian subjects (see Massaro, 1991, Figures 10 and 11).

Of special interest, the language parameters obtained from the model provided quantification for cross-linguistic comparison of the same informers in different languages. Animacy, for example, is more important in Italian, word order more important in English. This accords with linguistic intuition, but goes beyond to begin quantification of linguistic parameters and to compare them across different languages.

PROTOTYPES AND PROBABILITY QUANTIFIERS

Do words have a core, prototypical meaning, that is, a fixed lexical meaning that does not change with context? Many writers have adopted some concept of core meaning, but mainly on intuitive or esthetic grounds. That this assumption is questionable has been emphasized by a number of recent workers, some of whom have underscored the criticism by uncovering empirical context effects

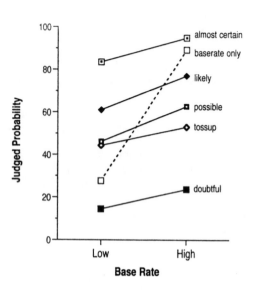

Figure 12.11. Cognitive reality of prototypes for probability quantifiers demonstrated by averaging rule. Solid curves represent pragmatic judgments of intended meanings of probability words conjoined with base rate information (movie scenario). Crossover of dashed curve for base rate alone supports averaging rule of integration. Functional measurement analysis of language parameters of Table 12.4 indicates invariance of prototype values. (From Zhu, 1991.)

that seem sharply contrary to the conception of invariant lexical meaning. *A few crumbs*, for example, are more numerous than *a few cookies*, as though the meaning of *a few* changes with context. Again, not only does *red apples* refer to a range of redness, but this range seems different from that for *red hair*.

Shu-Hong Zhu (1991) made a notable advance by providing definite evidence for cognitive reality of prototypes. The essential difficulty, Zhu notes, is that two levels of discourse are involved: representation and process. The concept of prototypical meaning refers to unobservable representation; the observable context effects must involve some process. Changeable surface meaning may stem from this process, with a changeable context being integrated directly with an invariant representation. By attacking both problems jointly, Zhu solved both, demonstrating the reality of prototypes by exhibiting their operation in a process model.

Zhu's first experiment studied probability quantifiers, such as *doubtful, possible*, and *almost certain*, in conjunction with context in the form of base rate. In one of his three scenarios, subjects saw sentences of the form:

It is [*probability word*] that a college student will go to the movies
[*base rate phrase*].

The phrase *once a week* defined a low base rate, since few students are expected to see movies on a weekly basis; the phrase *once a quarter* defined a high base rate, for most students see a movie at least this often. Subjects were told that each sentence represented the true opinion of some speaker; they were told to judge what likelihood the speaker had in mind.

An attractive assumption is that the prototype operates as a multiplier on the base rate:

Judged likelihood = Prototypical likelihood × Base rate.

Intuitively, the context-free, prototypical likelihood may be viewed as a proportion, relative to a certainty value of 100. This proportion would be used to modify the base rate that serves as context. This multiplication rationale for probability quantifiers is analogous to that for numerosity quantifiers studied in Figure 12.1. The multiplication rule predicts a linear fan, however, and the data shown in Figure 12.11 are definitely not a linear fan.

Instead, Zhu found a weighted averaging rule:

Judged likelihood = ω_P × Prototypical likelihood + ω_B × Base rate.

Operation of an averaging process in each of the three scenarios was shown by the marked crossover of the curve for base rate alone, illustrated with the dashed curve of Figure 12.11. Quantitative confirmation was found using the test of goodness of fit for nonlinear models cited in Chapter 2.

Success of the averaging rule implies the hypothesized prototypical likelihood is invariant across contexts—evidence for its lexical reality. Context affects the judgment directly through the averaging process, not indirectly by changing the meaning of the quantifier.

Invariance of the language parameters across the three scenarios provides further support for Zhu's theory. Parameters were estimated for each individual subject using the AVERAGE program, and their means are shown in Table 12.4. Especially striking is the near-constancy of prototypical values for each quantifier for all three scenarios (left half of table). Not only is the prototype invariant across context within each scenario, as shown by success of the model for each separate scenario, but it is also invariant across scenarios.

Weight parameters are also of interest, for they represent vagueness or fuzziness of the quantifiers. Lower weight means higher vagueness. These weight estimates agree with intuition, as may be seen in the right half of Table 12.4. Thus, *possible* has highest vagueness, with a weight around 15, whereas *almost certain* has lowest vagueness, with a weight 50% larger. Weights are more variable than values, a statistical property of the decision averaging model, but all three scenarios show similar patterns of weights.

Zhu's theory provides new scope for lexical analysis. Prototype value is only one element in his lexical representation. A second element is the weight parameter, ω_P, which represents fuzziness in the probability word. Zhu's theory not only provides evidence for the existence of both lexical parameters, but also provides quantitative measures of each.

The fuzziness weight parameter resolves a linguistic paradox. Strong arguments against the reality of prototypes had been made from findings that words

TABLE 12.4

PROTOTYPE PARAMETERS

	Prototypical meaning			Importance weight		
	Movie	Car	Jogging	Movie	Car	Jogging
Almost certain	95	96	96	22	26	25
Likely	73	74	73	15	15	15
Possible	51	52	52	14	15	16
Tossup	48	47	49	22	18	21
Doubtful	15	11	14	24	22	19
Base rate				3	4	3

NOTES: Meanings on 0–100 linear scale. Weights on ratio scale, normalized to sum to 100. Parameters estimated for individual subjects using AVERAGE program, and averaged across subjects. (After Zhu, 1991.)

of similar context-free meaning placed in the same context could yield different effects. Such seemingly paradoxical findings were taken by Hörmann (1983) to mean that the very process by which contextual meaning was determined was itself variable across context.

This paradox is resolved in Zhu's theory, for different effects can be produced by the fuzziness parameter. Thus, *possible* shows the same values as *tossup*, but lower weight. Correspondingly, base rate has greater effect with *possible*, shown by the greater slope in the movie scenario of Figure 12.11.

Zhu extended his investigation to consider context defined in terms of the confidence expressed by the speaker. Greater confidence caused the judged likelihood to be more extreme, positive or negative, according as the probability word was high or low. Zhu suggested polarity, positive and negative, as a third lexical element, which he incorporated in a serial integration model: Subjects begin with the prototypical meaning of the word, and adjust this according to the difference between the speaker confidence and a prototypical confidence for the word itself. This model did well in three experiments. The polarity concept is in line with the axiom of purposiveness and may extend to word classes other than probability quantifiers (see discussion of Figure 4.1).

Zhu's analysis is in the same spirit as the original studies of meaning invariance in person cognition (Chapters 1 and 4). There also the essential issue was whether the context influenced the meaning of the given word or was integrated independently, with the word itself being invariant. Zhu's theory is a signal advance, not only to new precision in the language–decision domain, but also to an analytical attack on general problems of lexical representation.[11]

COGNITIVE ALGEBRA OF LANGUAGE PROCESSING

Cognitive algebra represents a new kind of regularity and lawfulness in the language domain. Although the foregoing experiments may seem over-numerous, they make clear that a few simple integration rules operate across a spectrum of applications.

More broadly considered, the algebraic rules represent cognitive processes involved in social communication. Reflecting their base in the axiom of purposiveness and the concept of value, the algebraic rules are jointly related to the functions of language in social cognition and to the functions of social cognition in language.

CONTEXT

Context is integral to language processing. Context stimuli and focal language stimuli can be analyzed conjointly in an integration model. Context effects need not be an obstacle; instead, they can be a path of progress.

Zhu's thesis is a striking example of context analysis. His context integration theory provided evidence for the reality of prototypes and a means for measuring their parameters. With his theory, context and focal stimuli could be measured in common units. By expanding the inquiry to include context, Zhu obtained a theory at once more general and more powerful.

Context analysis was also a key in Oden's theory of disambiguation. In his thesis experiment, the context was verbal information about the physical situation pertaining to the ambiguous focal sentence. Similar analysis may be expected to hold with nonverbal context information that appears in everyday communication, including gesture and social role.

Context analysis exemplifies the functional perspective, which goes beyond language proper to the broader domain of communication. From this perspective, the term *context* is somewhat misleading; context provides information as pertinent as focal stimuli. All determinants of communication, nonlanguage and language, should be treated in a unified way. Integration theory can do this, as the foregoing experiments show.

MEANING INVARIANCE

Meaning invariance is a primary implication of cognitive algebra. Important in its own right, meaning invariance also shows the power of algebraic rules.

Demonstration of invariance depends on cognitive theory. Invariance cannot be defined at the surface level of observable effects. This point was clear in the original studies of person cognition, which showed that the same adjective could have opposite effects, positive or negative, depending on which other adjectives it was combined with (e.g., Figure 4.4). At a surface level, opposite effects implies stimulus interaction and meaning change. Integration theory, in contrast, revealed meaning invariance.

Similar necessity for cognitive theory is illustrated with the multiplication rule in the quantifier experiments of Table 12.1 and Figure 12.1. Under instructions to take *some* marbles out of the box, the actual number taken varies with the number in the box. At the surface level of behavior, *some* seems to have different meaning in these different contexts. In the cognitive integration rule, however, the language parameter is constant across contexts. At this underlying level of cognition, *some* has invariant meaning.

Invariance also reveals a twofold independence property in language processing. Valuation often proceeds independently for the various stimulus informers; there is no interaction among them prior to the integration operation. It follows further that valuation and integration are independent operations. Cognitive algebra thus provides a novel kind of evidence about how language processing is organized.

LANGUAGE PARAMETERS AND BEYOND

Language parameters attain reality through meaning invariance. That a word has a fixed meaning across different contexts argues that this meaning has cognitive reality. This implies corresponding reality of the language parameters, which represent functional values of the language stimuli. With functional measurement, as illustrated in Tables 12.1–12.4, true quantification of language parameters is possible.

This measurement analysis extends to diverse classes of context effects. Context may include semiverbal stimuli, such as intonation; nonverbal stimuli, such as gesture and facial expression; preverbal stimuli, such as affect; and extraverbal stimuli, such as may be contained in the physical environment. All such stimuli are potentially amenable to integration analysis, which can measure their effective parameters on a common scale. Although only feasible under certain conditions, such analysis can provide a useful approach to language processing and communication.

CONTINUOUS LANGUAGE CONCEPTS

The need to admit continuous concepts into language theory has been emphasized by many writers. Standard approaches, however, have usually begun with discrete categories and propositions, belatedly discovering that such discrete representations are not easily extended to continuity. IIT, in contrast, begins with continuous concepts as terms in the algebraic models. This approach does not force continuity. Quite the contrary, certain forms of discreteness are allowed, as indicated in the discussion of Oden's fuzzy logical model for phoneme identification.

Indeed, a novel line of evidence for discreteness developed from this theory of continuous representations. Meaning invariance argues for a discrete representation of the functional stimulus. The issue is whether such discreteness mirrors a deeper discreteness, not merely at the level of operating memory, but also at the level of long-term memory. Marshaling the evidence for discreteness may suggest ways to clarify the issue and pin it down.

Continuousness in response is easily compatible with discrete language parameters. Continuous response can come from variability in context. If a variable context is integrated with a discrete language parameter, the resultant response will vary along with the context. This process is nicely illustrated with the quantifier *some* in Figure 12.1.

Some form of continuousness, however, does seem required in long-term memory. A *sociable* person, for example, is sociable in some degree, as though the aspect of quantity is inherent in the word. A discrete representation, however, may be a particular value. Thus, *sociable* could represent a discrete, prototypical value of the quality of sociability.

Evidence for such discrete–continuous representation comes from the original studies of meaning invariance. The alternative hypothesis is that *sociable* has at bottom a fuzzy representation, as a continuous range of meaning, with a central tendency corresponding to the prototypical value. Under this hypothesis, however, meaning change would be expected, not meaning invariance. The degree or shade of meaning operative in any context would be one more fitting or consistent with the context—this was one rationale for the original change-of-meaning hypothesis in person cognition. The failure of this change-of-meaning hypothesis presents an explanatory problem for fuzzy representation.

This explanatory problem is amplified by a group of studies that tested whether the positive context effect in person cognition was caused by meaning change. When the subject is asked for the value of one adjective in a person description, the response varies directly with the values of the other adjectives— a positive context effect. At face value, this positive context effect is meaning change. And, since its size is continuously variable, it argues for a continuous representation. Several lines of evidence, however, supported an interpretation in terms of meaning invariance (see Figure 4.2).

One line of this evidence has present relevance as a direct test of the locus of fuzziness. Several investigators independently realized that if the positive context effect stems from meaning change, then it should be greater for words with greater ranges of meaning. This implication failed. Various indexes of range of meaning were used, but virtually all showed the same large positive context effect for words with narrow and wide ranges of meaning. Since range of meaning may be considered a measure of fuzziness, these results suggest that fuzziness is localized in generalized operating memory, with a discrete representation in long-term memory.

Understanding the discrete–continuous issue, as the foregoing discussion indicates, requires understanding of integration and of the role of context. A discrete stimulus representation may exhibit a continuous effect solely by virtue of integration of variable context. This point may be as important for general language analysis as it was for person cognition (Chapter 4).

The foregoing discrete–continuous representation differs from standard views of fuzziness, which envisage the basic representation as a continuous function. For normative theory, the locus of continuousness may not be pertinent; continuousness is clearly present at the level of action. But cognitive theory, as already indicated, requires a distinction between continuousness in operating memory and in long-term memory. Thus, the perceptual units in the Oden–Massaro studies were considered to be discrete representations in long-term memory. Fuzziness can arise from variability in the stimulus, which has correspondingly variable similarity to the discrete memory prototype. In this case, fuzziness is localized in operating memory, not in the underlying memory representation.

Zhu's analysis of probability quantifiers has further interest as evidence for a second discrete–continuous parameter, namely, weight. The weight is discrete in that it is constant across different experimental sentences. Lexically, it seems a discrete parameter. By virtue of the averaging process, however, weight can have continuous effects. Furthermore, weight simulates fuzziness: Lower weight can have effects similar to greater range or less exactness of meaning. This is a general property of the averaging model.

In this discrete–continuous view, continuousness is potential in the basic representation and becomes actualized in the task assemblage in operating memory. Thus, the averaging rule for person cognition corresponds to an averaging of particular quantitative values constructed from discrete informers. Similarly, the multiplication rule for semantic constraints of Figure 12.6 corresponds to multiplication of two particular quantitative values, constructed by the valuation process acting on the discrete representation. Continuousness can thus arise from function.

A pertinent qualification is that meaning invariance has so far been demonstrated only on a local basis, within the context of particular experiments. Valuation, however, is goal- and context-dependent; the same stimulus may have different values and/or weights in different tasks. Although task-dependent values and weights will appear even with invariant meaning, this task dependence suggests that change in meaning proper may appear across different experimental situations. The cited evidence for discreteness may thus be compatible with a continuous representation in long-term memory. Some mild evidence against this argument is provided by Zhu's finding of similar prototypical values across different scenarios. Even within-task invariance, however, raises some question for a fuzzy cognitive view.

The intuitive feeling of fuzziness requires consideration. The cited judgments about narrow and wide ranges of meaning, for example, seem direct perception of fuzziness. This interpretation has face validity, but similar face validity failed in the analysis of meaning invariance. An alternative interpretation is that intuitive judgments of fuzziness arise in general operating memory, referring to a class of potential context situations that create the fuzziness.

Often, of course, people wish to refer to some range of meaning. The intended referent of *doubtful* may thus be a range, for which the word is a makeshift substitute. Range usage, however, could be handled straightforwardly by treating the intended meaning as a range whose bounds depend on context in the same way as its central value, as in the discussion of quantifiers in the first part of this chapter. An alternative approach in terms of prototypical value and weight parameter by Zhu has already been discussed.

In language function, of course, continuousness is overwhelmingly clear. The various attempts to incorporate continuousness within a theoretical framework for language processing are a recognition of the common sense of everyday life. Cognitive algebra has provided an effective attack on continuousness, as illustrated in every experiment in this chapter. Among the many fundamental contributions by Oden, his measurement analyses have provided the first true quantification of fuzziness.

At the same time, the invariance property of cognitive algebra has provided clear evidence for discreteness in long-term memory—together with continuousness in operating memory. The foregoing discrete–continuous view is admittedly counterintuitive. Indeed, such concepts as *young–old* and *gray* are so intuitively continuous that it may seem obtuse to suggest the possibility of discreteness. Evidence for some form of discreteness seems clear from the foregoing experiments, however, even if its locus remains to be pinned down.

NORMATIVE THEORY

Cognitive theory and normative theory are fundamentally different. Normative approaches have been perennially attractive because they seem to promise an objective, rational foundation on which to erect psychological theory. Classical logic was perhaps the earliest normative approach. Experimental analysis, however, has repeatedly found that the laws of logic are not the laws of thought.

Later developments in normative theory have seen the introduction of cognitive-sounding terms such as subjective probability and fuzzy sets. These developments have occurred in reaction to normative shortcomings in the original normative formulations. They are commendable attempts to make these theories more generally applicable in their own normative domains. But they should not be confused with psychology.

Normative approaches aim for consistent, rational formulations in an essentially logical sense. They do not aim primarily to study how the mind actually works, as illustrated by their general indifference to experimental analysis. They live in an idealized world, not the real psychological world.

This cognitive–normative issue has already been discussed with respect to Bayesian probability theory in Chapter 10. That Bayesian theory incorporates a concept of subjective probability does not make it cognitive theory. It still seeks a rational, axiomatic base, just as classical probability theory.

Similar arguments apply to fuzzy set theory, which seeks to replace all-or-none set membership with continuous membership functions. This is more appropriate to everyday usage, which is replete with continuous categories, such as *young, good-looking*, and *cheerful*. But this does not make fuzzy set theory psychological, for it has an essentially different epistemological foundation. Fuzzy set theory can serve as a normative heuristic by suggesting algebraic rules, just as did Bayesian probability theory. Success of such rules, however, is as much a cognitive coincidence with fuzzy set theory as it was with Bayesian probability theory.

MOLAR–MOLECULAR ANALYSIS

Language processing involves a long progression of stages, ranging from feature perception to sentence understanding and beyond. Each stage involves valuation and integration; its integrated output constitutes a valuation for the following stage. Feature integration thus leads to phoneme perception, phoneme integration to word perception, and so on. A progression of stages is thus involved, $V–I \rightarrow V–I \rightarrow V–I \rightarrow V–I \ldots$, longer in language processing than perhaps any other form of cognition.

The idea of stage representations is perhaps universally accepted because it offers vital simplification. Progress would be most difficult if the entire processing sequence had to be analyzed all at once. If the stage representation is warranted, analysis can proceed at some given stage more or less independently of preceding and succeeding stages. This stage conception has already been discussed in relation to the unitization principle and the molar–molecular distinction of Chapter 1. Concepts applicable at any stage may be considered molar units, relative to more molecular representation of previous stages.

Cognitive algebra can place stage representations of processing on firmer ground. Stage representations are dangerous because there is no algorithm for defining appropriate stages. A given stage may not be unitary or understandable at its own level. Instead, it may be askew to nature, not a fruitful level of study. Success of an algebraic rule, however, supports the reality of the selected stage as well as its sufficiency as a base for theory. Such support is only suggestive, as previously cautioned, but it furnishes novel leverage on a problem that has largely been left to fend for itself.

It deserves reemphasis that cognitive algebra can provide molar boundary conditions on more molecular analysis. Any molecular theory must cohere with these constraints at its molar boundaries. These boundary conditions can thus serve as effective constraints on theory construction.

Qualitative boundary conditions appear in the algebraic structure of the integration rules, for this entails some analogous structure of processing. The algebraic structure may thus mirror the mental model for task performance assembled in operating memory. One example is the analogue fractionation rule noted in the last part of Chapter 2, which is presumably operative in the quantifier experiment of Figure 12.1.

Furthermore, success of a rule argues for cognitive reality of the concepts represented in that rule. Meaning invariance points to noninteractive processing, as in the positive context effect of Figure 4.2, and suggests discrete representation in long-term memory together with continuous representation in operating memory. Molecular theories may be testable by their ability to account for such qualitative, molar structure.

Quantitative boundary conditions are available with functional measurement. Stimulus scales, in particular, provide boundary conditions on more molecular stimulus representations. In this way, functional measurement can confer unique assistance for deeper levels of cognitive analysis (Anderson, 1981a, 1982). This role of boundary conditions has been nicely expressed by Oden (1988; Oden, Rueckl, & Sanocki, 1991) in saying that algebraic rules form a symbolic superstrate for connectionist level theories.

PERSON COGNITION AND LANGUAGE

Person cognition is a vital domain for language analysis. The studies of quantifiers in the first part of this chapter illustrate the flexibility of this class of tasks. Other examples appear among the studies of continuous language concepts in the second part of this chapter. This work extends the line of inquiry begun in the foundation studies of Chapter 4.

Intimate relations between person cognition and language should be no surprise. These relations stem from the social nature of communication and the communicational nature of society. Language use, as various writers have noted, is replete with assumptions that different participants share common understanding. The importance of interpersonal knowledge systems has received increasing attention in the development of language pragmatics.[12]

Language pragmatics may be carried further with cognitive algebra. A basic problem for pragmatics is to understand how social–physical context is integrated with focal language stimuli. One regularity in such integration processes is revealed in the studies of cognitive algebra. This work also demonstrates a new methodology, which allows exact measurement of the functional context, often extralinguistic, which could otherwise be difficult to define. The foundation of cognitive algebra in studies of person cognition makes it a fitting helpmate for language pragmatics.

COGNITIVE ALGEBRA AS LANGUAGE UNIVERSAL

Cognitive algebra may represent a universal mode of language processing. All language use rests on two basic processes: valuation and integration. Valuation operators are needed to process individual informers; integration operators are needed to combine these individual informers into an overall meaning. These two operations are the heart and mind of cognitive algebra. The studies of this chapter have shown a broad range of language applications.

Cognitive algebra is hypothesized to be a language universal on the ground that algebraic rules constitute a general mode of thought and action. The same algebraic rules discussed in this chapter have appeared repeatedly in other domains in previous chapters. The decision averaging rule of Chapter 10 has special relevance, for it mirrors the prevalence of judgment–decision processes in language. Algebraic rules of person cognition (Chapters 4 and 5) can help explore the pervasive role of social knowledge systems in language pragmatics and communication. Also relevant are the developmental studies of Chapters 6 and 8, for they suggest that algebraic rules have innate grounding. It may reasonably be expected, accordingly, that algebraic integration rules will hold across diverse languages, constituting a language universal.

NOTES

This chapter is dedicated to Gregg Oden, who has done ground breaking work on a range of problems in language processing, especially in development of his fuzzy logic model. This chapter is deeply indebted to his work and wisdom, although it is presented from my own perspective, which differs in certain respects from his. In particular, I have interpreted some results in terms of decision averaging theory, as with Table 12.2, instead of Oden's fuzzy logic formulation. I wish to thank Gregg Oden and Shu-Hong Zhu for helpful comments on earlier drafts.

1. A lucid, readable survey of pragmatics is given by Green (1989), who includes a discussion of Grice's (1975) conversational principles.

2. Value of course depends on the task; the same word may have different values along different judgment dimensions, that is, with respect to different goals. Judgments about a *clever thief*, for example, will differ along the three distinct dimensions of occupational proficiency, social value, and personal likableness (Anderson & Lopes, 1974; see also Chapter 4, Note 5). The *clever thief* will be a better thief than the *stupid thief*, thereby more negative in social value, but still more likable at a party, say, or as a cellmate should it come to that. This form of contextual dependence is related to the construction principle discussed in Chapter 1. The semantic meaning need not vary, however, and is presumably common for *clever thief* and *clever student*.

3. Adverb × Adjective multiplication was proposed by Cliff (1959), who also used a scaling task along the dimension of social desirability. Cliff's analysis lacked sensitivity, however, being based on discrete choice data and Thurstonian measurement theory. Hence he failed to detect the flat failure of the multiplication rule apparent in Figure 12.3 (see also Anderson, 1974b, pp. 18–19, Figure 3; 1974c, Section 7.9; 1981a, pp. 51–52, 328–333). The present analysis is expected to apply fairly generally, although further tests, with other judgment dimensions, for example, have yet to be done.

4. An interesting cross-check on adverb–adjective quantification could be obtained by combining two such adverb–adjective phrases in the manner indicated in the scaling experiment of Figure 4.1. Following that scaling analysis, the net value of each phrase could then be obtained from the averaging model. With suitable design, these derived values could be analyzed in the manner indicated in Figure 12.2. A common scale for different adverb–adjective phrases is also obtainable.

5. Relative quantifiers, such as *hot* and *large*, may also be viewed as (implicit) metaphors of the form:

large X : (average) X : : large : (average).

Functional measurement may thus be useful in metaphor theory.

6. An interesting historical use of the 1–10 scale was by William Tecumseh Sherman. Much was made in his day, as it is in ours, of his eastward march from Atlanta to the sea. The subsequent march northward through the Carolinas was far more difficult, being made in mid-winter rain through mainly swampy wilderness, and more important in ending the Civil War. Yet it was then and is now relatively unknown. Sherman himself commented (1875/1957, Vol. II, p. 221):

> Were I to express my measure of the relative importance of the march to the sea, and of that from Savannah northward, I would place the former at one, and the latter at ten, or the maximum.

7. Two factors seem required in general verb–object integration, as previously found in adjective–noun integration (Anderson & Lopes, 1974; see also Anderson, 1974b, pp. 60–64). *The man helps people*, for example, bespeaks a man of good character; also, it describes a sociable desirable action. One factor thus pertains to the personality of the man, the other to the social value of the predicate action.

Evidence for two factors appears in Table 12.5, which presents mean bad–good judgments of the man described by sentences of the form:

The man *(verbs) objects,*

with objects on the rows of the table, verbs on the column. The first two rows of data might seem to support the multiplication rule: The *people* row is more extreme, positive or negative, than the *physician* row. These two rows exhibit a crossover interaction, reminiscent of that seen with the multiplication rule of Figure 12.5. But *trust, reassure,* and *praise* are more extreme than *like* for *physicians*, less extreme for *people*. This disordinal pattern disagrees with the simple verb × object rule, but may be understandable in terms of two verb × object factors, one reflecting the personality of the man, the other the social value of his action.

TABLE 12.5

MEAN BAD–GOOD JUDGMENTS OF THE MAN DESCRIBED BY
SENTENCES OF THE FORM *THE MAN VERBS OBJECTS*

	Likes	Dislikes	Helps	Hinders	Harms	Trusts	Distrusts	Reassures	Criticizes	Praises
People	17.5	3.6	18.1	4.6	1.9	16.1	6.3	16.1	7.0	16.0
Physicians	13.9	8.2	16.2	5.0	2.8	14.4	8.9	14.5	8.8	14.3
Judges	13.4	8.2	15.1	6.2	2.8	14.8	8.9	14.1	9.4	13.8
Beggars	10.4	8.9	14.2	7.7	3.3	10.6	9.5	12.1	9.6	8.9
Vagrants	8.9	9.8	12.9	9.1	4.4	9.9	10.6	11.5	9.2	7.5
Alcoholics	9.4	9.4	16.4	10.4	3.6	10.0	10.3	13.2	9.9	6.2
Clerks	13.2	8.1	14.7	6.2	3.0	12.9	9.0	13.4	7.7	13.3
Plumbers	13.1	8.4	14.8	6.7	3.1	12.8	9.0	13.2	8.1	13.1
Garbage men	13.1	7.4	14.2	5.7	2.7	13.0	7.8	13.1	7.5	12.8

NOTES: *Objects* (classes of people) listed on rows, *Verbs* on columns. Entries are means over 28 subjects on 1–20, good–bad judgment scale. Some phrases, such as *helps criminals*, are ambiguous. (From N. H. Anderson, unpublished study, 1974.)

The personality factor should follow the multiplication rule of Equation 3. The verb proper defines a scale value, and the object defines the diagnosticity, or weight parameter. Thus, *likes people* is more diagnostic than *likes physicians* because *people* is a more comprehensive class.

Diagnosticity may have additional determinants. Of special interest is base rate, for an infrequent action may be more informative. Thus, the relatively negative judgment for *The man distrusts garbage men* presumably arises because there is better reason to distrust physicians or even plumbers than garbage collectors, who ordinarily have minor effect on one's life. Given that the subjective base rate of distrust is indeed lower for garbage collectors, a causal attribution schema (Chapter 5) implies that a man who does distrust them must be unusually distrustful and hence less likable.

The social value of the action may also obey a multiplication rule, specifically, the effectiveness of the action times the need of the object. The need term is taken in a general sense so that criminals need hindering just as alcoholics need help. In general, social value will depend on the verb–object configuration, but quantitative analysis may be possible by using quantified verbs as in the experiment of Figure 12.4.

8. Mathematical models and measurement of quantifiers received a decidedly negative evaluation by Moxey and Sanford (1993) on the premise that interpretation of a quantifier depends on context. They seemed to think that such dependence implies variability of meaning not amenable to quantification, as argued also by Hörmann (1983) and others.

Their conclusion does not follow from this premise. This was shown by the work on meaning invariance in Chapter 4. It is further shown by the quantifier studies in the first part of this chapter. Indeed, cognitive algebra actually capitalizes on context as a base and frame for measurement. Conceptually, the model analysis seems necessary to understand how context operates.

9. Feature averaging rather than multiplication may perhaps operate in the first stage of the Oden–Massaro fuzzy logical model for phoneme identification. This possibility seems plausible in view of the ubiquity of averaging processes for informers of similar quality. One approach is to study the pattern of the first-stage output parameters assessed by applying functional measurement to the integration operation of the second stage. The first step in this analysis is to determine the parameter values operative in the second integration stage. These values constitute the output, that is, the response, of the first integration stage. With suitable design, functional measurement may be applied a second time to these parameters to analyze the first integration stage (see Anderson, 1974a, Section II.B.11).

Both the multiplication and the differential weight averaging models can produce linear fan patterns. The averaging model, however, can produce nonfan patterns, including crossovers. Three-factor design may be useful for better discrimination.

This tactic was used with a Bayesian urn task by Leon and Anderson (1974), who found the first-stage output parameters to depend configurally on sample composition. This question deserves more serious consideration, especially as it may condition the meaningfulness of the estimated language parameters.

10. The probability model of Tulving et al. is a form of the classical high threshold model of psychophysics. High threshold theory has been massively disproved in signal detection theory, which assumes a continuous information variable underlying the all-or-none response (see *Signal Detection Theory with Functional Measurement* in Chapter 9).

11. In attempts to measure vagueness of probability terms and other quantifiers, subjects usually have been asked to give numerical equivalents for the terms and/or for their ranges of meaning. These attempts are unsatisfactory, as Wallsten, Budescu, Rapoport, Zwick, and Forsyth (1986) pointed out, in particular because they have taken the responses at face value, without providing a validity criterion. Wallsten et al. present a thoughtful attack on this issue, which, unfortunately, suffers two serious problems.

The first problem is that Wallsten et al. relied on weak inference. Although they recognized the need to establish an integration model, they used conjoint measurement, which, as is well known, lacks an error theory for testing goodness of fit. They report high correlations from the model analysis, but high correlations mean little in this context. In particular, these correlations have little bearing on the validity of the conjoint measurement axioms (see *Weak Inference* in Chapter 2).

Second, even if the conjoint measurement axioms were satisfied, this would not justify their application of metric scaling. This took the numerical responses at face value as a true linear scale, which does not follow from conjoint measurement.

This second problem is underscored by their finding virtually identical correlations, .75 and .77, for their difference and ratio models. These two models represent different psychological processes and treat the numerical response in quite different ways. Both models cannot be true. Yet the results fail to distinguish between them.

Wallsten et al. used a pair comparison procedure similar to that of Oden (1977a,b). Oden used functional measurement, however, which does provide a proper validity test with the given numerical response.

Zhu's work follows a different direction of attack, one based more directly on language usage. Previous studies have generally focused on membership functions. Thus, *possible* would be represented as a continuous function over the range from 0 to 1. Membership functions are intuitively attractive, but their psychological reality remains unclear.

Zhu used language tasks, in which the probability word was embedded in a context familiar from everyday life. The integration of probability word and context obeyed algebraic models. The parameters of these models provided psychological representations rather different from membership functions. Although prototype value may be considered a central tendency of a membership function, this central tendency need not have any simple mathematical form, such as mean or median. Prototype invariance, moreover, is not obtainable from membership functions.

A similar argument holds for Zhu's weight parameter. Intuitively, weight is analogous to the standard deviation or range of a membership function. These would certainly be correlated, but a simple mathematical relation can hardly be expected. Nor does Zhu's interpretation of weight as a lexical parameter seem derivable from a concept of membership function.

This comparison reemphasizes that measurement of language terms depends on establishing substantive language models. Zhu's work is exemplary in this regard, for he embedded his investigation within a context of everyday usage.

12. The close relations between person cognition and language have also been noted for Shakespearean drama: "In every dialogue the social order is a silent but essential partner; the simplest remark presupposes two analogously structured habit systems, and consequently the faith that the social order is coherent and pervasive enough to have instilled the same habits in the listener as in the speaker." (Burckhardt, 1968, p. 262; see further Green, 1989, Chapter 1, Sections 5 and 6.)

PREFACE

The theory of information integration is unified and general. Generality appears in the spectrum of preceding chapters, from person cognition to functional memory, and from social development to judgment–decision and language. Unity appears in the applicability of the same concepts and methods across all these domains.

The unity and generality of information integration theory derive from three interlinked features: purposiveness; information integration; and cognitive algebra. Purposiveness and information integration, in different ways, are basic givens of thought and action. Cognitive algebra provides effective analysis of information integration; functional theory of value measurement gives a cutting edge to the axiom of purposiveness.

The axiom of purposiveness entails a functional perspective: Thought and action are oriented toward goals. Functional perspectives have been advocated by many psychologists, but most have remained generalities, disappointingly weak for scientific analysis. Functional measurement of value provides an effective base for functional theory.

The functional perspective leads to a focus on phenomenology of everyday experience. Phenomenology is a priceless starting point, but it is inadequate in two respects. It can be obstinately mistaken, and it can do little with nonconscious processes. Cognitive algebra can help phenomenology find and resolve its mistakes, especially through measurement of the nonconscious.

Cognitive algebra can thus help transform everyday knowledge into science. Nearly all the concepts considered in integration theory are taken from everyday experience. The successes of the algebraic rules, together with their failures, are steps in transforming these phenomenological entities into scientific entities.

The integrationist approach has yielded new ways of thinking in many areas: memory, language, belief formation, judgment–decision, psychophysics, cognitive development, moral judgment, social attitudes, person cognition, and others. In part, this stems from analytical power of cognitive algebra. In part also, it stems from a foundation in structure of the internal world. With this shift to internal structure, many areas take on broader life and new vitality.

Cognitive algebra is not an end, but a new beginning. It can go beyond itself to help study nonalgebraic aspects of cognition. Indeed, the conceptual implications of cognitive algebra are in many ways more important than the quantitative capabilities, as itemized in the final section, *Beyond Cognitive Algebra*. The theory of information integration is incomplete in many ways, but it has considerable potential for analyzing structure of nonalgebraic cognition.

Chapter 13

UNIFIED THEORY

The theory of information integration, IIT, constitutes a unified, general theory. Its generality has appeared in the foregoing substantive chapters, which cover judgment–decision, functional memory, language processing, psychophysics, cognitive development, moral judgment, and social cognition. Its unity appears in the utility of three concepts, *purposiveness–value–information integration*, across all these domains. This unity appears further in similar modes of information processing across domains, most notably, modes of valuation and integration, especially in the form of cognitive algebra.

IIT has a primary concern with everyday thought and action. This entails a functional perspective, focusing on the goal-directed purposiveness of behavior. Primary concepts of the theory are taken from phenomenology, which provides both content and foundation for construction of scientific theory.

The unity and generality of IIT depend jointly on this functional perspective and on cognitive algebra. In the functional perspective, all thought and action are oriented toward goals. Goal directedness imposes a value axis of approach–avoidance that underlies functioning within all domains of psychology, from psychophysics to family interaction. Cognitive algebra makes the axiom of purposiveness effective through measurement of value. Cognitive algebra thus provides a cutting edge for functional theory. The phenomenology of everyday experience can be employed as a priceless starting point and an integral component in development of psychological science.

IIT is a working reality. It rests on an interlocking network of experimental studies within each domain covered in the foregoing chapters. Further interlocking appears in the cross-domain unity of concepts and methods.

INFORMATION INTEGRATION THEORY

Two basic concepts of IIT, as the paired Is indicate, are *information* and *integration*. The organism is a processor of information—signals utilized in pursuing purposes and goals. Initial processing of stimulus informers is required to construct goal-relevant values, the currency of purposiveness.

Further processing is required to integrate multiple informers into thought and action. This fundamental problem of multiple determination has received an effective solution in the form of cognitive algebra.

AXIOM OF PURPOSIVENESS

Purposiveness may be considered an axiom of psychology, for thought and action are basically goal oriented. Biological goals such as food are necessary to survival, and sensory–action systems have evolved for pursuing these goals. Social goals, especially with respect to status and offspring, become increasingly important in higher organisms. In human society, new classes of goals are found, in work, sports, religion, law, art, and science. Psychology thus requires a functional perspective, one that conceptualizes thought and action in terms of purposiveness.

Purposiveness has long been frowned on in scientific psychology, and with good reason, for it has suffered from teleological tautology. Purposiveness comes to be taken as the explanation as well as what is to be explained. Such reasoning underlies much discussion of need and motivation, as with motivational postulates in social–personality theory (Chapters 4 and 5). Such approaches are attractive because they point to important questions and promise answers. When scrutinized, however, their progress is seen to be circular. The concept of purposiveness thus remained a tantalizing closed door.

To unlock the promise of purposiveness requires a key. Such a key appears in the concept of value. Purposiveness imposes a one-dimensional representation on thought and action, manifested in approach and avoidance values of goals. Value embodies purposiveness, and can also serve a proper explanatory function. To turn value into a working key, however, requires a theory of measurement for psychological values. Such a functional measurement theory was developed with cognitive algebra. By solving this measurement problem, IIT provided a scientific key to purposiveness.

This functional measurement analysis may need emphasis because the language of purposiveness in IIT differs from other approaches. Traditional attempts to handle purposiveness have referred to needs within the organism or to incentives in the environment. In IIT, need and incentive are interactively represented in the concept of value. Motivation thus becomes manifest in value, and value becomes a means to analyze motivation.

A functional perspective leads naturally to a biosocial outlook. Theory construction must take account of the biosocial means with which goals are pursued. A primary means is motivation, conceptualized here in informational terms. At bottom, this information is biological, the evolutionary resultant of signal systems that facilitate goal attainment. At the human level, these biological bases are massively transformed through learning in society. Motivations, accordingly, are considered biosocial knowledge systems.

Functional perspectives have been employed by many previous writers. The biosocial outlook descends from Darwin, whose theories have recently had a renaissance. The concept of value, of course, has always been with us. What IIT contributes is a new way to capitalize on these concepts.

MULTIPLE DETERMINATION

Thought and action generally depend on multiple determinants. The same goal may have both positive and negative characteristics that need to be balanced off. Each positive and negative characteristic may itself have multiple aspects that need to be integrated to determine its value.

Here lies the fundamental problem of psychology. To predict behavior requires *synthesis* of multiple determinants, integrating them into a unitary response. To understand behavior requires *analysis* of multiple determinants, dis-integrating a unitary response to reveal its separate determinants. Synthesis and analysis are dual aspects of the fundamental problem of psychology.

How different theories handle—or fail to handle—synthesis and analysis conditions their focal concepts and sets bounds to their potential. Previous approaches have made little progress on the problem of synthesis. They have emphasized one kind of analysis, which seeks to identify certain kinds of concepts and processes. Without a dual capability for synthesis, this kind of analysis is too narrow for general theory.

> Previous approaches did not possess very good methods for analysis of stimulus integration. In the main, they had to bypass multiple causation [multiple determination] and develop issues and problems that could be studied with available tools. Naturally enough, the nature of theory was accommodated to these issues and these methods. Equally naturally, such approaches attained a conceptual existence and inertia that carried beyond their domain of usefulness.
>
> Conceptual orientations that lack effective methods for analysis of multiple causation are generally too narrow to permit growth of adequate theory. The need for theory that can handle multiple causation has appeared repeatedly in every empirical area that has been studied in this research program. Illustrative examples include continuous representations in semantic theory, additivity in decision theory, the psychophysical law, integrational capacity in children, and meaning-constancy in person perception. In all these areas, an integration-theoretical approach has led to restructuring of basic issues. (N. H. Anderson, *Foundations of Information Integration Theory.* Academic Press, 1981, p. 81.)

Without an integration theory, multiple determination must be treated empirically. Two variables can be manipulated jointly, and the resulting behavior treated as a two-variable, row × column table of data. Such tables can be useful for prediction—to the extent that the prediction situation is equivalent to that in which the data were collected. Change a single variable, the age of the subjects, their previous experience, the social context, and so on, and the table may become an irrelevant historical incident. As more variables are considered, the data table approach becomes exponentially more difficult. At best, this is an arduous path to knowledge. At worst, an arduous path into a morass.

Few investigators attempt a systematic data table approach, of course, but their combined efforts often amount to an unsystematic data table, as each adds some new variable to previous work. This is why the outcome of extended research inquiry so often seems more like disorder than order. This is why summary reviews so often conclude "it all depends"—on innumerable variables of task, stimulus materials, subjects, training, situation, and context.

Unified theory requires capability with both aspects of multiple determination, analysis and synthesis. Such dual capability has been developed with the theory of functional measurement in terms of the valuation and integration operations of cognitive algebra. This capability has been empirically fruitful.

COGNITIVE ALGEBRA AND FUNCTIONAL MEASUREMENT

Functional measurement, with its capability for measurement of values, opens a door to analysis of purposiveness. Value measurement, of course, has been controversial since the first attempts to measure psychophysical sensation well over a century ago. Value measurement is even more important in other psychological domains, as seen in previous chapters. But even simple sensations, such as loudness and grayness, have resisted true measurement.

Without a measurement theory, even the addition rule, almost the simplest form of multiple determination, could not be established. The many conjectures about algebraic rules of mind, which go back as far as Aristotle (Chapter 7), have thus remained conjectures. And most arguments for configurality and interaction, from the gestalt psychologists to contemporary theories in social–personality and in psycholinguistics, have also remained conjectural.

The path to success lay in a shift from valuation to integration. By good fortune, integration often obeys algebraic rules. This cognitive algebra solved the dual problems of value measurement and multiple determination. This functional measurement establishes the integration rule and the measurement scales simultaneously—lifting ourselves by our bootstraps.

A fundamentally new approach to psychological measurement is thus embodied in functional measurement theory. The foundation lies in algebraic structure of the internal world. Determining this structure was not simple. The averaging rule had to be unearthed and unraveled. Methodology for linear response had to be developed. Disagreements with other approaches had to be resolved in every area. The previous chapters, however, demonstrate the empirical value of this approach across many domains.

MEANING INVARIANCE AND **V–I** INDEPENDENCE

Meaning invariance is a primary implication of cognitive algebra. Observed parallelism, for example, is evidence both for an addition rule and for invariant informer values. The value of each informer is thus independent of which other informers it is combined with (see *Parallelism Theorem* in Chapter 2).

Meaning invariance provided a key to analysis of multiple determination. Context effects, in particular, are commonly interpreted in terms of bias, distortion, or other forms of meaning change and informer interaction. Such interpretations have been found incorrect in many cases when IIT was applied. What was taken as informer interaction was instead found to be noninteractive integration of information. This outcome has led to a different conceptual outlook in every field considered in the foregoing empirical chapters.

V–I independence is a related implication of cognitive algebra. The **V** and **I** operations can be separated, mathematically and psychologically, using functional measurement. The integration operation thus becomes a frame for measuring the outcome of the valuation operation. This independence makes effective the axiom of purposiveness by recognizing that values depend on momentary motivations and goals. Reflecting **V–I** independence, such value sensitivity can be handled with a few general integration rules.

Cognitive algebra is no easy road to knowledge. By addressing multiple determination, it shows how difficult it can be to understand and predict thought and action. It does, however, provide unique aid to the study of purposiveness. This opens up a new path for psychological science.

COGNITIVE THEORY

IIT follows a fundamental shift in strategy of inquiry—a shift from the external to the internal world. This shift was foreshadowed in *The Three Unobservables* of Figure 1.1. An integration function with algebraic structure allows a solution to all three unobservables. Structure of the internal world has thus provided a self-sufficient base for theory construction.

It is illuminating to scrutinize current theory and research with respect to the foregoing themes. Issues, concepts, and methods in every area have been constricted because of difficulties with multiple determinants. The conceptual base has been too narrow to allow growth of general theory. The continuing fragmentation between and within areas is both consequence and symptom of lack of capability with the dual problems of analysis and synthesis.

This too-narrow base can be seen in every area considered in this book. Most conceptual frameworks rely in essential ways on structure of the external world. This approach seems only sensible, and it is so useful that it came to determine the character of theory and method. It is too narrow, however, to solve the twin problems of value and multiple determination.

Cognitive algebra has provided a new way of thinking. This is bound up with the shift in strategy, from focus on the external world to focus on the internal world. This way of thinking has been effective, empirically and conceptually. This contrast in strategy is reviewed in the following sections for memory and language, judgment–decision, cognitive development, and perception.

MEMORY AND LANGUAGE

A functional conception of memory arises naturally from concern with purposiveness. Memory functions to subserve goal-directed thought and action. But memory is often not usable in its raw form; instead, memory must be processed to determine implications relative to operative goals. In such processing, past memory has a primary function in valuation of incoming information. These valuations are integrated in an operating memory for control of present thought and action. These integrations may in turn be stored for future use.

Functional memory differs from the traditional conception of memory as reproduction. Memory has been the subject of an enormous research enterprise, now into its second century. Yet virtually all this work has been governed by a monolithic conception of reproductive memory. This conception is characterized by its focus on accuracy in reproduction of given stimulus materials. A reproductive conception has limited relevance to the functions of memory in thought and action of everyday life.

One inadequacy of reproductive memory appears with valuation. Traditional memory theory lacks interest in or theory for measurement of value. Valuation may be a matter of taste, social, moral, or intellectual, to which the accuracy standard is irrelevant. A primary function of memory thus lies outside the scope of traditional memory theory.

A second inadequacy concerns integration of multiple determinants. In the functional memory view, much of long-term memory consists of integrated resultants from previous thought and action. Situational activation in long-term memory leads to further, online integration in operating memory. Neither kind of integration is generally amenable to the accuracy standard. With integration as with valuation, memory function and structure lie largely outside the scope of traditional memory theory.

Deep dissatisfaction with the progress of memory research has been expressed in recent times by some of the foremost workers in this field. One reaction has been to turn to studies of everyday memory. But this reaction, desirable in itself, remains trapped in the reproductive tradition.

A conceptual shift is needed. The conceptual framework that evolved with the reproductive orientation became fixated on the external world, represented in the accuracy criterion. Functional memory, in contrast, has primary concern with the internal world, as in the cited problems of valuation and integration. A functional approach thus seeks to integrate memory with its role in thought and action, especially social cognition and language processing. Memory is no longer considered an autonomous domain but part of functional cognition.

In language processing, memory functions both in valuation and integration. At each of many levels, separate linguistic and nonlinguistic stimuli have to be evaluated and integrated to determine overall meaning. Some of these integrations obey algebraic rules; this opens a new path for language analysis.

Meaning invariance is one implication of cognitive algebra. Meaning invariance, which appeared originally in person cognition, has been extended to general language processing. Meaning invariance is important for analyzing the structure and processing of information from memory and context.

Quantifiers, for example, have different effects in different contexts, a result often taken to imply that quantifier meaning depends on context. In the multiplication rule, however, quantifier meaning is context-invariant (e.g., Equations 1 of Chapters 10 and 12). Valuation and integration operators, V and I, were confounded in customary thinking. These operators were shown be distinct and independent through cognitive algebra. The different surface effects arise from the integration operation, not from change of meaning.

Meaning invariance is even more important with disambiguation, a pervasive process in understanding language. Disambiguation obeys a decision averaging rule in a number of tasks, ranging from phoneme perception to sentence understanding (Chapter 12). By virtue of V–I independence, this decision averaging rule can yield language parameters that are comparable across different kinds of language cues, including verbal and nonverbal.

Cognitive algebra provides a natural home for continuous semantic variables, replacing the common fiction of discreteness with the reality of continuous degree. Cognitive algebra thus provides a psychological foundation for fuzzy concepts, which can be well defined and measured.

Recent trends in psycholinguistics have emphasized the pervasive role of context, which conveys meaning not present in the literal communication. In particular, the listener must often attribute intention to the speaker to interpret a communication. Beyond syntax and semantics, therefore, lies a domain of pragmatics dealing with context and purpose.

Pragmatics thus leads into person cognition, as with attribution of intention. Current pragmatics, however, continues to be dominated by the accuracy standard—how correctly the listener interprets the speaker's intended meaning. But the listener's interpretation depends also on integration of prior information about the speaker, of general social stereotypes, and of the listener's desires and attitudes. These determinants cannot be understood in terms of accuracy standards. Pragmatics is a needed extension of traditional issues of syntax and semantics, but it requires a broader outlook. Theory of language—communication should be unified with theory of person cognition.

Two related points deserve consideration. First, speaker intention may not be well defined, even to the speaker. This fact has been obscured under the accuracy standard, which has been perpetuated by the hand-tailored examples customary in psycholinguistics. Second, the listener may have other goals besides understanding the speaker/communication. Thus, the listener may seek to judge the speaker's mood, intelligence, or dependability, for example, or amenability to some proposition. These goals are part of functional language processing, but hardly represented in conventional psycholinguistics.

Overall, information integration is important at every level of language processing. Some of these integrations obey algebraic rules, as has been shown with functional measurement theory. To demonstrate this, however, required a shift from externalist standards of accuracy to psychological structure in the internal world. This internal structure, especially in the form of algebraic rules, provides a new framework for the study of memory and language. This focus on internal structure is a necessary step toward development of general theory, unified with person cognition and judgment–decision.

JUDGMENT–DECISION THEORY

The judgment–decision field is foremost in recognizing multiple determination. Indeed, most approaches to theory construction have begun with algebraic rules: the rule of expected value, the Bayesian rule, multiattribute summation rules, and others. But effective analysis of these rules depends on capability for measuring subjective values. This measurement capability has been lacking in nearly all approaches. These approaches, accordingly, have made limited progress on either synthesis or analysis.

There is an algebra of judgment–decision, but it is cognitive, not normative. Whereas normative algebra was founded on structure of the external world, cognitive algebra is founded on structure of the internal world. Functional measurement theory thus solved the problem of *The Three Unobservables* (Chapter 1).

The measurement limitations of traditional approaches appear in the classical problem of subjective expected value. Some writers declared it insoluble. Others, relying on makeshift measurement, claimed support for a linear, additive model. With functional measurement theory, in contrast, the long-conjectured multiplication rule was put on solid ground.

A deeper obstacle to judgment–decision theory was the adoption of a normative rather than a cognitive framework. Thought and action were interpreted with reference to external standards of optimality. This normative framework is too narrow to accommodate the phenomena or allow general theory to develop.

Across the various areas surveyed in Chapter 10, cognitive algebra sometimes agrees, sometimes disagrees with normative algebra.

Of special interest is the ubiquitous averaging rule. It implies that adding a desirable good can decrease desirability of the whole—nonprobabilistic disproof of the sure-thing axiom, once a cornerstone for judgment–decision theory. At the same time, the decision averaging rule provides a viable alternative to the successive failures to press the normative Bayesian rule into a cognitive mold.

The strong grip of normative thinking appears in its self-perpetuating tendencies. Thus, discrepancies from the normative models, called "biases," were often misconstrued as genuine psychological phenomena. In a functional approach, the more or less arbitrary normative standard is replaced with a biosocial standard. The efficacy of this functional approach is indicated in the several sections of Chapter 10 entitled *Cognitive and Normative*.

Judgment and decision underlie thought and action in every domain. The normative approach, however, could not resolve the central problems of value measurement and multiple determination. Cognitive algebra, in contrast, has done well in many demanding tests.

The importance of nonalgebraic cognition is recognized in IIT (see *Beyond Cognitive Algebra* at the end of this chapter). In particular, cognitive algebra has emphasized operating memory and other aspects of assemblage, and can help in their analysis. Information integration theory thus offers a general approach to judgment–decision.

COGNITIVE DEVELOPMENT

Commonsense physics was pioneered by Piaget as a primary form of knowledge. Piaget relied on structure of the external world, claiming that the end state of cognitive development was isomorphism between internal and external worlds. Piaget was centrally concerned with integration; his standard choice task requires attribute integration for correct choice. IIT thus has a fundamental commonality with Piagetian theory.

But Piaget had no way to diagnose integration rules. All-or-none choice data, together with verbal justification, were his basic methods. These led to numerous important empirical discoveries that make Piaget one of the great psychologists of all time (see *Homage to Piaget* at end of Chapter 8). It also led to egregious blunders in theory.

For commonsense physics, his main concern, Piaget presented two explicit integration rules, both seriously incorrect. At younger ages, up to about 6 years, Piaget claimed that children centered on single attributes, quite unable to integrate two attributes. In fact, developmental integration studies have shown good integrational capacity as early as 3^+ years.

At the adult stage of formal operations, Piaget claimed that people have internalized the physical rule of the external world. Under this assumption of isomorphism—the linchpin of Piagetian theory—structure in the external world is the essential template for structure of the internal world.

Isomorphism was shown incorrect with functional measurement, which provided valid assessment of structure of the internal world. This approach demonstrated nonisomorphic structure of cognition. Also, it contributed a more powerful developmental methodology.

Developmental integration theory is thus very different from Piagetian theory. The concept of assemblage replaces Piaget's fundamental stage conception, which asserts that development proceeds through successive stages of qualitatively different character. Instead, assemblage theory considers that thought and action are generally heterogeneous in quality. Intuitive and symbolic thought, in particular, may function jointly and cooperatively.

Developmental integration theory also yields a unified treatment of knowledge of the external world and of the social world. Piaget's stage conception did not apply to the moral–social world, which thus lay outside his primary theoretical framework. Both worlds, however, involve the twin problems of value and multiple determination, and cognitive algebra applies to both.

INTEGRATION PSYCHOPHYSICS AND PERCEPTION

Consciousness tells us we have direct contact with the external world. Our internal world of objects, motions, and visual splendor seems direct perception of external reality. We fail to appreciate the senses, which code the external world into neural impulses and decode these neural impulses to construct our internal world. How the senses do this is the concern of psychophysics.

Psychophysics has wrestled with one question for well over a century: What is the algebraic relation between psychological sensation and the physical energy in the external stimulus? This psycho–physical law, as it was called, was seen as the first step toward understanding how the senses construct the internal world. Underlying this question is a preconception that structure of the internal world is derivative from structure of the external world.

This quest for the psychophysical law was doomed from the start because it ignored, almost denied, multiple determination. Instead, sensation was conceptualized as a function of single physical variables. This one-variable approach seemed to follow from the specificity of certain senses to single physical dimensions, as with the dependence of loudness and brightness on physical intensity of sound and light.

As one consequence of this one-variable limitation, classical psychophysics could not solve its own central problem of measuring sensation. Solving this problem required an integration psychophysics. A conceptual shift was needed, a shift from psychophysical law to psychological law, that is, to the integration function. Establishing the algebraic structure of these psychological laws finally resolved the problem of measuring sensation.

The other branch of psychophysics, namely, sensory psychophysics, is a flourishing, productive field, as noted at the end of Chapter 9. Sensory psychophysics, however, largely eschews the psychophysical law. This view is harmonious with the present integration psychophysics, which has argued that the concept of psychophysical law has been a historic misdirection.

From a functional standpoint, the branch of psychophysics that developed around the psychophysical law has a more serious inadequacy. It substantially isolated itself from the larger field of perception. Thus, its tendency to brush aside context effects flowed from its underlying conception of psychophysical law as a function of a single variable.

To the organism, however, the entire stimulus field is potentially relevant, not just some single psychophysical dimension. Perception based on the entire stimulus field is both common and useful. Integration psychophysics thus emphasizes perceptual more than sensory aspects of psychophysics, as shown in experimental studies presented in Chapter 9.

This functional inadequacy of the conceptual framework of psychophysical law appears also in the relative neglect of affect. To the organism, sensory affect often has greater importance than sensory intensity. In this functional view, taste and odor, temperature, pain, sex, and other affective senses take on importance comparable to vision and audition.

Integration psychophysics reemphasizes the shift from the external world to the internal world. The traditional psychophysical reliance on structure in the external world, like that in memory, language, and judgment–decision, was stymied by its need for psychological measurement. Only by shifting to structure of the internal world was this measurement problem resolved.

STRATEGY OF INQUIRY

Cognitive theory requires a broader horizon than has been recognized in mainstream cognitive psychology. Behaviorism, with commendable concern for empirically grounded concepts and conclusions, imposed severe restrictions on what could be studied. The cognitive movement was a step toward broadening the behaviorist horizon. It was a limited step, however, still ignoring most phenomena of everyday life.

This narrowness of mainstream cognitive psychology has appeared in all the foregoing areas. Much of this narrowness has been localized around two issues: functional perspective and multiple determination.

The functional perspective focuses on purposiveness and affect, both more or less passed by in mainstream cognitive psychology. Purposiveness and affect lead to a functional conception of memory, for example, qualitatively different from the traditional reproductive conception of memory.

Multiple determination involves integration operators, including the operators of cognitive algebra. Analysis of multiple determination cannot get far without capability for psychological measurement. Establishing even the simple addition rule depends on capability for measuring value on true psychological scales. Psychological measurement theory, however, is largely unknown terrain to mainstream cognitive psychology, which is accordingly limited in its capabilities for handling the fundamental problem of integration.

The narrowness of mainstream cognitive psychology also appears in its neglect of social cognition (Chapters 4–7). From a functional perspective, and from a cognitive perspective as well, social cognition would seem more fertile ground for development of cognitive theory than currently popular issues such as memory, attention, reaction time, and electrical brain potential. Indeed, social cognition is basic in language processing (Chapter 12) and was the origin of the functional conception of memory (Chapter 11).

The foregoing contrasts point up the macro–micro distinction that characterizes many differences between the functional and mainstream approaches to cognition. The functional focus on purposiveness leads to macrostructural, molar analysis, with concepts taken from everyday thought and action. These include pride of accomplishment, shame of failure, feelings of satisfaction and unfairness, gratitude, affection and resentment, right and wrong, attributions of traits and knowledge to self and others, as well as hope, expectancy, risk, and cost, taste, cold, and fatigue, and diverse pains and pleasures. The mainstream approach, in contrast, is heavily concerned with microstructure, far removed from phenomenal experience.

The macro approach can progress without undue concern for underlying microstructure. This claim follows the unitization principle of Chapter 1, and is validated in the success of cognitive algebra. In much analysis of memory, for example, it is only necessary to know what memory achieves, not how. For much of functional memory, accordingly, micro issues can be passed by.

The same point appears in cognitive algebra. For many purposes, it is enough to know the algebraic form of the integration operator, as revealed in observable thought and action, regardless of what mechanism (Chapter 2) underlies the integration. For many purposes, similarly, it is enough to be able to measure operative values, regardless of the detailed valuation processing.

One pertinent application is to schema theory, for which cognitive algebra has provided the only exact analysis. Only by passing over micro questions was cognitive algebra placed on a firm base. Now it constitutes a macro level of description and explanation that is in many ways self-sufficient.

Indeed, it is the molecular, micro approach that comes under question. The so-called cognitive revolution is still promissory. Beneath the bustle and glitter of its promises, they remain unfulfilled. Interesting work is being done on particular problems, but general theory continues to be a matter of hope and faith. There is nothing, it seems fair to say, comparable in scope, precision, and empirical foundation, with the theory of information integration.

The micro and macro approaches can help each other. Microanalyses are desirable for deeper understanding of the macro concepts of functional cognition. Macro concepts and results, on the other hand, can serve as boundary conditions on microanalysis, for micro theory must obey these boundary constraints at the macro level. The same point appeared in the analogous molar–molecular distinction of Chapters 1 and 12. For this purpose, however, the micro approach should become more cognizant of the functional perspective. Without addressing problems of affect and value, in particular, microanalysis cannot hope to rise to the macro level of thought and action.

Only at a macro level, moreover, can unified, general theory be expected. The great emphasis on microanalysis reflects a taken-for-granted reductionist view, which seeks an elementalist foundation for theory. But perception and sensory psychophysics, by far the most developed in microanalysis, give rather strong testimony against unified micro theory, even within a single sensory system. Despite its continual attractiveness, the elementalistic orientation deserves the skepticism that befits its disappointing historical record. The phenomenological macro approach adopted in IIT, in contrast, has had some success in working toward unified theory.

SOCIAL COGNITION

Social cognition has notable advantages for cognitive theory. Social cognition is basic to everyday thought and action and is extensively developed over a lifetime of experience. It is a primary locus of purposiveness and thus a primary concern for functional theory.

INFORMATION INTEGRATION

Information integration is basic in social cognition; multiple determinants underlie virtually all social thought and action. This central fact has been obscured, however, because most theories lack effective conceptualization of information as well as effective methods for studying valuation and integration of informers. This matter was illustrated with the seven issues of information integration in the foundation studies of person cognition in Chapter 4. These studies led to a unified theory that generalized far beyond person cognition.

A key finding was meaning invariance. To introspection, personality traits in a person description interact and change meaning. This intuition is so compelling that it continues to thrive three decades after the first of many disproofs. The success of the averaging rule, however, demonstrated meaning invariance; the introspective belief in meaning change, compelling though it is, was found to be a cognitive illusion.

Because of its foundation in information integration, IIT may seem stark compared to traditional approaches to social cognition, such as begin with specific motivational assumptions, for example, or with personality traits and typologies. These traditional approaches are intuitively attractive; they present high face validity. Primitive concepts in IIT, informers and information integration, in particular, lack similar intuitive appeal.

Face validity, however, is ultimately not relevant. Theoretical validity is needed. IIT has provided theoretical validity, but not the traditional approaches (see, e.g., *Unified Attitude Theory*, pp. 150–157).

This contrast was illustrated with the cognitive consistency theories in Chapter 4. Most began by assuming that people are driven by motivation for cognitive consistency. Their primary implication was that informers will change one another's meanings so as to reduce inconsistencies among them. This implication was shown to be incorrect by the finding of meaning invariance in the first study of the averaging model. Such conceptual implications, not merely algebraic precision, are why the averaging model is important.

The empirical failure of these cognitive consistency theories was matched with weakness in their concepts and methods. Cognitive consistency involves information integration in an essential way; an informer only becomes inconsistent by virtue of attempted integration with other informers. The consistency theories, however, lacked analytical power to study information integration. Hence they could not even attain clear understanding of the concept of cognitive consistency. Similar shortcomings apply to person–situation interactionist theories and contextualist theories.

Of course, much useful work has been and is being done within traditional approaches to social cognition. There are many domains to study, including person memory, attribution, attitude, roles, motivation, morality, self-concepts, psychodynamics, and many important problems within each domain. Recent decades have witnessed notable advances in conceptual understanding and in methodological soundness. Nevertheless, study of these problems has been handicapped by lack of general theory. These domains are compartmentalized from one another, and further compartmentalization holds within each domain.

A unified approach across all domains of social cognition has been provided by IIT. To attain this generality required a conceptual shift in which the basic theoretical concepts became information, valuation, and integration. Through functional measurement of value, this conceptual shift yielded an effective grip on the axiom of purposiveness.

Moreover, all the foregoing domains of general cognition appear in social cognition. Judgment–decision underlies all social thought and action. Social memory is basically functional memory. Language is heavily social, and essentially so, as shown by the rise of pragmatics. Social cognition is thus a prime domain for cognitive theory in a functional mode.

ATTRIBUTION

Attribution processes are common in social cognition, with behavior of another person or the self being attributed to some personality trait, predisposition, motive, mood, or other cause. Social attribution is par excellence a matter of information integration. This is clear in the attempts to conceptualize attribution in terms of schemas, such as the behavior–motivation–ability schemas.

By their own admission, however, previous attempts to develop a *theory* of social attribution have been stunted. A new way of thinking was required, one that could effectively analyze information integration. IIT provided a beginning, illustrated with the schema algebra of Chapter 5.

Attribution processes pervade the social–personal world. Recent work in psycholinguistics has revealed the importance in social communication of attributions about knowledge that others do or do not possess (Chapter 12). Self-attribution is prominent in psychodynamics of the ego (see third following section) and basic to being a person.

Outside the social realm, attribution is also important. A canonical problem in judgment–decision theory is to use available informers to make causal inferences about the true state of the world, as with the decision averaging model of Chapters 10 and 12. Much of perception and psychophysics, similarly, involves attributions from sensory informers to the external world (Chapter 9). Attribution about the external world is also fundamental in cognitive development, as in cognitive analogues of physical laws (Chapter 8).

Common to all these domains is information integration. Integrationist conceptualizations can be effective, as shown by experimental applications in the cited chapters. In particular, algebraic attribution schemas, previously conjectural in all the cited domains, have become testable and, in some cases, established reality. A general theory of attribution thus seems a realistic goal.

ATTITUDE

The concept of *attitude* has long been considered fundamental in the social-psychological field. Most social reactions seem to rest upon some attitude: liberal–conservative attitudes in politics, attitudes about right, wrong, and in-between, about women's roles and women's clothes, attitudes about crime, health, the environment, and diverse social issues from abortion and alcohol to the underclasses, are a few of the many that govern our thoughts and actions.

Information integration is central in attitude theory, both in learning of attitudes and in their functioning. Attitudes are a form of functional memory, containing stored outcomes of past integrations. Attitudes are thus a primary form of social learning. Attitudes function in operating memory for present thought and action through valuation and assemblage operations. Thus, they provide an adaptive, efficient means for guiding goal-oriented behavior.

Integration theory of attitudes differs from most approaches in several ways. Foremost is the conceptualization of attitude as a knowledge system instead of the common view of attitude as a one-dimensional evaluative reaction. Such evaluative reactions are a form of attitude function. They reflect the axiom of purposiveness. This form of attitude functioning is represented in the valuation operation of IIT.

But these one-dimensional reactions are not the attitude, only specific attitudinal responses, conditioned by the situation. IIT implies that attitude proper is a knowledge system (see, e.g., *Construction Principle* in Chapter 1).

A second difference between integration attitude theory and other attitude theories concerns motivation. Other approaches typically base themselves on assumptions about one or another particular motivation. These particular motivations have intuitive appeal and point toward important problems, but they led to fragmented, compartmentalized approaches (Chapter 5). At bottom, their explanatory power is mainly circular because of lack of measurement theory for motivation and value. A noncircular approach became possible with the discovery of a cognitive algebra of attitudinal reactions.

The idea of a cognitive algebra of attitudes has been rather popular. This idea concurred with the definition of attitudes as one-dimensional evaluative reactions. Various addition or summation rules were attempted, but these attempts were inconclusive because they lacked a theory of psychological measurement. Without a measurement theory, the addition and summation rules were untestable conjecture. In fact, they turned out to be false alleys.

Functional measurement theory showed that an exact algebraic rule did indeed govern many attitudinal responses. This rule was not addition or summation, however, but averaging, which is qualitatively different. The basic integration issues studied in person cognition in Chapter 4 appeared also in attitude theory—and they were resolvable using the same concepts and methods. These two domains of social cognition were thus unified.

Attitudes are as fundamental in general cognition as in social cognition. Attitudes are sources of values in judgment–decision across many domains. Attitudes are primary contents of learning–memory, and attitudinal responses are equally primary in operating memory. Outside social psychology, however, attitudes have been utterly neglected. This neglect stems in part from the predilection in mainstream cognitive psychology for issues and levels of analysis that move ever farther away from everyday thought and action, with little concern whether this is following a will-o'-the-wisp.

The conception of attitudes as knowledge systems embodies the axiom of purposiveness and helps understand its substantive representation. Integration theory offers a new way of thinking about attitudes, made effective through functional measurement. In this functional approach, attitude and judgment–decision are unified as a base for cognitive theory of everyday life.

AFFECT

Affect is the heart's blood of cognition. Positive and negative affect are vital in the control mechanisms for goal approach and avoidance. The affective senses, taste, temperature, pain, and others, continuously provide information for control of action. Through the diverse neural organizations of different senses, Nature utilizes one sovereign principle of affect as a universal means for survival of individual and species.

The principle of affect is variously extended in the person. In part, of course, this is amplification of sensory affect, as in likes and dislikes for food and sex. Nonsensory kinds of affect also appear, including parental care, friendship, admiration, jealousy, envy, aspiration, and joy.

Other extensions of the principle of affect appear throughout society. Socialized affects are prominent in morality, for example, and in politics. Morality is linked with self-esteem through pride, shame, and other self-affects, and with knowledge systems of right and wrong. Politics is also linked with moral knowledge systems, as well as with self-fulfillment and with blame, a pervasive social attribution. Such affects make person and society possible.

Affect, given its ubiquity in cognition and its function as a sovereign principle, should be prominent in general theory construction. On the whole, however, affect has had a Cinderella role with even less recognition than Cinderella herself. The most prominent attribution theories have deliberately avoided affect. Where affect is recognized, its nature is typically obscured. Traditional attitude theory, for example, seems to accord affect a central role as evaluative response, but this has been considered a response readiness directly connected to overt behavior, with minimal concern for its affective nature. The needs commonly postulated in attitude theories seem largely de-affected tendencies. Similarly, the stage theories of morality de-affect moral conflict into principled reasoning, losing much of the essential phenomena.

The utilitarian, Jeremy Bentham, thus stands out with his assumption of a pleasure–pain calculus as the foundation of his treatise, *Principles of Morals and Legislation*. Bentham gave detailed consideration to problems of measuring pleasure and pain, but his formulation could not advance far because methods for actual measurement were not forthcoming. This issue reappears in modern judgment–decision theory, one descendant of utilitarianism, which still relies largely on make-do methods of measurement (Chapter 10). This allows some progress on various practical applications, but it foregoes all hope of developing general theory.

Unified theory of affect seems possible if different affects follow similar integration rules, as present evidence suggests. There is much more to affect than integration rules, of course, but these rules provide a grip on an amorphous area. In particular, they can go beyond unsatisfying typologies to measure affects, thereby helping to establish them as scientific concepts.

PSYCHODYNAMICS OF EVERYDAY LIFE

The functional perspective looks to the psychodynamics of everyday life, a phrase chosen to contrast with Freud's psychopathology of everyday life. One difference between the two lies in the role of consciousness. To Freud, the ego defense mechanisms were unconscious. Much of everyday personality, however, is conscious. In making excuses, a prominent form of ego defense, people are both conscious and voluble.

Many other phenomena of everyday life are also accessible to consciousness, at least in part. These include various kinds of affection; other-esteem, positive and negative; self-confidence and diffidence; social obligation, honesty, fairness, and justice; winning and losing; envy—jealousy—faultfinding; conflict relations from bargaining in family and workplace to interpersonal negotiation for social status and roles; and many more.

Of special interest are phenomena that depend on relations with others, as with status; these are concrete issues for bringing interactionist approaches to personality down to earth. Also important are affective reactions such as happiness, sorrow, grief, anxiety, failure, dejection, pride, and hope.

As this partial enumeration indicates, psychodynamics of everyday life agrees with Adler and Horney much more than Freud. Freud's theory treats phenomenology mainly as darkly disguised symptoms of unconscious reality. Thus it misses most of personality. Freud's fixation on sex is replaced by better appreciation of other kinds of social relations and a more enlightened view of personality. A dominant theme is that of Adler, who stressèd the person's search for self-esteem and mastery of the environment.

Analysis of the nonconscious is also important; psychodynamics cannot be understood solely in terms of conscious manifestations. There is nothing mysterious about this; nonconscious determinants operate even in simple psychophysical tasks (Chapter 9). Determinants of functional memory may also be nonconscious (Chapter 11). Cognitive algebra can, under certain conditions, define and measure the nonconscious. The nonconscious can thus be put on an experimental basis, an essential tool for understanding consciousness (see also Note 10 of Chapter 4). The present conception of nonconscious thus differs from Freud's conception of unconscious.

The "self," in IIT, is construed in informational terms as a functional complex of knowledge systems. Attitudes as knowledge systems are thus defining characteristics of each individual self; attributions and affective reactions are functions of the self in operation. Such reactions can be analyzed with functional measurement under certain conditions, as illustrated in previous discussions of attitudes, attributions, and affective reactions. Within its limitations, this integration approach provides analytical capabilities not previously available. It does so, moreover, as part of a framework in which psychodynamics is an integral part of general cognition.

PERSON

A functional perspective has a natural focus: the person in everyday thought and action. This focus provides a unifying framework. Traditional areas of psychology, such as memory, cognitive development, and attitudes, have studied fragments of the person. Each area has been attacked opportunistically, without guidance from a unifying framework. This work has yielded many interesting results, but they are unconnected and noncongruent. We cannot hope to piece these fragments together to form a general theory.

A functional approach to the person has been exemplified with the four preceding concepts: psychodynamics, affect, attitude, and attribution. These concepts, and others, are not separate compartments of the person, but are inter-related in process and function. They need to be studied in a unified manner to achieve general theory.

This emphasis on the social person, it may be noted, is not intended to slur over the deep importance of animal psychology. Animals are functional systems with tremendous interest. By the biosocial heuristic, they can tell us much about ourselves, especially about biosocial knowledge systems of motivation. This animal–human unity is recognized in the many animal studies cited in introductory texts.

In theory of the person, however, unity is lacking. The roadblock is multiple determination. Personality theorists generally agree, even insist, on the com-plexity of thought and action, that is, on the multiple determinants of person and situation. It follows that any theory of personality must address and resolve this problem of multiple determination. Unable to surmount this roadblock, per-sonality theories have scattered in many directions. One path for unification is to treat personality traits like attitudes, specifically, as knowledge systems.

Knowledge systems are primary components of the person. It may seem odd to consider the trait of honesty, for example, as a knowledge system, but this accords with a functional perspective. *Honesty* is a cognitive system that under-lies thought and action in diverse situations of everyday social life (see Note 5 of Chapter 1). What is considered wrong in one situation, be it omission of relevant facts, lying, promise breaking, or theft, may be considered justifiable, even commendable, in another situation. Honesty usually refers to a conflict between self-interest and social obligation, both of which typically have multi-ple aspects, positive and negative. Resolution of such conflict thus depends on multiple determinants, not on some absolute rule about right and wrong. Tradi-tional personality theories, unable to solve the problem of multiple determina-tion, were unable to pursue the primary direction of inquiry.

This conception of traits derives from integration theory of attitudes. Just as attitude as knowledge system differs qualitatively from one-dimensional evalua-tive reactions, so also trait as knowledge system differs from traditional views of traits as unitary and one-dimensional. In hindsight, the dimensional view is seen to be a partial truth, certainly useful, but treated as a whole truth, for which it was critically insufficient. Extensions to multidimensional representations, as in factor analysis, further obscured the person. Understanding personality requires beginning with the functional nature of thought and action.

This integration perspective agrees with approaches that treat thought and action as interaction between person and social situation. The interactionist position is well-taken, but interactionist progress has been disappointing. Although multiple determination is basic to person–situation interaction, interactionists have not developed effective methods for analyzing multiple determinants (Note 17 of Chapter 5). Some interactionists even doubt that general psychological laws are attainable (see *Promise and Disillusion*, pp. 180*f*).

But general laws are attainable. Traits as knowledge systems underlie reactions in particular situations, and some of these reactions follow algebraic rules, just as with attitudes. Order and law cannot be expected at the surface level of behavior because of the multiplicity of situational factors and because these must be refracted through the knowledge systems of each individual.

There is order and law, however, at the integration stage. Cognitive algebra resolves the idiographic objection that general laws are precluded by the fact of individual differences. Values indeed differ across individuals—and across time and place for the same individual. But values are parameters in the integration rules. The rules themselves appear generally, in every substantive area. Cognitive algebra thus unifies idiographic reality with nomothetic law.

Attempts to construct personality theory must take the whole person as a unifying framework. Person is characterized not only by traits, but also by attitudes, affect, motivation, and memory. Characterization of person especially includes function, as with attribution, roles, and psychodynamics.

Experimental analysis can be usefully applied in all these areas, as illustrated in previous chapters. Such experimental analysis may be pursued at the level of the individual person, as in Figure 1.2, especially with personal design. Within its various limitations, personal design can bring some of the power of experimental analysis to bear on personality theory.

This approach also helps unify social–personality with general cognitive psychology. Person can be studied in a unified manner because similar processes of valuation and integration underlie all aspects of functioning. This unity extends to all cognition. These commonalities become clear in the present functional orientation.

In this way, as said previously, the concept of person constitutes a prime base for cognitive theory. Not only does person unify diverse areas of psychology, but it reveals them in new light, as with affect, memory, and social–cognitive development. In this functional perspective, psychology focuses on what many think should be its primary concern—the study of phenomenal experience and purposiveness in everyday thought and action.

SOCIETY

IIT takes a unified approach to the person in society. This began in Chapter 4, which gave a theoretical account of seven problems of person cognition. This theory has generalized to many other domains of social cognition, illustrated in Chapter 5 with attitudes, attribution, and group dynamics, in Chapter 6 with social development, and in Chapter 7 with moral judgment. Individual–society relations are implicit and explicit in all these domains. All have their existence and their function in the person in society.

A number of theories begin from the conception that person and society exist through mutual interaction. This idea was prominent in William James' treatment of the self and was propounded as a base for sociology by Cooley, Mead, and others. This blossomed into sociological schools of symbolic interaction, which sought to replace tables of sociological statistics with discussion of social symbols, including objects such as status symbols and national flags, events such as election campaigns and sports, and language, as the locus of socialization and social functioning. Individual–society symbolic interaction highlights social processes that psychologists mostly take for granted and neglect.

Sociologists, however, think in societal terms. Many are averse to psychological concepts. Sociological conceptualizations have been more or less alien to cognition. Attitudes, for example, a prime outcome and a prime determinant of symbolic interaction, are little acknowledged in sociology. The same holds for various other concepts of social psychology. Without roots in social cognition, the symbolic interactionist approach cannot flourish.

This need for interactive analysis of person and society is exemplified with moral development. Moral systems are essential in social functioning. They represent a great societal construction, ever continuing. They are a fine example of symbolic interaction. But sociology, although far ahead of psychology in family studies, has been far behind in concern with moral development. Although moral knowledge systems develop through family and society, they can only be understood at the individual cognitive level.

Experimental analysis of individual social cognition is essential as a foundation for sociology. Moral thought and action are in part amenable to experimental analysis at the individual level, as shown by the cited studies of moral algebra. Similar analysis is possible for roles, both intra- and interpersonal, as well as for attitude, attribution, and, of course, many affects and self-concepts.

Such experimental analysis is feasible in all social sciences: anthropology, economics, history, law, political science, and religion, as well as psychology and sociology. In each of these fields, IIT offers capability for experimental analysis within the value and knowledge systems of individual persons. Experimental analysis has obvious and strong limitations, of course, but it can provide a critical complement to observational data for theory construction in each social science.

PSYCHOLOGY AS SCIENCE

The goal of establishing psychology as a science has motivated innumerable workers, who have striven to discover general laws of thought and action. Much has been learned. Our understanding of the psychological world has increased steadily in breadth and depth. Fields as far apart as developmental psychology, judgment–decision, and language have undergone major transformation in the last two decades. The present time has unique potential as new phenomena are opened to investigation and old phenomena come under new scrutiny. Future generations will never have such opportunities as lie before us today. Future workers will look back on our era of boundless opportunity as

THE GOLDEN AGE OF PSYCHOLOGY.

PSYCHOLOGICAL LAW

General laws, however, have been lacking. General laws seem the premier characteristic of a science, but psychology compares poorly with chemistry or biology. This lack is everywhere visible in the extreme fragmentation in psychology. The different areas covered in the foregoing chapters have had little interaction; further fragmentation continues within each area. The more that is learned, the farther off general theory seems to recede.

Cognitive algebra is an exception. These algebraic rules are general laws of cognition. They hold throughout psychology. They provide a foundation for unified, general theory—general in its applicability across nearly all areas of psychology—unified in applying the same concepts and methods across all these areas. This approach is incomplete in major ways, but it is unified and general in concept and application. It is similarly unified in empirical support, a case of cumulative science.

The unity of cognitive algebra rests on the deeper unity of the functional perspective adopted in the theory of information integration. The person is unified in function, not fragmented by the boundary lines of academic areas and research traditions. This functional unity appears in the twin operations of valuation and integration, which underlie thought and action in every area. By a blessing of Nature, some of these integration processes can be represented as exact laws. This cognitive algebra provides a means to measure value and exploit the axiom of purposiveness.

The work on cognitive algebra covered in this book is a beginning. It is only a beginning, it is true, but it is a true beginning. It opens onto a new horizon.

BEYOND COGNITIVE ALGEBRA

Cognitive algebra has provided a foundation for unified, general theory. These studies have led to new ways of thinking in all the cited areas of psychology— conceptual implications no less important than the algebraic rules themselves. A partial itemization of these conceptual implications follows.

- Unified framework based on functional conception of information.
- Axiom of purposiveness placed on scientific base.
- Foundation of theory in structure of internal world.
- Phenomenology of everyday life incorporated into cognitive theory.
- Meaning invariance in person cognition—and in psycholinguistics.
- Independence of valuation and integration operators, **V** and **I**.
- Functional conception of memory, instead of standard reproductive view.
- Operating memory for online assemblage of thought and action.
- Context-cognizant approach to psycholinguistics.
- Definition of continuous semantic variables and fuzzy concepts.
- Normative to cognitive shift in judgment–decision theory.
- Unification of social and nonsocial attribution.
- Conceptualization of attitudes and traits as knowledge systems.
- Conceptualization of primacy–recency as serial integration.
- Cognitive–social structure of moral judgment.
- Nonstage view of moral development as continuous process.
- Assemblage alternative to Piagetian theory of knowledge.
- Integration psychophysics–welcoming context effects.
- Psychological law replaces psychophysical law.
- Affect and emotion integral to cognition.
- Measurement definition of nonconscious sensation and emotion.
- Motivations as biosocial knowledge systems.
- Nomothetic–idiographic unity and personal design.
- Information integration theory as tool for all social sciences.

Similar ideas have been considered by many previous workers, and the present approach is indebted to them in innumerable ways. These ideas deserve listing, however, to dispel the feeling that cognitive algebra is narrowly quantitative. On the contrary, cognitive algebra is more important for its qualitative, conceptual implications than for quantitative consequences.

Development of these conceptual implications is well along in some empirical domains, barely begun in others. In each domain, however, cognitive algebra goes beyond itself to be a guide and aide to unified, general theory.

References

Abele, A., & Petzold, P. (1994). How does mood operate in an impression formation task? An information integration approach. *European Journal of Social Psychology, 24*, 173-187.

Abelson, R. P., Aronson, E., McGuire, W. J., Newcomb, T. M., Rosenberg, M. J., & Tannenbaum, P. H. (Eds.). (1968). *Theories of cognitive consistency: A sourcebook.* Chicago: Rand McNally.

Adams, J. S. (1965). Inequity in social exchange. In L. Berkowitz (Ed.), *Advances in experimental social psychology* (Vol. 2, pp. 267-299). New York: Academic Press.

Anderson, N. H. (1959a). An analysis of sequential dependencies. In R. R. Bush & W. K. Estes (Eds.), *Studies in mathematical learning theory* (pp. 248-264). Stanford, CA: Stanford University Press.

Anderson, N. H. (1959b). Test of a model for opinion change. *Journal of Abnormal and Social Psychology, 59*, 371-381.

Anderson, N. H. (1960). Effect of first-order conditional probability in a two-choice learning situation. *Journal of Experimental Psychology, 59*, 73-93.

Anderson, N. H. (1961). Two learning models for responses measured on a continuous scale. *Psychometrika, 26*, 391-403.

Anderson, N. H. (1962a). Application of an additive model to impression formation. *Science, 138*, 817-818.

Anderson, N. H. (1962b). On the quantification of Miller's conflict theory. *Psychological Review, 69*, 400-414.

Anderson, N. H. (1963). Comparison of different populations: Resistance to extinction and transfer. *Psychological Review, 70*, 162-179.

Anderson, N. H. (1964a). An evaluation of stimulus sampling theory: Comments on Professor Estes' paper. In A. W. Melton (Ed.), *Categories of human learning* (pp. 129-144). New York: Academic Press.

Anderson, N. H. (1964b). Linear models for responses measured on a continuous scale. *Journal of Mathematical Psychology, 1*, 121-142.

Anderson, N. H. (1964c). Test of a model for number-averaging behavior. *Psychonomic Science, 1*, 191-192.

Anderson, N. H. (1965a). Averaging versus adding as a stimulus-combination rule in impression formation. *Journal of Experimental Psychology, 70*, 394-400.

Anderson, N. H. (1965b). Primacy effects in personality impression formation using a generalized order effect paradigm. *Journal of Personality and Social Psychology, 2*, 1-9.

Anderson, N. H. (1967). Averaging model analysis of set-size effect in impression formation. *Journal of Experimental Psychology, 75*, 158-165.

Anderson, N. H. (1968a). A simple model for information integration. In R. P. Abelson, E. Aronson, W. J. McGuire, T. M. Newcomb, M. J. Rosenberg, & P. H. Tannenbaum (Eds.), *Theories of cognitive consistency: A sourcebook* (pp. 731-743). Chicago: Rand McNally.

Anderson, N. H. (1968b). Averaging of space and number stimuli with simultaneous presentation. *Journal of Experimental Psychology, 77,* 383-392.

Anderson, N. H. (1969). Application of a model for numerical response to a probability learning situation. *Journal of Experimental Psychology, 80,* 19-27.

Anderson, N. H. (1970). Functional measurement and psychophysical judgment. *Psychological Review, 77,* 153-170.

Anderson, N. H. (1971). Integration theory and attitude change. *Psychological Review, 78,* 171-206.

Anderson, N. H. (1972a). Cross-task validation of functional measurement. *Perception & Psychophysics, 12,* 389-395.

Anderson, N. H. (1972b). Looking for configurality in clinical judgment. *Psychological Bulletin, 78,* 93-102.

Anderson, N. H. (1973a). Functional measurement of social desirability. *Sociometry, 36,* 89-98.

Anderson, N. H. (1973b). Information integration theory applied to attitudes about U.S. presidents. *Journal of Educational Psychology, 64,* 1-8.

Anderson, N. H. (1973c). Serial position curves in impression formation. *Journal of Experimental Psychology, 97,* 8-12.

Anderson, N. H. (1974a). Algebraic models in perception. In E. C. Carterette & M. P. Friedman (Eds.), *Handbook of perception* (Vol. 2, pp. 215-298). New York: Academic Press.

Anderson, N. H. (1974b). Cognitive algebra: Integration theory applied to social attribution. In L. Berkowitz (Ed.), *Advances in experimental social psychology* (Vol. 7, pp. 1-101). New York: Academic Press.

Anderson, N. H. (1974c). Information integration theory: A brief survey. In D. H. Krantz, R. C. Atkinson, R. D. Luce, & P. Suppes (Eds.), *Contemporary developments in mathematical psychology* (Vol. 2, pp. 236-305). San Francisco: Freeman.

Anderson, N. H. (1974d). Cross-task validation of functional measurement using judgments of total magnitude. *Journal of Experimental Psychology, 102,* 226-233.

Anderson, N. H. (1975). On the role of context effects in psychophysical judgment. *Psychological Review, 82,* 462-482.

Anderson, N. H. (1976a). *Integration theory applied to cognitive responses and attitudes* (Tech. Rep. CHIP 68). La Jolla, CA: Center for Human Information Processing, University of California, San Diego. (Shorter version published as Anderson, 1981b.)

Anderson, N. H. (1976b). *Social perception and cognition* (Tech. Rep. CHIP 62). La Jolla, CA: Center for Human Information Processing, University of California, San Diego.

Anderson, N. H. (1978a). Measurement of motivation and incentive. *Behavior Research Methods & Instrumentation, 10,* 360-375.

Anderson, N. H. (1978b). Progress in cognitive algebra. In L. Berkowitz (Ed.), *Cognitive theories in social psychology* (pp. 103-126). New York: Academic Press.

Anderson, N. H. (1979). Algebraic rules in psychological measurement. *American Scientist, 67,* 555-563.

Anderson, N. H. (1980). Information integration theory in developmental psychology. In F. Wilkening, J. Becker, & T. Trabasso (Eds.), *Information integration by children* (pp. 1-45). Hillsdale, NJ: Lawrence Erlbaum Associates.

Anderson, N. H. (1981a). *Foundations of information integration theory.* New York: Academic Press.

Anderson, N. H. (1981b). Integration theory applied to cognitive responses and attitudes. In R. E. Petty, T. M. Ostrom, & T. C. Brock (Eds.), *Cognitive responses in persuasion* (pp. 361-397). Hillsdale, NJ: Lawrence Erlbaum Associates.

Anderson, N. H. (1982). *Methods of information integration theory.* New York: Academic Press.

Anderson, N. H. (1983a). *A theory of stereotypes* (Tech. Rep. CHIP 119). La Jolla, CA: Center for Human Information Processing, University of California, San Diego. (Published as Anderson, 1991m.)

Anderson, N. H. (1983b). Intuitive physics: Understanding and learning of physical relations. In T. J. Tighe & B. E. Shepp (Eds.), *Perception, cognition, and development* (pp. 231-265). Hillsdale, NJ: Lawrence Erlbaum Associates.

Anderson, N. H. (1983c). *Psychodynamics of everyday life* (Tech. Rep. CHIP 120). La Jolla, CA: Center for Human Information Processing, University of California, San Diego. (Published as Anderson, 1991k.)

Anderson, N. H. (1983d). *Schemas in person cognition* (Tech. Rep. CHIP 118). La Jolla, CA: Center for Human Information Processing, University of California, San Diego. (Published as Anderson, 1991l.)

Anderson, N. H. (1986). A cognitive theory of judgment and decision. In B. Brehmer, H. Jungermann, P. Lourens, & G. Sevón (Eds.), *New directions in research on decision making* (pp. 63-108). Amsterdam: North-Holland.

Anderson, N. H. (1987). Review of *Political cognition*, R. R. Lau & D. O. Sears (Eds.). *American Journal of Psychology, 100*, 295-298.

Anderson, N. H. (1989a). Functional memory and on-line attribution. In J. N. Bassili (Ed.), *On-line cognition in person perception* (pp. 175-220). Hillsdale, NJ: Lawrence Erlbaum Associates.

Anderson, N. H. (1989b). Information integration approach to emotions and their measurement. In R. Plutchik & H. Kellerman (Eds.), *Emotion: Theory, research, and experience* (Vol. 4, pp. 133-186). New York: Academic Press.

Anderson, N. H. (1989c). Integration psychophysics. *Behavioral and Brain Sciences, 12*, 268-269.

Anderson, N. H. (1989d). Speech perception as information integration. *Behavioral and Brain Sciences, 12*, 755-756.

Anderson, N. H. (1990a). Integration psychophysics. In H.-G. Geissler (Ed.), *Psychophysical explorations of mental structures* (pp. 71-93). Göttingen: Hogrefe & Huber.

Anderson, N. H. (1990b). Personal design in social cognition. In C. Hendrick & M. S. Clark (Eds.), *Research methods in personality and social psychology: Review of personality and social psychology* (Vol. 11, pp. 243-278). Beverly Hills, CA: Sage.

Anderson, N. H. (1991a). A cognitive theory of judgment and decision. In N. H. Anderson (Ed.), *Contributions to information integration theory. Vol. I: Cognition* (pp. 105-142). Hillsdale, NJ: Lawrence Erlbaum Associates. (Reprint of Anderson, 1986.)

Anderson, N. H. (Ed.). (1991b). *Contributions to information integration theory. Vol. I: Cognition.* Hillsdale, NJ: Lawrence Erlbaum Associates.

Anderson, N. H. (Ed.). (1991c). *Contributions to information integration theory. Vol. II: Social.* Hillsdale, NJ: Lawrence Erlbaum Associates.

Anderson, N. H. (Ed.). (1991d). *Contributions to information integration theory. Vol. III: Developmental.* Hillsdale, NJ: Lawrence Erlbaum Associates.

Anderson, N. H. (1991e). Editor's Note 1. In N. H. Anderson (Ed.), *Contributions to information integration theory. Vol. II: Social* (pp. 90-94). Hillsdale, NJ: Lawrence Erlbaum Associates.

Anderson, N. H. (1991f). Editor's Note 2. In N. H. Anderson (Ed.), *Contributions to information integration theory. Vol. II: Social* (pp. 94-97). Hillsdale, NJ: Lawrence Erlbaum Associates.

Anderson, N. H. (1991g). Family life and personal design. In N. H. Anderson (Ed.), *Contributions to information integration theory. Vol. III: Developmental* (pp. 189-242). Hillsdale, NJ: Lawrence Erlbaum Associates.

Anderson, N. H. (1991h). Functional memory in person cognition. In N. H. Anderson (Ed.), *Contributions to information integration theory. Vol. I: Cognition* (pp. 1-55). Hillsdale, NJ: Lawrence Erlbaum Associates.

Anderson, N. H. (1991i). Moral–social development. In N. H. Anderson (Ed.), *Contributions to information integration theory. Vol. III: Developmental* (pp. 137-187). Hillsdale, NJ: Lawrence Erlbaum Associates.

Anderson, N. H. (1991j). Probability development. In N. H. Anderson (Ed.), *Contributions to information integration theory. Vol. III: Developmental* (pp. 111-134). Hillsdale, NJ: Lawrence Erlbaum Associates.

Anderson, N. H. (1991k). Psychodynamics of everyday life: Blaming and avoiding blame. In N. H. Anderson (Ed.), *Contributions to information integration theory. Vol. II: Social* (pp. 243-275). Hillsdale, NJ: Lawrence Erlbaum Associates.

Anderson, N. H. (1991l). Schemas in person cognition. In N. H. Anderson (Ed.), *Contributions to information integration theory. Vol. I: Cognition* (pp. 57-103). Hillsdale, NJ: Lawrence Erlbaum Associates.

Anderson, N. H. (1991m). Stereotype theory. In N. H. Anderson (Ed.), *Contributions to information integration theory. Vol. II: Social* (pp. 183-240). Hillsdale, NJ: Lawrence Erlbaum Associates.

Anderson, N. H. (1992a). Integration psychophysics and cognition. In D. Algom (Ed.), *Psychophysical approaches to cognition* (pp. 14-113). Amsterdam: Elsevier Science.

Anderson, N. H. (1992b). Integration psychophysics is *not* traditional psychophysics. *Behavioral and Brain Sciences, 15*, 559-560.

Anderson, N. H. (1993). Nonconscious sensation and inner psychophysics. *Behavioral and Brain Sciences, 16*, 137-138.

Anderson, N. H. (in press). Cognitive algebra versus representativeness heuristic. *Behavioral and Brain Sciences.*

Anderson, N. H., & Armstrong, M. A. (1989). Cognitive theory and methodology for studying marital interaction. In D. Brinberg & J. Jaccard (Eds.), *Dyadic decision making* (pp. 3-50). New York: Springer-Verlag.

Anderson, N. H., & Butzin, C. A. (1974). Performance = Motivation × Ability: An integration-theoretical analysis. *Journal of Personality and Social Psychology, 30*, 598-604.

Anderson, N. H., & Butzin, C. A. (1978). Integration theory applied to children's judgments of equity. *Developmental Psychology, 14*, 593-606.

Anderson, N. H., & Cuneo, D. O. (1978a). The Height + Width rule in children's judgments of quantity. *Journal of Experimental Psychology: General, 107*, 335-378.

Anderson, N. H., & Cuneo, D. O. (1978b). The Height + Width rule seems solid: Reply to Bogartz. *Journal of Experimental Psychology: General, 107*, 388-392.

Anderson, N. H., & Farkas, A. J. (1973). New light on order effects in attitude change. *Journal of Personality and Social Psychology, 28*, 88-93.

Anderson, N. H., & Farkas, A. J. (1975). Integration theory applied to models of inequity. *Personality and Social Psychology Bulletin, 1*, 588-591.

Anderson, N. H., & Graesser, C. C. (1976). An information integration analysis of attitude change in group discussion. *Journal of Personality and Social Psychology, 34*, 210-222.

Anderson, N. H., & Hubert, S. (1963). Effects of concomitant verbal recall on order effects in personality impression formation. *Journal of Verbal Learning and Verbal Behavior, 2*, 379-391.

Anderson, N. H., & Lopes, L. L. (1974). Some psycholinguistic aspects of person perception. *Memory & Cognition, 2*, 67-74.

Anderson, N. H., & Nakamura, C. Y. (1964). Avoidance decrement in avoidance conditioning. *Journal of Comparative and Physiological Psychology, 57*, 196-204.

Anderson, N. H., & Schlottmann, A. (1991). Developmental study of personal probability. In N. H. Anderson (Ed.), *Contributions to information integration theory. Vol. III: Developmental* (pp. 111-134). Hillsdale, NJ: Lawrence Erlbaum Associates.

Anderson, N. H., & Schlottmann, A. (1995). *Comparison of two models for belief integration.* Unpublished paper, University of California, San Diego.

Anderson, N. H., & Shanteau, J. C. (1970). Information integration in risky decision making. *Journal of Experimental Psychology, 84*, 441-451.

Anderson, N. H., & Shanteau, J. (1977). Weak inference with linear models. *Psychological Bulletin, 84*, 1155-1170.

Anderson, N. H., & Verdi, J. (1984). *Moral algebra of duty and obligation* (Unpublished manuscript). La Jolla, CA: Center for Human Information Processing, University of California, San Diego.

Anderson, N. H., & Wilkening, F. (1991). Adaptive thinking in intuitive physics. In N. H. Anderson (Ed.), *Contributions to information integration theory. Vol. III: Developmental* (pp. 1-42). Hillsdale, NJ: Lawrence Erlbaum Associates.

Anderson, N. H., & Zalinski, J. (1988). Functional measurement approach to self-estimation in multiattribute evaluation. *Journal of Behavioral Decision Making, 1*, 191-221. (Reprinted in Anderson, 1991b.)

Armstrong, M. A. (1984). *Attitudes and attitude change in marriage, studied with information integration theory.* Unpublished doctoral dissertation, University of California, San Diego.

Asch, S. E. (1946). Forming impressions of personality. *Journal of Abnormal and Social Psychology, 41*, 258-290.

Baddeley, A. (1986). *Working memory.* Oxford: Clarendon.

Bandura, A. (1986). *Social foundations of thought and action.* Englewood Cliffs, NJ: Prentice-Hall.

Bartlett, F. C. (1932). *Remembering: A study in experimental and social psychology.* London: Cambridge University Press.

Bates, E., McNew, S., MacWhinney, B., Devescovi, A., & Smith, S. (1982). Functional constraints on sentence processing: A cross-linguistic study. *Cognition, 11*, 245-299.

Bentham, J. (1907). *An introduction to the principles of morals and legislation.* London: Clarendon Press. (Originally published 1789 and revised 1823)

Berscheid, E. (1982). Attraction and emotion in interpersonal relations. In M. S. Clark & S. T. Fiske (Eds.), *Affect and cognition* (pp. 37-54). Hillsdale, NJ: Lawrence Erlbaum Associates.

Birnbaum, M. H. (1974). The nonadditivity of personality impressions. *Journal of Experimental Psychology, 102*, 543-561.

Birnbaum, M. H. (1976). Intuitive numerical prediction. *American Journal of Psychology, 89*, 417-429.

Birnbaum, M. H. (1982). Controversies in psychological measurement. In B. Wegener (Ed.), *Social attitudes and psychophysical measurement* (pp. 401-485). Hillsdale, NJ: Lawrence Erlbaum Associates.

Bogartz, R. S. (1978). Comments on Anderson and Cuneo's "The Height + Width rule in children's judgments of quantity." *Journal of Experimental Psychology: General, 107*, 379-387.

Bogartz, R. S. (1990). Evaluating forgetting curves psychologically. *Journal of Experimental Psychology: Learning, Memory, and Cognition, 16*, 138-148.

Bogartz, R. S. (1994). A window into children's minds. Review of *Contributions to information integration theory. Vol. III: Developmental* (N. H. Anderson, Ed.). *American Journal of Psychology, 107*, 449-453.

Borges, M. A., & Sawyers, B. K. (1974). Common verbal quantifiers: Usage and interpretation. *Journal of Experimental Psychology, 102*, 335-338.

Boring, E. G. (1950). *A history of experimental psychology* (2nd ed.). New York: Appleton-Century-Crofts.

Bower, G. H. (1981). Mood and memory. *American Psychologist, 36*, 129-148.

Boynton, R. M. (1979). *Human color vision.* New York: Holt, Rinehart and Winston. (Reprinted 1992 by Optical Society of America.)

Bransford, J. D., & Franks, J. J. (1971). The abstraction of linguistic ideas. *Cognitive Psychology*, *2*, 331-350.

Bruce, D. (1989). Functional explanations of memory. In L. W. Poon, D. C. Rubin, & B. A. Wilson (Eds.), *Everyday cognition in adulthood and late life* (pp. 44-58). New York: Cambridge University Press.

Burckhardt, S. (1968). *Shakespearean meanings*. Princeton, NJ: Princeton University Press.

Busemeyer, J. R. (1991). Intuitive statistical estimation. In N. H. Anderson (Ed.), *Contributions to information integration theory. Vol. I: Cognition* (pp. 187-215). Hillsdale, NJ: Lawrence Erlbaum Associates.

Bush, R. R., & Mosteller, F. *Stochastic models for learning*. New York: Wiley, 1955.

Butzin, C. A. (1978). *The effect of ulterior motive information on children's moral judgments*. Unpublished doctoral dissertation, University of California, San Diego.

Butzin, C. A., & Dozier, M. (1986). Children's use of ulterior motive information. *Child Development*, *57*, 1375-1385.

Carterette, E. C., & Anderson, N. H. (1979). Bisection of loudness. *Perception & Psychophysics*, *26*, 265-280.

Christensen, S. M., & Turner, D. R. (Eds.). (1993). *Folk psychology and the philosophy of mind*. Hillsdale, NJ: Lawrence Erlbaum and Associates.

Churchland, P. M. (1979). *Scientific realism and the plasticity of mind*. New York: Cambridge University Press.

Clavadetscher, J. E. (1977). Two context processes in the Ebbinghaus illusion (Doctoral dissertation, University of California, San Diego). *Dissertation Abstracts International*, *38*, 4500B.

Clavadetscher, J. E. (1991). Studies of a two process theory for geometric illusions. In N. H. Anderson (Ed.), *Contributions to information integration theory. Vol. I: Cognition* (pp. 217-257). Hillsdale, NJ: Lawrence Erlbaum Associates.

Clavadetscher, J. E., & Anderson, N. H. (1977). Comparative judgment: Tests of two theories using the Baldwin figure. *Journal of Experimental Psychology: Human Perception and Performance*, *3*, 119-135.

Cliff, N. (1959). Adverbs as multipliers. *Psychological Review*, *66*, 27-44.

Cliff, N. (1992). Abstract measurement theory and the revolution that never happened. *Psychological Science*, *3*, 186-190.

Cohen, G. (1989). *Memory in the real world*. Hillsdale, NJ: Lawrence Erlbaum Associates.

Colby, A., Kohlberg, L., Gibbs, J., & Lieberman, M. (1983). A longitudinal study of moral judgment. *Monographs of the Society for Research in Child Development*, *48*(Nos. 1-2).

Conte, H. R., & Plutchik, R. (Eds.). (1995). *Ego defenses: Theory and measurement*. New York: Wiley.

Cuneo, D. O. (1978). *Children's judgments of numerical quantity: The role of length, density, and number cues*. Unpublished doctoral dissertation, University of California, San Diego.

Cuneo, D. O. (1980). A general strategy for judgments of quantity: The Height + Width rule. *Child Development*, *51*, 299-301.

Cuneo, D. O. (1982). Children's judgments of numerical quantity: A new view of early quantification. *Cognitive Psychology*, *14*, 13-44.

Damon, W. (1977). *The social world of the child*. San Francisco: Jossey-Bass.

Dawes, R. M., & Corrigan, B. (1974). Linear models in decision making. *Psychological Bulletin*, *81*, 95-106.

Dixon, J. A., & Moore, C. F. (1990). The development of perspective taking: Understanding differences in information and weighting. *Child Development*, *61*, 1502-1513.

Dozier, M., & Butzin, C. (1988). Cognitive requirements of ulterior motive information usage: Individual child analyses. *Journal of Experimental Child Psychology*, *46*, 88-99.

Dreben, E. K., Fiske, S. T., & Hastie, R. (1979). The independence of evaluative and item information: Impression and recall order effects in behavior-based impression formation. *Journal of Personality and Social Psychology, 37,* 1758-1768.

Eagly, A. H., & Chaiken, S. (1993). *The psychology of attitudes.* Orlando, FL: Harcourt Brace Jovanovich.

Eich, E., Reeves, J. L., Jaeger, B., & Graff-Radford, S. B. (1985). Memory for pain: Relation between past and present pain intensity. *Pain, 23,* 375-379.

Ellis, B. (1966). *Basic concepts of measurement.* London: Cambridge University Press.

Estes, W. K. (1964). Probability learning. In A. W. Melton (Ed.), *Categories of human learning* (pp. 89-128). New York: Academic Press.

Estes, W. K. (1975). Some targets for mathematical psychology. *Journal of Mathematical Psychology, 12,* 263-282.

Eysenck, M. W., & Keane, M. T. (1990). *Cognitive psychology.* Hillsdale, NJ: Lawrence Erlbaum Associates.

Farkas, A. J. (1977). A cognitive algebra for bystander judgments of interpersonal unfairness (Doctoral dissertation, University of California, San Diego). *Dissertation Abstracts International, 38,* 4535B.

Farkas, A. J. (1991). Cognitive algebra of interpersonal unfairness. In N. H. Anderson (Ed.), *Contributions to information integration theory. Vol. II: Social* (pp. 43-99). Hillsdale, NJ: Lawrence Erlbaum Associates.

Farkas, A. J., & Anderson, N. H. (1979). Multidimensional input in equity theory. *Journal of Personality and Social Psychology, 37,* 879-896.

Farley, J., & Fantino, E. (1978). The symmetrical law of effect and the matching relation in choice behavior. *Journal of the Experimental Analysis of Behavior, 29,* 37-60.

Ferguson, A. (Chair.). (1940). Quantitative estimates of sensory events. *The Advancement of Science, 1,* 331-349.

Fiedler, K. (1983). On the testability of the availability heuristic. In R. W. Scholz (Ed.), *Decision making under uncertainty* (pp. 109-119). Amsterdam: North-Holland.

Fischhoff, B., Slovic, P., & Lichtenstein, S. (1979). Subjective sensitivity analysis. *Organizational Behavior and Human Performance, 23,* 339-359.

Fishburn, P. C. (1986). The axioms of subjective probability. *Statistical Science, 1,* 335-358.

Fiske, S. T. (1982). Schema-triggered affect: Applications to social perception. In M. S. Clark & S. T. Fiske (Eds.), *Affect and cognition* (pp. 55-78). Hillsdale, NJ: Lawrence Erlbaum Associates.

Frese, M., & Sabini, J. (Eds.). (1985). *Goal-directed behavior.* Hillsdale, NJ: Erlbaum.

Friedman, M. P., Carterette, E. C., & Anderson, N. H. (1968). Long-term probability learning with a random schedule of reinforcement. *Journal of Experimental Psychology, 78,* 442-455.

Gaeth, G. J., Levin, I. P., Chakraborty, G., & Levin, A. M. (1990). Consumer evaluation of multi-product bundles: An information integration analysis. *Marketing Letters, 2,* 47-57.

Gibbon, J., & Fairhurst, S. (1994). Ratio versus difference comparators in choice. *Journal of the Experimental Analysis of Behavior, 62,* 409-434.

Gibson, J. J. (1966). *The senses considered as perceptual systems.* Boston: Houghton Mifflin.

Gigerenzer, G., & Murray, D. J. (1987). *Cognition as intuitive statistics.* Hillsdale, NJ: Lawrence Erlbaum Associates.

Goldberg, L. R. (1968). Simple models or simple processes? Some research on clinical judgments. *American Psychologist, 23,* 483-496.

Graesser, C. C. (1978). A social averaging theorem for group decision making (Doctoral dissertation, University of California, San Diego). *Dissertation Abstracts International, 38,* 5647B.

Graesser, C. C. (1991). A social averaging theorem for group decision making. In N. H. Anderson (Ed.), *Contributions to information integration theory. Vol. II: Social* (pp. 1-40). Hillsdale, NJ: Lawrence Erlbaum Associates.

Graesser, C. C., & Anderson, N. H. (1974). Cognitive algebra of the equation: Gift size = Generosity × Income. *Journal of Experimental Psychology, 103*, 692-699.

Grant, D. A., & Hake, H. W. (1949). Acquisition and extinction of the Humphreys' verbal response with differing percentages of "reinforcement." *American Psychologist, 4*, 226. (Abstract)

Green, G. M. (1989). *Pragmatics and natural language understanding.* Hillsdale, NJ: Lawrence Erlbaum Associates.

Grice, H. P. (1975). Logic and conversation. In P. Cole & J. L. Morgan (Eds.), *Syntax and semantics (Vol. 3): Speech acts* (pp. 41-58). New York: Academic Press.

Gruneberg, M. M., Morris, P. E., & Sykes, R. N. (Eds.). (1988). *Practical aspects of memory: Current research and issues* (2 volumes). New York: Wiley.

Hartshorne, H., & May, M. A. (1928). *Studies in the nature of character (Vol. 1): Studies in deceit.* New York: Macmillan.

Hasher, L., & Zacks, R. T. (1984). Automatic processing of fundamental information: The case of frequency of occurrence. *American Psychologist, 39*, 1372-1388.

Hastie, R. (1983). Social inference. *Annual Review of Psychology, 34*, 511-542.

Hastie, R., Ostrom, T. M., Ebbesen, E. B., Wyer, R. S., Jr., Hamilton, D. L., & Carlston, D. E. (Eds.). (1980). *Person memory: The cognitive basis of social perception.* Hillsdale, NJ: Lawrence Erlbaum Associates.

Hastie, R., & Park, B. (1986). The relationship between memory and judgment depends on whether the judgment task is memory-based or on-line. *Psychological Review, 93*, 258-268.

Hastie, R., Park, B., & Weber, R. (1984). Social memory. In R. S. Wyer, Jr. & T. K. Srull (Eds.), *Handbook of social cognition* (Vol. 2, pp. 151-212). Hillsdale, NJ: Lawrence Erlbaum Associates.

Hawkins, R. D., Roll, P. L., Puerto, A., & Yeomans, J. S. (1983). Refractory periods of neurons mediating stimulation-elicited eating and brain stimulation reward: Interval scale measurement and tests of a model of neural integration. *Behavioral Neuroscience, 97*, 416-432.

Heider, F. (1958). *The psychology of interpersonal relations.* New York: Wiley.

Heit, E. (1993). Modeling the effects of expectations on recognition memory. *Psychological Science, 4*, 244-252.

Helson, H. (1964). *Adaptation-level theory.* New York: Harper & Row.

Hendrick, C. (Ed.). (1987a). *Group processes: Review of personality and social psychology* (Vol. 8). Newbury Park, CA: Sage.

Hendrick, C. (Ed.). (1987b). *Group processes and intergroup relations: Review of personality and social psychology* (Vol. 9). Newbury Park, CA: Sage.

Hendrick, C., & Costantini, A. F. (1970). Effects of varying trait inconsistency and response requirements on the primacy effect in impression formation. *Journal of Personality and Social Psychology, 15*, 158-164.

Herrnstein, R. J. (1970). On the law of effect. *Journal of the Experimental Analysis of Behavior, 13*, 243-266.

Himmelfarb, S., & Anderson, N. H. (1975). Integration theory applied to opinion attribution. *Journal of Personality and Social Psychology, 31*, 1064-1072.

Hogarth, R. M., & Einhorn, H. J. (1992). Order effects in belief updating: The belief-adjustment model. *Cognitive Psychology, 24*, 1-55.

Hommers, W., & Anderson, N. H. (1985). Recompense as a factor in assigned punishment. *British Journal of Developmental Psychology, 3*, 75-86.

Hommers, W., & Anderson, N. H. (1991). Moral algebra of harm and recompense. In N. H. Anderson (Ed.), *Contributions to information integration theory. Vol. II: Social* (pp. 101-141). Hillsdale, NJ: Lawrence Erlbaum Associates.

Hörmann, H. (1983). The calculating listener. In R. Baüerle, C. Schwarze, & A. von Stechow (Eds.), *Meaning, use, and interpretation of language* (pp. 221-234). Berlin: de Gruyter.

Howe, E. S. (1991). Integration of mitigation, intention, and outcome damage information, by students and circuit court judges. *Journal of Applied Social Psychology, 21*, 875-895.

Isen, A. M., Shalker, T. E., Clark, M. S., & Karp, L. (1978). Affect, accessibility of material in memory, and behavior: A cognitive loop? *Journal of Personality and Social Psychology, 36*, 1-12.

Jaccard, J., & Becker, M. A. (1985). Attitudes and behavior: An information integration perspective. *Journal of Experimental Social Psychology, 21*, 440-465.

Jaspars, J., Fincham, F. D., & Hewstone, M. (Eds.). (1983). *Attribution theory and research.* New York: Academic Press.

Jones, E. E., & McGillis, D. (1976). Correspondent inferences and the attribution cube: A comparative reappraisal. In J. H. Harvey, W. J. Ickes, & R. F. Kidd (Eds.), *New directions in attribution research* (Vol. 1, pp. 389-420). Hillsdale, NJ: Lawrence Erlbaum Associates.

Kahneman, D., Slovic, P., & Tversky, A. (1982). *Judgment under uncertainty: Heuristics and biases.* London and New York: Cambridge University Press.

Kahneman, D., & Tversky, A. (1972). Subjective probability: A judgment of representativeness. *Cognitive Psychology, 3*, 430-454.

Kahneman, D., & Tversky, A. (1979). Prospect theory: An analysis of decision under risk. *Econometrica, 47*, 263-291.

Kaiser, P. K., & Boynton, R. M. (in press). *Human color vision* (2nd ed.). Washington, DC: Optical Society of America.

Kao, S.-F., & Wasserman, E. A. (1993). Assessment of an information integration account of contingency judgment with examination of subjective cell importance and method of information presentation. *Journal of Experimental Psychology: Learning, Memory, and Cognition, 19*, 1363-1386.

Karpp, E. R. (1994). *Linking intuitive knowledge and symbolic knowledge in physics instruction.* Unpublished doctoral dissertation, University of California, San Diego.

Karpp, E. R., & Anderson, N. H. (in press). Cognitive assessment of function knowledge. *Journal of Research in Science Teaching.*

Kelley, H. H. (1972). Causal schemata and the attribution process. In E. E. Jones, D. E. Kanouse, H. H. Kelley, R. E. Nisbett, S. Valins, & B. Weiner (Eds.), *Attribution: Perceiving the causes of behavior* (pp. 151-174). Morristown, NJ: General Learning Press.

Kenny, D. A. (1994). *Interpersonal perception: A social relations analysis.* New York: Guilford Press.

Klatzky, R. L. (1980). *Human memory* (2nd ed.). New York: Freeman.

Klitzner, M. D., & Anderson, N. H. (1977). Motivation × Expectancy × Value: A functional measurement approach. *Motivation and Emotion, 1*, 347-365.

Koehler, J. J. (in press). The base rate fallacy reconsidered: Descriptive, normative, and methodological challenges. *Behavioral and Brain Sciences.*

Kohlberg, L. (1976). Moral stages and moralization: The cognitive-developmental approach. In T. Lickona (Ed.), *Moral development and behavior: Theory, research, and social issues* (pp. 31-53). New York: Holt, Rinehart & Winston.

Krantz, D. H., Luce, R. D., Suppes, P., & Tversky, A. (1971). *Foundations of measurement* (Vol. 1). New York: Academic Press.

Krueger, L. E. (1989). Reconciling Fechner and Stevens: Toward a unified psychophysical law. *Behavioral and Brain Sciences, 12*, 251-320.

Lakoff, G. (1972). Hedges: A study in meaning criteria and the logic of fuzzy concepts. *Papers from the eighth regional meeting of the Chicago Linguistic Society.* Chicago: University of Chicago Linguistics Department.

Lampel, A. K., & Anderson, N. H. (1968). Combining visual and verbal information in an impression-formation task. *Journal of Personality and Social Psychology, 9*, 1-6.

Lau, R. R., & Sears, D. O. (Eds.). (1986). *Political cognition.* Hillsdale, NJ: Lawrence Erlbaum Associates.

Leon, M. (1976). *Coordination of intent and consequence information in children's moral judgments.* Unpublished doctoral dissertation, University of California, San Diego.

Leon, M. (1980). Integration of intent and consequence information in children's moral judgments. In F. Wilkening, J. Becker, & T. Trabasso (Eds.), *Information integration by children* (pp. 71-97). Hillsdale, NJ: Lawrence Erlbaum Associates.

Leon, M. (1982). Extent, multiplying, and proportionality rules in children's judgments of area. *Journal of Experimental Child Psychology, 33,* 124-141.

Leon, M. (1984). Rules mothers and sons use to integrate intent and damage information in their moral judgments. *Child Development, 55,* 2106-2113.

Leon, M., & Anderson, N. H. (1974). A ratio rule from integration theory applied to inference judgments. *Journal of Experimental Psychology, 102,* 27-36.

Leon, M., Oden, G. C., & Anderson, N. H. (1973). Functional measurement of social values. *Journal of Personality and Social Psychology, 27,* 301-310.

Leventhal, H. (1982). The integration of emotion and cognition: A view from the perceptual-motor theory of emotion. In M. S. Clark & S. T. Fiske (Eds.), *Affect and cognition* (pp. 121-156). Hillsdale, NJ: Lawrence Erlbaum Associates.

Levin, I. (1986). (Ed.). *Stage and structure: Reopening the debate.* Norwood, NJ: Ablex.

Levin, I. P., Louviere, J. J., Schepanski, A. A., & Norman, K. L. (1983). External validity tests of laboratory studies of information integration. *Organizational Behavior and Human Performance, 31,* 173-193.

Lichtenstein, S., Earle, T. C., & Slovic, P. (1975). Cue utilization in a numerical prediction task. *Journal of Experimental Psychology: Human Perception and Performance, 1,* 77-85.

Lindzey, G., & Aronson, E. (1968-1969). *The handbook of social psychology* (2nd ed., Vols. 1-5). Reading, MA: Addison-Wesley.

Lindzey, G., & Aronson, E. (1985). *The handbook of social psychology* (3rd ed., Vols. 1-2). New York: Random House.

Lippmann, W. (1922). *Public opinion.* New York: Harcourt, Brace.

Loftus, E. F. (1979). *Eyewitness testimony.* Cambridge, MA: Harvard University Press.

Loftus, E. F., Donders, K., Hoffman, H. G., & Schooler, J. W. (1989). Creating new memories that are quickly accessed and confidently held. *Memory and Cognition, 17,* 607-616.

Lopes, L. L. (1976a). Individual strategies in goal-setting. *Organizational Behavior and Human Performance, 15,* 268-277.

Lopes, L. L. (1976b). Model-based decision and inference in stud poker. *Journal of Experimental Psychology: General, 105,* 217-239.

Lopes, L. L. (1987a). Between hope and fear: The psychology of risk. In L. Berkowitz (Ed.), *Advances in Experimental Social Psychology, Vol. 20* (pp. 255-295). San Diego, CA: Academic Press.

Lopes, L. L. (1987b). Procedural debiasing. *Acta Psychologica, 64,* 167-185.

Lopes, L. L., & Ekberg, P.-H. S. (1980). Test of an ordering hypothesis in risky decision making. *Acta Psychologica, 45,* 161-167.

Lopes, L. L., & Oden, G. C. (1980). Comparison of two models of similarity judgment. *Acta Psychologica, 46,* 205-234.

Louviere, J. J. (1988). *Analyzing decision making: Metric conjoint analysis.* Beverly Hills, CA: Sage.

Luce, R. D. (1959a). *Individual choice behavior.* New York: Wiley.

Luce, R. D. (1959b). On the possible psychophysical laws. *Psychological Review, 66,* 81-95.

Luce, R. D. (1962). Comments on Rozeboom's criticisms of "On the possible psychophysical laws." *Psychological Review, 69,* 548-551.

Luce, R. D., & Krumhansl, C. L. (1988). Measurement, scaling, and psychophysics. In R. C. Atkinson, R. J. Herrnstein, G. Lindzey, & R. D. Luce (Eds.), *Stevens' handbook of experimental psychology* (2nd ed., Vol. 1, pp. 3-74). New York: Wiley.

Macmillan, N. A., & Creelman, C. D. (1991). *Detection theory: A user's guide*. New York: Cambridge University Press.

Mandler, G. (1984). *Mind and body*. New York: Norton.

Marks, L. E. (1968). Stimulus-range, number of categories, and form of the category-scale. *American Journal of Psychology, 81*, 467-479.

Massaro, D. W. (1987). *Speech perception by ear and eye: A paradigm for psychological inquiry*. Hillsdale, NJ: Lawrence Erlbaum Associates.

Massaro, D. W. (1991). Language processing and information integration. In N. H. Anderson (Ed.), *Contributions to information integration theory. Vol. I: Cognition* (pp. 259-292). Hillsdale, NJ: Lawrence Erlbaum Associates.

Massaro, D. W., & Cohen, M. M. (1976). The contribution of fundamental frequency and voice onset time to the /zi/–/si/ distinction. *Journal of the Acoustical Society of America, 60*, 704-717.

Massaro, D. W., & Friedman, D. (1990). Models of integration given multiple sources of information. *Psychological Review, 97*, 225-252.

Massaro, D. W., & Hary, J. M. (1986). Addressing issues in letter recognition. *Psychological Research, 48*, 123-132.

McBride, R. L. (1989). Three models for taste mixtures. In D. G. Laing, W. S. Cain, R. L. McBride, & B. W. Ache (Eds.), *Perception of complex smells and tastes* (pp. 265-282). Sydney: Academic Press.

McBride, R. L. (1993). Integration psychophysics: The use of functional measurement in the study of mixtures. *Chemical Senses, 18*, 83-92.

McBride, R. L., & Anderson, N. H. (1991). Integration psychophysics in the chemical senses. In N. H. Anderson (Ed.), *Contributions to information integration theory. Vol. I: Cognition* (pp. 295-319). Hillsdale, NJ: Lawrence Erlbaum Associates.

McCloskey, M., & Zaragoza, M. (1985). Misleading postevent information and memory for events: Arguments and evidence against memory impairment hypotheses. *Journal of Experimental Psychology: General, 114*, 1-16.

McDougall, W. (1928). Emotion and feeling distinguished. In M. L. Reymert (Ed.), *Feelings and emotions: The Wittenberg Symposium* (pp. 200-205). Worcester, MA: Clark University Press.

McGuire, W. J. (1969). The nature of attitudes and attitude change. In G. Lindzey & E. Aronson (Eds.), *The handbook of social psychology* (2nd ed., Vol. 3, pp. 136-314). Reading, MA: Addison-Wesley.

McGuire, W. J. (1983). A contextualist theory of knowledge: Its implications for innovations and reform in psychology research. In L. Berkowitz (Ed.), *Advances in experimental social psychology* (Vol. 16, pp. 1-47). New York: Academic Press.

McGuire, W. J. (1985). Attitudes and attitude change. In G. Lindzey & E. Aronson (Eds.), *Handbook of social psychology* (3rd ed., Vol. 2, pp. 233-346). New York: Random House.

Mellers, B. A. (1982). Equity judgment: A revision of Aristotelean views. *Journal of Experimental Psychology: General, 111*, 242-270.

Mellers, B. A. (1985). A reconsideration of two-person inequity judgments: A reply to Anderson. *Journal of Experimental Psychology: General, 114*, 514-520.

Mischel, W. (1968). *Personality and assessment*. New York: Wiley.

Modgil, S., & Modgil, C. (Eds.). (1986). *Lawrence Kohlberg: Consensus and controversy*. Philadelphia: Falmer Press.

Morley, C. D. (1934). *The haunted bookshop*. Garden City, NY: Doubleday, Doran. (Original work published 1919)

Moxey, L. M., & Sanford, A. J. (1993). *Communicating quantities.* Hillsdale, NJ: Lawrence Erlbaum Associates.

Mullet, E., & Montcouquiol, A. (1988). Archimedes effect, information integration and individual differences. Paris, France: Université René Descartes, Laboratoire de Psychologie Differentielle, Document du Service du Recherches de l'I.N.E.T.O.P.

Mullet, E., & Vidal, E. (1986). La maîtrise intuitive des relations entre masse, volume et mass volumique chez des élèves du premier cycle. *European Journal of Psychology of Education, 1,* 47-65.

Münsterberg, H. (1909). *On the witness stand.* New York: Doubleday, Page.

Neisser, U. (Ed.). (1982). *Memory observed: Remembering in natural contexts.* New York: Freeman.

Neisser, U., & Winograd, E. (Eds.). (1988). *Remembering reconsidered: Ecological and traditional approaches to the study of memory.* New York: Cambridge University Press.

Nisbett, R. E., & Bellows, N. (1977). Verbal reports about causal influences on social judgments: Private access versus public theories. *Journal of Personality and Social Psychology, 35,* 613-624.

Nisbett, R. E., & Wilson, T. D. (1977). Telling more than we can know: Verbal reports on mental processes. *Psychological Review, 84,* 231-259.

Oden, G. C. (1974). *Semantic constraints and ambiguity resolution.* Unpublished doctoral dissertation, University of California, San Diego.

Oden, G. C. (1977a). Fuzziness in semantic memory: Choosing exemplars of subjective categories. *Memory & Cognition, 5,* 198-204.

Oden, G. C. (1977b). Integration of fuzzy logical information. *Journal of Experimental Psychology: Human Perception and Performance, 3,* 565-575.

Oden, G. C. (1978a). Integration of place and voicing information in the identification of synthetic stop consonants. *Journal of Phonetics, 6,* 83-93.

Oden, G. C. (1978b). Semantic constraints and judged preference for interpretations of ambiguous sentences. *Memory & Cognition, 6,* 26-37.

Oden, G. C. (1979). A fuzzy logical model of letter identification. *Journal of Experimental Psychology: Human Perception and Performance, 5,* 336-352.

Oden, G. C. (1988). FuzzyProp: A symbolic superstrate for connectionist models. *Proceedings of the IEEE International Conference on Neural Networks, 1,* 293-300.

Oden, G. C., & Anderson, N. H. (1971). Differential weighting in integration theory. *Journal of Experimental Psychology, 89,* 152-161.

Oden, G. C., & Anderson, N. H. (1974). Integration of semantic constraints. *Journal of Verbal Learning and Verbal Behavior, 13,* 138-148.

Oden, G. C., & Massaro, D. W. (1978). Integration of featural information in speech perception. *Psychological Review, 85,* 172-191.

Oden, G. C., Rueckl, J. G., & Sanocki, T. (1991). Making sentences make sense, or words to that effect. In G. B. Simpson (Ed.), *Understanding word and sentence* (pp. 285-303). Amsterdam: Elsevier Science.

Parducci, A., & Wedell, D. H. (1986). The category effect with rating scales: Number of categories, number of stimuli, and method of presentation. *Journal of Experimental Psychology: Human Perception and Performance, 12,* 496-516.

Paul, L. M. (1994). Making interpretable forgetting comparisons: Explicit versus hidden assumptions. *Journal of Experimental Psychology: Learning, Memory, and Cognition, 20,* 992-999.

Pervin, L. A. (Ed.). (1989). *Goal concepts in personality and social psychology.* Hillsdale, NJ: Lawrence Erlbaum Associates.

Petzold, P. (1983). Common components in information integration tasks: Individual differences investigation. In H.-G. Geissler (Ed.), *Modern issues in perception* (pp. 254-261). Amsterdam: North-Holland.

Piaget, J. (1965). *The moral judgment of the child.* (M. Gabain, Trans.). New York: Free Press. (Original work published 1932)

Piaget, J. (1969). *The child's conception of time* (A. J. Pomerans, Trans.). London: Routledge & Kegan Paul. (Original work published 1946)

Piaget, J. (1970). *The child's conception of movement and speed* (G. E. T. Holloway & M. J. Mackenzie, Trans.). London: Routledge & Kegan Paul. (Original work published 1946)

Piaget, J., & Inhelder, B. (1975). *The origin of the idea of chance in children* (L. Leake, Jr., P. Burrell, & H. D. Fishbein, Trans.). New York: Norton. (Original work published 1951)

Posner, M. I. (Ed.). (1989). *Foundations of cognitive science.* Cambridge, MA: MIT Press.

Pratkanis, A. R. (1994). A celebration for social psychology: On the contributions of functional measurement and information integration theory. Review of *Contributions to information integration theory. Vol. II: Social* (N. H. Anderson, Ed.). *American Journal of Psychology, 107,* 441-446.

Przygotski, N., & Mullet, E. (1993). Relationships between punishment, damage, and intent to harm in the incarcerated: An information integration approach. *Social Behavior and Personality, 21,* 93-102.

Rest, J. R. (1983). Morality. In P. H. Mussen, J. H. Flavell, & E. M. Markman (Eds.), *Handbook of child psychology: Vol. III: Cognitive development* (4th ed., pp. 556-629). New York: Wiley.

Riskey, D. R. (1979). Verbal memory processes in impression formation. *Journal of Experimental Psychology: Human Learning and Memory, 5,* 271-281.

Roediger, III, H. L., & Craik, F. I. M. (Eds.). (1989). *Varieties of memory and consciousness: Essays in honour of Endel Tulving.* Hillsdale, NJ: Lawrence Erlbaum Associates.

Rozeboom, W. W. (1962). The untenability of Luce's principle. *Psychological Review, 69,* 542-547.

Rumelhart, D. E., & Norman, D. A. (1973). Active semantic networks as a model of human memory. *Proceedings of International Joint Conference on Artificial Intelligence.* Palo Alto, CA.

Savage, L. J. (1954). *The foundations of statistics.* New York: Wiley.

Sawusch, J. R., & Pisoni, D. B. (1974). On the identification of place and voicing features in synthetic stop consonants. *Journal of Phonetics, 2,* 181-194.

Schachter, S. (1964). The interaction of cognitive and physiological determinants of emotional state. In L. Berkowitz (Ed.), *Advances in experimental social psychology* (Vol. 1, pp. 49-80). New York: Academic Press.

Schacter, D. L., Chiu, C.-Y. P., & Ochsner, K. N. (1993). Implicit memory: A selective review. *Annual Review of Neuroscience, 16,* 159-182.

Schlottmann, A. (1987). *Judgments of causality in the perception of launch events.* Unpublished master's thesis, University of California, San Diego.

Schlottmann, A., & Anderson, N. H. (1993). An information integration approach to phenomenal causality. *Memory & Cognition, 21,* 785-801.

Schlottmann, A., & Anderson, N. H. (1994). Children's judgments of expected value. *Developmental Psychology, 30,* 56-66.

Schlottmann, A., & Anderson, N. H. (1995). Belief revision in children: Serial judgment in social cognition and decision-making domains. *Journal of Experimental Psychology: Learning, Memory, and Cognition, 21,* 1349-1364.

Shafer, G. (1987). Probability judgment in artificial intelligence and expert systems. *Statistical Science, 2,* 3-44.

Shanteau, J. C. (1970). An additive model for sequential decision making. *Journal of Experimental Psychology, 85,* 181-191.

Shanteau, J. (1972). Descriptive versus normative models of sequential inference judgment. *Journal of Experimental Psychology, 93,* 63-68.

Shanteau, J. (1974). Component processes in risky decision making. *Journal of Experimental Psychology, 103,* 680-691.

Shanteau, J. (1975). Averaging versus multiplying combination rules of inference judgment. *Acta Psychologica, 39,* 83-89.

Shanteau, J. (1991). Functional measurement analysis of response times in problem solving. In N. H. Anderson (Ed.), *Contributions to information integration theory. Vol. I: Cognition* (pp. 321-350). Hillsdale, NJ: Lawrence Erlbaum Associates.

Shanteau, J., & Anderson, N. H. (1972). Integration theory applied to judgments of the value of information. *Journal of Experimental Psychology, 92,* 266-275.

Sherman, W. T. (1957). *Memoirs of General William T. Sherman.* Bloomington, IN: Indiana University Press. (Originally published 1875)

Siegler, R. S. (1981). Developmental sequences within and between concepts. *Monographs of the Society for Research in Child Development, 46*(2, Serial No. 189).

Siegler, R. S., & Richards, D. D. (1979). Development of time, speed, and distance concepts. *Development Psychology, 15,* 288-298.

Silverman, I. W., & Paskewitz, S. L. (1988). Developmental and individual differences in children's area judgment rules. *Journal of Experimental Child Psychology, 46,* 74-87.

Simon, H. A. (1982). Comments. In M. S. Clark & S. T. Fiske (Eds.), *Affect and cognition* (pp. 333-342). Hillsdale, NJ: Lawrence Erlbaum Associates.

Singh, R. (1985). A test of the relative-ratio model of reward division with students and managers in India. *Genetic, Social, and General Psychology Monographs,*

Singh, R. (1991). Two problems in cognitive algebra: Imputations and averaging versus multiplying. In N. H. Anderson (Ed.), *Contributions to information integration theory. Vol. II: Social* (pp. 143-180). Hillsdale, NJ: Lawrence Erlbaum Associates.

Singh, R., Sidana, U. R., & Srivastava, P. (1978). Averaging processes in children's judgments of happiness. *The Journal of Social Psychology, 104,* 123-132. *111,* 363-384.

Sjöberg, L. (1966). A method for sensation scaling based on an analogy between perception and judgment. *Perception & Psychophysics, 1,* 131-136.

Sjöberg, L. (1994). Integration theory: Applications to cognitive psychology. Review of *Contributions to information integration theory. Vol. I: Cognition* (N. H. Anderson, Ed.). *American Journal of Psychology, 107,* 446-449.

Slovic, P., Fischhoff, B., & Lichtenstein, S. (1977). Behavioral decision theory. *Annual Review of Psychology, 28,* 1-39.

Smelser, N. J. (Ed.). (1988). *Handbook of sociology.* Newbury Park, CA: Sage.

Stangor, C., & McMillan, D. (1992). Memory for expectancy-congruent and expectancy-incongruent information: A review of the social and social developmental literatures. *Psychological Bulletin, 111,* 42-61.

Stasser, G., Kerr, N. L., & Davis, J. H. (1989). Influence processes and consensus models in decision-making groups. In P. B. Paulus (Ed.), *Psychology of group influence* (2nd ed., pp. 279-326). Hillsdale, NJ: Lawrence Erlbaum Associates.

Stefurak, D. L. (1987). *Studies in chromatic induction.* Unpublished doctoral dissertation, University of California, San Diego.

Stein, N. L., & Trabasso, T. (1982). Children's understanding of stories: A basis for moral judgment and dilemma resolution. In C. J. Brainerd & M. Pressley (Eds.), *Verbal processes in children: Progress in cognitive development research* (pp. 161-188). New York: Springer-Verlag.

Stevens, S. S. (1975). *Psychophysics.* New York: Wiley.

Stich, S. P. (1983). *From folk psychology to cognitive science.* Cambridge, MA: MIT Press.

Suppes, P., Krantz, D. H., Luce, R. D., & Tversky, A. (1989). *Foundations of measurement* (Vol. II). San Diego: Academic Press.

Surber, C. F. (1982). Separable effects of motives, consequences, and order of presentation on children's moral judgments. *Developmental Psychology, 18*, 257-266.

Surber, C. F. (1985a). Applications of information integration to children's social cognitions. In J. B. Pryor & J. D. Day (Eds.), *The development of social cognition* (pp. 59-94). New York: Springer-Verlag.

Surber, C. F. (1985b). Developmental changes in inverse compensation in social and nonsocial attributions. In S. R. Yussen (Ed.), *The growth of reflection in children* (pp. 149-166). New York: Academic Press.

Surber, C. F. (1987). Formal representation of qualitative and quantitative reversible operations. In J. Bisanz, C. J. Brainerd, & R. Kail (Eds.), *Formal methods in developmental psychology* (pp. 115-154). New York: Springer-Verlag.

Tannenbaum, P. H. (1978). The congruity principle revisited: Studies in the reduction, induction, and generalization of persuasion. In L. Berkowitz (Ed.), *Cognitive theories in social psychology* (pp. 127-180). New York: Academic Press.

Thurstone, L. L. (1928). Attitudes can be measured. *The American Journal of Sociology, 33*, 529-554.

Thurstone, L. L. (1959). *The measurement of values.* Chicago: University of Chicago Press.

Tolman, E. C. (1959). Principles of purposive behavior. In S. Koch (Ed.), *Psychology: A study of a science* (Vol. 2, pp. 92-157). New York: McGraw-Hill.

Tukey, J. W. (1969). Analyzing data: Sanctification or detective work? *American Psychologist, 24*, 83-102.

Tulving, E. (1979). Memory research: What kind of progress? In L.-G. Nilsson (Ed.), *Perspectives on memory research* (pp. 19-34). Hillsdale, NJ: Lawrence Erlbaum Associates.

Tulving, E., Mandler, G., and Baumal, R. (1964). Interaction of two sources of information in tachistoscopic word recognition. *Canadian Journal of Psychology, 18*, 62-71.

Tversky, A., & Kahneman, D. (1973). Availability: A heuristic for judging frequency and probability. *Cognitive Psychology, 5*, 207-232.

Tyler, S. W., & Voss, J. F. (1982). Attitude and knowledge effects in prose processing. *Journal of Verbal Learning and Verbal Behavior, 21*, 524-538.

Verdi, J. (1979). *Integrating duty and need information in moral judgements.* Unpublished master's thesis, University of California, San Diego.

Vygotsky, L. S. (1978). *Mind in society: The development of higher psychological processes.* Cambridge, MA: Harvard University Press.

Wallsten, T. S., Budescu, D. V., Rapoport, A., Zwick, R., & Forsyth, B. (1986). Measuring the vague meanings of probability terms. *Journal of Experimental Psychology: General, 115*, 348-365.

Wang, M. S., & Yang, J. (1994). *A multicriteria experimental comparison of multiattribute weight ascertaining methods with an unfamiliar task of environmental impact.* Kaohsiung, Taiwan: Institute of Public Affairs Management, National Sun Yat-Sen University.

Weber, E. U., Goldstein, W. M., & Busemeyer, J. R. (1991). Beyond strategies: Implications of memory representation and memory processes for models of judgment and decision making. In W. E. Hockley & S. Lewandowsky (Eds.), *Relating theory and data: Essays on human memory in honor of Bennet B. Murdock* (pp. 75-100). Hillsdale, NJ: Lawrence Erlbaum Associates.

Weiss, D. J. (1972). Averaging: An empirical validity criterion for magnitude estimation. *Perception & Psychophysics, 12*, 3851-388.

Wilkening, F. (1982). Children's knowledge about time, distance, and velocity interrelations. In W. J. Friedman (Ed.), *The developmental psychology of time* (pp. 87-112). New York: Academic Press.

Wilkening, F. (1988). A misrepresentation of knowledge representation. *Developmental Review, 8*, 361-367.

Wilkening, F., & Anderson, N. H. (1982). Comparison of two rule-assessment methodologies for studying cognitive development and knowledge structure. *Psychological Bulletin, 92*, 215-237.

Wilkening, F., & Anderson, N. H. (1991). Representation and diagnosis of knowledge structures in developmental psychology. In N. H. Anderson (Ed.), *Contributions to information integration theory. Vol. III: Developmental* (pp. 45-80). Hillsdale, NJ: Lawrence Erlbaum Associates.

Wixted, J. T. (1990). Analyzing the empirical course of forgetting. *Journal of Experimental Psychology: Learning, Memory, and Cognition, 16*, 927-935.

Wolf, Y. (1995). Estimation of Euclidean quantity by 5- and 6-year-old children: Facilitating a multiplication rule. *Journal of Experimental Child Psychology, 59*, 49-75.

Wolf, Y., & Algom, D. (1987). Perceptual and memorial constructs in children's judgments of quantity: A law of across-representation invariance. *Journal of Experimental Psychology: General, 116*, 381-397.

Wright, W. A. (1995). *Accuracy of self-report*. Unfinished doctoral dissertation, University of California, San Diego.

Young, A. R., (1990). *Bidirectional influence in mother–child dyads*. Unpublished doctoral dissertation, California School of Professional Psychology, San Diego, CA.

Zadeh, L. A. (1965). Fuzzy sets. *Information and Control, 8*, 338-353.

Zadeh, L. A., Fu, K.-S., Tanaka, K., & Shimura, M. (Eds.). (1975). *Fuzzy sets and their applications to cognitive and decision processes*. New York: Academic Press.

Zajonc, R. B. (1980). Feeling and thinking: Preferences need no inferences. *American Psychologist, 35*, 151-175.

Zalinski, J., & Anderson, N. H. (1986). AVERAGE: A user-friendly FORTRAN-77 program for parameter estimation for the averaging model of information integration theory [computer software]. University of California, San Diego.

Zalinski, J., & Anderson, N. H. (1989). Measurement of importance in multiattribute models. In J. B. Sidowski (Ed.), *Conditioning, cognition, and methodology: Contemporary issues in experimental psychology* (pp. 177-215). Lanham, MD: University Press of America.

Zalinski, J., & Anderson, N. H. (1991). Parameter estimation for averaging theory. In N. H. Anderson (Ed.), *Contributions to information integration theory. Vol. I: Cognition* (pp. 353-394). Hillsdale, NJ: Lawrence Erlbaum Associates.

Zhu, S.-H. (1991). *Context effects in semantic interpretation: A study of probability words*. Unpublished doctoral dissertation, University of California, San Diego.

Zhu, S.-H., & Anderson, N. H. (1991). Self-estimation of weight parameter in multiattribute analysis. *Organizational Behavior and Human Decision Processes, 48*, 36-54.

AUTHOR INDEX

SUBJECT INDEX*

---

*Chapter and volume prefaces not specifically indexed.